LEO BAECK INSTITUTE
YEAR BOOK

2003

Theodor Herzl and his mother with delegates
from the 6th Zionist Congress held in Basle in 1903

LEO BAECK INSTITUTE

YEAR BOOK
2003

XLVIII

BERGHAHN BOOKS • OXFORD
PUBLISHED FOR THE INSTITUTE
LONDON • JERUSALEM • NEW YORK

FOUNDER EDITOR: ROBERT WELTSCH (1956–1978)
EDITOR EMERITUS: ARNOLD PAUCKER (1970–1992)

Editorial office: Leo Baeck Institute
4 Devonshire Street, London W1W 5LB
www.leobaeck.co.uk

THE LEO BAECK INSTITUTE
was founded in 1955 for the study of the history and
culture of German-speaking Central European Jewry

The Institute is named in honour of the man who was
the last representative figure of German Jewry in
Germany during the Nazi period

LEO BAECK INSTITUTE

JERUSALEM: 33 Bustanai Street
LONDON: 4 Devonshire Street
NEW YORK: 15 West 16th Street

Contents

ILLUSTRATIONS

Permission to reprint was sought for all illustrations. Copyright holders who could
not be ascertained will receive permission fees and acknowledgements if they contact the Leo Baeck Institute.

Preface

In his introduction to the "record of a discussion of Jewish questions" (*Niederschrift einer Besprechung über Judenfragen*) included in this volume, Jürgen Matthäus examines a crucial Weimar Republic debate about the policies to be instituted regarding Jewish immigrants and would-be immigrants to Germany from Eastern Europe. This debate—held on 31 March 1919 under the auspices of the German Foreign Office in Berlin—mirrors the fundamentally ambivalent situation of a great part of European Jewry in the age of nationalism. The concerns of the peace-makers in Versailles in 1919, as well as of the Jewish minorities in countries where they had previously been oppressed and threatened, was to establish minority rights through special treaties. Such a development, however, could not fail to have an impact on the status of Jews in the seemingly more progressive Western European states, where discrimination was generally not sanctioned by law. The majority of Jews in these states rejected the idea of being regarded as members of an ethnic minority, rather viewing themselves as German, French, or British. Within this conceptual framework, religion was understood to be a matter of personal choice. But at the same time, Western European Jews found themselves forced to act together in distinctive groups to protect themselves from those attacking them for being an alien element in the *Volksgemeinschaft*; such self-protection was, for instance, one of the important purposes of Germany's famous *Centralverein*, the "Central Association of Jewish Citizens of the Jewish Faith". It is striking that participants in the debate on "Jewish questions" contained in the *Niederschrift* seem already to have been well aware of something that seems much clearer from our twenty-first century perspective: that such ambivalence defines the position not only of Western Jewry, but in fact of many other minority groups as well (for participants in the debate, those in Eastern Europe; as we can now perceive things, those throughout the world). This underscores the vital role the history of German-speaking Jewry can play in our understanding of broader historical problems, and of the world we live in.

In addressing the issue of "Equality for Jews and Judaism in all countries of the world" during the debate, Walter Rathenau himself revealed a particularly strong awareness of the dilemma facing national minorities; the difficulties involved in trying to resolve it seem reflected in his rather convoluted contribution to the debate:

> Gentlemen! I regard this recommendation [to guarantee equality for the Jews in every country and to give them specific status as a national minority] as creating a serious [international] precedent [*Präjudiz*]. At the moment when the government of the German Reich interferes with the self-determination of other nationalities we have to expect reciprocity as a matter of course. ... If, however, one sees things from the perspective of this precedent, if one does not shrink from interfering with the setting-up of new nations and with their legal systems, then there is no reason to single out the Jews. In that case we must be the advocates of Ruthenians, Serbian minorities, and Walachian minorities in the other countries. Then raising these claims on behalf of Jews would constitute an exclusionary measure [*Ausnahmebestimmung*] in favour of a tightly defined national group. And this precedent goes further. For the German Reich would thus

stabilise the fact that at least elsewhere the Jews form a nation, even if by doing so the German Reich does not establish a precedent in the question of whether the Jews form a nation in Germany.

Was Rathenau afraid that defining Jews in the newly-created European states as a minority nationality with specific rights could backfire, leading to German Jews being regarded as a national minority, hence not totally German?

This political dimension has, to be sure, deep roots; it can also be analysed in a social context. In her article on the Jews in Imperial Germany, Marion Kaplan describes how Jews coped with their ambivalent situation in their daily lives. Drawing on memoirs and other sources, she provides a wealth of testimonies showing how Germany's Jews navigated between the Jewish and non-Jewish worlds. Jewish social life was, Kaplan suggests, predominantly centred on the family, but also, to be sure, around Jewish religious, communal and national institutions. But in both their professional and leisure activities, Germany's Jews likewise integrated with the non-Jewish majority, to varying degrees. They contributed to non-Jewish charities and cultural associations, and played an important role in state and national politics. For some, this involved tensions; others lived easily enough in both worlds, accepting the limitations this imposed without feeling great hardship. In general, it is clear that most German Jews were able to come to terms with the ambivalence underlying their situation, the older Jews tending to feel more in common with their non-Jewish neighbours than with the more recently arrived *Ostjuden*, but also recognising at the same time the link between their fates—as is shown in Jürgen Matthäus's contribution.

While we have focused here on two articles treating basic themes in the history of German-speaking Jewry, the other essays in the present volume address equally thought-provoking issues; many are interconnected in striking ways with those referred to above. As a complement to all the contributions, the *LBI Year Book* bibliography offers, as usual, a wider sense of the breadth and depth of current research than can ever be adequately reflected in a single volume. In this regard, we call the reader's attention to a new feature being planned: the publication of thesis-abstracts submitted by authors for inclusion in the *Year Book*.

It is always a pleasure to be able to thank our manuscript editors, bibliographers, and members of our advisory board, as well as external referees and, not least of all, our publisher. Generous financial support has again been provided by the *Bundesministerium des Inneren* and the *Ständige Konferenz der Kultusminister der Länder in der Bundesrepbulik Deutschland*. Without this support, maintaining both the scholarly standards and wide circulation of the *Year Book* would be far more difficult. We also wish to express our appreciation to the foundations listed on the first page of the bibliography for making its production possible.

John A. S. Grenville and Raphael Gross now jointly edit the *Year Book*.

John Grenville   *Raphael Gross*

Religious Renewal

Moses Mendelssohn's First Hebrew Publication: An Annotated Translation of the Kohelet Mussar

TRANSLATED BY EDWARD BREUER
EDITED BY EDWARD BREUER AND DAVID SORKIN

Moses Mendelssohn's first work in Hebrew, the *Kohelet Mussar* (The Preacher of Morals), was also his most obscure: there is uncertainty about the authorship, date of publication, and reception of this journal. Although Mendelssohn's authorship was never seriously questioned, the work appeared anonymously and some of his contemporaries did mention a co-author. Modern scholars have been divided on this issue. Some, adducing internal literary evidence, continue to accept that Mendelssohn had a collaborator; others, pointing to the unsuccessful attempts to identify such an individual, have suggested that Mendelssohn was the sole author. The editors of this translation subscribe to the latter position: a collaborator is likely to have been Mendelssohn's literary invention much like the other fictitious devices employed in the *Kohelet Mussar*.[1]

To add to the work's obscurity, the date of publication is also unclear. The text is undated, and while all evidence points to publication in the mid to late 1750s, there is no agreement about the exact year.[2] Finally, there is no record of how the work was received or why Mendelssohn ceased publication after two issues. Some commentators have maintained that it was suppressed by the communal authorities in Berlin. This claim invites our scepticism, since all the evidence that supports it is circumstantial. Moreover, it originated with an enterprising *maskil* who was only too happy to promote the now conventional narrative of rabbinic or communal opposi-

---

[1] The argument for a collaborator is based on the marginal notation in Salomon [Shlomo] Dubno's copy of *Kohelet Mussar* and Isaac Euchel's biography, *Toldot Rabeinu he-Hakham Moshe ben Menahem* (A History of our Teacher and Sage, Moses b. Menahem) Berlin 1788. Issachar Edelstein suggested that while Mendelssohn had inspired this work, he did not actually write any of it himself; see 'Ha-Hibbur Kohelet Mussar' (The Work *Kohelet Mussar*), in Ludwig Blau (ed.), *Festschrift zum 50 jährigen Bestehen der Franz-Josef-Landesrabbinerschule in Budapest*, Budapest 1927, pp. 60–61. Meir Gilon has argued that internal evidence supports the claim of a collaborator; see, *Kohelet Mussar le-Mendelson al Reka Tekufato* (Mendelssohn's *Kohelet Mussar* in its Historical Context), Jerusalem 1979, pp. 11–17, 89–97. Alexander Altmann, on the other hand, was the first to suggest that the collaborator may have been Mendelssohn's invention. See Alexander Altmann, *Moses Mendelssohn: A Biographical Study*, University, AL 1973, pp. 83–91.

[2] According to Gilon, pp. 9–11 and 83–89, the date of publication was sometime in the spring of 1755. Altmann, p. 84, following Simon Hochheimer, *Über Mendelssohns Tod*, Vienna and Leipzig 1786, p. 68, gave the date as 1758.

tion to the Haskalah.[3] Given these uncertainties, we have to base our knowledge of the *Kohelet Mussar* directly on the brief text of sixteen pages or one octavo.

The text exhibits all the defining characteristics of a "moral weekly". The moral weekly was an intimate journal (generally published monthly, but on the same day of the week) distinguished by a fictional narrator who used letters and essays, conversations and incidents, to discuss matters interesting to a predominantly middle class audience: manners, morals and aesthetics. The genre was popular in Germany in the second quarter of the eighteenth century, and Mendelssohn contributed to one such journal, *Der* [*sic*] *Chamäleon*, in the mid-1750s.[4]

The *Kohelet Mussar* consists of six sections or essays (in Hebrew: "gates") constituting two issues of a moral weekly in Hebrew, the only example of its kind. A number of Mendelssohn's friends in Berlin tried to establish journals in the 1750s; that he might try his hand at one is therefore not surprising.[5] Yet it is surprising that he tried to compose a moral weekly in Hebrew, since this was an innovation presenting significant obstacles.

The intimate, informal style of the moral weekly presupposed an ability to address readers in a direct colloquial prose. Although Hebrew had served continuously as the written language of the rabbinic and literary élite, it had not been a spoken language for many centuries and lacked the immediacy of everyday usage. Mendelssohn's strategy was to invent a colloquial Hebrew by exploiting the Bible as a repository of spoken language. His Hebrew prose was a pastiche of Biblical passages assembled through direct quotation, the recombination of quotations, and even reversals of meaning or context. In other words, he constructed sentences from prefabricated units of Biblical prose and verse. This pastiche style was to be used by most *Haskalah* prose authors until the end of the nineteenth century, and it contrasted sharply with the rhymed baroque prose of traditional Hebrew moralistic works of the eighteenth century.[6]

Such use of biblical quotation required virtuosity from the writer; it also made high demands on the reader. To understand, let alone fully appreciate, this creative borrowing one had to be thoroughly versed in the intricacies of the biblical books and their language. The audience was thus limited to cognoscenti such as Yeshiva students and scholars. Were there enough cognoscenti interested in a Hebrew moral weekly to sustain the *Kohelet Mussar*? Did Mendelssohn cease publication for lack of an audience?

---

[3] The claim has its origins in Euchel's *Toldot Rabeinu*. Gilon, p. 98, tries to support the claim with additional evidence.

[4] These contributions are reprinted in *Moses Mendelssohns Gesammelte Schriften. Jubiläumsausgabe*, vol. 2, Stuttgart 1972–, pp. 111–145. See Altmann, pp. 78–80. The standard study of the moral weekly is Wolfgang Martens, *Die Botschaft der Tugend: Die Aufklärung im Spiegel der deutschen Moralischen Wochenschriften*, Stuttgart 1968. The moral weekly was a German imitation of Joseph Addison's *Tatler* and Richard Steele's *Spectator*.

[5] Friedrich Nicolai and Gotthold Ephraim Lessing were both engaged with journals in the 1750s. See Gilon, p. 85.

[6] This sort of pastiche, sometimes referred to in Hebrew as *melitsah* (literally "florid" or "rhetorical"), remained the major form of Haskalah prose until the introduction of a style based on rabbinic or mishnaic Hebrew at the end of the nineteenth century, see Robert Alter, *The Invention of Hebrew Prose*, Seattle 1988. On the style of the eighteenth-century moralist works see Gilon, pp. 110–120.

The choice of subjects and the manner in which they were treated further limited the audience. The six sections addressed such related themes as the glories and order of God's creation and the vindication of providence (sections two, three and four); the nature of true pleasure and perfection (section four); as well as the beauties of the Hebrew language and the need to redress its recent neglect (sections two and six). With the exception of the last theme, these were the very ones that Mendelssohn discussed in his German works of the period.[7]

Mendelssohn treated the philosophical themes just as he had in his German writings: he derived the intellectual framework from Christian Wolff (1679–1754), the philosopher of the early German Enlightenment. Although Wolff is never mentioned in the *Kohelet Mussar*, Mendelssohn's unstated but unmistakable agenda was to show the congruence of Wolffian philosophy and Judaism. His method was to present an idea drawn from Wolff as if it were a dictum of sound reason and then support and illustrate it with passages from various Jewish sources such as the Bible, Talmud, Midrash, and philosophical treatises. Mendelssohn apparently thought that by introducing Wolffian concepts he could painlessly educate his readers in contemporary philosophy. His long-term aim was to revive the discipline of philosophy in Hebrew and with it to renew the study and use of the Hebrew language which, like the discipline of biblical exegesis, were on the margins of the curriculum of Central and Eastern European Jewry.

While Wolff goes unmentioned, a wide range of Hebrew texts – the Bible and biblical commentaries, Talmud and Midrash, philosophical and ethical works – is regularly cited and discussed. In this respect the *Kohelet Mussar* differed from German moral weeklies, which purveyed a sort of generic non-denominational Christianity or, in the idiom of the time, "natural religion": they at times discussed issues of Christian theology, but they never dealt directly with scripture or theological works.[8] In contrast, Mendelssohn presented a robust and textually rooted Judaism. Conspicuous among the philosophical and ethical texts Mendelssohn used were those of medieval Sephardic (Iberian) Jews, especially Maimonides and Jehudah Ha-Levi. To revive the tradition of philosophy in Hebrew it was imperative to bring these central works back into Jewish discourse.

With its optimistic themes and Wolffian approach, the *Kohelet Mussar* was clearly aligned with the moral weeklies and other Enlightenment literature. It stood apart from contemporary Hebrew moralistic works that focused on such dark themes as the fear of death and punishment, the power of Satan and the vanity of life.[9] The work was characteristic of the early *Haskalah* in aiming at intellectual renewal through the revival of neglected internal disciplines and engagement with the larger culture. Put differently, Mendelssohn used a current genre to fashion a Hebrew literature whose pious contents were consonant with contemporary philosophy. That Mendelssohn's effort was more pioneering than accomplished may be largely responsible for the work's obscurity. Yet the importance of the *Kohelet Mussar* should not be underestimated: some two decades after its publication the founders of the

---

[7]Gilon, pp. 55–74.
[8]Martens, pp. 170, 213–214.
[9]Gilon, pp. 120–139.

flagship journal of the *Haskalah, Hame'asef* (*The Gatherer*), looked to it as a model and point of departure.

THE TEXT AND ITS PUBLICATION HISTORY

The obscurity of the *Kohelet Mussar* is underscored by the paucity of original copies that have survived: there are only four extant copies of the first three sections, and only one extant copy of the last three sections. Sections one and three, and the latter half of section two, were reprinted in *Hame'asef* of 1785 (pp. 90–95, 103–105), and the same material was again reprinted in the early nineteenth-century maskilic journal *Bikkurei ha-Ittim* (1822, pp. 85–90, 96–98); the *Kohelet Mussar* appeared in its entirety in Issachar Edelstein's 'Ha-Hibbur Kohelet Mussar' and again a decade later in volume 14 of Mendelssohn's *Gesammelte Schriften* edited by Haim Borodianski (Bar-Dayan) with notes and textual emendations (Berlin 1938, pp. 1–21). It has also been reprinted as an appendix to Gilon's *Kohelet Mussar* (pp. 157–180); Gilon bases his text on photographic reproductions of the original, adding helpful annotations and some further emendations of his own.[10]

The selected translations presented below are, to the best of our knowledge, the first time large sections of this work have appeared in English. This English version is based on the virtually identical texts presented by Borodianski and Gilon, and has made judicious use of the emendations and annotations offered by both scholars. However, in a few instances, indicated here in the footnotes, the translation is based on further corrections of these Hebrew editions.

In general, the biblical citations in this translation are drawn from the Jewish Publication Society *Tanakh*, although they are often adapted or altered to capture the particular sense and tone intended by Mendelssohn. It should also be noted that Mendelssohn sometimes reversed the meaning of the biblical phrases he wove into his text; these are indicated in the translation with the abbreviation 'rev.' alongside the biblical citation.

SECONDARY LITERATURE

The most painstaking and authoritative study, unlikely to be superseded, is Gilon's *Kohelet Mussar*. Some of Gilon's conclusions, especially his insistence on the existence of a co-author alongside Mendelssohn and on the work's suppression by communal authorities, remain open to question. Alexander Altmann offers a judicious if brief account in his *Moses Mendelssohn* (pp. 83–91). Both Gilon and Altmann have addressed the conclusions of Jacob Toury, 'Die Anfänge des jüdischen Zeitungswesens in Deutschland', *Bulletin des Leo Baeck Instituts*, vol. 10, nos. 37–40 (1967), pp. 93–123, and Hermann M.Z. Meyer, 'Kohelet Mussar', *Bulletin des Leo Baeck Instituts*, vol. 11, nos. 41–44 (1967), pp. 48–65, regarding authorship,

---

[10]For both Edelstein and Gilon, see note 1.

dating, and publication. Finally, in his *Moses Mendelssohn and the Religious Enlightenment* (Berkeley 1996), pp. 15–18, David Sorkin sees the work as part of Mendelssohn's effort to revive the study of philosophy in Hebrew.

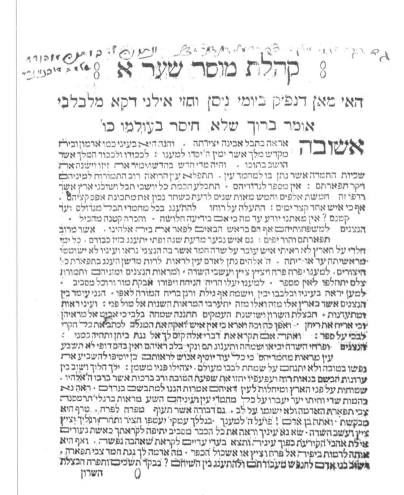

The first page of Moses Mendelssohn's *Kohelet Mussar*. This copy (preserved in the British Library) belonged to Salomon Dubno, who tutored Mendelssohn's son in Hebrew as well as participating in Mendelssohn's edition of the Hebrew Bible.

By courtesy of the British Library

KOHELET MUSSAR

SECTION TWO:

To ... greetings.[11]

I have clearly seen how our Jewish brethren have abandoned Hebrew[12] and I am *deeply grieved* [Jonah 4:9]. I do not know *how this evil happened* [Judges 20:3] *and what they experienced in this matter and what had happened to them* [Esth. 9:26], to fling to the ground *the proud crown of glorious beauty* [Isa. 28:1]. Is she not the finest of languages? The word of God that came through a vision to his prophets was in the Hebrew tongue,[13] and He conceived and shaped His world in this language. This is discussed in the fourth part of *Kuzari*, section 25, in his explication of *Sefer Yetzirah*, whose words I cite:[14] "The divine, created language (the *Kuzari* refers to Hebrew as "the created language" because it appeared at the very moment of God's creation of the world; other languages were human conventions that appeared after the dispersion [of the Tower of Babel])[15] that God taught man and placed in his heart and upon his tongue is without doubt the most complete of all languages and the most suitable to the objects they describe, as it is written: "And whatever the man called each living creature, that would be its name" [Gen. 2:19], meaning that each creature was worthy of its name, a name which was appropriate to it and indicative of its nature (that is, even though other languages assigned names to all objects, these nouns are no more appropriate to their nature than any other noun; this is not true with regard to Hebrew, in which the designation of nouns is appropriate to the nature of things). This demonstrates the superiority and advantage of Hebrew", etc., until "And it is said (in *Sefer Yetzirah*) with regard to writing".[16]

This *should not remain as it is* [Ez. 21:31] for we are obligated to learn Hebrew, as we see in Maimonides' statement in his commentary to *Pirkei Avot* II:1: "And afterwards the Mishnah stated that one must heed a *mitzvah* that appears to be less weighty – such as rejoicing on the festivals and learning Hebrew – as a *mitzvah* whose weightiness is clear."[17] Despite this, I set off in all directions and there is no one

---

[11]This entire section, including the essay entitled 'Everything that God does Is for the Good', is presented as a fictitious letter, a common eighteenth-century literary device.

[12]Mendelssohn consistently uses the prevalent rabbinic and medieval idiom *leshon ha-kodesh* (lit: the holy language) to refer to Hebrew.

[13]The term used here is the less common and post-rabbinic *leshon ever*.

[14]The *Kuzari* is a medieval philosophical classic written by the twelfth-century Spanish poet Judah ha-Levi; it appears to have garnered renewed scholarly interest in the eighteenth century. *Sefer Yetzirah* was probably composed between the third and sixth centuries and is a cosmological-mystical work that posits the letters of the Hebrew alphabet as the foundation of all creation.

[15]This awkwardly inserted parenthetical comment is Mendelssohn's own.

[16]Mendelssohn here skips a line of the *Kuzari* and concludes his citation with a reference to the *Kuzari*'s (and *Sefer Yetzirah*'s) subsequent discussion of the written alphabet.

[17]Maimonides (c. 1135–1204) was one of the most important and influential medieval rabbinic authorities, his legal, ethical, and popular writings occupying a central place in traditional Jewish learning. His first major work was an Arabic-language commentary to the Mishnah, including an extensive treatment of *Pirkei Avot* and its ethical teachings. His comment here is occasioned by the rabbinic exhortation that "one should heed a less-weighty *mitzvah* as much as a weighty one". Mendelssohn was obviously attracted by this comment because of its implied suggestion that the neglect of Hebrew was a long-standing problem that the Mishnah itself – at least in Maimonides' reading – was attempting to rectify.

endeavouring *to restore* the language *to its post as it formerly was* [Gen. 40:13]. Some may [explain this by] say[ing]: "with the four winds of heaven *the Lord has scattered us* [Lam. 4:16] in the lands of the nations who have not heard our language, and like slaves in the house of their masters we have learnt their language and have forgotten our own". This reply *should be dispersed as chaff is dispersed before* eastern *winds in the hills* [Ps. 68:3 and Isa. 17:13]; after all, despite the fact that our forefathers were *sold as slaves and maidservants* in Egypt [Esth. 7:4], they did not forget their language, as indicated in the passage of *Mekhilta* to Exodus.[18]

There are also those who *turned their head to bronze* [Isa. 48:4] and *look to the holy one of Israel* [Isa. 17:7], that being R. Solomon in his commentary to the rabbinic dictum (Babylonian Talmud, *Berakhot* 28b), "Restrain your children from *higayon*"[19], in which he explains that this [dictum] refers to the study of Scripture. Behold *they have made false-hood their refuge and taken shelter in treachery* [Isa. 28:15]. Aside from the fact that *they besmeared their eyes from seeing*, the explanation of Maimonides [Isa. 44:18], who suggest-ed that *higayon* was the study of logical demonstration and dialectics,[20] they also *mud-dled their vision and conceived lies* [Isa. 28:7 and 59:13] with regard to the words of Rashi. For his opinion was that we should not waste all our time in the study of Scripture and the Masorah,[21] like those men who delight in finding one letter or vowel-point never imagined by earlier scholars,[22] as he himself wrote: "do not be overly preoccupied with Scripture". It is better for us to study the [text of the] Torah transmitted to our sages, for this is our life and length of days. But to diminish the study of the language – far

---

[18]This oft-cited passage appears in the *Mekhilta, parashat bo*, section 5, as a commentary to Ex. 12: 6, "and you shall keep watch over [the lamb] [*ve-hayah lahem le-mishmeret*]" where the sages suggest a broader read-ing of what the Israelites preserved, or alternately, what virtues had preserved their national distinctive-ness: "R. Eliezer ha-Kappar Beribbi says: [The] Israelites [enslaved in Egypt] were in possession of four *mitzvot* more valuable than anything else in the world: they were above all suspicion with regard to sex-ual impropriety and with regard to tale-bearing; they did not change their names; and they did not change their language."

[19]R. Solomon b. Isaac (1040–1105), commonly known by his acronym Rashi, was the outstanding Ashkenazic commentator to Scripture and the Babylonian Talmud. The historical and scholarly ques-tion regarding this dictum was how to interpret *higayon* and by extension the basic intent of the Talmudic passage. Rashi famously explained the dictum as follows: "Do not allow [your children] to be overly pre-occupied with Scripture because it entices; another interpretation: [restrain them] from the prattle of children". This passage was also discussed in Mendelssohn's *Be'ur Millot ha-Higayon*; see *Moses Mendelssohns Gesammelte Schriften. Jubiläumsausgabe*, vol. 14, p. 27.

[20]While it is not clear that Maimonides had explicitly defined *higayon* in this manner, by the early eleventh century Jewish scholars living in Muslim lands had begun to use the word *higayon* to denote the Arabic word *mantiq*, usually understood as the science of logic. The most important Hebrew translators, mem-bers of the Ibn Tibbon family, consistently made this identification, and Maimonides' treatise on logi-cal terms appeared in its medieval Hebrew translation as *Millot ha-Higayon*. That Maimonidean text, in fact, served as the basis for some of Mendelssohn's earliest philosophical writings in Hebrew.

[21]The Masorah is a compilation of highly technical annotations from the early medieval period that sought to establish an accurate and authoritative text of the Hebrew Bible, including its vocalisation.

[22]Mendelssohn here seems to have understood *higayon* to be related to the Hebrew noun *hagahah*, i.e. anno-tation, such that he reads Rashi's interpretation as "do not allow your children to be overly preoccupied with textual annotations". His dismissive comment regarding "men who delight in finding one letter or vowel point never imagined by earlier generations" is a reference to modern Bible scholars, among them his German contemporaries, who pointed to the textual corruptions marking the traditional versions of the Hebrew Bible and were increasingly committed to scholarly-textual emendations. Mendelssohn's concern with biblical criticism of this sort is most evident in the introduction to his edition of the Bible, which appeared between 1780 and 1783.

be it from a saintly individual [i.e. Rashi] to have intended such a thing! On the contrary, [the study of Hebrew] is a *mitzvah*, and Rashi himself provides testimony and vindicates my point in his commentary to Deuteronomy 11:19, "[...and teach (these words) to your children], reciting them", to which he wrote: "From here our sages learn[23] that when an infant begins to speak, his father begins to speak with him in Hebrew and to teach him Torah; if he has neglected to do this, it is as if he has buried him."

Let us learn from the other nations, each with their own national language; they neither rested nor reposed until they fully developed their language. Why should we *lie sprawling* [Isa. 56:10] and not emulate their deeds with our own language, which is the finest and most ancient in time?

Behold, my beloved brother, from the day I first knew you I understood that you too were grieved at the abandonment of our language. About a month ago, when I was rejoicing with you in affection and we spoke about this matter, you suggested a *cure for this malady* [Hos. 5:13], to publish *the words of the wise and their riddles* [Prov. 1:6], *words upon words, some here, some there* [Isa. 28:10], words written with refined language so that it might please their readers. And Hebrews[24] *will look up and see* [Isa. 42:18] that our language can be employed on all occasions, giving voice to misery, *to sing soulful songs that rejoice to exultation* [Prov. 25:20 and Job. 3:22] or to admonish *evildoers at the gate* [Isa. 29:21]; *they will accept rebuke* [rev. Jer 2:30] and *speak* Hebrew *as a familiar language* [Jer. 23:31].

And now, my brother, *my hand is constantly with you and my arm will strengthen you* [Ps. 89:22]. Here are some refined words prepared on the *mitzvah* of trusting in God, which I have written down for reasons known to you; it is up to you to decide whether to *distribute them to Jacob and scatter them in Israel* [Gen. 49:7], or to consign them *to a devouring fire* [Isa. 9:4].

May the favour of the Lord our God be upon us; let the work of our hands prosper [Ps. 90:17]. May our words be acceptable to those who understand speech [Isa. 3:3] and may they join with us. Peace unto you [I Sam. 25:6].

EVERYTHING THAT GOD DOES IS FOR THE GOOD[25]

I observed that all living beings under the sun, the good and the pure, the foolish and the ignorant, can look to the Lord our God [Ecc. 4:7, 9:2, 9:4 and Ps. 49:11]. *They can be pleased with*

---

[23]The reference is to *Sifre* to Deuteronomy, *piska* 46.

[24]The text here has העברים (ve-ha-'ibrim: and the Hebrews), which is a homonymic play on the verse in Isaiah upon which Mendelssohn drew, הביטו לראות [ve-ha-'ivrim] העורים, "You blind ones, look up and see."

[25]Babylonian Talmud, *Berakhot* 60b. The full passage reads as follows: "A person should always accustom himself to say 'Everything that God does is for the good'. This is like the story of R. Akiba who was once travelling, and upon reaching a certain town, made inquiries in search of lodgings. He was refused, and declared: 'Everything that God does is good'. He went to sleep in an open field, and had with him a rooster, a donkey, and a lamp. The lamp was extinguished by a gust of wind, a wild cat came and ate the rooster, and a lion ate the donkey. R. Akiba declared: 'Everything that God does is good'. That very night a group of bandits took the residents of the town captive, and R. Akiba said to them: 'Did I not say to you that everything that God does is for the good?'" Rashi explains that the lamp and the animals belonging to R. Akiba would have attracted the attention of the bandits and resulted in his captivity; their loss ultimately saved him.

their own talk, selah,[26] [Ps. 49:14] [saying] all together: "*in God I will trust … what can a man do to me?* [Ps. 56:12]". I will explain that *as they grew proud, they sinned* in this fundamental principle [Hos. 4:7], and that *the wise is superior to the fool as the sun's brightness in the heavens* is superior *to a gloom with no dawn* [Ecc. 2:13, Job 37:21 and Isa. 8:22]. For the common man *will place his confidence in God* [Ps. 78:7] so that *he will become rich and that his wealth will endure* [rev. Job 15:29], and that he may have much *silver and gold … and the luxuries of commoners* [Ecc. 2:8], and that he may see *his children endure* and his *offspring plentiful enough for nations* [Job 21:8 and Gen. 48:19]. However, *if something were to try him* [Job 4:2] – *if thieves who plunder in the night were to come upon him* [Obad. 1:5] and *strip the mantle off the cloak* [Mic. 2:8]; or if a man, to whom he lent silver and gold, went to another land without repaying him; or if his ships raised their ensign in the Sea of Tarshish and God sent a stormy wind and *wrecked the ship* [Ps. 48:8], and all that was upon it *was overtaken by mighty rushing waters* [rev. Ps. 32:6]; *if the wrath of a lord flared against him to practice deeds of wickedness,* [Ecc. 4:10 and Ps. 141:4] *to lay his hands on all that was dear to him* [Lam. 1:10] whether ox or sheep – he will take it all away, *and put him at the bottom of a pit chained in bronze fetters* [Ps. 88:7 and II Kings 25:7]; when *death will climb through his windows* [Jer. 9:20] and *slay those who were dear to his eyes* [Lam. 2:4] – his son and daughter, brother and sister, *wife of his bosom or his closest friend* [Deut. 13:7].

Then *the fool sits desolate and folds his hands together* [Ecc. 4:5 and Ezra 9:4]; *he feels the pain of his flesh* [Job 14:22], *grumbling in his tent* [Deut. 1:27] "why did God do this to me? In vain *I put my confidence in Him* [Ps. 78:7], and my trust for naught. God cast a jealous eye on me, *poised His right hand like a foe* [Lam. 2:4] to destroy me."

The sweet light for those who behold the sun was darkened into night [Ecc. 11:7 and Amos 5:8]; the sadness of his heart felled him before his time, *and he went down to Sheol, head covered in mourning* [Gen. 37:35 and Esth. 6:12]. *Like a deaf viper* the fool *stops his ears; he will not listen to the voice of the wise who comes to contend with him* [Ps. 58:5–6 and Prov. 29:9]. For all of God's deeds are with us; He did not reject us. His ways are not like this, *to despise the toil of His hands* [Job 10:3] which He so magnificently fashioned. His only portion is in His world, and *He made everything for a purpose* [Prov. 16:4] – *how did all this become his enemy* [Isa. 63:10]?

It is not so. Rather, all of God's deeds are for our good and to sustain us. Either *sorrow and sighing will quickly flee* [Joel 4:4 and Isa. 35:10], *and relief and deliverance will come* from them [Esth. 4:14]; or through [these tribulations] one is delivered from far worse troubles. But *the fool* quickly *vents his rage and tests*[27] *the Holy One of Israel* [Prov. 29:11 and Ps. 78:41]. He says: "*By God who has deprived me of justice, to wrong me in his cause* [Job 27:2 and Lam. 3:36]; *surely His arm is not unable* [Job 24:25 and Isa. 50:2] to increase His goodness or to save me from the storm of troubles, and not to punish me with even greater afflictions."

My friends, *move away from the tent* of this fool [Num. 16:26], and do not *perish for his iniquity* [Jer. 51:6]. For he urges disloyalty against the Lord [Deut. 13:6] and has attributed[28]

---

[26]The Hebrew word *selah*, which appears at the end of a few dozen biblical verses (almost all in the book of Psalms), is of uncertain meaning; it may have served a liturgical or musical function.

[27]The meaning of the Hebrew יתור, adapting the biblical התור, is unclear.

[28]The text here has ויחפה, while the word that appears in II Kings [17:9] is ויחפאו, from the root חפא. Mendelssohn transposed חפא to חפה, meaning to concoct or fabricate, here taken to mean that the fool falsely attributes certain things to God.

to Him things that are not so [II Kings 17:9]. Turn your eyes towards the house of
Ahituv[29] our friend, and see how *the Lord singles out the faithful for Himself* [Ps. 4:4], how
He will *inflict extraordinary troubles upon him, smiting him with unceasing blows* [Deut. 28:59
and Isa. 14:6]. *A sword has passed through his land* [Ez. 14:17] and the [enemy] has laid
siege to the city and has taken it with a show of strength. *They entered the city, every man
heading straight to take its spoil and seize its booty* [Josh. 6:20 and Isa. 10:6], and *participants
of the military campaign, men oppressed by guilt blood* [Num. 31:14 and Prov. 28:17] came
even to his home. *Their swords were sharpened for slaughter* [Ez. 21:20] and they took all
his wealth and possessions by force, *taking even the bed from under him and stripping him of
his tunic* [Prov. 22:27 and Gen. 37:23]. His *beloved and cherished* children [I Sam. 1:23],
their appearance like sapphire [Lam. 4:7] were also *carried off in fish baskets* [Amos 4:2] into
another land, *sold there as slaves and miscreants* [Esth. 7:4] *and ruled over by their oppressors*
[Isa. 14:2]. His wife, *a loving doe and a woman of grace, wallowed in her blood* at his feet
[Prov. 5:19 and Ez. 16:6]. Because she did not want to abrogate the covenant she had
made with him in her youth, *she preferred strangulation, death to her wasted frame* [Job 7:15].
All this came upon him and still he keeps his integrity [Ps. 44:18 and Job 2:3]. He says: "*The
lines have fallen for me in pleasant places* [Ps. 16:6] and *I greatly rejoice in the Lord* [Isa. 61:10];
these blows are the blows of my friend [Zech. 13:6], from His desire to be generous with
me *to renew my youth like that of an eagle* [Ps. 103:5] or to save me from far worse evils
in the *pit of destruction* [Isa. 38:17]. This one can be properly called one who trusts in
God, and regarding him the prophets of Israel prophesied: *Happy is he who trusts in the
Lord* [Prov. 16:20].

   And lest you say to yourselves that *this man's heart is cast as hard as stone* [Job 41:16]
such that he would not complain about the loss of his friends; and that *his flesh is
bronze* [Job 6:12], that he would not weaken *to encourage the one who pounds the anvil* [Isa.
41:7]. Do not *allow your mouths to bring you into disfavour* [Ecc. 5:5] with regard to this
man. *For who feels* these wounds *but he* [Ecc. 2:25]. From the time *he sat on his mother's
knees* [Job 3:12] until the time that God's hand fell upon him, *his foot was so tender and
dainty that he never ventured to set it on the ground* [Deut. 28:56]. To the members of his
family *he showed pity and compassion* [rev. Ez. 7:4] *and provided for all who were failing* [II
Chron. 28:15]; *whoever touched them touched the pupil of his eye* [Zech. 2:12]. How, in one
moment, could *he turn into a cruel individual* [Job 30:21], *shutting his eyes from seeing and
his ears from hearing* their outcry [Isa. 33:15 and 59:1]? By God! *The sound of their wailing penetrated his inmost parts* [Zech. 11:3 and Prov. 18:8] and *out of his love and pity* for
them [Isa. 63:9], he would *give himself as ransom* for them [Ex. 30:12], if this is what
his adversaries desired.

   From his youth he was nourished by Torah and wisdom and he understood books
and *good sense* [Neh. 8:8]. He probed and understood that *the Lord is gracious and compassionate* [Ps. 111:4] and does good for all living things, *in accordance with* the individual's
ability [Lev. 14:22] to receive the abundance of His goodness. For that which perfects
us and our circumstances should be considered good, and conversely, the bad is that

---

[29]Although the name Ahituv appears in the book of Samuel and elsewhere, Mendelssohn has borrowed
   the name – which invokes both brotherhood (ahi) and the good (tuv) – and invented a character to represent those who truly understand God's goodness in the world.

which is a deficiency in ourselves and our circumstances.[30] We should know that God *cares for the work of His hands* [Job 14:15] as the Psalmist stated "May the Lord rejoice in His works" [Ps. 104:31], and from the rejoicing comes love; and that God's knowledge encompasses every occurrence[31] *and that which befalls* all things [Ecc. 9:11]. As such, one who ascribes miserliness to God – that He would be loath to grant His beloved creation *sufficient sustenance* [Deut. 15:8] – defames Him.

After I have told you all this, you should know *that God loves graciousness* to benefit His creatures [Mic. 7:18]. How can we delude ourselves *to defy the Lord of Hosts* [I Sam. 17:45] to think evil thoughts *to make Him our enemy* [Isa. 63:10]? *It must be bad thoughts* [Neh. 2:2] . Instead, *we should put our confidence in Him* [Ps. 78:7], *for He attacked and He can heal, He wounded and He can bind us up* [Hos. 6:1]. The evils will be the cause and means of bringing us the good.

And with regard to people saying "*Is His arm, then, unable to rescue* and not cause us pain?", [Ecc. 3:18 and Isa. 50:2] *say to them thus* [Jer. 10:11]: Should he *dislodge rocks from their place* on your behalf [Job 18:4]? *Who has stood in the council of God* [Jer. 23:18] and will reveal what is good for us? Are not *actions measured by God* alone [I Sam. 2:3]? *For He knows the way we take* [Job 23:10], that which He will bestow upon us at the end of our days.

Many statements of our sages support these ideas, and the following are the ones that, in my haste, I saw fit to put on paper. One statement is in the Babylonian Talmud, *Baba Kamma* 38a. "The daughter of R. Samuel b. Judah died, [and the rabbis said to Ulla: 'Let us go to console him.'] Ulla responded to them: 'I will have nothing to do with the consolation offered by Babylonians – it is blasphemous, since [in consolation] one says "what can one do?" but if something could have been done, it would have been done.'" Ulla understood that they would think that the evil inflicted upon us by God was an absolute evil, and *then this would be their consolation: who can contend with He who is stronger than himself?* [Job 6:10 and Ecc. 6:10]. In his eyes, the words of those offering consolation were inappropriate, and he considered them a blasphemy against the goodness of God. Ulla then went by himself *to console and comfort him* [Job 2:11], and he ended his words by saying:[32] "If our teacher's [that is R. Samuel's] daughter was worthy of producing good offspring, she would surely have lived." Ulla was explaining that God knows *the children who will follow after* his daughter [Deut. 29:21] – that *they will spurn the Lord and turn aside to shamefulness* [Num. 16:30 and Hos. 9:10] and would be an eternal disgrace for R. Samuel. Therefore God

---

[30]Wolffian ideas are introduced here as if they were the dictates of sound reason. Despite the loss of his family and possessions through a set of horrific Job-like (or Candide-like) experiences, Ahitov is rendered more spiritually perfect through his deepened trust in God. That increased perfection coincides with Wolff's definition of good and evil: "Whatever makes us and our condition more perfect is good; whatever makes us and our condition less perfect is evil." See *Vernünftige Gedanken über Gott, die Welt und die Seele des Menschen*, Frankfurt and Leipzig 1729, par. 426. In the same spirit, Wolff justifies adversity as a divine dispensation and a means to improve our well-being: "He [God] uses it as a means to beneficial ends" (par. 1060) and "God [allows] adversity [to come] as a means to promote our welfare" (par. 1064).

[31]This phrase, which might also be translated as "God's knowledge encompasses every accident", is used in medieval Jewish philosophical writings to suggest that God knows not only the essence of things, but their particular manifestation in time and space.

[32]Mendelssohn has skipped over a few lines of the Talmud to cite the conclusion of Ulla's remarks.

ended her life, since death with honour is preferable to life with disgrace. The reason for her death was to save her and the house of her father from a worse fate.

I will also point you to an even more striking passage in the Midrash: "And God saw all that He had made, and found it very good [Gen. 1:31]" – this is death.[33] Our sages, who have wisdom for an inheritance, taught that it is only due to our deficient understanding that we consider death the most bitter of evils. In truth, *it is a gift of God* [Ecc. 3:13], *for our good* [Deut. 6:24].

(The rest of the letter sent by my friend is in my possession, and I will publish it shortly.)

SECTION THREE:

A PERSON IS OBLIGATED TO ACCEPT THE BAD JUST AS HE ACCEPTS THE GOOD[34]

The *hardships that befall* mankind [Ex. 18:8] can be *divided into four parts* [Gen. 2:10]. Among them are (1) those [hardships] consequent to nature that happen to us *since we too are flesh, nipped from clay* [Gen. 6:3 and Job 33:6] and subject to generation and decay,[35] (2); those [hardships] whose roots lie in our choice of immoral conduct. Were it not for *the foolish thing that we did* [Gen. 31:28], and were it not *for substituting bad for good, or good for bad* [Lev. 27:10], these evils would not afflict us. (3) A third type are those evils that affect a man of God, *blameless and upright and shunning evil* [Job 1:1] when he is harassed by rebellious men who *ambush him for his blood* [Prov. 1:18]. (4) One cannot exclude from these [categories] words of *strife and contention* [Isa. 58:4] that cannot be escaped, for those living around us have different opinions, *one says thus and another says thus* [I Kings 22:20], all due to differing temperaments and moral qualities.

One of our divine *mitzvot* is that *we bend our shoulder to bear* [Gen. 49:15] the yoke of misfortunes that come to pass, *and wait patiently for His salvation* [Ecc. 3:26]. And if a person complains about the evil that has befallen him, his complaint is really against God and His providence. Aside from that fact that it is a sin, and highly rebellious, would it not be *good and pleasant for a man to bear a yoke* [Ps. 133:1 and Lam. 3:27] that was placed upon him and *not to sin with his lips* [Job 2:10]? It would make the burden [of misfortunes] lighter upon us and not too heavy to bear. The bitterness of *the cup of wrath* [Isa. 51:17] will be sweetened and *we will not be disgusted with our lives* [Gen. 27:46].

The natural hardships were affixed by the Lord God with a *strong bond* [II Sam. 15:12] that will not be removed with human endeavour and *their comings and goings*

---

[33]The source referred to here is Midrash *Rabbah* to Genesis, ch. 9 section 5, which reads: "In the Torah of Rabbi Meir they saw it written 'and found it very good [*ve-hineh tob me'od*]' – and found death good [*ve-hineh tob mavet*]".

[34]*Mishnah Berakhot* 9:5. I have translated the phrase in the sense in which it is understood in the Babylonian Talmud, *Berakhot* 60b, and by Mendelssohn's discussion that follows.

[35]This category closely follows the first of Maimonides' three categories of evil in the *Guide for the Perplexed*, III:12: "The first type of evil is that which befalls man because of the nature of generation and decay … because of his being endowed with matter."

[Ez. 43:11]. And if your complaints are with regard to these, *let us clarify the matter* [Isa. 1:18]! Surely you will admit that they are small in number. Stand and bear witness against me! Why will you speak against my God? Why *have you gone through all this trouble* [II Kings 4:13]? You bear witness to the weakness of *those who suckle at the breast, and the pain of their birth* [Joel 2:16 and Gen. 3:16]; the grief for the death of *men who were my friends* [Jer. 38:22], and *my strength that fails me in my hoary old age* [Ps. 38:11 and 71:18]; *my vigour that was destroyed* [Daniel 10:8], and this death that will be *my troubler* [Judg. 11:35]. For the other *evils that befall you* [Deut. 31:17] in your lifetime are either [due to] the imagined loss of the vanities of possessions,[36] or they are of the kind that reached you due to your foolishness and evil deeds – *this is what you have done* to yourself [Malachi 1:9]. This is also true with regard to *all sickness and all disease* that cause you pain [Deut. 7:15]; for the most part, *you have diminished your own strength* [Ps. 31:11], if also you have acted foolishly and did not pay attention to guard *your feet from stumbling* [Ps. 56:14]. Or perhaps *your arrogant heart has seduced you to swell your bones* [Obad. 1:3 and Prov. 15:30]; you went after the vain *luxuries of commoners*, and these *only for gain* [Ecc. 2:8 and Prov. 21:5]. *They wore away your flesh and skin; they shattered your bones* [Ecc. 3:4].

I have observed and taken to heart [Ecc. 8:9] that from all the hardships *whose names have passed your lips* [Ps. 16:4], there is none as *bad and bitter* [Jer. 2:19] as our death and that of *our kinsmen* [Obad. 1:7]. For these are *lashed tight and imposed upon our necks* [Lam. 1:14], *and even the most stout-hearted warrior will be flattened under their burden* [Amos 2:16 and Ex. 23:5]. Surely it will be easier for us to bear the weight of other evils that you mention, and even *a hollow man should not be dismayed by their noise* [Job 11:12 and Isa. 31:4].

It has been many years, and I have forgotten the *hardships that befell me* [Ex. 18:8] when I was young and had my mother's kind-heartedness. *No matter* [II Sam. 18:22]; why should I continue to speak about incidents pertaining to children? After all, *they lack discernment* [Deut. 32:28] and do not act with wisdom. *What can we gain or profit in searching the bundle* [Ps. 120:3 and Gen. 44:12] of endurance, if a person bears his yoke *before he learns to call his father and mother* [Isa. 8:4]? *Who will give a young child knowledge and foresight* [Prov. 1:4]? Desire alone rules him and soothes all his activities, from the least to the greatest.

No, A….[37] the hyena alone raised its hand to smite its nursemaid while still at the breast. However, *he and none like him* [Isa. 48:8] truly regretted that deed; *and he shall confess to that which he sinned* [Lev. 5:5]. *Only the simple will enter here* to do *as the fool with his nonsense* [Prov. 9:4 and 17:12].

The pangs and throes of a woman sitting on the birth stool *are beyond me* [Prov. 30:18 and Isa. 13:8]. I will never know how heavily the pain weighs upon her. But I would suggest that it is not too heavy to bear, in that I have seen widows, *forlorn and forsaken*[38]

---

[36]That is, people regard the loss of possessions, whose value is largely imagined, as an evil. The phrase here, *azivat hevlei ha-kinyanim ha-medumim*, is awkward and particularly difficult to translate. Mendelssohn would appear to have in mind Maimonides' reference in the *Guide of the Perplexed*, III:54, to the pleasure taken in the perfection of possessions – the lowest of the perfections – as purely imaginary.

[37]This is again a fictive device, as if the essay were addressed to someone in particular; the device is carried forward below with the use of the second person.

[38]Although the text reads עזובה ועצורה, the verse alluded to and the plain sense of Mendelssohn's words would indicate that the phrase should be עזובה ועצובה.

[Isa. 54:6], *remove their widow's garb and marry another man* [Gen. 38:14 and Deut. 29:7].
Or *beasts of the field and wild beasts born to their kind* [Joel 2:22, Gen. 1:24, and Num.
1:18]; *there is none to disturb him with all this trouble* [Lev. 26:6 and II Kings 4:13].

I reflected upon a man of hoary old age, and I have not found all these evils of
which you spoke. For as long as his strength diminishes and weakness prevails over
him; so *the caper bush will bud again* [Ecc. 12:5] and he will no longer continue to feel
his pains. Except for this, his life *will be pleasing to him* [Ps. 104:34] when he sees that *he
has long remained on the earth* [Deut. 4:40], even against *his diseases that the Lord has inflicted
upon him* [Deut. 29:21]. A person *in ripe old age* [Gen. 35:29] will not sigh except in facing death, and the sound of death that knocks at his door terrifies him more than a
younger man. However, if I have lost a beloved friend or brother, a father or son or
the wife of my bosom [Deut. 13:7], *I am distressed by what has happened* to me [Ecc. 2:17].
The hand of the Lord struck me [Deut. 2:15] and wounded my heart; *the tender and dainty*
in me [Deut. 28:56] has been severed. Were I incapable of being *strong and steadfast*
[Deut. 31:6] in the face of this misfortune, it would be almost too heavy to bear.

While *healing will come to the bruises and welts* of a strong and *healthy body* [Neh. 4:1,
Isa. 1:6 and Ps. 73:4], if the disease affects a downtrodden and suffering body, there
is no cure. This is true also with regard to psychological wounds. A strong individual
has self control [Prov. 16:32]; he will be steadfast and *hold his head high* [Ps. 110:7] in the
face of these troubles. *Seven times the righteous man falls and gets up* [Prov. 24:16]. *Like a
reed that sways in water to and fro* [I Kings 14:15 and 2:42], it will bend its head in the
face of *the sweeping wind and the tempest* until it passes [Ps. 55:9]. *All the sea-breakers and
billows will sweep over her* [Ps. 42:8]; and afterwards, she will rise and *stand like a wall*
[Ex. 15:8]. Not so *those devoid of sense* [Prov. 9:4], for they have reeled like *chaff dispersed by the wind* [Isa. 17:13]. *They melted on account of the evil* that has befallen them –
they shall fall and rise no more [Ps. 73:8 and Isa. 24:20].

What shall a man complain about [Lam. 3:39], and what will he protest with regard to
God, because He has taken *the wife of your bosom* [Deut. 13:7]. And you, when you *gave
your love to her* [Song 7:13], did you not know that she would surely die? God gave you
the light of your eyes, and God has taken away [Ez. 24:16]. *Lift up your hands to him and praise
the Lord for His steadfast love* [Lam. 2:19 and Ps. 107:8] for the days that *He granted you
the desire of your heart* [Ps. 21:3]. She was on loan to you from the Lord your God, and
now *her days have concluded* [II Sam. 7:12]; *the creditor is coming to collect,* and why *do you
have regrets in paying your debt* [I Kings 4:1, 7 and Deut. 15:10]?

Your heart moans [Jer. 48:36]: *who foretold from the start that her end is near* [Isa. 41:26
and Lam. 4:18]? Who believed that she would be taken from me in so short
a time?

Why did you not believe it? *Who foretold from the start* [Isa. 41:26] that you would
have many days *without invasion and without wailing* [Ps. 144:14]? Go and consider all
the good *that the Lord your God has wrought for you all along until this day* [Isa. 63:7 and
Num. 22:30], as against this evil. *Survey the course of your ways* [Prov. 4:26], the good
and the bad that you have done, and afterwards *bring charges* [Jer. 4:12] against the
Lord your God.

If, conversely, *the Lord has fulfilled your wishes* [Ps. 20:6], and *you went down with those
who go down to the grave* [Ez. 26:20], while she is still alive. Have your complaints
been removed? What more do you have to wail about? Beyond either of these two

possibilities,[39] what will you seek? For if you asked the Lord your God *to take both your lives on the same day* [Gen. 27:45] – by God, *you have not asked for this wisely* [Ecc. 7:10].

SECTION FOUR:

On a recent day, when I came home to do my work [Ps. 90:4 and Gen. 39:11], I found this letter on my doorstep, and now I will set it before you. *He has pronounced his verdict himself* [I Kings 20:40]. If only he had not kept his name from me, for now I have responded to him, as *your eyes will behold* [Ps. 17:2].

Here is the text of the letter:

To you, the *rod of discipline* [Prov. 22:15],[40] greetings.

How is it, my brother, that you have gone out today *to reprove your kinsman* [Lev. 19:17]? Will not *everyone who hears laugh at you* [Gen. 21:6]? Are we lacking admonishers? Those who go *in all directions, from town to town, province to province* [Ez. 40:5, II Chron. 30:10 and Esth. 9:28] *bitterly shrieking "Turn back, rebellious children"* [Zeph. 1:14 and Jer. 3:14]! We heard all this, but *we have not accepted correction* [Jer. 2:30]. *How did the spirit come to deceive you* [II Chron. 18:23 and II Sam. 3:25] that we should listen to your dreams and words? You wrote:[41] "And you,[42] if you will read these words; get up and go to *the palace garden* [Esth. 7:7]." *The mouth of the righteous utters wisdom* [Ps. 37:30]! See that I will not disobey you. I too *will betake myself* towards evening *to the mount of myrrh and to the hill of frankincense* [Song 4:6]. *You are a mighty prince among us! I will not withhold myself from complying with your request* [Gen. 23:6 and I Sam. 22:14]. *But may my lord*[43] *pardon your servant's iniquity in this: there will be no glory for me* to be like you [II Kings 2:18 and Judg. 4:9]. *I will not browse in the gardens parched with thirst* [Song 6:2 and Isa. 5:13]; *and I will not play over* an ant's hole [rev. Isa. 11:8] in order to search intensely after the consequence of things. But this has long been my way: *before the shadows of evening grow long* [Jer. 6:4], *a group of my friends* [Gen. 26:26][44] gathered *to the place we had chosen* [Deut. 12:5][45] the day before yesterday. And since we had long sur-

---

[39]That is, either you will predecease your spouse, or your spouse will predecease you.

[40]This appellation may have been doubly sarcastic, portraying the author of *Kohelet Mussar* as stern and abstemious, while also identifying him with the old-worldly piety of a moralistic tract of the same name, R. Elijah b. Solomon Abraham ha-Kohen's *Shevet Mussar*, Constantinople 1712.

[41]The reference is to the first section of *Kohelet Mussar*.

[42]In the original passage in the first section being cited, the extant texts have ואתה, "and you". In the one extant text of this section, the line here reads ועתה, "and now". Although both readings are plausible, the reading "and you" makes more sense in section one, and as such, I have assumed a typographical error here and emended the translation accordingly.

[43]The satirical intent of this imagined letter is readily captured in the textual substitution taking place here. The original biblical verse reads "may the Lord pardon your servant"; in replacing the reference to God with "my lord", the fictitious author mocks the pious and solemn tone of the biblical texts. The substitution is underscored in its Hebrew vocalisation, since it shifts the word reserved exclusively for God (*adonai*), traditionally uttered whenever the tetragammaton appears, to the formal appellation for a person (*adoni*).

[44]The translation draws upon the distinctly Ashkenazic interpretation of the biblical phrase אחזת מרעהו, which is otherwise read as "Ahuzzath his counsellor".

[45]The text is here displaying a witty irreverence, since all the permutations of the biblical phrase that is being employed, אל המקום אשר ב–ח–ר, "to the place that was/will be chosen", refer to God's designation of a sanctuary for worship.

veyed all the trees of the garden and their blossoms, no one among us *turns aside to see this sight* [Ex. 3:3][46] that he has seen *time and again* [Gen. 31:7]. *Let us by all means go up* [Num. 14:30], each man straightaway, to the place where the wine is to be found. *And what good is merriment* [Ecc. 2:2]; is it not that *wine cheers the hearts of men* [Ps. 104:15]? Then *we will treat ourselves to merriment* [Ecc. 2:1] until *our bellies are filled like a steaming water-skin* [Job 20:23 and 41:12]; *we will not be able to stop* [Jer. 36:5]. *We will dig with force and run with vigour* [Job 39:21], *we will yell and roar aloud* [Isa. 42:13] *and the earth will be split open by our uproar* [I Kings 1:40]. *It is not the sound of the tune of triumph, nor the sound of the tune of defeat* [Ex. 32:18] *but the loud sounds of gaiety and being merry with wine* [Jer. 8:16 and Esth. 1:10] to know *that they drank the deep drink of love* [Song 5:1].

A month ago I was sitting among my friends, happy and content, and *the seat* of A..., the chief of *wine guzzlers, was vacant* [I Sam. 20:18 and Prov. 23:20]. A moment later he ran towards us, *his mouth filled with laughter* [Ps. 126:2], and in his hand *a flying scroll inscribed on both its surfaces* [Zech. 5:1 and Ex. 32:15].[47] He laughed and said: "*It is not for you to drink* [Prov. 31:4]! *Accept discipline you most brutish people* [Ps. 2:19 and 94:8]; stand by *and I will show you the path that you should follow* [Jer. 42:3]." *Then he loudly read* [II Kings 18:28] the letter that you had written, and D. spoke up *saying "Then the matter is known* [Ex. 2:14]! I saw the [author] and *he looked ill-tempered* for several days [Dan 1:10]. It must be that these matters were *shut up inside him* [Jer. 20:9]." *The doorposts shook from the sound of the laughter* coming out of *our mouths* [Isa. 6:4 and Ps. 126:2].

And now, if not for the darkened *veil spread over your face* [Ex. 34:35 and Isa. 25:7], you would know *that he laboured in vain* [Isa. 49:4]. Even if *you call at the head of busy streets and cry aloud at every corner* [Prov. 1:21, 2:3 and 7:12], "*if only you would hear me out* [Gen. 23:13]"; place *a muzzle on your mouth* and do not *become a laughing-stock* [Ps. 39:2 and Gen. 38:23].

I know how stubborn you are [Deut. 32:27] that *you won't listen to my words* [rev. Ps. 103:20]. Perhaps *your arrogant heart has seduced you* [Obad. 1:3] to write things in order to publish them in the *Kohelet* [*Mussar*], for such is the way of essayists. But it is not this that saddens me. These words *are not of my own devising* [Num. 16:28], but from a gathering of all my friends who follow my way, that you should know that *you have become a laughing-stock to us, the butt of our jibes all day* [Lam. 3:14]. *Peace unto you* [I Sam. 25:6].

Response:
To my brother! We did not set out *to seize the corners of the earth to shake the wicked out of it* [rev. Job 38:13]. Who does not know *that they are like a heavy burden, more than we can bear* [Ps. 38:5]? It was not for *the money replaced in the mouths of our bags* [Gen. 43:12] *that we are in full cry after you* saying "*turn away, turn away* from your wicked ways [Jer. 12:6 and Isa. 52:11]". For it will *dull the nation's mind and stop its ears* [Isa. 6:10] when it sees that money puts words into the mouth of *one who speaks righteously* [Isa. 63:1]; when *he wraps his mantle around his face and raises his voice like a ram's horn* [I Kings 19:13

---

[46]The irreverence is again manifest in the use of a biblical phrase that in its original context, describes Moses' turn towards the wondrous sight of the burning bush.

[47]The irreverent satire is carried forward. The fictitious author of this letter identifies his addressee – i.e., the author of the *Kohelet Mussar* – with both Zechariah's prophetic rebuke and the two tablets borne by Moses.

and Isa. 58:1] and says "*how long will you simple ones love* ill-gotten gains [Prov. 1:22]!" – and then, when he concludes speaking, he says "*pay me my wages*" [Zech. 11:12].

You must see plainly that *I can imagine myself to be like you* [I Sam. 24:12 and Ps. 50:21]. You have given your heart over *to follow your eyes* [Num. 15:39] and to stray after all *the luxuries of commoners* [Ecc. 2:8]. You have gathered Jewish youth around you *to show them the practices they are to follow* [Ex. 4:15 and 18:20], and they are *like river-beds directing them to whatever you wish* [Job 6:15 and Prov. 21:1]. *I am not less than you* [Job 12:3]. I have also *put joy into my heart* [Ps. 4:8] since I became a man. *At nightfall I lie down* happy, *and in the morning there is joy* [Ps. 30:6]. *I call to my friends and I let them drink of the spiced wine of my pomegranate juice* [Lam. 1:19 and Song 8:2]. *We go early to the vineyards, we rest among the henna shrubs* [Song 7:12–13]. *Then our inclinations bear witness against us* [Isa. 3:9]; for merriment *entered our bodies like water, and like oil unto our bones* [Ps. 109:18]. None of us, however, *have feigned madness like a drunken man* [Ps. 34:1 and Jer. 23:9] *galloping like a steed, thundering his voice* at his acquaintances [Nah. 3:2 and Job 37:4] and responding to those who greet him with "*he-ach*"[48]. Neither with shaking nor noise *will a righteous man rejoice, but with brothers dwelling together in green pastures by still waters* [Ps. 58:11, 133:1, and 23:2]. The Sharon and the Carmel, the Plain and the Bashan; *the heights of heaven and the furthest parts of the earth* [Job 11:8 and Isa. 8:9] *will make all their goodness pass before them* [Ex. 33:19]. And all the trees of the field will *utter praises of the Lord* [Ps. 78:4]. On the right, *rams and sheep will skip* upon pastures, on the left *the birds of the sky will sing among the foliage* [Ps. 114:4 and 104:12]. *Tamed and wild beasts and creepy things will be glad to reach their pasture* [Ps. 148:10, Job 3:22, and I Chron. 4:40]. They will answer and say: "See that the hand of God makes us and *provides our food* [Job 38:41]."

Sweet was our fellowship [Ps. 55:15] with every man stirring the other saying: "*Let us be strong and resolute* [I Chron. 19:13]." See that *the Lord's steadfast love is for all eternity* upon *the creeping things that creep upon the earth* [Ps. 103:17 and Gen. 1:26], and all the more so upon mankind, the chosen of all creatures and the purpose of their existence. God drew *upon him a spirit from on high* [Isa. 32:15] *and set him high above all* living things [Deut. 26:19]. *How abundant is His good that He has in store* for humans [Ps. 31:20]! *The wise man will take note of these things; join in our jubilation* [Ps. 107:43 and Isa. 66:10]. He will contemplate the *perfect beauty* [Ps. 50:2] of the order of creation, and his own distinguished place in its hierarchy of gradations. *He will look below and gaze* [Isa. 5:30 and Gen. 24:21] at the multitude of beings that are below his feet *descending ever lower* [Deut. 28:43]; man, ape, and reptile; eagle, dove, and white owl; cedar, hyssop, and stones of the field. He will look up to the heavens, astonished at the plethora of creatures standing above him – *more than can be counted* [Ps 40:6.]! Tell me if you know of a joy greater than the joy of this contemplation.

I will set it before you! *I will rejoice in the Lord* [Ps. 104:34] because he has made me the chosen of living beings and caused me to dwell at a position established between nothingness and angels. *You rejoiced as over all riches* [Ps. 119:14], for you have gone down from the height of your station and *are like the beasts* [Ps. 49:13]. *For if a man will get drunk and expose his nakedness, he has no superiority over the beast* [Lam. 4:21 and Ecc. 3:19]. *Not by might nor by power will* man *be exalted and raised* above the living things on earth, *but by the spirit of the Lord of Hosts* [Zech. 4:6 and Isa. 52:13].

---

[48]Hebrew expression of joy.

If only you were to taste *but a small portion* [Num. 23:13] of the nectar of this delight. For *you had no rest and no quiet* [Job 3:26] until you chose Him over all human desires. *I censure you not for your* urges, for I know that *this is the Lord's doing* [Ps. 50:8 and 118:23], so that you may discern the sweetness of true pleasure and disdain the wormwood of lesser urges. And you, when you chose evil over good, you did not do so because of your evil nature, since your heart sought goodness. Rather, your knowledge was defective, *your predictions absurd* [Isa. 19:11].[49] You made foolish the ways of discernment *by taking the slag and separating the dross from the silver* [Isa. 1:25 and Prov. 25:4].

Consider that from the perfection of all things comes the pleasure that man experiences with regard to it, and if there is no perfection, there is no pleasure.[50]

When people notice an *exquisite object* [Isa. 2:16], why is their perception so pleasing to them, and why do they declare it to be so *pleasing to the sight* [Gen. 2:9]? This is only because of the perfection of the form and its realisation, as well as the substitution of different colours and the subtlety of shading of the illustrated object, for this, and nothing else, is its perfect beauty.

Why would *a wise man* rejoice *in his wisdom, a strong man in his strength, and a rich man in his riches* [Jer. 9:22]? Is it not because he considers it a value and a perfection of his being?

If a man looks upon royal palaces and their courtyards and the configuration of their *rows of hewn stone* [I Kings 6:36]; the ways in which stones are arrayed upon stones and the magnificence of the windows; the corners of the doorways of their houses and their dimensions; and the relation of the lowest storey to the upper one; – then *he will put joy into his heart* [Ps. 4:8], *for he will know and understand* [rev. Isa. 44:18] the science of architecture and the *glorious beauty* [Isa. 28:1] of the building and its design, because this is its perfection and its perfect beauty.

As such, if the perfection of the matter and its purpose *is hidden from a person* [I Sam. 3:17], he will not derive joy from it, *selah*.[51]

Put my words to the test [Gen. 42:16.]! If an ignorant man, who had no experience judging works of visual art, were to enter a nobleman's *mosaic-covered chambers* [Ez. 8:12]; or if a man who does not understand the methods of architecture will look upon the house of *the king's sanctuary* [Amos 7:13] – his eyes will grow weary of their delight and he will be astonished at those who rejoice in its magnificence.

I know that at times a person will enjoy himself with regard to something absent of all perfection; deficient in understanding, *his wilful heart made him wander* [Deut. 29:18 and Gen. 20:13], [causing him] to exchange the valuable for the worthless. Since it appears in his eyes to be perfect, *he will be happy to see it* [Ex. 4:14], but his joy will neither be enduring nor sure because *its foundation will be sunk* on false perfections and vain thoughts [Job 38:6].

If a man *shall be drained of spirit* [Isa. 19:3] such that he would take pleasure in abominable things and would rejoice in wickedness, thinking that it is good – is this

---

[49] A key to Wolff's optimism was that evil resulted from a lack of knowledge rather than innate evil or character; see his *Vernünftige Gedanken*, par. 1056.

[50] The Wolffian idea of perfection informs this letter. Perfection characterises God's creation, e.g., the beauty and order of the universe, including the great chain of being with its continuous gradations from the lowest to the highest. God, naturally, is the most perfect spirit. Our pleasure in apprehending creation is a product of that perfection. See *ibid.*, par. 702–719, 904, 964, 1083.

[51] In his use of *selah*, Mendelssohn is here mimicking the biblical style of the Psalms (see note 26 above).

what you call enjoyment? To me, it is like a *ravaging plague* [Deut. 32:24], like those who lay on their beds and in their midst *there will continue to burn a burning like that of fire* [Isa. 10:16]. They will rejoice because *they got what they craved* [Ps. 78:29] *not knowing that their lives are at stake* [Prov. 7:23].

Not so with the joy born from the lap of true perfection – its steadfastness will endure forever. The *strong bond* [II Sam. 15:12] of perfection, and the pleasure of its attainment, will not be severed; *the same fate* will extend to both [Ecc. 2:14].

Hear it and accept it [Job 5:27]: if a man rejoices in the perfection of his friend, his *desires will be towards him* [Gen. 4:7]. *He will not stir out of his tent* morning and evening, and if he is kept away from him *he will have no quiet nor rest until he finds the one he loves* [Job 3:26 and Song 3:4]. *And if he has it in his power to do him* good [Gen. 31:29], he will benefit him *as a mother nurses a child* [Ps. 131:2]. This was the love of David and Jonathan, which the sages have referred to as unconditional love.[52] This was because *the life of one was bound up with that of his friend* [Gen. 44:30] with regard to the true perfection and the unequalled excellence that he found in him, and not with an expectation for something else with which he wishes to fulfil his desire. And so, their love will never be terminated, and they would even say "*death* [alone] *will come between us* [Ruth 1:17]".

How great was the yearning of the wise for the source of the perfections and the purpose of them all? How shall the joy of discerning God's deeds and the work of His hands be weighed? Is there anything perfect other than Him? Is there anything that can be compared to His creations? Then, from the strength of his yearning, *he will fling away the idols of silver* to those devoid of sense [Isa. 2:20]. He will rejoice in God and be glad with the slight attainment of His perfection. And then it will be good for him, *selah*.

Consider well what is before you [Prov. 23:1], and know that love of God is the joy of knowing His perfection. And from it is born the desire to heed God and to observe His *mitzvot*, and this is worship stemming from love. (I have more to say on the subject of worship stemming from love, and at another time *I will speak glorious things of it* [Ps. 87:3].) For God cannot be opposed to the yearning to do well with Him, and if so, rejoicing in God and loving Him are one and the same.

This is what the sages stated in [the Babylonian Talmud] *Sotah* [31a], and these are their words: "Two students stood before Rava. One said to him: 'In my dream they read: "How abundant is the good, that you have in store for those who fear you [Ps. 31:20]."' The other one said: 'In my dream they read: "Let all who take refuge in you rejoice [Ps. 5:12]."' He responded to them: 'You are both completely righteous individuals – one from love and one from fear.'" Why did the end of that verse, "And let those who love Your name exult in You [Ps. 5:12]", not appear in his dream? (See Rashi).[53] Rather, *it*

---

[52]*Mishnah Avot* 5:16. "All love that is conditional – when the condition is removed, the love is removed as well; but love that is unconditional will never cease. … What is an example of unconditional love? The love of David and Jonathan." Mendelssohn is suggesting that Wolff's view of love coincides with the Mishnah. In *Vernünftige Gedanken*, par. 449, Wolff writes: "Love consists of the willingness to derive a marked pleasure from the good fortune of another. Therefore we take pleasure in the good fortune of those whom we love." "Good fortune" (or "happiness" – German: *Glück*) for Wolff is, of course, whatever contributes to our perfection. Hence Mendelssohn's definition of love as taking pleasure in another's increased perfection.

[53]The version of the Talmudic text Mendelssohn had in front of him appears to have included only the first part of Ps. 5:12, and Mendelssohn, following Rashi's comment to this passage, notes that the point being made here actually rests upon the final phrase of the verse.

is just as I have said [Gen. 41:28]; this pious student was informed by heavenly means that the love of God cannot be separated from rejoicing in God, and from it stems the yearning to serve Him. For the definition of love is rejoicing in the perfection of the object of love along with the yearning to earn its favour; and without joy, there is no love.[54]

But I would lay my case before you [Job 5:8]. I hope that you will not continue to mock my admonishments. *Do not spurn* [Lev. 26:11] with words you have measured in order to reprove. And if you insist upon placing joy into your heart, *let me enlighten you and show you which way to go; this is the resting place and this is the place of repose* [Ps. 32:8 and Isa. 28:12]. Without this, *I said of revelry: "It is mad* [Ecc. 2:2]. "

SECTION SIX:

THE FOLLOWING LETTER REACHED US RECENTLY

How much do *I yearn to sit with you together* [Ps. 83:4 and 133:1]? It has been a while since *I sat in the company of* my friends [rev. Jer. 15:17]; I saw that *your seats were vacant and I refused to be comforted* [I Sam 20:18 and Jer. 31:15]. *How good it is* for a man, *and how pleasant is his sitting* with *his kinsmen* [Ps. 133:1 and Obad 1:7], for *he will drink his fill of love* [Prov. 7:18] and pour into their bosoms all *the searchings of the heart* [Judg. 5:18]! However, when *I wandered far off and stayed in the outermost parts of the sea* [Ps. 55:8 and 139:9], even there *I always set you before me* [Ps. 16:8], and *until I die* [Job 27:5] I will surely remember you. From all his endeavours, *this is a man's* earthly *reward* [Job 20:29]; when the Most High gives him a trusted friend whose *soul is bound up with his own* [Gen. 44:30]. And *when the Lord is pleased with his conduct* [Prov. 16:7] the good will increase as those rejoicing in it will increase; and when he is distressed, his friends will also *bend their shoulders to the burden* [Gen 49:15]; *they will share his burden and make it easier for him* [Ex 18:22].

I cannot hide from you [Gen. 47:18], my brothers, that I have seen the beginning of your labours in the first issue of *Kohelet Mussar*. Since I found your words to be *straightforward to the intelligent man* [Prov. 8:9], I went to visit my friend, the scholar and physician S., for I know him as one who loves *a skilled tongue and beautiful words* [Isa. 50:4 and Gen. 49:21]. With him were the scholar B. and the enlightened patron H., all of them well-read and appreciative of the purity and magnificence of refined language, and they were in accord in praising the *sweetness of your speech* [Prov. 16:21]. B. spoke up and said that the editors were right (that our language can be employed on all occasions, to give voice to misery and *to sing songs* [Prov. 25:20]).[55] However, *our hands are incapable* [Isa. 50:2] of translating from foreign languages into Hebrew. The master of translators, R. Samuel ibn Tibbon, admitted that in translating a piece from Arabic into Hebrew, the beauty and magnificence of its refined language was lost.[56] And if this is true with regard to eastern languages [which developed] close to the

---

[54]Mendelssohn turns the idea of friendship, i.e. taking pleasure in another's increased perfection, into the basis for arguing that man must take joy in loving God but also in serving Him, i.e. obediently following his law.

[55]This parenthetical comment is citing from section two; see above, p. 10.

[56]Mendelssohn is here actually referring to R. Judah ibn Tibbon (d. 1190) and his translator's preface to Bahya ibn Pakuda, *Hovot ha-Levavot* (*Duties of the Heart*).

land of Israel and are almost the same tongue, what can we do with regard to languages of the west, north and south? Who would not be afraid to approach the task? The ways of the Hebrew tongue and its refined language are far removed from the refined language of those nations *according to their languages in their lands* [Gen. 10:20]; who will draw them close so that they be *joined together* [Ez. 37:17]?

I answered and said that the translator you mention was correct with regard to matters of Torah and philosophy, such as the *Commentary to the Mishnah*,[57] *The Duties of the Heart*,[58] *The Guide*,[59] *The Glory of God*,[60] and *The [Book of] the Apple*;[61] for in [translating] these books, one may not deviate in the slightest from the words of their authors. But then, *the same conclusion awaits all* languages [Ecc. 2:14]; *none of them shall be omitted* [Isa. 34:16].[62] If, however, *pleasant words* [Prov. 15:26][63] *are poured from vessel to vessel* [rev. Jer. 48:11], the translator should not preserve anything except the refined language. In this matter, the Hebrew tongue is well-established, and there is almost none like it. The *Epistle Concerning Animals*[64] and *The Prince and the Ascetic*[65] will prove my words to be correct. *Be so good as to turn to me* [Job 6:28]; we have before us a book written in A… (very far from the lands of the East), words of *lamentation, woe, and dirges* regarding *the plague with which the Lord smote* its author [Ez. 2:10 and Zech. 14:12]. Please put me to the test! I will write the beginning of his piece in Hebrew. [See] *whether I will be untrue to you* [regarding] *all that crossed his lips* [Job 6:28 and Num. 30:13].

To you, men, I have turned my intentions. You will decide if my words are correct; *deliver them to the overseers of the work* [II Kings 22:5]. *If not, I will take note and apply my hand again* to amend my errors [Gen. 18:21 and Isa. 11:11]. *Peace unto you* [I Sam. 25:6].

[What follows is a Hebrew translation of the first sixty-six lines of Edward Young's *Night Thoughts*.[66]]

---

[57]This commentary, Maimonides' first major scholarly work, was notable for being one of the few rabbinic texts focused primarily on mishnaic and talmudic sources to have appeared in Arabic.

[58]Bahya Ibn Pakuda's eleventh-century Arabic-language ethical treatise.

[59]Maimonides' *Guide for the Perplexed*, like almost all Jewish philosophical treatises written before the thirteenth century, also appeared in Arabic.

[60]Joseph ben Shem Tov Ibn Shem Tov's fifteenth-century philosophical treatise includes Hebrew translations of Aristotle's *Ethics*.

[61]A pseudo-Aristotelian book, translated from the Arabic into Hebrew in the thirteenth century.

[62]The problem of translation, in other words, affects all languages with regard to philosophical writings, and is not a deficiency of Hebrew alone.

[63]Mendelssohn clearly means belles-lettres.

[64]*Igeret Ba'alei Hayyim* was an early fourteenth-century Hebrew translation of one of the Arabic-language epistles of the Brethren of Purity, an Islamic group that flourished in the tenth and eleventh centuries. Although these epistles contain philosophical ideas drawn from Aristotelian and Neoplatonic traditions, Mendelssohn seemingly referred to this treatise as belletristic because of its literary rather than philosophical language and form of presentation.

[65]*Ben ha-Melekh ve-ha-Nazir* is a Hebrew version of the popular medieval tale known as 'Barlaam and Joasaph', in which a prince encounters an ascetic and adopts his ways. A Greek (Christian) version appeared in the early medieval period, an Arabic adaptation at some point later. The Hebrew version was produced in the early thirteenth century, by Abraham b. Samuel ibn Hasdai.

[66]Originally published in 1742–1746, this book appeared in its early editions under the full title of *The Complaint: or, Night-thoughts on Life, Death, and Immortality*. The book quickly gained popularity across Europe, and was translated into German in the early 1750s and shortly thereafter into French. Mendelssohn was undoubtedly attracted by the subject matter, but in choosing this piece, he was also trying to show that Jews could cultivate a Hebrew no less sophisticated than what fellow Europeans were producing in their native languages.

The Dialectics of Religious Reform: The Hamburger Israelitische Tempel *in Its Local Context 1817–1938**

BY ANDREAS BRÄMER

Tradition is an integral part of human culture, basically describing all rituals, customs and practices inherited from preceding generations and regulating the life of a social group. Every society in fact knows, uses and conforms to traditions, which help to preserve its memory of a collective past, its values and its character. Through constant repetition traditional practices establish such a continuity, and so strengthen social identity historically, rather than by rationally oriented means. Eric Hobsbawm, however, argues that the common picture of an unchanging and unvarying tradition is essentially an illusion. Traditions, Hobsbawm suggests, are indeed subject to change, and are often quite recent in origin despite appearing or claiming great vintage: traditions are sometimes "invented", thus firmly establishing themselves within only short spans of time. Hobsbawm notes that such invented traditions are most frequently manifest when rapid social transformation weakens or destroys the patterns for which more deeply rooted traditions had been designed or, conversely, when such older traditions and their institutional carriers no longer prove sufficiently adaptable to changing conditions.[1]

In not consistently adhering to its traditions but modifying some of their aspects and removing or replacing others, modern German Jewry would appear to exemplify Hobsbawm's insight. Basing her own approach on Hobsbawm's thoughts, Shulamit Volkov has thus characterised the "invention of a tradition" in Germany as the most comprehensive Jewish project of modern times.[2] While this invented tradition certainly did not confine itself to the domain of faith, religious aspects of Judaism were nonetheless highly important. The institutional beginnings of Jewish religious reform can be pinpointed to the second decade of the nineteenth century in the free city of Hamburg – the city where Germany's largest Jewish community was located. This was the city where German Jews had first gained status as equal citizens, only to lose it shortly after with the liberation of Hamburg from French

---

*This essay is a revised and expanded version of a paper presented at a seminar in honour of the late Julius Carlebach held at the University of Sussex on 13 March 2002.
[1]Eric Hobsbawm, 'Introduction: Inventing Traditions', in Eric Hobsbawm and Terence Ranger (eds.), *The Invention of Tradition*, Cambridge 1994, pp. 1–14.
[2]Shulamit Volkov, 'Die Erfindung einer Tradition. Zur Entstehung des modernen Judentums in Deutschland', in *Historische Zeitschrift*, vol. 253, no. 3 (1991), pp. 603–628.

occupation in 1813. On 11 December 1817, sixty-five mainly upper-middle class Hamburg Jews[3] met to sign the by-laws of the so-called *Neuer Israelitische Tempelverein* (New Israelite Temple Association), whose main goal was the organisation of its own religious service. As a product and symbol of opposition, it was to exhibit a great deal of unease regarding Jewish tradition. Describing recent developments in Jewish liturgy with metaphors of deterioration and decline, it presented itself as a timely alternative to the synagogue:

> Penetrated by the need to restore a suitable worth and significance to public prayer service – a service which had been neglected by so many, in part because of the ever-decreasing knowledge of the language in which it has been held, in part because of the many weaknesses that have set in as a result – and inspired by the desire to revive nigh-frozen feelings for our fathers' honourable religion, the signatories below have agreed to produce a worthy and organised rite in this city. for themselves and all those with the same sentiments. In doing so, we are following the example set by several Israelite congregations in Germany, specifically the Berlin congregation; the service shall be held according to this rite on the Sabbath and holidays as well as other festive occasions in a temple to be erected especially for this purpose.[4]

Only ten months later, the early enthusiasm of its members had enabled the *Tempelverein* to open a rented prayer house, located in the *Alter Steinweg*, where public services were held on Sabbaths and on holidays, conducted alternately by the preachers Eduard Kley and Gotthold Salomon. While from the outside the building did not reveal its identity as a place of Jewish worship, its interior design resembled that of other synagogues in Hamburg and elsewhere in Germany. Following the tradition of Ashkenazi Jewry, the Torah pulpit was located in the middle of the room, and women remained separate from men in a special gallery. At the same time, their view of the service was no longer impeded by a partition. A cantor was hired, a boys' choir established, and an organ installed; the organists, however, were exclusively Christian. New Jewish hymns in the German language were written, but the melodies were supplied by Christian composers. The result of the reforms was thus a somewhat peculiar Jewish prayer service accompanied by music in a style resembling that of the contemporary church.[5]

Regardless of such borrowings, the Jewish reform movement in Hamburg developed in a different direction from that of the Lutheran church in one important respect: the church was no longer following the same rationalistic impetus that had marked it at the start of the century; rather, it was now propagating strict belief in the Bible, something not generating much enthusiasm in the Hamburg Senate but

---

[3] Their yearly income averaged 4,500 Marks, thus exceeding the estimated bare subsistence level of a family of five by 900 per cent; see Andreas Brämer, *Judentum und religiöse Reform. Der Hamburger Israelitische Tempel 1817–1938*, Hamburg 2000, pp. 20f.

[4] 'Vereinigungs-Urkunde des Neuen Israelitischen Tempelvereins in Hamburg', 11 December 1817, *ibid.*, pp. 121–125.

[5] See Michael A. Meyer, *Response to Modernity. A History of the Reform Movement in Judaism*, New York–Oxford 1988, pp. 56f.; Edwin Seroussi, *Spanish-Portuguese Synagogue Music in Nineteenth-Century Reform Sources from Hamburg: Ancient Tradition in the Dawn of Modernity*, Jerusalem 1996, pp. 25–50.

First building used as prayer house by the *Hamburger Israelitischer Tempelverein*, Alter
Steinweg, Hamburg

Reprint from Andreas Brämer, Judentum und religiöse Reform

drawing many followers among both the clergy and general public.[6] The
Tempelverein's desire for changes of a progressive nature stood in marked contrast to
this trend towards reinforcing inherited forms of piety – without, to be sure, any conscious resistance to contemporary currents. The Jewish association's founding in fact
reflected a conviction that Judaism needed to make up for a considerable deficit in
modernisation. Hence at stake above all was bringing the larger society's values into
the synagogue without entirely abandoning Judaism's distinguishing features.

The modification of old religious traditio ns and the invention of new ones was in
full swing by 1819, when the *Tempelverein* created its own prayer book, representing
the first comprehensive reform liturgy ever published.[7] Some traditional prayers
were shortened or changed in wording and content, others were removed completely, replaced in the service by hymns or paraphrases in German. In this way, traditional aspirations connected to the Holy Land – hopes for the Messiah, redemption,
resurrection of the dead and reinstitution of the sacrificial service – were down-

---

[6]See Hans Georg Bergemann, *Staat und Kirche in Hamburg während des 19. Jahrhunderts*, Hamburg 1958, p.
40; Georg Daur, *Von Predigern und Bürgern. Eine hamburgische Kirchengeschichte von der Reformation bis zur
Gegenwart*, Hamburg 1970, p. 169.
[7]Mendel I. Bresselau and Seckel I. Fränkel (eds.), [*Seder ha'avoda.*] *Ordnung der öffentlichen Andacht für die
Sabbath- und Festtage des ganzen Jahres. Nach dem Gebrauche des Neuen-Tempel-Vereins in Hamburg*, Hamburg 1819.

played if not eliminated altogether. The partial departure from an eschatology considered overly particularistic was evidently designed to reflect a new identity: that of professing Jews who were also loyal citizens of the state.

The *Tempelverein* hoped to establish organisational structures largely resembling those of a *kehilla* – a traditional Jewish community. But unlike the *Deutsch-Israelitische Gemeinde*, which every Ashkenazi residing in Hamburg belonged to by law, the Israelite Temple was a free and voluntary congregation; its emergence reflected a general burgeoning of new clubs and associations throughout German society devoted to a wide range of ideas and purposes. The Jewish association's members were part of a small, bourgeois and élitist avant-garde, and reflecting this social position they made an effort to dissociate themselves from the rest of the Jewish community. At the same time, they were searching for new self-assurance as religious Jews.[8] Nevertheless, for Jewish orthodoxy the new congregation's founding was a provocative and highly controversial act.[9] In any event, despite the conviction of its conservative opponents that Reform Judaism was creating the problems it claimed to solve, the Israelite Temple had been founded explicitly to neutralise the effects of religious estrangement by developing modern patterns of piety. At the same time, the newly introduced framework of traditions harmonised with a private way of life in which obedience to Jewish law had lost much of its earlier significance. No effort was made, however, to develop a new system of religious ideas suitable for a Judaism no longer determining all aspects of a Jew's daily life. Meyer Israel Bresselau, one of the editors of the 1819 prayer book, acknowledged the ideological shortcomings of the *Tempelverein* when he indicated that he had always restricted himself to improving public worship and had never proposed becoming a reformer in the full sense of the word.[10] For Bresselau as for many of the association's rank and file, the measures taken to "Germanise" and simplify the congregational prayer book were congruent with limited expectations centred on a new image for Judaism.

Despite such limits, there are clear indications that the *Tempelverein*'s leadership intended more than just a renewal of the prayer service. In a short printed letter circulated to all members in 1819, the directorate was assertive regarding efforts to broaden the association's range of activities. In order to govern the religious life of its members in a way reflecting the new conditions, the association planned to take responsibility for all the basic rites of passage – circumcisions, confirmations, weddings, funerals. But the circular letter points to another reality as well – many members, it seems, lacked an urgently needed solidarity with the new congregation's aims, and some openly expressed contempt for them, viewing the reform measures as already violating the limits of a truly Jewish tradition. The directorate sensed that

---

[8]Cf. Thomas Nipperdey, 'Verein und soziale Struktur in Deutschland im späten 18. und frühen 19. Jahrhundert', in *idem, Gesellschaft, Kultur, Theorie. Gesammelte Aufsätze zur neueren Geschichte*, Göttingen 1976, pp. 174–205.

[9]Cf. *Eleh Dibre Ha-Berit* [*These are the Words of the Covenant*], Altona 1819 (reprint. Westmead, Hants. 1969); Michael A. Meyer, 'The Establishment of the Hamburg Temple', in Emanuel Etkes and Yosef Salmon (eds.), *Studies in the History of Jewish Society in the Middle Ages and in the Modern Period*, Jerusalem 1980, pp. 218–224 (in Hebrew).

[10]Meyer Israel Bresselau *et al.* (eds.), *Theologische Gutachten über das Gebetbuch nach dem Gebrauche des Neuen Israelitischen Tempelvereins in Hamburg*, Hamburg 1842, p. 25.

through their critique, such internal "enemies" could weaken what was, after all, a voluntary association, or even destroy it, and was thus prepared to threaten excommunication: with a small but loyal nucleus of families willing to accept the association's discipline, it would be easier to confront various orthodox opponents. Israelite Temple members were thus called on to either dispense with the *kehilla*'s religious services or else declare their withdrawal from the congregation:

> The directorate will thus pay back a half-year's fee for membership in the new temple to every member indicating that his inner sentiments or circumstances are not in harmony with being a member in the fullest sense (provided a written notice to this effect is delivered to the directorate by the following Easter at the latest). Furthermore, such members will be freed from any further obligations to the association. With the Temple itself and its officials determining the appropriate prayer-service rules, following this period, the directorate will consider every action related to the service carried out by a member of the New Temple Association in another manner than is found acceptable by the latter to be a definitive statement: to the effect that the member does not intend to remain in the Association. In this case, the directorate will remove his name from the list of members and dispose of his place in the Temple for best use of the Association without compensation for the remaining membership fee.[11]

It comes as no surprise that Hamburg's Jewish community board of elders was not ready to tolerate radical tendencies towards segregation among the Israelite Temple's leadership. What is remarkable, however, is the role of Adolf Embden – who served on the board of elders and was also a founding member of the Temple – in offering precise steps in 1819 to call that leadership to order. In expressing his distrust towards the new reform synagogue in a speech he gave to his fellow board members, Embden was calling into question his own engagement on behalf of religious progress. The Israelite Temple, he indicated, was the reflection of a new pluralism replacing the former unity of religious Judaism. But while such pluralism was a fact of contemporary life that had to be accepted, it was, he argued, at the same time necessary to subject the Temple to the laws of the community board, in order to prevent its unrestrained radicalism from harming the community.[12] Clearly, these efforts to reintegrate the reform Temple into the *kehilla*'s confines were in conflict with the *Tempelverein*'s self-definition as a voluntary body, free of obligations towards the Jewish communal corporation. However, fearing sanctions, the Israelite Temple had no choice but to accept the community's rules.[13]

Embden's engagement shows that there was a wide range of opinions concerning the observance of Jewish religious law within the *Tempelverein*'s congregation. In 1823, Gotthold Salomon, employed in the synagogue as a preacher since 1818, argued that this situation represented a major burden – that disagreement over the congregational reforms was responsible for the process of modernisation coming to a premature end. Salomon was also dissatisfied with the prayer book, which he called a

---

[11]Adolf Embden, 'An die geehrten Mitglieder des neuen Tempel-Vereins', Hamburg (1819). (Printed circular.)

[12]Sitzungsprotokoll des Gemeindevorstands, 26 June 1820, in State archives of Hamburg (STAH), 522–1 no. 273a vol. 2.

[13]See Brämer, pp. 28f.

quodlibet that lacked accuracy and was produced without care.[14] Salomon repeated his reproach in 1830. All hopes that the *Tempelverein* would be able to completely supersede the traditional Jewish community had come to nothing:

> There is no unity in this fragmented part [of the Jewish community]; enough freedom but no equality; one section allows the children to be confirmed, another is against this; marriage ceremonies occur rarely; the consecration ceremony for newborn children is in fact not very attractive; graveside sermons have simply not been held; opinions differ and deviate in the directorate itself, one director being in favour of moving forward, another maintaining we are already too advanced; no congregation could follow us, hence we stand alone.[15]

Salomon was not alone in his critique. Gabriel Riesser, who joined the *Tempelverein*'s board of directors in 1840, basically agreed with the preacher, remarking in private that many congregation members did not have the courage to push ahead with the reform of ritual. Without these "rascals and cowards", however, he knew it would be hard even to gather a *minyan* for prayer. "Any people possessing 'a notion of an idea'", he concluded, "will certainly always form an invisible church, and no sect or society".[16]

In 1839, plans to publish a second edition of the prayer book at long last saw fruition. Working together, the preachers and directors finally took the opportunity to review all the measures that had been taken to modify the synagogal service – changes that were far from welcomed by all the *Tempelverein*'s members. In fact, it was impossible for its leaders to ignore the resistance. In 1840, Marcus Samson Hertz, who had joined the Israelite Temple in 1818 at the age of forty-three, went as far as to appeal to the Hamburg Senate for support against the association, reporting that the synagogue had begun adding new liturgical elements and deleting others. These changes, he indicated, had caused great resentment and turmoil among High Holiday visitors to the synagogue services, nearly resulting in the intervention of the police authorities.[17] The probably exaggerated nature of his description notwithstanding, there are indirect indications that Hertz was acting on behalf of a whole bloc of protesters – the sort of men who much later, in 1847, would threaten to cancel their rented seats in the prayer house after rumours had spread that the reform synagogue was going to abolish Friday evening services completely.[18]

The older members in particular, erstwhile modernisers, were now content with the reform measures taken in the synagogue's earlier period; through continuous repetition year after year the resulting changes had themselves come to offer the comfort of a stable, seemingly unchangeable tradition. In contrast to the tradition-

---

[14]Gotthold Salomon to Isaak Noah Mannheimer, 10 January 1823, in Moses Rosenmann, 'Briefe Gotthold Salomons an Isak Noa Mannheimer', in *Jahrbuch für Jüdische Geschichte und Literatur*, vol. 22 (1919), pp 68–110, here pp. 74f.

[15]Salomon to Mannheimer, 1 June 1830, *ibid.*, p. 76; cf. Gotthold Salomon, *Kurzgefaßte Geschichte des Neuen Israelitischen Tempels in Hamburg während der ersten 25 Jahre seines Bestehens, nebst Anmerkungen und Beilagen*, Hamburg 1844, pp. 27f.

[16]Gabriel Riesser to M. Stern, 14 February 1842, in Gabriel Riesser, *Gesammelte Schriften* (ed. by Meyer Isler), vol. 1, Frankfurt am Main and Leipzig 1867, p. 383.

[17]Marcus Samson Hertz to Senator Martin Hieronymus Hudtwalcker, 1 September 1840, in STAH, CL VII Lit Lb no. 18 vol. 7b Fasc. 4 Inv. 3 ('Abgewiesene Beschwerden des M[arcus] S[amson] Hertz wider die Direction des Tempelvereins pcto Veränderungen des Ritualwesens, 1840').

[18]*Allgemeine Zeitung des Judenthums (AZJ)*, vol. 11, no. 37 (1847), p. 557.

alism of the orthodox, their own conservatism was not grounded in a logical theological line of reasoning but rather in emotion. At the same time, younger members of the Israelite Temple were not willing simply to put up with a tradition that had been invented for the synagogue in 1819.

Although Hertz could not convince the senate to intervene on his behalf, his fierce resistance to further changes in the liturgy was not without consequences. The second edition of the Israelite Temple prayer book that appeared in 1841 presented itself as the result of a compromise, the preparatory committee openly acknowledging the need to take a diversity of opinions into account. One member of the committee, Maimon Fraenkel, felt obliged to offer a public apology, asserting that "to please consistency, we would have had a book of strict unity, but no association; at the most we would have isolated ourselves completely".[19] This question of (real or imagined) isolation proved a serious, recurrent issue at the reform synagogue. Officially it was declared that a middle path between radical reform and orthodoxy had been taken without any intention of mediating opposing standpoints. Hence it was not surprising that the synagogue ended up satisfying neither party. Moses Haarbleicher, also a member of the prayer-book committee, was dumbfounded at the censure directed at the new prayer book. "Just because we once made a leap", he asked rhetorically, "do we have to keep on jumping?"[20]

In the early 1840s, Rabbi Abraham Geiger was one of the most important liberal critics of the Israelite Temple. Convinced that the Hamburg reform association had fulfilled a limited historical mission, Geiger characterised it as an "innocent institution". He did not expect salvation from an aestheticising reform to the prayer service, but wished, in fact, to see Judaism transformed from a law-centred to a confessional religion.[21] It is interesting that some of the reform institution's radicals actually concurred with Geiger, even Gotthold Salomon, obliged to defend the prayer book in public, judging it far from satisfying in more private moments. In the winter of 1847, a challenge arose to circumcision (the *brit mila*) as an essential rite of passage. Salomon favoured abandonment of the ritual as a superfluous and "bloody consecration"; he also wished to consider more sweeping possibilities for religious reform. When Salomon was confronted with the argument that religious practice in the Israelite Temple was grounded in *Halakhah*, that is rabbinic Judaism, he conceded this was partially the case, while stressing the extent to which the congregation had shaken off the yoke of Jewish religious law nevertheless. In an exchange of letters with the board of directors, he expressed regret that the Temple had come to a "rabbinic standstill", and strong opposition to accommodating "rabbinic intolerance". The abolition of circumcision, Salomon suggested, would prompt increased homogeneity, with conservatives abandoning their membership and younger members joining the congregation instead.[22] But Salomon's hopes would again be disappointed. Apart from the presence of its new prayer book, Israelite Temple practice

[19]Bresselau (ed.), p. 10.
[20]*AZJ*, vol. 6, no. 16 (1842), p. 235.
[21]Abraham Geiger, 'Der Hamburger Tempelstreit, eine Zeitfrage' (Breslau 1842), in *Abraham Geiger's Nachgelassene Schriften* (ed. by Ludwig Geiger), vol. 1, Berlin 1875, pp. 176–179.
[22]See Gotthold Salomon's assessment, 21 February 1848, in *STAH*, 522–1 no. 571c.

The new *Israelistische Tempel* in Poolstrasse, Hamburg, inaugurated in 1844.

By courtesy of Museum für Hamburgische Geschichte

remained basically the same. Clearly, the liberal synagogue's directors had no desire to further deviate from the limits of their previous deviation.

In any case, the general development of religious indifference did not call a halt at the Israelite Temple. The institution did inaugurate a new prayer house in 1844, but in the years that followed it ran into financial difficulties, only being able to avoid bankruptcy through yearly subsidies from Hamburg's Jewish community.[23] The Temple, in other words, was itself too much a product of religious estrangement to be able to fight the phenomenon successfully. Its members had now become well settled within secular bourgeois society, a process of cultural and social integration sharpening their sense that religious traditions and practices were becoming outdated. Moreover, the new traditions invented by the Temple Association were, appar-

[23]Israelite Temple board of directors to Hamburg Jewish community board, 28 February, 15 April, 25 November 1850, in *STAH*, 522–1 no. 571a vol. 1; *AZJ*, vol. 14, no. 27 (1850), p. 373; *Orient*, vol. 11, no. 37 (1850), p. 148.

ently, neither capable of transforming idealistic intentions into necessary deeds, nor producing new frameworks for authentic piety. Jewish religious activity, including Sabbath prayer, had surrendered to a great extent to economic and social exigencies. In defence of his colleagues, one association member insisted in 1857 that irregular attendance at the services had not been due to indifference, but, as he put it, life asserting its claim peremptorily, so that a less insistent religion simply had to stand back.[24] Economic and social necessities, in other words, did not favour concerns grounded in personal devoutness.

In the meantime, the controversies of the Israelite Temple's founding years had abated, the Jewish orthodox establishment having arrived at a more tranquil assessment of the reform institution. Nevertheless, tolerance had by no means evolved into esteem. When, for instance, *Jeschurun*, a monthly edited by Samson Raphael Hirsch, reported on the Temple in 1854, its anonymous correspondent felt confident enough to scoff at the resistance its liturgical changes had once sparked among traditional Jews. His conclusion was as follows:

> The intentions came to nothing; we may say they turned out a complete fiasco. During its almost forty year existence, it was, I could almost maintain, entirely impossible for the New Temple to alienate and win over even a single member of this old synagogue – despite the Temple's enticements; despite the well-known *cherem* [religious ban] having been shattered; despite the synagogue having remained on its old grounds. Those who joined the New Temple had already fully shared the views of its membership. For older members, the Temple went much too far and – herein lies the hollowness of the entire institution – for younger members it did not go far enough. For a long time now, song and preaching has propelled the senses of young people who grew up within the Temple beyond its confines. Only now and then, memories of a dear dead one, the old, involuntary awe in face of the New Year and – especially – the Day of Atonement, the need, at least on these days, to register oneself under some sort of religious rubric, impels a tender youthful spirit to enter the beautiful broad halls. Otherwise they remain closed on weekdays – and empty on *Shabbos* and holidays.[25]

Gotthold Salomon and Gabriel Riesser exemplify an early awareness that the reform institution was itself in need of reform. Still, without the consent of a majority it was impossible to launch any substantial changes. Whatever re-evaluation of invented traditions might have taken place during the years of the *Kaiserreich*, there were certainly no systematic attempts at radical reform. On the contrary, the few traces of such re-evaluation suggest a retrograde movement. "Re-reform" was, to be sure, not an easy task, requiring a radically new perception of the Jewish religion among the Israelite Temple's rank and file. In the absence of such a development, all efforts at improvement would be mere patchwork.

Nevertheless, over the years debates on the necessity of a fundamental shift in direction would intensify within the Temple.[26] New by-laws were passed in 1924,[27]

---

[24] *AZJ*, vol. 21, no. 46 (1857), p. 628.

[25] *Jeschurun*, vol. 1 (1854–1855), p. 216.

[26] Cf. Jacob Sonderling, 'Die neueren Bestrebungen des Hamburger Tempels', in *Neue Jüdische Monatshefte*, vol. 3, no. 1 (1918), pp. 12–18.

[27] 'Satzung des Israelitischen Tempel-Verbandes zu Hamburg, 2 März 1924', in Ina Lorenz, *Die Hamburger Juden zur Zeit der Weimarer Republik. Eine Dokumentation*, vol. 1, Hamburg 1987, pp. 652–658.

and for the first time in more than a century, a members' assembly was brought together to discuss the Temple Association's internal matters. In the course of a lively debate on revision of the reform synagogue's own tradition, Felix Schönfeld distinguished himself as the spokesman for "reform orthodoxy". In contrast to Marcus Samson Hertz's resistance to radical reform over eight decades earlier, Schönfeld feared conservative backsliding, arguing that the Temple had already gone much too far in a conservative direction over the years, for instance in cancelling a number of German prayers, reinstating the Ashkenazi pronunciation of Hebrew, and resuming reference to religious leaders as rabbis.[28] But in other respects, the objections of Schönfeld and Hertz were remarkably similar, both men claiming allegiance to an invented tradition that had proved questionable from both a historical and contemporary standpoint. Schönfeld's pious insistence on what had become the status quo in fact contradicted reformist principles, progressive Judaism's intent being not only to examine orthodox beliefs and concepts but in principle, to challenge elements of its own tradition.[29] Revealing little concern for such a liberal context, Schönfeld and other like-minded Israelite Temple functionaries would continue to press their case against "counter-reform".

A new Israelite Temple building had been under discussion for around forty years. It is surprising that the plan was actually realised in 1931, in a period of economic depression and high unemployment. The new synagogue in the Rotherbaum area corresponded to the needs of its congregation, which had long since moved from the Neustadt – the old synagogue's location – to the west side of the Alster river. But the new structure was clearly not simply a reflection of convenience. It seems those attending the dedication were strongly aware that the ceremony symbolically announced a new era. Enthusiasm for the future was accompanied by a more critical view of the past, with the chairman of the board, Heinrich Levy, openly referring to former areas of neglect such as scant synagogue attendance and limited social cohesion, while expressing his optimism that the tendency of regular members to only show up for Yom Kippur and Rosh Hashanah had come to an end.[30]

A lack of sources makes it difficult to draw an exact picture of developments in the Israelite Temple through the 1930s. But the few extant documents point to a striking process of reconsolidation. In 1932, Rabbi Bruno Italiener, who had been appointed to preside at the Temple a few years earlier (1927), reported that an increasing number of men and women had begun to attend Sabbath services. And for the first time since the reform institution's beginning in 1818, it was now open for prayer on Mondays and Thursdays. At the same time, very similarly to what was the case with other German Jewish communities, the institution no longer simply amounted to a "religious association", a *Kultusverband*, its focus limited to religious socialisation, but now represented a "cultural community", a *Kulturgemeinde*, organising a variety of extra-religious activities such as public lectures and study groups in the spirit of the *Freies Jüdisches Lehrhaus* in Frankfurt am Main. In this manner, the Israelite Temple helped its members strike new roots in Jewish culture at a time when

---

[28]Lothar Lubasch, 'Eine Aussprache im Tempelverband', in *Hamburger Familienblatt*, 10 April 1924, pp. 2f.
[29]See Max Dienemann, *Liberales Judentum*, Berlin 1935.
[30]'Der neue Tempel bei seiner Einweihung am 30. August 1931. Gedenkblatt des *Hamburger Familienblattes*.'

The new synagogue in Oberstrasse, Hamburg-Rotherbaum, 1931.

By courtesy of Landesmedienzentrum Hamburg

growing antisemitism had begun to shake the belief of many in a successful process of integration into German society.[31]

After the Nazi rise to power, a new attraction to the Jewish religious heritage became evident in the Israelite Temple, as in the wider Jewish community throughout Germany. Between 1934 and 1936, membership grew by twenty-five per cent – this despite Hamburg's Jewish community already suffering great losses due to emigration abroad. While the Temple now presented itself as a place of security and comfort, the renewed stress on positive religious belief did not always lead to success in the eyes of those with liberal convictions: young people often found it more appropriate to revive older traditions and rituals which had been dropped a century earlier.[32] While it is an exaggeration to speak of a return to orthodox Judaism, an ideological change involving critical re-assessment of the past was definitely taking place. There was a growing recognition that classical liberalism's faith in a constant amelioration of human soci-

---

[31]In 1931, the Nazi Party won 26.2 per cent of the votes in Hamburg; in 1932 it became the strongest faction with 31.2 per cent. Cf. Bruno Italiener, 'Predigt bei der Einweihung des neuen Israelitischen Tempels am 30. August 1931', in *Gemeindeblatt der Deutsch-Israelitischen Gemeinde zu Hamburg*, 2 October 1931, pp. 2f.: "Our present times are marked by a deep unease. It is the narrowness that is tormenting us. The material narrowness: no longer any real room for work, for our and our children's development. The narrowness of ideas: how much oppressive prejudice in social, political, and religious life. … You have lost your faith in the midst of all this hate by which you are surrounded? Here you can find your faith again."

[32]See 'Der Israelitische Tempelverband (Rundschreiben an seine aus Hamburg abgewanderten früheren Mitglieder)', in *Gemeindeblatt der Deutsch-Israelitischen Gemeinde zu Hamburg*, 26 September 1935, pp. 4f.

ety had been an illusion. In describing her own relation to the liberal synagogue, its founding fathers, and its invented traditions, Eva Stiel spoke for the generation she was a part of. She viewed liberalism's central task as synthesising tradition and reform:

> Like the first liberal Jews, we have acquired our profession of faith from the world of doubt. We have learned to see and judge in the course of confronting the old. Every new step demands independence in both thought and decision from us. If we gave up this independence and instead surrendered to tradition, we would give up the best part of our activity, our inner vivacity and honesty. We want to adopt from tradition only what we can realise as whole human beings with both heart and reason. At present, we cannot have an overview of the range of what will be adopted. But it is certain that we do not wish to simply imitate without having our own inner sense of affiliation – something that would only bring back the old rigidity against which the first Temple-founders were struggling.
>
> This finally, is the proper venue to say what separates us from the Temple founders and what ties us to them. The new and separating element is the revived belief in the Bible's living God and a higher estimation of Jewish tradition. What unites us with them, is our inner independence in face of tradition, and we intend to take up this independence as a legacy and nurture it further.[33]

Starting in the autumn of 1938 the living conditions of German Jews worsened at a dramatic pace. During the November Pogrom (*"Reichskristallnacht"*) the liberal synagogue's exterior escaped destruction, but the interior was to a great extent ruined. Soon after, the building was confiscated by the Gestapo. Liberal services continued, however, in the former local B'nai B'rith lodge until 1942. In 1943 the communal organisation formed by the Nazi bureaucracy in 1937 for the Jews of greater Hamburg (the *Jüdischer Religionsverband*) received an official letter announcing that the Israelite Temple had been removed from the list of Jewish associations in Hamburg.[34] By this point most members who had not been able to leave Germany had been deported to the ghettos and death camps in the East.

The fact that liberal Judaism in Hamburg was destroyed because of racist persecution rather than in the course of any internal developments, makes it difficult to draw definitive conclusions regarding the Israelite Temple's history. What is clear is that the *Tempelverein* must be accorded pioneering status within German Jewry, even if there were preceding reformist endeavours in Berlin and other places. But such a judgment requires a further distinction: the modern era of religious pluralism in Judaism started with but not through the Israelite Temple. In his reappraisal of Germany's liberal Judaism, Jacob Toury speaks of a reform that stopped short of a genuine revolution.[35] Toury's general observation is all the more valid for the Israelite Temple in particular, its initiators counting among the first participants in this transformation, but its members deciding at quite an early stage to dissociate themselves from the ongoing process of German Jewish religious reform. It is thus understandable that historians of modern religious reform have mostly focused on

---

[33]Eva Stiel, 'Unsere Stellung zum religiös-liberalen Judentum', in Jüdischer Tempel-Verband in Hamburg (eds.), 'Rundschreiben 6 an seine Mitglieder, ehemaligen Mitglieder und Freunde', Hamburg, April 1938, p. 8.

[34]Official notice of the Jüdische Religionsverband, 7 May 1943, in STAH, CL. VII Lit. Lbno. 18 vol. 7b Fasc. 4 Inv 14.

[35]Jacob Toury, 'The Revolution that Did Not Happen (A Reappraisal of Reform-Judaism)', in *Zeitschrift für Religions- und Geistesgeschichte*, vol. 36, no. 3 (1984), pp. 193–203.

the Temple's formative years. All the same, the history of Reform Judaism in Hamburg did not end with the dedication of the new synagogue building in 1844, even if the institution would for a time receive scant public attention. Especially after the First World War, it would again emerge as part of a dynamic process that may best be understood in the context of an apprehensive contemporary climate. The Temple's invented traditions had become unsuitable in an age of crisis, with Hamburg's liberal Jews searching for a renewed sense of security. In the ensuing years of forced dissimilation, the Temple was, however, able to stand by its followers. But tragically, by the time the institution's renaissance had set in, the fate of German Jewry was sealed.

*Jewish Social Life, Antisemitism
and Jewish Reactions in Imperial Germany
and During the Weimar Republic*

Unter Uns: *Jews Socialising with other Jews in Imperial Germany*

By Marion Kaplan

For Jews in Imperial Germany, leisure time meant family time.[1] This was not unusual in a society in which Catholics and Protestants assumed the same. Daily and weekly family gatherings, special family celebrations for life cycle events such as marriages, and family observance of the religious holidays meant that most leisure time was family time. Jewish families provided more than sociability, however. In a society plagued by recurring antisemitism, they offered social and psychological support. Also, in a society on the move – Jews migrated from small towns and villages to larger urban centres at rates far exceeding those of other Germans[2] – families sustained social and economic safety nets as bonds stretched over distances.

Despite intense family connections, a lively Jewish social life flourished beyond it. Jews were part of Jewish friendship circles engaged in activities ranging from private coffee visits to dinner parties and dance classes. They also joined Jewish associations, which, like non-sectarian organisations, burgeoned on the local and national levels in late nineteenth-century Germany.[3]

Jews nonetheless navigated two worlds. Even as they maintained an inner circle of intense familial relations and strong bonds with Jewish friends, they increasingly acquired and cultivated another circle, mixing with non-Jewish society. At work, Jews had many – some had mostly – non-Jewish business contacts. These relationships could lead to social contacts, to sharing some leisure time, to a weekly beer, to a professional organisation that offered evening lectures and annual excursions, and to some lasting friendships, including marriages. In fact, some historians now suggest that the era around 1900 was the high point of Jewish social integration.[4] Still, on a

[1] I would like to express my gratitude to the Leo Baeck Institute, New York and to the Dorothy and Lewis B. Cullman Center for Scholars and Writers of the New York Public Library for supporting the research for this article. Thanks as well to my friends in the German Women's History Study Group, New York for their careful critique of this essay.
[2] In 1871, about 70 per cent of Jews (and about 88 per cent of the general population) lived in towns with under 20,000 inhabitants. Forty years later, about 32 per cent of Jews (and 65 per cent of the general population) resided in towns that small. Especially Berlin's Jewish population grew in leaps and bounds. In 1871, greater Berlin housed about 36,000 Jews. By 1910 their number had grown fourfold to 144,000.
[3] Peter Pulzer, *Jews and the German State*, Oxford 1991, pp. 13–14; Jakob Thon, *Die jüdischen Gemeinden und Vereine in Deutschland*, Berlin 1906 (Veröffentlichungen des Bureaus für Statistik der Juden, Heft 3), pp. 58–59.
[4] Ulrich Baumann, *Zerstörte Nachbarschaften: Christen und Juden in badischen Landgemeinden 1862–1940*, Hamburg 2000, p. 113. See also Thomas Michel, *Die Juden in Gaukönigshofen/Unterfranken (1550–1942)*, Wiesbaden 1988, p. 328 and Till van Rahden, *Juden und andere Breslauer: Die Beziehungen zwischen Juden, Protestanten und Katholiken in einer deutschen Grossstadt von 1860 bis 1925*, Göttingen 1999.

day-to-day basis, Jews took each other's company for granted. The vast majority socialised – found companionship and friendship – within their extended families and with Jewish friends. "Socialise" here has a more narrow sense than "establish social contacts", implying a greater degree of intimacy, trust, and reciprocity. There may even have been some differences in how Jews interacted with other Jews compared to how they interacted with non-Jews. The sociologist Werner Cahnmann has argued that intra-Jewish relationships were *gemeinschaftlich*, or communal and intimate, and that inter-faith relationships were *gesellschaftlich*, or societal and more formal.[5] This has generally been borne out by the research presented below, which focuses on the *primary* social world of Jews – the Jewish social milieu – along with its rich and varied textures.

Memoirs provide the most abundant sources for understanding Jewish social life in Imperial Germany. In particular, women's memoirs offer important details of everyday sociability. Unlike memoirs by men, which tend to focus on public life, those by women highlight closer relationships and private emotions – home, family, leisure, birth, marriage and death. They detail physical and emotional minutiae, the quality of daily life. These are the strengths of memoirs, which, however, also present methodological dilemmas: since they are often written for children or grandchildren, they focus heavily – perhaps excessively – on family themes. Whether in the form of contemporary platitudes, a nostalgic glow surrounding Jewish families and friends, or attitudes towards non-Jews tainted by the Nazi experience, writers' conscious and unconscious self-representations and motivations surely colour these texts. The spotlight cast by memoirs on the family may also lead to an understating of the extent to which Jews interacted with both other Jews outside the family and non-Jews. Furthermore, it is well-known that memoirs have a middle class bias, since it was the middle class that had the leisure time to reflect on its past. This, to be sure, is not as large an obstacle as might be thought, since most Jews – estimates go as high as eighty per cent – belonged to the middle classes in Imperial Germany. In addition, since many memoirs were written during or after the Nazi era, some writers may have read their greater present-day isolation as Jews back into their earlier social lives. Finally, memoirs tend to present the family as an institution solving problems rather than creating them, providing a safety net of sociability and security rather than an ambivalent or problematic environment. Still, they offer us rare and often superior glimpses into the Jewish middle classes' social networks and the emotions connected with them.[6] More specifically, practical living, emergency and vacation arrangements, Jewish children's experiences at dance classes, and the growth of Jewish organisations – not just nostalgic

[5]Werner Cahnmann, 'Village and Small Town Jews in Germany', in Joseph Maier, Judith Marcus and Zoltán Tarr (eds.), *German Jewry: its History and Sociology: Selected Essays by Werner J. Cahnmann*, New Brunswick, NJ 1989, p. 58.

[6]For a discussion of these issues, see Jaclyn Jeffrey and Glenace Edwall (eds.), *Memory and History: Essays on Recalling and Interpreting Experience*, Lanham, MD 1994, especially the essays by Paul Thompson, Marigold Linton, and Karen Fields. For an example of the problems posed by memoirs, see Stefanie Schüler-Springorum, '"Denken, Wirken, Schaffen": Das erfolgreiche Leben des Aron Liebeck', in Andreas Gotzmann, Rainer Liedtke and Till van Rahden (eds.), *Juden, Bürger, Deutsche*, Tübingen 2001 (Schriftenreihe wissenschaftlicher Abhandlungen des Leo Baeck Instituts 63), pp. 369–393.

and sentimental material – all indicate that families came first and that most Jews socialised with other Jews as a close second.

THE ALL-EMBRACING JEWISH FAMILY

In a manner typical of most German Jews Betty Lifschütz, born in 1905 into a middle class Berlin family, spent the most intimate and regular part of her social life with her family. She had "lots of relatives", so her immediate family "didn't really mix much with other people".[7] From this and similar examples, it is clear that, with German Jews deeply enmeshed in their extended families, family gatherings occupied much of their social life.

From simple weekend visits to more elaborate vacations, Jews continually reinforced a web of informal social ties with their kin. Where families lived in physical proximity they shared daily contact. Occasionally relatives provided one's only social life, Hugo Marx, for instance, relying on his aunt and uncle for companionship when he lived in Karlsruhe during the First World War. Although he worked in the public prosecutor's office and thus could have presumably made some friends his own age, he spent a great part of his free time with his relatives, taking part in their active social life.[8] But the main form of contact remained that between grown children and their ageing parents. The family of Norbert Elias (born 1897) moved to his maternal grandparents' Breslau neighbourhood so that his mother could easily visit them.[9] Another example from Breslau is offered by Lotte Hirschberg (born 1898), who as a young adult found herself surrounded by family. Her grandparents and their siblings, her own uncles and aunts and their children (her cousins), all lived nearby.[10] Hirschberg's father called on his widowed mother every day, "and mostly fell asleep during her anecdotes". He insisted that his children see their grandmother once a week.[11] And in Berlin, Marie Munk's maternal grandmother lived only a few houses removed from her own house. From the street, the child could see the old woman as she sat "at the bay window…[and played] solitaire".[12] Munk's mother and children visited Marie's grandmother almost daily. Her father saw his father, who lived twenty minutes walking distance from his son, every two weeks, with or without the children in tow. Munk's parents also held regular Sunday family gatherings with her mother's sisters and cousins. Although the Munks had themselves and their children baptised in the 1880s, there was, it seems, no ensuing variation in the schedule of

---

[7]Citation of Betty Lipton (née Lifschütz) in John Foster (ed.), *Community of Fate: Memoirs of German Jews in Melbourne*, Sydney 1986, p. 24.

[8]Hugo Marx, *Werdegang eines jüdischen Staatsanwalts und Richters in Baden (1892–1933)*, Villingen 1965, p. 104. For family relations in Frankfurt, see Andrea Hopp, *Jüdisches Bürgertum in Frankfurt am Main im 19. Jahrhundert*, Stuttgart 1997, pp. 184–187, 192–193, 198, 235.

[9]Norbert Elias, *Reflections on a Life*, Cambridge 1994, p. 7.

[10]Lotte Hirschberg, 'Mein Leben', Memoir Collection, Leo Baeck Institute, NY (henceforth memoirs, LBI), p. 6.

[11]*ibid.*, p. 6. See also Toni Ehrlich, 'Kindheitserinnerungen', memoirs, LBI, p. 16. Ehrlich was born in 1880 in Breslau; she recalls that her mother visited her parents and parents-in-law daily; Hopp, p. 184.

[12]Marie Munk, untitled memoirs (2 volumes), vol. 1, memoirs, LBI, p. 20.

family get-togethers.[13] They had changed their religion, but not their ethnic and familial culture.

Villages provided even closer proximity and more frequent contacts than cities. In Hochberg am Neckar (Württemberg), a location with five hundred inhabitants including a total of five Jewish families, Alice Ottenheimer's grandparents "lived two houses away across the street". Their daughter, her husband and three children occupied their "big house" with them. Another relative had a house nearby and ate his meals with Alice's grandparents. Living closely with one set of relatives during the year, the Ottenheimers spent every summer in her mother's birthplace, Ichenhausen (Bavaria), visiting "aunts, uncles, and cousins galore. ... On the other hand, our aunts came to visit us in Hochberg also."[14]

The Ottenheimers were hardly unique. In other villages, too, several generations of one family might reside in the same house or in separate apartments in the same building. In the village of Nonnenweier (Baden), three generations of one family occupied one building, and the case was similar in Ellar (Hesse), with two generations living in the same house.[15] In towns and smaller cities such as Rheda (Westphalia) and Heidelberg, parents might build a house in which they occupied one floor and one of their children's families the other.[16] This arrangement was occasionally made in big cities as well. In Frankfurt, some wealthy families built big houses in which several of their married children or an elderly parent resided.[17] In Nuremberg, the different branches of the Elsas family lived in separate apartments in the same building. As a child, a non-resident relative recalled, "it seemed strange that everyone in the big house was somehow related to us".[18]

Practical considerations such as lower rents played a role when young couples moved into buildings owned by parents or widowed parents moved into buildings owned by their married children. Moreover, family businesses made the living together of extended families practical. Julie and Abraham Herzfeld (married in 1867 in Grätz, Posen) lived with Abraham's parents for the first nine years of their marriage. He travelled a great deal, she helped out in the business and shared the housekeeping with her sister-in-law, who also lived with them. Julie Herzfeld notes that she and her husband accumulated substantial savings as a result and recalls that "although some difficulties arose from the joint household", the family provided companionship, especially during her husband's business travels "when I would have been alone quite often".[19] In this case, it seems the financial benefits and companionship outweighed the "difficulties" (which she does not describe). We do not know how many families separated angrily because of such tensions.

As Jews migrated from country to town or city and as wealthier Jewish families began to move to the outskirts of the bigger cities, daily visits no longer became prac-

[13]*ibid.*, pp. 17, 20 and *passim*.
[14]Alice Ottenheimer, untitled memoirs, memoirs, LBI, pp. 3, 5.
[15]Louis Liebmann, 'Notes on my Life: Dedicated to my Children', memoirs, LBI, p. 5; Elfie Labsch-Benz, *Die jüdische Gemeinde Nonnenweier*, Freiburg im Breisgau 1981, p. 29.
[16]On Heidelberg circa 1890 see Marx, p. 18.
[17]Hopp, pp. 222–223.
[18]Malka Schmuckler, *Gast im eigenen Land: Emigration und Rückkehr einer deutschen Jüdin*, Cologne 1983, p. 6.
[19]Julie Herzfeld, 'Familiengeschichte', memoirs, LBI, pp. 18–19.

Portrait of a large, extended Jewish family in Germany on the occasion of a wedding anniversary in 1917. (Stefan Zweig Collection)

By courtesy of the Leo Baeck Institute, New York

tical. Despite significant distances between parents and their married children, the Sabbath, or Sundays for more secular Jews, were the occasion for weekly family gatherings. Extended families living in the same town or city would assemble on Friday evenings or Saturdays for a Sabbath meal, or for its secular equivalent. When Rahel Straus (born in 1880) moved to Munich after marrying, she encountered her husband's large family there. On the Sabbath, he would declare, only half-jokingly, that "Today we have to visit Uncle Moritz, Uncle David, Aunt Sarah, Uncle Angelo, Uncle Lothar." She would cover her ears as the list droned on.[20] For some German Jews, Sunday visits now came to replace previous Sabbath social calls. In the words of Betty Lifschütz: "Family life was very strong … and Sundays were specially for the family."[21]

Ceremonies such as marriages or bar mitzvahs also led to gatherings of both immediate and extended families. Large families would assemble for such special events, the Diamant family's, for example, generally involving over sixty family members.[22] Emergencies such as births, sickness or death would also bring family members from near and far. In these circumstances, mostly female relatives sprang into action. One example among many furnishes a good idea of what these emergencies sometimes involved. When Julie Herzfeld's first child was born in Grätz in 1868, her mother hurried to her bedside from out of town. Her father arrived for the circumcision ceremony a week later. Her in-laws, in whose house she lived, and especially her sister-in-law also helped out. The following year, when her second child was born, her sister-in-law assisted her again. At that time, she noted, no one from "bet-

[20]Rahel Straus, *Wir lebten in Deutschland: Erinnerungen einer deutschen Jüdin*, Stuttgart 1962, p. 122.
[21]Lipton in Foster (ed.), p. 24.
[22]Sophie Diamant, 'Familiengeschichte Schlessinger', memoirs, LBI, p. 15.

ter houses" in Posen hired aides when recovering from childbirth, female relatives helping out instead.[23] The death of one son in 1870 caused the young Herzfeld couple enormous pain, and their parents and in-laws grieved with them.

Another child died suddenly in 1872. This time an aunt came to comfort the couple, and Julie also travelled to her parents with her remaining child for a longer visit: "The love and sympathy of my parents and siblings helped me a great deal."[24] When she gave birth for the fourth time, her sister took over the household. The same sister visited her regularly, spending many weeks in Grätz to help her. In 1878, her mother again took over the household while Julie gave birth to another child. When two of her children came down with whooping cough, Julie took them to her parents' home to recuperate, both for a "change of air" as recommended by the doctor and for family comfort. Julie Herzfeld gratefully reflected: her in-laws "could be called upon repeatedly, just as her dear mother rushed to her when worries and sorrow approached".[25] When, at different times, her in-laws lay dying, the Herzfeld couple and the husband's siblings alternated caring for them. Herzfeld explains that "there were no [private] nurses in Grätz yet", but one imagines that she was also trying to reciprocate for the years of care the relatives had showered on her immediate family.[26]

As urbanisation increasingly pulled families apart, the younger generations moving into the big cities, visits preserved bonds across greater distances; the urbanites spent vacations "back home" in the countryside;[27] younger people living in the countryside visited siblings and cousins who had relocated to the big cities. Marie Munk's mother spent her summers at her parents' vacation home in the countryside with many of her siblings and cousins – meetings that became part of family lore.[28] Lotte Paepcke recalls her ambivalence when her relatives, "country bumpkins" (*kleine Dörfler*), visited her parents in Freiburg. The visitors dressed less fashionably than her parents and had names like Shelomo, Jeinkef, and Sara: "They didn't fit into our by this time citified-modern house." Nor did they "eat as nicely as one had taught us children to eat. … And when they left, father gave them a significant amount of money." But despite her own feelings of distance, Lotte noticed how delightedly her father greeted them and how much they meant to him.[29]

Family visits could also, of course, cross international borders. Henriette Necheles Magnus (born in Berlin in 1898) had a "divided family" located in Brussels, Hungary and England: "How nice it always had been to visit each other! One got to know other lands, one maintained family ties." During the First World War, in fact, some of these same cousins fought each other: "When a Belgian cousin died, our bonds with Brussels were torn, and the relationship was never effectively restored."[30] Where in

---

[23]Herzfeld, p. 24.

[24]*ibid.*, p. 27.

[25]*ibid.*, pp. 34, 37.

[26]*ibid.*, p. 42. Cf., for instance, Diamant, p. 15. After her siblings married, Sophie Diamant remained with her widowed mother until she was thirty-one. Then she married and took her mother into her new home. She also took in her niece until the child's father remarried.

[27]Herzfeld, p. 74.

[28]Munk, vol. 1, pp. 5, 8.

[29]Lotte Paepcke, *Ein kleiner Händler, der mein Vater war*, Heilbronn 1972, pp. 15–16.

[30]Henriette Necheles Magnus, 'Reminiscences of a German Jewish Woman Physician', unpublished manuscript (Chicago 1940), Houghton Library, Harvard University, p. 6.

this case nationalism and war severed international family bonds, one might also wonder whether such family ties ever tempered the martial enthusiasm of some Jews.

International familial connections could boost business relationships and provide a familiar base abroad. Visiting or apprenticing with relatives, boys learned newer commercial methods and made useful contacts in countries still more advanced than Germany. As Germany became more active in international trade, the former visitors could take advantage of the associations made during their stays abroad: "No wonder ... that the young Jew was ready much sooner to go by himself to foreign countries – as an apprentice or on business trips."[31]

How did families spend their leisure time together? Memoirs describe typically bourgeois pastimes: parents playing games or doing riddles or drawing with their children,[32] taking long walks (not always beloved by the children) in nearby woods,[33] and conversing or reading to each other.[34] Even if daytime brought a "great deal of turmoil" with it, Johanna Meyer Loevinson (born in Berlin in 1874) recalls that her parents tried to "create an atmosphere of peace and general relaxation" in the evenings. Her parents and siblings read each other stories, often novels appearing in serialised form in the *Berliner Tageblatt*.[35] Margarete Sallis (born in Frankfurt am Main in 1893) speaks of evenings sitting with her parents, grandparents and uncle roasting chestnuts while discussing world events like the Boer War (1899), the Agadir Crisis (1911), and the sinking of the Titanic (1912).[36]

Playing cards was, it seems, a favourite entertainment. Betty Lifschütz reminisces that when her extended family got together on Sundays, her father played cards (*Skat* or poker) with the other men, her mother with her female relatives, the children with their cousins. The family frequently visited cafés on Berlin's famous *Unter den Linden* boulevard where they would sit over their coffee and cream cakes "for as long as three hours".[37] Special food constituted an important element at these gatherings. Toni Ehrlich's mother, who had fifty-two cousins in Breslau alone, held regular "cousins' cafés" at which she served tropical delicacies such as dates, figs, raisins and almonds.[38]

---

[31]Arthur Prinz, *Juden im Deutschen Wirtschaftsleben, 1850–1914*, edited by Avraham Barkai, Tübingen 1984 (Schriftenreihe wissenschaftlicher Abhandlungen des Leo Baeck Instituts 43), pp. 9–10.

[32]Drawing and blocks recorded in Ehrlich, p. 12; games in Ottenheimer, pp. 3–5; riddles in Henriette Hirsch, untitled memoirs, memoirs, LBI, p. 2.

[33]Margarete Sallis, untitled memoirs, memoirs, LBI, p. 24.

[34]If the number of reviews in the popular *Allgemeine Zeitung des Judentums* (hereafter *AZJ*) is any indication of readers' interests, then Wilhelminian-period German Jews favoured books by, among others, the following authors (in order of popularity): Heine, Berthold Auerbach, Lessing, Goethe, Ludwig Börne, Karl Emil Franzos, Shakespeare, Karl Gutzkow, Gustav Freytag, Richard Wagner (!) and Schiller. More modern authors are mentioned less often; they include Grillparzer, Tolstoy, Fanny Lewald, Disraeli, Georg Hermann, Arthur Schnitzler, and Jakob Wassermann. Theodor Fontane, although not mentioned in the *AZJ* until his death, was also much loved. See Hans Otto Horch, *Auf der Suche nach der jüdischen Erzählliteratur*, Frankfurt am Main 1985), p. 35. On Fontane, see Paul Mendes-Flohr, *German Jews: A Dual Identity*, New Haven 1999, pp. 6–8.

[35]Johanna Meyer Loevinson, untitled memoirs, memoirs, LBI, p. 39. Loevinson also refers to "light reading" such as Julius Stinde's series of novels about the fictional Buchholz family, set in the Berlin of the 1880s and 1890s, as well as the works of Fontane. See also Hirsch, p. 2, who describes reading the *Gartenlaube* and other illustrated magazines, along with two children's journals.

[36]Sallis, p. 15.

[37]Lipton in Foster (ed.), p. 24.

[38]Ehrlich, p. 14.

Family interactions were, to be sure, not always idyllic, and were sometimes a source of serious tensions.[39] In time-honoured fashion, Hedwig Wachenheim's mother often complained about her own mother and later Hedwig complained similarly. Children, especially, chafed under too much parental control. Hedwig Wachenheim's happier moments occurred when her mother went to one of Wagner's operas. Then Hedwig could spend up to five hours with the books her mother had locked away.[40] Similarly, Arthur Prinz's adolescent diary rants against his mother's stifling love.[41] Even Margarete Sallis, while enjoying her family get-togethers, recalls her parents' absences with delight. Several times a week when they attended lectures, she had a few treasured hours to herself for reading or dressing up.[42]

In his memoirs, Victor Klemperer, who was born in Landsberg an der Warthe in 1881 and grew up in Berlin, exemplarily conveys such mixed feelings. Written with a sharp eye for familial foibles, the memoirs still express Klemperer's deep attachments, especially his love for his parents and sisters. On the other hand, he repeatedly quarrelled with his brothers, who prompted feelings of inferiority and anger – even as, or because, they subsidised his studies. One occasion in particular underscored the enduring nature of such feelings. While visiting his mother, who was in failing health, Klemperer was obliged circa 1905 to attend a formal family dinner planned by one of his brothers in his honour. His brother toasted the family's accomplishments and his nephew took photographs of all four "successful" siblings. Klemperer deplored the formality and pretentiousness of the entire event. He also disliked parting from his wife after dinner as the men and women entered separate rooms: "the women, to gossip among themselves in the salon ... the men to engage in more serious male conversation [*Männerworte*] in the smoking room ... I found this arrangement so artificial."[43]

Then as now, various forms of tension could naturally make themselves manifest in individual families. Nora Rosenthal's paternal grandfather, for example, insisted that her parents, happily ensconced in London, move back to Frankfurt am Main. As Rosenthal indicates, the older man "did not see why his only son should live so far away". "This was a harsh and dreadful change for my mother", she continues. "Also it is always very hard for a wife, if the husband is so attached to his parents, that there is hardly any chance for other social contacts. She had to have treatment by a famous neurologist."[44]

At times, families would reinforce their businesses and bonds by forcing their offspring down paths they would just as soon not have taken. Else Gerstel (born in 1890) indicates that her father would have loved to practice law but had to take charge of the family firm.[45] Likewise, in the 1890s Lotte Paepcke's grandfather apprenticed her

---

[39]On this theme for the period from 1900 through the Weimar Republic, see Claudia Prestel, 'Youth in Need: Correctional Education and Family Breakdown in German Jewish Families', in Michael Brenner and Derek Penslar (eds.), *In Search of Jewish Community: Jewish Identities in Germany and Austria, 1918–1933*, Bloomington 1998, pp. 200–223.

[40]Hedwig Wachenheim, *Vom Grossbürgertum zur Sozialdemokratie: Memoiren einer Reformistin*, Berlin 1973, pp. 7–10.

[41]Prinz, pp. 83–84 (for 1915).

[42]Sallis, p. 23.

[43]Victor Klemperer, *"Curriculum Vitae": Jugend um 1900*, 2 vols., Berlin 1989, vol. 2, p. 47.

[44]Nora Rosenthal, 'Opus One', memoirs, LBI, pp. 4–5.

[45]Else Gerstel, 'Blick zurück ins Kaiserreich', in Andreas Lixl-Purcell (ed.), *Erinnerungen deutsch-jüdischer Frauen 1900–1990*, Leipzig 1992, pp. 37–48, here p. 41.

father into the leather trade so that he might eventually take over the family shop. The young man, however, loved the piano. The battle between *Lied und Leder* – song and leather – ended with a three-year apprenticeship to a Jewish leather merchant.[46]

In addition, both gender and order of birth within the family could interfere with individual dreams and desires. Sisters generally had to forego education in favour of brothers – and by the turn of the century many resented this – while parents placed higher expectations on their sons. First-born sons sometimes gave up on their educational intentions in order to send younger (male) siblings to university. Conversely, parents expected girls to marry in birth order, which sometimes meant that the younger daughters had to forgo their opportunities until a suitable spouse came around for an older sister. Furthermore, when it came to marriage "many a young man and woman … would mutely bow to parental commands" rather than face the consequences of insisting on a partner of choice.[47] We have no way of knowing just how many unhappy marriages resulted from family pressure.

Why Jews maintained their particularly intense family attachments is a subject for both historical contemplation and nostalgic reminiscence. Remaining, here, within the former realm, we may suggest several reasons for the phenomenon:

(1) In the "bourgeois century",[48] the family remained a powerful social institution – an object of fascination and idealisation for, in particular, the Protestant, Catholic, and Jewish middle classes, "central to [their] cultural life and value system"[49] – despite worries about it being undermined by modernity, especially urbanisation, industrialisation, and an emphasis on the individual.[50] In this context, the concept of the family served to enhance Jewish self-esteem and enrich collective memories.[51] Jewish writers, scholars and artists thus depicted the traditional Jewish family proudly, using it in Jewish apologetics and as a strategy against antisemitic calumnies[52] – even enemies of the Jews conceded the vitality and virtue of Jewish family life.[53]

(2) Even when times were relatively good antisemitism continued to limit Jewish aspirations and achievements and restrict social integration; the family thus provided refuge from and solace for bigotry and rejection.

---

[46]Paepcke, p. 14. See also Hopp, pp. 58–59 for another example of a son who had to go into the family business.

[47]Peter Gay, referring to the bourgeoisie in general but, I would argue, especially relevant to the Jewish bourgeoisie, in *idem*, *The Bourgeois Experience: Victoria to Freud*, vol. 2, *The Tender Passion*, New York 1986, p. 98.

[48]*idem, ibid.*, vol. 1, *Education of the Senses*, New York 1984, p. 423.

[49]See Richard J. Evans, 'Family and Class in the Hamburg Grand Bourgeoisie, 1815–1914', in David Blackbourn and Richard J. Evans (eds.), *The German Bourgeoisie*, London–New York 1991, pp. 115–139, here p. 115.

[50]During this period, social theorists like Ferdinand Tönnies and Georg Simmel were describing society in binary terms, with family and community on one side and atomisation and individualism on the other. A general theme was that the city bred individualism and that its relationships, more formal, contractual, or self interested in nature, would replace the warmth and reciprocity of social bonds in previous communities and families.

[51]Paula Hyman, 'The Modern Jewish Family: Image and Reality', in David Kraemer (ed.), *The Jewish Family: Metaphor and Memory*, New York 1989, pp. 179–193.

[52]*ibid.*, p. 186.

[53]Cf. Paula Hyman's introduction to Steven M. Cohen and Paula Hyman (eds.). *The Jewish Family: Myths and Reality*, New York 1986, pp. 3–4.

(3) The Jewish minority's religious, cultural, occupational and educational distinctiveness played a practical role in maintaining borders with the non-Jewish world, raising the family to an especially prominent position in the lives of its members.

(4) In Imperial Germany the German-Jewish family frequently provided sustenance and material assistance, not just moral support. Most young men depended on family contacts for their apprenticeships and family support for their job placements. Many depended on family subsidies for their new businesses or practices. Unclear about his future Hugo Marx, for example, used his uncle's connection to work at a bank as an apprentice, remaining there a year and a half though he soon hated the job, while the bank "put up with him" thanks to his uncle. When he finally quit, he lasted only two months in the next job until another uncle promised to subsidise his legal studies.[54] And Victor Klemperer's increasing unhappiness in an apprenticeship (also acquired through family connections) led to similar familial intervention.[55]

(5) What might be considered the inverse side of material family support also held true: family businesses obliged families to maintain ties, to cooperate and communicate. Such businesses often brought fathers and sons, brothers, or other male relatives together for a lifetime of teamwork.[56] A glance at Jewish textile entrepreneurs in Silesia shows a pattern of businesses passed on in individual families from generation to generation.[57] Arranged marriages, in particular, cemented business alliances.[58] Moreover, marriages between cousins as well as those between two sets of brothers and sisters kept both "family within the family" and business within the family, solidifying social, class and business networks at the same time.[59]

It is the case that the non-Jewish German bourgeoisie may have behaved similarly, especially with regard to arranged marriages[60] but also in drawing younger generations into family businesses and maintaining commercial networks. Non-Jews, however, could also seek a broad array of civil service positions as well as university or army careers barred to Jews; they consequently had access to far more avenues independent of direct family intervention, although wealth and connections certainly helped the aspiring civil servant, military officer, or aca-

---

[54]Marx, pp. 48, 53.

[55]Klemperer, vol. 1, p. 141.

[56]Examples are the Herrnfeld brothers' theatre company; see Marline Otte, 'Eine Welt für sich? Bürger im Jargontheater von 1890 bis 1920', in Gotzmann *et al.* (eds.), pp. 121–145, here pp. 130–131, and the Hirschfeld brothers; see 'Isidor Hirschfeld', in Monika Richarz (ed.), *Jewish Life in Germany: Memoirs from Three Centuries*, University of Indiana Press 1991, pp. 228–234, here pp. 231–234.

[57]John Foster, 'The Jewish Entrepreneur and the Family', in Konrad Kwiet (ed.), *From the Emancipation to the Holocaust: Essays on Jewish Literature and History in Central Europe*, New South Wales 1986, p. 17.

[58]*ibid.*, pp. 21–22; Hopp, pp. 193–215 ; Morten Reitmayer, 'Zwischen Abgrenzung und Ausgrenzung: Jüdische Grossbankiers und der Antisemitismus im deutschen Kaiserreich', in Gotzmann *et al.* (eds.), pp. 147–170, here pp. 151–152. That this was not only a Jewish business practice can be seen in the work of Dolores Augustine, *Patricians and Parvenus: Wealth and High Society in Wilhelmine Germany*, Oxford and New York 1994, chap. 3; Hansjoachim Henning, *Das westdeutsche Bürgertum in der Epoche der Hochindustrialisierung 1860–1914*, Wiesbaden 1973; and Evans, 'Family and Class', pp. 115–139.

[59]For examples, see Hopp, p. 198.

[60]On business marriages in the Amsinck family, see Evans, 'Family and Class'. There were, however, proportionately fewer cousin marriages among non-Jews.

demic. In contrast, for newly established Jewish businessmen or professionals, the family frequently provided the only capital, the employees, the (mostly Jewish) connections, and even the first customers. Hence while important for the economic life of Imperial Germany's middle classes in general, the role of the family was nothing less than crucial for that society's Jewish middle class.

(6) As has certainly been the case for diaspora Jews in general, the desire to carry forward Jewish identity was in itself an important source for the family's centrality in German-Jewish life of this period. This desire is evident, for example, in Moritz Oppenheim's widely circulating portraits of Jewish family life and religiosity.[61] It is also evident in the contents of many contributions appearing in the *Israelitisches Familienblatt*, the most widely read national Jewish newspaper (founded in 1898). As public religious observance declined in the course of the Wilhelminian period, the family would become even more of a repository of religious values and symbols.[62]

(7) Lastly, Jews maintained their profound family attachments because the family served social and cultural goals – in other words, it facilitated the embourgeoisement of German Jewry, hence its acceptance into German society. German advocates of Jewish emancipation had wanted Jews seeking equality to become enlightened members of the bourgeoisie like themselves, which is to say they were meant to acquire the German ideal of *Bildung*. Jews responded by adapting to the German expectations of education and cultivation, but also refashioned these expectations to fit their own culture and needs. A family with *Bildung*, with its good taste, polish, and manners, was a symbol of "Germanness"; but it was also a symbol of Jewish respectability and breeding.[63]

In making family a central value, German Jews resembled other middle class Germans in Imperial Germany. But unlike the latter, Jews saw *Bildung* as an essential vehicle for fulfilling the family's aspirations of integrating into class and nation. Herein lies a paradox. The German Jewish family may have prized both *Bildung* and notions of bourgeois "Germanness", but the same family's very vitality inhibited the desire and ability of most Jews to integrate more fully with other Germans. Moreover, *Bildung* was an elastic concept, not only being closely tied to such Germanness, but – as George Mosse has noted – at the same time becoming *synonymous* with Jewishness.[64] In this manner, many German Jews accepted *Bildung* as a new form of Jewish faith, a tendency reflected in both Berthold Auerbach's call for religion to become *Bildung* and in Walter Benjamin's praise of his friend Ludwig Strauss's declaration that "above all, in a study of Goethe one finds one's Jewish substance".[65] A cultivated German Jewish family was thus not only bourgeois and

[61]Often reprinted as postcards, these portraits were collected in a volume, first published in 1882, that in the end "may have been one of the most popular Jewish books ever published in Germany"; see Ismar Schorsch, *Moritz Oppenheim: The First Jewish Painter*, Jerusalem 1983, p. 31.

[62]See Marion Kaplan, *The Making of the Jewish Middle Class: Women, Family and Identity in Imperial Germany*, New York 1991, pp. 64–84.

[63]The standard discussion of the German-Jewish ideal of *Bildung* remains George L. Mosse's *German Jews Beyond Judaism*, Bloomington 1985.

[64]*ibid.*, p. 4.

[65]*ibid.*, pp. 4, 14.

German but bourgeois and Jewish – Imperial Germany's Jewish family was consequently instrumental in providing a passport for becoming "German" and an anchor
for remaining Jewish.[66] In this sense, the family facilitated what has been termed the
"situative ethnicity" of the German-Jewish minority.[67] As a result of the new
German-Jewish identity, most German Jews and German-Jewish families could lay
claim to either Jewish ethnicity or German heritage, depending on the circumstances
– and this in a way that was neither manipulative nor even fully conscious.

SOCIAL RELATIONS OF GERMAN JEWS BEYOND THE FAMILY

Although family provided the primary focus of social interaction, imperial
Germany's Jews also socialised, of course, with other Jews, both informally and in
more formal, communal organisations. As is to be expected, such relationships ran
the gamut from intimate ties stemming from childhood friendships to weekly card
playing among male neighbours or business associates to more formal monthly meetings of women's or men's organisations.

Making and Meeting Friends

For more traditionally religious Jews, the Sabbath provided a regular pause for relaxation and short visits. In towns and cities, both observant and non-observant Jews participated in more formal Saturday coffee visits, similar to the occasions marking
Imperial Germany's bourgeois "visiting culture".[68] We read, for instance, that in
Berlin, Henriette Hirsch (born in 1884) would regularly dine on Friday evenings with
her grandfather, the well-known Orthodox rabbi Esriel Hildesheimer, and his immediate family (this until the single relatives married) as well as with whatever guests had
been invited.[69] The meal would be followed by "genuine *Schabbat-Menucha*", the
Sabbath respite, all those present sitting around, chatting and reading. On Saturday
after synagogue, the "entire large family and many friends and acquaintances" would
visit.[70] In villages, where circumstances were less formal, relatives would drop by
unannounced; unrelated people would pay far less frequent visits but might meet in a
beer garden or drop by when a friend's relatives were visiting from Berlin or Paris.[71]

---

[66]On the complex new German-Jewish identity developed by German Jews, see also Marion Berghahn,
German-Jewish Refugees in England, London 1984, p. 45. The emergence of a Jewish familial "inside" and
German "outside" would appear to have been anticipated by Jewish Enlightenment thinkers from Moses
Mendelssohn in Germany to Judah Leib Gordon in Russia who, drawing on the European
Enlightenment distinction between private and public, sacred and secular, urged Jews to privatise their
Judaism. Gordon (1831–1892) suggests in a poem that the Jew be "a man in the streets and a Jew at
home". See: Michael Stanislawski, *For Whom do I Toil? Judah Leib Gordon and the Crisis of Russian Jewry*, New
York 1988, pp. 49–52.
[67]Till van Rahden has used this term in *Juden und andere Breslauer*, pp. 19–21.
[68]Ulrich Baumann, *Nachbarschaften*, p. 75.
[69]Hirsch, p. 1.
[70]*ibid.*, p. 3.
[71]Ulrich Baumann, '*Nachbarschaften*,' p. 78.

As is to be expected, urban Jews entertained guests more often than their rural counterparts on days other than the Sabbath.[72] In a typical bourgeois and cultivated German-Jewish family, one might spend the evening at home with friends over dinner, playing music together, or reading aloud from classical or popular plays.[73] Lotte Hirschberg informs us that her family in turn-of-the-century Breslau played chamber music regularly with other Jewish friends at one or another of their homes. This habit was itself often rooted within the family: in the 1990s, Hirschberg explained to her grandchildren that "in the same way we sit nowadays in front of the radio or television, we would sit in the evenings in the so-called salon and listen to grandma's piano music".[74]

Urban cultural events provided another inviting venue for Jewish middle and upper middle class friends and family to meet. In Posen, for example, Jews supported the theatre, which served as a propitious setting for combining *Bildung* and sociability. Holding subscriptions, they would mingle with relatives and other Jewish theatre enthusiasts during intermissions.[75] In 1910, wealthy Königsberg Jews likewise helped subsidise the *Neues Schauspielhaus*.[76] In any event, starting at the turn of the century, younger Jews had begun to meet in more casual locales such as beer halls and restaurants. Newly-weds Rahel Straus and her husband met their friends, for example, in Munich beer halls: "That seemed strange to me at first. But there were wonderful, huge beer cellars. … One drank beer, ate … in innocent, cheerful company." For a wife and a full-time physician, she noted, "this type of socialising had the advantage that it spared exertion … in the household".[77]

Further opportunities for sociability could be found in a rather famous milieu: "taking the waters". Those spas which made Jews feel welcome, as opposed to those known to be antisemitic,[78] provided a place in which relatives could gather to enjoy each other's company; for younger visitors, the spas helped set the stage for suitable marriages.[79] Attestations to that effect are abundant: we are informed, for example, that in 1894 the Hirschfeld brothers from Hamburg planned spa vacations for the sake of meeting prospective Jewish brides,[80] and that spas as marriage markets had a long tradition in the family of Philippine Landau (born in 1869) – she expresses

---

[72]Cf., for instance, Straus, p. 121; Sophie Dann, untitled diary, memoirs, LBI, p. 7 (for the late 1880s).

[73]Compare the "tea evenings" described in Anne-Charlotte Trepp, *Sanfte Männlichkeit und selbständige Weiblichkeit: Frauen und Männer im Hamburger Bürgertum zwischen 1770 und 1840*, Göttingen 1996, p. 375.

[74]Hirschberg, p. 6.

[75]'Adolph Asch', in Monika Richarz (ed.), *Jüdisches Leben in Deutschland. Selbstzeugnisse zur Sozialgeschichte* (3 volumes), Stuttgart 1976–1982, vol. 2, *Selbstzeugnisse zur Sozialgeschichte im Kaiserreich*, pp. 221–235, here p. 229. See also Jenny Wierusowski, untitled diary, May 3, 1905, memoirs, LBI, pp. 162–163 and Ehrlich, pp. 6, 15.

[76]See Yoram K. Jacoby, *Jüdisches Leben in Königsberg/Pr. im 20. Jahrhundert*, Würzburg 1983, p. 18.

[77]Straus, p. 121.

[78]On this topic, see Frank Bajohr, *"Unser Hotel ist judenfrei". Bäder-Antisemitismus im 19. und 20. Jahrhundert*, Frankfurt am Main, forthcoming.

[79]Herzfeld, pp. 41, 53; Philippine Landau, *Kindheitserinnerungen: Bilder aus einer rheinischen Kleinstadt des vorigen Jahrhunderts*, Dietenheim 1956, p. 124; Jacob Epstein, untitled memoirs, memoirs, LBI, p. 5; Erika Bucholtz, *Henri Hinrichsen und der Musikverlag C.F. Peters: Deutsch-jüdisches Bürgertum in Leipzig von 1891 bis 1938*, Tübingen 2001, (Schriftenreihe wissenschaftlicher Abhandlungen des Leo Baeck Instituts 65), p. 36.

[80]See 'Isidor Hirschfeld', in Richarz, (ed.), *Jewish Life*, p. 232.

thanks that her grandparents had met at one such watering place.[81] But spas offered a variety of possible contacts. In spas such as Bad Ems, Jews from Eastern and Western Europe mingled.[82] Jews also met other Jewish guests in exclusively Jewish hotels that offered kosher meals, or in other hotels friendly to a Jewish clientele. Betty Lifschütz succinctly summarises the situation as follows: "Even when we went on holidays … we only came together with other Jewish people. There was a strong Jewish bond."[83]

There is considerable documentation showing that the social life of Jews in Imperial Germany was often self-consciously set in a Jewish milieu. This tendency could already be manifest in the social parameters set for children: in the 1880s, Paul Mühsam's family was one of a few Jewish families in the small town of Zittau (Saxony). For the sake of providing Jewish companionship for their own child, the parents of a Jewish schoolmate frequently invited Paul to their home.[84] Decades later, in Alex Bein's village in Lower Franconia, "Jews and Christians were closely connected in daily life … but went their separate ways socially".[85] Similarly, in the villages of Baden, where up to one third of Jewish newly-wed women had moved from other towns, the natural propensity was to approach relatives and other Jewish residents when trying to make new friends.[86]

Cities showed comparable patterns. In Lübeck, the Mühsams associated primarily with Jewish families in the 1880s and 1890s, "even though, in daily friendly-neighbourly interactions there were no barriers".[87] Contacts between Jews and non-Jews would take place somewhat more often – if still rather infrequently – among people with somewhat higher social status. In the last century's first decade, for example, there were meetings once or twice a week in Alex Bein's village between the Catholic priest, forestry official, doctor, and Christian and Jewish school teachers to discuss material in the journals, chat, and play cards. The priest also enjoyed stopping in at Bein's household during Passover to enjoy *mazzekaffee*, that is, a cup of coffee with *mazot* in it.[88] In the very different setting of the Karlsruhe *haute bourgeoisie* during the First World War, Hugo Marx's aunt and uncle also mingled with some non-Jews – but in this case the interaction was also due to the uncle's position as *Geheimrat* and the aunt's charitable work. Marx believed, in fact, that his relatives lived in the same "ghetto-like conditions" he endured in Heidelberg, the only difference being that the Jewish community in Karlsruhe included more academics and members of the upper middle class.[89]

In general, one can assume that strictly observant Jews had even less contact with non-Jews than did their secular counterparts. One memoir does point to broader opportunities for mixing in the liberal Jewish community. In Stettin, Rosa Vogelstein

[81]Landau, pp. 29–30.
[82]David Blackbourn, 'Taking the Waters: Meeting Places of the Fashionable World', in Martin Geyer and Johannes Paulmann, eds., *The Mechanics of Internationalism: Culture, Society and Politics from the 1840s to the First World War*, London 2001, p. 452.
[83]Lipton in Foster (ed.), p. 24.
[84]'Paul Mühsam', in Richarz (ed.), *Jewish Life*, pp. 252–257, here p. 255.
[85]Alex Bein *"Hier kannst Du nicht jeden grüssen": Erinnerungen und Betrachtungen*, Hildesheim 1996, p. 19.
[86]Ulrich Baumann, *Nachbarschaften*, p. 79.
[87]Charlotte Landau-Mühsam, memoirs, memoirs, LBI, pp. 22, 29.
[88]Bein, pp. 19–20; 47.
[89]Marx, p. 104.

and her husband Rabbi Heinemann Vogelstein interacted with a wide variety of non-Jews. Rosa was engaged in a range of educational and feminist activities and the rabbi, a liberal Jewish leader, taught Greek philosophy in one of her continuing education projects; in this and other ways both were meeting people well beyond their immediate Jewish circle. Rosa herself brought home non-Jewish friends and the couple regularly entertained people regardless of faith. Reflecting on the relationships that grew from these gatherings, their daughter notes that "at such events, people behaved differently from the way they did in their more closed circles. That this kind of sociability was to be found in a rabbi's home probably amazed many Jews who had been trying in vain to make contacts with their fellow [non-Jewish] citizens."[90]

In any event, such sociability had its limits; several examples offered by memoirs illuminate the boundaries between Christians and Jews even when they interacted socially. Frankfurt's Heilbrunn family provides a striking example: although the professional and political activities of the head of the family involved considerable contact with non-Jews – he was a mayoral candidate in 1913 – he never invited a non-Jew into his home.[91] In Berlin, the banker Carl Fürstenberg (born in 1850) observed that even among the most integrated Jews, including those who had converted or intermarried, "people knew each other personally and formed, in a sense, a large family".[92] Several decades later, the situation seems not to have changed much among fully acculturated bourgeois Berlin Jews. In her memoir, for instance, Lily Pincus (born in 1898) recalls that she "got together essentially, but not exclusively, with young Jewish people" and that "my parents had only Jewish friends, and almost all the people with whom they had anything to do, like doctors, dentists, tailors, were Jews."[93] Outside limited socialist-intellectual and bohemian circles, where Jews and non-Jews mingled with greater success, "one could not speak of a sociability that erased the boundaries between the confessions".[94]

Nor could one speak of confessional mixing that erased the boundaries between the private and public spheres. Insofar as current historiography argues that "sociability at home" created such fluid boundaries, it did so for Jews primarily *within* Jewish society.[95] There was really not enough mixing between Jews and Christians within the home to eliminate the boundaries between private Jewish and public non-

[90]Julie Braun-Vogelstein, *Was niemals stirbt: Gestalten und Erinnerungen*, Stuttgart, 1966, pp. 75, 80.
[91]Hopp, p. 153.
[92]See Cella-Margarethe Girardet, *Jüdische Mäzene für die Preussischen Museen zu Berlin*, Egelsbach 1997, p. 21.
[93]Lily Pincus, *Verloren-gewonnen: Mein Weg von Berlin nach London*, Stuttgart 1980, p. 10. See also pp. 17, 24, 27, 33.
[94]Hopp, p. 151; *idem*, p. 153, also cites a 1902 survey by the Berlin Attorneys' Association indicating that non-Jews preferred Jewish lawyers for cases of "intimate family affairs" because, generally, Jews "stood further removed from their social circles". Cf. Bucholtz, whose argument that Hinrichsen's "open house" reveals social integration seems less than convincing to me, the arrangement rather appearing to reflect convivial business contacts. Another non-memoir source should be cited here: one set of interviews in the late 1980s and early 1990s with sixty Jews formerly living in Königsberg. Of those whose parents had been active in socially mixed settings, more than half believed these parents had "mainly Jewish and a few individual Christian acquaintances". Jews rarely had "very close Christian friends". See Stefanie Schüler-Springorum, *Die jüdische Minderheit in Königsberg/Preussen, 1871–1945*, Göttingen 1996, p. 81.
[95]Cf. Gisel Mettele, 'Der private Raum als öffentlicher Ort. Geselligkeit im bürgerlichen Haus', in Dieter Hein and Andreas Schulz (eds.), *Bürgerkultur im 19. Jahrhundert: Bildung, Kunst und Lebenswelt*, Munich 1996, pp. 156, 168.

Jewish domains. Jews could venture across these boundaries, but only so far. In part, they hoped to avoid private, drawing-room antisemitism, being snubbed or made to feel unwelcome. However, their defensiveness should not be overstated. Jews had a strong sense of mutual affinity and sought comfort among their own.

Communal Social Life: Organisational Solidarity

From the smallest villages to major urban centres, Jews reached out to each other. Many met at the synagogue for reasons that were not only religious but also social. Thus Isidor Hirschfeld's family, situated in a small West Prussian town called Kasparus, felt obliged to join the few other Jews "on occasions of joy and sorrow".[96] In Stargard, another West Prussian town (located near Danzig), "Jewish life was centred around the synagogue", where "young people could walk about ... and exchange looks" in its courtyard and women could "chat undisturbed by any household duties" in its women's gallery.[97] For some people, it seems, "the most important part of the service was the conversation after it, the *Schwaetz*, when Jewish men stood in the synagogue yard and chatted".[98] Photos of Jewish women and men milling around in front of the synagogue after services may attest to somewhat more far-ranging, if fleeting, relations; opportunities in this regard were also being offered by religious structures such as the traditional *chevrot*, the male and female burial societies.

Just as its non-Jewish equivalent, Jewish club life blossomed on the local level in the latter part of the nineteenth century.[99] In mid-nineteenth century south Baden, Jewish men organised their own reading groups (sometimes led by Jewish teachers), as a reaction to being barred from non-Jewish clubs and out of a desire for both German *Bildung* and Jewish learning. Some of these groups lasted into the Weimar years; others dwindled as Jews moved to the cities.[100] In 1864, the Jewish community in Sulzburg, a town in Baden with 416 Jews among 1,296 inhabitants, amounting to a 32 per cent Jewish population, supported a reading society, a glee club, a

---

[96]'Isidor Hirschfeld', in Richarz (ed.), *Jewish Life*, p. 229.

[97]'Charlotte Popper' *ibid.*, pp. 266–270, here p. 266.

[98]See Oded Heilbronner and Jacob Borut, 'Leaving the Walls or Anomalous Activity: The Catholic and Jewish Rural Bourgeoisie in Germany', in *Comparative Studies in Society and History*, vol. 40, no. 3 (1998), pp. 475–502, here p. 496 (the authors do not cite the memoirs from which they draw this conclusion).

[99]For clubs and associations in Protestant regions, see essays in Otto Dann (ed.), *Vereinswesen und bürgerliche Gesellschaft in Deutschland*, Munich 1984 (*Historische Zeitschrift*, Beiheft 9 [neue Folge]). For those formed by Catholics in the Schwarzwald and Allgäu, see Oded Heilbronner, 'Die Besonderheit des katholischen Bürgertums im ländlichen Süddeutschland' in *Blätter für deutsche Landesgeschichte*, vol. 131 (1995), pp. 249–250. Protestants and Catholics may have interacted even less than Christians and Jews. In 'Religion and Conflict: Protestants, Catholics, and Anti-Semitism in the State of Baden in the Era of Wilhelm II', *Central European History*, vol. 27, no. 3 (1994), p. 293, Helmut Walser Smith quotes references to "peaceful segregation" between the denominations, with Catholics forming a "dense web of Catholic organisations" and Protestants joining members of their faith in social groups. Smith presents a careful analysis of intra-Christian tensions in his *German Nationalism and Religious Conflict: Culture, Ideology, Politics, 1870–1914*, Princeton 1995.

[100]Ulrich Baumann, *Nachbarshaften*, p. 100.

women's club and several charities.[101] Even tiny villages could sometimes boast of having more than one Jewish club – some of course proliferating as a result of disputes: "It was like this: there was one club and then they fought among themselves, and then there were two clubs."[102] Some clubs competed with one another, making social life even livelier.[103] Cities with a significant Jewish population could offer even richer possibilities for club activities. Berlin had at least 62 Jewish clubs in 1896, and Frankfurt am Main had 137 clubs and foundations by 1911.[104] By the 1890s, approximately 5,000 local Jewish clubs functioned in Germany.[105] Moreover, organisations for rabbis, Jewish teachers, and other religious employees grew nationally and regionally so that by 1905 there were 36 such organisations with about 7,300 members.[106]

Nationwide Jewish organisations especially emerged in the 1890s.[107] A brief survey of a few of the more prominent national organisations shows the breadth of their offerings. Jews could choose among groups subsidising Jewish culture, promoting Jewish philanthropy, and supporting Jewish self-defence – such activities often also being accompanied by participation in non-Jewish associations.

Jewish leaders founded the *Deutsch-Israelitische Gemeindebund* (the Union of German-Jewish Communities) in 1869 to provide some kind of united structure to the disparate Jewish communities. Its mandate focused on education and welfare, but it was meant more generally to promote the "common interests of German Jewry".[108] Regional associations such as the *Verband der Synagogengemeinden Ostpreussens* (Association of Synagogue Communities of East Prussia) also provided organisational structure.

In 1882, antisemitism that had sprung up again in the late 1870s, and that was limiting Jewish entry into Freemason lodges, prompted the founding of a lodge-organisation for Jewish men, the now well-known *B'nai B'rith* ("Sons of the Covenant").[109] A typical early member was Gustav Tuch, who had belonged to non-Jewish organisations most of his life and, although a member of the Jewish community board, did not attend synagogue.[110] *B'nai B'rith* had swelled to 1,200

---

[101]Lesegesellschaft "Eintracht", founded 1846; Sängerbund, founded 1862; and the Israelitische Frauenverein, founded 1885. See Ingeborg Hecht, *"Ich bin doch geborener Sulzburger und Deutscher": Aus der Geschichte der israelitischen Gemeinde Sulzburg*, Sulzburg 1994, pp. 16, 19. For Gailingen, which had four Jewish clubs in 1867, see Ulrich Baumann, *Nachbarschaften*, p. 108.

[102]*ibid.*, p. 74 (referring to the village of Breisach).

[103]*ibid.*, pp. 72–74. The assertion by Borut and Heilbronner, pp. 488–489, that the Jewish village bourgeoisie "abandoned [its] system of traditional societies and tried to integrate into the system of bourgeois societies in [its] places of residence", appears to be an overstatement.

[104]For Berlin see photograph of page from 'Der Berliner Vereinsbote' in Richarz (ed.), *Jüdisches Leben*, p. 82; for Frankfurt am Main see Hopp, pp. 138–140, 299.

[105]Thon, p. 59.

[106]*ibid.*, pp. 56–57.

[107]*ibid.*, p. 59. See also Pulzer, pp. 13–14; Andreas Reinke, *Judentum und Wohlfahrtspflege, Das jüdische Krankenhaus in Breslau, 1726–1944*, Hannover 1999, p. 181. About 40 per cent of the approximately 5,000 Jewish clubs in Germany in 1906 had formed in the last quarter of the nineteenth century.

[108]*Mittheilungen vom Deutsch-Israelitischen Gemeindebunde*, no. 34, Berlin, May 1892 (Gesamtarchiv der deutschen Juden, Centrum Judaicum, Berlin, A Al 1, no. 17, Allenstein [film 26, frame 213.])

[109]The organisation had originally been established by Jewish communities in the United States in 1843.

[110]Sabine Knappe, 'Jüdische Frauenorganisationen in Hamburg zwischen Assimilation, jüdischer Identität und weiblicher Emanzipation während des Kaiserreichs', M.A. Thesis, University of Hamburg 1991, p. 124. Tuch was born in Hamburg in 1834.

members by 1885, multiplying to 8,600 members in 79 lodges by 1912.[111] With its goals including philanthropy and education, the *B'nai B'rith* was an élitist organisation, acceptance as a member signalling bourgeois social status. Inversely, in small towns rejection by the lodge "was tantamount to social ostracism".[112] Many now joining lodges in the larger towns had previously lived in villages. Cahnmann suggests that these Jews did not feel comfortable joining the large urban Orthodox synagogues, with their "top-hatted worshippers", preferring "philanthropy", which had begun "to assume the place that formal piety had occupied at an earlier period".[113]

After a decade of political and social antisemitism, leading Jewish and non-Jewish liberals founded the *Verein zur Abwehr des Antisemitismus* (Association for the Defence Against Antisemitism) in 1890. Its formation signalling the need for a more open, public approach to the problem of antisemitism, the organisation attracted over 12,000 members;[114] it drew on Jewish grassroots organisations for financial support. In a small town in East Prussia in 1893, the Jewish community collected sums ranging from one to six marks per person to send to the Association's headquarters in Berlin.[115] Established in 1893 and representing Jews who avowed a German identity, the largest and most successful Jewish civic organisation in Imperial Germany, the *Centralverein deutscher Staatsbürger jüdischen Glaubens* (henceforth C.V.), saw its main goal as defending Jewish civic rights and interests.[116] The C.V. also provided a social context for Jews who may have belonged to non-sectarian organisations but wanted to socialise in expressly Jewish circles as well. Claiming about 200,000 members in 1916 (including affiliated societies and some 40,000 individual members), it had invited women onto its board in 1908, when the Prussian law that banned women from political organisations was rescinded.[117] Another way to measure the success of the C.V.'s position is to note the scant attraction that Zionism held for German Jews before the First World War.[118]

In any case, the fight against antisemitism did not absorb most of the time Jews spent socialising. Many also joined the *Verband der Vereine für jüdische Geschichte und Literatur* (United Associations for Jewish History and Literature). Founded, like the C.V. in 1893,

[111]Hopp, p. 132.

[112]'Samuel Spiro', in Richarz (ed.), *Jewish Life*, p. 208.

[113]Werner Cahnmann, 'Village and Small-Town Jews in Germany: A Typological Study', in *LBI Year Book*, vol. 19 (1974), pp. 107–130, here p. 128.

[114]Barbara Suchy, 'The Verein zur Abwehr des Antisemitismus (I)', in *LBI Year Book*, vol. 28 (1983), pp. 205–240 and 'The Verein zur Abwehr des Antisemitismus (II)', in *LBI Year Book*, vol. 30 (1985), pp. 67–104.

[115]'Zur Abwehr des Antisemitismus', Gesamtarchiv der deutschen Juden, Centrum Judaicum, Berlin, A AI 1, no. 13, "Generalakten des Vorstandes 1888–1899".

[116]Thon, p. 58.

[117]Ismar Schorsch, *Jewish Reactions to German Anti-Semitism, 1870–1914*, New York 1972, p. 119. The law, known as the *Vereinsgesetz*, was passed in 1851; similar laws in Bavaria and Saxony were even stricter.

[118]In 1914, Zionism had roughly 10,000 followers in Germany, including a substantial number of Russian nationals. Zionist groups grew in response to local appeals and attacks against Jews. See, for example, the case of Duisburg in Ludger Heid, 'Harry Epstein. Zionistischer Politiker und Anwalt der Ostjuden', in Jan-Pieter Barbian, Michael Brocke and Ludger Heid (eds.), *Juden im Ruhrgebiet*, Essen 1999 pp. 105–132. Only four Zionist organisations for women existed in Germany before the First World War: those in Hamburg, Berlin, Posen and Königshütte.

this organisation began with 29 branches, attracting about 15,000 members by 1903 and encompassing more than 200 branches before 1914. On a local level, in Westphalia, for example, as many as five to six per cent of Jews were members, a relatively significant portion when one takes account of the fact that children could not join.[119] Focusing on Jewish knowledge in order to promote Jewish self-awareness,[120] the organisation supported libraries, lectures, and a popular yearbook.[121]

From local singing groups on upwards to the national level, segregation of the sexes seems to have been taken for granted in such organisations, as was the case in their Catholic and Protestant equivalents;[122] it influenced the character of Jewish leisure time. Both before and after 1908 men were at the head of all the main mixed-sex Jewish organisations. Women did, of course, attend public lectures, and even deliver them. They also took part in celebrations with their husbands or brothers and (in both the C.V. and *B'nai B'rith*) joined women's auxiliaries. As a result of the pervading sexual segregation, Jewish women's organisations, growing out of traditional women's charities, flourished in this period – more than half of all women's organisations in existence in 1908 had been founded after 1900.[123] Like Christian groups of the same sort, Jewish women's groups had begun to reshape the public sphere to reflect broader female concerns; the Jewish women also joined non-sectarian women's organisations.[124] One Hamburg association, the *Israelitische humanitäre Frauenverein* (Israelite Humanitarian Women's Society), typified their popularity: a small group at its inception in 1893, it had grown to 176 members by 1895 and to over 750 by 1912.[125] In Frankfurt, Bertha Pappenheim founded the *Jüdischer Frauenbund* (League of Jewish Women) in 1904, encompassing many of the social welfare efforts of Jewish women under its aegis.[126] The League's emphasis on women's education and equality and its alliance with the German women's movement gave a political, feminist form to what could otherwise be seen as an organisation comprising social welfare projects alone.

By 1905 a total of twelve leading Jewish organisations stretched across Germany; there were also twenty-three major Prussian regional associations.[127] When taking national, regional and local groups into account, tens of thousands of Jews belonged to Jewish organisations. These groups offered conviviality as well as the opportunity to pursue special interests. Jews could get together to support Jewish teachers or defend Jewish rights, to learn about Jewish poets, or simply to go hiking with other Jews.

---

[119]Trude Maurer, *Die Entwicklung der jüdischen Minderheit in Deutschland (1780–1933)*, Tübingen 1992, p. 58. Statistics on the United Associations are taken from *Jüdisches Lexikon*, Berlin 1927–1930, vol. 4, 2, col. 1169.

[120]Awareness of the need to inform non-Jews about Judaism also marked the organisation's spirit. See Chaim Schatzker, *Jüdische Jugend im zweiten Kaiserreich*, Frankfurt am Main 1988, pp. 109–110, citing *AZJ*, vol. 10 (10 March 1899).

[121]*AZJ*, vol. 22 (29 May 1903), pp. 257–59; 'Max Daniel', in Richarz (ed.), *Jewish Life*, p. 223. Daniel recalls the excitement with which he attended his branch in Stettin around 1905 ("I didn't skip a single meeting").

[122]Heilbronner, p. 251.

[123]Kaplan, *The Making of the Jewish Middle Class*, p. 202.

[124]On Christian participation in such organisations see Ursula Baumann, *Protestantismus und Frauenemanzipation in Deutschland, 1850 bis 1920*, Frankfurt am Main 1992; Gisela Breuer, *Frauenbewegung im Katholizismus*, Frankfurt am Main 1998.

[125]Knappe, pp. 129–133.

[126]Marion Kaplan, *The Jewish Feminist Movement in Germany*, Greenport 1979.

[127]Thon, p. 58.

The first board of the *Weibliche Fürsorge*, a Jewish women's organisation in Frankfurt am Main (1907), including Bertha Pappenheim, Henriette Fürth, Henny Elkan, Sidonie Dann, and Mrs. Epstein. (Bertha Pappenheim Collection)

By courtesy of the Leo Baeck Institute, New York

Jewish organisations provided more than conviviality, special interests, or Jewish knowledge; for many individuals, they provided the community they no longer sought from the synagogue alone. In other words they became "their principal mode of Jewish identification".[128] Others actively sought a Jewish bourgeois social milieu for its familiarity and useful social and business connections, or because of a perception of shared values and culture. Finally, as has already been noted, the burgeoning of Jewish organisations was also a response to antisemitism.

Communal Social Life: Fissures and Fault Lines

Class prejudices influenced the nature of Jewish sociability. Adolph Asch, for example, describes Posen's society in the 1880s and 1890s as divided into three groups: the Polish population of workers and craftspeople, the "Christian-German" population of professionals and businessmen, and a Jewish middle class that had been there for

---

[128]Steven M. Lowenstein, 'The Community', in Michael A. Meyer (ed.), *German-Jewish History in Modern Times*, vol. 3, New York 1997, p. 144.

several generations.[129] Within the last group, Asch portrays eight different rungs on the social ladder, from the most elegant and fashionable to the lowest, noting that the boundaries had weakened somewhat since his grandmother's days.[130] And Max Daniel points to the class prejudices he saw among Jewish academics "who fancied themselves superior" in Stettin, "a very liberal city, friendly to the Jews".[131]

Urban dance classes for young people both solidified Jewish cohesiveness and reinforced inter-class distinctions. In Munich the sons of the "elegant" Jewish families, those with money or titles, attended the mixed, Jewish and non-Jewish dance lessons. The children of "ordinary" Jewish business people attended lessons in which only Jews participated. As a young teenager, Philipp Löwenfeld preferred the Jewish lessons because his friends attended them, but his parents insisted that he take part in the "better" lessons in the hope that he would meet up with young people of his social standing.[132] In other cities as well, dance lessons remained segregated by class, ethnicity, or both. In Frankfurt am Main, Margarete Sallis went to lessons for boys and girls from the "top" Christian and Jewish families; in Berlin, the Eycks also provided class-appropriate lessons for their sons and daughters, clearing their own dining room occasionally so the young dancers could meet at home.[133] And in Breslau, the Baer and Reif schools attracted the Jewish middle class. Adolf Riesenfeld attended the Baer Institute, "entirely Jewish" but not as "distinguished" as the dance lessons at the Reif school.[134]

Some small-town Jews, with even fewer co-religionists to choose from, also maintained class biases. Although they united in political situations, they otherwise lacked social cohesiveness. About a hundred Jewish families lived in Stargard in the first decades of the twentieth century. According to Charlotte Popper, born there in 1898, "in everyday life, class rules were sacrosanct. … We had it good because we belonged to the middle class, which represented the broadest section. The 'wealthy' had it bad in their isolation, while the poor in their parts of town cultivated neighbourly relations in solidarity with the non-Jews".[135] In villages with few Jews, class differences stood out even more markedly,[136] Jews praying together, participating in charities as givers and receivers, but having little else in common. It was quite easy to identify the poor, and those "work-worn, tired men" who continued their Jewish learning impressed the others.[137]

Children, too, noticed these hierarchies. In Stargard, for example, the Hebrew school teacher allowed the children of wealthy Jews to sit in the front rows, relegat-

---

[129]'Adolph Asch' in Richarz (ed.), *Jüdisches Leben*, p. 221.

[130]*ibid.*, p. 223.

[131]'Max Daniel', in Richarz (ed.), *Jewish Life*, p. 222.

[132]'Philipp Löwenfeld', *ibid.*, p. 235.

[133]Sallis, p. 22; Eyck, untitled memoirs, memoirs, LBI, pp. 72, 75 (1896).

[134]"[T]hose who wanted to count themselves among the 'better' circles went to Reif, that means there were just purely Jewish participants, but also what one would call today in Germany 'Mischlinge', and people who had become richer and had hoped to assimilate through baptism. At Baer [one found] exclusively the Jewish middle class". Adolf Riesenfeld, untitled diary, memoirs, LBI, entry of 12 February 1941.

[135]'Charlotte Popper', in Richarz (ed.), *Jewish Life*, p. 267.

[136]Michel, p. 268.

[137]'Samuel Spiro', in Richarz (ed.), *Jewish Life*, p. 202.

ing the poorest children to the rear. Wealthy children could transgress without reproach, but the teacher often punished the pupils in the last rows to the point of thrashing.[138] Henry Buxbaum of Friedberg (Upper Hesse) recalls how these class differences affected him, the son of a peddler. He was invited to his richer friends' homes but

> I was never able to overcome my feelings of inferior status within the social life of the community. .... [E]ach time I was invited to a birthday party ... I remember with what awe and discomfort I entered such a house. ... All the brightness and riches made me feel small. ... I never knew where to turn, where to stand, or where to sit.[139]

Wealth was not the sole criterion dividing people; often place of origin counted as much or more. Born in 1885, Samuel Spiro describes Jewish "society" in the small city of Fulda (Hesse-Nassau), where

> [T]here already existed a so-called upper class of university graduates, educated merchants, some industrialists, bankers, and some officials. Then there was the class of the old-established families, who by virtue of their Fulda roots thought that they were better than their brethren who had moved from the villages. The latter formed the third social layer, and it was almost impossible for them to be accepted into so-called high society.[140]

These tensions escalated when native Jews derided either the Eastern European origins of newcomers or their rural roots. Buxbaum notes that Friedberg's Jews, some of whom had lived there three hundred years or more, "considered themselves nobility and looked down with contempt ... at the 'yokels'" who had arrived more recently from the east or from surrounding villages.[141] Moreover, German Jews often felt threatened by either the Orthodoxy or the political radicalism that some Eastern Jews brought with them. Hugo Marx notes that their "deficient German and peculiar clothing" set them apart.[142] Nevertheless, class counted for more than such factors. Within one generation, middle-class Eastern European Jewish immigrants came into close contact with the German-Jewish middle classes – in social clubs among other places: "All of the mutual-aid societies, trade associations, *B'nai B'rith* lodges and Masonic lodges include[d] Eastern European Jewish members."[143]

In view of these social divisions, can one speak of a cohesive Jewish community at all? The answer is arguably in the affirmative. Wealthier Jews clung to their class pretensions, creating fissures in, but remaining part of, a larger whole. Even with class differences and the presence of snobs, all understood themselves to be part of one community brought together by religion, tradition and history. Moreover, obliged to maintain a solid front against antisemitism, Jews accepted responsibility for each other across class lines, supporting charities so that their poor would not call nega-

---

[138]'Charlotte Popper', *ibid.*, pp. 267–268.
[139]'Henry Buxbaum', *ibid.*, p. 302.
[140]'Samuel Spiro', *ibid.*, p. 208.
[141]'Henry Buxbaum', *ibid.*, pp. 301–302.
[142]Marx, p. 46.
[143]Klara Eschelbacher, 'Die Ostjüdische Einwanderungsbevölkerung der Stadt Berlin', in *Zeitschrift für Demographie und Statistik der Juden* , nos. 1–3 (1923), pp. 17–18.

tive attention to themselves. These charities, a "separate Jewish culture of welfare", strengthened connections among Jews (even if that culture may have contributed to a further distance between Jews and non-Jews).[144] In addition, providing for their co-religionists in the company of other Jews also allowed Jews who were increasingly secularised to maintain links to Jewish causes and Jewish identity.[145] Furthermore, in small towns and villages wealthier Jews lived in relatively close proximity to their poorer coreligionists. They often went to the same schools and worshipped in the only synagogue available. Finally, rapid Jewish upward mobility produced a certain fluidity between classes.[146] In sum, these national, regional and local Jewish organisations provided a *Teilkultur* – a "partial subculture",[147] inviting Jews to join – in numbers never before seen in German-Jewish history – but also remaining porous enough to allow them to leave.

Non-Jewish Friendships

This essay has focused on the textures and qualities of intra-Jewish relationships. Yet, as indicated, Jews participated avidly in the civic, cultural, and social lives of their local communities and maintained personal and business relationships with non-Jews.[148] Jews increasingly belonged to both Jewish and non-sectarian organisations. This was a sign of increased integration compared to previous generations, but also a reflection of normal bourgeois associational patterns in imperial Germany. With more leisure time and wealth at their disposal, many middle class people in general were joining more than one organisation.[149] Jewish integration into both formal and informal urban and rural life, from the *Kränzchen* or *Stammtische* in small town taverns to the clubs in big cities, reached its high point around 1900.[150]

In Imperial Germany, Jews and non-Jewish Germans mingled as neighbours, schoolmates and business associates, and in social situations ranging from informal gatherings to formal organisations. Some intimate life-long friendships developed from this interaction. The rising rate of intermarriage verifies the increasingly intimate contact between Jews and non-Jews. Young people generally do not marry the first person to whom they are attracted and all the less so if that person is of anoth-

[144]Rainer Liedtke, 'Jewish Welfare in Hamburg and Manchester', in Michael Brenner, Rainer Liedtke and David Rechter (eds.) (co-ordinated by Werner E. Mosse), *Two Nations: British and German Jews in Comparative Perspective*, Tübingen 1999 (Schriftenreihe wissenschaftlicher Abhandlungen des Leo Baeck Instituts 60), p. 271.

[145]*ibid.*, p. 262. See also Derek Penslar, 'Philanthropy, the "Social Question", and Jewish Identity in Imperial Germany', in *LBI Year Book*, vol. 38 (1993), pp. 51–74.

[146]'Joseph Lange' in Richarz (ed.), *Jewish Life*, p. 185.

[147]Borut and Heilbronner, p. 488.

[148]See Marion Kaplan, 'Friendship on the Margins: Jewish Social Relations in Imperial Germany', in *Central European History*, vol. 34, no. 4 (2001), pp. 471–502.

[149]In mid-1870s Mannheim, 39 per cent of Music Society members and 44 per cent of Art Society members belonged to the "Harmonie", the city's most élite association. Dieter Hein, 'Soziale Konstituierungsfaktoren des Bürgertums', in Lothar Gall (ed.), *Stadt und Bürgertum im Übergang von der traditionalen zur modernen Gesellschaft*, Munich 1993, pp. 179–180.

[150]Kaplan, 'Friendship', pp. 471–502.

A group portrait of volunteer firefighters (*Freiwillige Feuerwehr*) of the Linnich
Community comprising Jewish and non-Jewish members. Photograph dated
1914–1918. (Linnich Community Collection)

By courtesy of the Leo Baeck Institute, New York

er religion or ethnicity.[151] It can thus be assumed that many of the Jewish partners
in these intermarriages had previously had non-Jewish friends and, possibly, romantic attachments with non-Jews, finding intimacy, trust and reciprocity with them.

Intermarriage notwithstanding, social recognition did not necessarily imply total
social acceptance. The rules of sociability were complicated. Encounters with non-
Jews tended to be more formal, less intimate,[152] and far more likely to take place in
public rather than at home. Interactions remained ambivalent: Jews and other
Germans enjoyed contact with one another while remaining distinctive and apart.

Many relationships between Jews and non-Jews would fall into what Georg
Simmel has called "differentiated friendships" that connect individuals according to
common intellectual interests, common experiences, common careers or situations in
life. As opposed to his notion of (non-qualified) "friendship", seen as "more apt than
love to connect a whole person with another person in its [*sic*] entirety", most of the
relationships between Jews and non-Jews maintained a degree of reserve, avoiding

[151]In 1903, 8.5 per cent of Jewish grooms and 7.3 per cent of Jewish brides intermarried. Intermarriages
reached a highpoint during the war – in 1915, 27 per cent of Jewish women and 40 per cent of Jewish
men intermarried. These percentages dropped thereafter. Thus, the majority of Jews remained endog-
amous. For an excellent study of this topic, see Kerstin Meiring, *Die Christlich-Jüdische Mischehe in
Deutschland 1840–1933*, Hamburg 1998 (statistics on p. 95).

[152]Cahnmann, p. 58.

certain areas of intimacy, interest and feeling.[153] Jews understood this and, to some extent, accepted and fostered it as well. Hedwig Wachenheim's mother sought non-Jewish friendships and had her children baptised after her husband's death. Yet when her mother made new acquaintances during her summer vacations, her grandmother would ask, "'De nous' [meaning Jews] or 'de vous' [non-Jews]?"[154]

In her account of life in Germany, Charlotte Wolff, born in 1901 near Danzig, observes that

> The family is a circle, turning round on itself with little room for friendships. Jewish families were ... a closely-knit community, bound together by mutual help and affection. Rarely did they let their relations down, even when feelings were antagonistic.

She then remarks that

> Friendships with other Jews were redolent of pleasant family ties but on a rather casual level, and contacts with non-Jews did not go further than acquaintanceships. A certain separateness between Jews and Gentiles was self-chosen, as no sign of antisemitism reared its ugly head in my early surroundings. The truth is that German Jews had an emotional affinity with each other, which drew them together and tended to exclude Gentiles.[155]

Although antisemites successfully excluded Jews from memberships in some organisations in Imperial Germany, this was, as we have seen, only one of several reasons why Jews remained a relatively tightly knit social group. Despite significant successes within non-Jewish circles, for most Jews the first – innermost – circle of social life consisted of the family, the next of other Jews, and the last of non-Jewish society. The possibilities offered for Jewish integration were thus in a state of dynamic tension with Jewish affinities and traditions. Jews, in other words, were simultaneously drawn towards two strong poles of attraction – integration, on the one hand, and the desire to retain some degree of Jewish connectedness and identity on the other.

---

[153]George Simmel, *The Sociology of Georg Simmel*, transl. by Kurt Wolff, New York 1950, p. 326.
[154]Wachenheim, p. 2.
[155]Charlotte Wolff, *Hindsight*, London 1980, p. 6.

Ahlwardt on Trial: Reactions to the Antisemitic Agitation of the 1890s in Germany*

By Christoph Jahr

One can learn a great deal about the political culture of a country through the analysis of sensational trials. This is even more the case when the issue at stake in the proceedings was regarded by contemporaries as an important social problem – such as the relationship between "Christian" and "Jewish" Germans – and was therefore of direct political significance. One such closely followed trial was the so-called "Jewish rifles trial" (*Judenflinten Prozeß*) against Hermann Ahlwardt which took place in late 1892. Through numerous speeches and pamphlets Ahlwardt shot to fame becoming the new "star" among the antisemites; indeed, Hellmuth von Gerlach has described him as "the most powerful demagogue Germany possessed before Adolf Hitler".[1] Since Ahlwardt's attack also extended to the Prussian Army and its officers, the "Jewish rifles trial" received much attention in the press, but also from the state authorities and the political parties. Furthermore, the fact that the "headmaster of all the Germans"[2] was simultaneously sentenced to five months in prison for libel *and* elected as a deputy to the *Reichstag* forced all political camps to redefine their relationship to antisemitism and to confront the question of how to respond to it. At the same time this case provides an opportunity to study how the authoritarian imperial state dealt with political dissent – or rather, with a person defined as a political opponent – in the courts; and, in turn, how its conduct of the trial was evaluated in the press organs of the various political factions. In this regard, the case is particularly illuminating because the prosecution of political dissent was directed not against the Left – that is, against the labour movement – but rather against *Radauantisemitismus* ("violent" or "rowdy" antisemitism).

Nineteenth-century antisemitism was above all a reaction to the perceived threat posed by concomitant forms of socio-economic and political modernisation.[3] During its first phase, which began around 1878–79, "modern antisemitism" was still

---

*Translated from the German by Deborah Cohen.

[1] Hellmut von Gerlach, *Erinnerungen eines Junkers*, Berlin 1926, p. 114.

[2] Ahlwardt was nicknamed *Rektor aller Deutschen* since he carried the title *Rektor a.D.* – i.e., *Rektor außer Dienst* (retired) after his dismissal from office. Whereas Ahlwardt's supporters took this nickname seriously, his opponents used it ironically.

[3] The latest, if rather brief, overview can be found in Werner Bergmann, *Geschichte des Antisemitismus*, Munich 2002. For other general treatments of the subject see Peter Pulzer, 'Die Wiederkehr des alten Hasses' and 'Die Reaktion auf den Antisemitismus', in Michael A. Meyer and Michael Brenner (eds.), *Deutsch-Jüdische Geschichte in der Neuzeit*, vol. 3, *Umstrittene Integration 1871–1918*, Munich 1997, pp. 193–277; Helmut Berding, *Moderner Antisemitismus in Deutschland*, Stuttgart 1988.

a largely conservative phenomenon, whereas it underwent an increasing radicalisation after 1890. One wing of the antisemitic movement developed into an uncontrollable, radically right-wing fundamental opposition to the existing order of the *Kaiserreich*. Aggressive agitators with mass appeal like Otto Böckel, Ernst Henrici, and Hermann Ahlwardt not only availed themselves of modern propaganda methods but also petitioned rhetorically for, among other things, greater political participation by the *Volk*, without of course being democratically minded in an emancipatory sense. However, this antisemitism directed against "Junkers and Jews" could successfully appeal to the emancipatory promise of the nation state, which had been only insufficiently realised in Imperial Germany; it could denounce the obvious deficit in democracy and legitimacy of the existing social order. The Conservatives, on the other hand, continued trying to use antisemitism as an instrument for the stabilisation of the existing order. The "Tivoli Programme" of the *Deutschkonservative Partei*, into which an antisemitic passage was inserted in late 1892, can only be understood within the context of the electoral success of antisemitic candidates like Ahlwardt.

While the connection between the antisemitic movement and the Conservatives is well established, there has as yet been no systematic analysis of the effects of state and, above all, judicial action against antisemitism.[4] This fact is surprising inasmuch as the early 1890s were a turning point in the history of the struggle against antisemitism. In the 1880s the hope had still persisted that it would be just a fleeting phenomenon. In addition German Jews saw the danger that, in actively resisting, they might truly cut themselves off from non-Jewish Germans, thereby inadvertently reinforcing antisemitic stereotypes even further.[5] Hence the most important anti-antisemitic initiative was initially launched by Christians in the shape of the *Verein zur Abwehr des Antisemitismus*, in which educational counter-propaganda played a central role.[6] An effective and systematic resistance by legal means, on the other hand, only began with the foundation of the *Centralverein deutscher Staatsbürger jüdischen Glaubens* in the spring of 1893.[7] The existing laws, it must be said, were not ideally suited to com-

---

[4]In this regard see Arnold Paucker 'The Jewish Defence against Antisemitism in Germany, 1893–1933', in Jehuda Reinharz (ed.), *Living with Antisemitism. Modern Jewish Responses*, Hanover–London 1987, pp. 104–132; Sanford Ragins, *Jewish Responses to Anti-Semitism in Germany, 1870–1914. A Study in the History of Ideas*, Cincinnati 1980, pp. 60ff.; Richard S. Levy, *The Downfall of the Antisemitic Political Parties in Imperial Germany*, New Haven–London 1975, pp. 130–165; Ismar Schorsch, *Jewish Reactions to German Anti-Semitism, 1870–1914*, New York 1972, pp. 123–132. The state of research on this theme in the context of the Weimar Republic is better; cf. Dirk Walter, *Antisemitische Kriminalität und Gewalt. Judenfeindlichkeit in der Weimarer Republik*, Bonn 1999; Cyril Levitt, 'The Prosecution of Antisemites by the Courts in the Weimar Republic: Was Justice served?', in *LBI Year Book*, vol. 36 (1991), pp. 151–167; Udo Beer, 'The Protection of Jewish Civil Rights in the Weimar Republic. Jewish Self-Defence through Legal Action', in *LBI Year Book*, vol. 33 (1988), pp. 149–176; *idem*, *Die Juden, das Recht und die Republik. Verbandswesen und Rechtsschutz 1919–1933*, Frankfurt am Main 1986; Donald L. Niewyk, 'Jews and the Courts in Weimar Germany', in *Jewish Social Studies*, vol. 37, no. 2 (1975), pp. 99–113. The theme of antisemitism, the law, and the justice system is the subject of further research by the author.
[5]Cf. Jacob Toury, 'Anti-Anti 1889/1892', in *LBI Year Book*, vol. 36 (1991), pp. 47–58; Jacob Borut, 'The Rise of Jewish Defence Agitation in Germany, 1890–1895: A Pre-History of the C.V.?', in *LBI Year Book*, vol. 36 (1991), pp. 59–96.
[6]Cf. 'The Verein zur Abwehr des Antisemitismus', in *LBI Year Book*, vol. 28 (1983), pp. 205–239 and vol. 30 (1985), pp. 67–103.
[7]Cf. Avraham Barkai, *"Wehr Dich!" Der Centralverein deutscher Staatsbürger jüdischen Glaubens 1893–1938*, Munich 2002, which includes references to older literature.

bating antisemitism, as the holding of antisemitic views was not, of course, in itself a crime.[8] The main problem, however, was that the aim of the emancipation process had been the attainment of formal legal equality as a stepping stone for the integration of Jews into the nation and bourgeois civil society, while the antisemites regarded Jews as non-assimilable. For this reason, special "protective laws" for Jews seemed anachronistic and were harmful to the process of nation building. Leopold Auerbach noted this in 1893:

> No specific protection under criminal law exists against the public libel of the *Jewish tribe*, just as no such special protection against public defamation is extended to any of the nationalities [*Volksstämme*] existing in the German Empire. And the legal authorities were right to dispense with such special protection, as the state has no interest in the conservation and isolation of these tribes, but rather regards its primary objective as their unification into one nation.[9]

The "Jewish rifles trial" of Hermann Ahlwardt and the reactions to it need to be understood against this historical background. The case also provides an opportunity to make some further-reaching reflections on the question of the continuity of antisemitism in the *Kaiserreich* and the Weimar Republic. As Richard S. Levy has decisively demonstrated,[10] party-political antisemitism during the Wilhelminian era failed: completely fractured, it did not achieve its goal of rescinding the legal equality of Jews. Nevertheless, Peter Pulzer sees the success of the antisemitic parties in the fact that they permeated society with their ideas;[11] this notion has been further advanced by Werner Jochmann.[12] The latter has emphasised that it was precisely the fractured nature and weakness of party-political antisemitism that led both to its being underestimated and to its success in penetrating deep into society. Indeed antisemitism, together with radical nationalism and imperialism, was spread through organisations like the *Alldeutscher Verband*, the *Deutschnationaler Handlungsgehilfenverband*, and the *Bund der Landwirte*, such that it ultimately developed into something like a "cultural code"[13] in Wilhelminian Germany. On the one hand, the debates triggered by Hermann Ahlwardt's trial over whether and how antisemitism could be fought by legal means and whether it should be fought in that manner, make it possible to draw conclusions about the capacity of the *Kaiserreich* for social and political integration. On the other

---

[8]Cf. Maximilian Parmod (i.e. Max Apt), *Antisemitismus und Strafrechtspflege. Zur Auslegung und Anwendung der §§ 130, 166, 185, 193, 360¹¹ des Straf-Gesetz-Buchs in höchstrichterlicher und erstinstanzlicher Praxis*, Berlin 1894.

[9]Leopold Auerbach, *Wie ist die Judenhetze mit Erfolg zu bekämpfen?*, Berlin 1893, p. 9 (emphasis in the original). The connection between nationalism, citizenship, and antisemitism is underscored in Peter Pulzer, 'Why was there a Jewish Question in Imperial Germany?', in *LBI Year Book*, vol. 25 (1980), pp. 133–146; see also Klaus Holz, *Nationaler Antisemitismus. Wissenssoziologie einer Weltanschauung*, Hamburg 2001 and Peter Alter, Claus-Ekkehard Bärsch and Peter Berghoff (eds.), *Die Konstruktion der Nation gegen die Juden*, Munich 1999.

[10]Cf. Levy, pp. 254–265.

[11]Cf. Peter Pulzer, *The Rise of Political Anti-Semitism in Germany and Austria*, rev. edn., London 1989, pp. xii-xxiii.

[12]Cf. Werner Jochmann, 'Struktur und Funktion des deutschen Antisemitismus', in Werner E. Mosse and Arnold Paucker (eds.), *Juden im Wilhelminischen Deutschland 1890–1914*, Tübingen 1976 (Schriftenreihe wissenschaftlicher Abhandlungen des Leo Baeck Instituts 33), pp. 389–477.

[13]Cf. Shulamit Volkov, 'Antisemitism as a Cultural Code. Reflections on the Historiography of Antisemitism in Imperial Germany', in *LBI Year Book*, vol. 23 (1978), pp. 25–46.

hand, they make it possible to consider the effects of court action on the antisemitic movement. It will be argued below that many judicial, party-strategic, and political factors played a role here. There was one question, however, that interested hardly any of the parties involved in this debate, apart from the Jews: the question of what form effective protection of a minority against systematic defamation might take.

I. "JEWISH RIFLES" – THE ANATOMY OF A POLITICAL TRIAL

Hermann Ahlwardt was born on 21 December 1846 in Crien, near Anklam.[14] In 1881 he became headmaster of a girls' school in Berlin; in 1890, he was dismissed from this post for embezzlement. In the period that followed he rose to prominence as an antisemitic speaker and journalist, reaching the peak of his popularity in 1892 and 1893.

Ahlwardt's speciality was the spreading of bizarre and sensational stories characterised by insane conspiracy theories through public speeches and pamphlets. These activities earned him his first prison sentence, a term of four months, in February 1892. The next of Ahlwardt's "revelations" was not long in coming. He alleged that the Loewe rifle factory in Berlin had been commissioned by the *Alliance Israélite Universelle* to despatch over 400,000 defective rifles to the German Army in order to render the nation defenceless. As proof of his claims, Ahlwardt zealously gathered witness testimonies from former Loewe factory employees, these testimonies being meant to show that the inspection process at the factory left much to be desired. Alongside the factory owner, Isidor Loewe, the Christian gun inspector and retired lieutenant colonel Kühne was alleged to be co-responsible. At Ahlwardt's request, Friedrich Ernst Freiherr von Langen (a mediator between conservatives and antisemites, and a conservative *Reichstag* deputy from 1893 to 1903) appealed to the Berlin chief of police, Bernhard Freiherr von Richthofen, to launch an investigation into Loewe and Kühne, which the official refused to do for fear of being "used as a relay horse, as it were, for an antisemitic affair".[15] Subsequently von Langen complained to the Prussian War Ministry, which agreed to study the allegations. But without waiting for the results of such an investigation, Ahlwardt decided at the beginning of April 1892 to publish his *New Revelations – Jewish Rifles*[16] with the Dresden publisher F.W. Glöß, well-known for his antisemitic list. This pamphlet went through thirty-three printings and over 100,000 copies were sold. The public attention it attracted now spurred the Prussian and Saxon War Ministries to launch an investigation into the Loewe rifles. At the end of May 1892 the Prussian Minister of

[14]Cf. Uwe Mai, '"Wie es der Jude treibt." Das Feindbild der antisemitischen Bewegung am Beispiel der Agitation Hermann Ahlwardts', in Christoph Jahr, Uwe Mai and Kathrin Roller (eds.), *Feindbilder in der deutschen Geschichte. Studien zur Vorurteilsgeschichte im 19. und 20. Jahrhundert*, Berlin 1994, pp. 55–80; Barnet P. Hartston, *Judaism on Trial: Antisemitism in the German Courtroom (1870–1895)*, PhD thesis, University of California, San Diego 1999, pp. 305–341; Thomas Gondermann, *"Der Rektor aller Deutschen" Hermann Ahlwardt und der politische Antisemitismus im deutschen Kaiserreich*, Diplomarbeit (unpublished), Hamburg 2000.
[15]Cf. Richthofen's testimony at the trial, *Das Kleine Journal*, 7 December 1892.
[16]Hermann Ahlwardt, *Neue Enthüllungen. Judenflinten*, Dresden 1892; Hermann Ahlwardt, *Judenflinten, II. Theil*, Dresden 1892.

War Georg von Kaltenborn declared that the Loewe rifles met all of the require-ments "that military deployment might place upon them".[17]

Ahlwardt's "Jewish rifles" only reached the courts on 12 May 1892, when Loewe and Kühne initiated legal proceedings for libel. Independently of this, the Prussian Ministry of Justice simultaneously pursued its prosecution of Ahlwardt. The Chief Public Prosecutor at District Court I (*Landgericht I*) in Berlin, [Karl?] Drescher, called for the "Jewish rifles" pamphlets to be confiscated and for Ahlwardt himself to be arrested.[18] The presiding examining magistrate agreed to hear the libel case, but rejected both of these requests. The public prosecutor successfully appealed against this judgement, with the result that Ahlwardt was arrested on 2 June 1892.[19]

Due to the scope of Ahlwardt's allegations, which he reaffirmed in a second "Jewish rifles" pamphlet that appeared at the end of May 1892, his case was han-dled not only by the courts but also by the Ministry of Justice and by both the Prussian and Imperial governments. On 29 May, a Sunday, Imperial Chancellor (and Prussian Foreign Minister) Leo Graf von Caprivi and Prussian Justice Minister Hermann von Schelling held a meeting with the Imperial Director of Public Prosecutions (*Ober-Reichsanwalt*), in order to deliberate over further proceedings against Ahlwardt. Caprivi's explanation for the government's interest in this case is enlightening:

> The damage that the appearance of these pamphlets and the absence of any satisfactory official explanation for this has already done to the reputation of the military prepared-ness of our army and that of the solidity of our industry abroad is ... so great that I feel obliged to seek redress by the means at my disposal.[20]

Thus the decisive factor in the intervention of the Imperial Chancellor and Prussian Foreign Minister was not the concern that Ahlwardt's allegations defamed German Jews but the fear that the reputation of the army and of German industry could be damaged. In Caprivi's view, a decision reached by the Berlin District Court on 23 May 1892 was especially problematic for the public perception of the case. In that decision, the chamber did decide to initiate proceedings on the grounds that Ahlwardt's "utterly baseless" allegation that the parties involved had acted with trea-sonous intent met the criteria for libel; on these grounds any further publication of the defamatory remarks about Loewe and Kühne in the "Jewish rifles" pamphlet was prohibited. But Caprivi judged problematic a passage in the *ratio decidendi* in which Ahlwardt's allegations were characterised as being not obviously untrue. For this rea-son, Ahlwardt was conceded the "pursuit of legitimate interests" under § 193 of the Criminal Code (StGB), which offered protection against prosecution for libel.[21] Indeed, this fact was interpreted by Paul Förster, among others, as proof of the truth-

---

[17]*Deutscher Reichsanzeiger und Königlich Preußischer Staats-Anzeiger*, no. 126, 30 May 1892. The Imperial Chancellor Georg Leo Graf von Caprivi and the Saxon Minister of War von der Planitz only made a statement to this effect before the *Reichstag* on 12 December 1892, and then only in response to a ques-tion from the *Nationalliberale Partei*; cf. *Verhandlungen des Deutschen Reichstages* (*VDR*), vol. 127, pp. 253–256.

[18]Geheimes Staatsarchiv Preußischer Kulturbesitz (GStA PK), Rep. 84a/55741, pp. 7ff.

[19]*ibid.*, p. 14 and pp. 31ff.

[20]*ibid.*, pp. 18ff., here p. 18.

[21]*ibid.*, pp. 29f.

fulness of Ahlwardt's accusations, which "appear to be credible or proved".[22] As one Prussian Ministry of Justice official noted with resignation in a memo, there was no recourse against this misuse of judicial rulings.[23]

The judges of District Court I demonstrated little personal initiative, despite the fact that the government clearly welcomed Ahlwardt's prosecution, and despite the political significance of the case being obvious. It took a complaint from the public prosecutor to effect Ahlwardt's arrest. Likewise the confiscation of the entire second instalment of the *Jewish rifles* pamphlet was only authorised at the request of Chief Public Prosecutor Drescher via both the Local Court (*Amtsgericht*) in Dresden and the Local Court I (*Amtsgericht I*) in Berlin.[24]

In any event, on 13 June 1892 the District Court I in Berlin decided, in agreement with the examining magistrate, to release Ahlwardt from pre-trial custody on 10,000 marks bail, on the grounds that his allegations were not "not demonstrably true" and that Ahlwardt subjectively believed them to be justified; therefore no intentional defamation could be demonstrated. But Ahlwardt was only able to enjoy his freedom for a few days, because, based on the new complaints by the public prosecutor, the Berlin Court of Appeal (*Kammergericht*) ruled on 22 June to increase the bail to 50,000 marks. Nevertheless Ahlwardt's supporters were able to raise this sum of money as well, so once again he was released from prison on 1 July. However, after the earlier four-month sentence came into force, Ahlwardt was once again obliged to return to Plötzensee Prison in Berlin at the end of October 1892.

It took a new initiative from the Prussian Ministry of Justice for the case against Ahlwardt to be moved forward. The ministry warned that the investigation against him, which "has, as is well known, attracted a high degree of popular attention, should in the public interest be pursued with the greatest dispatch".[25] For this reason the chief public prosecutor of the District Court and the president of the Court of Appeal were advised to carry on with proceedings. The investigations uncovered certain irregularities within the inspection process at the Loewe factory but no evidence of the intentional manufacture of defective rifles. On this basis, the entire first instalment of the *Jewish rifles* pamphlet was confiscated.[26]

The question of whether the court should proceed as quickly as possible to an indictment or first complete its investigation pointed clearly to the various starting-points. In agreement with Chief Public Prosecutor Drescher of District Court I, the Court of Appeal recommended, "at the risk of prolonging the proceedings, that the preliminary investigation be conducted on a broad scale, so as to provide a secure basis for the future trial". Nevertheless the Prussian Ministry of Justice decided in favour of a speedy initiation of proceedings.[27]

Despite this, the bill of indictment against Ahlwardt was not completed until the beginning of October. Ahlwardt was charged with repeated public defamation and

---

[22]Paul Förster, *Der Fall Ahlwardt in der öffentlichen Meinung und im Lichte der Wahrheit. Eine Streitschrift*, 3rd edn., Berlin 1893, p. 22.
[23]GStA PK, Rep. 84a/55741, pp. 27f.
[24]*ibid.*, pp. 31ff. and p. 46.
[25]*ibid.*, p. 54.
[26]*ibid.*, p. 56.
[27]*ibid.*, pp. 58ff. and pp. 61f.

libel. With respect to the *Jewish rifles* pamphlets, the complaint states: "In their general content, these two pamphlets are directed in particular, apart from certain remarks and suspicions relating to Jews as a whole, against ... the enterprise Loewe & Co."[28] However, according to the indictment Ahlwardt's accusations were completely untenable. As evidence, the public prosecutor presented no fewer than sixty-four witness testimonies and expert opinions. The fact that the Chief Public Prosecutor not only himself acted as prosecuting counsel but also kept the Ministry of Justice informed about the state of the proceedings via regular telephone reports underlines the political significance of this trial. For his part, Justice Minister von Schelling kept the Prussian Ministry of State abreast of the case's progress.[29]

The proceedings were held before the Berlin District Court between 29 November and 9 December 1892. Hoping to profit from the immunity Ahlwardt would receive as a *Reichstag* deputy, he and his defence lawyer Hertwig tried to draw out the trial by continually calling for new motions to take evidence. To this end, new witnesses were continually named who either happened to be abroad or whose whereabouts still had to be established. A guilty verdict was nevertheless reached, Ahlwardt being sentenced to five months in prison for libel. However, as he had won the final ballot in the parliamentary elections in the constituency of Arnswalde-Friedeberg on 5 December – he had run as an independent candidate – he did indeed fall for a time under the protection of the immunity clause. Based on a motion proposed by Liebermann von Sonnenberg and which was also supported by sixteen Social Democratic parliamentarians, Ahlwardt was released from prison and the proceedings against him were suspended for the remainder of the current parliamentary session. Not until September 1893 – in the middle of the parliamentary recess – did the Supreme Court of the German Reich reject a motion for judgement in an appeal submitted by Ahlwardt, with the result that he finally had to serve out his sentence in Berlin's Plötzensee Prison from 4 October 1893 to 6 March 1894. A motion for his re-release from prison after the start of the new parliamentary session in mid-November 1893 was withdrawn by its petitioners, revealing how weak the support for Ahlwardt had grown by this time, even among his fellow antisemites.[30]

The conduct of the proceedings was not a model of objective justice, the presiding judge often responding to statements by the defendants with personal remarks. Nor did the confessed antisemite's attempts to distance himself from the agitators of the labour movement by repeatedly emphasising his pro-monarchist and conservative credentials help him in any way. When Ahlwardt stated that his information about the Loewe rifles was not passed on within the War Ministry because a high-ranking officer there was a Jew, the following exchange ensued:

> Judge: "That, once again, is certainly untrue."
> Defendant: "That the party concerned is a Jew, I can prove. He is a baptised Jew."

[28]*ibid.*, pp. 79–125, here p. 81.
[29]*ibid.*, p. 128.
[30]*ibid.*, pp. 198, 210 and *VDR* vol. 135, p. 2298 and vol. 136, p. 474. The claim, widely repeated since its first appearance in Paul W. Massing, *Rehearsal for Destruction. A Study of Political Anti-Semitism in Imperial Germany*, New York 1967 (first published 1949), p. 94, that Ahlwardt was never compelled to serve the full term of the sentence imposed at the "Jewish rifles trial" is incorrect.

Judge: "That cannot be accepted as being right. Either a person is a Jew, and that is what he is; or he has become a Christian, in which case he *is* a Christian."[31]

The presiding judge openly sneered at Ahlwardt's motion to question soldiers of the *Landwehr* whose weapons had allegedly proved to be defective: "You [Ahlwardt] cannot be so foolish as to think that the expert opinion of a cab driver or some convicted criminal could be of greater value than that of the highest military authorities and specialists? Such matters are not for the headmaster of some school to decide."[32]

When Ahlwardt expressed doubt as to the correctness of the statements given by a witness who was a member of the *Alliance Israélite Universelle*, Chief Presiding Judge Georg Robert Brausewetter once again intervened directly: "You appear to have a strange conception of the sanctity of the oath if you think that someone would just stand here and commit perjury out of sheer malice. ... We have not yet sunk so low here that witnesses would perjure themselves just for the sake of ruining you."[33]

A further example of the presiding judge's prejudiced conduct of the proceedings is the examination of a witness, the antisemite Karl Paasch, who alleged that officers of Jewish descent had participated in the awarding of contracts to the Loewe factory:

Judge: "You don't know the names of any such officers? Then why are you casting such suspicions?"
Paasch: "This is a racial matter. We've also had a Jewish Education Minister."
Judge: "Are the ministries now supposed to be pilloried as well?"[34]

On the penultimate day of the hearings, the judge expressed his firm – and correct – belief that the defendant was making new applications to take evidence solely for the sake of protracting the proceedings, at which Hertwig, in a theatrical gesture, withdrew from the case, appealing to the public as a higher authority:

For my part, I declare that I must refuse to continue with the defence of a man who was already condemned before the hearings began and who is being deprived of his evidence. Whatever the judgement may be, we are not afraid, and leave it to the public to criticise these proceedings.[35]

Drescher, the Public Prosecutor, who was calling for a sentence of one-and-a-half years, made it clear in his closing arguments that Ahlwardt's agitation went beyond the bounds of what could be claimed to fall under the protection of freedom of speech:

Every party, including the Antisemitic Party, must be accorded the right to criticise and to rebuke; but no party may in doing so abandon one fundamental principle: the fundamental principle of truth and truthfulness. ... He who operates by illegal means cannot claim the protection of the law.[36]

---

[31]Otto Bähr, 'Der Prozeß gegen Ahlwardt', in *Die Grenzboten*, vol. 51, no. 52 (1892), pp. 609–620, here p. 611.
[32]*ibid.*, p. 612.
[33]*ibid.*, p. 615.
[34]*ibid.*, p. 618.
[35]*ibid.*, p. 619.
[36]*Das Kleine Journal*, 10 December 1892.

It is strange, however, that Drescher thought it appropriate to give the antisemitic movement some good advice for the future: "Political scandal-makers who are only concerned with attracting attention will do your party more harm than good and they will become a cancer to your party."[37]

Presiding Judge Brausewetter also gave the "moderate" antisemitic movement a clean bill of health in the judicial sense when he stated during the trial:

> I consider antisemitism to be in a certain sense not entirely unjustified, or rather to be just as justified as all other political tendencies. Someone who is an antisemite should be allowed to express his views, but he should do so in a different manner from that of the defendant.[38]

This statement openly proposes that it is permissible to propagate antisemitism as long as it is not done in a demagogic and defamatory way.

The courtroom was used as a stage by the different parties involved in the trial. Naturally, this applies particularly strongly to Ahlwardt and his defence lawyer, but also to the chief presiding judge and the public prosecutor, who took pains to demonstrate a serious will to prosecute through their "brisk" demeanour. What they above all demonstrated, however, was their authoritarian conception of the law. It is noteworthy that this authoritarian behaviour on the part of the court was not only directed against Social Democrats but, as in this case, also against radical antisemites. However, despite the court's unmistakable bias against Ahlwardt, his antisemitic stance was not fundamentally challenged but rather was in a certain sense affirmed. This took place by distinguishing between "justified" and "unjustified" forms of antisemitism and setting the two in opposition to one another. "Justified antisemitism" was thus in a sense removed from the realm of judicial judgement, thereby lending it an air of legality and ultimately of legitimacy. This way of thinking harmonised with that of Imperial Chancellor von Caprivi, who in the *Reichstag* expressed his understanding for the position "that one can be an antisemite" and stated that he could even find rescinding the emancipation law of 1869 "comprehensible". However, he continued, "if there is public agitation for this endeavour [*draußen betrieben*], then I will oppose it by all the means at my disposal".[39] For the Chancellor, therefore, the problem with antisemitic agitation lay not with it being *antisemitic* but rather with it being *agitation*; this did not fit in with the conservative image of society in which the concepts of "order", "authority" and "state authority" loomed large.[40]

II. THE "JEWISH RIFLES TRIAL" IN THE PRESS AND IN POLITICAL JOURNALISM

The positions regarding antisemitism that emerged in the various press organs hold few surprises. What is interesting, however, is how the "Jewish rifles" trial proceed-

---

[37]*ibid.*
[38]Bähr, p. 617.
[39]*Reichstag* session, 12 December 1892, *VDR* vol. 127, p. 273.
[40]This fact is often emphasised; see, for example, Peter Pulzer, *Jews and the German State. The Political History of a Minority, 1848–1933*, Oxford 1992, p. 119: "Most states were concerned more with public order than with justice."

ings were evaluated judicially and politically. Minds were divided over the question of whether one should respond to agitators like Ahlwardt by tightening press laws or by giving priority to freedom of speech. Thus it was neither a Social Democratic nor a Liberal paper but the Conservative *Norddeutsche Allgemeine Zeitung* that demanded, at the beginning of May 1892, that Ahlwardt be dealt with more severely. The paper complained of a "very alarming hole in our entire legal system", because "one-sided allegations are permitted to be spread for weeks over the widest area, while the rectification and refutation of such allegations can only follow so much later, after complicated and difficult proceedings for the introduction of evidence".[41] In order to avoid such episodes in the future, the paper called for a tightening of the press laws.

The liberal *Vossische Zeitung* strongly opposed this viewpoint. In its opinion, the problem arose not through a "hole in the legal system" but through hesitation on the part of the War Ministry.[42] Similar arguments were put forward by the *Börsen-Courier* when it concluded that Ahlwardt's attacks had "not been aimed at a Jew" but at state institutions, above all the army. The *Norddeutsche Allgemeine*, it alleged, was just taking advantage of an opportunity "to set a trap for freedom of speech by means of a law directed against Ahlwardt". The Liberals, so the argument continued, could not allow themselves to be fooled by the hypocrisy of the Conservative-governmental antisemites. A "hole" was not gaping in the legal system "but in our administrative practice".[43]

The debate triggered by the *Norddeutsche Allgemeine* reveals at first glance a surprising opposition of forces, with the conservative papers calling for decisive judicial action against Ahlwardt and the liberal newspapers viewing this as merely a conservative tactic to restrict press freedom. Here we see a reflection of an old clash between conservatives and liberals. But what was *not* at stake was antisemitism and its effects on the Jews. Instead, the Ahlwardt controversy was viewed in the context of the conflict within the Conservative Party over how to combat organised party-political antisemitism, which had already begun to make inroads into its own base of support.

The argument that allowing Ahlwardt to continue for so long unimpeded might reinforce the impression that there "was something" to his allegations was also invoked by the committed foes of antisemitism. Thus Josef Feuerring concluded that so long as the officials remained inactive, the people would "assume that you [Ahlwardt] must be right about your defamatory allegations".[44] In this respect a dilemma arose as to whether antisemitic agitation should be tolerated or repressed, since either course of action could be construed as indirect evidence of the plausibility of the agitators' claims. Indeed, the antisemites appropriated both arguments in marketing their pamphlets. Thus the caption "has been confiscated" adorning the title page of the third edition of Paul Förster's *Der Fall Ahlwardt in der öffentlichen Meinung und im Lichte der Wahrheit* (*The Ahlwardt Case in Public Opinion and in the Light of Truth*) was meant to give the impression that an antisemitic publication had been sup-

---

[41] *Norddeutsche Allgemeine Zeitung*, 7 May 1892. A similar argument was made in the *Kreuzzeitung*, 27 May 1892: Alongside Loewe and Kühne, "Ahlwardt himself should have been arrested and his 'Revelations' confiscated. This would have spared the German people much misfortune and turmoil".

[42] *Vossische Zeitung*, 9 May 1892.

[43] *Börsen-Courier*, 18 May 1892.

[44] Josef Feuerring, *Der Antisemitenapostel! Ein Wort der Entgegnung an Rektor Hermann Ahlwardt auf seine letzte Broschüre: "Neue Enthüllungen Judenflinten"*, Berlin 1892, p. 2; cf. also Schorsch, pp. 84f.

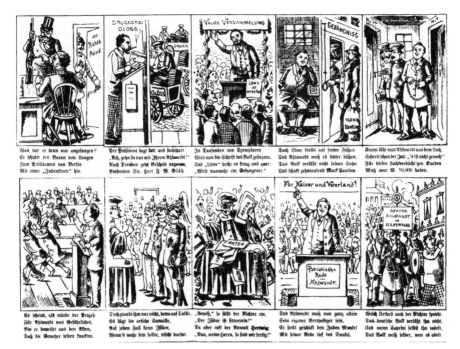

Excerpt from a cartoon strip entitled "Ahlwardt's Heldenthaten" published in *Politischer Bilderbogen No. 7*, (1892), commenting on the "Jewish Rifles Trial".

"Puffed-up Ahlwardt in the *Reichstag*". This cartoon was published in *Lustige Blätter*, vol. VIII (1893). The caption reads:
Reich Chancellor: "What's the peculiar smell?"
Minister of War: "What do you expect – with that windbag blowing his own trumpet!"

pressed by the state not because it contained lies but rather monstrous truths. On the other hand, a clear example of the axiom that lack of punishment serves as proof of veracity is found in the publisher Gustav Adolf Dewald's advertisement for Ahlwardt's text *Schwerin und Bleichröder oder Edelmann und Jude* (Schwerin and Bleichröder or Nobleman and Jew): "Generally one would expect this book to be confiscated; that this has not taken place is a sign that its contents are only too true."[45]

The Ahlwardt trial before the Berlin District Court afforded all the large daily newspapers an opportunity for further illuminating discussions. Among the antisemites themselves, the complaint of alleged persecution by the "Jewified" judicial authorities formed part of their efforts to style themselves "persecuted innocents". This is clearly in evidence in the case of Rudolf Plack-Podgòrski, who, in connection with the "Jewish rifles trial", spoke of the "so-called rule of law in Prussia",[46] which he contrasted with the "feeling for justice" of the German *Volk*, a feeling "that cannot be killed, not even by means of the most blatant application of Roman-Jewish law by our jurists".[47] In this spirit Paul Förster posed the rhetorical question: "Was this simply a civil case for libel, or a state trial [*Staatsprozeß*]? More likely the latter!"[48] In point of fact, Förster was not far from the truth: the trial against Ahlwardt was sanctioned by the highest levels of political authority; in the trial, both the public prosecutor and the presiding judge knew what was "expected" of them and acted accordingly.

And yet criticism of the conduct of the proceedings not only came from the radical antisemitic camp. The lawyer Otto Bähr, who had represented the *Nationalliberale Partei* in both the Prussian *Abgeordnetenhaus* and the *Reichstag* between 1867 and 1880, conducted a detailed study of the "Jewish rifles trial", which left him with "strange and far-from-pleasant impressions".[49] By this, Bähr was referring to, in his view, the numerous formal deficiencies of the proceedings, which he saw as orientated too much towards the audience: "The judge's chair is not a rostrum from which the judge is called upon to lecture the audience."[50] Citing a variety of examples, he complained of Presiding Judge Brausewetter's biased conduct of the proceedings and, despite the rather mild sentence of five months in prison, he subjected the *ratio decidendi* to severe criticism: Even Ahlwardt "had a right to an objective hearing of his case. … [A]fter the one-sidedness with which the case was prosecuted and conducted, one might suspect all the more that an element of truth was meant to be suppressed here".[51] Thus Bähr reached the concluding judgement: "We should hope that proceedings such as these never take place again. It would cause inordinate harm to the justice system."[52]

Like Bähr, the conservative *Schlesische Zeitung*, published in Breslau, came to the conclusion that Brausewetter did not fulfil his obligation to appear "as the embodi-

---

[45]The advertisement was printed on the last page of Rudolf Plack-Podgòrski's pamphlet *Pharisäer und Heuchler oder die Leuchten des deutschen Parlaments und die Stützen des Staates*, Berlin 1893.
[46]Rudolf Plack-Podgòrski, *Ahlwardt vor Gericht. Eine kritische Beleuchtung des Judenflinten-Prozesses*, 6th edn., Dresden 1893, p. 12.
[47]*ibid.*, p. 14.
[48]Förster, p. 53.
[49]Bähr, p. 609.
[50]*ibid.*, p. 610.
[51]*ibid.*, p. 620.
[52]*ibid.*, p. 620.

ment of the administration of justice, untouched by any hint of emotion". "The worst thing", the paper continued, "is that through this discussion the entire trial appears removed from the grounds on which it was supposed to have been conducted and [now] seems to have been branded a battle between Judaism and Antisemitism."[53] Hence the factor that Otto Bähr had noted positively – namely "that here a great battle against antisemitism was being fought"[54] – was criticised in the *Schlesische Zeitung*, which denied that the "Jewish rifles trial" had been a judicial confrontation with antisemitism.

The Catholic newspaper *Germania* was equally contemptuous of the biased conduct of the proceedings and of the behaviour of the defendant.[55] Strikingly, while of very different political inclinations, the liberal *Frankfurter Zeitung* also argued that the presiding judge had been derelict in his duty to be objective, thus offering Ahlwardt and his supporters "an apparent right to complain… about the administration of justice". To judge irrespective of the person concerned, so the paper continued, is also necessary in the case of a person like Ahlwardt. "Our opinion of Ahlwardt has been stated often enough; we see in his person the embodiment of the most disastrous goings-on that have ever sought to drape themselves in the cloak of honesty and patriotism." Nevertheless "we feel that it is necessary for us to raise our voice in protest when his rights are infringed upon even in the slightest. What obliges us to do this is the principle that we uphold for friend and foe alike: that of 'equal rights for all!'"[56]

The Social Democratic press went one step further, likening the conduct of the case against Ahlwardt to its own recent experiences with the anti-socialist legislation known as the "Socialist Laws" (*Sozialistengesetze*). In this spirit the *Berliner Volkstribüne* wrote: "All of Berlin is acquainted with Herr Brausewetter and his administration of office. Above all we Social Democrats have all too often experienced first-hand how this presiding judge regards all defendants as guilty from the outset and then behaves accordingly. Herr Brausewetter would not have been Herr Brausewetter had he shown a different face in this trial. … If the judges are already convinced that a defendant is guilty, what is the point of the weeks of proceedings? Perhaps to strengthen the people's trust in the administration of justice in a state governed by one class?"[57] The accusation that a state governed by one class also exercises class justice was here simply transferred to an antisemite who was behaving like a social revolutionary. The long-lived nature of the reputation District Court Judge Brausewetter earned himself is illustrated by a comment Hellmut von Gerlach offered in 1926: Brausewetter was a "mad hanging judge who was in office for years".[58]

It would certainly be unreasonable to suspect the SPD or its press organs of harbouring any sympathies for Ahlwardt.[59] Nevertheless his claim that *Vorwärts*, togeth-

---

[53]*Schlesische Zeitung*, 11 December 1892.
[54]Bähr, p. 609.
[55]*Germania*, 15 December 1892.
[56]*Frankfurter Zeitung*, 5 December 1892.
[57]*Berliner Volks-Tribüne*, 10 December 1892.
[58]*Welt am Montag*, 22 February 1926.
[59]Cf. Reinhard Rürup, 'Sozialdemokratie und Antisemitismus im deutschen Kaiserreich', in Micha Brumlik Doron Kiesel, and Linda Reisch (eds.), *Der Antisemitismus und die Linke*, Frankfurt am Main 1991, pp. 17–31.

er with the *Staatsbürger-Zeitung*, the *Berliner Lokalanzeiger*, and the *Tägliche Rundschau*, represented a "laudable exception"[60] because it attempted to provide an objective report is not entirely wrong. Thus, for example, *Vorwärts* did conclude that the conduct of the trial "gave Ahlwardt's supporters ample ammunition". Still, *Vorwärts*' criticism of the presiding judge's behaviour was structured differently from that of the newspapers cited above. Its initial complaint was not that Ahlwardt was placed at a disadvantage before the court, but, on the contrary, that "so broad a marshalling of evidence as was offered to the defendant in this trial is unheard of in the history of judicial practice in Germany. This we reproach in the least. But we draw comparisons with trials that have been conducted against Social Democrats." Yet because the behaviour of the presiding judge was not neutral, "Ahlwardt, however much leeway he was given, still appears as a martyr with limited defence resources". *Vorwärts* did admit that the motive behind the court's accommodating behaviour was nothing less than a desire to establish full clarity. This could not, however, be achieved by such means, for "even the subtlest attempt to influence the conduct of the trial, even if it stems from the best motives", places "the good name of the administration of justice" at risk.[61] In the view of *Vorwärts*, the principles of an objective judiciary that the *Kaiserreich* liked to claim for itself had not been maintained in court, but were willingly sacrificed on the altar of political utility.

Mincing its words even less than *Vorwärts*, the *National-Zeitung* claimed to see through the strategy of the antisemites: they did not simply want to draw out the trial, but to use the court of justice as a platform for their agitation. The theatrical departure from the courtroom by Ahlwardt's lawyer Hertwig – "a prepared scene in a theatrical performance intended for their friends in the audience" – was an example in point. The court's hope that in permitting a thorough marshalling of evidence, the charge of bias against the defendant might be refuted was in vain: "in the face of an agitation bent on scandal. …. The criminal proceedings are being … degraded into an instrument of agitation by those against whom they are directed and by their comrades."[62] In this way the *National-Zeitung* made it clear that Ahlwardt's agitation was not merely a judicial but above all a political problem. The *Frankfurter Zeitung* had already recognised this in June 1892, when it accused the government of lacking "the right political sensibility to judge Ahlwardt's actions and their consequences. … With a few strong words one could have nipped the scandalous deception in the bud." The judicial review, on the other hand, was an issue "of secondary importance as compared to that of greatest political importance: namely, that untruth be identified from the beginning and publicly combated".[63] The "purely judicial" treatment of Ahlwardt was inappropriate, the *Frankfurter Zeitung* concluded, as it did not grasp the political implications of his case.

The *Börsen-Courier* tackled the subject of the above-mentioned decision by the Berlin District Court, asserting that Ahlwardt was "filled with so fanatical a zeal against the Jews" that "he has often lost his objectivity", and declaring that "from the standpoint

---

[60]Ahlwardt, *Judenflinten, II. Theil*, p. 6.
[61]*Vorwärts*, 8 December 1892.
[62]*National-Zeitung*, 8 December 1892.
[63]*Frankfurter Zeitung*, 2 June 1892.

of the court… the suspect is not a slanderer". The paper judged this line of argumentation, which implies a privileging in criminal law of the expression of political opinions, as having extremely negative implications, since by this means "the excessiveness of an insult creates the presumption of good faith, and precisely the immoderation of a slander lends it the milder character of an insult". According to this logic, the judges were objectively encouraging all slanderers to prove the sincerity of their allegations through outrageous statements guaranteeing freedom from punishment:

> A person makes a slanderous allegation without evidence, which becomes all the more dishonourable in that it is meant to apply not simply to specific individual persons but rather to a community of hundreds of thousands [the German Jews], whose members may, through a peculiarity in our legal system that is difficult to comprehend, be insulted and slandered without fear of punishment – and if this slanderous allegation be truly outrageous, the slanderer has the presumption of good faith on his side; and if he adds the further slanderous allegation that he regards the community as a public ill and himself as the physician competent to remedy this ill, then he can claim protection under § 193 of the Criminal Code, which relates to the perception of legitimate interests![64]

Finally, the *Börsen-Courier* noted the fact that the existing laws were structurally insufficient to deal with a political movement such as antisemitism. The "perception of legitimate interests" (§193 of the Criminal Code), for example, was in point of fact a legal regulation that, within a certain framework, protected the free expression of political opinions, including those of antisemites, from criminal prosecution.

The "Jewish rifles trial" also provided an opportunity for a fundamental press critique of the legal system. If the antisemitic *Staatsbürger-Zeitung* complained about the conflict existing "between popular and judicial notions of the law", then it was defending a critique of the justice system that formed part of the standard repertoire of the antisemites. "The layman", the *Staatsbürger-Zeitung* continued, "therefore has no idea what to make of the results of this implementation of the law; the cases pile up in which the people are not in agreement with the judicial proceedings because they do not understand them and indeed find them to be in contradiction with their common sense [*natürlicher Verstand*]".[65] Roman law was here considered simply a further instrument of "Jewish domination", a view that Ahlwardt himself often expressed.[66] From this point, only a small step was needed to redefine the duties of the "good citizen". Consequently, the antisemite Paul Förster wrote: "We must learn to elevate the bourgeois concept of honour. The duty of the good citizen is not only to obey and trust in the authorities; he should also freely participate in matters of state and concern himself with the state's economic and moral existence."[67] Förster equated the defence of the state against alleged internal "Jewification" with its mili-

---

[64] *Börsen-Courier*, 14 June 1892.

[65] *Staatsbürger-Zeitung*, 11 December 1892.

[66] For example in a speech given in Essen on 29 October 1892, in which, according to the police protocol, he stated that the justice system was, in his view, "in and of itself disagreeable"; that it was based on Roman law; that Roman law followed a strict logic incomprehensible to the German people; that the great Germanic people was utterly incapacitated in the courts; that the Jews took advantage of this situation – the explanation for the strong predominance of Jewish elements in the justice system; and that anyone who did not have sacks of money was powerless. GStA PK, Rep. 84a/55740, pp. 3f.

[67] Förster, pp. 33.

tary defence. Yet while in the external defence of the country the leadership role of
the aristocracy was still acknowledged, in its "internal defence" this was expressly
ascribed to the citizen: "We are not only the defenders of our country in the King's
uniform, but also defenders of the law in civilian dress."[68] This appeal to the "people" to take the initiative should the authorities "fail" was also part of Ahlwardt's
repertoire as an agitator.[69]

Yet criticism of the judicial system did not come from the antisemitic camp
alone. The *Allgemeine Zeitung* especially rebuked the behaviour of Ahlwardt's
defence lawyer Hertwig, since "the defence lawyer is an organ of justice, not of
injustice, and sophistic support of the criminal reduces the defence lawyer to a
criminal's crony and rogue's accomplice". Because the antisemitic press's systematic defamation of the German courts "leads to the undermining of the latter's
good name," one needed to consider how "this progressive mocking of state
authority can be countered".[70]

Once again, the *Norddeutsche Allgemeine Zeitung* stated this even more clearly when it
characterised the left-liberals' "malicious penchant for criticising and fault-finding,
joking and mocking" as "preparing the ground for Ahlwardt". Part of the blame for
Ahlwardt's rise, the *Norddeutsche Allgemeine* continued, resided with those, alongside his
supporters, who "instead of suppressing his dangerous and hypocritical behaviour,
stood idly by and allowed him to continue as he might". Like Caprivi, the *Norddeutsche
Allgemeine* was not as much bothered by the hateful content of the antisemitic agitation as by its potential to encourage "insubordination", which "must not be allowed
to proliferate".[71]

Strikingly, the *Allgemeine Zeitung des Judenthums*, apparently reflecting its need to find
allies against antisemitism, underestimated this problematical aspect of the
Norddeutsche Allgemeine's line of argumentation, instead welcoming the supposed
"about-face which the entire antisemitic cause must undergo as a result of this trial
and its aftermath. Is it really still the Jews against whom the outrages of Ahlwardt
and his ilk are directed? In place of Jewry, the German army and German justice
have become targets of the antisemites and have suddenly provided the Jews with
allies that their opponents least anticipated."[72]

An anonymously published brochure by a "German" (non-Jewish) military officer
characterising Ahlwardt's allegations as not only unpatriotic but also factually untenable indicates that the assessment of the situation in the *Allgemeine Zeitung des
Judenthums* stemmed more from unfortunately misplaced optimism than from sober
analysis. But it also indicates in virtually paradigmatic fashion that there could be no
talk of a hoped-for "about-face" to the Jewish side on the part of the conservatives.
"You, Headmaster Ahlwardt, seek to harm a Jew", the officer wrote, "and you do this
in such a way that you thoroughly dupe a number of Christians." The goal had to

---

[68]*ibid.*, p. 47.

[69]Ahlwardt, *Neue Enthüllungen. Judenflinten*, p. 6: "the people can only be saved by the people".

[70]*Allgemeine Zeitung*, 11 December 1892.

[71]*Norddeutsche Allgemeine Zeitung*, 11 December 1892.

[72]*Allgemeine Zeitung des Judenthums*, vol. 55, no. 51 (16 December 1892), supplement entitled *Der Gemeindebote*,
pp. 2f.

be to keep the civil service and the officers corps, "our bulwarks" against the excessive influence of the Jews, "warm for antisemitism" – "not to alienate them through rowdyism [*mit seinem Radau*]".[73]

III. ANTISEMITISM, POLITICAL JUSTICE AND SOCIAL CONSENSUS

The hope of the *Allgemeine Zeitung des Judenthums* that the trial against a *Radauantisemit* could lead all political camps to show solidarity with the actual victims of this hate-filled agitation, the Jews, was illusory. The press reaction to the Ahlwardt trial makes clear that what from today's perspective seems central to the Ahlwardt phenomenon – his malicious antisemitic agitation – was not the decisive factor for most contemporary observers. The Conservatives did call for Ahlwardt's rigorous prosecution, but not because he was an antisemite. Rather they used the "Jewish rifles trial" as a welcome opportunity to attack a "liberal penchant for criticism" that allegedly threatened state authority, as well as to demand restrictions on press freedom. The Liberals, for their part, used the trial to demonstrate the contradictory and tactically motivated attitude of the Conservatives towards antisemitism. In this they were certainly correct; however in thus proceeding they unintentionally thwarted the realisation of a political consensus against antisemitism.[74] The Social Democrats likewise focused less on Ahlwardt's antisemitism than on the authoritarian state's repression of political dissent, from which they also suffered. And the conduct of the trial had indeed shown that an authoritarian understanding of state and society also formed the impetus for prosecuting Ahlwardt, the radical antisemite. For this reason, the imperial state only made enemies for itself with this trial. Social integration and any consensus on values proved weak and highly fragmented. Liebermann von Sonnenberg's successful motion in the *Reichstag* that parliamentary immunity be extended to Ahlwardt shows the surprising nature, more tactical than substantive, of the political alliances that the confrontation with antisemitism had generated.[75] Alongside the antisemites, those supporting the petition were the Centre Party and the Social Democrats: probably as a result of their shared memory of state persecution during the *Kulturkampf* and under anti-socialist legislation (*Sozialistengesetze*), the value they placed on parliamentary immunity outweighed their reservations about Ahlwardt. On the other hand, those opposing immunity for Ahlwardt represented an unusual alliance of Conservatives, National Liberals and left-liberal (*freisinnige*) members of parliament. Here, if from varying motives, an astonishing temporary coalition formed for the purposes of keeping Ahlwardt out of the *Reichstag* and preventing him from evading punishment.

The "Jewish rifles trial" against Ahlwardt can also be understood as an example of political justice in the *Kaiserreich*, for the highest echelons of politics exerted influ-

---

[73]Anon., *Ahlwardt und seine Judenflinten. Ansichten eines deutschen Waffenoffiziers,* Berlin 1892, pp. 12f.

[74]To this extent, Marjorie Lamberti's praise for the left liberals' dedication to principle in 'Liberals, Socialists and the Defence against Antisemitism in the Wilhelminian Period', in *LBI Year Book,* vol. 25 (1980), pp. 147–162, should be qualified.

[75]Cf. the plenary session of the *Reichstag* on 14 December 1892, in *VDR* vol. 127, pp. 339–347.

ence on it in order to suppress political dissent by judicial means.[76] In this trial, much more was at stake than the question of whether or not the criteria for libel were present. Rather, the trial involved an ultimately doomed effort to demonstrate a basic consensus between the regime and society. As has been argued in these pages, Ahlwardt was not condemned because he was an antisemite, but because his radical methods appeared to challenge state authority. The government was only too happy to make an example of him, because in the figure of Isidor Loewe he had attacked not just an important industrialist and a Jew but above all the army. In addition, even within the ranks of the antisemites Ahlwardt was a controversial figure; and even the Conservative press – down to the *Kreuzzeitung* – ultimately withdrew its support for him after a long phase of friendly disposition. Through this trial, the state authorities were able to prove that they were willing to severely punish not only attacks from the left but also from the right-wing, antisemitic camp. But a tacit presupposition at play in this demonstration was that antisemitism was in itself a legitimate political-social movement. To this extent the harsh judicial prosecution of the *Radauantisemit* had the paradoxical consequence of making allegedly moderate antisemitism appear serious, legal, and therefore potentially legitimate. The distinction between a putatively "justified" antisemitism that sought to achieve its goals by "purely legal means" and a *Radauantisemitismus* of which the social élite wishes to wash its hands, although it shares its premises, is as old as "modern" antisemitism itself. From this perspective, sensational trials against antisemites constituted the further development of "respectable antisemitism" into a Wilhelminian cultural code.

These trials also formed part of a learning process for radical antisemites. The judicial prosecutions did not modify their hate-filled beliefs. Instead they sought to propagate their ideas by more subtle means. Paul Förster offered the following instructions: "Mind you, if one does not want to make oneself ridiculous, one cannot say everything that one feels and thinks. The reader learns the art of reading between the lines. In corrupt times, one must use one's head."[77] This change was also described by the chairman of the *Verein zur Abwehr des Antisemitismus*, Theodor Barth, in October 1908, when he noted that "Brutal antisemitism, as was embodied in the figures of Ahlwardt and Graf [Walter] Pückler, has disappeared. The dangerous kind – antisemitism in kid gloves – has remained."[78] As future developments would show, Barth's assessment of the situation was on the mark. "Brutal antisemitism" was repressed during the *Kaiserreich* but its grounding in society and its broad backing were not checked – quite to the contrary. In this context, it is useful to take note of the dialectic contradictory situations Walter Grab has identified as facing German Jews before 1914 and after 1918:

> Before 1914 the authoritarian upper strata had permitted antisemitism and regarded it as socially acceptable; its most brutal excesses, however, ... were not tolerated. The

---

[76]According to Otto Kirchheimer, *Politische Justiz. Verwendung juristischer Verfahrensmöglichkeiten zu politischen Zwecken*, Frankfurt am Main 1985, p. 11, one can speak of political justice "when courts are used for political purposes ... The way political justice works is that the political behaviour of groups and individuals is subjected to legal scrutiny."

[77]Förster, p. iv.

[78]*Berliner Tageblatt*, 19 October 1908.

republican government after 1918 did recognise the equal rights of Jews in the political and social arenas; on the other hand, however, they refrained from taking decisive steps against *völkisch* racist antisemites and their murder-mongering.[79]

There are many reasons for things reaching such a point. One reason is surely that during the *Kaiserreich* the state viewed the struggle against antisemitism as a problem to be solved by above all judicial means. In taking such an approach, the state availed itself of precisely those authoritarian methods against which not only the left-liberals, the Social Democrats, and the Centre Party but also antisemites could agitate successfully. Thus the real problem, one might conclude, was not a lack of political will to suppress antisemitism, but rather a lack of will within the wider society to do so. This reality appears manifest in the fact that a criminal conviction did not necessarily have a stigmatising effect, but actually came to be seen as proof of the veracity of the antisemites' claims, thereby solidifying the group identity of the radical antisemites.[80] To this extent, trials such as the "Jewish rifles trial" can lead us to reflect on the extent to which it is possible to fight a social movement like antisemitism by judicial means.

In addressing the question of why efforts to deprive antisemitism of its social base did not succeed in the *Kaiserreich*, one must take into account many factors. The observation that politically the legal profession was largely anti-liberal and antisemitic is not sufficient in itself. Perhaps the Austrian lawyer Josef Kopp – who represented Joseph Bloch, the *Reichsrat* member and District Rabbi of Floridsdorf, in the 1884 libel case brought against him by August Rohling – was correct. For Kopp there was "no less appropriate a forum" for combating antisemitism "than a state court … whose decisions … will never contribute in the slightest to bringing us even one step closer to solving political, national, confessional or social questions or to curing the ills of our age".[81]

---

[79]Walter Grab, *Die jüdische Antwort auf den Zusammenbruch der deutschen Demokratie 1933*, Berlin 1988, p. 7.
[80]Cf. Massing, pp. 94f.
[81]Josef Kopp, *Zur Judenfrage nach den Akten des Prozesses Rohling-Bloch*, Leipzig 1886, p. 1.

Tagesordnung: Judenfrage
*A German Debate in the Early Stages of the Weimar Republic**

BY JÜRGEN MATTHÄUS

The following "record of a discussion of Jewish questions" (*Niederschrift einer Besprechung über Judenfragen*) is based on a meeting held on 31 March 1919, from 11:30 until 13:15, at the *Geschäftsstelle für Friedensverhandlungen* in Berlin, Behrenstrasse 21. Presided over by Johann Heinrich Graf von Bernstorff, former ambassador to the United States, the meeting was attended by high-ranking politicians, bureaucrats, and representatives of Jewish organisations in Germany. Among the participants were the future Foreign Minister Walter Simons, Professor Moritz S. Sobernheim (according to the record associated with the *Reichswirtschaftsministerium*, but acting here in his capacity as *Referent für jüdisch-politische Angelegenheiten* at the *Auswärtiges Amt*), several officials involved in German occupation policy during the First World War including Hermann Struck, former *Dezernent für jüdische Angelegenheiten* on the staff of the *Oberbefehlshaber Ost* and later adviser to the German delegation to the Versailles peace conference, Eugen Fuchs of the *Centralverein deutscher Staatsbürger jüdischen Glaubens* (henceforth C.V.), Richard Lichtheim of the *Zionistische Vereinigung für Deutschland* (henceforth ZVfD), and – speaking more for themselves than for any particular organisation or institution – Eduard Bernstein, James Simon, and Walther Rathenau. Designed as a prelude to further debates in preparation for the Versailles peace conference, this seems to have been the only meeting held in 1919 under the auspices of the Foreign Ministry to discuss the Jewish Question for which the records have survived. After May 1919, further discussions seemed pointless in view of Allied refusal to consider German demands for a revision of the peace terms. In combining a broad range of subjects and opinions – some outspoken, some muted – the *Niederschrift* allows an insight into the German state's attitude towards the Jews as well as into the general perspective of German-Jewish functionaries regarding a traumatic past and an uncertain future.

The First World War had been a crucial experience for German Jews: the illusion of a fatherland united against a common foe had quickly evaporated to reveal old antisemitic stereotypes. These overlooked the sacrifice of Jewish soldiers and civilians for the German cause while blending with new racial slogans widely held among the

---

*The opinions presented here are those of the author and do not necessarily reflect the opinions of the United States Holocaust Memorial Museum.

ruling élites and the middle class. Already in October 1914, German-Jewish soldiers could again hear "the old, hated ways of speaking",[1] once the "spirit of 1914" had been replaced by the trauma of total war, Jews found themselves marginalised as shirkers, war-profiteers, and enemies of *völkisch* grand designs. German military victories against Tsarist Russia and the occupation of vast areas in Eastern Europe had brought millions of Jews living in the former Pale of Settlement, as well as everything associated with them, closer to home. Some German Jews found the roots of their identity in their encounter with the *Ostjuden*; others sensed the danger lurking behind the confrontation of a prejudiced and politically disillusioned German gentile population with what it perceived as the revolting image of "the eternal Jew".[2] In its official proclamations the *Kaiserreich* supported the claim for Jewish self-determination in the East, as well as in Palestine – albeit in the latter case half-heartedly and only in the last stage of the war. At the same time, however, it helped propagate antisemitic slogans at home. The German army's "Jews' census" (*Judenzählung*) in the autumn of 1916 and the "border closure" (*Grenzsperre*) enacted against Eastern Jews in the spring of 1918 dealt a deadly blow to the hopes of the German-Jewish majority, tossing it back into the trenches of a war against antisemitism in which it could count on few allies.[3]

Before August 1914, organised German Jewry had been polarised between mainstream and radical opinions, represented by the C.V. with its large membership on the one hand and the small, but highly active ZVfD on the other. Only months before the beginning of the war, both organisations had declared the aims of the other incompatible with their own: for the Zionists, the C.V.'s programmatic orientation towards "cultivation of a German sentiment" (*Pflege deutscher Gesinnung*) was inimical to an assertive acceptance of Jewish identity; in turn, the C.V. perceived such an ideal as a potential threat to the delicate balance between *Deutschtum* and *Judentum*.[4] The debate, undertaken by both organisations in the hope of gaining the backing of German public opinion, was aborted at the war's outset in favour of assurances, echoing official government proclamations, that Jewish and German interests overlapped. Avoiding the controversial issue of national versus Jewish identity, the main strata in German Jewry worked towards a common policy to relieve the plight of the Eastern Jews, for this purpose even forming an unprecedented though short-lived umbrella organisa-

---

[1]"*Die alten, verhassten Redensarten*"; Julius Marx, *Kriegs-Tagebuch eines Juden*, Zürich 1939, p. 32 (entry for 5 October 1914).

[2]On the German-Jewish experience of war – its *Kriegserlebnis* – see Clemens Picht, 'Zwischen Vaterland und Volk. Das deutsche Judentum im Ersten Weltkrieg', in Wolfgang Michalka (ed.), *Der Erste Weltkrieg. Wirkung, Wahrnehmung, Analyse*, Munich 1994, pp. 736–757; Ulrich Sieg, *Jüdische Intellektuelle im Ersten Weltkrieg. Kriegserfahrungen, weltanschauliche Debatten und kulturelle Neuentwürfe*, Berlin 2001, pp. 109–172; Gregory A. Caplan, *Wicked Sons, German Heroes: Jewish Soldiers, Veterans, and Memories of World War I in Germany*, Ph.D. thesis, Georgetown University 2001, pp. 60–102.

[3]Still useful for the broader context: Egmont Zechlin and Hans Joachim Bieber, *Die deutsche Politik und die Juden im Ersten Weltkrieg*, Göttingen 1969; Werner E. Mosse and Arnold Paucker (eds.), *Deutsches Judentum in Krieg und Revolution 1916–1923*, Tübingen 1971 (Schriftenreihe wissenschaftlicher Abhandlungen des Leo Baeck Instituts 25).

[4]Avraham Barkai, "*Wehr Dich!*" *Der Centralverein deutscher Staatsbürger jüdischen Glaubens 1893–1938*, Munich 2002, presents the first comprehensive study on the history of the C.V. On the conflict between the Zionists and mainstream German-Jewish organisations see the essays by Jehuda Reinharz, 'Advocacy and History: The Case of the Centralverein and the Zionists' in LBI Year Book, vol. 33 (188), pp. 113–122; and Marjorie Lambertie, 'The Centralverein and the Anti-Zionists – Setting the Historical Record Straight', *ibid*, pp. 123–128.

tion, the *Vereinigung jüdischer Organisationen Deutschlands zur Wahrung der Rechte der Juden des Ostens* (Union of Jewish Organisations for the Preservations of the Rights of Eastern Jews), with Eugen Fuchs as one of its most avid supporters. The hegemonial aims of the *Kaiserreich*, however, left little room for real improvement in occupied Eastern Europe, even in regions such as the Baltic that had been under German rule for years.[5] The same was the case in Palestine, where Richard Lichtheim was trying, on behalf of the ZVfD and with the support of prominent German Jews, to get the backing of Germany's ally Turkey for post-war settlement plans. The Balfour Declaration and the turn of the tide in favour of the Western allies thwarted the efforts of German Zionists, whose role as the leading faction within the international Zionist movement would end with the war.[6]

For both sides of the German-Jewish spectrum, Germany's defeat had far-reaching consequences. Deep-rooted loyalty to the defunct *Kaiserreich* merged with feelings of confusion and shame about the national humiliation experienced after the war was lost; there was likewise deep disillusionment over the rise of antisemitism as the stock-in-trade of right-wing populism. At the same time, the unceremonious vanishing of the old regime's figureheads and the prospect of a new world order opened the view towards a brighter future within democratic structures – a hope shared by Zionists and non-Zionists despite their differences on how to reconcile *Deutschtum* and *Judentum* in times of rapid transition.[7] The most pressing questions for the Jewish future in Germany were whether the continuity of antisemitic discrimination could be broken and whether the fledgling democracy would grow strong enough to secure the Jewish minority's vital rights and interests better than during the *Kaiserreich*. This was the subtext of the discussion on 31 March 1919. Ideologically charged terms like *nationaldeutsch*, *Volkstum*, and *Judentum* had taken on new meanings and reflected the ongoing search for Jewish identity in the Diaspora. On the issue at hand, the interests of the participants differed. The representatives of Jewish organisations who had jointly drafted the peace-conference proposals serving as the meeting's agenda were looking for an opportunity to address what they regarded as key issues of Jewish future life – and to do so without sacrificing their own individual programmes. For Fuchs and the C.V., the German perspective was obviously more important than for Lichtheim and the ZVfD, who were concerned with strengthening the foundations for Jewish settlement in Palestine; nevertheless, the two sides presented a united front at the meeting by demanding equal Jewish rights in "all countries of the world" and by calling for a Jewish commonwealth in Palestine.

This consensus would erode as quickly as the prospect of a peace conference at which the new *Reich* government would be able to present its own ideas about the

---

[5]Jürgen Matthäus, 'German Judenpolitik in Lithuania During the First World War', in *LBI Year Book*, vol. 43 (1998), pp. 155–174. For an in-depth analysis of German occupation policy in the Baltic region and its impact on the occupiers see Vejas Gabriel Liulevicius, *War Land on the Eastern Front. Culture, National Identity and German Occupation in World War I*, Cambridge 2000.

[6]See Hagit Lavsky, *Before Catastrophe: The Distinctive Path of German Zionism*, Jerusalem 1996, pp. 18–39.

[7]See Avraham Barkai, Paul Mendes-Flohr, and Steven Lowenstein, *Deutsch-Jüdische Geschichte in der Neuzeit*, vol. 4: 1918–1945, Munich 1997, discussion by Flohr, pp. 28–35. Caplan, pp. 103–151, develops an interesting interpretation of a "culture of militarism", nurtured by the emerging *Reichsbund jüdischer Frontsoldaten*, that presented a "third possibility" for German-Jewish identity in the early post-war period.

postwar world order. During the Weimar years, both the C.V. and the ZVfD focussed intensively on strengthening the core areas of their organisational mission; in the process, the time of rapprochement vanished from memory in favour of a re-emergence of the pre-war rivalry.[8] Outside pressure was the key factor for dissent within organised German Jewry. The massive rise of antisemitism in German political culture, in combination with the inability – in many cases unwillingness – of state institutions to defend democratic freedoms and minority rights, made one hope in particular seem increasingly doubtful: that the *Judenfrage* would one day be perceived in Germany as anything other than a question for which *völkisch* ideas could provide an answer. Already during the meeting, the draft proposal presented by the representatives of Jewish organisations found a mixed reception with state officials: Bernstorff welcomed it as a tactical weapon to counter the demands of the "enemies", that is the victorious Allies; Sobernheim tried to reconcile his vision of prudent state policy with Jewish demands, but met resistance from his colleagues in the Prussian and Reich ministerial bureaucracy. The latter openly expressed their eagerness to maintain the same positions that had driven the *Kaiserreich*'s attitude towards the *Judenfrage* – positions that would thus facilitate future anti-Jewish measures.

As an attempt at dialogue, trust-building, and reconciliation between entrenched groups, the meeting represents a forgotten episode in German-Jewish history. Despite official statements regarding a "new spirit" in post-war Germany, the prejudices of the past would prevail in a time of radical change. In their rejection of democratic values, the majority of state bureaucrats would particularly contribute to the demise of the Weimar Republic and the rise of Nazism to power.[9] Transformed from a political issue into a right-wing dogma not to be discussed with Jews but solved at their expense, the *Judenfrage* would remain an element of continuity in German policy-making until its culmination in the Holocaust. In discussing the question in 1919, those later involved – as perpetrators, victims, or bystanders – in its attempted "solution" were sitting around the same table: Walter Rathenau, foreign minister of the Weimar Republic in 1922, would be murdered by members of a right-wing organisation; as representative of the Jewish Agency in war-time Geneva, Richard Lichtheim would gather first-hand evidence on the "Final Solution" in German-occupied Europe; Franz Eugen Fuchs, the son of Eugen Fuchs, would be among the millions to perish in it; while *Geheimrat* Hering from the Reich Interior Ministry, like numerous other German state officials, helped to draft and implement the anti-Jewish measures after 1933.[10]

---

[8]For the C.V. see Barkai, *Wehr Dich*, pp. 126–138.

[9]On the role of bureaucratic élites in the Weimar period see Hans Mommsen, *Die verspielte Freiheit. Der Weg der Republik von Weimar in den Untergang 1919 bis 1933*, Frankfurt am Main and Berlin 1990.

[10]See *ibid.*, p. 169; Barkai, *Wehr Dich*, p. 212; Richard Lichtheim, *Rückkehr. Lebenserinnerungen aus der Frühzeit des deutschen Zionismus*, Stuttgart 1970, especially pp. 379–381 with reference to the meeting; Uwe D. Adam, *Judenpolitik im Dritten Reich*, Düsseldorf 1972, p. 163; Raul Hilberg, *Die Vernichtung der europäischen Juden*, vol. 1, Frankfurt 1990, p. 69.

Conference Record (Niederschrift)[1]

AGENDA: *THE JEWISH QUESTION*

President [Graf Bernstorff]: Gentlemen, although it is not yet certain whether the Jewish Question will be discussed at the preliminary peace conference, it is still desirable that we express our views on this issue, especially since this is one of the questions where we might be in a position – as is similarly the case with the issue of the League of Nations and the social question – to face our enemies with a positive programme in hand, a programme that will solve the problem in principle, through which we will regain world-wide sympathy, and which will prove that a new spirit is at large in Germany.

In agreement with the *Referent für jüdische Angelegenheiten* [Official responsible for Jewish Affairs] [Sobernheim], the commission in charge of working on the Jewish question for the peace negotiations, whose representatives were selected from all sections of the Jewish community, has suggested putting forward the following demands at the peace conference:

1) Equality for Jews and Judaism in all countries of the world.
2) Abolition and prohibition of all laws, decrees and regulations containing restrictive measures applicable exclusively to Jews, especially bans on immigration and the closing of borders to Jews.
3) National and cultural autonomy within the new states to the extent demanded by the majority of Jews living in those parts, while safeguarding minority rights and arranging for the Sabbath to be taken into account within the legal framework.
4) Laying down of such political, administrative and economic conditions for Palestine that its development as an autonomous common wealth [*sic*], supported by all Jews, is ensured.
5) Compensation for victims of pogroms by the state concerned.
6) The setting-up of an international committee to watch over the enforcement of peace-conference principles and decisions that apply to Jews.

I would now like to ask Professor Sobernheim to present his report on the question. After that it might be best to go through the points one by one.

---

[1]Translated from the German by Gabriele Rahaman.
This document is located in the *Sächsische Hauptstaatsarchiv* Dresden (*Sächsisches Ministerium der Auswärtigen Angelegenheiten, Varia Juden betr., 1910–19*); a microfilm copy (which served as the basis for this publication) is available at the Archives of the United States Holocaust Memorial Museum in Washington, DC (RG 14.011M, reel 9). Editorial annotations have been restricted to material necessary for an understanding of the document. Additions to the text are printed in square brackets, emphases in italics. Where the original German contains phrases with different connotations from comparable English terms, these phrases have been retained or added in brackets.

[marginal note:] Point 1.

Dr. Sobernheim: Equality for Jews is, generally speaking, a principle firmly established in the constitutions of the Western countries. However, Jews have not always been successful in obtaining it fully.

In the East European countries, especially in those that used to constitute the former Russia and also in Roumania, the situation is quite different. There, even preparations for genuine equality for Jews have not as yet started. Thus the whole of Jewry [*Judenheit*] must strive to bring about equality. This matter gains further importance with point 6, which calls for an entirely new method to implement this.

As far as equal status for Jewry [*Judentum*] as such is concerned, there is a claim for legal equality of the Jewish religious community with other church communities, such as in financial regard and with respect to the position their officials hold within the religious community.

[marginal note:] Point 2.

Although equal status implies the abolition and prohibition of all laws, decrees, and regulations containing restrictive measures applicable exclusively to Jews, it must nevertheless be stressed that during the war, bans on immigration combined with the closing of borders to Jewish workers, for instance, were implemented in several countries. In Prussia, as well as in other countries, such prohibitions existed either openly or clandestinely during the war. This is why a special formulation is needed, particularly because at the international Socialist conference in Berne the demand has already been made that countries which prohibit immigration for economic reasons must submit their reasons for doing so to the League of Nations.

Dr. Lenz [Prussian Ministry of the Interior]: I am sorry that the points presented to us here could not be communicated to the participants of this meeting before. Under these circumstances I am in no position to comment on behalf of the Prussian Ministry of the Interior in any way on point 2. However, may I ask the chairman or the *Referent* whether the intent was perhaps to exert influence with point 2, directly or indirectly, on the German states, in particular on Prussia, regarding the immigration of 8 million *Ostjuden*, especially the 2 million Polish Jews, that is, those 2 million Jews living in *Kongresspolen*[2] at present? I need to know these basic facts in order to report to my superior authority and obtain a comment on this point.

Since it is my turn to speak I would like to take this opportunity to correct the information presented by the *Referent*. It was indeed the case that in Prussia a prohibitive regulation regarding the recruitment and employment of Jewish workers from *Kongresspolen* was enacted in April 1918, but this was just an [unforeseen] consequence of a measure taken by the German administration in the Warsaw

[2]The term *Kongresspolen* refers to that part of the former Polish kingdom that since 1815 was dominated by Tsarist Russia and that was occupied by the German and Austrian armies during the First World War; see Paul Roth, *Die politische Entwicklung in Kongreß-Polen während der deutschen Okkupation*, Leipzig 1919.

Generalgouvernement[3] prohibiting Jewish workers from being recruited for work in Germany. It was therefore inevitable that their employment in Prussia would not be allowed either. Both measures, the Prussian one and the one by the *Generalgouvernement*, are based solely on the fact that in *Kongresspolen* typhoid had appeared in an extremely dangerous form and that according to medical expert opinion the Jewish community represented the category of inhabitants most likely to increase the danger of typhoid [infection].

Chairman: I would like to comment on this as follows. As already set out in the introduction of this memorandum and as I have also said previously, these are proposals by the commission in charge of dealing with the Jewish Question whose representatives were selected from all sections of the Jewish community. The recommendations of this commission are to be put before the various government departments on this very day so that they may comment. It is perfectly clear, after all, that instructions to the peace delegation can only be issued when all government authorities are in agreement on this. Instruction will only be issued when agreement has been reached. This meeting has been called for the purpose of initiating such an agreement. We shall, of course, be most grateful if we could have the response of the Prussian Ministry of the Interior later.

Dr Fuchs: I am the leader of the *Centralverein der deutschen Staatsbürger jüdischen Glaubens*, which has roughly 200,000 members standing on *nationaldeutsch* soil.[4] I am a member of the executive commission of the *Verband der deutschen Juden* and the representative of the *nationaldeutsche* Jews elected by the *Vereinigung der jüdischen Organisationen*.[5] As you

---

[3]Following the advance of the German army into *Kongresspolen*, on 24 August 1915 the Reich government established a civil administration (*Generalgouvernement*) in Warsaw under General Beseler. Within this *Generalgouvernement Warschau*, subordinated to both the Kaiser and the Reich Ministry of the Interior, a department for Jewish affairs was created as a result of political pressure generated by German-Jewish organisations (see Zechlin, *Deutsche Politik*, pp. 155ff.). In the Second World War, the term *Generalgouvernement* described those Polish territories not annexed to the Reich and administered by Hans Frank.

[4]The terms *deutsch-national* and *nationaldeutsch* have been retained as these cannot be meaningfully translated into English; for a discussion of how these terms were often misinterpreted particularly as applied to the *Centralverein*, see Arnold Paucker 'Zur Problematik einer jüdischen Abwehrstrategie in der deutschen Gesellschaft' in Werner E. Mosse and *idem*, *Juden im Wilhelminischem Deutschland 1890–1914*, 2nd edn., Tübingen 1998 (Schriftenreihe wissenschaftlicher Abhandlungen des Leo Baeck Instituts 33), pp. 479–548, here p. 526. "Zudem nannte man sich noch lange Jahre hindurch 'deutsch-national', was ursprünglich, in sachlicher Gegenüberstellung zu 'jüdisch-national' durchaus legitim war . Damals war das eben noch kein Parteibegriff und beweist nur die Realität eines Bedeutungswandels in der politischen Terminologie. Allerdings fuhr man fort, sich dergestalt zu bezeichnen, auch noch als es den Deutschnationalen Handlungsgehilfenverband schon bald eine kleine Ewigkeit gab und fast schon eine Deutschnationale Volkspartei. Wenn eine spätere Historiographie den Centralverein zuweilen fälschlich unter die konservativen und gemäßigt reaktionären Organisationen einreihte (also dort, wo eben das deutsche Bürgertum stand, und gerade nicht die Juden), so ist sein eigener Sprachgebrauch für diese Verwirrung nicht völlig ohne Verantwortung."

[5]Fuchs is referring here to the *Vereinigung jüdischer Organisationen Deutschlands zur Wahrung der Rechte der Juden des Ostens* (the Association of Jewish Organisations in Germany for the Preservation of the Rights of Jews in the East) founded in January 1918 in Berlin. At the time of the meeting, however, this organisation seems to have been already disbanded; see Jürgen Matthäus, 'Deutschtum and Judentum under Fire: The Impact of the First World War on the Strategies of the Centralverein and the Zionistische Vereinigung', in *LBI Year Book*, vol. 33 (1988), pp. 144–147.

gentlemen will know, three sections of the German-Jewish communities are represented in this commission: a representative from the Orthodox section, a representative from the Zionist section, and a representative from the non-Zionist section,
that is, from the *nationaldeutsch* section, and I am speaking to you as the latter.

I am sorry, too, that the Prussian Ministry [of the Interior] did not respond just
now, for I would have been eager to hear what the Prussian Ministry has to say about
this point which, in my opinion, accords with human rights generally. I have said
repeatedly that the extent to which a people or a nation state wishes to close itself off
from other countries is a matter everyone has to settle with his own political or social
conscience. If the German Republic and Prussia were to come and say, we wish to
cut ourselves off from all those who are not German or Prussian – I think there
would be thousands and thousands of my co-religionists who would say, yes, we want
to remain amongst ourselves, we want to stay German or Prussian. But if you wanted to institute prohibitive measures and regulations, or close borders exclusively to
keep Jews out of this country, than that would be a point of view not in keeping with
humanity [*Menschlichkeit*]. It would also not be justified by simply stating that somehow typhoid and lice, by their very nature, have a particular faith and that one has
to keep lice away from borders whenever they are Jewish, but will let them pass if
not. As you no doubt know, typhoid is caused by lice. According to the experience I
have had, I must say that the experts on whom *Geheimrat* Lenz relies have produced
a report which is dubious to the highest degree. I would very much like to wait and
see if it is indeed necessary to protect oneself in particular against Jews infected with
typhoid. I also believe that the Prussian Ministry will come around to the view that
if somehow there has been typhoid in a certain country, perhaps in Lithuania or in
Volhynia, the infectious agent causing it will not have been limited to Jews, in which
case one will do well to exclude everyone from this country. It is possible that the
Völkerkongress[6] will not permit countries to shut themselves off from each other. It is
also possible that the national consciousness of various nations [*Völker*] will rise in
such a way that they perhaps will feel the need to shut themselves off; but if they wish
to do so they may only do so on a national and not on a religious basis. Should such
ideas be uttered again I would then come to the following conclusion and say: I
would like to concede as little influence on the states as possible to the *Völkerkongress*;
in particular I would not like to see Germany bent under the yoke of the congress.
That is why, as the representative of the *deutschnational* Jews, I have simply stated the
point of view and the thesis that we wish to submit only those questions to the
League of Nations which are general questions of humanity with international significance; nothing that is exclusively relevant to our German fatherland should be
left to the competence of the *Völkerkongress*. I therefore urge you to agree to the prohibition of all exclusions based on religious denomination. The world will not understand this.

---

[6]The term *Völkerkongress* (congress of peoples [or: nations]) refers to an envisaged international peace conference with a much broader mandate than the Versailles proceedings and to a conference of Jewish representatives from Europe and the U.S. proposed by American Zionists as early as 1914. While Fuchs and
the *Centralverein* opposed the idea of a congress of German Jews advanced by the ZVfD, they accepted
the need for discussions on the fate of Jews outside Germany (see Zechlin, *Deutsche Politik*, pp. 501–502,
566–568; Barkai, *Wehr Dich*, pp. 126–131).

Bernstein: Although I differ in my opinion from Dr Fuchs and in contrast to him wish the League of Nations to have responsibility with regard to the various nations and although I have no fear that this responsibility might lead perhaps to Germany, the German Republic, the German nation being in a worse position than other nations, I essentially concur with his protest and declarations. I do not, however, believe that this is a question of religious denomination. I also do not believe that this was on *Geheimrat* Lenz's mind. This is about much more. Judaism [*Judentum*] as a faith is not the question uppermost in our minds here; it is rather ethnicity [*Volkstum*], or race – whatever you want to call it – that is at issue here. I think I do not misinterpret *Herr Geheimrat* Lenz when I assume this. We know each other very well from *Reichstag* times when we debated the laws regarding citizenship [*Reichs- und Staatsbürgerrecht*] and when the question arose whether members of other nations [*Völker*] who had lived in Germany for a long time, and impeccably so, should be granted naturalisation rights for which my faction [the Social Democrats] and others then fought in vain. It is not a question of which religion one belongs to but rather a question of ethnicity.

The figure of 8 million Jews which *Geheimrat* Lenz mentioned – whether they are to be let loose on Prussia [*Preußen-Deutschland*] – sounds threatening from a certain point of view. But one should know at least to some extent how things really are. We have talked in a previous meeting about the immigration question, which is going to be very important indeed. I would recommend every sensible protective measure possible against the mass exportation of immigrants. However, with respect to workers coming into the country of their own free will – they will be looking for work and will return home when they do not find any. I think the question of immigration from the East is vastly exaggerated. We must not forget: what is claimed here on behalf of Jews will most probably have to be claimed for Germans, too. In various countries a strong counter-movement will spread against the immigration of Germans. It is still quite obscure how employment opportunities will develop for our people. We do not know whether a large number of our industrial workers might not be forced to emigrate, to go to other countries in order to find employment elsewhere. It is possibly the case – of course I do not wish for such a thing, but it is possible perhaps because of a lack of raw materials, or because of industrial decline – that a number of our workers will be forced to emigrate. In many countries, in England, in America, there are laws against immigration, [which is to say] precisely in those countries where German workers might conceivably find employment conditions that accord with their cultural expectations. If we do not display justice here how can we fight the other [discriminatory] laws [of the other countries] successfully! One could possibly – although this is not my point of view but one developed by the Chairman – test the others [the other countries] as follows: if they allow freedom here [in their own countries], they must also allow it elsewhere. For this reason I think one would have to support this matter.

Sanitary measures – [applied] when epidemics begin to spread somewhere – are not the same as emergency laws. Dr Fuchs was right when he said that typhoid was not limited to the Jewish population. I know that typhoid was rampant with devastating effect here in Germany in the Russian camps; a whole camp was decimated by the epidemic. But those were Russians of all denominations, of all races, if you want to call it that. Of course one would have to ask for an expert opinion and declare oneself willing to consider it, if that is what is wanted. But these are points of view which also make me take the side of Dr. Fuchs in the matter concerned.

Hering: I, too, cannot as yet respond on behalf of the Reich Ministry of the Interior regarding point 2 since it was not known to us beforehand. I would only like to point out that in its own national interest a country with a long eastern border, shared with a country in which a great number of *Ostjuden* live – who, because of hundreds of years of cultural neglect by the Russian government have sunk to a great extent to an extremely low cultural level – would have to be especially careful in the interest of preserving the culture of its own people, before it opens up its eastern border completely to this part of the Eastern population.

Regarding the prohibition on employing Jewish-Polish workers I can only confirm what *Geheimrat* Lenz said, namely that this regulation was exclusively based on considerations of public-health policing [*medizinalpolizeiliche Gesichtspunkte*] and that it grew out of the practical experience of the Warsaw *Generalgouvernement* at the time: typhoid, despite most carefully worked out counter-measures, could not be eliminated from the quarters of the poor Jewish population in Warsaw, Lodz, or elsewhere. It flared up time and again, especially in these quarters. The prohibition on recruiting workers from these areas, then on transporting such workers to Germany, emerged from these practical experiences.

Dr. Lenz: I can only confirm the statements the previous speaker made and say that the medical department of the Ministry of the Interior was also responsible for the regulation of April last year ["the closing of borders"] and that it was not based on a denominational distinction between Jewish and non-Jewish lice. That much is quite obvious. I thought I would be spared from stressing this point. The matter is indeed as *Geheimrat* Hering has shown: it is a fact that in a particular quarter of Warsaw and Lodz – you, gentlemen, will know that the Jewish communities [*die Judenschaft*] in Warsaw and in Lodz are living separately from the rest of the population to a certain extent and one may indeed still call these ghettos in a way – that in this quarter typhoid had grown in such a way – because of the particular uncleanliness of the Jewish population, as may indeed be emphasised since it is a known matter of fact – as to suggest that there was indeed a particular danger for Poland as well as her neighbours. That was the reason why the medical department of the Ministry of the Interior took this measure in agreement with the Reich Ministry of the Interior and the medical experts.

In addition I would like to draw your attention to the fact that in its present radical formulation point 2, which I cannot discuss in detail here, represents an interference with the general policing of aliens [*allgemeine Fremdenpolizei*], an interference with sovereign state powers, an interference which presents itself, frankly, as special legislation for Jews. Seen from this point of view one may not be able to justify general agreement. Essentially the principle of equal status for Jews has been stated in point 1. I am convinced that the Prussian Ministry of the Interior will not object to point 1. In contrast to this, point 2 presents itself as a clause which allows an exception [*Ausnahmebestimmung*] in the sphere of competence of the Alien Police in such a radical form that I, for one, am of the opinion that a great many things speak against it.

Herr Bernstein referred to the negotiations regarding the naturalisation law taking place in the Reichstag in 1912. From the tone of his comments, I discerned with satisfaction, if I may say so, that he is somewhat favourably inclined towards the views held by the Prussian authorities at the time. To a great extent I can agree to what he has said here, and I could point out in particular that a sharp distinction has to be made – I do not need to explain this further to you, gentlemen, who are representatives of the Jewish community – between Jews as a religious community and Jews with regard to nationality [*in nationaler Beziehung*]. It is well known that in *Kongresspolen* in particular, and especially during the war, the Jewish community there, that is the *Ostjuden*, claimed and still claims to be a nation and demanded to be recognised as such. Here I may emphasise, although I think it is almost superfluous, that whenever measures were taken in Prussia against Eastern Jews, denomination never played a decisive role in any way, but descent, race, nationality did. It is a widely believed superstition that especially in the realm of naturalisation policy, foreign Jews in Prussia are caused particular difficulties. For this reason I have endeavoured for years to prove the opposite with the help of statistics. At the time when the naturalisation law was debated, the same proof was given to the *Reichstag* commission. I am in the position to communicate the latest figures about this; you, gentlemen, may find them interesting – they prove that the Jewish community has not done too badly, at least as far as our naturalisation policy is concerned. I have here in front of me figures from 1914 to 1918. According to these, naturalisation applications made by foreign Jews [living] in Prussia were granted as follows:

in 1914, 263 applications out of a total of 311 were granted, only 48 were declined
" 1915 397 " " " 486 " " 89 "
" 1916 207 " " " 245 " " 38 "
" 1917 120 " " " 155 " " 35 "
" 1918 100 " " " 107 " " 7 "

(figures [for 1918] apply almost to the end of the year). In total there were 1,304 applications between 1914–1918 of which 1,087 were granted and 217 declined. If one were to calculate the percentage – I could only have this done for 1914, 1915 and 1916 because the statistics for 1917 and 1918 are not as yet obtainable – then the following results are obtained: out of 5,324 persons naturalised in Prussia in 1914, 349 were Jewish, that is 6.56%; in 1915 out of 7,938 persons [naturalised in Prussia], 604 [were Jewish], that is 7.61%; in 1916 out of 7,946 persons [naturalised in Prussia], 353 [were Jewish], that is 4.44%. When you consider that the percentage of the Jewish population in Prussia in relation to that of other denominations is roughly 1, then you will probably agree with me and regard the percentage of Jews obtaining citizenship in Prussia as quite high.

Chairman: Gentlemen! As I mentioned earlier, these proposals were put forward by the commission and not by the government. The position of the government will only become clear through this meeting and perhaps later ones. I would like to point out – in order to come to an agreement – that in my view the emphasis in point 2 lies on the term 'exclusively'. (Quite so!) The intention is not to introduce emergency laws [*Ausnahmegesetze*] but rather to avoid them. (Quite so!) In this instance we might perhaps come to an agreement to find a format so that emergency laws no longer remain or so that they are not introduced. If it were the case, for example, in the matter of hygiene that one part of Warsaw were more contaminated than another, and that this particular part were inhabited by Jews, then the regulations could say: from this geographical area emigration must not take place – or some similar formulation. I only want to submit this question for your consideration because I hope that we will eventually agree on a positive agenda.

Dr Fuchs: Herr Bernstein concluded with the statement that he would have liked an expert opinion regarding this question. But, gentlemen, I ask you, what could an expert tell you? Could he tell you that Jews in Poland as such were more affected by typhoid than others? And if he were to tell you that, do you think that you would ever come to the conclusion: the Jews are exclusively afflicted by typhoid? And if no expert could tell you that because it would contradict factual logic, you would, based on your own human experience, come away with the sentence: there was a certain type of typhoid in Poland and Jews were more afflicted by it than Christians. With this, you wish to justify opposition to a regulation which simply intends to abolish the closure of borders *exclusively* to Jews.

It is said that we demand preferential treatment. We have very carefully considered whether we need point 2 in addition to point 1. The very practice exercised by the Prussian authorities and the points of view uttered by *Geheimrat* Lenz just now make it a matter of urgency to give this regulation a somewhat different grounding and to submit it to the peace congress, because we do not have the necessary trust in how the authorities have acted up to now. Gentlemen, I am a representative of the *nationaldeutsch* Jews and the representative of those Jews whose circles include many thousands opposed to an influx from the East, for reasons of their [own] equal status. As leader of the *Centralverein* I would, however, consider myself as pursuing old antisemitic policies if I were to tolerate the borders of my fatherland being exclusively closed to Jews; and even if that meant my social standing being threatened with damage, I, as a man, as a Jew, as a man of law and justice, would never be able to agree with the following: to pursue antisemitic policies and close the borders to Jews, to pursue antisemitic policies which in the end have gained our German fatherland the dislike of the neutral powers and the inability to have friendly relations with the whole world. That is why it is important to me that this point is included.

Gentlemen, in the times of Tsarist Russia many Jews wished to leave and enter a land of freedom. Now that Russia is no longer Tsarist you can be sure that Jews will not be much interested in coming to us, to our land of freedom. I do not know if you are sufficiently familiar with history to know that in 1914 and 1915 the Polish Jews saw the Germans as liberators, going over to the German camp with drums beating and banners flying high, but that they later said: rather [be] Russian than German-Prussian. That is the first point which will put your minds at rest.

The second point is as follows. It has been said: here we do not mean denomination but merely race, nationality. I would have to speak for an hour to correct this course of thought for you. The great majority of the Jews in Germany are not part of a foreign race, a foreign nationality, but are German nationals [*deutschnational*], and this is based on hundreds of years of history; they took part in the wars of liberation and other wars. That is the view I have represented for decades, where I am located within the movement, at least in the last few decades. The Jews from the East, the Jews of Poland, do have a kind of nationality in addition to being members of a community of faith: they speak a different language, namely Yiddish, they have a different culture, they close themselves off in a ghetto-like manner. That is why the Jews from the East are part of national and religious communities [*nationale und Religionsgemeinschaften*], whereas the Jews in the Western states – this is the opinion held at least by my friends; the Zionists differ on this point – belong to the German nation [*Nation*], are part of the German people [*sind deutschvölkisch*], as German as the Beringers and the Dubois-Reymonds, who have lived here for hundreds of years and have become part of German culture. If at the peace congress the Polish Jews achieve recognition as a nation according to the law of self-determination – and I will be happy if they do, although I am not sure if this will be to their benefit – then Prussia and Germany, if they shut themselves off from [all] nations, will [also] shut themselves off from this nation. But we don't want to stop them doing this at all. I have already said so quite openly: if you believe that Germany wishes to be autochthonously German and wants to shut itself off, I have nothing against that – then we will stay amongst ourselves. But they [Prussia and Germany] should not say: the Jews are to be excluded. They may reject anyone in Poland who wishes to be Jewish-national according to principles by which they reject other nationalities.

I am grateful for this discussion as it has opened my eyes to something which – according to the new spirit allegedly at large in the *Reich* and the state – I would not have believed possible, namely that one should regard the prohibition of restrictions aimed at Jews as preferential treatment of Jews and as interference with the business of police departments dealing with foreign nationals.

Dr. Cohn: Honoured gentlemen! I would like to add one item to the comments that have been made supporting this point. The commission which came up with this agenda was of course wholly of the opinion that it had to submit proposals to the circles that were in favour of German interests. In this I must touch on the chairman's introductory remarks: if it is a matter of reawakening sympathies for Germany in wider circles, then it is pressing to somehow put right, in the eyes of the world, the Prussian regulations of that time. For anyone who has experienced what happened in Warsaw – how this regulation in particular removed even the last remnant of faith in German justice (even in the Polish population) – has to say: it is a very wise and good thing if it is now realised that such differences, be they denominational or national, no longer matter. At that time in Warsaw, it was said that there were so many wonderful delousing centres at the border, and that one might, after all, prohibit the importation of labour originating from certain streets in Warsaw; but this general prohibition caused immense annoyance not only in Jewish circles; a large number of Poles as well were simply stunned and did not understand, although they might have understood in their heart of hearts, how these regulations could have been passed at a time when it was essential to gain world-wide sympathy. Just stating that the German *Reich* no longer recognises denominational and national differences with regard to its police regulations would be the minimum one could do to make up for the injustice perpetrated at that time.

Dr. Pick: Everything that has to be said has already been said, I think. I just want to add a few observations based on my four-year experience in Poland as the *Dezernent* at the police headquarters in Lodz and as deputy director of the press department. What purpose might our conclusions have? They are to show the world that our former policies regarding the Jewish Question, how it has been dealt with in Germany so far, has not been right, and that Germany has learned to mend its ways. We regard it as an essential task for Germany to show the world that the old ways have gone. And they have to go with regard to the Jews as well.

What *Geheimrat* Lenz said is something with which I do not think I ought to delay the deliberations of this meeting any longer, as this gathering surely has no intention of discussing Prussian matters and things of the past, but will be of the opinion that we want to ensure justice and law and, above all, Germany's standing in the eyes of the world! We have to try and cover up the sore point in the history of this occupation, namely the exclusion [*Absperrung*] of the Polish Jews, so that we rekindle the interest and good opinion of Jews world-wide. It has been said that there should be no preferential treatment but that there is to be no special legislation introduced exclusively for Jews. In the whole of Poland, as has already been mentioned several times, and not only in Poland but in an area reaching far into Russia, the first months of the occupation of Poland meant great success for German policies. Everywhere one could hear: the Germans have taken the oppressed, the Jews, under their care and protection. After a year the situation had changed completely, the spirit amongst Jews had sunk to its lowest level, and later we had no opportunity at all to make good the damage in the eyes of the international community.

I would also like to correct something else: it did not matter how the gentlemen in Berlin envisaged things but what impact the regulation had in reality. Jews felt that this regulation was directed especially against them. I have to state here that a large portion of the working class Jews in particular did not live in the quarter of Lodz mentioned here; a certain kind of long-robed orthodox Jew lived there. Members of the Socialist Party in particular suffered because of this regulation. Unskilled labourers were also expressly held back.

If the points we have raised today were to gain influence on world politics as a German initiative, then the situation of Jews in the East European countries would improve so much that they would never have any intention of emigrating to Germany. (Quite so!) If today's discussion were to have the side effect of making Prussia careful with regard to certain things, however well-meant they might have been originally, that would be most pleasing. Let us hope that the fear of being swamped by *Ostjuden* will turn out to be baseless. We know the circumstances only too well and know that it is simply a question of a small percentage. For reasons of general policy and bearing in mind the experience I have had with *Ostjuden* I would therefore urge you to accept this point as it is.

Bernstein: *Geheimrat* Lenz misunderstands me if he believes that I expressed positive sentiments regarding the negotiations at that time. I have tried to speak somewhat urbanely and went a bit too far. I believe in those negotiations we were very much opposed to each other. The new statistics cannot convince me either that the view taken by my party and myself was unjust. I do not want to go into this, however, because in that case one might have to discuss motivations and it is better they are left out of the game.

I am not a Jew by faith, neither do I belong to a specific Jewish association and I am not a national Jew either. I grew up as part of the German people and I feel German, but I know that I am Jewish by descent, and wherever Jews are oppressed I regard it as my duty to stand up for them. The question of exclusion cannot be justified by the arguments that have been put forward. The previous speaker has quite rightly pointed out that Jews who migrate are very different from the Jews who are meant to be the object of these measures here. I also have to take issue with the belief that the Jewish population, even in Poland, is particularly unclean. If you force people into a limited space without any provision for hygiene, then even the cleanest people will have to abandon cleanliness. In London, where marked uncleanliness reigns in some districts, I have seen German housewives, whom I knew to be immaculately clean by upbringing, abandon the fight against uncleanliness because the surrounding circumstances made it impossible for them. In any case according to my experience the Jewish population is not particularly unclean. If it were so, I would admit it, because I am completely unprejudiced.

It has already been pointed out by the chairman, and quite rightly so, that in this point the emphasis lies on the word "exclusively". Taking certain sanitary measures cannot be denied to any nation. But the passing of special legislation [*Ausnahmebestimmungen*] should not follow from this. I did not ask for an expert opinion although Dr. Fuchs seems to think so. I only said that there should be the opportunity to consult such an opinion.

Otherwise I can only confirm what has been said here about the effect the measures taken by the German administration in Russian Poland had on the whole Jewish community. It is quite true that at the beginning of the war the Russian and Polish Jews were passionately in favour of Germany – which also was obvious in America. You know that many Jews live in New York. There was also jubilation in Russia and Poland when the Germans marched in. In 1916 we were visited by a gentleman who travelled as the representative of a charity. He talked with us in detail about the situation of the Jews in Russian Poland and in the occupied area and told us, among other things, that an old Jew in Vilna had said the following: I have only committed one sin in my whole life and that is weeping tears of joy when the Germans came. – That is how the mood had changed. If you knew what we were told then you would understand. Here is something for which we need to make amends and that can happen by being in favour of this point [point 2].

Regarding the dangers related to the treatment of the Jews, please do not forget the advantages. I had the opportunity to observe that when a number of Jews fled from Russia and, I think in 1891, arrived in England. I lived in England at that time. These Jews were a means for England to stop importing ready-to-wear garments from Germany. Just ask in New York how much the Jewish immigrants contributed to raising whole industries to a new level. Then you will understand that there can be no talk of danger when you obtain a labour force.

[marginal note:] Point 3.

Dr. Sobernheim: Point 3 is mainly about the states which have yet to be established. National autonomy makes use of the principle of the right to self-determination for national minorities and is based on principles which the present *Staatskanzler* Renner

worked out many years ago with the purpose of enabling the many peoples of
Austria to live together within a monarchy. With these measures, he intended to
avoid certain frictions between the various nationalities which had come about
because of the election campaign and the establishment of schools. The Jewish
minority would accordingly be treated as a nation in its own right like, for instance,
the German minority in Hungary, or Bohemia, or Moravia; that means they would
have their own election register for the legislative authorities and for the local government administration, with the number of seats being in proportion to their percentage in the population and with representation at all higher administrative
authorities on a percentage basis as well. A special national ministry might well be
set up for each minority, the Jewish one included. The minorities would also be
allowed to represent their communities by forming local and regional associations
headed by a high council. Their language[s] would be accepted as the language[s]
of a minority state [*Nebenstaatssprache*]. Members of the minority, that means Jews
too, would have the right to have an interpreter in court and all other official administrative offices. In areas where minorities represent the majority, judges from that
minority, which means Jewish judges as well, should be appointed to the civil courts.

The question now is whether these principles have as yet ever been put into practice
anywhere. And in this case I have to answer: yes, they have been put into practice in
the Bukowina. There the Roumanian nationals, the Ruthenian nationals, the German
nationals have lived side by side with their own election registers, their own school
administrations. The election register of the German nationals was tacitly split in two:
the German and the Jewish register. These four nationalities have lived together peacefully. In a town like Czernowitz, the Roumanian, German, Ruthenian and Jewish may-
ors have taken turns; they have visited each others' festivals and taken part in the
national life of their various communities. When naming streets and squares the great
figures of each nationality have been taken into consideration, so we have the *Herzl-
Platz*, named after the great Zionist leader, in Czernowitz. At present this principle is
being put into practice by a special ministry in the Ukraine. This demand [for self-
determination] has also been made for Lithuania, and for the West Ukrainian
Republic, which is Eastern Galicia. It was made during the presidency of Kerenski for
Greater Russia. One always has to keep in mind that this demand was indeed of great
importance in Galicia and Russia. There are towns there with a Jewish population of
up to 90%. In Poland itself only a small party is demanding national autonomy. In
Germany such demands are not made by anyone.

Cultural autonomy demands – of course under general supervision of the state –
freedom in matters of schooling – elementary schools, secondary schools, and spe-
cialised schools – and freedom in all cultural domains. Institutions serving the
minorities would be maintained either by their own taxes, collected by the community – in this case minorities would sometimes demand permission to deduct a pro-
portionate amount for this cultural tax [*Kultussteuer*] against the tax they pay the state
– or by direct support from the state government, which, for example, is the case in
Germany at the moment. Cultural autonomy also means freedom to observe the
Sabbath and the holy days and includes the right to work on all other days without
hindrance. For example, in smaller towns in Poland and in the Lodz and Warsaw
ghettoes, an attempt is being made to stop Jews from working on Sundays so that

people sometimes have two non-working days a week and thus sustain damage to their social and commercial life. Thus, a resolution has already been passed at the Berne Socialist Conference to the effect that all workers should have a 36 hour rest-period and that those communities [*Völker*] for whom Sunday is not a holy day should be permitted to observe another day instead.

This type of cultural autonomy may be considered for Poland, *Deutsch-Österreich*, Czechoslovakia, and Yugoslavia. In some countries there are also demands for national autonomy. In the Western countries cultural autonomy for the sake of educational freedom and the possibility of religious practice essentially exists already, for instance in Germany, and this must remain so.

Dr. Rathenau: Gentlemen! I regard this recommendation as creating a serious [international] precedent [*Präjudiz*]. At the moment when the government of the German Reich interferes with the self-determination of other nationalities we have to expect reciprocity as a matter of course. If we advocate that a part of the population in certain states receives autonomy then we have opened the door to the same claim by minorities on us. I think that particularly at the peace conference, we should try to prevent any precedent that could be used against us. If, however, one sees things from the perspective of this precedent, if one does not shrink from interfering with the setting-up of new nations and with their legal systems then there is no reason to single out the Jews. In that case we must be the advocates of Ruthenians, Serbian minorities, and Walachian minorities in the other countries. Then raising these claims on behalf of Jews would constitute an exceptional measure [*Ausnahmebestimmung*] in favour of a tightly defined national group. And this precedent goes further. For the German Reich would thus stabilise the fact that at least elsewhere the Jews form a nation, even if by doing so the German Reich does not establish a precedent in the question of whether the Jews form a nation in Germany. I am of the opinion that such a series of grave international questions is going to unfold under these circumstances – and they are not at all going to be raised in the interest of the German Reich – that I would ask you to desist from this claim.

Dr. Fuchs: The concerns expressed by the previous speaker were significant [only] as long as we had the hope that Germany would occupy a dominant position in the East, that Germany would be responsible for the fate of the *Ostjuden* and for Eastern Europe altogether. Even from my viewpoint as a good German I asked myself: should our Jews in the East have the right to demand autonomy? And then I was faced with the question: should they be Germanised or Polonised? That is when my scruples started. As a good German I cannot allow these Jews to be Polonised and thereby remove support from my fatherland, which lies in the fact that the Jews in the East, the Jews of Poland, love Germany more and that their love for Germany is greater than their hatred for Poland, because Jews and Poles do hate each other. After many deliberations with my friends I came up with the formula that we do well to say: the Jews should not be Germanised, not be Polonised, they should keep their national distinctiveness; and according to the principle which is now at large in the world, the principle of the right of self-determination, we should give them the right to stay in the East with Jewish nationality.

Everything has changed now because Germany has lost its influence in the East and because it will not be possible to gain a dominant position there. That means we have to rescue whatever can be rescued of German interests there and this leads me, a *nationaldeutsch* Jew, to think in the same way as the Zionist Jews: if we want the Jews there not to be Polonised or incorporated into Polishness [*Polentum*] by force, then it would be in the interest of Germanness [*Deutschtum*] to grant them national autonomy. Then they do not need to become Polish, and having their own nationality – because of their sympathies for Germany and because of their language – will lead to them becoming a buffer against the Poles. Gentlemen, why are the member countries of the *entente* interested in the fate of the Jews? Surely not for the sake of the Jews! I cannot imagine that England loves the Jews that much, that out of love for the Jews it is giving them Palestine; rather, it is giving them Palestine in order to drive a wedge into Turkey and the Orient, in order to have a population there which is sympathetic to England. Similarly, why will the member countries of the *entente* be willing to grant Jews national autonomy? Because they will not want Poland to become too powerful. The thought of preventing Poland from becoming too dominant is congruent with the demand made here to allow the Jewish community cultural autonomy and the right to self-determination. A number of my friends have said they will regret it, they will be killed by the Poles. I say *item* to that, as a politician I do not personify destiny, I must not interfere with destiny, if they wish to become a nation according to the right of self-determination I shall give it to them. In any case the right of self-determination is today a greater fortune to them than would be my saying: you must become Poles. I grant them the right of self-determination from a *deutschnational* standpoint and say: stand up against the Poles as a nationality in your own right. That would be to the profit of *Deutschtum*.

I would regard regulation of cultural autonomy in Germany by the *Völkerkongress* as interference with the sovereignty of the German people, an interference with which I could not have any truck. If, however, the *Völkerkongress* allows new states to be created, then I would wish them to be shaped in our interests, in which case they should be granted national autonomy. This way we would kill two birds with one stone: we would safeguard German national interests by avoiding the Polonisation of the Jews and we would offer the *Völkerkongress* something which would give it powers over the fate of the nations it has created. We do not, however, wish the congress to interfere in any way with Germany's national or cultural autonomy or that of any other country it has not created; in such cases we create our own autonomy.

These are the considerations and I would ask you to approve these *deutschnational* considerations which coincide with Jewish interests. I would like to close with these words: while being in charge of the association for the last 25 years I have always found that the well-understood interests of *Deutschtum* have never excluded the justified claims of the Jews. These well-understood interests, provided they are based on justice, truth and freedom, are unanimously accepted throughout the world.

Chairman: Gentlemen, I will have to report to the government about this meeting and therefore cannot say which position the government will adopt on such an important question. However, I believe that, generally speaking, questions of national and cultural autonomy will be incorporated into the greater question of national minorities which has already been discussed by the cabinet. This would, however, be an admission that the Jews constituted a nation – [an admission] which Herr Dr. Rathenau regards as dangerous. Whether we can escape this danger once Palestine has been reshaped by the Zionists is extremely questionable. But that is a question we shall have to leave for the future.

Dr. Fuchs: I have forgotten to mention something. I do not accept the claim that the Jews should be recognised as a nation. I make a strong distinction between Western and Eastern Jews because the *Ostjuden* are a nation but the *Westjuden* are not. The decisive criterion for the concept of nationality, in my opinion, is will, putting aside the objective aspects of language, history, and baptism of blood on the battlefields, and we maintain that, roughly calculated, 500,000 Jews have the will to belong to Germany [*Deutschtum*] as a people.

Dr. Lichtheim: I am not going to enter into the discussion about the nature of a national race [*nationale Rasse*] or religion. From a Jewish point of view that would appear to me to be wrong. I represent the Zionist point of view here. We understand Jews to be what all the gentlemen here understand. We mean that religion and community [*Volksgemeinschaft*] which, based on common descent and cultural history, has endured for 4,000 years of world history. I do not wish to define the particulars here in more detail.

Regarding the question of autonomy I would like to say the following. We Zionists, who represent this position in public, are very clear about the fact that dangerous or unfavourable consequences may arise from this stance. In particular I have personally felt concern that national autonomy for a national minority, realised completely, could have very dangerous economic consequences for such a minority. If one agrees to grant a smaller group [*Volksgruppe*] within a larger [such] group special status in all areas, if one grants them special schools, a special judiciary system, separate election registers and so on, that might lead to economic exclusion and cultural alienation. This is a danger – we will not deny it. But we are confronted by the fact that 6 million Eastern European Jews demand national or cultural or national-cultural autonomy. They claim this to be the only means they can think of to protect themselves against encroachment by the Slav peoples amongst whom they live. We have to take the desire of this mass of people into account and we will have to represent them. I do not think, however, that Germany will be forced to take the initiative in this question at the peace conference. Regarding this point I think I can dispel Dr. Rathenau's concerns. There will not be a situation that will force Germany to broach this question. The question will be raised by others. At this moment the conference of the national Jewish councils of Eastern Europe is taking place in Paris. Founded during the war, these bodies represent all the Jews in the various Eastern European countries. In the Ukraine, where approximately 3 million Jews live, a congress has taken place attended by all Jewish parties. This congress demanded national autonomy. In Roumania cultural autonomy is being demanded, along with protection against attacks by the Roumanians. The situation is similar in Poland and other Eastern European countries. The conference is taking place in Paris [*sic*]. Wilson has agreed to listen to the requests made at this conference at the peace conference and to discuss them. Here it is only a matter of the German delegation being informed about this question and having at least something of a guideline on how to react when the question is raised. I do not think that the German delegation will harm German interests if it bases its comments on general humanitarian principles, on the idea of freedom, and if it says: this demand, put forward by the Jews, to be protected against encroachment by others, to maintain their cultural autonomy, is justified, and one should consider it sympathetically. That is the real content of the claim we have been making.

At present we cannot assess how the details will be arranged. I would only like to point out the following. The League of Nations conference in Berne has agreed unanimously that the Jews are to be admitted to the League of Nations as a nation. Hence regardless of the fact that Palestine is to become a Jewish country, the Jews are to be recognised as a nation. At this moment, it is also impossible to say how this formula is going to be transformed into practice at [the] Paris [conference]. But there is indeed a world-wide tendency to understand the Jews as a national community and to recognise, as Jews themselves [*die Judenheit*] wish to do, their right to national self-determination. Looking at the figures, it is certain that out of 15 million Jews worldwide, 12 million think this way. It may be the case that the smaller Jewish groups scattered amongst the Western European countries, like, for instance, the 600,000 Jews in Germany, do not regard themselves, in the main, as belonging to the Jewish nation. But when working out such a formulation one has to go by the wishes of the overwhelming majority.

Bernstein: I have to say again that I can support Dr. Fuchs's claims, albeit from a different point of view, and those of the preceding speaker, again from a point of view that is closer to though not congruent with his. For me this is about natural law, if I may express it that way. As I have said before, I am not close to these national aspirations but I cannot deny that they exist. For Jews in certain countries, it is perhaps a necessity, although not one that will last, thus a transitory one, to elevate their people, their nation, to show them new aims, to unite them in some way. To this extent I am of the opinion their claim should be granted. The claim, after all, is limited by the fact that national and cultural autonomy will only be granted to the extent demanded by the majority of the Jewish population in a given country. This presupposes that there is a majority which does not identify with the nationality within which it finds itself. This will not be the case in areas where a complete mutual acculturation [*ein vollständiges Hineinleben in die Kultur*] has taken place, which, in any case, I think should be striven for. I consider this a transitory standpoint. I cannot agree with the apparently Machiavellian argument to do this in order to create a nation within a nation, thus perpetuating an existing conflict. In Poland Jews and Poles may be hostile towards each other, but certainly not exclusively so, at least not in Galicia. There are great exceptions in Galicia. I remind you of Seckel's [*sic.*] book[7] (interjection: rubbish!) – You may reject it, but it is a Jewish voice, after all. (Dr. Lichtheim: bought

---

[7]Binjamin Wolf Segel (1867–1931), author of, among other works, *Die polnische Judenfrage* and *Der Weltkrieg und das Schicksal der Juden: Stimme eines galizischen Juden an seine Glaubensgenossen in den neutralen Ländern, insbesondere in Amerika*, both published in Berlin c. 1916 and supporting an active German role in post-war Eastern European affairs.

by the Poles!) Well, [I am] not sure about 'being bought' – there is a lot of passion in this book, I have read it, in any case it contains a protest against this conflict. I must add that I also spoke with a great number of Polish Jews – albeit Socialists of the international kind – for whom this conflict did not exist. I can only see it as a transitory state of affairs that minorities living scattered among various countries and nations feel themselves to be something special. As long as circumstances are such, I myself am of the opinion that national and cultural autonomy must be granted.

Since national and cultural autonomy may indeed be given great scope, it is perhaps very good that within the definition there is a more accurate formulation: provided the rights of the minority are safeguarded.

Regarding the consideration of the Sabbath in the legislation, I could only decide with great difficulty to agree to this demand. For me Sunday is a secular day of rest [*bürgerlicher Feiertag*]. This one day of the week should, if at all possible, be separated from religion and prescribed as a day of rest. I found that when I was young nothing brought me closer to my Christian environment – I grew up amongst Christians – than the fact that my family observed the same day of rest as the general population. I do not think that the denominational element suffered because of this. That was the feeling of commonality, on which the League of Nations is based, which we should aim to bring about not only in one country but in all nations [*Völkern*]. By demanding that the observance of the Sabbath is taken into consideration, a strongly divisive element is being introduced. I would like to support this demand only where there is a pressing need – and only then.

Chairman: Gentlemen! These questions are extraordinarily profound and discussing them would most probably take a very long time. To shorten the debate I might perhaps be allowed to say a few words which, I think, will influence the negotiations considerably. There is no question but that President Wilson, who will have a great influence on the discussion of this question, is under strong Zionist influence. His good friend, Supreme Court Judge Brandys,[8] is going to be in Paris or will at least influence the negotiations. As you gentlemen will know better than I do, 90% or perhaps even 99% of the 3 million Jews living in America have moved towards Zionism in the last few years and this tendency is absolutely predominant there. I take it therefore that points 3 and 4 in particular will only be relevant to us insofar as we will either have to agree to them or reject them. I do not think that by doing so we are taking on responsibility for these points being implemented. They will no doubt be implemented. The crucial matter will be which attitude we adopt.

Dr. Cohn: Gentlemen! Dr. Rathenau sensed correctly that the formulation of point 3 is a compromise, the result of long discussions. We said to ourselves that the German delegates must somehow take a position on the Jewish questions outside Palestine and it seemed to us unthinkable that German delegates would reject the national Jewish question *a limine*. As a result, a formulation was chosen which actually says as

---

[8]The reference here is of course to Louis D. Brandeis (1856–1941), US Supreme Court judge, close associate to President Woodrow Wilson, and since 1914 chairman of the Provisional Committee for General Zionist Affairs and supporter of an American Jewish congress.

little as possible and only grants Jews in each respective country, and – even more tightly defined – in the newly created countries, the right to self-determination to a quite limited degree.

It would, however, be a mistake – this opinion must be dispelled now, at the very start – if one were to think, like *Geheimrat* Fuchs, that fashioning national minorities into constitutional entities guarantees that German interests would be served. Firstly, *Geheimrat* Fuchs is in error if he believes that there is a great demand for such national autonomy in Poland. Secondly, based on my own experience, I have to completely agree with Mr. Bernstein that there are many Polish Jews who would reject it totally if one were to say that culturally they are inclined more towards some other country than towards Poland and that they would prefer, if they had to accept a non-Jewish culture, to opt for the Polish rather than the German one. For historical reasons it has to be made clear that the German Reich should not and must not have any particular expectations in connection with the establishment of national autonomies in the East.

With respect to considering the Sabbath in the legislation, the following speaks in favour of it: the few sympathies which the German administration in the East gained from the Jews are based on the fact that the German administration, in as far as it was competent to do so, advocated with exceptionally moving and anxious care, the preservation of the religious aspect [*des religiösen Moments*]. Germany will gain much more sympathetic support if it stressed and demanded consideration of the religious aspect before an official authority such as the peace conference or the League of Nations. This will surely gain it the sympathies of 6 million Jews in the East, which will have an effect one way or another. In all honesty I also have to confess that that would somehow be quite prejudicial for German [internal] affairs. Even if we do not demand what the Socialists' conference in Berne demanded for the Jews in the settlements of the East, the suspicion has been raised by the German religious Jews, in view of the possibility that schools and perhaps also social legislation might be made uniform, that this might be an interference with freedom of will – an interference which they would like to at least try to prevent. It is believed that if Germany does demand consideration of the Sabbath in the legislation for newly created states, then this should be implemented, if possible, in the German state as well.

Dr. Sobernheim: Gentlemen! For the sake of clarification I would like to say that these demands have already been conveyed to the peace conference in a similar way by other sections of the Jewish community. It is only a matter of what position Germany is going to take in this regard. Also point 4: the laying down of such political, administrative and economic conditions for Palestine etc. has on the whole been set up according to the American model. We only left out that Palestine should be put under the mandate of the League of Nations, especially under the mandate of England. The development of the Palestinian question is well-known. The Committee of Ten at the Paris conference has already accepted the demand for a Jewish commonwealth [*Gemeinwesen*] in Palestine. The formulation proposed by the commission roughly follows the American one. The main demand of the German Jews is that no Jew – regardless of nationality or orientation – should be excluded from settling and working in Palestine, from visiting or migrating to Palestine. The

London Zionist conference, too, has already passed a resolution to this effect. The London Zionist conference went as far as to say that all those organisations that have already considered this matter, even if they are not Zionist, should be asked to join, and all those organisations that are presently considering it, no matter which country they are from, should join as well.

Chairman: Does any of the gentlemen wish to speak on this matter?

Dr. Fuchs: This point, too, only came about because of mutual concessions which all sections of the Jewish community have made in order to reconcile Jewish and German interests. That is why it was purposely not defined as a national home [*nationale Heimstätte*], but rather as a commonwealth.

[marginal note:] Point 5

Dr. Sobernheim: Gentlemen! Point 5: Compensation for victims of pogroms by the state concerned – that is surely to be taken for granted. It does not apply to Germany at all and simply serves as a support for the whole of the Jewish community in those countries where it has suffered so extraordinarily until now. Dreadful pogroms have taken place in Galicia which have also been acknowledged in the press here,[9] and there were pogroms in the Ukraine perpetrated by uniformed gangs which the press and the [Foreign] Office have not singled out for mention because it is less the fault of the Ukrainian government, which shows extraordinary good will towards the Jews, but rather because it is a phenomenon of war. At the peace conference, compensation must of course be claimed for all these victims of pogroms – to be paid for by the state in whose territory they have occurred.

Dr. Fuchs: In this instance we have also found a formulation which allows everyone to agree to it. The words "by the state concerned" is necessary because we in Prussia, as you know, according to the law of 1838, I think, have the problem of whether it is the local authorities [*Gemeinden*] [that should pay] and extensive legal proceedings have arisen from this. The local authority says: the facts are otherwise, therefore we will not pay. That is why we are saying: the state should take on the responsibility. [However,] it is doubtful which state is the one concerned [here]. The *Referent*, Professor Sobernheim, thought it should be the state on whose territory the pogroms occurred. Please come to an agreement on whether this needs further specification. Just think: Haller's army perpetrated a pogrom in Danzig or elsewhere. I would not think it right if recourse were taken to the state where this happened, rather one should take recourse to the state whose institutions have made it possible for the pogrom to be carried out.

---

[9]These Russian pogroms in the Pale of Settlement during the First World War were documented by Shloime Ansky, best known as the author of *The Dybbuk*, during a relief-organising tour of the region he took under the auspices of the International Red Cross between 1914 and 1917; his findings would be published posthumously in Yiddish as 'Der Yudisher hurbn fun Poylen, Galitsye un Bukovina' in Sh. An-Ski, *Gezamelte shriften in fuftsehn bender*, vols. 4–6, Warsaw and New York 1925–1927. For extensive selections in English, see S. Ansky, *The Enemy at His Pleasure: A Journey Through the Pale of Settlement During World War I*, transl. by Joachim Neugroschel, New York 2002.

[marginal note:] Point 6

Dr. Sobernheim: Claim number six has seldom been raised until now. The Jewish Question is seen as a uniform one, as a question of humanity of world-wide significance which has to be solved by all nations co-operatively. Only establishing a commission offers certainty that the first four demands are really going to be implemented. The pretext of interference with the internal matters of other countries, so popular until now and always put forward by Roumania, should be made impossible by this.

Paul (Prussian Ministry of Science, Art, and Education): I may perhaps point out here that like *Geheimrat* Lenz, I received these points [of the agenda] only at the last moment and have therefore been unable to comment on behalf of the Prussian Ministry for Science, Art and Education. I would like to ask you, however, not to draw any conclusions from my silence during today's proceedings.

Chairman: Gentlemen! We only submitted the issue to the ministries today and would be very grateful if in the near future we were to receive a written or oral response from the relevant ministries, either verbally to the *Referent* or by written communication addressed to me.

Thank you, the meeting is now closed.

Leopold Jessner: German Theatre and Jewish Identity*

BY ANAT FEINBERG

When one looks back on the history of the German stage in the so-called Golden Twenties of the Weimar Republic, three directors repeatedly come to mind: Max Reinhardt, Leopold Jessner, and Erwin Piscator. Of the three, Jessner has drawn relatively little attention, although his politically oriented "topical theatre" (*Zeittheater*) paved the way for the political theatre of Piscator and Brecht. In fact, it is impossible to think of the work of leading directors like Jürgen Fehling, Erich Engel and Erwin Piscator without what has been termed "Jessner's radical republican functionalisation of the stage".[1]

Likewise, three names tend to dominate every discussion of the Jewish contribution to the modernisation of German theatre, and of these – Otto Brahm, Reinhardt, Jessner[2] – it is Jessner again who remains in the shadows. There is, in fact, not a single monograph on this German Jew, and no discussion of how his background influenced his work. Overshadowed by Reinhardt, Jessner – while inaugurating, in the words of the late *Habima* actor Shimon Finkel, "a new era in world theatre" – "has been forgotten by non-Jews and Jews alike".[3]

This article is meant to make amends by shedding light on Jessner's "way as a German and a Jew", to borrow the title of Jakob Wassermann's famous book. This will involve exploring Jessner's Jewish heritage, reviewing his firm conviction that a German-Jewish synthesis was possible and desirable, registering the fractures this idealised viewpoint suffered and the effects it had on his professional development, and tracing his changing attitudes towards Jewishness during his years in Germany and later in exile. The following discussion will not constitute a detailed examination of the many productions Jessner directed – several efforts in this direction have

---

*I am grateful to Marje Schuetze-Coburn and Claude Zachary of the Feuchtwanger Memorial Library, University of Southern California, for making available to me invaluable material on Jessner and other exiled authors and artists, collected by the sociologist and art-historian Marta Mierendorff. I likewise wish to thank William Abbey from the Institute of Germanic Studies, London, for his kind assistance in archival matters. Manuscripts and letters by Jessner are also found in the "*Sammlung Leopold Jessner*" at the *Stiftung Archiv der Akademie der Künste* in Berlin. See also *Handbuch des deutschsprachigen Exiltheaters 1933–1945*, edited by Frithjof Trapp, Werner Mittenzwei, Henning Rischbieter and Hansjörg Schneider, Munich 1999, vol. 2: *Biographisches Lexikon der Theaterkünstler*, pp. 460–461.

[1]Jost Hermand and Frank Trommler, *Die Kultur der Weimarer Republik*, Munich 1978, p. 196.
[2]See for example Klaus Siebenhaar, ' … "dass der Schaubühne künstlerischer und geistiger Neuwert entquelle". Juden auf dem deutschen Theater', in Julius Schoeps (ed.), *Juden als Träger bürgerlicher Kultur in Deutschland*, Bonn 1989, pp. 91–108.
[3]Shimon Finkel, *Bama ve-Klaim*, Tel Aviv 1968, p. 172. Finkel recounts how disappointed he was when he visited the Schiller Theater in Berlin in 1957 and did not find a bust of Jessner next to those of other prominent theatre personages of the Weimar period; *ibid.*, p. 119.

Leopold Jessner

The *Staatstheater am Gendarmenmarkt* in Berlin (now the *Konzerthaus*) where Jessner
was *Intendant* from 1919 to 1930

already seen print.[4] It will, however, address Jessner's theoretical and practical theatre work in as much as it is related to or correlates with his convictions.

It is hardly surprising that Jessner's name was frequently mentioned in internal Jewish discourse, mostly by advocates of a German-Jewish symbiosis.[5] Appointed *Intendant*, or general director, of the leading theatre house of the Weimar Republic, the Prussian *Staatstheater*, Jessner was one of a handful of Jewish *Intendanten* in Germany.[6] Jessner sought to interweave humanistic ideas and heightened political awareness with modern staging concepts and modes of acting; his career might have thus served as a shining example of successful German-Jewish symbiosis had it not been accompanied from its very outset by antisemitic defamation. Truly, the extent of Jessner's tragedy can best be appraised in relation to the hope and promise that his arrival on the theatrical scene represented.

THE PERSON AND PERSONA OF JESSNER

One of the reasons for the absence of a Jessner biography is doubtlessly the lack of material about the private man as distinguished from the renowned director.[7] The material we have discloses the persona, not the person. Jessner left behind neither a diary nor autobiographical sketches.[8] His essays and articles are matter-of-fact and

---

[4]See Manfred Brauneck, *Klassiker der Schauspielregie*, Hamburg 1988, pp. 180–193; David F. Kuhns, *German Expressionist Theatre. The Actor and the Stage*, Cambridge 1997, esp. pp. 195–217; *idem*, 'Expressionism, Monumentalism, Politics: Emblematic Acting in Jessner's "Wilhelm Tell" and "Richard III"', in *New Theatre Quarterly*, vol. 7, no. 25 (February 1991), pp. 35–48; Michael Patterson, *The Revolution in the German Theatre, 1900–1930*, Boston 1981, pp. 88–95; Günther Rühle, *Theater in unserer Zeit*, Frankfurt am Main 1976, pp. 47–81; *idem*, 'Der Freiheitsschrei – laut und gesetzlich: Leopold Jessner, die Revolution und das ganz andere Regietheater', in *Theater Heute*, vol. 32, no. 2, pp. 27–35; Klaus Siebenhaar, 'Das perikleische Zeitalter der Republik. Der Theaterregisseur Leopold Jessner', in Hermann Haarmann (ed.), *Berliner Profile*, Berlin 1993, pp. 91–105.

[5]See for example, Felix Goldmann, *Der Jude im deutschen Kulturkreis*, Berlin 1930; Erwin Kalser, 'Über die Juden und das Theater', in *Jahrbuch für jüdische Geschichte und Literatur*, vol. 28 (1927), pp. 63–83; Siegmund Kaznelson (ed.), *Juden im deutschen Kulturbereich*, 2nd edn., Berlin 1959.

[6]Cf. Henning Rischbieter, 'Theater als Kunst und als Geschäft. Über jüdische Theaterregisseure und Theaterdirektoren in Berlin 1894–1933', in Hans-Peter Bayerdörfer (ed.), *Theatralia Judaica: Emanzipation und Antisemitismus als Momente der Theatergeschichte von der Lessing-Zeit bis zur Shoah*, Tübingen 1992, pp. 204–217. According to the historian Esra Bennathan, there were sixty Jewish directors in Germany in June 1933; cf. *idem*, 'Die demographische und wirtschaftliche Struktur der Juden', in Werner E. Mosse and Arnold Paucker (eds.), *Entscheidungsjahr 1932: Zur Judenfrage und der Endphase der Weimarer Republik*, Tübingen 1966 (Schriftenreihe wissenschaftlicher Abhandlungen des Leo Baeck Instituts 13), pp. 87–131, here p. 112.

[7]The only author dedicating an entire study to Jessner is Horst Müllenmeister, who completed a Ph.D. thesis entitled 'Leopold Jessner: Geschichte eines Regiestils' for the University of Cologne in 1956. While mentioning some basic biographical facts, this unpublished thesis concentrates on Jessner's theatre, examining most of his productions. In January 2001, Dr. Müllenmeister indicated to me that his thesis supervisor, Professor Carl Niessen, had instructed him "to deal only with the theatrics of Jessner", thus avoiding references to Jessner's Jewish identity.

[8]According to Marta Mierendorff, 'Leopold Jessner', unpublished ms., Feuchtwanger Memorial Library, Department of Special Collections (henceforth FML), p. 26, Alfred Perry (Pinkus), Jessner's close friend in Los Angeles, possessed a diary that Jessner had written between 1942 and 1945, along with an incomplete manuscript of some thirty-five pages, presumably Jessner's notes on the political theatre in Germany. It was not possible to locate either manuscript.

succinct, focusing on professional issues and avoiding personal references.[9] Even his private correspondence is scant and unemotional: the most we can glean from it is the impression of a self-controlled, rather taciturn man. There is a short, undated account with the promising title 'Self-Portrait without Halo', but the account is itself disappointing; rather than an act of self-revelation, it is a placid meditation that leaves its author as enigmatic as before.[10] Recourse to accounts by colleagues and friends does not help much – there is perplexingly little about Jessner the man in a collection published on his fiftieth birthday in 1928, the critic Kurt Pinthus being the sole of fifteen contributors to mention Jessner's Jewishness.[11] This facet of his biography is also absent from Karl Bluth's study of Jessner's work, published in the same year.[12]

Who then was Leopold Jessner? The few known facts concerning his early life leave ample room for questions and conjectures. Born in Königsberg on 3 March 1878 to parents of Lithuanian descent,[13] he is said to have been "adopted from a Lithuanian orphanage by the Jessner family, probably distant relatives".[14] But the obituary published in *Die Westküste*, the West Coast section of the weekly *Aufbau*, has another version: the man later nicknamed the "Reinhardt of Königsberg"[15] was actually born in Tauroggen, the oldest son of East-European Jews who headed westwards.[16] In any case, nothing is known about his childhood years, the early death of his parents or the orphanage in Königsberg in which he allegedly grew up.[17] The distant relatives who apparently adopted him were Dr. Samuel Jessner – putatively Leopold's uncle, a well-established and highly respected dermatologist in the East Prussian capital – and his wife.[18]

There is another twist to this familial drama: Leopold married the doctor's daughter, Else (also named Elsa and Ellon). This marriage between cousins took place in 1919, when Leopold moved to Berlin as general director of the *Staatstheater*, and it involved Leopold's adoption of Lotte, the daughter from Else's first marriage. The Jessners separated after they had emigrated to London, but they never

---

[9]Jessner's essays were collected and published to mark his hundredth birthday as *Leopold Jessner: Schriften*, ed. by Hugo Fetting, Berlin 1979.

[10]See Leopold Jessner, 'Selbstporträt ohne Glorienschein', *ibid.*, pp. 283–284.

[11]Felix Ziege (ed.), *Leopold Jessner und das Zeit-Theater*, Berlin 1928.

[12]Karl Theodor Bluth, *Leopold Jessner*, Berlin 1928. Bluth was a physicist and author whose play 'Die Empörung des Lucius' premièred under Jessner's direction at the Berlin *Staatstheater* on 2 February 1924.

[13]Despite intensive attempts together with Stefanie Schüler-Springorum, I could not locate any information about Jessner's parents. Ruth Leiserowitz has kindly informed me that Jessner's grandfather, Hirsch Jessner, came from Plunge in Lithuania.

[14]See Herbert A. Strauss and Werner Röder (eds.), *International Biographical Dictionary of Central European Emigrés*, vol. 2, part 1, Munich–New York 1983, p. 569.

[15]Müllenmeister, p. 25.

[16]m.g., 'Ein grosser Verlust', in *Die Westküste*, 27, *Aufbau*, vol. XI, no. 51 (22 December 1945), p. 4. According to Marta Mierendorff, 'Eva Samson-Jessner: Die Jessner Dynastie in den USA', in *Die Mahnung*, vol. 35, no. 8 (1 August 1988), p. 6, Jessner's only sister, Sophie Gordon, disappeared in Theresienstadt after she had been refused an entrance visa to the United States.

[17]There were several orphanages in Königsberg, some run by the local Jewish community. See Stefanie Schüler-Springorum, *Die jüdische Minderheit in Königsberg/Preussen 1871–1945*, Göttingen 1996, pp. 119–120. All efforts by Schüler-Springorum and myself to discover which orphanage Jessner grew up in have failed.

[18]See Erwin Lichtenstein, *Bericht an meine Familie*, Darmstadt 1985, pp. 13–16.

divorced.[19] We can safely surmise that Leopold had a decisive influence on another child of his adoptive family, his reputation and connections paving the way for the theatrical career of his cousin Fritz Jessner. Fritz's two daughters followed the same path, though less successfully.[20]

Yet another version of Leopold Jessner's origins and early years also appeared in *Aufbau*'s West Coast section on the occasion of his sixty-fifth birthday. It is significant that Jessner, then on the advisory board of the weekly, never refuted this version. In a letter to the editor, Dr. Bernhard Borkon recounts that Jessner actually grew up in Russ at the delta of the Memel in northern East Prussia, and was trained as a timber-dealer in the sawmill owned by the author's family. According to Borkon, Jessner actually could often be found in the woods leaning against a tree, absorbed in one of the German classics. The author's father had grown up with Jessner and, we are informed, told his son how Jessner vociferously recited "*Hebe Dich hinweg, Unhold!*" ("make off, monster"), whereupon the Jewish teacher, who had just entered the classroom, took to his heels crying out "a *meschuggener!*"[21]

Jessner's own references to his childhood are both rare and circumscribed, mostly made during his years in American exile. In one of these late, unsentimental recollections, he emerges as a child suffering from being an outsider. German Jewish friends branded him a "Litwack Jew", while for his Lithuanian playmates he was a *Jecke*, the derisive term for a Western Jew.[22]

We know frustratingly little about the inner world of Jessner, his likes and dislikes, moods and habits. The photographs we have are all similar: a tall, portly man with an egg-shaped face, almost bald, always pedantically dressed – waistcoat, suit, high collar and necktie. Unlike other Jewish theatre celebrities such as Fritz Kortner or Alexander Granach, there was nothing "typically Jewish" about his looks. In fact, Jessner seems to have projected no particular aura, at least not insofar as posture is concerned. He looked like "an art-teacher, a chief librarian or a serious businessman".[23] The photos reveal a man keen to guard his privacy, a face that strives to

---

[19]Else Jessner-Caspary emigrated to America shortly after the start of the Second World War. While Jessner settled in Los Angeles in late 1937, she and her daughter Lotte Jessner-Thompson ("Leopold's secret love" according to Marta Mierendorff in 'Eva Samson-Jessner') chose to live in New York, where Else died, probably in 1960.

[20]Fritz Jessner (1889–1946), who took a law degree to please his father, started his theatre career as an actor with Reinhardt. Between 1925 and 1933 he was, like Leopold before him, theatre manager and director of the *Neues Schauspielhaus* in Königsberg, and between 1934 and 1936 director of the theatre section of the *Jüdischer Kulturbund* in Berlin. His oldest daughter Hannelore (by his first wife, the actress Lilli Schmahl) studied in Leopold Jessner's acting school in Berlin and participated in the *Jüdischer Kulturbund* before emigrating to Holland, from where she was eventually deported to Bergen-Belsen. She survived and is reported to have lived afterwards in Casablanca. Her younger sister, Eva, hoped as well to be an actress, but had to abandon her dream. She reached Los Angeles in March 1939, where, for a time, she was a member of a company of actors run by Ernest Lenart, before opting for family life. See Marta Mierendorff, 'In memoriam Fritz Jessner, zum 25. Todestag (1889 bis 1946)', in *Die Mahnung*, vol. 18, no. 13 (1 July 1971), p. 8; Herbert Freeden, *Jüdisches Theater im Nazideutschland*, Tübingen 1964, pp. 68–81.

[21]See letters to the editor section in *Aufbau*, 23 July 1943.

[22]Jessner, 'Jüdische Politik', in *Aufbau*, 1 October 1943.

[23]Alfred Mühr, *Rund um den Gendarmenmarkt: Von Iffland bis Gründgens*, Oldenburg 1965, p. 267. Similar observations are to be found in Eckart von Naso, *Ich liebe das Leben*, Hamburg 1953, p. 436, and in Bernhard Reich, *Im Wettlauf mit der Zeit*, Berlin 1970, p. 179.

betray nothing. And yet the eyes appear to tell a different story, gazing into the distance with a touch of melancholy. The theatre critic Alfred Mühr recalls the "subdued sharpness" in Jessner's eyes, and Eckart von Naso, Jessner's assistant in Berlin, remembers "very agile, completely round eyes which looked into the world fairly cleverly and shyly, not really nervous or unstable and yet one could rarely repose in that glance. The security was missing".[24] As we will see, lack of self-confidence was a basic feature of Jessner's character. He was, we read, kind and good-hearted, ready to help friends and colleagues and loyal to old acquaintances; yet he seems to have had very few close friends.[25] Although he had not fathered any children himself, he liked children and let himself go in their company – von Naso goes as far as to describe him as "a *Kindernarr* of overflowing goodness" (in this regard, von Naso offers other remarks in the same effusive vein).[26]

Jessner is said to have been an excellent public speaker and a "raconteur of rare charm" – as well as a reputed gourmet who easily charmed restaurant personnel.[27] In contrast to Reinhardt, he never became prosperous through his work in the theatre. Out of necessity and conviction his habits were modest, in exile even frugal.[28] There are no known episodes of love affairs in his life story, no sensational or extravagant adventures. The drama of his life emerged through the theatre – and, of course, through the turbulent times.

Similarly to Reinhardt, Jessner began his theatre career as an actor. Working in various theatres in the provinces, he played in comedies and so-called folk-plays without making any particular impression on critics or spectators. Notably, his writings include only a single reference to his stint as an actor, a recollection of how he was repeatedly given the sack for being "totally untalented". His formal dismissal in Graudenz read: "Leopold Jessner! We would like to give you a good piece of advice, not to continue with the stage career you have taken up, since you are absolutely unsuited for the theatre profession".[29] In typical fashion, Jessner does not waste a word in order to describe the effect this letter had on him. Instead he points out that other famous actors shared a similar experience. Was he considered a poor actor

---

[24]von Naso, p. 436.

[25]The theatre director Karl Heinz Martin describes Jessner as follows: "As a colleague he is the example of a comrade who is fully aware of his profession's dignity; as a boss – the ideal leader, who out of this self-respect runs [the theatre] wisely and cautiously; also the ideal boss for those directors who work under him." *idem*, *Die Scene*, vol. 18 (March 1928), special issue marking Jessner's fiftieth birthday, p. 79. One of his few close friends was Heinz Lipmann (1897–1932), who, like Jessner, grew up in Königsberg; Lipmann would become Jessner's dramatic adviser in Berlin, settling all misunderstandings in the theatre and helping Jessner write the speeches defending himself against his increasingly vehement detractors. When Jessner was appointed head of the important Union of Artistic Stage Directors in 1924, he appointed Lipmann editor of *Die Scene*, the union's official journal. For Jessner's activity in the union, see Wolfgang Ebert, 'Die Vereinigung künstlerischer Bühnenvorstände und deren Organ *Die Scene*', Ph.D. thesis, Berlin 1967. Jessner's obituary for his prematurely deceased friend is reprinted in Fetting (ed.), pp. 202–204.

[26]von Naso, pp. 436, 446.

[27]Alfred Perry, 'Ein Denkmal für Leopold Jessner', unpublished ms., FML.

[28]One example is the five-day vacation in Santa Barbara shortly before he died, which he allowed himself after receiving 6,000 dollars in indemnity for a car accident he had suffered three years earlier. See Mierendorff, 'Leopold Jessner', p. 20.

[29]Jessner, 'Hinter dem Vorhang', in Fetting (ed.), pp. 258–260, here p. 260.

because he failed to fit into the entrenched formalism of Wilhelminian drama? Or was he simply unable to implement his original ideas of vigorous acting – ideas that would later help launch actors like Fritz Kortner and Werner Krauss? In any event Jessner was at his best in Ibsen plays which matched his own interest in contemporary society and its problems. "Considering his ability to play Ibsen characters, one is inclined to feel sorry that there is no permanent Ibsen Theatre. Mr. Jessner would be a great credit to such a theatre", writes one critic.[30]

Reinhardt gave up acting in favour of directing; so did Jessner. Reinhardt played in Otto Brahm's *Deutsches Theater* before he dissociated himself from Brahm's directorial concepts to forge his own theatre of magic. While Jessner never acted under Brahm's direction, the latter was nevertheless his decisive role-model (not Carl Heine, despite Heine having introduced him to the art of directing).[31] Following Jessner's initial directorial experience in Hamburg and Dresden, he was invited to Hamburg's *Thalia Theater*, where he presided between 1904 and 1915. Comedies and farces featured prominently in his repertory; still, he managed to introduce the local public to names like Ibsen, Gorki, and Wedekind. Between 1911 and 1914, he had a concurrent appointment as manager and artistic director of the *Volksschauspiele* in Hamburg, a theatre founded by the labour unions for the purpose of ensuring some sort of income for actors during the summer months. Presenting a new production nearly every fortnight, Jessner included works by Ibsen, Strindberg, and Shaw, along with plays by Wedekind and Büchner. In 1915 he returned to Königsberg, this time as manager and artistic director of the *Neues Schauspielhaus*; despite the war, Jessner was able to make this one of the leading German theatre houses.

Jessner's reputation as a revolutionary director and precursor of the political theatre, "the most accomplished of late Expressionist directors",[32] rests upon his period as general director of the *Staatstheater* in Berlin (1919–1930). In this role he was a constant target of antisemitic and nationalistic attacks, and he finally resigned his leading position in 1930, though he still directed new productions until March 1933. The last twelve years of his life were spent in exile, first in London (1934–35), where he founded an unsuccessful film company (*Jesba*); then in Palestine (1936), where he directed two productions at the *Habima* theatre; a short spell in Vienna (1937), where he directed a dramatic poem on contemporary Jewish strife; and finally in the United States, where he failed to establish himself in the Hollywood film industry and was unable to repeat his success as a theatre director. His main activities there would be in the local immigrant organisation known as *The Jewish Club* of 1933. Many of his fellow exiles had witnessed his rise and fall in Germany. In their community, he remained highly esteemed, even revered, but at the time of his death he was a lonely man living in a two-room apartment.

He had requested burial in an orthodox Jewish cemetery in an eastern suburb of Los Angeles, and he explicitly asked for an anonymous funeral with no speeches. The

---

[30]Cited from Müllenmeister, p. 100 (n. 1).

[31]The actor Paul Bildt told Horst Müllenmeister that "Brahm was his [Jessner's] inner schooling, even if he had never seen anything by him", and another actor, Hans Wyneken, described Brahm as Jessner's "great model"; *ibid.*, p. 101.

[32]Kuhns, 'Expressionism, Monumentalism, Politics', p. 36. A revised version of the article is part of the discussion of Jessner's theatre work in Kuhns' *German Expressionist Theatre*.

requisite ten-man prayer group was made up of Eastern European Jews, as he had requested, the prayer of mourning thus also being recited by an Eastern Jew "whom I didn't know, who didn't know me and didn't know anything about me but the fact that he was burying a Jew."[33] This gesture, Jessner felt, would symbolise his life having come full circle, meaning back to the world from which he came. Dr. Jacob Sonderling, the liberal rabbi conducting the memorial ceremony a few days later, indicated that Jessner's views had become "so orthodox that they nearly conflicted with mine"; Jessner, we are told, had written his will, with its precise if somewhat unexpected burial instructions, during his last days in "gloomy loneliness".[34] But this information is in fact far from accurate. In his unpublished 'Ein Denkmal für Leopold Jessner', Alfred Perry (Pinkus), probably Jessner's closest friend in Los Angeles, recounts that the will was drafted years earlier, during Jessner's days of fame in Berlin. Jessner had asked to be laid to rest in Berlin's orthodox cemetery because he wanted to oblige the "more or lesser antisemitic officials of the state to publicly follow the funeral procession from the government residence through the Jewish quarter ... so that they pay their last respects according to the Jewish rituals".[35]

THE TRIBULATIONS OF SUCCESS

Jessner was at the zenith of his career when he argued that a German-Jewish social and cultural synthesis was not only possible but also fruitful. With his sensational *Wilhelm Tell* (1919), the production of *Richard III* (1920) incorporating "Jessner steps" in its stage design, and the sombre ballade-like *Othello* (1921) to his credit, he had become the leading director of the young Weimar Republic.[36] He made the argument in an article entitled 'Das "verjudete" Theater' ('The "Judaised" Theatre') published in the *CV-Zeitung*, the widely circulated publication of the liberal German Jewish establishment.[37] This was a month before the political murder of Walter Rathenau, one of the paragons of that establishment. Jessner was one of twenty honorary members invited to join the board of the C.V. "By race a Jew, politically though and by disposition – a German" is how he described himself – in line with the self-definition of so many German Jews of the time. Jews enriched the German stage, he asserted, "the strong-bloodedness [*Starkblütigkeit*] of their temperament imbues the theatre with vigour and animation".[38] This argument was echoed by others, including Arnold Zweig in his study *Juden auf der deutschen Bühne* (1928). Slipping

---

[33]See m.g., 'Ein grosser Verlust', in *Aufbau*, 21 December 1945; f.k. "Totenfeier für Jessner", in *Aufbau*, 11 January 1946. Fetting indicates in *idem* (ed.), pp. 287–288, that the tombstone was erected in the Bet David Cemetery thirteen years later (November 1958).

[34]Quoted in f.p. 'Tragische Heimkehr', in *Die Westküste, Aufbau*, 28 January 1949.

[35]Alfred Perry, 'Ein Denkmal für Leopold Jessner', unpublished ms., FML, p. 1.

[36]Following Jessner's triumphal production of *Richard III*, Max Reinhardt left Berlin for Vienna while the directors Rudolf Bernauer and Carl Meinhardt gave up the management of the Lessing Theater.

[37]See Reiner Bernstein, 'Zwischen Emanzipation und Antisemitismus – Die Publizistik der *C.V.-Zeitung*, Organ des "Centralvereins deutscher Staatsbürger jüdischen Glaubens", 1924–1933', Ph.D. thesis, Berlin 1969, p. 67. For the *Centralverein* see also Ruth Pierson, 'German Jewish Identity in the Weimar Republic', Ph.D. thesis, Yale 1970. Avraham Barkai, *"Wehr Dich!" Der Centralverein deutscher Staatsbürger jüdischen Glaubens (C.V.) 1893–1938*, Munich 2002; Jessner, 'Das "verjudete" Theater', in *CV-Zeitung*, vol. 1, no. 3 (18 May 1922), p. 37; reprinted in Fetting (ed.), pp. 61–62.

[38]Jessner, 'Das "verjudete" Theater", in Fetting (ed.), p. 62.

into ever-new fictitious identities, losing and reshaping the self in endless metamor-
phoses, was the expression of Jewish longing, a kind of homecoming for a restless
pariah, Jessner maintained. For the director, then, theatre was a kind of *Wahlheimat*,
to use the wording of one of his prominent actors, Alexander Granach.[39] Like
Granach, who never forgot his Jewish origins in Galicia, Jessner – an "ardent socialist ... and passionate Republican"[40] – tenaciously held onto his Jewish roots.[41] "I am
not merely a Jew, I am a religious Jew" he is reported to have proudly stated in Berlin,
and to an audience in Palestine in 1936, he confessed: "I have been a Jew, and consciously so, all my life, though in all my endeavours I served the German republic."
In the Palestine setting, he also recounted his childhood love of the Sabbath rituals,
which he had then encountered in Heine's works as an adult, and which he would
observe throughout his life.[42]

Miriam Bernstein-Cohen recalls how she visited Jessner on the Sabbath while she
was in Berlin as a young *Habima* actress in 1923.

> Jessner considered the Sabbath a holiday and had the privilege of time off. He always
> used to say 'The job I hold forces me to work and write on the Sabbath, but on the other
> hand I don't smoke! That's my own decision!' He used to greet me with avuncular affec-
> tion: 'Ah, here she is, the little Portuguese!' He called me Portuguese because of my
> Sephardic accent in Hebrew. The Bible was always there, in his desk drawer. He would
> take it out and hand it to me: 'Read me something from the Psalms, but with Portuguese
> intonation'. He would listen with his eyes half-closed as if he were dreaming, resting his
> big head on his hand.[43]

And the account of Shimon Finkel, who initially made his way in the theatre with
Jessner's help, points in the same direction: once Jessner was nearly half an hour late
for an official meeting at the Reichstag, his explanation being that attending Yom
Kippur services came first.[44]

Once in exile, having been forced to give up his German citizenship, Jessner's
observance of Jewish rituals became more pronounced; and yet it would be wrong
to maintain that he only discovered a Jewish identity during his last years, in
America.[45] An "insider" who strove for recognition in German society, Jessner may
in fact be regarded as one of countless examples of a phenomenon Frederic
Grunfeld discusses in his seminal *Prophets Without Honour*. Addressing the momentous
contribution of the "marginal Jews" to intellectual and cultural life in Germany,
Grunfeld maintains that the "very precariousness of their position astride two cultures gave them an extraordinary vantage point from which to survey the European

[39]Cited in Albert Klein and Raya Kruk, *Alexander Granach: Fast verwehte Spuren*, Berlin 1994, p. 109.

[40]Ludwig Marcuse, *Mein zwanzigstes Jahrhundert: Auf dem Weg zu einer Autobiographie*, Munich 1963, p. 54.

[41]See Kurt Pinthus, 'Wunsch aus Kritik', in Ziege, pp. 40–42, here p. 40.

[42]Cf. Finkel, p. 118; 'Me-Sichot Chug Habima Banoar: al chagey haam be-Eretz Israel', in *Bama* 3 (May
1936), pp. 56–58.

[43]Miriam Bernstein-Cohen, *Ketipa bajam*, Ramat Gan 1971, p. 129.

[44]Finkel, p. 69.

[45]This argument is voiced by Rabbi Sonderling as cited in f.p., 'Tragische Heimkehr', and is likewise
expressed by Marta Mierendorff, 'Leopold Jessner'.

cultural landscape".[46] The tragedy of Jessner, a theatre innovator who wholeheart-
edly believed in a fruitful German-Jewish synthesis, is perhaps best expressed by
Alfred Kerr, the prominent Jewish theatre critic of the Weimar Republic who was
himself an insider turned exile. Standing up for Jessner in his moment of crisis in
1929, Kerr describes him as having "turned a stable into a temple [meaning the
Staatstheater] ... what has he made out of this contemptible stage during the past ten
years! He has offered an unprecedented wealth of great directors and actors. Such
abundance, such flourishing! There was no such thing in Europe or America. Berlin:
centre of the world! How will this phase be considered? No doubt, as the Periclean
era of the Republic."[47]

Jessner's appointment as the *Staatstheater*'s general director in September 1919 was
actually a political and not an artistic decision. He was the right man for a fresh
beginning: a staunch Republican who advocated political engagement; a long-standing Social Democrat and union activist who had campaigned for the improvement
of actors' working conditions.[48] His "outstanding economic and organisational abilities were of substantial importance", wrote Felix Ziege in 1928, adding that "as a
performing artist Leopold Jessner did not count for much as far as the Berlin
Staatstheather was concerned".[49] This statement is as telling as it is startling – particularly in light of the fact that Jessner's professional record in Hamburg and
Königsberg had served, already, as a striking testimony to his original, innovative
approach to the theatre. The essentials of his approach were amply evident in the
productions he directed in those cities; his rise to fame in Berlin was due to the fact
that the Weimar Republic capital offered the perfect ambience for the kind of theatre he had set out to direct – the timing was simply right. In an article on new concepts of directing he wrote in 1927, Jessner himself speaks of the pre-Berlin years as
seminal for his development as a director.[50]

Looking back on this earlier period, it is easy to see all of Jessner's interests taking
shape. Among these are (1) the pursuit of a stage devoted to both the classics and
modern drama; (2) the idea of a *Volkstheater* in the sense of Schiller's *Schaubühne* as
moral tribunal;[51] (3) an emphasis on the social critique expressed in contemporary
plays – by Ibsen, Gerhart Hauptmann, Maxim Gorki and others – and on political
theatre as the expression of the time;[52] (4) the role of the director as "guide to the
play" (*Spielleiter*),[53] as an intermediary between playwright and actor, in search of

[46]Frederic V. Grunfeld, *Prophets without Honour: A Background to Freud, Kafka, Einstein and their World*, New York
    1979, p. 5.
[47]Alfred Kerr, 'Jessner', in *Berliner Tageblatt*, 5 April 1929.
[48]Jessner was the first German director to pay actors for overtime; see Müllenmeister, p. 25. He introduced
    working contracts, raised the basic salary, and pressed for better co-operation between actors and direc-
    tors. See Jessner's articles 'Probleme des Provinztheaters' (1918), in Fetting (ed.), pp. 49–51, and 'Der
    Schauspieler als Bürger' (1919), *ibid.*, pp. 56–58.
[49]Ziege, p. 24; Reich, p. 179, points out that the social-democrat Jessner was preferred to younger direc-
    tors like Karl Heinz Martin, Gustav Hartung, Richard Weichert, and Berthold Viertel.
[50]Jessner, 'Neue Regie', in Fetting (ed.), p. 167.
[51]Jessner, 'Meine Bewerbung um die Leitung des Neuen Volkstheaters in Berlin' (1913), *ibid*, pp. 13–16.
[52]This is apparent in the list of productions in Hamburg and Königsberg, especially in the choice of pro-
    ductions for the *Hamburger Volksschauspiele*. Cf. *ibid.*, pp. 306–308.
[53]Cf. Jessner, "Die künstlerische Verantwortung des Regisseurs, seine Rechte und Pflichten" (1913), *ibid.*,
    pp. 144–149.

Lothar Müthel and Fritz Kortner in Jessner's 1920 production of Franz
Wedekind's *Marquis von Keith*

Stage set with *Jessnertreppen* designed by Emil Pirchan
for Jessner's production of *Richard III*.

what he had first termed an overriding "directorial concept" and would later term a "basic motive" (*Grundmotiv*);[54] (5) the trimming of dialogue, pruning of scenes, and omission of figures, in an attempt to focus on the underlying "basic motive", thus stressing the play's universal message and ensuring a rapid pace;[55] (6) the conflation of word, gesture, and movement and the accentuation of speech and mime; (7) the gradual shift from an illusionistic stage-design to an "architectonic" set – culminating in the famous Jessner steps[56] – using light and colour as denotative images; (8) the advancement of ensemble work, furthering the career possibilities of promising new actors and actresses;[57] (9) and finally, the founding of an actors' school with a systematic training programme, which Jessner ran in Hamburg long before heading the *Schauspielschule* in Berlin.[58]

Indeed, the 1919 production of Schiller's *Wilhelm Tell*, which marked the beginning of a new era in German theatre,[59] was the product of a long process unfolding within Jessner's mind. In 1913 he indicated that he "would also like to avoid producing that outcry of freedom, *Wilhelm Tell*, this wonderful folk-poem, as a realistic, pleasant comedy".[60] In 1916 he directed his first rendering of the play in Königsberg. This early production embodies the core elements of the 1919 version: the predominant idea of freedom, the renunciation of a nationalistic, romanticised atmosphere, the trimming and condensation of the text, the depiction of Tell as a non-heroic, introverted, and haunted man. Fritz Kortner, who played Tell's diabolical foil Gessler in 1919 and 1923, describes the 1919 *Tell* as "revolutionary and anti-nationalistic"; he does not hide his disappointment with the 1923 production, which

[54]Jessner first maintained that every drama had its own style which the director was obliged to recognise in order to interpret the play appropriately. Thus when he directed Maeterlinck's *Palleas und Melisande* in Hamburg in 1908, he concentrated on the semi-pathetic style in tone and movement, in this way underlining the idea of longing. The notion of an inherent style soon generated that of a "basic motive". See *ibid.*, p. 146. He elaborated the notion of the "directorial concept" in Königsberg; see the review in the *Königsberger Hartungsche Zeitung*, 16 October 1916, by the paper's critic Ludwig Goldstein, of Jessner's production of Wedekind's *Karl Hetmann*. For later reference to the "basic motive" see Jessner, 'Der Regisseur' in Fetting (ed.), pp. 178–180, and *idem*, 'Regie', *ibid.*, pp. 171–177, especially p. 173.

[55]This process is evident already in his Hamburg productions of Büchner's *Dantons Tod* (1910) and Ibsen's *Peer Gynt* (1910) and in the Königsberg production of *Peer Gynt* (1915), where the text was reduced from 170 pages in the original to some ninety pages in the production. The Königsberg *Tell* (1916) consisted of twelve instead of fifteen scenes and Hauptmann's *Florian Gayer* (1917) was reduced by fifty per cent. Correspondingly, Jessner attributed great importance to the producer; in Königsberg he made Julius Bab responsible for the production work along with Hans-Hermann Cramer and Max Feldmann.

[56]Jessner mentions that he had used a variation of the steps before moving to Berlin, in *Peer Gynt* (1915) and *Karl Hetmann* (=*Hidalla*) (1916). See Jessner's 'Die Treppe – eine neue Dimension' (1922), *ibid.*, pp. 154–155. For his objections to an over-valuation of "the wrongly named *Treppe*", see 'Das Theater' (1928), *ibid.*, p. 99. Importantly, using steps as a set was influenced by Appia's stage-design and had already found expression in Reinhardt's 1908 productions of *Lear* and *Lysistrata*. In 1917, Georg Kaiser's *Die Bürger von Calais* had also been performed on the steps leading to a Frankfurt church.

[57]Jessner advocates ensemble work as early as 1913, in 'Meine Bewerbung', *ibid.*, pp. 13–16, esp. p. 15. Among the young actors he discovered was the seventeen year old Luci Mannheim, whom he invited to Königsberg.

[58]Jessner speaks of the urgent need for such a school in 'Meine Bewerbung'. While in Hamburg before the First World War, he headed the actors training programme integrated into the local conservatory Früß-Färber. See Manfred Brauneck, *Klassiker der Schauspielregie*, Hamburg 1988, p. 184.

[59]Cf., for instance, Günther Rühle, 'Leopold Jessner', in *Theater in unserer Zeit*, Frankfurt am Main 1976, p. 47ff.

[60]Jessner, 'Meine Bewerbung', in Fetting (ed.), p. 15.

he describes as a "total break" with the earlier version, a kind of "bowing" to extra-theatrical coercion.[61]

One of the striking things about the 1919 *Tell* was the nervous reaction of a "panic-stricken Jessner", prepared to cancel the performance when protests were heard in the audience.[62] This anxiety was in fact a central feature of Jessner's personality. Eckard von Naso recalls that "he often made the impression of someone about to face a catastrophe".[63] Especially in Berlin, the anxiety had artistic implications. For Alfred Mühr, he "was a man with potential, competent and of high reputation … but there was something tragic: this aggressive director tended to compromise as soon as minor resistance came up. … He would virtually condemn himself, becoming more and more passive."[64] The anxiety was thus mixed with passivity and indecision and undoubtedly contributed to Jessner's reluctance to promote and stage new drama. Fritz Kortner, one of Jessner's principal actors and a friend, suggests as much in a severe recollection:

> Jessner was a religious Jew, a Socialist and at the same time sympathetic to the Centre [Party]. He was a man of opportunistic placability. After he had attained his high position, he grappled with nothing else. He wasted his own power in the futile and ultimately unworthy attempt to maintain his position, and this by all means, including prayer. [In the end] nothing was holy to him but his own position, the social amenities which it comprised. He sacrificed his professional conviction in favour of his craving for recognition. The weaker, more opportunistic, and more unsteady he became, the more stress he placed on God.[65]

Observations by other contemporaries are in a similar vein: Wilhelm Reich registers a conversation with Bertolt Brecht in which the aspiring dramatist maintained that "Jessner evades decisions and tends to search for compromises."[66] And Kurt Tucholsky, summarising the Berlin theatre scene of 1929, quips that "Jessner wants to please everybody – and pleases no one. Who is he afraid of?"[67] It would thus appear that with his observation of 1928, "when the revolution reaches the stage of evolution, the thesis becomes synthesis", Jessner is attempting to explain his own artistic compromises "with a seeming approximation to the earlier style".[68] This tendency to compromise was certainly connected to the repeated personal attacks and attacks on his directorship, laced as they were with nationalistic and antisemitic slander. It is here useful to recall Eckard von Naso's recollection that "as the first Jewish *Intendant* of the *Staatstheater*, Jessner was a thorn in the side of the right and the cen-

[61]Fritz Kortner, *Aller Tage Abend*, Munich 1959, pp. 354–362.

[62]On this episode see Kuhns.

[63]von Naso, p. 436.

[64]Mühr, p. 274.

[65]Fritz Kortner, *Letzten Endes. Fragmente*, Munich 1971, p. 189.

[66]Reich, p.198. Brecht was impressed by the way Jessner used lighting in his productions. Watching *Othello* (1921), he had the feeling that the characters on stage resembled figures by Rembrandt; see Bertolt Brecht, *Schriften zum Theater, Gesammelte Werke*, vol. 17, Frankfurt am Main 1967, p. 949. Herbert Ihering, *Reinhardt, Jessner, Piscator oder Klassikertod*, Berlin 1929, pp. 22ff., was one of the first to recognise the influence Brecht had on Jessner.

[67]Kurt Tucholsky, *Werke*, vol. 7, Reinbek 1975, p. 244.

[68]Jessner, 'Das Theater unserer Zeit', in Fetting (ed.), pp. 95–97, here p. 96.

tre parties until his overthrow".[69] Jessner was accused of "Judaising" the state-sub-sidised theatre and of political, Bolshevist agitation; he was criticised for being unpa-triotic and *volksfremd*, for casting Jews in leading roles, and for forcing "Jewish images" on the audience. In a pernicious article about Jessner's production of Hauptmann's *Florian Geyer* (1927), Mühr suggested that "German literature is being ruthlessly rav-aged by the *Intendant* of the Prussian *Staatstheater*".[70] Reflecting in 1930 on his Berlin years, Jessner acknowledged being insecure, yet stressed that "the crises were not a result of insecurity; rather, whenever insecurity arose, it was the result of incessant crisis".[71] Harassed and slandered despite his best efforts to modify some of the artis-tic principles and innovations that had made his name, Jessner nevertheless was always open and forthright about his Jewishness.

Was he "staging Jewish theatre" (his words), as his opponents alleged? Hardly. In his early production of Hebbel's *Judith* (Königsberg 1917), he did choose to end the tragedy on a "victorious note" with "a Jewish Chanukah song", for which he was promptly criticised.[72] But nothing of the kind is apparent during the Berlin period, though he seems to have made a habit of annually accepting one Eastern European Jewish actor – "to incense the Goyim".[73] Unlike Reinhardt, Jessner did not person-ally direct *The Merchant of Venice* on a German stage, leaving the job to Jürgen Fehling, appointed as one of his two house-directors in 1922. Performed at the *Staatstheater* in 1927, with Kortner as Shylock, the production prompted a malicious review in *Der Stürmer*.[74]

In this context, Jessner's decision to première Paul Kornfeld's *Jud Süß* on 7 October 1930 – only a month after the sensational success of the National Socialists in the Reichstag elections – is quite surprising. The drama about the precipitous rise and fall of court Jew Joseph Süß Oppenheimer in the 18th century Dukedom of Württemberg was not produced at the *Staatstheater*, from which Jessner had had to resign,[75] but at the *Theater am Schiffbauerdamm*. Writing for the *CV-Zeitung*, Alfred Hirschberg aptly maintained that Kornfeld's historical drama should be regarded as *Zeittheater*,[76] and this was surely the way Jessner perceived the play and staged it. He pruned the original text, concentrating on "the man Süß",[77] a scapegoat whose peri-patetic life "was perceived by the audience as a summary of highly topical events and

---

[69]von Naso, p. 437

[70]Cf. Fetting, 'Notizen zu Jessner', in *idem* (ed.), p. 298. Mühr's article 'Walter Frank spielt Florian Geyer', in *Deutsche Zeitung*, Berlin, 19 April 1927, is reprinted in Günther Rühle, *Theater für die Republik. Im Spiegel der Kritik*, vol. 2, Frankfurt 1988, p. 822.

[71]Jessner, 'Staatliches Schauspielhaus', in Fetting (ed.), pp. 31–36, here p. 32.

[72]Marcuse, p. 53.

[73]Finkel, p. 117.

[74]For reviews of the production see Günther Rühle, *Theater für die Republik*, pp. 823–830. Kortner reports that he developed his portrayal of Shylock against Fehling's directorial concept. Fehling wanted to pres-ent a "more humanity-loving Shylock", so as not to deliver more antisemitic arguments, but Kortner was seeking "requital, the exposure of Christian hatred". Kortner, *Aller Tage Abend*, pp. 377ff. and p. 411.

[75]Upon Jessner's resignation in 1929, Kornfeld wrote an article commending him as "the higher type of the erudite, versatile man of the world", see *idem*, *Das Tagebuch*, 11 January 1939, pp. 56f., cited in Wilhelm Haumann, *Paul Kornfeld: Leben–Werk–Wirkung*, Würzburg 1996, p. 603.

[76]Alfred Hirschberg, 'Jud Süß. Zugleich eine Betrachtung über das Zeittheater. II. Politisches Theater', in *CV-Zeitung*, vol. 9, no. 42 (1930), pp. 449–450.

[77]Sandra Nuy, *Paul Kornfeld: Jud Süß*, Anif–Salzburg 1995, p. 143.

anticipations".[78] In the title role, Jewish actor Ernst Deutsch sought to shun "all repulsive traits", fascinating the audience with his "expressive silent acting, supple, witty delivery and magnificent élan".[79] Caspar Neher's set created a sense of timelessness, though allusions to Hitler could easily be discerned in the Duke's rhetoric.[80] Süß appeared in the first act with side-locks and in traditional Jewish garb. Imprisoned, he cries out "The Jew, the Jew! But this is surely not the only thing. Something isn't right here. … What kind of a man is he whom everybody wrongs?" Did Jessner feel affinity with the scapegoat he staged so sympathetically? And why did he omit the aggressive mass scenes, in which the "people's anti-Semitism is pilloried",[81] much to the author's dismay?[82] Was he apprehensive that the crowd's antagonism and rancour might spill over from the stage to the auditorium, stirred by latent antisemitism?

THEATRE AS SYNAGOGUE, OR MOULDING THE NEW JEWISH IDENTITY

As he witnessed his dream of a German-Jewish social and cultural synthesis crumbling before his eyes, Jessner became increasingly estranged from his political-cultural milieu, increasingly allied to his Jewish background. As it turned out, he would be one of the few German-Jewish theatre celebrities (directors or actors) to try his luck in Palestine after being chased out of Germany. Though his contract to serve as *Intendant* had been extended in 1929,[83] following the scandal connected with his production of Ferdinand Reyher's *Harte Bandagen* (premièred on 31 December 1929), he was forced to agree to serve as director only. The young dramatist Arnolt Bronnen, by then close to the German Nationalists, had maintained in his critique of the play that "Mr. Jessner has long been a rotten tooth in a rotten body";[84] and the prominent critic Herbert Ihering had referred to "the hesitant tactics of a weak *Intendant*", demanding that Jessner give up his other position as director of the *Schauspielschule*.[85] Accompanying such brickbats was a growing influence of the Nazis within the Prussian state.[86] His last production for the theatre he had once steered was Richard Billinger's *Rosse* (premièred on 1 March 1933). Partly because it was clear this marked Jessner's farewell, the applause lasted nearly fifteen minutes. "It is useless to campaign against him. He is a fallen 'great man' (*eine gestürzte 'Grösse'*). This staging is his last 'deed'", wrote the critic Ludwig Sternaux.[87]

   With a company of thespians who, like himself, had become jobless overnight or had been forced into exile, Jessner went on tour in Belgium, Holland, and England.

[78]Hirschberg, p. 449.
[79]Cf. Wilhelm Haumann, p. 604.
[80]Felix Hollaender, 'Kornfelds "Jud Süß"', in *8–Uhr-Abendblatt*, 8 October 1930.
[81]Rühle, *Theater der Republik*, p. 34.
[82]Rühle, *ibid.*, argues that Jessner did so "out of fear"; Nuy, pp. 141ff., takes issue with this.
[83]Müllenmeister, p. 133.
[84]Arnolt Bronnen, 'Das Loch am Gendarmenmarkt', in *Berliner Lokalanzeiger*, 13 January 1930.
[85]Herbert Ihering, 'Jessners Abschied als Intendant', in *Berliner Börsen-Courier*, 19 January 1930.
[86]Müllenmeister, p. 39.
[87]*Berliner Lokalanzeiger*, 2 March 1933 (article untitled).

The troupe performed Schiller's *Kabale und Liebe* in 1933 and in the following year augmented the programme to include Hermann Sudermann's *Heimat* and Bruno Frank's *Nina* as well as a version of *Tell*, which premièred in the Hague on 4 February 1934. The plays Jessner chose to present on the tour had – like most of his earlier productions – a political message.[88] Jessner received a warm reception in Holland, and the local press intimated he would be engaged as director of a Dutch theatre. However, there were apparently no negotiations. He left Holland in late February 1934, after the première of *Tell*, heading north.

The next station of his exile was England (between 1934 and 1935), and he may well have eventually left for Palestine because his various endeavours in London failed so miserably: The *Jesba* Film Company he had founded with the Swiss banker G. E. Bacher managed to produce only one film, *The Children of the Fog*. Planned German(!) productions of Schiller's *Kabale und Liebe* and Sudermann's *Heimat* at the Duke of York Theatre never materialised.[89] And "Jessner's famous *Treppen* were gazed at in disbelief."[90] He arrived in Tel Aviv in February 1936, during the heyday of German-Jewish emigration to Palestine, the so-called Fifth Aliya. He had been invited by the *Habima* company to direct "one tragedy by Shakespeare and a historical Jewish play"[91] with the possibility of an appointment as the theatre's artistic director. Margot Klausner of the theatre's management, who had met him in Lucerne in 1935 on the margins of the Zionist congress, recalls that "Jessner talked to me at length about the repertoire and all the conditions of directorial work".[92] That professional prospect surely attracted Jessner, who had met a good number of *Habima* actors in Berlin, and had revealed "great interest in developments in Palestine".[93]

"Leopold Jessner should go to Palestine, where he belongs," Pastor Koch, an active member of the *Deutschnationale Volkspartei*, had proclaimed in Berlin[94] – one of many suggestions of the same sort. Marta Mierendorff indicates that early childhood experiences played a strong role in his decision to opt for Palestine.[95] Nevertheless, soon after arriving in Tel Aviv, he overheard a revealing exchange: "With all due respect to the accomplishments of our guest, it cannot be denied that we in Palestine wish

---

[88]Cf. Fetting, 'Notizen zu Jessner', in *idem* (ed.), p. 300.

[89]See William Rose, "German Literary Exiles in England", in *German Life and Letters*, New Series, vol. 1, 1947–1948, pp. 175–185, here p. 178. Rose was Jessner's closest friend in London. He observes that "the English did not take advantage of a unique opportunity to recruit his constructive mind and vast experience" (*ibid.*, p. 178).

[90]Günter Berghaus, 'The Emigrés from Nazi Germany and their Contribution to the British Theatrical Scene', in Werner E. Mosse, Julius Carlebach, Gerhard Hirschfeld, Aubrey Newman, Arnold Paucker, Peter Pulzer (eds.), *Second Chance*, Tübingen 1991 (Schriftenreihe wissenschaftlicher Abhandlungen des Leo Baeck Instituts 48), pp. 297–314, here p. 298. Jessner also gave three lectures (one on portraits of actresses), according to his letter to Rose, 22 January 1936, and an informal talk at the University of London. Archive of the Institute of Germanic Studies, London, William Rose Papers, WRO5.

[91]Jessner, 'Yediot', in *Bama* 7 (June 1935), p. 56.

[92]Margot Klausner, *Yoman Habima*, Tel Aviv 1971, p. 211.

[93]Finkel, p. 113; *idem*, p. 83, recounts how Jessner came to the *Habima* rehearsals of 'Balthazar' in Berlin and "gave some good advice".

[94]As Jessner indicates in 'Jüdische Politik'. Cf. Manfred Gailus, *Protestantismus und Nationalsozialismus. Studien zur nationalsozialistischen Durchdringung des protestantischen Sozialmilieus in Berlin*, Cologne 2001.

[95]Marta Mierendorff, 'Leopold Jessner im Exil', unpublished ms. (proposed research project), FML, p. 4. Mierendorff indicates that Jessner had to decide between Palestine and Russia, to which he had been invited in 1936. Jessner refers to this invitation in 'Jüdische Politik'.

to have a director for Habima who comes not from Berlin but from Russia."[96] Branded an outsider as a child, caught between East and West, Jessner now had to once more absorb the fact – this time in a non-German context – that Jews too could be guilty of discrimination, and that there was no such thing as "a [uniquely] Jewish fate".[97] The Palestine interlude would last six months.

Jessner's production of *The Merchant of Venice* opened in Tel Aviv on 14 May 1936; his version of the Shakespeare play constituted a meditation on the collective diasporic experience. Far away from Europe, in an incipient renewed Jewish homeland, Shylock was portrayed as a man more sinned against than sinning; not an individual victim, but a symbol of the maltreated, downtrodden Jew. And yet, Jessner indicated, "the defeated [Shylock] leaves the battlefield not as a broken or humiliated person, but as one who feels contempt for this society"; with his production, he appears to have intended a proud and self-assured response to the Jewish agony he had experienced so personally. "Here then is Shylock the fighter ... not the man who endures, but the tragic hero".[98]

The summer of 1936 in British Mandate Palestine, fraught as it was with violent clashes between Jews and Arabs, was not an ideal time for theatrical ventures. Still, holding fast to his initial plans, Jessner proceeded with a German classic – a première of *Tell* on 28 July 1936. As in his previous renderings of the play, he was more intrigued by the idea of freedom than by the fate of individual characters. *Tell* should be perceived as "a human manifesto against enslavement and tyranny", he maintained. Nevertheless, he accepted the allusions to current political affairs that some spectators recognised in his "primordial, Biblical" production:[99] the brown colour (of Gessler's costume, for instance) reminiscent of Nazi uniforms, or the analogy between the play's Swiss freedom declaration and "the political promise given to us – the Balfour Declaration".[100]

The productions of both the *Merchant* and *Tell* had a mixed reception from critics and spectators, and nothing came of the prospect of directing the company.[101] "Until this very day I believe that we theatre people in Israel did great injustice to this man, who wished whole-heartedly to stay in the country and strike roots in it", states Shimon Finkel, adding that "he came with no demands ... he did not ask to be the manager or as-it-were director but wanted to stand by the cradle of the country's young theatre, to serve as a loyal tutor, guide, and educator, by virtue of his

---

[96]*ibid.*

[97]*ibid.*

[98]Jessner, "Al ha-Teatron ha-Eretz Israeli ve-Teudato", in *Bama* 3 (May 1936), pp. 3ff., here pp. 3–7. On the production and reception of the play see Shelly Zerzion, "Shylock ole le-Eretz Israel", in *Cathedra*, 2004 (forthcoming).

[99]Jessner, 'Mi-Sichot chug Habima La-Noar', in *Bama* 1–2 (October 1936), pp. 76–77; Yaacov Fichmann, 'Al ha-Teatron ha-klasi', *ibid.*, pp. 3–13, here p. 13.

[100]Jessner, 'Mi-Sichot', p. 77.

[101]Marta Mierendorff asked the *Habima* management why Jessner had stopped working with them but never got a reply, see *idem*, "Memorabilia", unpublished manuscript, 3 October 1972, FML. The theatre historian and critic Mendel Kochansky, *Ha-Teatron ha-Ivri*, Tel Aviv 1974, p. 119, argues that by inviting Jessner, *Habima* went against its own principle of "internal directorship", i.e. the principle that the actors chose the director from amongst themselves. Klausner, pp. 211–212, maintains that this principle had been undermined by the actors.

enormous experience. ... Before he left, he told me, 'It's easier to stage *Nathan the Wise* for the Goyim than for the Jews'."[102]

In fact, Jessner's short career with *Habima* exemplifies his belief that Hebrew theatre could serve as a vehicle for moulding a new Jewish identity. He gave several lectures in German, accompanied by Hebrew translation, in which he expounded his cardinal belief in topical, political theatre as a vehicle for producing a national consciousness.[103] Like the classics of world drama, the emerging Hebrew drama was meant to reflect the spirit of its time and place, thereby contributing to an authentic political and cultural awareness: "The theatre of *Eretz Israel* should not go along the paths of Russian, German, or Yiddish theatre. It should discover its own spirit and find its own form, stemming from the spirit of *Eretz Israel*".[104]

The context for the above citation is the dramatically controversial reception that Jessner's production of *The Merchant of Venice* received in Palestine. Many spectators felt offended, wondering why the play had to be produced in the first place. The heated debate between the play's opponents and supporters culminated in what was termed a public "literary trial", taking place in Tel Aviv on 23 June 1936.[105] The prosecutor, Mr. Klinov, opened the "trial" by accusing the "great English dramatist William Shakespeare" of "heedlessly incorporating anti-Jewish matter" into his play, thereby wilfully or inadvertently creating "a demonic, impossible figure", tinged with extreme antisemitism. The second fault, he argued, lay with the *Habima* Theatre for having produced the play on the Hebrew stage. And finally, the director was at fault having "interpreted the figure of Shylock in a way that neither suits reality nor fulfils the proposed intention, thus arriving at the opposite".[106]

The witnesses on behalf of the "prosecution", among them the poet Alexander Penn, argued that Shylock was a repulsive figure, mirroring antisemitic *topoi*. Furthermore, Shylock was an *anti-Zionist* figure in that as a petty-minded money-lender he posed a potential threat to the emerging Jewish state. The appointed "defence-counsel", Dov-Beer Malkin, based his arguments on observations and comments made by prominent German Jews such as Heine, Heinrich Graetz, and Gustav Landauer. Following some fifteen minutes of consultation, the judges, among them the poet Shaul Tschernichowsky, announced their verdict: Shakespeare was innocent, as was the *Habima* Theatre. As for Jessner, the judges evoked the director's own notion of *Zeittheater* in confirming his presentation of the play "according to the spirit of the time"; moreover, they indicated, Jessner had done his utmost to underscore the two major aspects of the play: "The moral stance of the suffering and proud Shylock" and the "heedlessness and flawed conscience of his foes".[107]

In general, Jessner viewed the young local theatre as having a constitutive role in the new nation's development. Religion, that cementing factor which held the Jews

---

[102]Finkel, p. 118.

[103]Jessner, 'Al ha-Teatron', p. 4. Cf. Curt Wormann's report 'Leopold Jessner über das palästinensische Theater', in *Mitteilungsblatt der HOG*, 1 July 1936, pp. 11–12.

[104]Jessner, 'Neum ha-Neesham Professor Jessner', in *Bama*, vols. 1–2 (October 1936), pp. 34–37, here pp. 36–37.

[105]For an account of the entire trial, see 'Ha-Mishpat ha-Sifruti al Shylock', in *Bama, ibid.*, pp. 23–41.

[106]*ibid.*, p. 24.

[107]*ibid.*, p. 41.

together in the Diaspora, could not serve as the programme for "a crowd becoming a people", he argued.[108] "The synagogue is not the platform ... let the theatre be the platform". This little aphorism shows clearly just how far his views had travelled: from his early faith in a German-Jewish synthesis in the spirit of the *Centralverein* to a nationalist ideal of the "new Jew" in Palestine[109]; from an Orthodox-liberal stance to secular Zionism. At the time of his stay in Israel, Jessner felt strongly that theatricality, as a fuel for ceremonies and rituals, was vital to the formation of the symbols without which no nation could exist. The word "synthesis" here figured strongly for Jessner, although in anything but a *Centralverein* context: "I see in the synthesis of new ideas, the Bible and tradition, an elementary principle in the shaping of holidays in *Eretz Israel*".[110] With similar Zionist ardour, he approved a kibbutz Passover *seder* in which the Exodus story was compared to the mass immigration from Nazi Germany; he advocated the celebration of *Shavuot* as the feast of Hebrew pioneers; he praised the carnival-like ambience of a children's *Purim* procession; and he endorsed the notion of dedicating one day of *Chanukah* to a contemporary Maccabee – Joseph Trumpeldor. "I would like to see the symbolic and concrete expression of my conviction that there are not only suffering Jews, but also fighting and victorious Jews", he informed young people in Palestine, in whom he now invested all his hopes and longings.[111]

Jessner's ardour did not wane after the mixed reception given his *Habima* productions. He continued collaborating and investing in the emerging Israeli theatre, offering dramaturgic assistance to kibbutz playwright Shulamit Bat Dori, who was working on a play entitled *The Trial* to be premièred at *Habima*.[112] He also invested efforts in negotiating with the Jewish Agency for regular production of Jewish holiday plays and ceremonies – most likely in the vein of his new approach to Jewish history. The plan did not materialise: "Habima functionaries among the actors led a campaign against us in the Agency", Klausner notes.[113]

In the autumn of 1936, Jessner left the country for Vienna – but he did not give up his new theatrical trajectory. Along with lectures in Zionist circles, he got involved with Jewish amateur actors, whom he considered "an indispensable instrument in the formation of a Jewish nation".[114] Once again, theatre converged with political conviction; it addressed contemporary problems: the tragedy of exile, the return to folklore, state-building. "The seeds of a national religious drama are latent in the responses of the synagogue service, which in turn influenced the ecclesiastical service and consequently also medieval amateur drama", he maintained.[115] The result of this engagement was a production, with a group of eighty young amateurs, of the dramatic poem *Chronicle of 1936* in Vienna on 22 June 1937. The highly emotive,

---

[108]Jessner, 'Al ha-Teatron', p. 7 and *idem*, 'Mi-Sichot', p. 56.
[109]*ibid.*, pp. 57–58.
[110]*ibid.*
[111]*ibid.* Arnold Zweig, who lived in Palestine between 1933 and 1948, also harboured hopes for a Zionist rebirth through young Jews in Palestine. See Jost Hermand, *Arnold Zweig*, Reinbek 1990, pp. 35 and 41. A parallel with the Maccabees is also to be found in Zweig's writing; *ibid.*, p. 85.
[112]The play was in the end directed by Leopold Lindtberg. "We felt that Lindtberg had the greater talent for this purpose", writes Klausner, p. 212.
[113]*ibid.*
[114]See Hilde Haider-Pregler, *Überlebenstheater: Der Schauspieler Reuss*, Vienna 1998, p. 167.
[115]*ibid.*, p.168.

pathos-ridden text of Malka Locker, a Yiddish poetess and wife of leading Zionist politician Berl Locker, was perfectly aligned with Jessner's pursuit of Jewish *Zeittheater*: the play interweaves history and current politics, verse dialogue and radio announcements, Hitler Youth slogans and parts of an antisemitic speech by Goebbels.[116] Underscoring the idea of a Jewish bond with Jerusalem, viewed as the eternal city, it depicts the life of the Hebrew pioneer in his newly resettled homeland, applauds the return to the soil and its cultivation, and dramatises both violent clashes with hostile Palestinian Arabs and the ongoing rescue operation of European Jews from the "divine comedy of hell". The dramatic poem concludes on a confident and hopeful note. Persecuted Jews from Germany and Poland, representatives of diasporic suffering, come together with pioneers as "new Jews" in a budding Jewish state to struggle resolutely for a new existence: "with the good and the honest/ we shall gather every remnant/ and build our holiest hand in hand".[117]

AMERICA: "HUMANITY HAS ARISEN"[118]

Jessner never returned to Palestine. On 26 October 1937 he arrived in New York aboard the *Ile de France*. The last station in his trajectory of exile was Los Angeles, where he settled at the end of 1937. Unlike Reinhardt, who was at least partly successful in American theatre, Jessner's ventures in both film and theatre foundered time and again.[119] He chose *Tell* for his American debut on 25 May 1939, trusting in the theatre's capacity to generate a powerful political impetus. From the sidelines, one could have easily foreseen the disaster: the American public had little interest in European classics, and despite three diction coaches, the actors, all German immigrants, had severe language problems. Above all – and this is crucial – "modernity was missing".[120] The one-time innovator had become a traditionalist – not overnight, but as this essay has tried to show, in a gradual process that began in Berlin. Rudi Feld, who designed the set for the American production of *Tell*, recalls that "we urgently advised him not to stage *Tell* of all plays for the Americans. But

---

[116]The text of the play in Hebrew translation by Avigdor Hameiri is published in *Bama* 1 (December 1937), pp. 28–42, and shows that *Habima* followed Jessner's activities outside Palestine with interest.

[117]*ibid.*, p. 42. A review of the play, "'Palästinakalender'': Jessners Volksspiele``, first published in *Die Stimme* (Vienna), 25 June 1937, is reprinted in Brigitte Dalinger, *Quellenedition zur Geschichte des jüdischen Theaters in Wien* (Conditio Judaica, vol. 42, Tübingen 2003), pp. 60–62. Jessner was registered in Vienna with the police until 15 March 1938, though he left the city earlier.

[118]Jessner, '1942', in *Die Westküste*, *Aufbau*, 9 January 1942.

[119]He emigrated to the US with the help of a working contract by MGM, according to which he was to serve as a "technical advisor" in the film production of "The Great Waltz". As it turns out, he did not do much during the first year. The contract was not extended, and he was "unemployed and without means". He then received, like other European colleagues, fifty dollars per week from film producer Walter F. Wanger. Later, after the *Tell* flop, he received monthly payments from the European Film Fund, which was run by Mr. and Mrs. William Dieterle. Among the papers collected by Marta Mierendorff, there is a heart-breaking letter by Jessner (4 August 1945), in which he admits that he has to give up his "hope and ambition" of paying back the "generous" sum. Instead, he offers his services as a manuscript reader.

[120]Marta Mierendoff, 'Leopold Jessner', p. 6.

Mr. *General-Intendant* wanted no advice, only his *Tell* and his steps."[121] The play had to be cancelled after three performances, its producer, William Dieterle, lost 30,000 dollars, and the troupe *The Continental Players* was disbanded. Jessner would direct one more production, Victor Clement's *The Marseillaise*, with the troupe *France Forever* (premièred on 16 January 1943).

Professionally frustrated, Jessner now channeled his energies to matters Jewish. He became an active member of the Fairfax Temple Community, was on the advisory board of the weekly *Aufbau*, and served for three years, until his resignation in August 1940, as president of the main West Coast immigrant organisation, *The German-Jewish Club of 1933*. It was during his presidency that the word "German" was deleted from the club's official title, the German name of its newspaper, *Neue Welt*, being replaced, in turn, by the English *New World* – all in line with his suggestions. The man who had once written that "in the German *Volkstheater*, our mother tongue should at long last regain recognition"[122] now distanced himself from this mother tongue, urging émigrés to master the English language and favouring English as the language of club events.[123] His article 'The Zion Soul' ('Die Zions Seele'), which for years would be considered the "Magna Carta of immigrants"[124], is an appeal for integration into American society. In any event, the title's Zionistic tenor is misleading, in that Jessner's flirtation with Zionism was actually relatively short-lived. His later ideas in fact rather resemble his earlier belief in a German-Jewish synthesis, with one major difference – in striking contrast to his critical view of "Americanisation",[125] Germany had now been replaced by America.

Nations that give refuge to the persecuted are rewarded with an enriched culture, Jessner argues, extolling the ethnic and religious heterogeneity he observed in America. It is the "task" of the newcomer to fulfil his civic duties "in order to merit confidence and WÜRDE [*sic*], self-respect, to prove worthy of liberty".[126] But it is no less important to sustain and nurture one's religious conviction: "It is useless to deny it. The denial did not help before", he contends, alluding to the fate of Germany's assimilated Jews. "The make-up of assimilation will be suspected of concealing a misshapen face by the antagonist [*sic*], hence, he will wipe it off with a single blow and with that same blow destroy the face behind it." Hence, although considered a staunch Zionist by friends and colleagues in America,[127] Jessner's "Zion soul", was not permanently orientated towards the Land of Zion. Rather, it was now expressed as an acknowledgement of the Jewish religion and its traditions; as the

---

[121]Marta Mierendorff, 'German Jewish Club of 1933, Los Angeles: Ein vergessenes Kapitel der Emigration', radio presentation on Süddeutsche Rundfunk, 1966. Cf. Walter Wicclair, *Von Kreuzberg bis Hollywood*, Berlin 1975, pp. 139–140, and Kortner, *Aller Tage*, p. 420.

[122]Jessner, 'Meine Bewerbung', p. 15.

[123]This demotion of the German language led to a debate in the club and the founding of a German-speaking theatre group, the *Freie Bühne*. See Wicclair, pp. 149–159.

[124]The article was published in both English and German in *New World*, October 1940. Marta Mierendorff, 'Leopold Jessner', p. 13.

[125]Cf. Jessner, 'Theater und Publikum' , in Fetting (ed.), p. 47 (written in 1917), and 'Hinter dem Vorhang' (written in 1925).

[126]Leopold Jessner, 'The Zion Soul', *New World*, October 1940, pp. 1–2, here p. 1. The same article is printed in the original German , entitled 'Die Zions Seele', on p. 3.

[127]Perry, p. 3.

recognition of a "spirit [that has] never ceased longing, neither from Moshe Rabbenu to the Nazarene, nor from Baruch Spinoza to the present day"; as pride in a faith that "began with the meditation of [*sic*] the moral laws, the ten commandments".[128] Indeed, for Jessner the Jewish and American spirits meet in a yearning and struggle for freedom, tolerance, and humaneness. "Americanisation" as he now understands it denotes first and foremost "democratisation on the basis of tolerance".[129] And he seems to fully return to his initial *Weltanschauung* , even to his dramatic concept of the "basic motive", when he addresses an audience of émigrés as follows:

> Prevailing opinion should not insinuate that because of Jewish experience the Jew must live in isolation. We have learnt that Jewry ... [as] an organised group is not isolated, but thinks and fights with the army of freedom. We are fighting not only against a person, not only against a system, but against an *idea*, and when the system and persons are long extinguished, the struggle against the idea which made this system and these persons possible should go on. *An idea against an idea.*[130]

Significantly, one of Jessner's last projects was a planned oratorio, a *Peace Chorus* meant, as the name implies, to promote international understanding and reconciliation. The first part of the proposed work was intended to introduce the large family of nations in times of peace; the second to survey "developments since the Hitler tragedy", expounding the horrors of war "from the concentration camp to Lidice" in word, rhythm, music, and movement.[131] The work's unifying element was to be the Unknown Soldier, who was to have the final word, underlining "present-day slaughter". This testimony of a politically engaged artist would never be written.

Writing in exile in the summer of 1932, the German-Jewish poet Ernst Lissauer, an embittered and disillusioned sometime believer in a German-Jewish synthesis, opined that "the characteristic flaws of Judaism have made themselves manifest in many Jews, like Kerr, Tucholsky, Krauss [*sic*], Jessner, Reinhardt. ...The decline of the theatre cannot be imputed to the Jews, but the theatre directors are mostly Jewish".[132] But with a review of Jessner's life, taking in his deeply felt convictions and his profound and sincere involvement in Jewish matters, it would appear that Lissauer's opinion of the director was at the least unfair. Jessner could neither be considered a self-hating Jew – of the kind often seen as represented by Karl Kraus – nor an estranged Jew – of the sort often seen as represented by Kurt Tucholsky. Throughout his life, and not merely after the rise of Nazism, he remained self-aware regarding his Judaism, and he was prepared to freely acknowledge it. Before his exile, this never conflicted with a capacity to share hopes for a German-Jewish social and cultural synthesis with the mass of fellow German Jews who were far more acculturated.

---

[128]Jessner, 'The Zion Soul', p. 1.

[129]Marta Mierendorff, 'Leopold Jessner', p. 15.

[130]Leopold Jessner, 'Einleitende Worte zu einem Döblin Abend', in Fetting (ed.), pp. 206–210, here pp. 207–208.

[131]Letter by Jessner to Dr. Hans Sahl and Mr. Heilbut, 19 September 1942, FML.

[132]Ernst Lissauer's diary, 3 July 1932, quoted in Robert Weltsch, 'Entscheidungsjahr 1932' in Mosse and Paucker (eds.), pp. 535–562, here p. 551.

In light of Jessner's theatrical innovations and his dynamic belief in the political role of the theatre, he should be considered an invigorating force within his contemporary German cultural scene – by no means an agent of cultural decline. Rejecting illusionist traditions and theatrical extravagance, Jessner struggled to realise an emotionally charged and intellectually provocative theatre. He anticipated Brecht and differed from Reinhardt in maintaining a belief in the theatre's political energies: its power to influence the *Zeitgeist* in Weimar Germany, its ability to invigorate Jewish life and mould Jewish identity in Palestine, and its capacity to promote reconciliation and tolerance in America.

Portrait of Leopold Jessner by Siegfried Sebba (Königsberg).

Fritz Rathenau (1875–1949).
On Antisemitism, Acculturation and Slavophobia: An Attempted Reconstruction*

BY CHRISTIAN SCHÖLZEL

"I personally believe that I have done my duty as a Jew. … That I did not see the coming storm in time or appreciate its full gravity was a failure of intellect but not one of character! Nor was I alone in this!"[1] The author of this statement, the jurist Fritz Rathenau (a cousin of Walther Rathenau; 1867–1922), was a leading official in the Prussian Ministry of the Interior in Berlin during the years of the Weimar Republic. His responsibilities included administering matters concerning the immigration of Eastern Europeans to Prussia and dealing with questions pertaining to ethnic minorities in Eastern Prussia. Forced from this post and persecuted as a Jew by the Nazis, he began to grow sceptical regarding the acculturationist approach to life that he had previously espoused.[2]

The following pages will focus on who Fritz Rathenau was and the extent to which his biography might furnish some paradigmatic insights, particularly with regard to the failure of his concept of Jewish acculturation and to the blending of questions he had related to his own Jewish identity with stereotypical notions about "the East".[3]

---

*This article was translated from the German by Deborah Cohen.

[1]Fritz Rathenau, unpublished autobiography, Leo Baeck Institute (New York) (henceforth LBI), MM 62, roll 104, ME 530, p. 107, cf. p. 126. I would like to thank Deborah Cohen, Barbara Danckwortt, Paul Martin, and Jörg Rudolph for translating, editing, and improving the text. Special thanks go to Esther Schulz-Goldstein. Note should be taken of a book published after submission of this essay, Thomas Rink, *Doppelte Loyalität: Fritz Rathenau als deutscher Beamte und Jude*, Hildesheim 2002. Rink's study sometimes uses other sources than this author's, and addresses separate questions.

[2]Throughout this essay, variants of the term "acculturation" will be used in preference to variants of the term "assimilation".

[3]On the latter see Hans Lemberg, 'Zur Entstehung des Osteuropabegriffs im 19. Jahrhundert. Vom "Norden" zum "Osten" Europas' in *Jahrbücher für Geschichte Osteuropas*, new series, vol. 33, no. 1 (1985), pp. 48–91; John M. Efron, 'The "Kaftanjude" and the "Kaffeehausjude": Two Models of Jewish Insanity. A Discussion of Causes and Cures among German-Jewish Psychiatrists', in *LBI Year Book*, vol. 37 (1992), pp. 169–188; *idem*, 'Scientific Racism and the Mystique of Sephardic Racial Superiority', in *LBI Year Book*, vol. 38 (1993), pp. 75–96.

THE LIFE OF FRITZ RATHENAU

A large if scattered body of sources has made it possible to reconstruct the biography of Fritz Rathenau, about whom little has as yet been written.[4] For his early years, his autobiography, statements by his children, and the curriculum vitae attached to his dissertation are the most informative sources.[5] He was born in Berlin on 9 July 1875 as the son of Oscar Rathenau (1840–1926), a textile merchant and judge in a commercial court and his wife Hermine (née Goldberger, 1849–1906). By the time his son submitted his doctorate, the elder Rathenau had already retired.

Having initially received a private education at his parents' home, Fritz Rathenau attended the *Königliches-Wilhelms-Gymnasium* in Berlin from 1882 until 1892, when he took his *Abitur* exams.[6] Familiarly known as the "patent-leather-boot gymnasium" due to its high percentage of boys from wealthy homes, the school was also frequented by a number of children from upper-class Jewish families.

After his school examinations, Rathenau studied law for one year in Berlin, continuing in Munich before returning to the *Friedrich Wilhelms Universität* in Berlin for his final two semesters. Among the professors whose lectures he attended were the jurist and legal philosopher Josef Kohler (1849–1919), whose assistant he would soon become, and Otto von Gierke (1841–1921), one of the "founding fathers" of the German Civil Code. However, it might have been the "lectern socialist" Gustav Schmoller who first kindled Fritz Rathenau's interest in social and economic questions. In 1895 he took his first *Staatsexamen* in law, going on to pass his oral Ph.D. examinations on 28 July 1896. Since his dissertation, entitled *Zur Lehre vom fortgesetzten*

---

[4]The most important source is Fritz Rathenau's roughly 200 page unpublished autobiography. It was written in approximately 1939–1940; he clearly made various additions shortly before his death. In 1989 the manuscript was made available for scholarly access by the LBI (signature: ME 530). Further sources are the files of *Ministerialrat* Fritz Rathenau in Geheimes Staatsarchiv Preußischer Kulturbesitz (Berlin) (henceforth GSA), Rep. 77 (Ministerium des Innern), Tit. 4036, no. 7–13; some papers from the Walther Rathenau Collection in the Moscow Central State Archives (henceforth ZA) F. 634, Walther Rathenau Collection; papers in the Political Archive of the German Foreign Office (Berlin) (henceforth PA); papers from Department III "*Jüdisch-Politische Angelegenheiten*" and from the Prof. Kurt Sobernheim Collection, as well as from the Department IV "Polen" in the Bundesarchiv Koblenz (henceforth BAKO), Nl 1062, Maximilian Harden Collection, file 85 as well as documents from the Central Zionist Archives (Jerusalem) (henceforth CZA); from the Archive in the Zentrum für Antisemitismusforschung of the Technische Universität Berlin (henceforth ZAF); from the Archive in the Centrum Judaicum – Stiftung Neue Synagoge (Berlin) (henceforth ACJ); from the Manuscripts Department of the Staatsbibliothek Preußischer Kulturbesitz (Berlin), Haus 2 (henceforth SPK), Kurt Breysig Collection, box 3 (Kurt Breysig [presumably] to Fritz Rathenau, 20 March 1917); *ibid.*, Hans Delbrück Collection, box 131 (three letters by Fritz Rathenau to Hans Delbrück); as well as a series of publications by Fritz Rathenau. Marginal references to Fritz Rathenau can be found in Salomon Adler-Rudel, *Ostjuden in Deutschland 1880–1940. Zugleich eine Geschichte der Organisationen, die sie betreuten. Mit einem Vorwort von Siegfried Moses*, Tübingen 1959 (Schriftenreihe wissenschaftlicher Abhandlungen des Leo Baeck Instituts 1), p. 69; Trude Maurer, *Ostjuden in Deutschland 1918–1933*, Hamburg 1986, pp. 251f., 325, 471, 845; Werner Röder and Herbert A. Strauss (eds.), *Biographisches Handbuch der deutschsprachigen Emigration nach 1933*, vol. 1: *Politik, Wirtschaft, Öffentliches Leben*, London 1980, pp. 584f. Cf. The collection of material for this entry: ZAF Research Foundation, Jewish Immigrants, MF 51, shoots 2121–2157. Cf. Bildarchiv Preußischer Kulturbesitz (eds.), *Juden in Preussen. Biographisches Verzeichnis. Ein repräsentativer Querschnitt von Ernst G. Lowenthal*, Berlin 1981, p. 186.

[5]LBI, MM 62, roll 104, ME 530, pp. 2ff.; ZAF Research Foundation, Jewish Immigrants, MF 51, shoots 2121ff.; Fritz Rathenau, *Zur Lehre vom fortgesetzten Verbrechen mit besonderer Berücksichtigung seiner Geltung nach dem Reichsstrafgesetzbuch.* Ph.D. thesis, Friedrich-Wilhelms-Universität Berlin, 1896, n.p.

[6]LBI, MM 62, roll 104, ME 530, pp. 5f.

Verbrechen mit besonderer Berücksichtigung seiner Geltung nach dem Reichsstrafgesetzbuch (*On the Theory of Habitual Criminality with Special Attention to its Status in the Imperial Penal Code*), earned him only a *rite*, the lowest pass in a doctoral examination, an academic career for Rathenau was now effectively ruled out.[7]

After attaining the status of a graduate civil servant (or *Assessor*) in 1900, he travelled to England, where he spent five months on a study visit.[8] In 1904 he married Sophie Clara Dannenbaum, with whom he would raise three sons.[9] Until the end of 1905 he was employed at the Imperial Patent Office in Berlin (the *Kaiserliches Patentamt*).[10] During the next three years Rathenau worked as a county and state judge in Berlin, despite the fact that posts in the capital were highly sought after and only rarely offered to Jews.[11] From 1909 until 1917 he held the title of senior civil servant at the Imperial Patent Office.[12] From 1915, following a very brief deployment at the front, Rathenau, by now an expert on patent law, served in the wartime economic administration.[13] From 1917 until 1920 he worked at the National Office of Statistics (the *Statistisches Reichsamt*).[14]

By the end of the First World War, Fritz Rathenau already had a long list of publications to his name on questions of patent and copyright law.[15] In these publications he repeatedly emphasised his own "patriotic leanings", sentiments that he brought to bear in his presentation of the subject matter at hand.[16] Thus in 1908 he foresaw a danger for the "administration of the law" and for the "fatherland" should special courts for patent law be instituted,[17] calling instead for such disputes to be dealt with within the framework of the existing courts and speaking out in favour of an "organic structuring of the German administration of justice".[18] In a legal opinion that he drafted for the 30th annual German jurists' day in 1910, he appealed for "a German

---

[7]*ibid.*, p. 10; Fritz Rathenau, *Lehre*.

[8]LBI, MM 62, roll 104, ME 530, pp. 11f.

[9]*ibid.*, p. 14. With data on the family members: ZAF Research Foundation, Jewish Immigrants, MF 51, shoots 2121–2157. Sophie Rathenau was of Jewish birth.

[10]LBI, MM 62, roll 104, ME 530, pp. 7, 12ff..

[11]*ibid.*, pp. 15ff.; ZAF Research Foundation, Jewish Immigrants, MF 51, shoot 2128; Fritz Rathenau, *Das Sachverständigenwesen in Patentprozessen zugleich ein Beitrag zur Frage der Errichtung eines selbständigen gemischten Patentgerichtshofes*, Berlin 1908, p. 60.

[12]LBI, MM 62, roll 104, ME 530, pp. 21f.

[13]*ibid.*, pp. 13, 30ff.

[14]*ibid.*, pp. 30ff.; ZAF Research Foundation Jewish Immigrants MF 51, shoot 2128.

[15]Fritz Rathenau, *Sach- und Schlagwortverzeichnis in Buchstabenfolge zum Handbuch des Deutschen Patentrechts von Josef Kohler*, Mannheim 1904; *idem*, 'Die Entwicklung eingetragener Wortzeichen zu Warennamen mit besonderer Berücksichtigung des Wortzeichenschatzes für Arzneimittel', in *Archiv für bürgerliches Recht*, vol. 27 (1905), pp. 1–54; *idem*, *Sachverständigenwesen*; *idem*, *Patent- und Gebrauchsmusterprozesse in Preußen im Lichte der Statistik*, Leipzig 1908; *idem*, 'VIII. Gutachten des Herrn Regierungsrat Dr. Rathenau, Berlin über die Frage: Empfehlen sich Sondergerichtshöfe in Streitigkeiten aus dem Gebiete des gewerblichen Rechtsschutzes?', in Schriftführer Amt der ständigen Deputation (eds.), *Verhandlungen des Dreißigsten Deutschen Juristentages 1910*, vol. 1, *Gutachten*, Berlin 1910, pp. 302–488; see *ibid.*, vol. 2, Berlin 1910, pp. 200ff., esp. pp. 251, 263–273; *idem*, 'Rezension zu: Georg Wilhelm Häberlin, Der Anspruch auf ein Patent und das Recht der Erfindung', in *Deutsche Juristenzeitung*, vol. 18 (1913), col. 1393; *idem.*, 'Gewerbliche Schutzrechte während des Krieges', in *Weltwirtschaftliches Archiv*, vol. 7, no. 1 (1916,), pp. 53–78. LBI, MM 62, roll 104, ME 530, pp. 13, 18, 22.

[16]LBI, MM 62, roll 104, ME 530, p. 11.

[17]Fritz Rathenau, *Sachverständigenwesen*, p. 63. Cf. LBI, MM 62, roll 104, ME 530, p. 20.

[18]Fritz Rathenau, *Sachverständigenwesen*, p. 6.

sense of duty" on the part of judges.[19] In 1916 he tackled the subject of "commercial property rights during wartime".[20] Especially in England but also in France, Fritz Rathenau argued, German patents and trademarks were wrongfully being used in a context of "economic war". To prevent such abuse, he demanded that trademarks and patents no longer be regarded as aspects of private law but rather dealt with in the framework of public law. For the jurist, the conflict over norms had become, as it were, a front-line battle: "If one surveys the battlefield of commercial property rights … one cannot ward off a feeling, one less astonished than bitter … that our enemies do not even draw a line at that."[21] From 1915 until 1922 Fritz Rathenau served as editor of the Berlin-based legal-political journal *Recht und Wirtschaft. Monatsschrift des Vereins zur Förderung zeitgenössischer Rechtspflege und Verwaltung* (*Law and Economics. Monthly of the Association for the Promotion of the Administration of Justice*). He would remain a member of the association until 1930.[22]

In 1919 Fritz Rathenau's first longer piece of political writing appeared under the title *Parlament und Räte*.[23] The author understood the brochure – which he drafted on 3 May 1919 under the impact of his experiences in the wartime economy[24] at the end of the war and during the workers' uprisings of 1918–1919 – as an attempt to formulate a bourgeois position vis-à-vis the integration of the concept of workers' councils into Germany's constitution (the *Reichsverfassung*). The brochure was meant "to point out a way promising reconciliation of additional segments of society within our unhappy Fatherland".[25] A reform-orientated bourgeois aspiration towards coalition-building merged with the "hunger for wholeness" (Peter Gay). According to Fritz Rathenau, the creation of a standardised system of workers' councils also offered protection against the threat of Bolshevism in Germany. As this threat was not to be fought with weapons, he called for giving workers an equal stake in the means of production.[26] The economy was everyone's concern and was not to be organised as the dictatorship of a single class.[27] In his opinion, it was a matter of "recognising that only the complete fulfilment of the duties of the individual towards the whole, including in the economic arena – that is, the relinquishing of the slogan about the free play of forces – can help us get back on our feet economically".[28] As one of the lesser-known representatives of the

[19]Fritz Rathenau, *Gutachten*, p. 302.

[20]Fritz Rathenau, 'Schutzrechte', pp. 63ff., 67ff., 71ff.

[21]*ibid.*, p. 71.

[22]GSA, Rep. 77 (Ministerium des Innern), Tit. 4036, no. 13, pp 153–166. The association "Recht und Wirtschaft" was already founded in 1911: SPK, Hans Delbrück Collection, box 131 (Fritz Rathenau to Hans Delbrück, 28 March 1911).

[23]Fritz Rathenau, *Parlament und Räte*, Berlin 1919. Cf. LBI, MM 62,. roll 104, ME 530, p. 26.

[24]BAKO, Nl 1209, Rudolf Wissell Collection, file 17, pp. 316–318, esp. p. 316 (Fritz Rathenau to Rudolf Wissell, 18 July 1919). Rathenau was working as the "Referent des Reichskommissars für Aus- und Einfuhrbewilligungen". In 1919 he still was deputy commissioner of the *Reichswirtschaftsministerium* at the *Weinhandelsgesellschaft*. Cf. David E. Barclay, *Rudolf Wissell als Sozialpolitiker 1890–1933*, Berlin 1984, p. 133.

[25]Fritz Rathenau, *Parlament*, p. 4. Cf. LBI, MM 62, roll 104, ME 530, p. 32. Rathenau rejected the Versailles Treaty.

[26]Fritz Rathenau, *Parlament*, pp. 52ff., also thought about establishing a second chamber of the *Reichstag* representing the different professions. Concerning the "anti-Bolshevism" of Rathenau in the early 1920s: GSA, Rep. 77 (Ministerium des Innern), Tit. 4036, no. 13, p. 165.

[27]Fritz Rathenau, *Parlament*, pp. 6f., 37f.

[28]BAKO, Nl 1209, Rudolf Wissell Collection, file 17, pp. 316–318, esp. pp. 317f. (Fritz Rathenau to Rudolf Wissell, 18 July 1919).

"co-operative economics movement" (*gemeinwirtschaftliche Bewegung*) – a school of thought already doomed to fail in any practical sense shortly after the end of the First World War – he was in contact with Wichard von Moellendorff, Rudolf Wissell, and other proponents of the movement.[29] Fritz Rathenau attributed the demise of the idea to insufficient publicity on the part of its adherents.[30]

In 1920, despite his initial opposition to serving in a "left-leaning" government, Fritz Rathenau allowed himself to be persuaded to enter the Prussian Ministry of the Interior, first as an assistant and then as a ministerial counsellor with responsibility for foreign residents and problems arising from the Treaty of Versailles.[31] Here his primary concern was with the immigration to Prussia of both Jews and non-Jews from Eastern Europe – an unenviable task, as the policies of the Prussian ministerial bureaucracy towards immigrants from the East were neither pro-foreigner nor free of antisemitic prejudices.[32] Later on, his principal area of responsibility shifted to the problems of the German and Polish minorities in the Prussian border regions. In his publications on this topic, *Deutschlands Ostnot* (1931) and *Polonia irredentia?* (1932), he propounded anti-Polish views motivated by hostility towards the terms of the Versailles Treaty.[33]

Fritz Rathenau remained at the Prussian Ministry of the Interior until 1933.[34] For two years he worked for the building authorities in Berlin, but in 1935, under pressure from the Nazis because of his Jewish origins, he was forced to give up his post once and for all. In 1939 he emigrated to the Netherlands, from where he was deported to Theresienstadt in 1943. After being liberated in 1945 he returned to Holland, where he died in 1949.

---

[29]BAKO, Nl 1158, Wichard von Moellendorff Collection, files 34, 169; *ibid.*, Nl 1209, Rudolf Wissell Collection, file 17, pp. 317–323 (correspondence between Fritz Rathenau and Rudolf Wissell, July-December 1919).

[30]BAKO, Nl 1209, Rudolf Wissell Collection, file 17, pp. 316–318, esp. pp. 317f. (Fritz Rathenau to Rudolf Wissell, 18 July 1919).

[31]LBI, MM 62, roll 104, ME 530, pp. 33ff.; GSA, Rep. 77 (Ministerium des Innern), Tit. 4036, no. 13, pp. 109–111, esp. p. 109 (Fritz Rathenau to Friedrich Freund – *Staatssekretär* in the Prussian Interior Ministry – 4 September 1920): he, Fritz Rathenau, has been employed in this office for the past seven months. For a differing statement see W. Röder *et al.*, *Handbuch*, p. 584. Fritz Rathenau was *Ministerialrat* and head of the division for minorities and foreign residents from 1927 onwards. See Preußisches Staatsministerium (ed.), *Handbuch für den Preußischen Staat*, vol. 128 (Berlin 1922), p. 57; *ibid.*, vol. 131 (Berlin 1925), p. 133; vol. 132 (Berlin 1926), p. 151; vol. 133 (Berlin 1927), p. 164; vol. 134 (Berlin 1928), p. 172; vol. 135 (Berlin 1929), p. 176; vol. 136 (Berlin 1930), p. 181; vol. 137 (Berlin 1931), p. 180. After 1930 *Ministerialrat* Rathenau was assigned to Department III, responsible for "Zoll-, Paß-, Grenz- und Einwanderungsfragen", in the Prussian Ministry of the Interior. According to his own statement he was promoted in 1923.

[32]Cf. Maurer; Jack Wertheimer, *German Policy and Jewish Politics: The Absorption of East European Jews in Germany (1868–1914)*, Ph. D. thesis, Columbia University 1978; *idem*, *Unwelcome Strangers: East European Jews in Imperial Germany*, New York–Oxford 1987; Steven E. Aschheim, *Brothers and Strangers: The East European Jew in German and German Jewish Consciousness 1800–1923*, Madison, WI 1982; Ludger Heid, *Maloche – nicht Mildtätigkeit. Ostjüdische Arbeiter in Deutschland 1914–1923*, Hildesheim 1995.

[33]Fritz Rathenau, *Deutschlands Ostnot*, Berlin 1931; *idem*, *Polonia irredentia?*, Berlin 1932. Cf. *idem*, 'Die Nationalitäten in den Staaten Europas', in *Der Heimatdienst*, vol. 11 (1931), p. 353; *idem*, 'Staat und Minderheiten', in *Der Heimatdienst*, vol. 12 (1932), pp. 70f. Cf. LBI, MM 62, roll 104, ME 530, pp. 65ff., 71, 80, 88, 92ff.

[34]W. Röder *et al.* (eds.), p. 584.

It is possible to demonstrate at least fragmentary connections between the lives of Fritz Rathenau and his first cousin Walther Rathenau (their respective fathers, Oscar Rathenau and the AEG-founder Emil Rathenau, were brothers).[35] For three years they attended the same gymnasium[36] and, given their close family ties, it is likely that they had some personal contact there, although we have no documentary evidence of this.[37]

In 1911 Walther Rathenau was engaged in a journalistic controversy with Josef Kohler, one of his cousin's former professors. This was most probably the occasion for the documented contact between the two Rathenaus at this time. In subsequent years we have evidence of communication between the two men only for the years 1919 and, probably, 1921.[38]

Fritz Rathenau resembled his cousin Walther both in his adoption of the model of Jewish acculturation and in his adherence to the idea of co-operative economics. He also supported Walther Rathenau's *Erfüllungspolitik* (the policy of unconditional fulfilment of the terms of the Versailles Treaty). However, as an eminent industrialist, philosopher, and politician, Walther Rathenau cast a long shadow, and it bothered Fritz that he was always perceived as a relative of his more successful cousin.[39]

FRITZ RATHENAU'S ATTITUDE TOWARDS JUDAISM

Fritz Rathenau's familial environment was the first major influence on the development of his complex sense of identity. Oscar Rathenau was an active member of the Jewish community in Berlin, serving as director of various charitable organisations. Hermine Rathenau also appears to have participated in such activities. For a time, Fritz Rathenau's parents, both adherents of reform Judaism, would occasionally take their son to synagogue.[40]

In general Fritz Rathenau shared the view expressed by the philosopher Max Dessoir (himself one of Walther Rathenau's classmates) that Jewish pupils at the *Königliches-Wilhelms-Gymnasium* had remained largely untouched by the everyday antisemitism otherwise prevalent in Wilhelminian Germany.[41] Nevertheless he did describe an incident in 1883 or 1884 – that is, while he was still at school – in which the son of the architect Paul Wallot was forbidden to play with him because he was Jewish.[42] This was, it seems, his first encounter with antisemitism.

In considering his own future career path, Fritz Rathenau no doubt took the antagonism against Jews in Imperial Germany into account. Thus a career as an officer would have quickly been ruled out, as Jews rarely managed to attain such

---

[35]LBI, MM 62, roll 104, ME 530, p. 3.
[36]Walther Rathenau's exercise books in ZA, F 634, Walther Rathenau Collection finding aid (henceforth Fb.) 1, file 10.
[37]But cf. LBI, MM 62, roll 104, ME 530, pp. 3, 7.
[38]ZA F. 634, Walther Rathenau Collection, Fb. 1, file 32, p. 2 (Walther Rathenau to Fritz Rathenau, 26 December 1919); *ibid.*, file 798, p. 49. In 1932 Fritz Rathenau was a member of the *Walther Rathenau-Gesellschaft*, founded four years previously; LBI, MM 62, roll 104, ME 530, p. 99.
[39]LBI, MM 62, roll 104, ME 530, pp. 33, 51, 57.
[40]*ibid.*, p. 5; Julie Braun-Vogelstein, *Was niemals stirbt. Gestalten und Erinnerungen*, Stuttgart 1966, pp. 59, 325.
[41]LBI, MM 62, roll 104, ME 530, p. 6. Max Dessoir, *Buch der Erinnerung*, 2nd edn., Stuttgart 1947, pp. 26, 138.
[42]LBI, MM 62, roll 104, ME 530, p. 6.

positions. While Oscar Rathenau wanted his son to become a rabbi, Fritz managed to overcome his father's opposition and studied law. Among the professors whose lectures he attended was the historian Heinrich von Treitschke. As a lecturer at the University of Berlin, Treitschke had written a series of essays, beginning in 1879, which had set the signal for the so-called *Antisemitismusstreit* (the "antisemitism controversy) in Berlin.[43] Together with other scholars, he emphasised the "danger" posed by Jewish immigrants to the German Reich, especially Jews from Eastern Europe. Alongside this scholarly debate, the subsequent "academisation of antisemitism" – the palpable spreading of an increasingly anti-Jewish mood among non-Jewish students,[44] including those at the *Friedrich-Wilhelms-Universität* – provided the ideological background for Fritz Rathenau's student years in Berlin. "Gentlemen! When I get onto the subject of Englishmen and Jews you must take what I say with a grain of salt. I get so angry that I lose my head!"[45] Fritz Rathenau recalls Treitschke making this remark in one of his seminars.

After completing his university studies, Fritz Rathenau's professional life began. Already as a trainee, however, he was slighted by his superiors because of his Jewish birth. "Years later, when I had occasion to view a part of my personal file, I saw that the word 'Jew' had been written in green ink in the margin of the first sheet of paper. … Thus I was branded … No further 'sign-posting' was necessary to know where my career as a state official was heading!"[46] This was his retrospective judgement. Even during his early years as an official at the Imperial Patent Office, he had experienced setbacks as a result of everyday antisemitism. In one case, superiors advised him to convert if he wanted to advance professionally. He refused.[47] Already at this point in time – just after the turn of the century – it seems that while taking a positive stand towards his own Jewishness, Fritz Rathenau also supported Jewish acculturationist strivings vis-à-vis the non-Jewish German majority.

The question may be left open as to whether Fritz Rathenau's emphasis on German interests in his publications after the pre-war period was symptomatic of a more general contemporary nationalist attitude, or whether it offers evidence of a personal effort to acculturate; subjectively at least, this may have seemed necessary.[48]

Visible evidence of a positive stance towards Jewishness can be seen in Fritz Rathenau's decision in November 1910 to add his signature to the appeal of the Berlin Jewish community's *Liberaler Verein* for votes in the elections to the Assembly of Representatives.[49] In addition (and strikingly), throughout his professional career,

[43]LBI, MM 62, roll 104, ME 530, pp. 8ff.; ZAF Research Foundation, Jewish Immigrants MF 51, shoot 2128; Walter Boehlich (ed.), *Der Berliner Antisemitismusstreit*, Frankfurt am Main 1988.

[44]Norbert Kampe, 'Jews and Antisemites at Universities in Imperial Germany (II) – The Friedrich-Wilhelms-Universität of Berlin: A Case Study on the Students' "Jewish Question"', in *LBI Year Book*, vol. 32 (1987), pp. 43–101.

[45]LBI, MM 62, roll 104, ME 530, p. 10.

[46]*ibid.*, p. 11.

[47]*ibid.*, pp. 7, 12ff.

[48]Cf. BAKO, Nl 1062, Maximilian Harden Collection, file 85, sub-file 2, pp. 11, 13.

[49]ACJ 1, 75 A Be 2, Gesamtarchiv der deutschen Juden, Jüdische Gemeinde zu Berlin, file no. 4; Elisabeth Kraus, *Die Familie Mosse. Deutsch-jüdisches Bürgertum im 19. und 20. Jahrhundert*, Munich 1999, p. 347. The signature is falsely assigned to Walther Rathenau in ZAF Research Foundation, Jewish Immigrants, MF 51, shoots 2126, 2130. Presumably Fritz Rathenau was not able to read Hebrew.

Rathenau seems to have observed the Jewish holidays, even if this meant staying away from work.[50]

One passage from Walther Rathenau's journal refers directly to Fritz Rathenau's position with regard to his own Jewishness. The entry for 9 January 1911 reads: "Monday. Published … article in *Montags-Zeitung* on 'Jewish conversions' (*Judentaufen*). Fritz Rathenau in agreement."[51] The text referred to here was first published as a separate article but later that same year would reappear as the first third of the essay *Staat und Judentum*.[52] With which of his cousin's statements did Fritz Rathenau allegedly agree? As in his first important essay on the subject of Jewry, 'Höre Israel'[53], Walther Rathenau continued in this piece to regard German Jews and non-Jewish Germans as belonging to separate "races".[54] He argued that the co-existence of these two groups led to antisemitism and to discrimination against German Jews. He summed up the situation in the following way:

> One can scarcely hope for this aversion [of non-Jews towards Jews] to disappear so long as the state continues to condone, extol and justify it through differential treatment and so long as certain tribal peculiarities continue to make the Jewish German recognisable and suspect in the eyes of his Christian compatriot.[55]

With regard to the question of how this deplorable state of affairs in society might be rectified, Walther Rathenau offered two suggestions: On the one hand, the Jews should "reform" (*erziehen*) themselves, a proposal that ultimately implied nothing short of their renouncing Jewish cultural traditions in favour of an extremely far-reaching acculturation to the Christian environment. However, he feared that this approach would entail great sacrifices and therefore could be pursued only very gradually.[56] On the other hand, he demanded that the Prussian state revise its policies towards Jewish citizens by granting them legal equality with Christian Prussians. Jews should be given the same access to state office and to the military as non-Jews. After considering whether the conversion of German Jews to Christianity could serve as a means of remedying antisemitism and discrimination,[57] he rejected this option[58] – the adoption of another faith was not necessarily a way to leave discrimination behind. In addition, it appeared opportunistic, as everyone knew that it was

---

[50]LBI, MM 62, roll 104, ME 530, p. 14.

[51]Walther Rathenau, *Tagebuch 1907–1922. Herausgegeben und kommentiert von Hartmut Pogge von Strandmann. Mit einem Beitrag von James Joll und einem Geleitwort von Fritz Fischer*, Düsseldorf 1967, p. 121.

[52]Walther Rathenau, *Tagebuch*, p. 121 (comment by Pogge von Strandmann); idem, 'Staat und Judentum. Eine Polemik´, in *Walther Rathenau, Gesammelte Schriften*, vol. 1, Berlin 1925, pp. 183–207, esp. pp. 185–191. LBI, MM 62, roll 104, ME 530, p. 168. Cf. Rudolf Kallner, *Herzl und Rathenau. Wege jüdischer Existenz an der Wende des 20. Jahrhunderts*, Stuttgart 1976, pp. 337ff.

[53]Walther Rathenau, 'Höre Israel!', in Walther Rathenau, *Impressionen*, Leipzig 1902, pp. 1–20. This text was published the first time in 1897.

[54]Ernst Schulin, 'Walther Rathenau und sein Integrationsversuch als "Deutscher jüdischen Stammes"', in Walter Grab (ed.), *Jüdische Integration und Identität in Deutschland und Österreich 1848–1918*, Tel Aviv 1984, pp. 13–41, esp. pp. 14ff., 25f.

[55]Walther Rathenau, 'Höre Israel', p. 186.

[56]Walther Rathenau, 'Staat', p. 185; Christian Schölzel, *Walther Rathenau 1867–1922 in Auseinandersetzung mit den Widersprüchen seiner Zeit*. Ph.D. thesis, Leipzig University 2002.

[57]Walther Rathenau, 'Staat', pp. 189f.

[58]In 1895 Walther Rathenau had filled out the appropriate form but did not sign it.

motivated by a desire to secure social advantages and not out of inner spiritual conviction. Walther Rathenau saw the conversion of Jews as tacit confirmation of the Prussian policy of treating Jews unequally. Instead of putting pressure on the state to change its policies, by converting one simply circumvented social barriers that were allowed to remain in place. Clearly, Fritz Rathenau's refusal to convert had motivations intersecting, at least in part, with Walther Rathenau's ideas on conversion – ideas with which the diary entry informs us Fritz Rathenau at least partly agreed.[59]

Both during and after the war, Fritz Rathenau would continue to be confronted by the antisemitism of his day. In 1918 his attempt to join the *Reichswirtschaftsamt* (Reich Ministry of Economics) failed – due, he claimed, to the antisemitic prejudices of the officials there.[60] Against this backdrop, what attitude had Fritz Rathenau developed towards Judaism by the end of the First World War? While before the war he spoke out in favour of a change in Prussian domestic policy towards the establishment of real equality between Jews and non-Jews, he regarded his own Jewishness in a context of acculturation. He rejected conversion as a means of achieving equal social status. His agreement with Walther Rathenau's ideas suggests he may well have himself regarded Jews as a "race". Fritz Rathenau's nationalist utterances throughout the war might be understood as not merely typical of their time but also as a sign of inclinations towards acculturation that his early experiences of antisemitism had led him to perceiving as necessary. For all his efforts to "adapt" to non-Jews, however, there are instances in which an affirmation of his Jewish identity can be seen: in his observance of Jewish holidays and in his rejection of conversion.

In the face of this attitude, both his strong public stand in defence of bourgeois society and his clear self-distancing from Bolshevism in 1918–1919 can be read in the context of his self-image as a Jew. The former could serve as a means of securing equal citizenship rights between Jews and non-Jews, while the latter coincided with a wish to dissociate himself from the stereotype of the Eastern European "Jewish Bolshevist".

This simultaneous attempt to affirm his own Jewishness while representing himself as both a devoted son of the Fatherland[61] and as a Jewish German orientated towards non-Jewish society would continue to characterise Fritz Rathenau's attitude into the post-war period, as would his efforts to distance himself from cultural and religious traditions seen as Eastern European Jewish. This is also demonstrated by his behaviour during the Kapp Putsch, which took place shortly after he began his work for the Prussian Ministry of the Interior.[62] With rebellious troops moving into position in Berlin, Jewish organisations feared that antisemitic riots might follow.[63] In the

---

[59]See LBI, MM 62, roll 104, ME 530, p. 7.

[60]LBI, MM 62, roll 104, ME 530, pp. 26f.

[61]Cf. the antisemitic stereotype of the *vaterlandslose Juden* since the Napoleonic wars in George L. Mosse, *Jüdische Intellektuelle in Deutschland. Zwischen Religion und Nationalismus*, Frankfurt am Main–New York 1992, p. 29f.; Sander L. Gilman, *Rasse, Sexualität und Seuche. Stereotype aus der Innenwelt der westlichen Kultur*, Reinbek 1992, pp. 181ff.

[62]CZA, Alfred Klee papers, A 142/87/40 (Alfred Klee [?], Report concerning the "Kapp-Putsch", probably after mid-March 1920). Cf. LBI, MM 62, roll 104, ME 530, pp. 49–52. Cf. Walther Rathenau, *Tagebuch*, pp. 230–234, describing Walther Rathenau's role as a negotiator during the coup.

[63]For this kind of raid see BAKO, Kl. Erwerbung 719–2, n.p., (Julius Hirsch, Friedrich Ebert, 1959); Hjalmar Schacht, *76 Jahre meines Lebens*, Bad Wörrishofen 1953, pp. 214f.

so-called *Scheunenviertel*, an area in which many Jews from Eastern Europe had settled, street patrols were set up to protect the local inhabitants. Jews who wore kaftans were advised to stay off the streets. As a member of the Jewish community's Assembly of Representatives, Alfred Klee appealed to Fritz Rathenau for troops to be stationed in the *Scheunenviertel* to protect the residents. Rathenau, who was in personal contact with Wolfgang Kapp during those days,[64] initially denied this request on the grounds that the units were untrustworthy and that their presence would only increase the risk of plundering. His own worry was that anti-Jewish riots might break out in Halensee or on the Kurfürstendamm, areas in which more successful, socially established Jews lived. But ultimately, he agreed to put some police and army units at Klee's disposal. Looking back, Klee observed of Rathenau: "He made a thoroughly assimilated but for the most part very reasonable and calm impression. He repeatedly emphasised that he himself was Jewish, but at the same time declared the mass immigration of *Ostjuden* to Germany to be a misfortune [*ein Unglück*]."[65]

Despite Rathenau's acculturationist and patriotic stance, he would not be immune to antisemitic hostility over the following decade as well. This is demonstrated by the story of his membership in the National-Liberal *Deutsche Volkspartei*, which he joined in 1926. After his attempt to stand as a candidate for the post of *Regierungspräsident* in Potsdam failed, in the course of discussions with party members, due to his Jewish background, Rathenau resigned from the party, protesting against its discriminatory treatment of Jews.[66] He also continued to suffer disappointments when it came to promotions within the bureaucratic hierarchy.[67]

Despite such experiences, Rathenau continued to link both his sense of duty as an official and his unconditional loyalty to the state apparatus to his own Jewishness. He was serving not only the German Reich but also the republican Fatherland. To fulfil one's duty in the interest of the state, and this to the furthest extent possible, was, in his opinion, also a virtue to be displayed by the Jewish official.[68] This attitude would also influence his later dealings as a ministerial counsellor with the "East" and with issues involving both Jewish and non-Jewish Eastern Europeans.

FRITZ RATHENAU AND THE "EAST"

Already before the outbreak of the First World War, we see indications that Fritz Rathenau's attitude towards Eastern Europe was influenced by widely spread negative stereotypes. In a comparative legal report on the development of patent law he

---

[64]LBI, MM 62, roll 104, ME 530, pp. 49–52.

[65]CZA Alfred Klee papers, A 142/87/40. Cf. LBI, MM 62, roll 104, ME 530, p. 34.

[66]LBI, MM 62, roll 104, ME 530, pp. 79, 99ff.; ZAF Research Foundation, Jewish Immigrants, MF 51, shoot 2129. Apparently Rathenau was a member of the National Liberal party before the First World War. Cf. the antisemitic encyclopaedia article 'Rathenau, Fritz', in E. Ekkehard (ed.), *Sigilla Veri. Stauff's Semi-Kürschner, Lexikon der Juden, -Genossen und -Gegner aller Zeiten und Zonen, insbesondere Deutschlands, der Lehren, Gebräuche, Kunstgriffe und Statistiken der Juden sowie ihrer Gaunersprache, Trugnamen, Geheimbünde usw.*, 2nd rev. edn., vol. 5 (Berlin 1932), pp. 228f.

[67]LBI, MM 62, roll 104, ME 530, pp. 57f., 61; in 1931 Rathenau was attacked in antisemitic fashion in the *Völkischer Beobachter*.

[68]LBI, MM 62, roll 104, ME 530, p. 52.

wrote: "It should come as no surprise that patent legislation in Russia is quite unde-veloped, even if Russia does have a new patent law (from 1896).[69] Here the old stereotype of the inability of "the Slavs" – in this case, "the Russians" – to build a state was being rehashed. After the end of the war and in the face of the October Revolution and the revolution in Germany, he warned: "Therefore, before the flood-waters [of Bolshevism] rise any further we must act quickly and energetically."[70] His rejection of the Soviet social model may well have itself been spurred by strong doubts about the ability of the "Slavs" to organise any viable society. In actuality, behind the fear of the "threat from the East" lurked a concern shared by many acculturated upper-class Jews about the wave of Jewish immigrants from Eastern Europe, whose presence in Germany threatened to revive antisemitism.[71]

After 1920, the immigration of both Jewish and non-Jewish Eastern Europeans to Prussia would become one of Rathenau's central areas of responsibility at the Prussian Ministry of the Interior.[72] Since the founding of the Weimar Republic, the principle of equal treatment for that which is essentially equal and unequal treat-ment only for that which is essentially unequal (*wesentlich Gleiches gleich und nur wesentlich Ungleiches ungleich zu behandeln*)[73] had been reinforced in numerous edicts from the ministry regarding immigration to Prussia of both non-Jewish and Jewish Eastern European foreigners. Inherent in the Enlightenment principle of the equality of all before the law was the notion that "unequal people" – in acknowledgement of their individuality – should be treated unequally (for example in the area of access to social welfare services). What remained to be resolved was the question of what def-inition of "difference" would appear to justify such unequal treatment in accordance with the principle of equality.

Subliminal antisemitic images of Jews influenced the way this basic democratic tenet was implemented by members of the bureaucratic apparatus. On the one hand, the tacit assumption of the racial inequality of Jews with respect to non-Jews and of Slavs with respect to non-Slavs appeared to justify discrimination against cer-tain people within the permitted constitutional framework. On the other hand, the prohibition, also deriving from constitutional law, placed on discrimination against citizens on the basis of their religious affiliation (Weimar Republic Constitution, arti-cles 135 and 136) imposed normative limitations on the Prussian administration.[74]

The groups of persons affected by these legal regulations and administrative prac-tices included Polish Jews who had been brought to Germany during the First World War to serve as labourers in the German wartime economy, military prisoners of war, refugees from pogroms in Poland at the end of the war, Poles in transit through Germany on their way overseas, war refugees, and immigrants who had fled from con-

---

[69]Fritz Rathenau, *Patent- und Gebrauchsmusterprozesse*, p. 483.

[70]Fritz Rathenau, *Parlament*, p. 37.

[71]Maurer, p. 174; Jacob Toury, 'Gab es ein Krisenbewußtsein unter den Juden während der "Guten Jahre" der Weimarer Republik, 1924–1929?', in *Tel Aviver Jahrbuch für deutsche Geschichte*, vol. 17 (1988), pp. 145–168.

[72]For example GSA, Rep. 77, Minsterium des Innern, Tit. 856, no. 37, pp. 364ff., 452ff.

[73]For example PA, file R 78705, pp. L 348566f., L348570, L348573.

[74]The Weimar *Reichsconstitution* did not incorporate protection against racial discrimination like the pres-ent-day Basic Law (*Grundgesetz*).

tinued fighting between Russia and Poland after the war, as well as those who had previously emigrated from Eastern Europe. In the minds of the representatives of
German officialdom, these Eastern Europeans were associated with threatening
images of "foreigners" (namely Jews and Slavs) flooding the country, of revolution and
economic collapse, as well as of the introduction and spread of infectious diseases.[75]

In the early years of the Weimar Republic, Eastern European Jews were not infrequently sent back to their countries of origin.[76] However, when it became apparent
in 1920 that many of those sent back to war-ravaged Poland were being refused
entry, officials at numerous departments throughout the German Reich and in
Prussia – Fritz Rathenau among them – decided to set up internment camps for such
refugees.[77] At a meeting of the representatives of various state authorities held in
August of that year, a proposal for establishing a labour camp was put forward by
the *Abeiterfürsorgeamt der jüdischen Organisationen Deutschlands* (Workers' Relief Bureau of
the Jewish Organisations in Germany). Initially it was envisioned as holding 700 people for five months; this number could rise to 2,000 at the most. The internees would
be charged five marks a day for food and lodging. It was hoped that the American
Jewish Joint Distribution Committee would provide the means for the maintenance
of the camp as well as raw materials for the workshops. The goods manufactured
would be sold in Poland and Lithuania. A site for the camp would have to be sought
close to Berlin. The protocol of the meeting stated:

> In the ensuing discussion about the advisability of this plan, the doubts that needed to be
> raised were not dismissed out of hand. In particular, it was pointed out that the setting up
> of a labour camp might [inadvertently] serve as a welfare measure that would encourage
> the immigration of Eastern-European Jews. Likewise the proposal to locate the camp near

---

[75]PA A. 78657, Bll. L. 329497–L 329507; *ibid.*, R 78705; GSA, Rep. 77 (Ministerium des Innern), Tit.
1814, no. 10, pp. 34–36, esp. p. 34; *ibid.*, Tit. 4036 no. 8, p. 7. Cf.: Ludger Heid, 'Die Pestbeule
Deutschlands: Ostjuden zwischen Erstem Weltkrieg und Weimarer Republik', in Wolfgang Dreßen (ed.),
Jüdisches Leben, Berlin 1985, pp. 24–43, esp. pp. 33f.

[76]GSA, Rep. 77 (Ministerium des Innern), Tit. 1814, no. 10, p. 34. PA, file R 78656, p. L 329158, file R
78660, file R 78705, from file R 82786 to file R 82789 (referring to Bavaria and Mecklenburg) and file
R 82781; Heid, *Maloche*.

[77]Maurer, pp. 416ff.; PA, file R 78656, pp. L 329206–329210; cf. *ibid.*, pp. L 329211–L 329213. Cf. in the
same collection, file R 78704 and file R 78705, pp. L 348545–L 348549, pp. L 348570–L 348573; Eike
Geisel, *Im Scheunenviertel. Bilder, Texte und Dokumente. Mit einem Vorwort von Günter Kunert*, Berlin 1981, p. 69.
Besides the camp in Cottbus-Sielow, further camps were established in former POW-camps in Stargard
and in Eydtkuhnen/East Prussia. For Stargard: GSA, Rep. 77 (Ministerium des Innern), Tit. 4036 no.
8, esp. pp. 39ff.; Eydtkuhnen: *ibid.*,p. 57; *ibid.*, p. 14 (Fritz Rathenau to the *Ministerialdirektor* Edgar Georg
Loehrs, 17 December 1920). On internment of foreigners in POW camps of the *Reichswehr* see Maurer,
p. 420; Geisel; PA, file R 78705, p. L 348728; GSA, Rep. 77, Ministerium des Innern, Tit. 4036 no. 9,
pp. 42f.; Yale University Library 1560, Moritz Schlesinger Papers, fol. 159 (Erich Köhrer, 'Besuch im
Interniertenlager', in *Berliner Börsen-Zeitung*, 25 December 1920). For Quedlinburg see Maurer, p. 426; for
Schneidmühl see PA, file R 82788, n.p. (Deutsches Generalkonsulat Posen to the Deutsche Konsulat
Thorn, 30 January 1924). On internment camps for East European Jews in Bavaria see Maurer, pp.
434f.; Dirk Walter, *Antisemitische Kriminalität und Gewalt. Judenfeindschaft in der Weimarer Republik*, Bonn 1999;
PA, file R 78716, pp. L 350234–L 350238. Cf. Wertheimer, *Strangers*, p. 51. On placement of the camp
in Cottbus under the control of the Prussian administration see PA, file R 82782, n.p. (the
Reichskommissar für Zivilgefangene und Flüchtlinge to the Foreign Office, "Abteilung IV. Polen", 12
December 1923). Cf. GSA, Rep. 77 (Ministerium des Innern), Tit. 4036, no. 8, pp. 2ff.

Berlin was considered inadvisable, as it was feared that a problematic situation would result from the anticipated participation of the internees in illegal businesses in Berlin.[78]

This passage quite clearly demonstrates the presence of antisemitic ideas in the discourse of the state officials. "*Ostjuden*" appeared as "greedy" and "criminal".[79] Assistance was to be coupled with the obligation to work. Alongside fiscal considerations, we can here see reflections of a "work ethic" passed down in antisemitic discourse over centuries, an ethic stipulating that Jews needed to perform physical, agricultural, or manual labour in order to become "useful" members of society.[80]

The labour camp, which was to be jointly administered by Prussia and the Reich, was only intended as a temporary measure; originally it was to close after at most one year, at the end of 1920. However, the forced internment of foreigners would simultaneously help to redress local housing shortages by freeing up flats for the "native-born" population. Thus it was planned to move entire families into the barracks. At the same time, arrangements were to be made to avoid any negative impact on the "German" labour and sales markets by the sale of products produced in the camp.

Against this background Rathenau, who had been involved in the discussions, drafted a text for Ministerial Director Edgar Georg Loehrs of the Prussian Ministry of the Interior, offering his perspective on the 'State of the Question of the Eastern European Jews'.[81] This document shows that, on the one hand, Rathenau sought to ease the suffering of many of the Eastern-European Jewish immigrants living in the German Reich. It also shows, on the other hand, that he did not entirely reject the position of the German authorities in favour of a restrictive immigration policy – a policy that was, as suggested, based on economic self-interest and strongly influenced by a brand of antisemitism shaped by racial ideology.[82] According to the decrees already issued by the Prussian government, Rathenau argued, any separate treatment of Eastern-European Jews vis-à-vis other foreigners was impermissible. There were five areas in which this had nevertheless taken place: 1) the issuing of identity cards; 2) placement in employment; 3) the limitation of reasons for deportation; 4) the restriction of authorisation for arrest in order to facilitate deportation; 5) the requirement of the administrative authorities to co-operate with Jewish relief organisations in looking after Eastern-European Jewish immigrants. Rathenau concluded:

> For the most part, however, this does not amount to preferential treatment for Eastern-European Jews. Rather the aim is to bring the bad situation of Eastern-European refugees into line with that of other foreigners, especially since, for reasons of language

---

[78]PA, file R 78656, pp. L 329207f.

[79]In this context cf. the antisemitic topic of the "Jewish Gold and Jewelry dealer": PA, file R 78705, pp. L 348530–L 348541, quotation: p. L 348532. Cf. *ibid.*, pp. L 348562, L 348724. Cf. these stereotypes in the files of the "Kaiserlich deutsche Kolonialverwaltung"in Bundesarchiv Berlin, R 151 F, Kaiserliches Gouvernement in Deutsch-Südwestafrika, MF FC 15063 file R XIV b. 1, pp. 6, 9.

[80]For this antisemitic work ethic see Christian Wilhelm Dohm, *Über die bürgerliche Verbesserung der Juden*, 2 parts, Berlin and Stettin 1781–1783. Cf. Maurer, pp. 419f.

[81]GSA, Rep. 77 (Ministerium des Innern), Tit. 4036, no. 8, pp. 15–24 (Fritz Rathenau, exposé, after 8 October 1920); cf. LBI, MM 62, roll 104, ME 530, pp. 34f.

[82]LBI, MM 62, roll 104, ME 530, p. 34.

and custom, they are in some cases not in a position to make themselves understood by the German authorities.[83]

At another point he continues: "The special measures ... were only intended to serve the purpose of integrating the Eastern-European Jews into the German economy as smoothly as possible and of keeping an eye on them while they are in the country, but also of protecting them from harassment by lower-level bureaucrats."[84] All told, Rathenau was appealing for help for the Eastern-European Jews without either abandoning the widely held stereotype about their "backwardness" or violating the principle of equality enshrined in the Weimar Constitution. The Ministry of the Interior, he continued, was determined to limit the influx of Eastern European Jews into Prussia. Foreigners with a criminal record as well as those who were "less than irreproachable"[85] should be deported. However, just as had been the case with conscientious objectors and deserters, this was unlikely to succeed, since there were no contractual agreements with the Polish authorities regarding the repatriation of these deportees. Such deportations were also forbidden under international law, but a possibility had recently been found for initially interning in such camps "all Eastern-European Jews, irrespective of rank, property or position, who are either criminals or are residing here despite already having been deported".[86] The national government would cover two-thirds of the cost of running the camps, while Prussia would come up with the remaining third. The supervision of the inmates would be carried out by units of the security police. To avoid social problems, Rathenau indicated, Eastern-European Jews were to be integrated into the German labour market, although, as before, priority was to be given to native Germans; alternatively, their passage on to third countries such as Palestine or Canada was to be facilitated.

Writing in 1922, in the face of the worsening economic situation, Rathenau would argue, in the same spirit, that it was important to prevent the "flooding of the German labour force by foreign workers".[87] He would end his remarks with a sort of argumentative "borderline position" between engagement on behalf of the Jews and sentiments fed by his own concept of acculturation, which, as has been suggested, he was trying to adapt to the anti-Jewish discourse within the Prussian administration. In the years that followed, he would make many efforts to balance these opposing tendencies in his self-image. Despite all the problems that the immigration of Eastern-European Jews may have caused, he maintained, under no circumstances were they to be subjected to worse treatment than other groups of migrants. Otherwise, one risked provoking a storm of indignation abroad – especially in Great Britain and the United States – over the "reactionary" (anti-Jewish) policies of the German state. The result might be that "the economic damage to our Fatherland would be greater than the potential damage caused by all the 80,000–100,000 Eastern-European Jews".[88] The number of such Jews in Germany was small, even if

[83]GSA, Rep. 77 (Ministerium des Innern), Tit. 4036, no. 8, pp. 15, 16.
[84]GSA, Rep. 77 (Ministerium des Innern), Tit. 4036, no. 8, pp. 15, 16.
[85]*ibid.*
[86]*ibid.*, p. 22.
[87]*ibid.*, no. 9, p. 131 (Fritz Rathenau during a meeting in the Prussian Ministry of the Interior, 18 October 1922).
[88]GSA, Rep. 77 (Ministerium des Innern), Tit. 4036, no. 8, p. 23.

this group included "criminals" and "Bolsheviks", who added new fuel to anti-semitism.[89] Rathenau argued not in terms of human dignity or tolerance, but in terms of "national reason", economic damage-limitation through a balancing of values, and the purported threat of pressure on Germany by the victorious powers. His arguments for the establishment of an internment camp were similar: legal, economic, and security aspects weighed more heavily than any potential moral objections to the internment of human beings in camps.[90] However, a central motivation behind this was fear of antisemitism spreading in Germany.

Apart from the internment camp at Cottbus, additional camps for "persons of foreign origin" were set up at Stargard (for 2,700 people, including women and children)[91] and at Eydtkuhnen in East Prussia (also for women and children).[92] After a time, the existence of such internment camps also became a topic of public discussion. On 15 January 1921 Mathilde Wurm, member of parliament for the *Unabhängige Sozialdemokratische Partei Deutschlands*, spoke out in the main committee of the *Reichstag* against the establishment of what she referred to as "concentration camps". The Jewish welfare organisations could just as easily keep the potential inmates occupied, she argued. The *Deutschnationale Volkspartei* demanded that relief services be left to private organisations, and the Minister of the Interior defended himself against the accusation that he was promoting antisemitic policies.[93] At around the same time, the cultural journal *Die Zukunft* – or, most likely, its publisher Maximilian Harden – also took a position on the subject.[94] The author of the article warned against the setting up of "concentration camps". By taking such repressive measures against immigrants, he argued, Germany would damage its reputation abroad, especially among Jewish organisations. This could also harm the country's foreign trade balance, which was just beginning to recover from the war. In addition it seemed to him that the policy towards Eastern-European Jews was primarily a class issue. The task at hand was to fight "racketeers" (*Schieber*), both large and small, of all religions and "races". Harden's own "Jewish self-hatred" is doubtlessly displayed in this opinion.

In reality, the decrees of the Prussian Ministry of the Interior on the internment of persons in camps contained racist clichés directed against Jews and Slavs. As a cost-saving measure, *fremdstämmige Ausländer* (foreigners of alien stock), for example,

---

[89]GSA, Rep. 77 (Ministerium des Innern), Tit. 4036, no. 8, pp. 37f. In a directive by Prussian Interior Minister Carl Severing to the Prussian Regierungs- und Oberpräsidenten dated 17 November 1920; Severing took the same position as Rathenau concerning the treatment of Eastern European Jews in Prussia.

[90]PA, file R 78705, pp. L 348733f. (Report about a meeting in the Prussian Ministry of the Interior, 17 November 1920). Rathenau referred to the thinking of officials at both the Prussian and the Reich Ministries of Justice regarding the implementation of forced labour in the internment camps and, if necessary, a shortening of the internees' rations.

[91]GSA, Rep. 77, Ministerium des Innern, Tit. 4036, no. 8, p. 42; PA, file R 82779, file R 82780, file R 82782, and file R 82785; Maurer, p. 424.

[92]For the expression "*Fremdstämmigen-Lager*" see GSA, Rep. 77, Ministerium des Innern, Tit. 4036, no. 8, p. 40, in the context of the discussion regarding the disinfection of the Stargard camp.

[93]PA, file R 78657, pp. L 329360f. Cf. detailed: Heid, *Maloche*, pp. 172ff., 178ff., 191ff.

[94]Anonymous [Maximilian Harden?], 'Von Bebel zu Babel. Juden, Ungarn, Unrecht, Militärputsch', in *Die Zukunft*, vol. 29 (1921), pp. 41–51; cf. Maurer, p. 422.

were to be interned in the camp at Stargard if they had either recently arrived in Germany or had committed crimes there. "Foreigners" could also be interned if they could not be deported because their home country would not accept them back. The note that "[t]his measure is also not to be applied with undue severity to Eastern-European Jewish immigrants" suggests antisemitic prejudices within the state administration that were not to be openly expressed.[95] At the end of 1922 the Prussian Minister of the Interior, Carl Severing, recommended to the German Minister of Foreign Affairs, Friedrich von Rosen, that rapid deportation proceedings be introduced and border controls intensified. In addition, Eastern-European immigrants should only be allowed to work on a temporary basis.[96] Severing feared that

> Even energetically and impeccably conducted police measures … must necessarily be inadequate in light of the dangers that threaten us from the flood of people of alien stock to whom Germany offers hospitality and asylum. This is not a racial question, let alone a question of Eastern-European Jewry as such.[97]

From this perspective, what was at stake was a migratory movement of world-historical significance, as well as the protection of the embattled German national economy against outside influences. In terms of state policy, the treatment of *Ostjuden* was not to be considered from the standpoint of race.[98] Importantly, these arguments, structured as they were in terms of racial ideology and economics and based in part on the historical theories of Count Gobineau and Houston Stewart Chamberlain, were not to be too openly publicised as the official stance of the state authorities. A confidential letter from Fritz Rathenau to Moritz Sobernheim of the Foreign Office, written around the same time, reflected similar motivations.[99] Following speculation in the *Jüdisch-Politische Nachrichten* concerning a decree by the Bavarian Ministry of the Interior directed against the proliferation of antisemitism in Bavaria, Rathenau had the text of the legal document in question reviewed. As he wrote to Sobernheim, he considered it unnecessary to discuss such a regulation publicly. The decree contained a warning that public order was threatened by increasing antisemitic propaganda calling for violence against Jews. Particularly in the countryside and in smaller towns, the police authorities were admonished to exercise special vigilance in order to inhibit such propaganda or to prevent assemblies of antisemites; the churches, schools and the press were instructed to combat hatred of Jews through appropriate education of the population. Rathenau recognised the explosive significance of this circular. As he had done in 1920, he now again took measures against antisemitic tendencies. At the same time, he was concerned with not overemphasising the

---

[95]PA, file R 78657, p. L 329525. Cf. *ibid.*, R 78705, pp. L 348558–L 348565 (Carl Severing to the Arbeiterfürsorgeamt der jüdischen Organisationen Deutschlands, 1 June 1920); cf. p. L. 348523. Cf. *ibid.*, R 78660, p. L 330013. Ruth Louise Pierson, *German Jewish Identity in the Weimar Republic*, Ph. D. thesis, Yale University 1970, pp. 34f.; Walter; Heid, *Maloche*, pp. 168f., 192ff.

[96]GSA, Rep. 77, Ministerium des Innern, Tit. 4036 no. 8, pp. 84–88 (27 December 1922).

[97]GSA, Rep. 77, Ministerium des Innern, Tit. 4036 no. 8, p. 84.

[98]GSA, Rep. 77, Ministerium des Innern, Tit. 4036 no. 8, p. 84.

[99]PA, file R 78657, pp. L 329758–L 329760 (Fritz Rathenau to Moritz Sobernheim and appendix, 9 September 1922).

presence of such tendencies. In this manner, he continued to vacillate between standing up for Jews and rigidly adhering to an acculturation-centred perspective.

After the peace treaty between Russia and Poland in March 1921 (the Treaty of Riga), the attitude of the Prussian Ministry of the Interior towards the immigration of Eastern Jews relaxed. According to the terms of the treaty, Germany was no longer bound to neutrality towards the formerly warring nations.[100] In a decree of 4 July 1921, the Prussian Minister of the Interior, Alexander Dominicus, ordered a review of the possibilities for facilitating the deportation of Eastern Europeans. According to the text only deserters should continue to be interned directly, in the Cottbus-Sielow camp.[101] Further stipulations of a similar nature followed until the middle of 1923. What remained was the consistent latent antisemitism or racism in the formulations.[102]

At the end of August 1921, the camp at Stargard was closed. However, this occurred less because of altered political circumstances than because of public protests over poor hygienic conditions, which had led to the outbreak of epidemics among the inmates. Additional factors included government spending cuts[103] and antisemitically motivated physical and verbal abuse of internees by guards. In 1923 the other internment camps were also closed.[104] Rathenau was involved in both the closing of the camps and the deportation of internees.[105]

A meeting held in early January 1923 between representatives of the Foreign Office, the Prussian Ministry of the Interior, and the German delegate to the League of Nations with responsibility for Russian refugees sought new possibilities for solving the "Eastern immigrant problem".[106] During the meeting Fritz Rathenau stated: "The issue here is not just the so-called *Ostjuden* but the numerous immigrants from the East more generally. The problem must be divested of its hateful character of a racial question. It can no longer be mastered by means of police measures."[107] Rathenau, who at that time was personally involved in police raids against Eastern European Jews in Berlin, was anxious to keep antisemitic prejudices out of the discussion. He nevertheless emphasised that "the question of the foreignisation (*Überfremdung*) of Germany is becoming increasingly urgent. In Breslau alone, 36.5% of all landed property is now in foreign hands."[108] On the one hand, Rathenau thus shared the criticism of this alleged "foreignisation"; on the other hand, he now increasingly translated the anti-Jewish discourse into an anti-Slavic one, or at least blended the

---

[100]Heid, *Maloche*, p. 154.

[101]PA, file R 78657, p. L 329526. Cf. *ibid.* R 78705, pp. L 348506f.

[102]For a detailed discussion see Maurer, pp. 427ff. PA, file R 78705, pp. L 348530–L 348541, quotation p. L 348532.

[103]Heid, *Maloche*, p. 154.

[104]GSA, Rep. 77, Ministerium des Innern, Tit. 4036 no. 8, p. 55. Cf. PA, file R 82781, n.p. ('Deutsch-polnischer Ausweisungskonflikt', in *Deutsche Rundschau*, 21 August 1923); *ibid.*, n.p. (Fritz Rathenau to the Foreign Office, 4 September 1923). Cf. *ibid.* R 82782; Heid, *Maloche*, pp. 203ff., 209ff.

[105]PA, file R 82781, n.p. (Fritz Rathenau to the Foreign Office, "Abteilung IV Polen", 13 September 1923). The letter also offers indications of internees escaping from the camp at Cottbus-Sielow. Cf. *ibid.*, file R 82782, n.p. (Fritz Rathenau to the Foreign Office, "Abteilung IV Polen", 17 November 1923).

[106]PA, file R 78705, esp. pp. L 348515–L 348518.

[107]*ibid.*, p. L 348515.

[108]*ibid.* Rathenau had already thought of the Jews in this context in 1920: LBI, MM 62, roll 104, ME 530, pp. 35f.; on razzias in the *Scheunenviertel* in 1920 see PA, file R 78705, pp. L 348721– L 348732; Heid, *Maloche*, p. 202.

two together. He hoped that Germany could "rid itself of Eastern immigrants".[109] Here his effort to combine acculturation with a stronger Jewish identity once again became evident. In the years leading up to 1933 Rathenau intensified this aspiration by incorporating the confrontation with the "East" into discourses both anti-Slav and hostile to the terms of the Versailles Treaty. The subjects of Jewry and anti-semitism retreated into the background. The confrontation with the topos of the "East" remained, however – facilitated no doubt by the expansion of his sphere of responsibilities after 1923, since Rathenau was by then increasingly preoccupied with "minority questions" in Prussia's eastern provinces.[110]

One form of "national delimitation" from the "East" that Rathenau was involved with after 1926 in the Prussian Ministry of the Interior was the distribution of funds for Prussia's Eastern aid programmes.[111] The general guidelines for subventions by the national and state governments in 1926 describe in some detail the type of projects with which he was concerned.[112] "This assistance ... can ... only be claimed for the support of purposes involving removal of the consequences of the war or the Treaty of Versailles and strengthening the present-day border region economically or ethnically [*volkspolitisch*]." In contemporary parlance, the term *volkspolitisch* meant a strengthening of "Germanness", *Deutschtum*. Fritz Rathenau was pursuing the policy target of revoking the terms of the Treaty of Versailles.[113] Discussions between representatives of Prussia and the relevant national authorities revealed substantial conflicts surrounding the subsidies that the national government was expected to pay.

In these discussions, Fritz Rathenau consistently promoted Prussian interests as a representative of his government department.[114] In a consultation of 9 May 1927 between representatives of the national and Prussian governments concerning the level of national-government subsidies for Eastern aid for 1927, he stated that there must be no cuts in the funds promised to Eastern Prussia by the national government.[115] The stipulations of the Treaty of Versailles had functioned as a kind of tourniquet, cutting off circulation to parts of the Prussian East:

> The state of the economy and of culture in the German border region should be the unifying moment for ethnic Germans [*Deutschstämmige*] living on foreign territory, whose eventual return to the territory of the German Reich we all hope for. For that reason, the German Reich must also contribute in its own interest to creating a cultural wall

---

[109]The transfer of the discourse is clearly visible in LBI, MM 62, roll 104, ME 530, p. 36. PA, file R 78705, p. L 348516. Cf. LBI, MM 62, roll 104, ME 530, p. 35.

[110]Cf. LBI, MM 62, roll 104, ME 530, pp. 67ff., 73, Cf. Rathenau's former concern with questions regarding the Paß-, Zoll- und Grenzwesen: PA, file R 78705, pp. L 348515–L 348518; *ibid.* R 82781f.; GSA, Rep. 77, Ministerium des Innern, Tit. 4036, nos. 11 and 13.

[111]LBI, MM 62, roll 104, ME 530, pp. 44ff., 60f., 73ff. GSA, Rep. 77 (Ministerium des Innern), Tit. 4036, no. 7. Cf. Martin Broszat, *Zweihundert Jahre deutsche Polenpolitik*, Frankfurt am Main 1972, pp. 226–233; Norbert Krekeler, *Revisionsanspruch und geheime Ostpolitik der Weimarer Republik. Die Subventionierung der deutschen Minderheit in Polen 1919–1933*, Stuttgart 1973.

[112]GSA, Rep. 77 (Ministerium des Innern), Tit. 4036, no. 7, p. 150, also for the following quotations.

[113]For example, *ibid.*, pp. 217–219, quotation p. 218.

[114]*ibid.*, pp. 321f. (Fritz Rathenau to the chargé d'affaires of the Schlesische Städte- und Handelskammern in Berlin, 16 May 1927).

[115]*ibid.*, pp. 274–283; for the following quotations: pp. 278, 281; *ibid.*, pp. 284–298.

Raid in Grenadierstrasse, Berlin-Mitte on 25 February 1920 - entry to premises is being blocked. (Picture ref. 183/H1030/500/2N)

By courtesy of Bundesarchiv (Koblenz)

Raid in Grenadierstrasse, Berlin-Mitte on 25 February 1920 - women arrested during the raid are taken to the 'Alexander' barracks. (Picture ref. 183/R98627)

By courtesy of Bundesarchiv (Koblenz)

in the East and the North, which will repel the Slavic and Danish flood and bring it to a standstill.[116]

This revisionist objective[117] was linked to the classic, stereotypical topos of the "German cultural wall" against the "Slavic flood", with its "lower capacity for culture". That this could also be associated with a defence against the Eastern Jews has already been indicated.

Rathenau's contacts, made in connection with his work distributing Eastern aid funds, with *Geheimer Regierungsrat* Professor Wilhelm Volz and the *Deutsche Mittelstelle für Volks- und Kulturbodenforschung* (DMVK; from early 1927 onwards known as the *Deutsche Stiftung für Volks- und Kulturbodenforschung*, or DSVK) in Leipzig were also bound up with his confrontation with ethnic policy – *Volkstumspolitik* – in the East. The organisation was founded in Berlin in January 1922 by *Volks- und Kulturboden* researchers Albrecht Penck and Wilhelm Volz, along with Karl Christian von Loesch,[118] and Rathenau's dealings with the DMVK reveal the extent and limitations of the influence exerted by an institution of German "research on the East" (*Ostforschung*) on his position as a ministry official. These dealings also reflect the particular notions of research held by the participants.[119]

The surviving correspondence between Wilhem Volz and the Prussian Ministry of the Interior, above all with Fritz Rathenau, begins in 1924.[120] Attempting to outline the DMVK's theoretical understanding, Volz indicated that the organisation had emerged out of a necessity to close knowledge gaps regarding the "Fatherland" and *Deutschtum*: "The enemy [Germany's former enemies in the First World War] was more farsighted and had worked purposefully long before the World War." Thus he formulated the objectives of his work as: "rooting out enemy literature and checking enemy work; the unmasking of incorrect and tendentious work. We [the DMVK] do not want to produce propaganda but must for our part provide flawless, irreproachable material for our government offices, etc.".[121] In these formulations, scholarly research, understood in the sense of, for instance, Max Weber, was subjected to nonscholarly determinants – political consulting and the legitimisation of nationalist-ideological arguments. Volz here defined efforts at empirical objectivity in negative

---

[116]With the term "Danish flood" Rathenau was indirectly referring to the problems of minorities and *Deutschtumspolitik* in Schleswig-Holstein with which he was also temporarily occupied; see GSA, Rep. 77 (Ministerium des Innern), Tit. 4036, no. 12; LBI, MM 62, roll 104, ME 530, esp. pp. 37ff., 45f., 62.

[117]GSA, Rep. 77 (Ministerium des Innern), Tit. 4036, no. 7, p. 564 (Fritz Rathenau, 'Der Widerstandswille des Ostens', in *Kölnische Volkszeitung*, 12 February 1930, p. 2.

[118]Karl Christian von Loesch, 'Das Ostproblem in der Aussenpolitik', in Arnold Killisch von Horn (ed.), *75 Jahre Berliner Börsen-Zeitung*, Berlin 1930, pp. II 3–II 7; Loesch demanded a revision of the Versailles Treaty.

[119]LBI, MM 62, roll 104, ME 530, pp. 44f. Cf. Michael Burleigh, *Germany turns Eastwards: A Study of Ostforschung in the Third Reich*, Cambridge 1988; Bernd Faulenbach, 'Nach der Niederlage. Zeitgeschichtliche Fragen und apologetische Tendenzen in der Historiographie der Weimarer Zeit', in Peter Schöttler (ed.), *Geschichtsschreibung als Legitimationswissenschaft 1918–1945*, 2nd edn., Frankfurt am Main 1999, pp. 31–51; Willi Oberkrone, 'Geschichte, Volk und Theorie. Das "Handwörterbuch des Grenz- und Auslandsdeutschtums"', *ibid.*, pp. 104–127, esp. pp. 106ff.

[120]GSA, Rep. 77 (Ministerium des Innern), Tit. 856, no. 298, pp. 1–29 (Wilhelm Volz to the Prussian Ministry of the Interior, 18 December 1924, and protocols of the conference).

[121]*ibid.*, pp. 3f., quotations: pp. 3, 4.

terms: "So-called German objectivity daily commits countless scholarly sins and all too often breaks the windows of its own Fatherland's house."[122] The self-definition of the DMVK thus taking shape both emerges from and furthers a central, ideologically distorted line of German research on "the East" since the turn of the twentieth century. Non-scholarly factors, diverting attention from an empirical exploration of autonomous areas of research, were at work here to varying degrees; we need only think of the appointment in 1892 of the German-Baltic historian Theodor Schiemann, with the strong support of Wilhelm II, as a professor of Russian History at the *Friedrich-Wilhelms-Universität* in Berlin.

Such ideological factors run, in fact, like a red thread through the general history of German scholarship down to the early post-Second World War period (and sometimes beyond) in both German states – albeit with many differences in intensity, context, and content that cannot be detailed here. The extent to which the objectives of scholarly political advice formulated by Volz harmonised with the inclinations of the state authorities concerned is documented by a letter from the Reich Ministry of the Interior to Volz.[123] Referring to the DMVK conference in the autumn of that year, the Ministry welcomed the results of the conference and the nature of the *volkspolitische* activities of the DMVK that had become evident there.[124] Both the Reich Ministry of the Interior and the Prussian Ministry of Science, Art, and Education would consistently offer financial support for the meetings and publications of the DMVK/DSVK.[125] The same cannot, however, be said of the Prussian Ministry of the Interior.[126] Nevertheless contacts between Volz and Rathenau as representatives of, respectively, the DMVK/DSVK and the Prussian Interior Ministry did initially became closer. Volz regularly invited Rathenau to DMVK/DSVK events, and Rathenau generally accepted. In the summer of 1925 the director of the DMVK requested Fritz Rathenau's assistance in influencing the local authorities to allow the organisation to hold its conference of 10–12 October 1925 at the historic Marienburg Castle, and Rathenau granted the request, emphasising his own willingness to support the DMVK, since he was "convinced of the extraordinarily beneficial and fruitful work" it was doing. Ultimately he succeeded in securing some of the rooms for the conference.[127] In so doing, he was making the castle of the Teutonic Order – the Prusso-German national symbol of the "German struggle in the East"[128] – available to the DMVK, once again demonstrating his approval of their work – and also his own "national sentiments".

---

[122]GSA, Rep. 77 (Ministerium des Innern), Tit. 856, no. 298, p. 3.

[123]*ibid.*, pp. 30f.

[124]*ibid.*, p. 30.

[125]*ibid.*, p. 166 (Wilhelm Volz to Fritz Rathenau, 7 February 1927).

[126]*ibid.*, pp. 236, 362f. Concerning this support see *ibid.*, pp. 64, 269; *ibid.*, pp. 236, 362f.

[127]*ibid.*, p. 68 (Wilhelm Volz to Fritz Rathenau, 13 July 1925); *ibid.*, p. 69 (Fritz Rathenau to the Regierungspräsident [?] Brauweiler, 31st July 1925); *ibid.*, p. 72 (Fritz Rathenau to Wilhelm Volz, 17 August 1925).

[128]Concerning the symbolism of the Marienburg from about 1800 onwards see Sven Ekdahl, 'Denkmal und Geschichtsideologie im polnisch-preussischen Spannungsfeld', in Klaus Zernack (ed.), *Zum Verständnis der Polnischen Frage in Preussen und Deutschland 1772–1871. Referate einer deutsch-polnischen Historiker-Tagung vom 14. bis 16. Januar in Berlin-Nikolassee*, Berlin 1987, pp. 127–218, esp. pp. 128ff., 192ff.; Wolfgang Wippermann, *Der Ordensstaat als Ideologie*, Berlin 1979.

After attending the organisation's 16th conference, held in Glogau from 4–6 October 1928, on the subject of "Greater Poland", Fritz Rathenau became less enthusiastic about the scholarly qualities of the DSVK's work.[129] In a letter to Volz written a few days after the conference, Rathenau laid out his criticisms of the increasingly evident self-understanding of the *Ostforscher* in Glogau.[130] "Both the choice of individual themes and their treatment by some speakers and discussion participants have given me cause for severe misgivings." Rathenau continued: "I believe that the conferences are descending from the heights of objective scholarly observation into the dangerous waters of current political struggle." He thus recommended that the agendas and choice of speakers for future conferences be discussed in advance with the Prussian Ministry of the Interior.[131] Volz responded within a few days.[132] He was apologetic but avoided expressing any clear position on the points Rathenau had made. In closing, Volz underlined the significance of the task of guiding scholars towards patriotism and agreed that for him, scholarship continued to be unpolitical; however, it was obliged to at least keep the political side of its activities in mind.

Through his reply, Volz in fact succeeded in securing Rathenau's continued support of the DSVK, since the ministerial counsellor was not able to formulate a clear counter-position on the definition of scholarliness. For years he had looked favourably upon the DMVK/DSVK's politicised notion of scholarship and now was criticising its excessive orientation towards current politics. Despite its sharper tone, Rathenau's critique did not actually represent a fundamental rejection of his previous position towards the DSVK's brand of scholarship.[133] In a report to the Prussian Ministry of the Interior on the DSVK's autumn conference of 1929 on the 'Border-region of Silesia', he commented on the lectures presented there by stating that "naturally not all of them were on the same high scholarly level".[134] The low quality of the political lectures, which Rathenau criticised, was attributed to wrong choices on the part of the DSVK. But despite all such misgivings, he did not sever his ties with the DSVK, but rather joined its board of directors.[135] In this capacity, he succeeded in securing tax-free status for the organisation.[136]

Why did Rathenau continue to offer his services to the DMVK/DSVK, despite his repeated criticisms of its work? Did this reflect attitudes typical of the era, an embrace of nationalist-revisionist models of scholarship, the desire to retain the influence of the Prussian administration on this particular area of scholarship – or were there other motives? Presumably, membership in a coalition of the "patriotically minded" such as the DMVK/DSVK meant an acceptance of his patriotic-acculturative aspirations in a way that could not be matched by either Wilhelminian or even Republican German society. Quite clearly, the anti-Slavism often present in the DSVK's scholarship allowed a transfer of the negative image of the Eastern-

[129]GSA, Rep. 77 (Ministerium des Innern), Tit. 856, no. 298, pp. 321–346, here: p. 324.
[130]*ibid.*, pp. 347f., quotations: p. 347 (Fritz Rathenau to Wilhelm Volz, 9 October 1928).
[131]*ibid.*, p. 347.
[132]*ibid.*, pp. 349–352 (Wilhelm Volz to Fritz Rathenau, 17 October 1928).
[133]*ibid.*, pp. 359ff., 364.
[134]*ibid.*, pp. 367f., here p. 367.
[135]*ibid.*, p. 371.
[136]*ibid.*, pp. 376ff., 407.

European Jew onto the Slav. In this manner, it would appear, Rathenau could avoid a personal confrontation with the potentially compromising problem of Jewish existence in Germany, while at the same time maintaining his specific, acculturative self-definition and a correspondingly dissociated counter-image: the "Slav" as replacement for the Eastern-European Jew.

Into the early 1930s, Rathenau's publications continued to advocate an anti-Slavism directed mainly against Poles, with a clearly German-nationalist and anti-Versailles tenor.[137] Here, too, we see signs of the displacement of an internal Jewish discourse onto the contemporary anti-Slavic discourse. Germans were of a different "race" from the Poles, and were superior to them in civilisation and culture. German "cultural ground" (*Kulturboden*) needed to be "defended": "German culture is powerful enough, German *Volkstum* is strong and youthful enough, to compete successfully with other cultures."[138]

Elsewhere, he asserted that "In terms of constitutional law, the Polish minority in Prussia can thus only be referred to as 'Polish Prussians' in the sense of Prussian nationals of Polish stock [*Stamm*]."[139] Was not Rathenau's attempt to claim rights for minorities in Prussia under German-national premises – that is, to emphasise his own tolerance of minorities and at the same time call for the integration of Poles in Germany – also an attempt to attain equality as a "patriot", and as a member of the long-disadvantaged Jewish minority, within the context of acculturation?

THE FAILURE OF ACCULTURATION AND THE CHANGE IN FRITZ RATHENAU'S JEWISH SELF-IMAGE

Despite his continued adherence to the concept of acculturation and to nationalistic ideas, Fritz Rathenau continued to be confronted repeatedly with the problem of antisemitism.[140] Even before the end of the Weimar Republic, he advocated the participation of the Nazi Party in the government, hoping that in this way it would exhaust its appeal and those capable of insight would abandon their antisemitism.[141] Later he wrote: "I encountered complete rejection [of this view] only amongst my Zionist colleagues, who pointed out in no uncertain terms that, once in the saddle, the Nazis would never voluntarily dismount. They [the Zionists] were right!"[142]

On 31 January 1933 he went to work as usual. While a crowd singing the "*Horst-Wessel-Lied*" and chanting "*Juda verrecke!*" gathered outside the Prussian Ministry of the Interior demanding to see Hermann Göring, Rathenau watched from inside the building. In retrospect, he noted with regret that

> Despite these expressions of the most abject hatred, I was infected by the enthusiasm of the masses and was extremely impressed. ... I saw in it the realisation of the democratic

---

[137]Fritz Rathenau, 'Staaten'; LBI, MM 62, roll 104, ME 530, pp. 65ff., 70f., 80, 88, 92ff.; *idem*, 'Nationalitäten'; *idem*, *Ostnot; idem, Polonia.*

[138]Fritz Rathenau, *Polonia*, p. 76; cf. pp. 73ff.

[139]Fritz Rathenau, *Polonia*, p. 3. The expression *Stamm* is used synonymously with *Rasse*; cf. *ibid.*, p. 10.

[140]LBI, MM 62, roll 104, ME 530, p. 89.

[141]*ibid.*, pp. 111ff.

[142]*ibid.*, p. 111.

idea that the people … must be able to create that form of government which appears most appropriate to them! Today, I can only lament: Oh, what a fool I was![143]

After the National Socialists came to power, Fritz Rathenau remained in office. He did not wish to allow himself to be forced out, resolved to "stand fast", and insisted on upholding the duties of a civil servant bound by the democratic rule of law – even under Minister Hermann Göring.[144] But increasingly, he recognised the hopelessness of his conduct, that National Socialism would be no mere interregnum. He managed to protect a colleague from arrest by the Gestapo, hoped to "save what [could] be saved", protested to his superiors about the expropriations and other assaults on Jews. Then in August 1933, he was forced to resign from his post in the Ministry of the Interior.[145] In November he was placed, as a *Regierungsrat*, in a less important position in the office of the president of Berlin's building and finance authority.[146] In 1935 he was dismissed from that position in the wake of an antisemitic defamation campaign. Shortly after his forced retirement, the Nuremberg Laws came into effect, which would have made it impossible for him to remain a civil servant in any event.[147] Later Rathenau believed that he "had done his duty" as a Jew. At the beginning of the Nazi period he had still hoped that he could be of some use as a civil servant. However, like many others he ended up acknowledging that he should have recognised the regime's nature earlier.[148]

In retirement in Nazi Germany, Fritz Rathenau felt, not surprisingly, at a loss and marginalised.[149] In any case, he had been actively involved in the *Reichsvertretung der deutschen Juden* from its creation in July 1933, secret meetings of the organisation actually being held at his home. Through his contacts with Leo Baeck, Max M. Warburg, Heinrich Stahl and others, he did his best to protect Jews from attacks within Germany and make it easier for them to emigrate. But organisational problems within the *Reichsvertretung* prompted rebukes on his part of fellow members, along with a call for more unity between competing Jewish organisations, from different regions and with differing aims, in face of the Nazi threat. What mattered, Rathenau argued, was that Jews preserve a self-assured sense of honour in their dealings with the outside world. At the same time, he recommended that Jews living abroad be excluded from participation in the *Reichsvertretung* – either, he indicated, they protested too openly or too little against antisemitism in Germany, thus endangering the German Jews.[150]

---

[143]*ibid.*, p. 115.

[144]*ibid.*, p. 159.

[145]*ibid.*, pp. 81ff., 115ff., 118ff.

[146]Cf. in this context and for the following: *ibid.*, pp. 81, 124ff.; ZAF Research Foundation, Jewish Immigrants, MF 51, shoot 2128; Röder *et al.* (eds.), p. 584; Preußisches Staatsministerium (ed.), *Handbuch für den Preußischen Staat*, vol. 138 (1934), p. 335.

[147]LBI, MM 62, roll 104, ME 530, pp. 124ff.

[148]*ibid.*, p. 107, cf. p. 126.

[149]*ibid.*, pp. 139ff., 151.

[150]*ibid.*, pp. 123, 137ff., 141ff. On the founding process and first years of the *Reichsvertretung* see Avraham Barkai, 'Organisation und Zusammenschluß', in Michael A. Meyer *et al.* (eds.), *Deutsch-Jüdische Geschichte der Neuzeit*, vol. 4, *Aufbruch und Zerstörung 1918–1945*, Munich 1997, pp. 249–271, here pp. 250ff.; Michael A. Meyer, 'Im Schatten der Verfolgung und Vernichtung. Leo Baeck in den Jahren des NS-Regimes', in Fritz Backhaus and Georg Heuberger (eds.), *Leo Baeck 1873–1956. Aus dem Stamme von Rabbinern*, Frankfurt am Main 2001, pp. 77–102; Wolfgang Benz (ed.), *Die Juden in Deutschland. Leben unter nationalsozialistischer Herrschaft*, Munich 1988, pp. 49–75.

Put forward in the spring of 1935, Rathenau's recommendation was rejected by the *Reichsvertretung*. A few months later, Julius Hirsch, Warburg, and Baeck also rejected his idea of organising a protest by distinguished German Jews to be presented to Hitler, Göring, the Reich government, the world – put into practice, this notion was likely to endanger the remaining Jews in Germany. Instead, they decided to have a declaration from the *Reichsvertretung* concerning the situation of the Jews in Germany read aloud in all synagogues. But the Gestapo intercepted the text, and this plan had to be abandoned. At the end of 1935 Rathenau, more pessimistic than he had ever been about the future of Germany's Jews, distanced himself from the *Reichsvertretung*.[151] While himself inclined to encourage an at least partial measure of Jewish solidarity, he likewise felt that as a group, the Jews should not present themselves too publicly as that might have had a compromising effect, thus further inciting antisemitism.[152]

In Rathenau's eyes, the concept of acculturation he had believed in had failed. His attitude towards the *Reichsvertretung*, and thus to an alternative concept of Jewish solidarity, nevertheless remained ambivalent. With the threat to life and limb growing in Nazi Germany, he did gradually place more emphasis on his Jewish identity. His unpublished autobiography, *1895–1935. Als Jude im Dienste von Reich und Staat*, probably largely written in the period leading up to his emigration in 1939–1940, with some smaller sections written shortly after his emigration, is a reflection of such a complex shift in Rathenau's sense of core identity.[153] Basing his comments on his own experience as both a German Jew and a civil servant, Fritz Rathenau expressed the desire to "test whether we could or ought to have sensed our impending fate at least more clearly. Is it not our fault that the majority of us were caught unawares and for that very reason were hit doubly hard?"[154] Unlike other passages written somewhat later,[155] he here placed responsibility not on society's antisemitic majority but rather on a purported failure of the discriminated minority to have seen the dangers sooner. In some formulations, he continued to lapse into racist generalisations about Jews. He cited their "different nature", their "appearance, manner [*Gebahren*], knowledge and abilities, industriousness and activity [*Aktivität*], great eloquence and a certain theatrical talent" as among the factors that had generated the current antisemitism.[156] Such attitudes contrasted sharply with a basic question posed at the beginning of his work: would it not have been better to have succumbed earlier to the Zionist demands and emigrated to Palestine? Both the German-Jewish middle class and more recent Jewish immigrants from the East should, he insisted, have developed a common national feeling far sooner. Their error had consisted in not developing a sense of mutual solidarity, an awareness of the dangers posed by anti-

---

[151]LBI, MM 62, roll 104, ME 530, pp. 150ff. Cf. the declaration by, presumably, Rathenau in Benz (ed.), *Juden*, p. 64.

[152]LBI, MM 62, roll 104, ME 530, pp. 20, 61, 110.

[153]*ibid.*, pp. 6, 8, 42, 72, 164f., 175ff., 180f., 193ff.

[154]*ibid.*, p. 1.

[155]*ibid.*, on p. 165 he states that the German people supported Hitler and are responsible for the misery of the Jews. Rathenau probably wrote this portion of the text in 1940.

[156]*ibid.*, pp. 177f. *ibid.*, p. 19, regarding the question of specific technical abilities of Jews; *ibid.*, p. 148 regarding the "Jewish appearance" of the economist Julius Wolff; *ibid.*, p. 155 regarding the question of a possible trait of "oriental fatalism" in Jews.

semitism for Jews across the board.[157] In taking this position, Rathenau was, of course, also calling into question his own work as a civil servant, his long struggle to fulfil his duty to the German nation while remaining an unconverted Jew.[158] At this late point, he had thus come to the conclusion that the emancipation of the German Jews had failed.[159]

These reflections were bound up with thoughts of emigration:

> Today, now that the word has been spoken that WE [the Jews] are the enemy, even the elderly and those who have been deeply rooted in the country for centuries will scarcely be able to wait much longer. I myself had indeed always believed that I would find my final resting place in this soil, sooner or later. Today I no longer dare to believe this. ... Very hard, very bitter! For we were devoted with every fibre of our being to the people and the land in whose midst we, like our fathers, lived, for which we worked and, like everyone else, made sacrifices, whose language we spoke and in whose surroundings we grew up! We wish neither to complain nor to accuse! It is fate, not even a new one, but one we have borne and ... yet survived for thousands of years! But an inner voice keeps asking: Why has the world not changed in all this time? And why was my generation blind? There is probably no answer to these cruel doubts. ... In my opinion, at least, there can be but one slogan: pack carefully and march off! IMMEDIATE programmes must be set up! We must avoid all fragmentation and combat every partisan standpoint (Zionist or non-Zionist). Not flight but retreat with honour![160]

Fritz Rathenau did not know when he and his wife would emigrate. He did not want to go to Palestine, feeling too old. But perhaps he would have no other choice.

In 1939, with the deterioration in the living conditions of Germany's Jews and the arrest of his brother Kurt, Fritz Rathenau and his wife followed their children's example and emigrated to the Netherlands, a step that had been proceeded by long discussions.[161] Once in that country, he despaired at not being able to find any appropriate work. Fritz Rathenau studied Dutch, but both he and his wife felt uprooted.[162] Some four years later, in the spring of 1943, Fritz and Sophie Rathenau were deported to Theresienstadt.[163] Here he met judicial counsellor Julius Magnus,

[157]*ibid.*, pp. 1, 175ff. Cf. *ibid.*, pp. 181ff.

[158]*ibid.*, pp.191ff.

[159]*ibid.*, pp. 193f.

[160]For here and below see Yad Vashem S 26/9703 (Fritz Rathenau to Werner Senator, undated copy, between 1935 and 1939). The recipient was a member of the *Arbeiterfürsorgeamt*. Similar passages in LBI, MM 62, roll 104, ME 530.

[161]*ibid.*, pp. 87, 157, 159; ZAF Research Foundation, Jewish Immigrants, MF 51, shoots 2122, 2127–2129, 2132, 2137, 2147, 2157. LBI, MM 62, roll 104, ME 530, pp. 118f., 151f., 157.

[162]LBI, MM 62, roll 104, ME 530, pp. 8, 157, 164.

[163]List of the survivors of the concentration camp Theresienstadt], Terézin, n.d., pp. IX, XXII, 372. Fritz Rathenau was deported with the first transport from the Netherlands to the camp. The transport carried the number XXIV/1 and was dated 22 April 1943. Cf. Käthe Starke, *Der Führer schenkt den Juden eine Stadt. Bilder – Impressionen – Reportagen – Dokumente*, Berlin 1975, pp. 248, 252; H[ans] G[ünther] Adler, *Theresienstadt 1941–1945. Das Antlitz einer Zwangsgemeinschaft. Geschichte. Soziologie. Psychologie*, 2nd rev. edn., Tübingen 1960, p. 811. According to Adler, Rathenau wrote a memorandum about the camp. Information received in response to a request has indicated that no documentation concerning Fritz Rathenau is available in the archives of the Terézin memorial site. For information concerning the arrival of the 295 individuals in the transport that included Rathenau, see Miroslav Kárny, 'Theresienstädter Dokumente II', in *Judaica Bohemiae*, vol. 18, no. 2 (1982), pp. 65–87, esp. p. 69.

whom he had known from the time when he had been a judge and whose death in the camp in 1944 he would witness.[164] As a so-called *Prominenter*, Rathenau would be forced to participate in the filming, in August and September 1944, of the Nazi propaganda piece *Theresienstadt. Ein Dokumentarfilm aus dem jüdischen Siedlungsgebiet* (*Theresienstadt. A Documentary from this Jewish Place of Settlement*) directed by the German-Jewish Theresienstadt inmate Kurt Gerron.[165] Barbara Felsmann's comment about Gerron also holds true for Fritz Rathenau's participation in the film: "Under the circumstances, surrounded by the SS, which oversaw every stage direction, every gesture, every glance, with suspicion, it was unthinkable to undermine the intentions of those who had commissioned the film, to inscribe oppositional messages from the position of a victim, a position of absolute defencelessness."[166]

After the liberation of Theresienstadt by Soviet troops at the end of the war, the Rathenaus moved back to the Netherlands, settling in Bilthoven. Shortly before his death, Fritz Rathenau appears to have revised his autobiography. It remains an open question whether it was only then, or already in 1939–1940, that he decided to explain his behaviour to his sons, above all concerning his long hesitation about emigrating.[167] He did not mention his time in the concentration camp.[168] He died on 15 December 1949.[169]

CONCLUSION

Against the background of his oscillation between Jewish acculturation and Jewish identification, Fritz Rathenau distanced himself to a great extent from Eastern-

---

[164]LBI, MM 62, roll 104, ME 530, p. 19.

[165]On the *"Prominente"* see Ruth Bondy, *"Elder of the Jews": Jakob Edelstein of Theresienstadt. Translated from the Hebrew by Evelyn Abel*, New York 1989, pp. 322f.: The so-called "prominents" received certain privileges in the camp. Those were, among other things, not having to do forced labour and for some of them, alleged protection from being deported to an extermination camp. On the "prominents' houses", see Starke, pp. 47ff. (Käthe Starke was temporarily a member of the *Kommando* that had to clean these accommodations.) Dokumentationsarchiv des Österreichischen Widerstandes (ed.), *Totenbuch Theresienstadt. Damit sie nicht vergessen werden*, Wien 1987, pp. 1.11, 1.18. Cf. Ludmila Chládková, *Ghetto Theresienstadt*, Terezín 1991, p. 24.

Most of the Jews deported from Holland were accommodated in the ghetto's "Hamburger Kaserne". See H. G. Adler (ed.), *Die verheimlichte Wahrheit. Theresienstädter Dokumente*, Tübingen 1958, pp. 324–330, esp. pp. 328, 330. During the filming in the middle of August 1944, Fritz Rathenau was filmed according to the director's stipulations. He sat on a terrace together with former Czechoslovakian Secretary of Justice Alfred Meissner, former French Premier Léon Blum, and Georg Gradnauer, earlier Minister of the Interior of the Reich and Saxonian Prime Minister. About the film production and its history, see Starke, pp. 128ff., 211f.; Karl Löwenstein, *Theresienstadt*, typescript without location or date (manuscript of the Bibliothek der Jüdischen Gemeinde zu Berlin), pp. 52ff.; Felsmann, esp. pp. 88ff., 104ff. On Gerron see Barbara Felsmann and Dieter Prümm, *Kurt Gerron – Gefeiert und gejagt 1897–1944. Das Schicksal eines deutschen Unterhaltungskünstlers: Berlin, Amsterdam, Theresienstadt, Auschwitz*, Berlin 1992, p. 230: The original title of the film was not, as is commonly thought, 'Der Führer schenkt den Juden eine Stadt'.

[166]Felsmann *et al.*, p. 230.

[167]LBI, MM 62, roll 104, ME 530, pp. 8f., 11, 41, 94, 109, 165. Rathenau continued to maintain that if his policies on Poland had been implemented, attacking the country could have been avoided.

[168]LBI, MM 62, roll 104, ME 530, p. 19.

[169]Starke, pp. 162ff.; ZAF Research Foundation, Jewish Immigrants, MF 51, shoot. 2124.

European Jews whom he defined as an out-group. Frequently confronted with anti-semitism, he sought to keep the theme of discrimination against Jews away from centre stage, displacing discourses on *Ostjuden* onto views of Eastern European foreigners and "Slavs" that were typical of the era. In Rathenau's case, the use of concepts that would eventually be appropriated by his, and the Jewish people's, fanatical persecutors thus did not merely reflect a reception of contemporary clichés, but also sprang from a desire to avoid being subjected to discrimination.

In his "identity as a search for an identity" and his demonstration of a "situational ethnicity" that, in retrospect, can be understood as having permitted only a temporary duality between Germanness and Jewishness, between the majority and the minority, Fritz Rathenau was paradigmatic of the Jewish middle class in late Imperial Germany and the Weimar Republic. The same may be said for the failure of his concept of acculturation after 1933, a failure that he himself would, in the end, confirm.[170]

---

[170]Till van Rahden, 'Weder Milieu noch Konfession. Die situative Ethnizität der deutschen im Kaiserreich in vergleichender Perspektive', in Olaf Blaschke *et al.* (eds.), *Religion im Kaiserreich. Milieus – Mentalitäten – Krisen*, Gütersloh 1996, pp. 409–434. Rahden's term "situative ethnicity" is most sustainable in a comparative perspective focusing on the collective identity of Jews in Germany. Cf. Anthony Kauders, 'False Consciousness? "German-Jewish" Identity after Emancipation', in *Tel Aviver Jahrbuch für deutsche Geschichte*, vol. 28 (1999), pp. 459–475, warning against an excessively rigid and bipolar presumption of a "German majority" and a "Jewish minority". Cf. Pierson; Yfaat Weiss, *Deutsche und polnische Juden vor dem Holocaust. Jüdische Identität zwischen Staatsbürgerschaft und Ethnizität 1933–1940*, Munich 2000, pp. 11ff., 219ff.; Jacques Ehrenfreund, *Mémoire juive et nationalité allemande. Les juifs berlinois à la Belle Époque. Préface d´ Etienne François*, Paris 2000, pp. 3ff.; Shulamit Volkov, 'Jüdische Assimilation und jüdische Eigenart im Deutschen Kaiserreich. Ein Versuch', in *Geschichte und Gesellschaft*, vol. 9 (1983), pp. 331–348, esp. pp. 332, 347; Dolores L. Augustine, 'Die jüdische Wirtschaftselite im wilhelminischen Berlin Ein jüdisches Patriziat?', in Reinhard Rürup (ed.), *Jüdische Geschichte in Berlin. Essays und Studien*, Berlin 1995, pp. 101–116; David Sorkin, 'The Impact of Emancipation on German Jewry: A Reconsideration', in Jonathan Frankel *et al.* (eds.), *Assimilation and Community: The Jews in Nineteenth-century Europe*, Cambridge 1992, pp. 177–198. Dolores L. Augustine, *Patricians and Parvenues. Wealth and High Society in Wilhelmine Germany*, Oxford and Providence 1994, p. 11. The questions debated in this context are connected with the older discussion of a "German-Jewish symbiosis".

Shattered Hopes under National Socialism

Emancipation and Assimilation in the German-Jewish Discourse of the 1930s*

BY GUY MIRON

I

In the December 1931 issue of *Der Morgen*, the monthly of the *Centralverein deutscher Staatsbürger jüdischen Glaubens* (C.V.), Selma Stern published an article concerned with basic issues of Jewish emancipation and assimilation.[1] The problems with these two concepts, Stern wrote, were not merely historical, but remained part of the reality of German Jewish life, and would continue to do so. Stern distinguished between emancipation – the process of Jewish social and cultural integration into the body of the state – and assimilation. Emancipation, she explained, was based on a non-Jewish movement and the Jews had only accepted it passively. It was a lengthy process, already begun in the absolutist state before the end of the eighteenth century, motivated by the state's self-interest.[2] The modern constitutional state of the nineteenth century merely completed and formalised this process by granting the Jews equal rights.

Unlike emancipation, Stern continued, assimilation was an inner-Jewish phenomenon, one that "stands before the [Jewish] individual every day and every hour and demands from him a new answer and a solution time and again".[3] Whereas the processes of Jewish emancipation in the modern state could be examined in an objective-scientific manner, Stern regarded the enduring dynamics of the assimilation question as interfering with any cogent explanation of the integration of the Jews into their surrounding world.[4] She described the struggles and identity dilemmas of Moses Mendelssohn, Rahel Varnhagen and Henriette Herz, Heinrich Heine, Moses Hess, and Ferdinand Lassalle as personal experiences that reflected different balances in the tension between Judaism and Germanness, and she concluded with a description of the present generation as torn between two worlds, while nevertheless searching for new ways to link them.

*This article was written with the support of the Warburg fund of the Institute for Jewish Studies at the Hebrew University of Jerusalem. My English translation of the original Hebrew text was made possible through the kind support of the university's Richard Koebner Center of German History. The author thanks Dr. Arieh B. Saposnik for editing the translation, and Dr. Jacob Borut and Ms. Havi Ben Sasson for their helpful comments.

[1]Selma Stern, 'Probleme der Emanzipation und der Assimilation', in *Der Morgen*, vol. 7, no. 5 (1931), pp. 423–439.
[2]This was Selma Stern's thesis in *idem, Der preussische Staat und die Juden*, Berlin 1925.
[3]Stern, 'Probleme der Emanzipation', p. 424.
[4]*ibid.*, pp. 437–438.

Stern was associated with German Jewry's liberal wing and expressed a corresponding position. Jewish liberals were not willing to identify themselves as "assimilating", a title that both Zionists and Orthodox Jews pinned on them. At the same time, they refused to see the assimilation process itself in a negative light. The ethos of the C.V. presented the maintenance of a proper balance between Germanness and Judaism – a responsible regulation of the assimilation process – as a life mission.

The upheavals that rocked Germany in 1933 were interpreted by many witnesses, including prominent German historians, as a historical turning point.[5] In the atmosphere of the first months of Hitler's regime it became common not only to speak about the decline of the Weimar Republic but also to interpret contemporary events as marking the close of an era that had lasted a century and a half: a development marked by defeat of Enlightenment and bourgeois liberal values.[6] As a consequence, prominent Jewish historians such as Stern, as well as Jewish publicists and politicians who self-consciously adhered to the heritage of emancipation, experienced a deep crisis. Various writers from the Jewish liberal milieu – among them a number of key figures in the C.V. – gradually began to share this perspective. "The past weeks have freed German Jewry from its illusions", wrote the C.V. activist Alfred Hirschberg in July 1933. "At the end of a Jewish development in Germany which lasted 120 years and was founded on the ambiguous concept of emancipation, we are confronted today with a situation more difficult in many respects than was the starting point."[7]

Hirschberg rejected the belief by some other Jews that they would be able to integrate into the "German national revolution", German Jewish youth being called upon to produce figures serving an analogous purpose in the new age to that of Mendelssohn and Gabriel Riesser in the old.[8] Nothing could be more fallacious, Hirschberg claimed, than to say that German Jews were again beginning a process of emancipation from the same starting point as long before. It was true, he added, that men such as Mendelssohn and Riesser and their heritage would continue to serve as models for German Jews, but the present age had entirely new requirements. While Jewish emancipation had meant an improvement in the Jews' political standing, the process at play now was one of political decline. Moreover, the bourgeois ideals of *Bildung* and *Besitz*, which had served as the bases of German Jewry's cultural and economic achievements, had themselves declined in the general German set of values.

Hirschberg's article reflected an early stage in the liberal Jewish internalisation of the new German reality. It seems, however, that although he called for a new formula for Jewish life in Germany and for a "new emancipation", he also continued to speak

---

[5]On the decline of liberal concepts in German historical discourse during the Weimar Republic, see Hans Schleier, *Die bürgerliche deutsche Geschichtsschreibung der Weimarer Republik*, Cologne 1975; Bernd Faulenbach, *Ideologie des deutschen Weges, Die deutsche Geschichte in der Historiographie zwischen Kaiserreich und Nationalsozialismus*, Munich 1980.

[6]Karen Schönwälder, *Historiker und Politik. Geschichtswissenschaft im Nationalsozialismus*, Frankfurt am Main–New York 1992, pp. 20–26.

[7]Alfred Hirschberg, 'Sammeln und Richtung nehmen', in *C.V.-Zeitung* (henceforth *CVZ*), vol. 12, no. 28 (13 July 1933), pp. 269–271, here pp. 269, 271.

[8]Heinz Kellermann, 'Ende der Emanzipation', in *Der Morgen*, vol. 9, no. 3 (1933), pp. 176–177.

in the name of integrative values associated with the "old emancipation". It is note-worthy that Hirschberg's article provoked a great deal of criticism, primarily from lib-eral readers who were not willing to accept what seemed to be his renunciation of the "old emancipation". Two weeks later, in an answer to these criticisms, he made clear that he had not meant to claim that German Jews should not aspire to "re-emanci-pation" (*Wiederemanzipation*); rather he had simply called for the formation of a new synthesis between Germanness and Judaism, one more in tune with the new reality.[9]

In the following months, appeals to renew the formula for Jewish integration with-in Germany continued to appear in the *C.V.-Zeitung*. In some articles, especially those written by younger contributors, the appeals were accompanied by attempts to explain the decline of the liberal "old emancipation".[10] Thus, in an article directed at German-Jewish youth, Robert Wohlheim attributed the failure of the emancipa-tory project to the fact that the Jews had not been strong enough in their Judaism.[11] Wohlheim saw the strengthening of Jewish identity as part of a new integrative strat-egy that would enable most German Jews to stay in their homeland. The "new emancipation" would be possible, he wrote, only if Jewish ties with the non-Jewish world had a stronger Jewish foundation. The Germanness of Jews should no longer be accompanied by a renunciation of their Judaism.

Another liberal writer, Heinz Warschauer, stressed even more powerfully the need to break free from the "rubble of the old assimilatory Jewish shadow-life" in order to form a new German-Jewish type.[12] What was at stake was not returning to ghetto life, he stressed, but rather opening new horizons for Jewish consciousness. German Jews needed to change the paradigm of their existence as their ancestors had one hun-dred and fifty years earlier, when the liberal-assimilationist emancipation movement made its way into the ghetto.[13] Such articles displayed an effort to use the concept of a "new emancipation" in the search for practical solutions to the new problems fac-ing German Jewry. Some of these solutions – changes in vocational structure, a movement of Jews from the cities to agricultural work in the country, the formation of a more communal Jewish life with a stronger Jewish consciousness – were already being discussed during the Weimar Republic.[14] It is important to note that even though such proposals were in some sense reminiscent of those made by Zionist speakers, there was still a gap between them. The C.V. activists continued to uphold

---

[9]Alfred Hirschberg, 'Ein Brief an die Breslauer *Jüdische Zeitung*', in *CVZ*, vol. 12, no. 30 (27 July 1933), p. 296.

[10]For an earlier discussion of the use by C.V. authors of concepts like "new emancipation" in this period, see Avraham Margaliot, *Between Rescue and Annihilation: Studies in the History of German Jewry 1932–1938* (in Hebrew), Jerusalem 1990, pp. 183–193.

[11]Robert Wohlheim, 'Jüdische Jugend Deutschlands sucht ihren Weg', in *CVZ*, vol. 12, no. 31 (3 August 1933), p. 312.

[12]Heinz Warschauer, 'Innere Wandlung', in *CVZ*, vol. 12, no. 36 (20 September 1933), n.p.

[13]See also: Friedrich Brodnitz, 'Um eine neue Emanzipation', in *CVZ*, vol. 13, no. 4 (25 January 1934), n.p. Brodnitz also raised the concept of *group emancipation*, tying it to the previous generations' tradition of "all [those in] Israel are sureties one to the other". Concerning the discussion by CV spokesmen of the con-cept of "group emancipation" in 1933 see Avraham Barkai, *"Wehr Dich!" Der Centralverein deutscher Staatsbürger jüdischen Glaubens 1893–1938*, Munich 2002, pp. 317–330.

[14]See Claudia Prestel, 'Population Policy in Jewish Society: An Expression of Jewish Identity?', in Oded Heilbronner (ed.), *Weimar Jewry and the Crisis of Modernization* (in Hebrew), Jerusalem 1994, pp. 214–262.

their organisation's heritage and espouse principles of Jewish integration, despite having conceded that the "Old Emancipation" had failed.

A fuller formulation of these concepts appeared in an article by the Bielefeld jurist Willy Katzenstein, a member of the earlier generation of the C.V., Katzenstein directed his criticism at those claiming that the Jewish gravitation towards distinct organisations and their cultivation of their heritage were leading them back to the ghetto. He reminded his readers that "The ghetto lives in the memory of us all as a reality to which nobody wishes to return. ... Hundreds of years of dark shadows. ... [The ghetto] alienated the Jews ... from the soil and from nature ... and filled them with feelings of inferiority towards their environment." In contrast with this representation of ghetto life, Katzenstein tried to present a path towards a positive Jewish consciousness that could lead, in turn, to the "new emancipation". This path would be even more remote from ghetto life than the one hundred and fifty years of "old emancipation" had been. The latter form of emancipation had been associated with a lack of inner freedom, religious conversions for some Jews and a tendency among others to obscure their Jewishness – phenomena that Katzenstein presented as "the shadows of the ghetto". This had eventually led to the collapse of the "first emancipation".[15] In his proposed "new emancipation", which was to be based on the lessons of the first one, the Jews would no longer aspire to be loved by the Germans, but rather to be respected. This respect, moreover, could only be gained if they first respected themselves.

Notwithstanding Katzenstein's attack on certain Zionists who tried to present the ghetto as a Jewish alternative to failed emancipation, his article is a striking example of the growing similarity between ideas that were being raised by some C.V. members and traditional Zionist ideas. Both the characterisation of the age of emancipation as a deliberate effort to escape from Judaism and the claim that the escape had led to the tragic situation now facing German Jewry were very popular among Zionists. Likewise, Katzenstein's search for a new, more honourable form of integration of Germany's Jews is reminiscent of the Zionist plea to create "distance" between Jews and Germans.[16] It must be stressed, however, that such similarity did not bring a halt to the ideological and organisational struggle between the C.V. and the Zionists. To the contrary, it seems that the intensified concern with Jewish history among representatives of liberal Judaism was in large measure an act of self-defence against Zionist assaults.

II

In the years 1933–1934 the liberal Berlin rabbi Joachim Prinz, a Zionist activist in his early thirties, held a series of lectures that filled the halls with hundreds of Jewish listeners. In these lectures, Prinz challenged the basic assumptions that had moulded

[15]Willy Katzenstein, "Ghetto, Emanzipation und jüdische Gegenwart", *CVZ*, vol. 13, no. 9 (1 March 1934), n.p.

[16]On the Zionist leader Kurt Blumenfeld's concept of a need for *Distanz* between Jews and Germans see Jehuda Reinharz, *Fatherland or Promised Land*, Ann Arbor 1975, p. 156; see also Peter M. Baldwin, 'Zionist and Non-Zionist Jews in the Last Years before the Nazi Regime', in *LBI Year Book*, vol. 27 (1982), pp. 87–108. The arguments against escape from Judaism were also put forward by the C.V.'s established leaders but they believed in a proud Jewish integration within Germany, without any need for "distance".

the period of German-Jewish emancipation, in the process attacking the historical picture presented by the C.V.[17] His analysis was then presented in his book *Wir Juden*.

The exodus of European Jews out of the ghetto had been extremely abrupt, Prinz argued. The ghetto Jews, who had lived peacefully in a traditional society, were like prisoners whose cell bars had suddenly been removed.[18] A Jewish generation that had nurtured a naïve faith in Enlightenment and French revolutionary ideas had shown little reflective propensity in the speedy abandonment of its traditional surroundings. In this context, Prinz vividly described Solomon Maimon's wife and children, left behind in the ghetto, as cursing Maimon for his treason – and the similarly situated relatives of Moses Mendelssohn as condemning Mendelssohn for his translation of the Bible.[19]

Within the ghetto, Prinz continued, Jews had enjoyed freedom in their inner lives, their names and origins only becoming sources of distress as a result of emancipation. Prinz thus interpreted the emancipatory process as an attempt by Jews to escape not only from tradition but through this, from themselves: "In this way emancipated Jews lived on the margins. They took a wide detour around their Judaism and missed the path to a true life."[20] The principle encapsulated in Clermont-Tonnerre's saying, "the Jews should be denied everything as a nation, but granted everything as individuals" had led Western Jews to disintegration and deadlock.[21]

One central theme in Prinz's thesis was the price of emancipation. The tragedy of the modern Jew involved the state's offer of a solution (*Lösung*) at the price of disintegration (*Auflösung*) – the demand for an absolute renunciation of all manifestations of Jewish exclusiveness.[22] Quite unmistakably, Prinz's critique of Emancipation Jewry reverberates with the language of the contemporary *völkisch* critique of modernity. These echoes are most audible in his claim that the mass urbanisation of the Jews had cut them off from the soil and the *Volk*, installing them instead in what he termed an "anonymous" ghetto, far more oppressive than the old one, in which the Jews had at least been able to maintain self-respect and inner confidence.[23]

Prinz was, to be sure, not alone in attacking the heritage of Emancipation Jewry and the fundamental Enlightenment values of the nineteenth century. The most famous such Zionist attack was of course Robert Weltsch's editorial, published in the *Jüdische Rundschau* following the countrywide April 1933 boycott of Jewish businesses, the first Nazi organised anti-Jewish act on a nation-wide scale.[24] Another Zionist

---

[17]On Prinz's activity in the Nazi period see his memoir: Joachim Prinz, 'A Rabbi under the Hitler Regime', in Herbert A. Strauss and Kurt R. Grossmann (eds.), *Gegenwart im Rückblick*, Heidelberg 1970, pp. 231–238; see also Jacob Boas, 'The Shrinking World of German Jewry: 1933–1938', in *LBI Year Book*, vol. 31 (1986), p. 247.

[18]Joachim Prinz, *Wir Juden*, Berlin 1934, pp. 19–21.

[19]*ibid.*, p. 23.

[20]*ibid.*, p. 31.

[21]For Count Clermont-Tonnerre's speech, delivered in the French revolutionary national assembly on 23 December 1789, concerning the eligibility of the Jews for French citizenship, see Paul Mendes-Flohr and Jehuda Reinharz, (eds.), *The Jew in the Modern World*, New York and Oxford 1995, pp. 114–115; above citation from p. 115.

[22]Prinz, p. 36.

[23]*ibid.*, p. 147.

[24]Robert Weltsch, 'Tragt ihn mit Stolz, den gelben Fleck!', in *Jüdische Rundschau* (henceforth *JR*), vol. 38, no. 27 (4 April 1933), pp. 131–132.

essayist described the reality that the Jews encountered when the ghetto gates were opened as an "assimilationist fiction" that had damaged the foundations of the Jewish entity. Some Orthodox writers also used concepts such as *fata morgana* to characterise the way in which nineteenth-century Jews viewed their environment, while others described the rights that had been granted them as nothing more than "illusory emancipation".[25]

Many Zionist writers thus defined the concepts of "emancipation" and "assimilation" in the context of the price Jews had had to pay for emancipation. In this manner, one writer referred to assimilation as the "purchase price" (*Kaufpreis*) of emancipation – a conscious disavowal of Jewish collective identity.[26] The Zionist educator Hugo Rosenthal argued that this pact had been misguided from the beginning – the Jews should have rejected the very idea of assimilation as a condition for emancipation, since they should have understood that their citizenship would be meaningful only if their ethnic uniqueness was recognised. The misunderstanding in the pact, Rosenthal claimed, lay at the base of the Jews' current distress.[27]

When the Jews became Europeans, claimed another Zionist publicist, they should have understood that they were being accepted at the very best like salt in soup. The extent of European society's willingness to absorb them was therefore a matter of good taste and proportion.[28] But either most Jews refused to admit this fact or did not even understand it; instead, they grasped at every opportunity for outward advancement without taking sufficient note of the reluctance to accept them, until that reluctance became forcefully evident in the Nazi period. The solution had therefore to be based on admission of past failures and on a realistic recognition that there was no place for assimilation. Jews had to instead seek a return to Jewish history.

Another notable aspect of the Zionist critique of the German-Jewish past was related to the figure of Moses Mendelssohn. Whereas Prinz presented Mendelssohn as the chief representative of the erroneous assimilationist path, other Zionists described him as a pioneer who had tried to direct the emancipation process in a responsible and balanced way. Rather than throwing accusations at him, they instead placed the blame on his disciples. Hugo Rosenthal, for example, claimed that unlike those Jews who agreed to give up their ethnic uniqueness for emancipation, Mendelssohn attempted to pave the way for a true Jewish integration that would not blur the ethnic boundaries between Jews and Germans. In the bi-centenary of Mendelssohn's birth, the Munich publisher and writer Ludwig Feuchtwanger described him as someone who had not lost his heritage and who had avoided the errors committed by many Jewish figures after him.[29] According to Feuchtwanger, Mendelssohn's friendship with Christian scholars did not lead him to the sorts of illu-

---

[25]'Sturm über Europa', in *JR*, vol. 39, no. 14 (16 February 1934), p.1; Dr. Elias, 'Das Ende einer Illusion. Teil 1', in *Der Israelit*, vol. 73, no. 32 (4 August 1932), pp. 1–2; Saly Geis, 'Wie ist es gekommen? Teil 1', in *Der Israelit*, vol. 74, no. 32 (10 August 1933), pp. 4–5.

[26]Anon., 'Die Zukunft der Juden', in *JR*, vol. 39, no. 5 (16 January 1934), p. 1.

[27]Hugo Rosenthal, 'Die deutsche Judenheit im neuen Deutschen Reich. Teil I', in *JR*, vol. 38, no. 42 (26 May 1933), pp. 217–218.

[28]Anon., 'Echte oder scheinbare Wandlung?', in *JR*, vol. 38, no. 37 (9 May 1933), pp. 185–186.

[29]Ludwig Feuchtwanger, 'Der Streit um den Geist Moses Mendelssohns', in *JR*, vol. 41, no. 1 (3 January 1936), p. 5.

sions later nurtured by other Jews – he was very aware of the distinctions between himself and his Christian friends, it thus being unfair to link him to concepts more appropriately associated with the nineteenth-century emancipation struggle. It would appear that for Feuchtwanger, Mendelssohn embodied the ideal of a Jewish-Christian relationship in which the Jewish side maintains a clear and solid connection to its heritage. In contrast to Prinz, Rosenthal and Feuchtwanger did not feel alienated from the symbolic starting-point of Jewish modernisation in Germany. Instead, they called for a distinction between proper and erroneous paths in the unfolding of this process, a distinction that became common in essays by the German-Jewish liberals as well.

III

In the difficult circumstances of the 1930s, the C.V.'s representatives and other liberal Jewish publicists were forced to cope with a range of challenges and threats. First and foremost, of course, they had to confront the ongoing destruction of Jewish emancipation. They also had to confront, more concretely, the anti-Jewish defamations that were ubiquitous in the Nazi media.[30] At the same time, the fundamental values of the liberal Jewish camp were being exposed to attacks by the Zionists, whose influence was increasing rapidly, especially among the younger generation.

As has already been shown, in the first months after the Nazi accession to power, writers for the C.V. already began to express acceptance of the loss of emancipation in the traditional liberal sense and called for a search for alternative solutions. However, despite this new awareness, they still refused to accept the argument that the emancipation process had been wrong from the outset, its fall inevitable. This insistence on the legitimacy, at least in its own time, of the fundamental principles of the emancipatory era reflected the latitude that the situation in Nazi Germany still allowed the Jews until 1935.

Within certain Zionists groups, wrote Eva Reichmann-Jungmann, it had become fashionable to attack the entire emancipation era as erroneous, with Jews achieving their rights at the price of treason and dishonor.[31] This, she argued, was in fact a black and white approach, reading and judging history from the currently bleak perspective. The opening of the ghetto gates and the gift of freedom had offered Germany's Jews a simultaneously hopeful and hazardous fate; many Jews had chosen hope. Reichmann-Jungmann maintained that the fruitful synthesis at work in German-Jewish emancipation had no parallel in any other country. She tried to explain the defeat of emancipatory values as a result of an unbridgeable gap between the legal status now enjoyed by the emancipated Jews and their image in society (as a result of the level of their assimilation)

---

[30]See in this regard Jacob Boas, 'Countering Nazi Defamation – German Jews and the Jewish Tradition, 1933–1938', in *LBI Year Book*, vol. 34 (1989), pp. 205–226.
[31]Eva Reichmann-Jungmann, 'Vom Sinn deutsch-jüdischen Seins', in *CVZ*, vol. 13, no. 22 (31 May 1934), n.p.

The most prominent representative of the C.V. view on such matters was the Berlin historian Fritz Friedlander.[32] In an article published in the *CVZ* in August 1934, Friedlander followed Ranke in asserting that all eras are equally close to God – every past period thus needing to be approached without the imposition of present-day values on it.[33] A scholarly discussion of the problems of assimilation and emancipation "as they actually were" – a citation, of course, of Ranke's *Wie es eigentlich gewesen ist* – should consequently be based, Friedlander insisted, on nineteenth-century political values.[34]

Friedlander expressed his view most clearly in a confrontation with a Nazi scholar in November 1935 that can only be termed courageous. Earlier that year, Wilhelm Grau, a German historian in charge of the "history of the Jewish problem" in the *Reichsinstitut für die Geschichte des neuen Deutschlands*, had published a book about Humboldt and the "Jewish problem". Grau presented Humboldt's positive attitude to Jewish integration within Germany as a demonstration of deficiency from a German-national point of view. He argued that by not considering the Jews on the basis of racial ideology, Humboldt had done severe damage to the German nation. As Friedlander described it in his critique, Grau's criticisms of Humboldt were part of a broader attack upon what Grau referred to as assimilationist and liberal Jewry.[35]

Friedlander attacked not only Grau's anti-liberal concepts, but also what he regarded as their positive reception in some Zionist circles. Just as Napoleon's defeat at Waterloo, he indicated, should not make us forget his great victory at Austerlitz, Jewish emancipation had had its moment of greatness and historical significance, notwithstanding the possible defeat of emancipatory ideals that was transpiring. In a general manner, Friedlander's article shows that even in a situation where open political struggle against the Nazis had become impossible, one could still criticise them indirectly through a defence of nineteenth-century Enlightenment ideals.[36]

In addition to insisting that emancipation had in fact been the right course, liberal Jewish speakers did increasingly show openness to critical discussions of its shortcomings. In April 1935 Gerhardt Neumann published an article in *Der Morgen* describing the 1880s as the beginning of the end of emancipation.[37] In retrospect, Neumann argued, German Jews appeared to suffer from self-deception and a failure

---

[32]Fritz Friedlander was active in the Berlin Jewish education system in the 1930s; see *idem*, 'Trials and Tribulations of Jewish Education in Nazi Germany', *LBI Year Book*, vol. 3 (1958), pp. 187–201.

[33]On this notion in Ranke see George G. Iggres, *The German Conception of History: The National Tradition of Historical Thought from Herder to the Present*, Middletown, CN 1983, pp. 63–89.

[34]Fritz Friedlander, 'Jüdische Assimilation im Zeitalter der Emanzipation', in *CVZ*, vol. 13, no. 35 (30 August 1934), n.p.; cf. *idem*, 'Eine Idee und ihre Zeit, 2. April 1806 – Gabriel Riesser – 2. April 1936', in *CVZ*, vol. 15, no. 14 (2 April 1936), n.p. For a similar approach see Jacob Jacobson, 'Das Emanzipationsedikt von 1812', in *Gemeindeblatt der Jüdischen Gemeinde zu Berlin*, vol. 24, no. 49 (29 December 1934), pp. 4–5.

[35]Fritz Friedlander, 'Eine Charakterbild in der Geschichte, Zu Wilhelm Grau: "Wilhelm v. Humboldt"', in *CVZ*, vol. 14, no. 45 (7 November 1935), n.p. About the institute see: Helmut Heiber, *Walter Frank und sein Reichsinstitut für Geschichte des neuen Deutschlands*, Stuttgart, 1966; and *ibid.*, pp. 411–412 on Grau's book about Humboldt and the reactions it evoked.

[36]For another Jewish attack on Grau see Hans Liebeschütz 'Zur Frage des jüdischen Geschichtsbildes von heute', in *Gemeindeblatt der Deutsch-Israelitischen Gemeinde zu Hamburg*, vol. 12, no. 6 (12 June 1936), pp. 4–6.

[37]Gerhardt Neumann, 'Das Emanzipationsproblem vor 50 Jahren', in *Der Morgen*, vol. 11, no. 1 (1935), pp. 39–41.

to understand the popular mood. The Jewish entry into the German economy at the beginning of the 1870s had been too quick and impulsive, the Jews exploiting all the formal rights granted them by law, thus arousing deep social hostility, the root of the present misfortune. Hence the events of the 1880s – and, by implication, those of the 1930s – emerged from the narrowness of the emancipatory foundations themselves.

Beyond such interpretations of the purported mistakes that German Jews had made in forging their relationship with their non-Jewish environment, liberal writers began to discuss the price that the Jews had paid for emancipation. One of the starting points for this discussion was the publication in 1933 of Max Wiener's book *Jüdische Religion im Zeitalter der Emanzipation*. Wiener, a Berlin rabbi and scholar, claimed in his introduction that he had finished writing the book before German Jewry was affected by "the tragic events of these days", the events consequently having "no influence on the formation of the book".[38] The circumstances of the book's appearance, however, had a major influence on its reception. According to Hugo Hahn, from the point of view of an era in which the age of emancipation appeared to have come to an end, Wiener did not leave that age's failures unnoticed, but rather exposed the influence of opportunistic motives on the integration of Germany's Jews.[39] And the Hamburg teacher and rabbi Alberto Jonas suggested that Wiener's book had clarified the limits of Jewish regeneration. Jonas called upon German Jews to read the book, since recognising the errors of the past might teach them a lesson regarding the formation of a "new emancipation" – one that would not be assimilationist but rather attentive to Jewish roots.[40]

The discussion of the price German Jews had paid for emancipation prompted a double response on the part of various liberal Jewish writers. On the one hand, they rejected Prinz's analysis, since it went as far as to reject the heritage of Moses Mendelssohn; in contrast, they tended to present Mendelssohn's path as the healthy and balanced choice for an emancipated Jewry. On the other hand, they condemned what was presented as the alternative to Mendelssohn, a mistaken emancipatory path marked by self-denial and thorough assimilation and understood to be associated with figures like David Friedländer. This distinction between two types of emancipation was made clear in a late 1935 lecture by the historian Ismar Freund.[41] Freund directed his attack at those presenting emancipation as "the biggest error in the history of the diaspora". He nevertheless admitted that plans such as the one presented by David Friedländer in the early nineteenth century, involving a sacrifice of Judaism for the sake of integration, were historical mistakes that should be condemned.[42] Freund's major point was to stress the gap between ideas like Friedländer's and more balanced views of emancipation, which, he argued, were

[38]Max Wiener, *Jüdische Religion im Zeitalter der Emanzipation*, Berlin 1933, p. 4.

[39]Hugo Hahn, 'Jüdische Religion im Zeitalter der Emanzipation: Zu dem gleichnamigen Buche von Max Wiener' in *CVZ*, vol. 12, no. 47 (7 December 1933), n.p.

[40]A. Jonas, "Zu Max Wieners Buch: Jüdische Religion im Zeitalter der Emanzipation", in *Israelitisches Familienblatt* (henceforth *IFB*), no. 8 (22 February 1934), p. 11.

[41]'Jüdisches Leben und jüdischer Geist. Aus den Vortragssälen', in *CVZ*, vol. 14, no. 45 (7 November 1935), n.p.

[42]On David Friedländer's proposal see, for example: Jacob Katz, *Out of the Ghetto, The Social Background of Jewish Emancipation, 1770–1870*, Cambridge, MA 1973, pp. 116–119.

linked to Mendelssohn's heritage. Mendelssohn was being presented unjustly as "the father of the Jewish disaster", whereas in fact his model of emancipation was developed in order to provide diaspora Jewry with the best possible chance to preserve its heritage. The seeds of the tragedy which, Freund implied, involved both an accelerated assimilation process and the eventual demise of emancipatory hopes – could be tied to those who, unlike Mendelssohn, did not maintain the boundaries between Jew and Gentile, and were thus willing to completely forego their tradition.[43]

This liberal Jewish tendency to present a more critical picture of the past was also manifest in a programmatic article by C.V. president Ernst Herzfeld which was focussed on the significance of changing the name of the association from *Centralverein deutscher Staatsbürger jüdischen Glaubens* to *Jüdischer Central Verein*.[44] Herzfeld defined the old name as representing the nineteenth century and, in particular, the idea of a union between Judaism and European culture. But this idea, he indicated, had negative as well as positive aspects – during the emancipatory process Judaism had been neglected, various Jewish traditions, and even Jewish history, put aside. Herzfeld thus called for a return to Judaism in the spirit of the association's new name. But at the same time, he insisted that the light and shadow of the emancipatory age should be viewed in balanced proportions, leaving a space for the fruitful results of those one hundred and fifty years, including the emergence of modern Jewish scholarship (*Wissenschaft des Judentums*).[45]

IV

Another strategy used by liberal Jewish authors in their struggle to reshape the past involved endowing emancipatory values with historical depth, liberating them from an exclusive link to the nineteenth century and its political liberalism. This attitude was expressed in noteworthy fashion as early as February 1933, in an article by the Düsseldorf rabbi Max Eschelbacher. "For fourteen years", he wrote, "we have been conducting the struggle for our rights on the foundation of the Weimar Constitution … [according to which] all Germans are equal before the law", and it seemed that there was no reason to stop relying on that constitution.[46] But in the final lines of his article, Eschelbacher touched on the possibility that a basic shift in Jewish history was now taking place. He consequently suggested a fresh response to changed circumstances:

> Constitutions can change. If the upheavals of history lead to the unbelievable and the National Socialist programme is realised, and if a new constitution determines that a Jew can no longer be a citizen, then we will no longer be able to rely on the constitution. In such a case, however, we will not give up our rights, but rather derive them from a deep, eternal foundation. Our ancient Jewish past and our history of almost two thousand

---

[43]For a similar view see also Fritz Friedlander, 'Jüdische Assimilation im Zeitalter der Emanzipation', *CVZ*, vol. 13, no. 35 (30 August 1934), n.p.

[44]Ernst Herzfeld, 'Jüdischer Central Verein', in *CVZ*, vol. 15, no. 33 (13 August 1936), n.p.

[45]For a similar argument cf. Alfred Hirschberg, 'Der Centralverein deutscher Staatsbürger jüdischen Glaubens', in *Wille und Weg des deutschen Judentums*, Berlin 1935, p. 16.

[46]Max Eschelbacher, 'Der deutsche Jude und der deutsche Staat', in *Der Morgen*, vol. 8, no. 6 (1933), p. 414.

years in Germany bear powerful witness to God's will. … Then we will finally lead our struggle for full civil rights in Germany as German Jews, on the basis of God's will.[47]

Rabbi Eschelbacher tied his proposed solution to both a religious destiny and an historical horizon. The real possibility of the Republic's collapse took him much further back than the beginnings of the emancipation period, to the real or invented starting-point for almost two thousand years of Jewish life in Germany. This historical continuum, which Eschelbacher presented as an expression of divine will, served as a deeply rooted, durable moral foundation for the future of Germany's Jews.

Quite possibly, the tendency in this period of crisis to hearken back to the early period of Jewish settlement in Germany was a reflection of *völkisch* neo-romanticism, as well as being a kind of despairing counterpart to the Nazi mythologising of a distant past. There were, in any event, clear and significant differences between the two mythologising structures. The Nazis used Germany's pagan past and Middle Ages in positive juxtaposition to negatively charged concepts such as rationalism, liberalism – and of course Jewish emancipation.[48] For Jewish writers, on the other hand, a deepening of the historical horizon was a way to support values that were, in fact, deeply rooted in the modern, liberal world. Hence in September 1933 Alfred Hirschberg argued that for the past two thousand years Jews around the world had lived as "citizens with equal rights whose countries' laws were as meaningful to them as their religious laws", and that a synthesis between Jews and their surroundings had existed at virtually all times and in almost every location.[49] Two years later, Hirschberg claimed that "the meaning of emancipation for us today is to cling to the places of work and rest for the present generations and for those to come within Germany's borders, where the graves and the living places of Jews have been already for forty generations".[50] One can here discern an effort to redefine emancipation in a way better adapted to present needs and as something upon which Germany's Jews could depend in their troubles.

In 1935, the *CVZ* published a series of articles about the history of the Jews in Germany.[51] Many of these articles themselves reveal a desire to reach into past eras for the sake of present needs. Thus Ismar Elbogen, rector of the Berlin liberal rabbinical seminary, did not define the period between the eleventh and thirteenth centuries exclusively in terms of growing hatred towards the Jews. Rather, he laid some stress on the protection offered Jews during the crusades by many Christian city dwellers, including clerics. Likewise, he noted that the hatred and fanaticism indeed marking this period had not prevented a further expansion of Jewish settlement in expanding towns where relations between Jews and non-Jews were marked by equality of civic status – *Gemeinbürgerschaft*.[52] According to Elbogen, although the Jews con-

---

[47]*ibid.*

[48]Karl Ferdinand Werner, *Das NS Geschichtsbild und die deutsche Geschichtswissenschaft*, Stuttgart 1967, p. 40.

[49]Alfred Hirschberg, 'An der Schwelle des Jahres', in *CVZ*, vol. 12, no. 36 (20 September 1933), n.p.

[50]Hirschberg, 'Der Centralverein', p. 20. Boas, 'The Shrinking World', p. 251, has described Hirschberg as "the most consistent champion of the German Jewish way".

[51]*CVZ* 17 May, 14, 28 June, 12, 26 July, 9, 30 August 1934, n.p.

[52]Ismar Elbogen, 'Jüdisches Schicksal in Deutschland im 11. bis 13. Jahrhundert', in *CVZ*, vol. 13, no. 26 (28 June 1934), n.p.

tinued to develop their distinctive interpretation of the Bible and Talmud, this common life led to a similarity in language, values, and cultural tastes and sensibilities. However historically accurate his account may be, it would seem that in his depiction, and especially in his choice of terms such as "citizenship", Elbogen was particularly concerned with balancing a description of the period's pogroms with images of normality in Christian-Jewish relations – a picture harmonising well with nineteenth-century aspirations towards Jewish integration into German society and culture.

The memory of the Middle Ages was also prominent in the lectures and publications of C.V. activist Bruno Weil, responding in 1934 to Prinz's ideas. In Weil's critique, Prinz viewed the ghetto as the Jews' natural way of life, considering the emancipation era as a century-long marginal diversion doomed to fail from the very outset. Prinz, Weil claimed, was unaware of the real meaning of the ghetto and the nature of the developments leading to emancipation. This lack of understanding, he continued, had to do with the need for a much broader historical perspective – one stretching over a millennium – in order to examine the salient historical problems.[53] Weil claimed that the emancipation had not been an abrupt and unexpected event in Jewish history, but rather a deep-rooted, complicated, and tumultuous process, and that one needed to understand the ghetto, the historical antithesis to emancipation, in historical perspective. Thus there were many years of free Jewish settlement in Worms before the city's Jews were forcibly ghettoised in the second half of the fourteenth century. This period, Weil continued, was the beginning of five hundred years of humiliation and contempt directed at the Jews throughout Germany, but it began after more than one thousand years of legal equality (*Rechtsgleichheit*).[54] Hence ghetto existence was strictly a product of the late middle ages. Civil equality on the other hand, according to Weil, had much deeper roots in the early middle ages, which he presented as a period of proto-emancipation.[55]

Weil's choice of Worms as a model for Jewish life in medieval Germany was not accidental. That year (1934), German Jewry had marked the nine-hundredth anniversary of the city's ancient synagogue, where Rashi had once been active. The anniversary was marked by a series of events and articles. Offenbach's liberal rabbi Max Dienemann suggested that the history of the Worms community revealed not only Jewish suffering during pogroms, but also Jewish participation in Germany's bourgeois life in better times.[56] In an editorial which appeared in the special anniversary volume of the *C.V.-Zeitung*, Hirschberg described the Jews who prayed in the medieval synagogue as citizens who had enjoyed full equal rights in their city.[57] It was

---

[53]Bruno Weil, 'Rechenschaft und Ausblick', in *CVZ*, vol. 13, no. 45 (8 November 1934), n.p.

[54]Bruno Weil, *Der Weg der deutschen Juden*, Berlin 1934, pp. 178–180.

[55]On Weil's approach to the early middle ages see also 'Dr. Bruno Weil spricht im Central Verein', in *IFB*, no. 2 (11 January 1934), p. 9.

[56]Max Dienemann, "Die Geschichte der Einzelgemeinde als Spiegel der Gesamtgeschichte", in *Zeitschrift für die Geschichte der Juden in Deutschland*, vol 5 (1934), pp. 115–121.

[57]Alfred Hirschberg, '900 Jahre Wormser Synagoge', in *CVZ*, vol. 13, no. 22 (31 May 1934), n.p. Similarly Ismar Elbogen, 'Neunhundert Jahre Wormser Synagoge (1034–1934)', in *Gemeindeblatt der Jüdischen Gemeinde zu Berlin*, vol. 24, no. 20 (2 June 1934), pp. 2–4; for an additional description of the synagogue's period of establishment as a culminating point of Jewish integration see S. K., 'Haus des Schicksals. Die Wormser Synagoge im Wandel der Zeiten', in *CVZ*, vol. 13, no. 22 (31 May 1934), n.p.

true, he indicated, that their rights were later undermined, but the synagogue would continue to exist over the centuries, serving as a symbol for Jews of the integration of homeland and faith (*Heimat und Glaube*), even when their legal status had been impaired. The values that Hirschberg associated with the medieval community of Worms were in fact a reflection of the liberal Jewish world of the C.V. Beyond his use of the expression "citizenship", one can say that his very usage in the article of the term *deutsche Juden* – a term Zionists rejected and the Nazis banned after passage of the Nuremberg Laws – was a symbolic affirmation of the emancipatory ideal. For its part, "faith and homeland" (*Glaube und Heimat*) was at that time a well-known formula in the C.V.[58] All in all, Hirschberg's vocabulary seems to reflect an effort at establishing a line of continuity between the Jews of medieval Worms and the modern German Jews – both rooted in their homeland, at peace with their civic affiliation, and loyal to their faith both in good times and times of crisis.

The heritage of Worms was discussed by the Zionists as well, but from a different point of view. In a *Jüdische Rundschau* editorial, Kurt Loewenstein, a Zionist journalist and youth movement activist, cited Worms as proof of the Jews' unique bond with Germany, hence a counter to the antisemitic claim that the Jews had always been unwanted guests.[59] It was the case that the city's Jews had been restricted in various realms, but they also shared various public responsibilities with non-Jews, hence were not to be seen as guests but as a resident minority. It seems that in contrast to Hirschberg, Loewenstein consciously chose not to use the term "equal citizens", preferring to describe Worms' medieval Jews as a "minority" – a concept better reflecting Zionist aspirations of the 1930s.[60] In addition, he argued that the integration of Worms' Jews into their surroundings was based on their own recognition of their "distance" from the German people – as suggested, a major concept in the Zionist critique of modern emancipated Jewry. The balanced path of integration displayed in medieval Worms faded during the nineteenth century, he claimed, to be replaced by a drive for radical assimilation.

Both Loewenstein and Hirschberg suggested that the heritage of Worms Jewry offered a proper model of Jewish integration into the German environment – a justification offered in the past for what each conceived as the correct path in the present. But whereas Hirschberg spoke in terms of continuity between medieval Worms and nineteenth-century Germany, Loewenstein stressed the vast difference between the two periods. Nevertheless, despite the significant differences between the two writers, their ideas did have some important parallels. As a Zionist, Loewenstein did not deny the value of Jewish integration, as long as it did not turn towards radical assimilation; and Hirschberg, too, rejected such an extreme. Putting aside the organisational competition informing the two viewpoints, it would appear that the implicit disagreement

---

[58]It was coined by the association's leader during the First World War, Eugen Fuchs; cf. *idem*, 'Glaube und Heimat', in *Im Deutschen Reich*, September 1917, pp. 338–351.

[59]Kurt Loewenstein, 'Das Judengespenst. Vor 900 Jahren – und heute", in *JR*, vol. 39, no. 44 (1 June 1934), pp. 1–2.

[60]On the Zionist desire to fix the status of Germany's Jews as a minority with rights see Margaliot, pp. 232–243. It is noteworthy that a more scholarly contribution to the same *JR* issue refers to the Jews of thirteenth- and fourteenth-century Worms as "citizens"; see: Guido Kisch, 'Zur Geschichte der Wormser Juden', in *JR*, vol. 39, no. 44 (1 June 1934), p. 9.

between Hirschberg and Loewenstein centred on the meaning of both Jewish uniqueness and the nineteenth-century German-Jewish heritage.

                                        V

In April 1934, the *Völkischer Beobachter* published an article on "the problem of dissimilation".[61] The author, Lutz Lenders, described both "emancipation" and "assimilation" as products of the French Revolution and indicated that they had been adopted by the European peoples for doctrinal reasons. Liberalism, he wrote, had demanded that the Jews renounce their national uniqueness and the Jews, for their part, had chosen to blur the national component in their tradition out of purely opportunistic motives. Defining the distinction between Jews and non-Jews as purely religious, he insisted, was "a Jewish trick". The Nazi state, he continued, determined the boundaries between Jews and non-Jews in a legal way, but a positive solution to the Jewish problem depended simply on choices made by Jews in the course of their "dissimilation" from the Germans. The Third Reich, Lenders suggested, had proved its willingness to help the Jews by enabling them to establish the Jewish *Kulturbund*. It seemed, however, that the Jews, who had decided to present Lessing's *Nathan der Weise* at the *Kulturbund's* theatrical premiere, still tended towards assimilationism.

Lenders' article received a great deal of attention in the Jewish press.[62] In their reactions, Jewish publicists attempted to redefine the concepts of "assimilation" and "dissimilation" in order to clarify their points of disagreement with the Nazi writer. This kind of critical discussion, which included implied disapproval of the Nazi anti-semitic measures, was still possible in 1934.

The immediate Zionist reaction to the article was rather simple. Kurt Loewenstein agreed with Lenders that the era of assimilation had come to an end, and that in the new dissimilationist period every social group had to preserve its uniqueness.[63] Loewenstein chose not to touch on the nefarious motives that Lenders attributed to Jewish assimilation, preferring to indicate simply that Zionism had always been opposed to assimilation and had considered Jewish education and a connection to the traditional Jewish homeland as the foundation for a renewal of Jewish uniqueness.

For liberal Jews, Lenders' article represented a more difficult challenge and induced a more complex reaction. True, Hirschberg indicated, the German Jews of the C.V. (himself included) aspired to assimilate into "Germanness". At the same time, however, they wished to dissimilate from racist ideas.[64] Both assimilation and dissimilation were positive forces in the life of the Jewish community, which needed to find a proper balance between them. Whereas various groups in history such as the ten lost tribes of Israel, the mediaeval Teutons, and many of the ethnic groups that immigrated to America had assimilated to the point of complete disintegration,

[61]Lutz Lenders, 'Zum Problem der Dissimilation', in *Völkischer Beobachter*, vol. 47, no. 115 (25 April 1934).
[62]For a detailed report on the article with extensive citations, see 'Zum Problem der Dissimilation', in *IFB*, no. 18 (3 May 1934), p. 2.
[63]Kurt Loewenstein., 'Dissimilation', in *JR*, vol. 39, no. 34 (27 April 1934), p. 1.
[64]Alfred Hirschberg, 'Assimilation oder Dissimilation?', in *CVZ*, vol. 13, no. 18 (3 March 1934), n.p.

Jewish history displayed a thousand-year pattern within which dissimilation was encouraged as an unconsciously preservative force, one balancing out assimilationist tendencies.[65] Hirschberg conceded that German Jewry had accepted assimilationist ideas in the nineteenth century, but at the same time he of course rejected Lenders' interpretation of the process as a "Jewish trick", describing it instead as a natural reaction to the nineteenth-century *Zeitgeist*. At present, with the German nation undergoing a process of dissimilation and focusing on the differences between itself and other nations, the Jews would themselves be forced to adapt to the new dissimilationist *Zeitgeist*.

In fact, a close examination of Hirschberg's argument shows that he was trying to adapt the new, prevalent "dissimilation" to his own liberal views. Dissimilation, he insisted, could not turn back the clock – the concept had to incorporate the history of the nineteenth century, hence could not produce a complete separation between Germany and the Jews. Instead he proposed a formula that would fuse the German Jews into a distinct spiritual community while still leaving them room on the margins of the German nation.

Hirschberg's reservations regarding what he termed unbalanced assimilation reflected an important element in the self-consciousness of the liberal Jews. Even before 1933, notable liberal Jewish speakers had opposed extreme assimilation and had seen it as detrimental to Jewish dignity.[66] It seems, however, that in the post-1933 era, with the increase in Zionist power, the liberals had become more sensitive about being associated with assimilation. At the same time, they did not wish to dissociate themselves from the integrationist vision. This situation led them to redefine the terms "assimilation" and "dissimilation" and reinterpret the historical processes through which they developed. Thus, another C.V. publicist proposed a distinction between "assimilation" as a superficial and harmful path of integration on the one hand and "synthesis" as a deeper and more mutual path on the other hand.[67] Another, anonymous commentator distinguished between "positive assimilation" and "negative assimilation".[68]

The most systematic discussion of this theme in liberal circles can be found in Fritz Friedlander's articles. All of world history, Friedlander insisted in August 1934, could be interpreted as a process of continuous renewal and assimilation; that history was riddled with examples of a dominant environment influencing closed cultural groups. Assimilation was thus a general and inevitable human process, one not concerning Jews alone and with roots extending much further back than the nineteenth century. This process, he added, inevitably had its tragic aspects; it always led to the disappearance of noble and valuable traditions for the sake of a higher unity – this was the case with the assimilation of the Germanic Franks in France, and it was the case with Jewish assimilation in Germany. Assimilation, Friedlander argued, had laid the groundwork for the demand for emancipation, since only minorities that had reached a certain level of assimilation aspired to emancipation.[69]

---

[65]Cf. Hirschberg, 'Der Centralverein', p. 18.

[66]See for example Ludwig Hollaender, *Deutsch-Jüdisch Probleme der Gegenwart*, Berlin 1929, p. 6.

[67]Hans Rosenfeld, 'Assimilation oder Synthese', in *CVZ*, vol. 12, no. 34 (7 September 1933), n.p.

[68]Anon., 'Von der Vergangenheit zur Gegenwart', in *Der Schild*, vol. 14, no. 49 (6 December 1935), pp. 1–2.

[69]Fritz Friedlander, 'Jüdische Assimilation im Zeitalter der Emanzipation', in *CVZ*, vol. 13, no. 35 (30 August 1934), n.p.

A year later, Friedlander addressed the concept of "productive assimilation" during his debate with the Nazi historian Wilhelm Grau.[70] While he depicted figures such as the Rahel Varnhagen and Henriette Herz, Heinrich Heine and Ludwig Börne as victims of the emancipation process, Friedlander described Leopold Zunz, Isaak Marcus Jost, Gabriel Riesser and others who had worked for a development of Jewish consciousness alongside Jewish integration within Germany as models of "productive assimilation". He also suggested that the *Centralverein* was the legitimate successor to the tradition represented by such figures, stressing that the century of assimilation that had now come to an end had not been in vain. In an argument that would become common for liberal Jewish writers in the second half of the 1930s, Friedlander explained that young Jews now emigrating from Germany were taking the fruits of the German Jewish heritage with them to their new homelands.

Several Zionist writers also addressed the concept of assimilation, arguing against the liberal interpretation. In March 1934, Kurt Loewenstein took a stand against what he saw as the superfluous use of the concept, in particular by non-Zionist groups appropriating it for ideological ends from the Zionists, who had been using it for decades in their condemnation of the liberals.[71] Loewenstein was thus struggling to regain the monopoly on a "correct" interpretation of the concept of assimilation.

According to Loewenstein, every integration of a minority group within a majority society, and every tendency of the minority to accept the majority's norms, was to be understood as an inevitable "natural assimilation". However, German Jews were mistaken when they turned the liberal norms of their environment into their primary source of values, adopting them not only as an outcome of natural considerations of benefit, but as the key to their destiny. Recent events, he continued, had caused great shock to the natural assimilation process and had rendered void the German-Jewish assimilative ideology. This ought to have led German Jews to recognise that they shared a "fate of exile" (*Galuthschicksal*), and to understand that the intensively discussed "new emancipation" could only be a collective process involving a Jewish commitment to leave Germany for Palestine.

It seems that beyond his pronounced reservations, Loewenstein here in fact reveals an acceptance of basic liberal assumptions about assimilation. The process, according to Loewenstein, is in itself not wrong; indeed, all the nineteenth-century ideologies of assimilation contained an element of striving to preserve Judaism in a largely non-Jewish world. The problem with assimilation, Loewenstein thus claimed, was not the process itself but rather its radicalisation and transformation into a self-contained ideology.[72]

---

[70]Fritz Friedlander, 'Eine Charakterbild in der Geschichte. Zu Wilhelm Grau: "Wilhelm V. Humboldt"' in *CVZ*, vol. 14, no. 45 (7 November 1935), n.p.

[71]Kurt Loewenstein, 'Zeichen des Untergang, Gefahren der Assimilation', in *JR*, vol. 39, no. 18 (2 March 1934), pp. 1–2. It seems that Loewenstein was reacting to claims raised by *CV* speakers that Jewish nationalism was in fact a way of assimilating the original religious form of Judaism to a context of German nationalism and even racism; see for example Hirschberg, 'Assimilation oder Dissimilation?', in *CVZ*, vol. 13, no. 18 (3 May 1934), n.p. Other CV speakers blamed Zionism on "brown assimilation"; see Jacob Boas, 'German-Jewish Internal Politics under Hitler 1933–1938', in *LBI Year Book*, vol. 29 (1984), p. 22. For Orthodox claims that Zionism was a path to assimilation see Anon., 'Deutsche und jüdische Kultur', in *Der Israelit*, vol. 75, no. 18 (3 May 1934), pp. 1–3.

[72]Kurt Loewenstein, 'Assimilation und Dissimilation', in *JR*, vol. 38, no. 78 (29 September 1933), p. 590.

Despite the considerable gap between Loewenstein's confirmation of "natural assimilation" and Fritz Friedlander's idea of "productive assimilation", conceptual parallels between the two authors are quite evident, both writers claiming that there was a natural, inevitable, and perhaps even positive assimilative path. Both also noted that German Jewry's problems had originated in the choice of a different, negative path towards assimilation, which involved the willingness to sacrifice the very foundations of one's tradition and collective existence. Both agreed, moreover, that this erroneous path needed to be abandoned. To be sure, Friedlander, the liberal, identified the negative path with figures such as Varnhagen and Herz, Heine and Börne, whereas Loewenstein, the Zionist, identified it with the vast majority of nineteenth-century German Jewry. But in their fundamental acceptance of the process, both implicitly took issue with Prinz's total rejection of the emancipatory heritage, as well as with his positive assessment of ghetto life.

Another illustration of shared assumptions held by liberals and Zionists in the assimilation question is offered by Zionist interpretations of the Prinz-Weil debate. Weil, according to one anonymous Zionist author, had not understood the Zionist attitude in claiming that Zionism had been opposed to emancipation from the very outset.[73] To the contrary, all Jewish nationalists saw emancipation as a necessary historical process, recognising the fact that Zionism itself was an offspring of emancipation. To be sure, the same author conceded, one might ask if emancipation had to take the historical course that it did, and whether it was necessary for the Jews to react with such intense "characterless assimilation" (*charakterlose Assimilation*). It was regarding this particular point, he indicated, that Zionists were in fact critics of emancipation, but this did not mean they opposed the process of integration itself. Zionists had no nostalgia for the ghetto, he wrote, but simply aspired to new paths towards emancipation. They were not considering abandoning the linguistic and cultural heritage of the Jews in Germany. Ideas of dissimilation were solely aimed at developing a new and more positive Jewish identity, something, he insisted, with which even Weil should be able to identify.

It seems that starting in 1935, the deteriorating situation of the Jews in Germany, and especially their growing isolation, encouraged an increased proximity of Zionist and liberal approaches. Another expression of such proximity can be found in an article by David Schlossberg in the *Jüdische Rundschau* of March 1936. Schlossberg stressed that Zionism had never rejected the natural and unconscious adjustment of Jews to their environment, and that there were positive aspects even to "conscious" assimilative processes.[74] Schlossberg maintained that one could speak about "positive assimilation" – for instance, the assimilation of the Enlightenment period, which had led to a Jewish renaissance – as opposed to negative assimilation, which had threatened the continuity of Jewish existence in the Diaspora. A further resemblance between Schlossberg's ideas and those of the C.V. can be found in his cyclical model of history, according to which every assimilation process had to be followed and balanced by a process of dissimilation. Schlossberg appears to have been aware of this resemblance, prompting him to lay stress on the differences between him and the liberals:

[73]Anon., 'Um die Emanzipation: Zu einer Rede Bruno Weils', in *JR*, vol. 39, no. 88 (2 November 1934), p. 5.
[74]David Schlossberg, 'Assimilation und Dissimilation', in *JR*, vol. 41, no. 26 (31 March 1936), p. 2.

The lasting exchange between assimilation and dissimilation should not be allowed to tempt us Jews to a fatalism holding that "it will soon change again". Assimilation cannot annihilate us, since it will be brought to a halt in time from the outside. Nor can dissimilation be deadly for us, since in the eternal course of *Auf und Ab* it will have to surrender its proper place to its opposite element.

At the same time, Schlossberg attacked an approach that, based on the recurrence of specific patterns within Jewish history, predicted that the current evil – forced dissimilation – would necessarily be followed by a return of better times, meaning the renewal of free assimilation. He defined this approach – held by a number of liberal writers at the time – as destructive.[75] The periods of dissimilation, he wrote, were actually becoming increasingly longer, leading to an uprooting of Jews from the places they had lived for centuries. Assimilation also had an accumulative price – the disappearance of many Jews. Schlossberg saw the realisation of the Zionist vision in Palestine as the sole way out of this otherwise endless pattern: disintegration as part and parcel of assimilation, followed by the indignities of dissimilation. Zionism meant active Jewish participation in world culture without a loss of what was unique in Judaism and of the Jewish communal character.

VI

On 23 March 1933, the Orthodox journal *Der Israelit* published an article under the pseudonym Nechunia.[76] In an introductory comment the editors noted that they had decided to publish the article because of its call for repentance, although they were not in agreement with all of the author's claims. The article took an extremely radical approach in addressing the reality of the emancipatory ideal's collapse. For a century, the writer observed, German Jews had only felt the cold wind of exile, so typical of Jewish history, from a distance. God had provided them with a respite in order to examine their loyalty to his *Torah* outside of the ghetto, and had now decided, after the vast majority of them had failed the test, to send them the current misery as an educational tool. Liberals, Zionists, and even some Orthodox Jews were described by Nechunia as sinners. His conclusion was clear: German Jews had to recognise and confess their fundamental sin – desertion of the laws of the *Torah*. A great wave of repentance had to now flood German Jewry.

In an additional article published five months later, the same author sought to examine the origins and meaning of that same sin as originating in the eighteenth and nineteenth centuries.[77] One hundred and fifty years ago, he wrote, "the poison of assimilation" (*das Gift der Assimilation*) had begun to emerge. The meaning of assimilation for Nechunia was treason against God and against divine law. When the

---

[75]For a liberal presentation of such ideas see Bruno Weil's discussion of what he terms, in a chapter title *Wellenlinie jüdischen Schicksals* ("the ups and downs of Jewish fate"); see *idem*, *Der Weg*, pp. 11–43. A similar theme was raised by Ernst Herzfeld, 'Assimilation, Dissimilation, Auswanderung', in *CVZ*, vol. 16, no. 8 (25 February 1937), n.p.

[76]Nechunia, 'Die Losung der Stunde', in *Der Israelit*, vol. 74, no. 12 (23 March 1933), pp. 1–3.

[77]Nechunia, 'Die grosse Abrechnung', in *Der Israelit*, vol. 74, no. 35 (31 August 1933), pp. 1–3.

German Jews chose this path, they broke down the barriers between them and their environment, relinquishing the totality of Jewish ghetto life. This poisonous reality, whose clearest expressions could be found in Jewish religious liberalism, treason against the Sabbath, and mixed marriages, had even penetrated into the ranks of German Jewish Orthodoxy, whose majority, according to Nechunia, had turned to the path of "partial assimilation" (*partielle Assimilation*). But God's hand had now put an end to this poisonous process – the nineteenth century emancipation had been left in ruins and assimilation had been robbed of meaning within the new state. Nechunia viewed the popular turn towards Zionism as a substitution of one version of assimilation for another. The useless effort to create a Jewish nation like all other nations, and that to continue the life of Germany's Jewish communities – to organise sports and cultural activities with messages like "we will never return to the ghetto" – only demonstrated that the proper historical lesson had not been learnt.

With a comparative glance, one can observe an interesting similarity between Nechunia's interpretation and the radical Zionist approach formulated by Prinz. Both Prinz and Nechunia differed from other writers on the assimilation question by completely rejecting the assimilation process – each of course for his own reasons. The two writers also shared a positive attitude to the ghetto – its era identified with suffering and misery, but also with an original, productive, and proud Judaism. To be sure, it would be difficult to find any deeper similarities. For Nechunia, Prinz's attitude was only another version of assimilation, perhaps even more dangerous than the liberal version at the moment, while Prinz would probably have claimed that Nechunia did not understand the fundamental national forces directing Jewish history. In our context, it is important to understand that in their radical rejection of the emancipation tradition, both writers represented exceptions even within their own, orthodox and Zionist, camps.

Nechunia's radical separatism was doubtless all the more a minority position among contributors to *Der Israelit*. To be sure, there were others who expressed similar positions. Simon Schwab, for example, challenged the entire path towards modernisation which German Jewry had embarked on, claiming that all the solutions to current problems emerged from the pre-Mendelssohnian period.[78] The contrasting, far more commonly held moderate Orthodox approach, its representatives generally seeing themselves as part of Rabbi Samson Raphael Hirsch's tradition, was presented in, among other places, an anonymous article published in *Der Israelit* in July 1934.[79] The article's author stressed the millennium-old connection of Orthodox German Jewry with the German homeland. He defined this connection, moreover, as an "active force of assimilation" (*Aktive Assimilationskraft*). This force, he stressed, did not conflict with full devotion to God's laws; rather, it was an expression of the aspiration to adopt surrounding spiritual values without abandoning Jewish tradition or turning it into an abstract entity. As soon as the Jews had stopped actively directing their assimilation process, they were exposed to the "assimilating forces of their surrounding culture", which posed a threat to their Judaism. Even those who maintained the principle of "*Torah* with *derech eretz*" (allying the Jewish religion with

---

[78]Simon Schwab, *Heimkehr ins Judentum*, Frankfurt am Main 1934. For a similar position see Anon.,'Deutsche und Jüdische Kultur', in *Der Israelit*, vol. 75, no. 18 (3 May 1934), pp. 1–3.
[79]Anon., 'Der Aufruf der Geschichte', in *Der Israelit*, vol. 75, no. 30 (26 July 1934), pp. 1, 3–4.

progress) were not free from this danger, since only a small minority of Jews ever succeeded in properly implementing such a synthesis, thus fully realising the ideal of
"active assimilation".[80] God's powerful voice had once again made itself heard in
history through the failure of German Jewry's emancipatory striving. The reaction
to this, however, the anonymous author continued, should not be a complete renunciation of love for Germany, its landscapes, its culture, but rather to recognise that
the German Jews, and the Orthodox among them, had gone too far in their adoption of the general culture.

In any event, the representatives of the central Orthodox camp in German Jewry,
those indeed associated with the heritage of "*Torah* with *derech eretz*", continued to uphold
the idea of emancipation and oppose the call for a return to ghetto life. Such principles
were manifest in Orthodox representations of the figure of Moses Mendelssohn.
According to one Orthodox publicist, the boundary between Jewish culture and general culture was at present a reality within each individual German Jew; the community
was not ready to once again erect ghetto walls. Retracing Mendelssohn's footsteps, tra-
versing the road back from Berlin to Dessau, was no longer possible.[81]

In his programmatic book *Das gesetzestreue Judentum*, Rabbi Joseph Carlebach, one
of the most prominent leaders of German Orthodoxy, presented Mendelssohn as a
founding father. Mendelssohn, he claimed, had been the first to define the boundaries
of the assimilation process and to determine in an acceptable fashion the price
Germany's Jews would be willing to pay for emancipation. Carlebach focused on
Mendelssohn's well-know declaration that if the civil rights offered the Jews were conditional on their renunciation of religious laws, then they would be unable to accept
the offer. The rabbi presented this position as the starting point for traditional Jewry's
struggle with the challenges of civil freedom.[82] Mendelssohn, he indicated, had
wished to free the Jews from their state of alienation from their surrounding culture
through a process of "inner emancipation" – cultural renewal based on projects such
as his translation of the Bible – even before the advent of the "external emancipation".[83] Carlebach thus pointed to Mendelssohn's route towards modernisation as the
proper one. At the same time, he suggested that Mendelssohn had nevertheless presented his plans too early, then passing his leadership position on to other figures who
had generally preferred "external" to "internal" emancipation" – thus viewing their
religion as an obstacle to political progress. In calling upon traditional Judaism to cope
directly with the challenge of emancipation, Hirsch would remain an isolated figure.[84]

VII

Announced by the Nuremberg Laws, the final destruction of German Jewry's emancipatory ideals also marked a turning point in the thinking and modes of actions

---

[80]For an excerpt from Samson Raphael Hirsch in which he discusses his concept of "*Torah* with *derech eretz*"
see Paul Mendes-Flohr and Yehuda Reinharz (eds.), pp. 197–202.
[81]M. Elias, 'Rückblick und Ausblick', part 3, in *Der Israelit*, vol. 76, no. 3 (17 January 1935), pp. 3, 5–6.
[82]Joseph Carlebach, *Das gesetzestreue Judentum*, Berlin 1936 (Jüdische Lesehefte, vol. 15), pp. 15–16.
[83]*ibid.*, p. 27.
[84]*ibid.*, p. 34.

adopted by its various ideological camps. It is important also to note here that in the late 1930s German Jews, especially those still believing in a Jewish future in Germany, had less and less latitude to express their opinions in a free way.

In this unmistakably radicalised situation, the *Centralverein* activists, and even those of the National League of Jewish Frontline Soldiers (the *Reichsbund jüdischer Frontsoldaten*) could no longer ignore the growing need for emigration. Some of these individuals now began devoting most of their efforts to promoting emigration, now considered a mission. The Zionists, on the other hand, had to cope with the contradiction between the pressure for emigration and Palestine's inability to absorb all of the emigrants. They were thus forced to acknowledge the need to emigrate to other destinations.[85]

These changes in the agendas of the various German-Jewish political groupings were given prominent expression in their publications. Instead of the political commentaries and discussions of internal politics, emigration and surrounding issues now emerged as central. Even the discourse regarding the German-Jewish heritage had now begun to focus on the question of the potential for continuity in new Diasporas. The terms "emancipation" and "assimilation" were beginning to be used in this new context as well.

Among German Jews, the South African Alien Act of early 1937, which made immigration to that country conditional on the immigrant's potential for assimilation into local white society, evoked a new discussion regarding the connection between immigration and assimilation.[86] With the great need for immigration having now become, at least formally, dependent on their "assimilation", liberal speakers were offered a new opportunity to re-evaluate the concept. Thus, Ernst Herzfeld, president of the C.V., used the chance to propose a conceptual and historical interpretation adequate for the C.V.'s agenda.[87]

"Assimilation" (*Assimilation*), Herzfeld indicated, was a Latin-based expression whose direct German translation was *Anähnelung* (resemblance). A certain level of assimilation – mostly an adjustment to the environment's language and modes of thought– was an inevitable part of any civilisation process. Beyond this, however, Herzfeld proposed a new distinction between two forms of assimilation – "assimilation in the accusative", which he presented as the effective suicide of the minority, its knowing absorption into the majority, and "assimilation in the dative", which he presented as a process essential for "life itself". The role of Jewish leadership was therefore, he continued, to delineate the boundaries of the process, thus preserving essential elements in the future of Jewish existence.

Herzfeld went farther than any of his predecessors in his view of the extent and depth of the assimilation process in Jewish history and his detailed description of the assimilationist-dissimilationist cycle. Several outstanding eras in Jewish history, he argued – the Alexandrian within the Roman empire, the Spanish under the Arabs,

---

[85]Abraham Margaliot, 'The Reaction of the Jewish Public in Germany to the Nuremberg Laws', in *Yad Vashem Studies*, vol. 12 (1977), pp. 75–107.

[86]On the South African Alien Law see L. Hotz, 'South Africa and the Refugees En Route. Restrictions on Immigration', in Frieda H. Sichel, *From Refugee to Citizen: A Sociological Study of the Immigrants from Hitler-Europe who Settled in Southern Africa*, Capetown 1966, pp. 17–18.

[87]Ernst Herzfeld, 'Assimilation, Dissimilation, Auswanderung', in *CVZ*, vol. 16, no. 8 (25 February 1937), n.p.

the German during the early middle ages – were characterised by advanced assimilation. In each of these periods, however, there had also been contrary forces facilitating recreation of the Jewish communities. The crusades, for example, had prompted a strong dissimilating tendency among Ashkenazi Jews – a clear hint at the current situation of the Jews under the Nazis.

Like Weil and other Jewish liberal observers, Herzfeld disagreed with the view that the modern development of European Jewry was unprecedented in Jewish history. The assimilation process that began in Western Europe in the late eighteenth century was not essentially different from these earlier processes. Modern Jews had gained their rights with a clear expectation that they would respond with willing integration (*Verschmelzung*) into the general society, to the point of disappearance (*Verschwinden*). Throughout the nineteenth century, those who chose to remain Jewish in Germany were thus rejected by the state, whereas many doors were opened to those who were baptised. In what, to the present author, appears to be its underestimation of the scope of Jewish integration in Germany, Herzfeld's approach seems quite different from that of C.V. speakers of the pre-Nazi era. It served as the backdrop for Herzfeld's presentation of the C.V. as an organisation aspiring to steer the assimilation process in the right way, even now, during the crisis-driven emigration. The C.V., he claimed, differed from the body of radical assimilationists (*Assimilantentum*), who had no desire to preserve Judaism in any form. It had actually become the major agency for preserving Jewish existence in Germany.

The Nazi politics of dissimilation had once more placed the question of assimilation and dissimilation on the German-Jewish agenda – this time in radicalised form. All of the Jewish factions in Germany now recognised the importance of bringing about change. There was, however, no possibility of erasing the past 150 years and returning to the ghetto. Furthermore, Herzfeld observed, most of the Jews who had left Germany had emigrated to other countries than Palestine, which would continue to be the destination of only a limited number of Jews. The demand made by various countries, such as South Africa, for a willingness and capacity of the immigrants to assimilate thus had clear implications for the Jewish leadership concerned with preparing young people to leave Germany. The leaders needed to avoid discounting the question of loyalty to Judaism; but it was no less crucial to be able to immigrate, hence to assimilate.

Herzfeld's distinction between "assimilation in the accusative" and "assimilation in the dative" was rejected by the Zionist press as both strange and groundless. Zionism, a certain H.F. indicated, had established the more relevant distinction between a natural, inevitable "unwilled assimilation" (*ungewollte Assimilation*) and a "willed assimilation" (*gewollte Assimilation*) that Zionists rejected. Herzfeld had avoided the crux of the problem by ignoring these key concepts.[88] The typical "German citizen of the Mosaic faith" tended towards "willed assimilation", reducing Jewish identity to the religious element. This eventually led to religious indifference, in some cases even to conversion or self-hatred. In contrast, the Zionists opposed the trans-

---

[88]H.F., 'Assimilation, Dissimilation und neue Assimilation: Eine Erwiderung', in *JR*, vol. 42, no. 20 (12 March 1937), pp. 1–2; for an additional Zionist response see Hans Pomeranz, 'Erneuerung der jüdischen Begriffsbildung, Mut zur Entwicklung', in *JR*, vol. 43, no. 38 (13 May 1938), p. 4.

formation of German citizens of the Mosaic faith into Brazilians and South Africans of the Mosaic faith, since they understood that what had failed in Germany would eventually fail in Brazil and South Africa. Given present circumstances, the author was not opposed to the idea of such Jewish immigration. But he stressed the need to construct a basis for integration into the new countries in terms of a synthesis between two equal partners.

The initial Zionist response to the South African Alien Act also included an anonymously authored article with a different, more apologetic tone.[89] The article's starting point was South Africa's approach to Zionism as evidence of a Jewish unwillingness to assimilate, this used as an argument against Jewish immigration to the country. A full solution, the author argued, to Jewish problems could not be achieved solely by granting civil rights to Jewish individuals. The Jews in Germany had learnt that devotion to "unfettered and total assimilation" (*hemmunglose und restlose Assimilation*), which ignored all distinctions between groups, lead to a sharp anti-Jewish reaction. On the other hand, he added, modern history had proven that Jews were able to assimilate when not met with surrounding opposition. And there had also always been Jews who managed to preserve their Jewish self-consciousness while still successfully integrating into their various homelands, adjusting to the new ways of life and developing a sense of local political loyalty, as in Western Europe and the United States. The American Zionists were no less proud of their American identity as a result of their Zionism, and if this was the kind of assimilation demanded by the South Africans, then all Jews could be assimilated. However, he concluded, over a century after the Napoleonic Sanhedrin, past errors had to be avoided; it was important not to demand once again that the Jews give up their traditions as the price for integration.

The response to the South African laws by Herzfeld and the anonymous Zionist author points again to both similarities and differences between C.V. and Zionist standpoints. Both authors drew a distinction between two kinds of assimilation, and both insisted that Jewish emigration would be possible due to the ability of the Jews to assimilate in the right way. Under the circumstances of 1937, when the problem of emigration was extremely urgent and the option of Palestine seemed unrealistic for most German Jews, even the Zionists had to come up with a formula allowing Jewish emigration to diaspora countries. Hence both liberals and Zionists aspired to create a new form of Jewish integration laying stress on a balanced relationship with the wider society, thus rendering maintenance of the Jewish collective entity possible. In the context of an ever-worsening daily reality, the disagreements between the two sides had an increasingly rhetorical nature, without clear practical implications.

VIII

A significant portion of the Jewish public discourse during the 1930s regarding the questions of emancipation and assimilation was clearly influenced by a variety of external challenges. It seems that at least some of these challenges were having little

---

[89]Anon., 'Assimilierbarkeit', in *JR*, vol. 42, no. 12 (12 February 1937), pp. 1–2.

real impact on the Jewish situation in Germany. Lutz Lenders, for instance, was only a marginal Nazi writer and South African policy was far from determining the fate of Jewish emigration from Germany. The fact that both Lenders' article and the South African Alien Act evoked responses by key Jewish figures, prompting them to reopen the basic problems of modern Jewish history for discussion, demonstrates the depth of confusion of German Jewry and the ideological crisis it was undergoing at the time.

An overview of the major German-Jewish approaches to assimilation and emancipation in this period reveals a gradual blurring of the traditional division between the major camps – Liberal, Zionist, and Orthodox. Notwithstanding the preservation of the old organisational frameworks, the new circumstances had led to the emergence of new ideological divisions between a radical minority, which rejected any form of assimilation, and a moderate majority, which favoured a number of moderate models of assimilation, rejecting only the more radical ones.

Most Liberal, Zionist, and Orthodox authors displayed a tension between the need to maintain a bond with past achievements, in order to find a measure of security there, and the need to interpret the current crisis. The resemblance here between liberals like Fritz Friedlander and Ismar Freund, Zionists like David Schlossberg, and an Orthodox individual like Joseph Carlebach, is striking. They all described, or at least implied, two paths of assimilation. The original assimilative route, associated mainly with the founding figure of Mendelssohn, was described in terms of "positive", "productive", and "active" assimilation, or in one case, "inner emancipation". This route was defined as preserving Jewish uniqueness accompanied by an integration of the Jews into German society. The other, negative route was defined as the renunciation of fundamental Jewish qualities – one involving religious conversion according to the liberals, denial of the national element in Judaism according to the Zionists, and abandonment of Jewish law according to the Orthodox. All these authors thus remained loyal to an original ideal of leaving the ghetto for the sake of integration and emancipation without, however, renouncing the foundations of Judaism – foundations each author understood in accordance with his own world view.

It appears that in the discussions surrounding the South African Alien Act, the principal gaps between the Liberal and Zionist concepts of history became less central than previously. The main Zionist discomfort with assimilation diminished significantly, the dynamic of assimilation in Western countries being now described as successful and contrasted with the situation in Germany. Zionists, in fact, seem to have even assumed that if things went the proper way, the German-Jewish immigrants would become successfully integrated into their new countries. This position was clearly different from that expressed by Joachim Prinz, who not only rejected the processes of emancipation and assimilation in Germany from their very outset, but also claimed, in 1934, that the same eternal Jewish fate would eventually be visited upon the Jews of France, England and the United States. Emancipation, in other words, would collapse there as it had in Germany.[90]

The changes that took place in the liberal camp are equally evident. In the circumstances of 1937, Herzfeld did not hesitate to connect the essential shortcomings

---

[90]Prinz, p. 54.

in the Jewish situation emerging from the nineteenth century to both the assimilation process and German emancipation policy itself, which was not inclined to accept the Jews as Jews. With this claim, Herzfeld was moving in the direction of the more sceptical, Zionist evaluation of Jewish emancipation in Germany.

In the final analysis, one basic historical picture was manifestly shared by a majority of German Jewish writers concerned with the assimilation question in the 1930s. Most German Jews in general felt extremely uncomfortable with the memory of the ghetto and with declarations calling for a return to ghetto life. Even with emancipation collapsing before their eyes, they continued to identify in principle with its values and symbols. A total rejection of emancipation and assimilation, and complete alienation from the values of the Enlightenment, far from uncommon in non-Jewish German society during this period, were quite rare among German Jews. Those articulating such views, the Zionist Prinz, the Orthodox Nechunia, were clearly exceptions even in their own milieus. However, representatives of all the German Jewish factions did share a recognition that something had gone wrong in the emancipation and assimilation process. Zionists and Orthodox Jews tended, each side in its own way, to blame the entire nineteenth century, and especially liberalism, for irresponsible assimilation, and even for Jewish self-denial. In their view, the assimilative path, beginning with Mendelssohn's best intentions and actions, was transformed in the course of the nineteenth century into something destructive – this mainly being due, according to these depictions, to a destructive process, primarily caused by a facile willingness on the part of German Jews to renounce their traditions for the sake of equal rights. This destructive route, they maintained, had led not only to the decline of German Jewry, but also to the eventual collapse of emancipation, either because of a non-Jewish unwillingness to accept Jews who had abandoned their dignity, or – according to some renditions – because of God's intervention in human history.

Liberal publicists avoided such a sweeping rejection of the nineteenth century heritage. Many believed that the values of the period had been good then, even if they were untenable now. But the liberals did tend to consider certain forms of Jewish integration in Germany as expressions of a destructive form of assimilation, a form departing from Mendelssohn's heritage. Certain liberal authors went so far as to voice regret at the lack of awareness German Jews had shown to the depth of hostility felt towards them by non-Jewish Germans, or laid stress on the historical limitations of the emancipatory project in Germany, which, even in its heyday, had in fact hardly been ideal.

It is difficult to draw a clear conclusion from these historical discussions, but it seems that the combination of acceptance, in principle, of the values of emancipation and assimilation and criticism of the manner in which these processes unfolded, implies an expectation that emancipation might be regained if lessons could be drawn from past errors. An increasingly clear awareness by liberal publicists that this was actually not the case, and a growing Zionist awareness that Palestine would be unable to offer a full solution to the plight of the German Jews, led to a growing focus on the promise held by emigration to other diaspora countries. There, it was hoped, German-Jewish immigrants might be able to implement the lessons of their past and fulfil the processes of emancipation and assimilation in a better, more stable fashion.

Kurt Singer's Shattered Hopes

By Adam J. Sacks

The hopes referred to in the above title were twofold: on the one hand those of maintaining German-Jewish culture in the Third Reich, on the other those of transplanting German-Jewish culture to the United States. The medium of German-Jewish culture Singer's hopes were pinned on was the *Jüdischer Kulturbund* (Jewish League of Culture). A neurologist and musician, Kurt Singer was the *Intendant* (general director) of the *Kulturbund*. Two letters by Singer, written in Amsterdam in the aftermath of the German pogrom night of 9–10 November 1938 ("*Kristallnacht*") and appended below in translation, illuminate his attitude. One was sent to his *Kulturbund* colleagues, the other to Hans Hinkel, *Reichskulturwalter* (Reich Administrator of Culture), the Nazi official who oversaw the *Kulturbund* and with whom Singer had a particularly close working relationship. It is worth considering Singer's aims in light of these letters.

George L. Mosse's *German Jews Beyond Judaism*,[1] and Saul Friedländer's more recent *Nazi Germany and the Jews*[2] have both offered an appraisal of the *Kulturbund*. The arguments in these books make a useful starting point. For Mosse, the *Kulturbund* represented an oasis of Weimar humanism in the desert of Nazi culture. Although, he indicates, the German-Jewish dialogue no longer existed, the Jews nevertheless carried forward and became the sole custodians of Humboldt's ideal of *Bildung*. From this perspective, the German Jews embodied the "true spirit of Germany",[3] raising the banner of *Bildung* high in Nazi Germany. In contrast, Friedländer sees the *Kulturbund* as a Jewish undertaking that suited Nazi plans for isolating the Jews, while serving as a cover for what might have proved embarrassing in executing the policy of exclusion. Friedländer thus sees the *Kulturbund* as foreshadowing the Nazi ghetto, where the pretence of autonomy camouflaged total subjugation. He asserts that the "ongoing misunderstanding of the true meaning of the situation was compounded by the ambition of some of its founders".[4] The last sentence of Friedländer's book refers to the "doomed" audience members at a *Kulturbund* performance.

The idealising tendencies in Mosse's reading may be summarised in his characterisation of the *Kulturbund* as the grand last act of Weimar culture, which he defines as largely determined by the German-Jewish dialogue. Yet portraying the participants of the *Kulturbund* as essential vehicles for enlightenment and tolerance does not take into account the complex use the Nazis themselves made of the proponents of

---

[1]George L. Mosse, *German Jews Beyond Judaism*, Cincinnati 1985
[2]Saul Friedländer, Nazi Germany and the Jews, vol 1: *The Years of Persecution*, 1933–1939, New York 1997.
[3]Mosse, pp. 16–17, 43.
[4]Friedländer, p. 66.

enlightenment. In contrast, Friedländer's hard judgment exchanges a post-Weimar for a pre-Holocaust context. It defines the *Kulturbund* as a *Judenrat avant la lettre*.

This judgment of the *Kulturbund* treats Kurt Singer as something like a "fall guy". In general, one is tempted to explain the sporadic and belated scholarly coverage of this cultural organisation as an implicit verdict of condemnation by neglect. The attempt to discredit the *Kulturbund* begins with Singer and singles Singer out as uniquely responsible. An example is Mark Goldsmith's journalistic work, *The Inextinguishable Symphony*.[5] In contrast to the author's depiction of the musicians' valiant efforts, Singer is portrayed as ego-obsessed, at times tyrannical, and even as obstructing the efforts of the organisation's members to escape from Nazi Germany.

In actuality, more than any other person involved in the organisation – and his colleagues included Julius Bab and Joachim Prinz – Singer elevated the *Kulturbund* beyond an emergency rescue effort to a cultural movement, one that at times articulated a critique of the culture of emancipation. In this manner, the *Kulturbund* carried forward the German-Jewish secular tradition of engaging in aesthetic and cultural pursuits in the face of political disappointments and setbacks. For Singer, the nightmare of the deteriorating conditions of German Jewry had to be turned into an opportunity. His efforts eloquently demonstrated the persistence and will to live of a culture that would not so easily renounce what had been assiduously acquired over decades of emancipation. It is important to recall that at this time Auschwitz was not only unforeseeable but inconceivable.

KURT SINGER'S VISION FOR THE *KULTURBUND*

An address by Kurt Singer entitled '*Jüdischer Kulturbund: Rückschau und Vorschau*', delivered at a *Kulturbund* symposium in September 1936, demonstrates the organisation's ambitions, programmatic content, and goals.[6] In the course of this address, Singer revealed his basic reaction to the isolation of the German Jews – a sense that this predicament needed to be made productive through a fundamental change of attitude. A synthesis was possible, he maintained, between Jewish folk cultures and Western culture. He would attempt to bridge the differences and even harmonise the competing Zionist and non-Zionist visions of Jewish life. He regarded this as a necessity for the continuation of German-Jewish cultural activity in Hitler's Germany.

"Bread and circuses" was Singer's term for the situation the *Kulturbund* initially faced – and even indulged in to some extent. His example was Lessing's *Nathan the Wise*, the organisation's first production. Singer viewed the play less as a continuation of Weimar humanism than as a backward glance, lacking constructive content and not reflecting any new Jewish ideas. His message implicitly conveyed a critique of the culture of German-Jewish emancipation as unsuitable for confronting contemporary challenges. Singer pointed to the *Habima*, the Hebrew-language theatre of the *Yishuv*, as an alternative to the theatre of Wilhelminian Germany – an alterna-

---

[5]Mark Goldsmith, *The Inextinguishable Symphony*, New York 2000. See chapter 9, 'Kurt Singer'.
[6]Akademie der Künste, Fritz Wisten Archives (henceforth Adk, FWA', 74/86/5032). The translation and publication of this address is part of a larger research project by the author.

Kurt Singer speaking at the conference of the *Reichsverband der jüdischen Kulturbünde* in Berlin on 5 September 1936. From left to right: Werner Levie, Benno Cohn, Kurt Singer and Joachim Prinz.

By courtesy of the Jewish Museum, Berlin. Photograph Herbert Sonnenfeld

tive serving as an ideal closely related to his ideas for the future of the *Kulturbund*. He opened the symposium at which his address was delivered by announcing the dispatch of telegrams of solidarity to both the *Habima* and the Jewish Palestine-Orchestra of Bronislaw Huberman.

Co-operation, assistance, and a process of mutual learning, not conflict, envy, and obstruction, were to become the norm in relations between the *Kulturbund* and other Jewish cultural institutions.[7] At the same time, in distinction to an institution such as the *Habima*, the *Kulturbund* was a vehicle for conserving and preserving two cultures threatened with obliteration: the wider European German-language culture and the specific culture emerging from the German-Jewish symbiosis. Both these traditions suffered grievous damage in Germany during the Nazi period. Singer's vision of progress for future decades included creating an archive of Yemenite and Palestinian (Jewish) folk music, as well as an institute for translating Hebrew and Yiddish texts into German.[8] Yet at one point in his address, he does allude to the possibly inevitable, gradual embrace of another, unspecified language as the official working language of the *Kulturbund*.[9]

---

[7]Kurt Singer. 'Die Arbeit der Jüdischen Kulturbünde: Rückschau und Vorschau'. Adk, FWA, 74/86/5032, 26.
[8]*ibid.*, 35.
[9]*ibid.*

TRANSPLANTING GERMAN-JEWISH CULTURE

A few years before Singer tried to transfer the *Kulturbund* to the United States, he made Palestine the goal of a similar effort. Alice Levie has provided testimony showing that her husband, Werner Levie – a Dutch citizen, a Zionist, and General Secretary of the *Kulturbund* – spoke with Hinkel about the possibility of moving the organisation's technical and administrative personnel and artists to Palestine.[10] She offers a positive portrait of the relationship between her husband and Hinkel. In 1936, on one of several visits by members of the *Kulturbund* to Palestine, Levie spoke with Huberman and Arturo Toscanini about his plan to organise concerts on the model of those the *Kulturbund* sponsored.[11] A follow-up visit took place in early 1938.[12] Apparently, Toscanini agreed to direct the first, German opera as a protest against the Nazis. There were also negotiations with the *Habima* theatre regarding its possible expansion through addition of the *Kulturbund*'s opera company. Alice Levie recalls that she had already rented an apartment for her family for the move.[13] Upon returning to Berlin in the summer of 1938, the Levies were told by the German authorities that neither funds nor instruments could be taken out of the country.

THE CONTEXT OF SINGER'S AMSTERDAM LETTERS

In October 1938 Kurt Singer travelled to the United States with money from Jewish organisations to help get out more people from Germany, one of his main intentions being to raise funds for the emigration of the *Kulturbund*.[14] A recently discovered message from Singer to *Kulturbund* members, written before his departure on the occasion of the fifth anniversary of the group's first theatrical production, reads like a coded farewell message.[15] The message makes clear that Singer planned the American visit as the first step in a process of emigration by himself and the *Kulturbund*, with the help of American Jews. During his trip, he saw his sister in Boston, gave lectures at Harvard, and discussed the possibility of a teaching appointment with both Yale University and the New School.[16] Against the wishes of his family, Singer insisted on returning to Berlin as he did not want to abandon his colleagues in the *Kulturbund*. Ernest Lenart, a *Kulturbund* actor who had already emigrated, recalls visiting Singer in his New York hotel room the day after "*Kristallnacht*". His bags were already packed for his return from New York when he learned of

---

[10]See testimony of Alice Levie, 'Wer ist die blonde Frau? Das ist doch keine Jüdin!' in Eike Geisel and Henryk Broder (eds.), *Premiere und Pogrom: Der Jüdische Kulturbund 1933–1941, Texte und Bilder*, Berlin 1992, pp. 153–160.

[11]*ibid.*, p. 156.

[12]*ibid.*, p. 157.

[13]*ibid.*

[14]Eike Geisel, 'Ein Reich, ein Ghetto: Zwei Karrieren', in *idem* and Broder (eds.), pp. 326–327.

[15]Akademie der Künste (ed.), *Drei Leben für Das Theater: Fritz Wisten*, Berlin 1990, p. 83.

[16]See testimony of Margot Wachsmann-Singer, 'Mein Vater hat den Kulturbund so ungeheuer geliebt', in Geisel and Broder (eds.), p. 196.

Germany's wide-scale pogrom. But the news appears to have strengthened his resolve to return.

The *Kulturbund*'s theatre, located on Berlin's Kommandantenstrasse, was one of the city's few Jewish institutions left unharmed that night.[17] In fact, an armed unit of SS troops guarded the building, with orders to defend it against an SA group from Magdeburg sent to destroy it. After the pogrom, those *Kulturbund* members remaining in Berlin received special orders and protection letters from the propaganda ministry to return to work, along with a promise that colleagues in concentration camps would be released.[18] Hinkel had insisted that the performance of an English comedy, *Rain and Wind* by Merton Hodgson, premièred on 2 November 1938, be resumed; but in one of a number of acts of resistance, the *Kulturbund* used a "deceptive manoeuvre", "in the presence of Hinkel and foreign journalists", to arrange a memorial service for the victims of the November pogrom.[19] The comedy was therefore only performed again ten days later.[20] The *Kulturbund* would not be closed down by the Gestapo until September 1941. Hence whereas, in line with the hopes he pinned on America, Singer viewed "*Kristallnacht*" as necessarily marking the end of the *Kulturbund*'s German existence, in actuality the pogrom precipitated not so much the end as a direct abuse of the organisation and those connected with it.

Singer arrived in Amsterdam practically without baggage at the end of 1938. He actually had had no previous intention of going to Holland.[21] At first, he believed it would be possible to return to Germany. Soon after his arrival, obeying a Gestapo order, some members of the *Kulturbund* travelled to Amsterdam to persuade him to return to Berlin, but news that he would be arrested had been relayed to him by friends and Singer's brother had already been taken into custody. The *Intendant* thus now became a refugee.[22]

Singer's commitment to his supporters and co-workers before going into exile evoked Leo Baeck's determination to remain in Germany as long as there were people who needed his help. After some years in Holland – as will be detailed, beyond all hope of escaping to America – Singer may well have clung in solace to his former

---

[17]Stephan Stompor, *Jüdisches Musik- und Theaterleben unter dem NS-Staat*. Schriftenreihe des Europäischen Zentrums für Jüdische Musik, vol. 4, edited by Andor Izsák with the assistance of Susanne Borchers (Europäisches Zentrum für Jüdische Musik 2001), Hannover 2001, p. 142.

[18]*ibid.*

[19]In this memorial service, Leo Baeck delivered "an address in memory of the martyrs of Kristallnacht, of the 60,000 prisoners, and of the burning of the synagogues". For this and additional details, all of which have apparently been overlooked, see Kurt Baumann Memoirs, Leo Baeck Institute Archives, New York, pp. 81–83. The memorial service has itself often been overlooked in the literature on the subject.

[20]Eike Geisel. 'The Cultural League is Formed', in Sander Gilman and Jack Zipes (eds.), *Yale Companion to Jewish Writing and Thought in German Culture, 1096–1996*, New Haven 1997, p. 510. Cf. Kurt Baumann Memoirs, pp. 181–183.

[21]Christine Fischer-Defoy (ed.), *Paula Salomon-Lindberg* [testimony], Berlin 1992, p. 119.

[22]Levie and Fischer-Defoy (ed.). There are conflicting versions of this incident. Alice Levie recounts that she herself had travelled to Amsterdam at the behest of her husband and the authorities. Paula Salomon-Lindberg contends rather that Singer had received a telegram from an underground organisation warning him not to return. According to Baumann, p. 93, Singer had actually received a handwritten letter directly from Hinkel urging him to return to Berlin; it contained a guarantee he would not be harmed and would be allowed to prepare for emigration. Singer's letter to Hinkel is a reply to that letter, which remains unaccounted for.

German career of "service" with the *Kulturbund*. Eventually, he would give up, agreeing to board one of the last transports to Theresienstadt on 20 April 1943, with special treatment as a *Prominenter* – one of the *Juden mit Verdiensten* ("Jews who have earned merit"). He was accompanied by Gertrud Ochs, the daughter of Siegfried Ochs who had been Singer's mentor and the founder of the Berlin Philharmonic Choir. Singer wrote a personal history of Siegfried Ochs and the choir which was published in 1933. He had asked Albert Salomon, former chief surgeon at the Jewish Hospital in Berlin, and his wife Paula Salomon-Lindberg, an acclaimed contralto and one of the *Kulturbund*'s stars, to accompany him. On her knees, Paula Salomon had fruitlessly begged Singer not to leave.[23]

In Theresienstadt, Singer gained a reputation as a sort of cultural apostle, offering spiritual nourishment to inmates who were starving for it.[24] He gave lectures on music with titles such as 'Development of the Sonata' and 'Music as Expression of its Creator', ultimately with piano accompaniment. Helped by friends from Berlin such as Kurt Gerron, Singer became involved in the "free time" programme of cultural activities in what was claimed to be a "model camp." He issued reviews – distributed on individual sheets of paper – of vocal music performed in Theresienstadt: Verdi's *Falstaff* and *Requiem* and the children's operetta *Brundibar*. The reservations he expressed regarding the choice of the requiem attest to the survival of his sense of the *Kulturbund*'s function regarding the promotion of Jewish art. At the same time, they show that Singer was under no illusions about the Jewish situation in Europe under Nazi occupation. He wrote as follows:

> Certainly an artistic experience [referring to the performance of Verdi's *Requiem*], yet unfortunately distant from all that which should concern Jews as long as they live in Theresienstadt. The library of Theresienstadt contains the oratorios "King Salomon", Esther", and "Joshua", all three equally great in conception and powerful in musical design. …That would truly be a great artistic event and a Jewish event. Did none of those responsible feel this? Did the suggestion not occur to anyone? If not today, then when? If not in Theresienstadt, then where? There is no country and no city in Europe where "Israel" or "Judah Maccabee" could be performed. Only Theresienstadt had this chance. It is not being used.[25]

Months after his arrival Singer contracted a lung infection. He died in Theresienstadt on 30 January 1944 at the age of fifty-eight. The Red Cross informed his daughter in Palestine soon after his death.[26]

Kurt Singer saw the *Kulturbund* as opening a new cultural era for German Jewry and as an idea that had the potential to outlast the Third Reich, both in Germany and elsewhere. His failed plans to transfer the group to America represent an unfulfilled chapter in the history of German Jewry's emigration. Had the plans succeeded, the evolution of German-Jewish culture as a distinct phenomenon outside Germany may have followed a different path. Not only would hundreds of distin-

---

[23]Fischer-Defoy (ed.), p. 124. Albert and Paula Salomon-Lindberg were the parents of the artist Charlotte Salomon. Charlotte had already been sent to her grandparents in the South of France when she completed her monumental work *Leben? Oder Theater?* Her main exposure to culture was through the *Kulturbund*.
[24]Stompor, p. 208.
[25]Kurt Singer, 'Musikkritischer Brief nr. 4. Verdis Requiem', in Ulrike Migdal (ed.), *Und die Musik spielt dazu*, Munich 1986, p. 170.
[26]Stompor, p. 179.

guished artists and scholars have enriched American cultural life, as was indeed the case, but a medium would have been available for a specific type of German-Jewish cultural and communal continuity. A successful transplant of the *Kulturbund* may thus have helped delay the inevitable absorption of emigrated German-Jewish culture into American – and American-Jewish – society by at least a generation.

Written in December 1938, Kurt Singer's two letters to Berlin from Amsterdam are addressed to, respectfully, Hans Hinkel – supervisor of the *Kulturbund* and *Reichskulturwalter* of the *Reichskulturkammer* – and the managers of the *Kulturbund*.[27] The message in both letters is clear: although he had indeed come back from his American journey with the hope of continuing the *Kulturbund* elsewhere, after "*Kristallnacht*" such a hope was unrealisable, and this had to be recognised. The letter to the *Kulturbund* reveals Singer's keen awareness of imminent danger and calls into question the widespread perception of leading German Jews having kept their eyes shut when faced with catastrophe. The problems are reviewed in both letters: people, financial means, facilities, repertoire. In both, Singer conveys a sense of peril, along with his knowledge that the vision of a post-emancipatory German-Jewish cultural movement belonged to an era before the German-Jewish symbiosis had been destroyed, with the resulting split between German Jewry's culture and Nazi terror. The letters also express Singer's deep dismay and incomprehension at the resumption of activities by the *Kulturbund* after "*Kristallnacht*".

In his letter to Hinkel, Singer explains that his nerves have still not recovered from the pogrom. Nevertheless, his stated reasons for not returning to Germany do not involve concerns for personal safety but rather the view that the *Kulturbund* has no chance of continuing successfully. He bases his decision not to return on official reports in the German press, rather than mentioning his contacts with underground, non-German or Jewish sources. Though clearly aware that no distraction could possibly conceal the terror of a nation-wide pogrom, he merely cites an absence of the audience excitement necessary for successful theatrical performances as a reason for not returning to Germany. He also informs Hinkel of his advice to colleagues that the *Kulturbund* be brought to an end as quickly as possible. Without explicitly mentioning the pogrom, he states that he is suffering together with his co-religionists. He does make one veiled reference to "*Kristallnacht*", writing that the *Kulturbund* has fallen victim to "circumstances". It is notable that he describes his fellow Jews as *Glaubensgenossen*, referring to a shared religion and refusing to adopt the Nazi terminology of race.

Although the valuable work of Alan Steinweis on Hans Hinkel remains a vital contribution to understanding that figure, his role with regards to the *Kulturbund* needs further explanation.[28] Hinkel's close relationship with the leaders of the Jewish organisation, in particular with Singer, was as ambivalent as it was singular in the Third Reich. The existence of the *Kulturbund* offered enrichment to this self-serving

[27]Kurt Singer to *Reichskulturwalter* Hans Hinkel, Amsterdam, 8 December 1938. Bundesarchiv Koblenz, R56I?113 Bl. 7. Kurt Singer to the Vorstand des Jüdischen Kulturbundes Berlin, Amsterdam, 8 December 1938. Adk, FWA, 74/86/1276.

[28]Alan E. Steinweis, 'Hans Hinkel and German Jewry, 1933–1941', in *Leo Baeck Institute Yearbook*, vol. 38 (1993), pp. 209–219.

and opportunistic Nazi official, earlier a mere school teacher; he could now interact closely with highly cultured Jewish artists. Strikingly, there is much evidence to suggest that Singer and Hinkel enjoyed a cordial working relationship.[29] Kurt Singer, it appears, believed in Hinkel's commitment to Jewish culture. In his address two years earlier, Singer had carefully articulated the *Kulturbund*'s ambivalent relationship with the state, understood as representing both control and protection. While Hinkel enforced harsh censorship in his feudal enclave, he also fought for recognition of *Kulturbund* activities and the organisation's security.[30] It is worth noting that in his memoirs, Singer's assistant, Kurt Baumann, records a general perception of Hinkel as belonging to a left-wing faction of the Nazi party.[31] Other testimonies, including that of Alice Levie, avoid labelling Hinkel an antisemite. It would appear that the career of Hinkel – an early Nazi Party member and leader of the *Kampfbund für deutsche Kultur* – in the first five years of the Nazi regime reflect an attempt by the regime to "collaborate", after a fashion, with some Jews.

In his letter to the *Kulturbund* members, Singer records the losses inflicted on the pogrom night – the artists and audience will soon have to emigrate. Possibly alluding to the destruction of the synagogues, which often served as performance venues, he indicates that adequate performance space no longer exists. He equates returning to Germany to the situation of a captain on a sinking ship, in vain seeking to halt rising waters. For Singer, even maintaining the organisation at a standstill would have been a sign of decline. Prevailing circumstances, he insists, for immediate dismantling. His disappointment with what has become of Germany is shown by the fact that when referring to the country, he is only able to write its first letter.

Singer also confirms his hope of rebuilding the *Kulturbund* outside Europe – hence indirectly his conviction that the *Kulturbund* was a viable expression of a new German-Jewish culture, not merely a temporary response to the extraordinary conditions of the first years of Nazi power. He points to the United States as his desired location for the future *Kulturbund*, a choice confirming his general cultural stance, which had broken with Zionist strictures. To the last, then, Singer's Jewish self-identification remained rooted in religion and shaped by fate. In the letter, he thus exhorts those left in Berlin to continue to hold their Jewish beliefs high.

In this note of farewell and thanks in one, Singer lets his former co-workers know that he is ready to write references needed for emigration purposes. This practical gesture points to the resistance undertaken by Singer as not only being of a spiritual or cultural nature. Testimonies by members of the *Kulturbund* who survived the Holocaust, refer to several instances where politically persecuted individuals lacking any specific qualifications were given make-shift jobs or otherwise engaged by the organisation in order to avoid their arrest.[32] Much of the impetus behind taking amateur or unusually young artists into the group involved providing training to facilitate emigration. Before "*Kristallnacht*", the *Kulturbund* did not "evolve" according to Nazi plans. At its start, the organisation revealed itself as strikingly "German"

[29]*ibid.*
[30]Kurt Singer, 'Die Arbeit der Jüdischen Kulturbünde', Adk, FWA, 74/86/5032, 27.
[31]Baumann, p. 35.
[32]Fischer-Defoy (ed.), pp. 103–104 and Geisel and Broder (eds.), p. 133.

Kurt Singer in Amsterdam

By courtesy of Stiftung Archiv der Akademie der Künste, Berlin, Kurt-Singer-Archiv, 20.55.11

when the Nazis expected something "Jewish". When it did turn to the problem of the "Jewish culture" of German Jews, this was linked with the effort to move elsewhere equipped with a viable program of post-emancipatory German-Jewish culture.

Photographs of Singer in Amsterdam reveal him as prematurely worn and aged. He was met at the Amsterdam airport by the Salomons – Albert and Paula had escaped from Berlin after Albert's release from Sachsenhausen. Singer and the Salomons would live together in Amsterdam in a double apartment located for them by the director of the Spinoza Gymnasium. In Amsterdam, Singer gave private music lessons and held literature discussions for children, who included Anne and Margot Frank. His private lectures focused on musical analysis, featuring excerpts from his work on the history of opera, the choir music of Bruckner, and Bach's cantatas.[33] He also organised a choir, evoking his "doctors' choir" in pre-1933 Berlin, which practised regularly. One month before the choir's last meeting in June 1942, Singer was appointed to Amsterdam's Jewish Council (the *Joodse Raad*), in existence since the German invasion in the spring of 1940. Singer's specific duty was administrating the affairs of the non-Dutch Jews living in the Netherlands – specifically

[33]Geisel and Broder (eds.), pp. 328–331.

German Jews and Jews from non-European countries protected by the Swiss government. Documents marked "internal information" addressed to Singer contain references to deportation of German Jews to "work camps in Germany".[34] In addition, Singer oversaw the organisation of Jewish vocational education.

For members of the *Kulturbund* in Berlin, deportation and forced labour began immediately after the organisation's closure by the Gestapo in September 1941. The *Kulturbund* in Amsterdam was allowed a one year reprieve. Kurt Singer refused any leadership position – this role was assumed instead by Werner Levie. At this point, the actors had to appear on stage in Amsterdam wearing the Jewish star. The theatre would later be used as a deportation centre.

After the German invasion of the Netherlands in spring 1940, all that remained of the hopes of transferring the *Kulturbund* to America were Singer's own desperate attempts to leave.[35] But these attempts were made too late. Born in Danzig, a territory allotted to Poland by the Treaty of Versailles, Singer was assigned to the Polish quota in the birthplace-based administration of American visas. The waiting time for this quota was decades longer than the German one. With references from Albert Einstein and Wilhelm Furtwängler among others, he tried to obtain a "non-quota" visa,[36] spending his time filling out dozens of forms while going through various stages of the bureaucracy. He began translating his book on Bach's cantatas into English, in preparation for his emigration. More than once, in the morass of administrative details, he failed to obtain just one vital document that was still missing. In the summer of 1941, he finally secured permission to travel and obtained a ticket as well as the necessary transit visas. But the American consulate had now closed. His visa never arrived, and his chance to flee Europe had passed.

APPENDIX: TWO LETTERS FROM KURT SINGER

Amsterdam, 8 December 1938

Most Esteemed Herr Reichskulturwalter

Herr Dr. Levie will have informed you of the reasons leading me to wait for the calming of my nerves here in Holland. Despite all entreaties, I left America to return to my work as head of the Kulturbund. It was only in Europe that, based on the official reports of the German press, I became convinced that the continued existence of the Kulturbund is no longer possible. We lack the people, the financial means, the repertoire, the performance spaces; in a short time we will also lack the artists who could maintain the ensemble of an orchestra, choir, theatre, or cabaret. We certainly lack the excitement and the atmosphere of the audience, without which effective

---

[34]'Joodse Raad voor Amsterdam, Interne Informatie 22, 9. December 1942', Akademie der Künste, Kurt Singer Archives, 1.55.25,1.

[35]Geisel, pp. 327–331.

[36]An unlabelled letter in the Kurt Singer Archives, Akademie der Künste, refers to his efforts to obtain a non-quota visa through the Chief Consulate in Rotterdam.

theatre cannot emerge. Therefore I see practically no artistic or economic possibility of reconstructing Jewish cultural work in Berlin or of the Reichsverband in Germany. Therefore my opinion and advice to Dr. Levie is the following: to liquidate the enterprise jüdischer Kulturbund as soon as possible. If I saw even the slightest possibility of assisting my co-workers and artists, the employees and workers of the jüdischer Kulturbund in Berlin, then I would even now continue to regard my return as a moral duty. Until now, no argument has been able to alter my disbelief and hopelessness in any way. I suffer with my co-religionists and mourn the fact that such work—for which I would have liked to have sacrificed my whole life—must, after such a marvellous beginning, now silently fall victim to circumstances.

I close with the expression of sincerest and highest esteem, and I remain

With devotion:

Dr. Kurt Singer

To the Members of the Managing Committee of the jüdischer Kulturbund in Berlin

My dear honourable friends!

If I complete this letter without it breaking my heart than I know I have nerves of steel. But I know at this moment and have felt it for weeks: your strength to carry on must be tremendous. And in such a terribly difficult time, when everything threatens to falter, I stand removed from you, even if I am in spirit amongst you! I take no direct part in your work, your troubles, and your distress. Until the end of my days, this will remain for me a secret, a riddle, and a paradox. But no matter how hard I think, I can neither lift the veil of secrecy, nor solve the riddle, nor explain the paradox. Without being able to help, I observe you, my most valuable assistants, from a lonely, wholly isolated distance, helpless like a wild bird with broken wings. The comparison may easily be extended: my heart of hearts has been wounded to the core. The Kulturbund without me, I without the Kulturbund: that is the end.

I am tied up in knots when I choose to call up the memories of the beginnings of our work, the heroic start, the stormy ascent, the struggles and victories, the moments of failure and encouragement, the initial steps taken, the musings and the wrestling for the spirit and meaning of the work of the Jüdischer Kulturbund. What unity even in contradiction! What courageous self-support, while the ground was shaking! What a collegial, mutual challenge, what a prize for us, even greater for the Jews in their totality! That has become our unforfeitable possession for all times.

We have overcome many crises together, and I would like to express my thanks to you for that. The crises were largely of an economic nature, which sometimes perhaps also touched the goals and the substance. Nevertheless: we mastered them. However the crisis that has now arisen appears to me to be so elementary that I can no longer fathom a solution. My collected, continually active optimism has collapsed. In the face of this elementary shock to our Jewish being, I have become powerless and unsteady. I mourn this work, that had to fall victim to circumstances, and suffer with the people who carry the wreck on their strong shoulders. And so, after a long period of consideration and waiting, I now have to call out to you:

> "Take away my glory and crown,
> But not the sufferings of which I am King."

From this distance, I cannot see into your souls. I hope, at least I believe, that all of you still believe in what remains of your task, and that you devote your artistic will to it. I myself have become completely unbelieving and hopeless in the last weeks of my despair. I departed from America to be with you in the hour of hardest struggle and of endurance; departed, although everything held me back, and although I could have remained. In the time of gravest emergency, I could not and did not want to be a private person on safe shores. It was only in Europe that I reckoned with the possibility of the work of the jüdische Kulturbund. The result of this reckoning was crushing. I had to and continue to believe that in a short time, there will be, in Germany, no more Jewish actors, musicians, or artists at all able to form a high-quality ensemble. In the provinces, there are no performance spaces. Every evening there is an absence of people receptive to concerts, theatre, and cabaret. The financial means and the possibilities of support by the Jewish communities are also missing. I see before me a slip into petit-bourgeois primitivism in decorations, scenes, and costumes, and I see a deadly scarcity in repertoire and a lack of performers in all domains. The press remains silent. The resonance amongst the people is missing, as their distress does not permit them to enjoy such performances. Were I to return, that would be like a captain who attempts to remove the water from an already sinking ship with a hollow hand. I do not believe that I would be able to set right what is falling or to raise what has sunk. I do not believe any longer that I could be anything more for the people I lead than a fellow sufferer. Perhaps you may succeed one more time in raising the sinking ship; my blessings accompany a rescue in which I myself cannot participate. Yet I would not like to burden my conscience with the guilt that although having returned, I could no longer make the enterprise function, despite all our efforts and despite summoning up the very last reserves of energy. If the Kulturbund perishes – and I see no other image before me – that would not come to pass through your efficiency and courage, but even your greatest talent cannot maintain it as it once was. Even a standstill would signify decline. But standstill is less the law of the hour, it is regression. The idea of the Kulturbund now belongs to history. Your names, [those of members of] my managing committee, engraved as if in marble in the great pages of the book I will write.

We want to remain faithful to the idea of the jüdische Kulturbund. Perhaps I will build it up again outside Europe. Then you should be – that I state with celebratory praise—the most important guarantors of the new work, its goals and purposes. And in this new work across the ocean in America – you can see that I believe in this.

Thus though removed from you, I wish to remain amongst you. No longer the leading figure, [I am] rather one of many. I will prepare you and support you and all of our artists, employees, and workers. Let me know [your] plans, wishes, applications, general and personal. I will write recommendations for individuals and attempt to give them weight through my name and [the reputation of] my artistic work established over decades. As long as I am in Holland, I will provide honorary service in the cultural department of the committee, [by] remaining attentive, cultivating relations, and conveying your wishes to the various centres of the artistic world. Collect these requests, and send them all to me. I will work, work, work for you. And my soul, which is filled with worry and grief, is lightened by the feeling of being able to work better for you here than I ever could in G.

Thus I do not feel separated from you. And I know: I have not been disloyal. Every sign of thought and memory, of loyalty, trust, and hope, that I have received from you and your co-workers, will enable me to carry on. And this accumulation of spiritual strength will and should accrue to your good benefit.

As soon as I have rest, I will write to each one of you individually. In this hour of external division, accept my thanks, and take my pledge to your, our communal work; take my vow that I will not forget a single person, be they assistants at the box office, wardrobe staff, department heads, artists, musicians, secretaries, actors, or singers. Put these and all the others together, I loved them all. And I [will] treasure this love until my last breath.

If the administration remains the same, if Wisten directs our theatre, Schwarz and Sander our music, Bab our "lectures", Sondheimer the stage – then I am replaced.[1] And I go on calmly with my work.

Farewell! Keep hold of your strength. Remain united. And hold the faith, the Jewish faith up high!

With unswerving loyalty – despite it all: Yours

sign. Kurt Singer

Amsterdam
Minervalaan 82
bei Manasse

---

[1]Fritz Wisten (1890–1962), actor, theatre director and successor to Kurt Singer as general director of the *Kulturbund* in 1939; slave labourer during the Holocaust; in 1945 director of the first post-war theatrical première of *Nathan the Wise*, later *Intendant* of both the *Theater am Schiffbauerdamm* and the *Volksbühne*. Rudolf Schwarz: (b. 1905), last musical director of the *Kulturbund* (1939–1941); survived Auschwitz, Sachsenhausen and Bergen-Belsen; conductor of the BBC and Birmingham Symphony Orchestras after his emigration to the UK. Julius Bab (b. 1880), active in the *Volksbühnebewegung* and one of Weimar Germany's most prominent theatre directors; cofounder and dramaturge of the *Kulturbund*, emigrated to the United States in 1940. Hans Sondheimer, stage and technical director of the *Kulturbund*, emigrated to the USA in 1939, later worked for Piscator's Drama Workshop and for the City Center Opera of New York City. Berthold Sander, *Kapellmeister* and choir director of the *Kulturbund*, deported and murdered in Auschwitz.

Hans Litten 1903–2003:
The Public Use of a Biography*

BY STEFANIE SCHÜLER-SPRINGORUM

A strange sight in autumn 2001 in the bohemian *Scheunenviertel* of Berlin: boys and girls in khaki scout uniforms are looking for traces of the life of Hans Litten after whom their Hamburg scout group is named. Three years ago they chose this name on the advice of staff at the Buchenwald *Gedenkstätte* although they knew little of Hans Litten's biography. It was above all important to the young people to make sure that the name symbolically represented the aim of their scout movement: "To openly support justice and encourage others to oppose injustice." This basic attitude is, according to them, a link with the life of Hans Litten. Hence the members of the group are now trying to "broaden their knowledge of the man whose courage and engagement for justice and law is an example to us".[1]

The scouts from Hamburg are the latest addition to a quite disparate group of people and organisations linked solely by a shared interest in Hans Litten, a Berlin lawyer who was born in Halle, spent his youth in Königsberg, and only lived to the age of thirty four. Since his early and violent death many different aspects of his personality – the activist who was strongly influenced by the youth movement, the committed lawyer, the upright concentration camp inmate – have attracted renewed attention for various reasons. In this respect, the history of the reception of Hans Litten's biography could be read as an example of how memory is influenced by different interests, how it is instrumentalised for political purposes, and how members of successive generations use it to express their need for identification.

At the turn of 2000–2001, the German Federal Association of Lawyers (*Bundesrechtsanwaltskammer*) moved its headquarters to the Hans Litten Haus in Littenstraße 9, located in Berlin Mitte – an address that "honours with its name a lawyer who among German jurists was one of the outstanding, early fighters against National Socialism".[2] In previous years both the naming of the street and the naming of the building in honour of Litten had not been uncontested. East Berlin's for-

*Translated from the German by Gabriele Rahaman. For some time I have been working on a biography of Hans Litten for which I have received support from, among other sources, the Axel Springer Foundation. My special thanks to Knut Bergbauer, Cologne, and to Sabine Fröhlich, Frankfurt am Main, with whom I have shared an interest in Hans Litten for many years; this article was conceived during our many discussions regarding the "Litten projects".
[1] E-mails by Horst Schröder to Margot Fürst, 3 and 4 July 2001, private estate of Max and Margot Fürst, Stuttgart. See also the website of the scout group: http://www.stephanus-pfadis.de.
[2] http://www.rak-berlin.de/menschenrechte/Litten.htm; cf. http://www.brak.de.

mer Neue Friedrichstrasse had been renamed Hans Litten Strasse in 1951. In the early 1990s, only a rather large protest action by politically engaged lawyers prevented the street from falling victim to the renaming mania arising after the fall of the East German regime. In 1992 a conservative Berlin city councillor suggested renaming the street 'An der Klosterkirche' in order to help erase any presence of Communism in the city's memory.[3] A few years later, after the established streetname had been successfully defended, a fresh controversy arose under very different and rather unusual circumstances. This time, the name of the new headquarters of the Federal Association of Lawyers was at issue, with lawyers such as Gerhard Jungfer, who had fought for years to commemorate Hans Litten, now arguing against using his name again.

They thought, and not without reason, that doing so meant being on the safer side – especially as the street was already named after Litten. This was the precise motive for representatives of the *Arbeitskreis historisch interessierter Rechtsanwälte und Rechtsanwältinnen* (Study Group of Historically Interested Lawyers) pleading for a chance to "commemorate another lawyer" who could represent the liberal and democratic values of Weimar Germany equally well, but in a less polarising way. Without intending to diminish Litten's achievements, Gerhard Jungfer and Tillman Krach – the latter probably the most knowledgeable expert on Weimar Republic jurists – rightly pointed out that at the time Litten's colleagues accepted neither his personality nor his professional conduct.[4] That Litten was in fact chosen – rather than for instance, Julius Magnus, the editor of the *Juristische Wochenschrift* who died of starvation in Theresienstadt in 1944 – might have reflected the politics of memory as much as simple expedience: Litten's rise to the status of a left-wing juridical icon in West Germany had started in the late 1980s. Two essays on Litten were published in 1988; at the same time, in an impressive commemorative ceremony at the Dachau concentration camp *Gedenkstätte* on the occasion of the fiftieth anniversary of his death, the Hans Litten prize was awarded for the first time by the *Republikanische Anwältinnen- und Anwälteverein* and the *Vereinigung Demokratischer Juristinnen und Juristen e.V.* The prize had been established to honour "jurists who have shown exceptional democratic commitment".[5]

---

[3]Citations from the *Tagesspiegel* and from a letter by Margot Fürst to the lawyer Stefan König, reprinted in Annette Wilmes, 'Hans Litten – Portrait eines engagierten Strafverteidigers der Weimarer Zeit', broadcasting manuscript, Sender Freies Berlin, 21 April 1992; cf. the letter of the president of the *Landgericht*, Berlin, addressed to the president of the *Kammergericht*, 22 November 1990, copy in: private estate of Kurt Neheimer, Institute for the History of German Jews, Hamburg.

[4]Tillmann Krach and Gerhard Jungfer, letter regarding the renaming of the "Anwaltshaus" in Littenstrasse, July 2000, in www.anwaltsgeschichte.de/Aktuelles1_1.htm. See also Gerhard Jungfer, 'Hans Litten zum 50. Todestag, Eine Dokumentation', in *Anwaltsblatt*, no. 4 (1988), pp. 213–216; *idem*, 'Zur Erinnerung: Hans Litten – ein Lebenslauf', in *Berliner Anwaltsblatt*, no. 272 (1991), p. 13–15; Tillmann Krach, *Jüdische Rechtsanwälte in Preussen. Über die Bedeutung der freien Advokatur und ihre Zerstörung durch den Nationalsozialismus*, Munich 1991.

[5]The prize has been awarded five times. The website of the *Vereinigung* emphasises that "the tradition Hans Litten adhered to is also the tradition the *VDF* aims to follow". Cf. http://www.vdj.de and the report in the *Süddeutsche Zeitung*, 5 February 1988; Norman Paech, '"Ich habe nur als proletarischer Anwalt meine Pflicht den angeklagten Proletariern gegenüber erfüllt". Hans Litten, Rechtsanwalt (1903–1938)', in *Demokratie und Recht*, vol. 16, no. 1 (1988), pp. 70–78; Heinz Düx, 'Hans Litten (1903–1938). Anwalt gegen Naziterror', in Kritische Justiz (eds.), *Streitbare Juristen. Eine andere Tradition*, Baden-Baden 1988, pp. 193–203.

The Rote Hilfe lawyers Rosenfeld and Litten (2nd and 3rd from left,
back row) with workers involved in the "Röntgenstrasse" trial after
the successful conclusion of the case, 1932.

By courtesy of the Neheimer estate

The reason for so quickly coming up with Hans Litten's name in the search for, as
Norman Paech put it, a "tradition of German jurists … who in the juridical class
struggles did not stand on or defect to the side of those generally associated with the
concept of tradition, for whom the expression 'dreadful jurist' (Rolf Hochhuth) has
been forged"[6] – in other words, a tradition uncontaminated by Nazism – might have
been a rather banal one: Litten's adult life had already been described in four publications, two published in East Germany and two in the Federal Republic.[7] These
present the history of a left-wing lawyer who had engaged in spectacular court-room
duels with the Nazis in the Weimar Republic's last few years, had been promptly
arrested after the *Reichstag* fire in February 1933, and had paid for his resistance to
the Nazi regime with five years imprisonment in various camps and, ultimately, with
his life. Litten had viewed himself as a champion of the working class and had often
defended Communists at the request of the *Rote Hilfe* organisation, but he had never
been a member of the German Communist party (KPD). To the contrary, he had
defended both anarchists and opposition Communists against Communist party offi-

---

[6]Paech, p. 70.
[7]Irmgard Litten, *Eine Mutter kämpft gegen Hitler*, Rudolstadt 1947 (new edition 1985); Carlheinz von Brück,
Ein Mann, der Hitler in die Enge trieb. Hans Littens Kampf gegen den Faschismus, Berlin 1975; Max Fürst, *Gefilte
Fisch. Eine Jugend in Königsberg*, Munich 1973; *idem, Talisman Scheherezade*, Munich 1976 (new edition 2002).

cials. He thus represented the non-Stalinist wing of the German workers' movement, in spite of East German claims that he was one of their own.[8]

In the end, a second factor may have played a role in the choice of Litten's name for the award: he had been the protagonist in a memorable and dramatic court-room scene in the period before the Nazi accession to power; this scene was repeatedly recounted in the various versions of his biography.[9] The context was the so-called "*Edenpalast*" trial. In November 1930, a *Rollkommando* of SA storm troopers had attacked members of a workers' association meeting in a dance hall. Serving as a prosecutor in the ensuing trial, Litten tried to establish that the Nazi Party had employed terrorist tactics in a planned, methodical way. He succeeded in calling Hitler as a witness and, with the help of a large number of citations of Nazi sources, forced the future dictator to distance himself publicly from both his own party publications and his propaganda strategist Goebbels, this distancing being meant to preserve a semblance of legality and adherence to the constitutional order. Despite this spectacular development, the SA members received relatively short prison terms. Rumours began to circulate that Litten had attracted the personal enmity of Hitler, an enmity that would later prove fatal for clemency pleas on his behalf.[10]

The "*Edenpalast*" trial sheds light on the general approach Litten took to criminal proceedings – an approach that left-wing lawyers in West Germany of the 1980s liked to claim they were following. Deeply convinced that in a capitalist system the judiciary served the people in power, Litten consistently tried to demonstrate that trials in which he was involved were politically motivated, ultimate responsibility for the actions at issue lying with the highest echelons of the state. This argument was at play in both his prosecution of the SA members and his defence of workers involved in the central German uprisings of 1921 known as the *Mitteldeutscher Aufstand*, and in the litigation he initiated against police commissioner Karl Zörgiebel, accused of being responsible for the deaths occurring during the "bloody May" demonstration of 1929. Litten also knew about the power of publicity. In one case, defending the

---

[8]With regard to Litten distancing himself from Communism see the extensive letter he wrote, most likely in early 1934, in the Esterwegen concentration camp, in: Stiftung Archiv der Parteien und Massenorganisationen der DDR im Bundesarchiv (BA-SAPMO), Berlin, NL 11 (estate of Irmgard Litten), Nr. 3, Bl. 235–238. Cf. the letter by one of Litten's former partners, Ludwig Barbasch, to Lord Arnold-Forster, 7 September 1937, referring in detail to Litten's undogmatic political attitude and his difficulties with the KPD, in: BA-SAPMO, NL 11, Nr. 8, Bl. 59–61. There is a clear intention underlying this distancing, since English supporters were eager to confirm that Litten was not the "spiritual leader of Communism in Germany", as Ribbentrop had described him in an answer to Lord Hurtwood published in December 1935; but Litten's party-political independence is indisputable, particularly in light of his earlier activity in the youth movement and the articles he published in the anarchist paper *Die Schwarze Fahne* in 1929.

[9]Cf. Irmgard Litten, *Mutter*; v. Brück; Fürst, *Fisch*; idem, *Talisman*; Paech; Düx; the broadcasting script of Annette Wilmes; and another such script by Margot Litten, 'Ich hänge tot an meinen Träumen. Erinnerung an den Widerstandskämpfer Hans Litten', n.d., n.p., private estate of Max and Margot Fürst, Stuttgart. In February 1998, the part of the "*Edenpalast*" trial in which Hitler appeared as a witness was restaged, using original court records, at the commemoration at the Dachau *Gedenkstätte* of the sixtieth anniversary of Litten's death.

[10]The rumours are attested to by Litten's mother, quoting the notorious Nazi judge Roland Freisler and the Prussian crown prince August Wilhelm, both of whom she had asked, along with many others, to intervene on her son's behalf. The two men responded the same way to the appeal: "No one is going to be able to do anything for Litten. Hitler turned red with rage when he heard his name mentioned." See Irmgard Litten, *Mutter*, pp. 66f.

pacifist Ernst Friedrich against a libel action by *Reichswehrminister* Gustav Noske, Litten tried to show, in a lengthy motion to hear evidence, that Noske had indeed "committed a number of actions justifying terms such as scoundrel [*Lump*] and rogue [*Schurke*]".[11] He sometimes sought attention by examining witnesses in unusual venues like bars and by commenting in the press about ongoing trials; together with his unorthodox methods of investigation, such tactics seemed rather dubious to many of his colleagues, at least from a professional point of view.[12]

In any case, present-day jurists who have intensively studied Litten's handling of the code of criminal procedure are fascinated by both his erudition and virtuosity, as well as by the great personal support he offered his clients, sometimes extending to the limits of his strength.[13] In the depictions of Litten as "one of the outstanding ... fighters against National Socialism" it is usually forgotten that he certainly paid a high price for this role, which, for instance, often put his friendships under severe strain. His best friend, Max Fürst, whose wife at that time was Litten's secretary, recalls this time in Litten's life from a more intimate perspective:

> He was as fanatic as someone fighting his last battle. He had the strength to endure this battle for three years. I was probably a bad friend towards the end, distancing myself from him more and more. Often I was angry that Margot was captivated by him and his work so completely and that she hardly had time for me. I never have had limitless patience. Of course I knew what was at stake, but to know what is right and to tolerate it against one's own interests are two different things. I foresaw not only a political but also a human tragedy.[14]

Max Fürst's memoirs of his youth in East Prussia and the time he spent in the youth movement contain a sensitive portrait of his friendship with Hans Litten. Describing in detail the years he shared with Litten in Königsberg and the fate of other Communist friends, the memoirs were published in West Germany in the 1970s. It is therefore striking that Marion Gräfin Dönhoff, in her own words, "discovered" the story of Litten in 1986.[15] Deliberately ignoring the Fürst memoirs, it seems, Dönhoff based her article on Irmgard Litten's account of her fight for her imprisoned son, written in exile in England and published in 1940 in various countries in a German and an English edition.[16] Although the first West German edition of the book did

---

[11]Beweisantrag Litten, 4 March 1929, in Geheimes Staatsarchiv Preußischer Kulturbesitz, Reichsjustizministerium, 2.5.1., Nr. 12670, Bl. 10–16, quotation Bl. 10; cf. also the trial report in *Die Schwarze Fahne* , vol. 5, no. 11 (1929); cf. the report by Erich Cohn-Bendit, 'Kurzer Überblick über die Tätigkeit des Rechtsanwalts Hans Litten', BA-SAPMO, NL 11, Nr. 7, Bl. 1–7; and v. Brück; Fürst, *Fisch*; *idem*, *Talisman*; Paech; Düx.

[12]Cf. Litten's article on the 'Felsenecke' trial, 'Zugrunde gerichtet!', in *Arbeiter-Illustrierten Zeitung*, no. 37 (11 April 1932), and letter by Krach and Jungfer.

[13]While neither has published academic articles on Litten, the Berlin lawyer Tobias Abesser is most likely the most knowledgeable expert on Litten's legal style and the jurist and historian Cord Brügmann has also intensively researched Litten's life. Brügmann organised a second memorial ceremony for Litten on the sixtieth anniversary of his death at Dachau; cf. the report in the *Süddeutsche Zeitung*, 9 February 1998.

[14]Fürst, *Talisman*, pp. 355–356.

[15]Cf. *ibid.*, and *idem*, *Fisch*; see also Marion Gräfin Dönhoff, 'Der vergessene Opfergang, Eine Mutter kämpfte gegen Hitler', in *Die Zeit*, 5 December 1986, p. 74.

[16]Irmgard Litten, *Die Hölle sieht Dich an. Der Fall Litten*, Paris 1940; *idem*, *A Mother fights Hitler*, London 1940; *idem*, *Mutter*. Cf. Marian Malet, *Beyond Dachau. Irmgard Litten in England*, in Charmian Brinson (ed.), *Keine Klage über England? Deutsche und österreichische Exilerfahrungen in Großbritannien 1933–1945*, Munich 1998, pp.124–138.

Exiled to England, Irmgard Litten continued to fight for her son.

By courtesy of the Neheimer estate

not appear until 1984, it was published in censored form in East Germany in 1947; subsequently reissued in 1985, this edition contained some differences from that appearing in 1940.[17]

Written shortly after the death of her son, Irmgard Litten's book has had an enduring influence on the image of Hans Litten. This begins with his image in the literal sense – from the book's 1940 publication onwards, Litten's portrait, drawn by Gustav Hammermann, a fellow inmate in the Lichtenburg concentration camp, has been displayed in all publications, websites, and events concerning his life and writings. It shows him as a thin, bald man of almost spectral appearance, a man having the appearance of a "Franciscan [monk]", as Rudolf Olden puts it in his foreword to Irmgard Litten's book. But this ascetic figure bears little resemblance to the rather tubby, shy young man revealed in photographs taken before his arrest. Likewise, the book lays stress on Litten's decidedly bourgeois interest in art and his Catholic inclinations while merely touching on other aspects of his life, for example his relationship with Sulamith (Charlotte) Siliava, who had emigrated to Spain in 1933 with the photographer Walter Reuter and whom Litten, judging by his letters written from prison, loved passionately.[18] Although this type of desexualisation is first-rate material for speculating about the mother-son bond, what is clear is that Irmgard Litten's description of her son as a bourgeois-Christian martyr was aimed at the public in the various Allied countries where the book was published. While she does mention the

---

[17]Remarkably, the censored East German edition has now also been published by the Deutscher Anwaltsverlag, Bonn 2000. My thanks to Sabine Fröhlich for having drawn my attention to this.

[18]Letters from prison in BA-SAPMO, NL 11; a quite unflattering portrait of Siliava is found in Fürst, *Talisman*, pp. 344–346.

Hans Litten in front of the 'Bärenbrunnen' in Berlin-Mitte, early 1930s.

By courtesy of Margot Fürst

Portrait of Hans Litten; drawing by Gustav Hammermann, a fellow inmate in Lichtenburg concentration camp.

By courtesy of the Neheimer estate

fact that Litten's brother and his friends were also indefatigable in their efforts to obtain his release,[19] she apparently saw emphasising her own role as a Mother Courage-like figure as the most effective strategy. In their own stress on this particular theme, both Dönhoff's article and Mike Carmody's current preparation of a film script about Litten suggest that Irmgard Litten's instincts were in fact correct.[20]

In her book, Irmgard Litten describes her efforts to get her son released upon his arrest after the *Reichstag* fire; her arguments with low- and middle-ranking regime officials; her pleas on behalf of her son with highly-placed Third Reich dignitaries who had formerly been friends of her bourgeois and conservative family. She also reconstructs, in remarkable detail considering the emotional situation surrounding the book's writing, the suffering of her son in various prisons and concentration camps: Spandau, Sonnenburg, Moabit, Brandenburg, Esterwegen, Lichtenburg, Buchenwald and, finally, Dachau. She movingly describes the steady psychological and physical torture (including mock executions) that Litten had to endure, particularly at the beginning of his imprisonment – cruelties that led him to a first suicide attempt.

By the time he found some respite in the Lichtenburg camp – he would remain there for over three years, working in the library and book-binding workshop – he had become a man marked deeply by suffering; because of heavy beatings, he was half-blind and half-deaf, only able to move with crutches and suffering from blackouts and heart spasms. Litten nevertheless, continued with his reflections on philology and art theory during the years in Lichtenburg. The many accounts by fellow prisoners of his lectures and efforts to help others mostly stem from this period; the stay in one relatively tolerable place for several years allowed a solidarity to develop that formed the basis for crucial psychological and material sustenance. With a tearing apart of the personal relationships and the recommencing of physical brutality after Litten's removal first to Buchenwald in August and then to Dachau in October 1937, Litten's spirits appear to have crumbled. In the new camps, the other prisoners did their best to protect Litten – at this point he would have been one of the last survivors of the first wave of inner-German persecution. But in the wake of the torturing to death of one his friends and threats by the guards pointing in the same direction, he apparently decided to thwart his murderers. In the night of 4–5 February 1938, he was found hanged in a latrine at Dachau concentration camp.[21]

In the same month as Litten's death, his parents and younger brother Heinz emigrated to England, where Litten's father Fritz died in 1940. (Rainer, the youngest

---

[19]After the death of his fiancée, Brigitte Worringer, in May 1934, and after he had been dismissed from his post at the *Stadttheater* in Chemnitz, Heinz Litten dedicated himself entirely to supporting his mother and brother. Information based on interview with Lucinde Sternberg-Worringer, October 1997; and Irmgard Litten, *Mutter*, pp. 103–105. Hans Litten's friend in the youth movement, Leo Roth, first brought reports of his mistreatment in Sonnenburg to public attention; cf. Bundesarchiv Berlin (BA), NJ, Nr. 14220/2, Bl. 2–18. In England, Margot Fürst's sister, Hilda Monte, played her role in publicising Litten's plight through an article published only a few days before his death; see Hilda Monte, 'The Tragic Case of Hans Litten', in *Manchester Guardian*, 26 January 1938. (Monte would herself be shot to death in April 1945 during a resistance mission in Austria.)

[20]Carmody discovered Litten's story while reading through the journalistic work of Irmgard Litten written in exile.

[21]Cf. Alfred Dreifuß, 'Wie Hans Litten starb', in *Sonntag*, 12 September1948, pp. 4–5; and Irmgard Litten, *Eine Mutter*; v. Brück; Fürst, *Fisch*; *idem, Talisman*; Paech; Düx.

Commemorative plaque for Hans Litten at Burgstrasse 43 in Halle, the house where he was born

By courtesy of the Neheimer estate

Littenstrasse in Berlin-Mitte.

By courtesy of Knut Bergbauer

brother, who had earlier been a promising film star, had lived in Switzerland since 1933.) Irmgard and Heinz Litten returned to West Germany in 1947. When Irmgard Litten, well known because of her publications and her work for the BBC, was attacked in the Federal Republic for being a "traitor", and was denied a widow's pension, the family decided to move to East Berlin. With this move, Hans Litten's legacy was now located in East Germany as well.[22] There, as indicated, the book detailing his concentration camp imprisonment was republished, a commemorative plaque was put on the house where he was born and, in 1950, the first institution for

---

[22]Irmgard Litten died in 1953; two years later, Heinz committed suicide. One study has appeared concerned with Heinz Litten, see Birgit Radebold, *Exiltheater in der Tschechoslowakei und in Grossbritannien am Beispiel von Erich Freund und Heinz Wolfgang Litten*, Hamburg 2000.

training East German judges (the *Volksrichterschule*) was named in his honour in the presence of his mother and brother. The Neue Friedrichstrasse was renamed after Litten the following year.[23]

There was, however, a price paid for such commemoration: a smoothed-out version of Litten's biography, with the main emphasis placed on his legal work for *Rote Hilfe* and his resistance activities against Fascism; in contrast, his commitment to the Jewish youth movement received short shrift. This emphasis is apparent, for instance, in Carlheinz von Brück's *Ein Mann, der Hitler in die Enge trieb* (*A man who drove Hitler into a corner*, 1974), which focuses on the trials in which Litten played a role. It is also apparent in the East German versions of Irmgard Litten's book: they leave out the first edition's references to an important letter by Litten in which he distances himself from the KPD and the references to the radical pacifist Kurt Hiller, whom Litten had known since the last years of the Weimar Republic and who had been a prisoner with Litten for a few months in Brandenburg.[24] While one-sided, the East German commemoration did stir renewed interest in Litten relatively early, while in the West his life and work would be neglected for another thirty years. The East German jurist Gerhard Baatz, for instance, noticed the commemorative plaque on Litten's house in 1969 and from then on worked to uphold Litten's memory – work that would continue in post-unification Germany.[25] Likewise, Kurt Neheimer, a returned emigrant who would later be active as a journalist, became acquainted with Irmgard Litten at the inauguration of the *Volksrichterschule* in 1950. Deeply impressed by Litten's biography, he would spend decades collecting additional material, including accounts by witnesses. Neheimer died before being able to realise his plans for a comprehensive biography.

A few years earlier, in 1988, Neheimer had presented his research findings in West Germany at a lecture delivered at the above-mentioned commemoration in Dachau, which had been arranged with the help of Margot Fürst. She had been in touch with Neheimer for some time and has played a central role in the East and West German recognition of Litten. In this respect, Margot Fürst continues to play a dual role. As the wife of Litten's best friend and as – much beyond her work as secretary – Litten's close intellectual and spiritual collaborator, she lived and worked with him during his years in Berlin and knew him better than virtually anyone. After his arrest (she had just given birth to her second child) she tried to save Litten's legal practice; together with Irmgard Litten, she fought for permission to visit him and for alleviation of his prison conditions. For months she was the only person with access to Litten in her

---

[23]Cf. the following selection of East German articles on Litten: Wolfgang Weiss, 'Hans Litten zum Gedächtnis', in *Neue Justiz*, no. 2 (1950), pp. 54–55; Anon., 'Das Recht muß dem Frieden dienen', in *Die Tat*, no. 26 (1951), p. 26; Hilde Benjamin, 'Hans Litten', in *Weltbühne*, 19 June 1973, p. 788–89; Max Fürst, 'Zu Hans Litten', in *Sinn und Form*, no. 30 (1978), pp. 236–239; 'Hans Litten – Anwalt der Roten Hilfe', in *Der antifaschistische Widerstandskämpfer*, no. 6 (1988), pp. 18–19.

[24]Cf. Litten's letter from Esterwegen in BA-SAPMO, NL 11, Nr. 3, Bl. 235–238; Brück, and Irmgard Litten, *Hölle*, pp. 95–99, 125–127; in the East German version, the passage describing the persecution of Litten's brother Heinz is also slightly altered. Cf. *ibid.* pp 115–117 and Irmgard Litten, *Mutter*, pp. 103–105.

[25]Gerhard Baatz, 'Hans Litten', in *Mitteilungen der Bundesrechtsanwaltskammer*, no. 1 (2001), pp. 11–13; *idem*, letters to the author, 6 and 18 June 2002.

"secretarial" capacity. In the autumn of 1933, she travelled to Geneva to meet Hannah Arendt, who as a young woman had known Litten in Königsberg. In the hope of gaining international attention, Fürst handed Arendt documents on the conditions under which Litten was being held in prison. Finally, after Litten's attempted suicide, she and her husband decided to make a quite daring effort to free Litten (disguised as an SA-man) during a Christmas party for the guards. But the Fürsts and their friend Felix Hohl – affiliated with the Plättner group whose members Litten had once defended – fell into a trap laid by the Gestapo, were arrested, and imprisoned. A year later, in September 1934, Margot Fürst was freed, managing in 1935 to emigrate to Palestine together with her husband and children.[26]

Since the publication of her husband's memoirs, followed by his death in 1978, Margot Fürst has also become the guardian of Litten's legacy. Since the 1950s she has been living in Stuttgart, where all requests for information about Hans Litten now converge. Whether those making the requests are scouts or historians, journalists or teachers, film makers or law students, they all receive the same attentive responses from Margot Fürst. At times the parties involved have a chance to meet, and these connections occasionally produce new projects. A close collaboration thus developed between this author and the social educator Knut Bergbauer, who had come across Hans Litten and his youth group *Schwarzer Haufen*, a splinter group of the German-Jewish youth movement *Kameraden*, when researching anarchist traditions; the end result was an exhibition on this specific youth group, accompanied by an exhibition catalogue.[27]

Hans Litten's time in the Jewish youth movement and the political options developing from it were the main spur for both Bergbauer's and the author's interest in his life story.[28] In 1921, he joined the Königsberg branch of the youth group (self-defined as a *Wanderbund*) termed the *Kameraden* – an organisation that according to his former group leader Erwin Lichtenstein he soon began to dominate because of his "outstanding intelligence, exceptional knowledge, and purposeful will".[29] Litten was the son of a baptised Jewish father and a Protestant mother; his decision to join the Jewish youth movement thus was a statement in itself. Doubtlessly, the statement can be interpreted legitimately as a protest against his father – a distinguished professor of Roman and civil law who had also served as dean of the law faculty of Königsberg University and was that institution's rector. But Litten's motivation appears to have gone far beyond this, since he invested the time and effort to learn Hebrew, while urging the *Kameraden* to study Talmud and discuss Jewish topics.[30]

---

[26]Fürst, *Fisch*, pp. 389–438.

[27]Knut Bergbauer and Stefanie Schüler-Springorum, *"Wir sind jung, die Welt ist offen…". Eine jüdische Jugendgruppe im 20. Jahrhundert*, Berlin 2002; exhibition from 8 September 2002 to July 2003 in the Gedenkstätte Haus der Wannseekonferenz Berlin.

[28]Knut Bergbauer, 'Der "Schwarze Haufen" – Eine deutsch-jüdische Jugendgruppe zwischen pädagogischem Anspruch und politischer Realität', unpublished qualifying thesis, Fachhochschule Köln 1998; Stefanie Schüler-Springorum, 'Jugendbewegung und Politik. Die jüdische Jugendgruppe "Schwarzer Haufen"', in *Tel Aviver Jahrbuch für deutsche Geschichte*, vol. 28 (1999), pp. 159–200.

[29]Letter from Erwin Lichtenstein to Max Fürst, Tel Aviv 11 December 1972, estate of Max and Margot Fürst.

[30]Hans Litten, 'Was bedeutet uns der Talmud?', in *Deutsch-jüdischer Wanderbund Kameraden – Gau Nordost*, no. 4 (1924); Hans Litten, 'Reply to Franz Kälter (on the Jewishness of the "Kameraden")', in *Gau Nordost*, no. 3 (1924).

Felix Hohl in his 'Dixi' car used in the attempt to free Hans Litten from prison.

By courtesy of Knut Bergbauer

Max and Margot Fürst after their release from prison, autumn 1934.

By courtesy of Margot Fürst

Later, former youth movement friends would emphasise that Litten had not 'really' been Jewish, and that his group, the *Schwarzer Haufen* had not been Jewish either. But these statements need to be understood as reflecting both the discussion of 'Red assimilation' (an involvement with the labour movement seen as signifying a turn away from Judaism) and the search for Jewish identity after the Shoah, rather than as addressing the sensibility of the time.[31] In actuality, the Königsberg *Kameraden* grounded their sense of Jewishness on an idea of "inner experience" that was generally well established in the German youth movement; none of Litten's contemporaries would have questioned Litten's commitment to the Jewish stream within this movement.[32] As late as 1938 former members of the *Kameraden* who had by then emigrated to Palestine as the *Werkleute* group and founded Kibbuz Hazorea, wrote a moving obituary focussing precisely on this aspect of Litten's life.[33]

Hence Litten's provenance did not pose a problem for the umbrella organisation of the *Kameraden*; nor did his unusual, often quite extravagant concept of art.[34] Rather, it was the tone he frequently adopted, especially with those whom he regarded as opponents of his ideas, that was found objectionable. This tone would later help make him famous as a lawyer. In his letters to other members of the *Kameraden*, it shone through in all its juridical precision, but also in all its rigidity. Another contributing factor was Litten's obvious intellectual superiority – an asset that he used ruthlessly when necessary.[35] At the same time, Litten was something of a mystic and romantic who tried to defend a metaphysical notion of "leadership" in discussions with the young Communists in the *Schwarzer Haufen*. This provoked sharp protest, and the retrospective criticism of having mixed "utopian-socialist, anarcho-syndicalist, romantic views with, to say the least, proto-Fascist views".[36] Litten's appearance was itself somewhat provocative. As a young lawyer in his mid-twenties, he could be seen walking through

---

[31]Cf. Hermann Meier-Cronemeyer, 'Jüdische Jugendbewegung' (2 parts), in *Germania Judaica*, new series vol. 8, nos. 27/28 (1969), pp. 1–56, 58–96, 80f.; Erwin Lichtenstein, 'Der Sohn des verlorenen Sohnes. Erinnerungen an Hans Litten', in *Mitteilungsblatt der Organisation der Einwanderer aus Mitteleuropa*, no. 41 (10 October 1941), p. 3; in contrast: letter of Berthold Jacoby to Max Fürst, 20 February 1977, indicating that Litten "voluntarily identified with the Jews", estate of Max and Margot Fürst.

[32]Führerschaft der Ortsgruppe Königsberg, 'Aus Königsberg. In eigener Sache', in *Führerblatt der Kameraden*, no. 12 (1923), p. 6; Theodor Neumann and Martin Goldner, 'Zu den Königsberger Sätzen', *ibid.*, p. 8; Litten, reply to Franz Kälter; letter of Max Fürst to Erwin Lichtenstein, 31 December 1972, estate of Max Fürst. In contrast to the Ernst Wolff group that later developed into the *Ring* and then the *Schwarzes Fähnlein*, the Königsberg *Kameraden* rejected the admission of non-Jews; cf. lecture by Hans Litten at the "Führertag" in Merseburg, 12 June 1927, minutes in Neue Synagoge Berlin – Centrum Judaicum, Archives (= CJA) I, 75 C Wa 1, Nr. 1, Bl. 62–69, 65.

[33]'Le-zikhro shel Hans Litten', in *Shvuon Kibbutz Hazorea* (21 April 1938), Archives of Kibbutz Hazorea, 91/96, 91–7–2.

[34]See, for example, Hans Litten, 'Jugend und moderne Kunst', in *Bundesblatt der Kameraden*, new series, no. 3 (1925), pp. 33–36.

[35]Regarding Litten's role and his reputation in the *Kameraden*, see Schüler-Springorum, *Jugendbewegung und Politik*, pp. 172–193. Good examples of the above-mentioned features are offered by various articles and letters of Hans Litten, for example 'Gesetz', in *Gau Nordost*, no. 3 (1923); 'Vom Berliner Führertreffen', *ibid.*, no. 5 (1924); letter to Ernst Markowicz, 12 July 1923, Archives of Kibbutz Hazorea, 91/96, 91–7–2; and letters to Julius Freund on the "school question" (the fight for school reform), 20 April 1927 and 5 May 1927, in CJA I, 75 C Wa 1, Nr. 10, Bl. 81, 85ff.

[36]Siegbert Kahn, unpublished memoirs (typescript c. 1975) in BA-SAPMO, NY 4323/vorl. 10, p. 24c; the verbatim discussion of the "leadership question" is located in the transcript of the "Bundestag" of the *Schwarzer Haufen* in summer 1927; Staatsarchiv Leipzig, Polizeipräsidium, PP-V 4315, n. p.

Hans Litten

the streets of Berlin sporting the *Wandervogel* uniform of "open-necked shirt plus shorts below which bare knees were visible".[37] He also wrote incendiary articles advocating a "unified youth front" meant to "completely destroy this system, i.e. the system of the older generation having dominance over youth".[38] From our vantage point, such notions might be considered risible, but at the time they simply marked a logical continuation of youth-movement ideals into adulthood and professional life – something Litten had propagated in his arguably most prescient article, concerned with "the youth movement and politics". His demand that "a youth movement that means to be taken seriously has to be political"[39] would be put into practice by nearly all of his friends who had joined political parties, for the most part the KPD, but also some of the many breakaway groups on the Weimar left.[40]

Litten transferred his early political activity to his professional life; neither his dedication as a lawyer, nor the solidarity he showed his fellow prisoners, nor the spiritu-

[37]Irmgard Litten, *Mutter*, p. 5.
[38]Hans Litten, 'Revolte im Erziehungshaus', in *Die Schwarze Fahne*, vol. 5, no. 3 (1929), pp. 1–2.
[39]Hans Litten, 'Jugendbewegung und Politik', in *Bundesblatt der Kameraden*, new series, no. 3 (1925), pp. 40–43, here p. 42.
[40]For a more detailed discussion of the topic, see Bergbauer and Schüler-Springorum.

al counter-world he would create to sustain him in the camps, can be understood without taking into account his years in the youth movement. Understood against this backdrop, Litten's stormy and often contradictory nature, as well as the dogmatic radicalism of his intellect, would be described by the Weimar intellectual Kurt Hiller with particular clarity:

> In his complicated and baroque ideology, Socialist and Catholic-theocratic motives mingle. He is *for* Marx-Lenin and *for* the absolute monarchs of the seventeenth century, *against* Reformation and Enlightenment, *against* Goethe, but *for* Hölderlin, *for* Rilke; he simultaneously promotes (and in his case it is genuine) the cult of the proletariat and the cult of Mary.[41]

On 19 June 2003 Hans Litten would have been one hundred years old. The further we are removed from the narrative of his life, the easier it seems to select only those aspects of it that confirm our own collective tradition-building, as well as our own individual values. In all this, however, Litten's inner world, his feelings, hopes and motivations, remain quite opaque. Perhaps Margot Fürst summarised the essence of Hans Litten's personality most succinctly. Questioned at the memorial ceremony in Dachau regarding what she best recalled about him sixty-five years after their last encounter, she responded, after a lengthy pause, as follows: "His great fear – and his great courage".[42]

---

[41]Kurt Hiller as quoted in Irmgard Litten, *Hölle*, p. 99.
[42]Margot Fürst at the memorial celebrations in Dachau on 7 February 1998. Margot Fürst died on 2 July 2003.

Yad Vashem and the German "Righteous"

The German *"Righteous Among the Nations"*: An Historical Appraisal

By Daniel Fraenkel

Despite widespread popular interest, up to the present there have been few efforts to place the "Righteous Among the Nations" – a term used interchangeably with "Righteous Gentiles" in Holocaust historiography for non-Jewish rescuers of Jews – in their historical context. On the one hand, literary portrayals or film recreations of the careers of individual rescuers like Oskar Schindler tend to present them as larger than life, disregarding any methodological issues and comparative implications. On the other hand, a number of behavioural scientists who have done research on this topic have operated with assumptions and employed theoretical models that are largely ahistorical.[1] To cite the most notable study, Samuel and Pearl Oliner presume that given the right kind of socialisation and upbringing, people can be made to evolve personalities predisposed to altruism in times of crisis.[2] From a historiographical perspective, three basic objections to this hypothesis seem evident. Firstly, it is applicable (or inapplicable) in the same measure to rescue efforts undertaken during the Holocaust, any man-made catastrophe, and natural disasters such as earthquakes. Secondly, the notion of an altruistically predisposed personality not only presumes to predict the contents of human behaviour, but in a sense to predetermine it. But as both history and everyday experience abundantly teach us, there is an irreducible element of incalculability in such behaviour. Especially in extreme situations, people tend to behave very differently from the deterministic expectations produced by theoretical constructs. More than that, they frequently act against their own previously conceived intentions and beliefs. As we try to fathom the motives underlying the conduct of Holocaust rescuers, we often discover that the individual concerned was unaware of the full import and possible consequences of his or her initial decision to help. Frequently an unpremeditated gesture of help, performed spontaneously and unreflectingly, proved to be the trigger for a full-fledged commitment to rescue. The rescuers in these cases acted on the spur of the moment, responding to the force of the situation and the plight of the person seeking help. The third objection is that considering Holocaust rescuers as endowed with a special kind of personality tends to

---

[1]For a survey and cogent critique of research on Holocaust rescuers see David P. Gushee, 'Many Paths to Righteousness: An Assessment of Research on why Righteous Gentiles Helped Jews', in *Holocaust and Genocide Studies*, vol. 7, no. 3 (Winter 1993), pp. 372–393. See also *idem*, *The Righteous Gentiles of the Holocaust: A Christian Interpretation*, Minneapolis 1994; Mordecai Paldiel, 'The Altruism of the Righteous Gentiles', in *Holocaust and Genocide Studies*, vol. 3, no. 2 (1988), pp. 187–196. German Holocaust rescuers from the military are discussed in Wolfram Wette (ed.), *Retter in Uniform. Handlungsspielräume im Vernichtungskrieg der Wehrmacht*, Frankfurt am Main 2002.

[2]Samuel P. Oliner and Pearl M. Oliner, *The Altruistic Personality: Rescuers of Jews in Nazi Europe*, New York 1988.

make them into a unique human type, standing as it were beyond the bounds of time and place. There is, however, no convincing evidence for such "otherness". Arguably, the most striking feature of the German rescuers as a group is their utter "ordinariness": they were both "ordinary men" – and women – and "ordinary Germans". In other words, in their broad spectrum of differing social origins, religious beliefs, political affiliations, and occupations, they appear to constitute a cross-section of society as a whole: housewives, soldiers, labourers, industrialists, artists, doctors, scientists, peasants, city and country dwellers, clergymen, nuns, atheists, conservatives, Communists, Social Democrats, and so forth. It may be difficult to digest the fact that not being all that different from the mass of ordinary Germans included membership in the Nazi Party. In fact, we would be justified in inferring – tautologically in a way – that the only common characteristic *decisively* separating the rescuers from the rest of their compatriots was the fact that they put themselves at risk to help Jews.

THE YAD VASHEM DATABASE

The present article sets out to sketch a historically grounded picture of German Holocaust rescuers, based on a review of representative files in Yad Vashem. While far from complete, the Yad Vashem data-base for the "German Righteous" allows some quantitative and qualitative distinctions defining the historical context of rescue in both Germany and the Nazi-occupied countries. Clearly the rescue of Jews was at best a marginal phenomenon. The figures for those designated "righteous" by Yad Vashem are instructive, though far from exhaustive, in this respect. As of the time of this article's writing, some 17,433 individuals have been so designated, among them 5,373 Poles and 4,289 Dutchmen, but only 336 Germans. The latter figure in any case probably represents only a fraction of the Germans actually involved in helping persecuted Jews. Stipulating a certain degree of risk taken by the rescuers, the Yad Vashem criteria qualify a select circle of strongly committed individuals; there were, however, many Germans manifesting solidarity with persecuted Jews in various ways: closing their eyes to the presence of "illegals", contributing food coupons, transmitting information. It should also be noted that the Yad Vashem case files for "righteous" rescuers were not created in the framework of a systematic research effort aimed at tracking down every identifiable person. Rather, they were created in response to the spontaneous initiative of private individuals, for the most part the survivors themselves, but not infrequently independent sponsors and scholars. Some Jews who received aid were subsequently caught and were thus never able to tell their story, while for many survivors, testifying about their experiences during the Holocaust would have meant reviving memories suppressed with difficulty and opening unhealed wounds.

Some additional implications of Yad Vashem's criteria ought to be noted. Because of its focus on the individual rescuer, the Yad Vashem database tends to obscure cases where the rescue act was in fact the work of a group or network, small and informal as it may have been. Moreover, the Committee for the Designation of the Righteous does not consider cases where the person rescued was a first-degree relative of the rescuer. This leaves out of consideration the by far largest category of Jewish survivors in Nazi Germany: some 12,500 Jewish men and women saved thanks to the selfless loyalty and sacrifice of their non-Jewish spouses.[3] Also excluded are cases of rescue involving Christians of Jewish descent, that is, racially defined Jews who were either brought up as Christians or had converted to Christianity before the advent of the Third Reich. It is reasonable to assume that most of those able to escape deportation to the death camps by hiding 'illegally' in Germany – 3,000 survivors according to a commonly accepted estimate – were assisted at some point by the non-Jewish population.[4]

The quality of the documentation collected in the "Righteous" files is uneven. This has partly to do with the clandestine nature of the rescue activity, which meant it was not recorded when it took place. Furthermore, the Yad Vashem Righteous project is far more concerned with establishing a person's claim to that designation than with reconstructing the rescue story in its historical details. The Committee for the Designation of the Righteous attaches special weight to the corroborative testimony of the survivors. The latter, however, should not be regarded as unbiased observers – their understandable gratitude to the rescuer is likely to result in an idealised and over-simplified view of what took place. One perceptive witness has commented on the distortion at work in Holocaust testimonies furnished many years after the event as follows: "It is a daunting task to render the atmosphere and feelings from these horrific times and retain their authenticity; it is almost impossible to resurrect the memories without being affected by the perspective created by time and emotional distance."[5]

Even in those cases where the rescuers' own version of events is available, their retrospective explanation of their motivation is often no more than a collection of fond clichés and pat generalisations.

SOLIDARITY WITH JEWS AND THE NAZI *VOLK* COMMUNITY

In order to contextualise the description of the German rescuers, it is useful to replace the hypostatised concept of an "altruistic personality" with the empirically observable phenomenon of solidarity with persecuted Jews. Solidarity in a sociological-functional sense may be defined as the bonds of reciprocal responsibility arising

[3]Ursula Büttner, 'Bollwerk Familie; Die Rettung der Juden in "Mischehen"', in Günther B. Ginzel (ed.), *Mut zur Menschlichkeit. Hilfe für Verfolgte während der NS-Zeit*, Cologne 1993, pp. 59–71; *idem*, 'An Unknown Case of Resistance: The Rescue of Jews in Christian-Jewish Mixed Marriages', in Andrew Chandler (ed.), *The Moral Imperative: New Essays on the Ethics of Resistance in National Socialist Germany 1933–1945*, Boulder, CO 1998, pp. 105–117; See Also: Nathan Stolzfus, *Resistance of the Heart: Intermarriage and the Rosenstrasse Protest in Nazi Germany*, New York 1996. For a less heroic view of the role of the "Aryan" partners in mixed marriages during the Holocaust, see Beate Meyer, 'The Mixed Marriage. A Guarantee of Survival or a Reflection of German Society during the Nazi Regime?', in David Bankier (ed.), *Probing the Depths of German Antisemitism: German Society and the Persecution of the Jews, 1933–1941*, New York–Oxford, 1999, pp. 54–77.

[4]Günther B. Ginzel estimates the number of Germans assisting Jews threatened with arrest or deportation at 100,000. Cited in Gerhard Paul, '"Nein, den kenn ich, der ist Italiener!" – Wie Menschen aus Schleswig-Holstein verfolgten Juden beistanden', in Gerhard Paul and Miriam Gillis-Carlebach (eds.), *Menora und Hakenkreuz. Zur Geschichte der Juden in und aus Schleswig-Holstein, Lübeck und Altona, 1918–1998*, Neumünster 1998, pp. 573–589, here p. 574. A comprehensive project initiated by the Zentrum für Antisemitismusforschung der Technischen Universität Berlin has thus far identified 2,000 individuals involved in giving "life-saving help" to Jews in Germany. Cf. Beate Kosmala, 'Experiences of Jews who survived in Germany', paper delivered at the Yad Vashem Institute for International Holocaust Research (winter 2000).

[5]Henrietta (Kicia) Altman's testimony, *Yad Vashem*, Department for the Righteous (henceforth *YVR*), M-31, file 6239 (Alfred Rossner).

between members of a group. Although the term stems from early Roman jurispru-
dence, its modern ethical connotations only began to develop at the end of the eighteenth century, especially in the wake of the French Revolution and its proclaimed
ideal of universal brotherhood.[6] One scarcely needs to point out that the course of
European history since the French Revolution has often been irreconcilable with the
idea of universal solidarity. In a sense, the Nazi concept of the *Volksgemeinschaft*
reflected an effort to confront the social fragmentations and cultural dislocations of
modernity by reversing the ethical implications of that ideal, reverting instead to a
pre-modern morality of "blood".[7] On the one hand, from beginning to end the integrated national community remained a figment of Nazi propaganda; on the other
hand, the regime did succeed in destroying the bonds of human solidarity within
German society. As "community aliens" (*Volksfremde*) and "community pests"
(*Volksschädlinge*), the Jews can thus be understood as the first victims of a concerted
assault on the moral foundations of civilised society. From this perspective, their
German rescuers were individuals who resisted the Nazi attempt to redraw the lines
of human solidarity.

The unique dilemma of the rescuer was that solidarity with the Jews –
Judenfreundschaft in the Nazi jargon – was widely construed as treason to one's national community, a crime against one's own "blood". In Nazi Germany as distinct from
the occupied countries, the antisemitic campaign was not implemented by a foreign,
usurping power, but reflected the official policy of a regime accepted by the vast
majority of Germans as legal and legitimate. The root criminality of the anti-Jewish
measures was disguised by an elaborate cloak of sham legality, the Third Reich thus
being aptly characterised as a *legalisierter Unrechtsstaat* (a legalised unjust state)[8]. It has
been observed that in Germany Jewish victims of the Nazi regime did not only have
to contend with situations of extreme privation and abuse but had also to bear the
psychological burden of knowing that the legalised will of the legitimate state
authority stood behind such treatment.[9] This also constituted part of the dilemma of
the would-be rescuer or resister. One has only to recall how deeply ingrained the values of obedience and submission to authority were in German society and culture.[10]
And one should note the fact that Germans inside Germany were geographically,
hence experientially and emotionally, removed from the sites of torture and mass-
killing in the east. More than his counterpart in Eastern Europe, the typical German

---

[6]See Kurt Bayertz, 'Begriff und Problem der Solidarität', in *idem* (ed.), *Solidarität. Begriff und Problem*,
Frankfurt am Main 1998, pp. 11–53.

[7]For a good discussion of the relationship of National Socialism to modernity, see Detlev J. K. Peukert,
Inside Nazi Germany. Conformity, Opposition, and Racism in Everyday Life, transl. by Richard Deveson, New
Haven 1987.

[8]Günther B. Ginzel makes the observation in the discussion appended to Wolfgang Benz, 'Juden im
Untergrund. Vom Überleben in den Jahren 1943 bis 1945', in Ginzel, pp. 7–18; 'Diskussion', pp. 19–27,
here p. 24.

[9]*ibid.*

[10]The unwholesome mixture of subservience and conformism so typical of German society before 1945
is immortalised in Heinrich Mann's satirical character Diederich Heßling; see Heinrich Mann, *Der
Untertan. Roman*, Berlin 1918. For a 1960s perspective on German political culture and its alleged lack of
"civic culture", see Gabriel A. Almond and Sidney Verba, *The Civic Culture*, Princeton 1963. See also
Kurt Sontheimer, *Deutschlands politische Kultur*, Munich 1990, pp. 36–40.

rescuer thus had to rely on inference, hearsay, and imagination to grasp the true import of the deportations.

Even if for the vast majority of the German population – those who voted for the Nazis among them – a "solution of the Jewish problem" had never assumed the paramount, obsessive importance it had for Hitler and the hard core of Nazi radicals, six years of Nazi rule had succeeded in stamping out any remaining sense of solidarity with the Jews. On the one hand, the image of the Jew had undergone a progressively dehumanising and "depersonalising" transformation, catalysing and reflecting public internalisation of the antisemitic stereotypes of Nazi propaganda. A progressive "abstraction" of the Jewish problem was facilitated by the fact that physical contact with Jews had become rare with their increasing segregation and confinement in "Jew houses". On the other hand, the problem had became increasingly displaced from ordinary awareness, people being preoccupied with other matters such as the daily struggle to secure food and income, the safety of one's relatives at the front, and the escalating air warfare. The Jews had become aliens, in this sense literally beyond the pale of ordinary human solidarity. Their martyrdom was not regarded as a moral problem by the vast majority of ordinary Germans.

The German resistance movement was here no exception. Even if one were to accept the – disputed – assertion that it was their horror at the genocide of the Jews that drove the plotters of 20th July 1944 to their desperate last-ditch attempt on Hitler's life,[11] it remains true that the rescue of Jews never became a top priority on their political agenda. It would appear, moreover, that many of the conspirators were not only themselves infected by antisemitism but, moreover, deeply implicated in the "final solution".[12] To be sure, the relationship of the Polish underground to the Jews was also highly problematic. Still it did spawn, even if only indirectly and belatedly, an organisation like *Żegota*, which was specifically dedicated to the rescue of Jews. No less important, the Polish and other national resistance movements succeeded in preserving the vision of an alternative society, its moral impact transcending that of the actual armed insurrection. In Germany, the political vision of "another Germany" was only preserved – if at all – in each individual anti-Hitler conspirator's private realm.

To appreciate the burden that German Holocaust rescuers took upon themselves, we need to take note of their isolation. The individual rescuer had to rely on his or her own courage, his or her own sense of right or wrong, for guidance in confronting a social and existential dilemma.

---

[11]Peter Hoffmann, 'The Persecution of the Jews as a Motive for Resistance Against National Socialism', in Chandler (ed.), pp. 73–107; *idem*, 'The German Resistance to Hitler and the Jews', in Bankier (ed.), pp. 463–477.

[12]Amongst those executed for their part in the conspiracy were Arthur Nebe, the notorious commander of *Einsatzgruppe* B, and Count von Helldorf, Chief of the Berlin police under the Nazis. See Peter Steinbach, 'Antisemitismus und Widerstand' in *Tribüne. Zeitschrift zum Verständnis des Judentums*, vol. 39, no. 154 (2000), pp. 120–136, here p. 120.

THE RISK FACTOR

Because antisemitism was so central to the Nazi *Weltanschauung*, any act that tended to thwart the Nazi murder design, even when taking place on the non-political, non-heroic everyday level, merits recognition as an act of resistance.[13] There was a whole spectrum of non-political, non-organised dissent by ordinary Germans: refusing to believe various forms of Nazi propaganda, spreading gossip that was unkind to the regime, listening to foreign radio reports, avoiding productive work, hoarding food. Though the regime did its best to stamp out such activities, none posed a serious threat to achieving any of its main objectives.[14] Because of the centrality of anti-semitism within both Nazi ideology and Nazi political practice, showing solidarity with Jews, meaning any act that tended to thwart the extermination programme, represented an altogether different category of resistance. A reconstruction of some of the rescue stories may thus offer insight into the possibilities for non-political resistance open to rank and file Germans – people who, unlike the "20th of July" conspirators, had no chance of toppling the regime from within.

There is no simple answer to the question of what sort of risk German rescuers took upon themselves in helping Jews escape their ordained destruction. Undoubtedly, the degree of risk varied according to the evolution of Nazi Jewish policy and, of course, the type of help being rendered. The situation of the *Wehrmacht* sergeant smuggling arms to the Jewish underground in Belorussia was probably far more precarious than that of the prominent German industrialist in Stuttgart who, in 1938, provided secret funding for Jewish emigration, or of the *Wehrmacht* contractor in Berlin who tried to protect his "war-important" Jewish workers from deportation. While if caught the sergeant could expect summary execution, the industrialist and the contractor still had some manoeuvring room: the formidable corpus of laws, decrees, and ad-hoc regulations comprising the Special Law for Jews (*Sonderrecht*) in Nazi Germany does not include a single reference to help rendered by Germans to Jews. The closest thing is a decree by the Head Office for Reich Security, dated 24 October 1941, stipulating, "on educational grounds", up to three months imprisonment in a concentration camp for persons of "German blood" who openly displayed friendly relations with Jews.[15] This should be contrasted with the situation in Eastern Europe, where after October 1941 Poles caught helping Jews had to reckon with the death penalty – often together with their entire household.[16] The Nazi masters of Germany tended to be more lenient with their own offending "national comrades". In practice, the punishment inflicted on Germans caught helping Jews inside

---

[13]Peter Steinbach, '"Unbesungene Helden" – Ihre Bedeutung für die allgemeine Widerstandsgeschichte', in Ginzel, pp. 183–202 ; Wolfgang Altgeld and Michael Kissener, 'Judenverfolgung und Widerstand', in Michael Kissener (ed.), *Widerstand gegen die Judenverfolgung*, Constance 1996, pp. 9–40.

[14]Gerhard Paul, 'Everyday Acts of Dissent and Disobedience', in Wolfgang Benz and Walter H. Pehle (eds.), *Encyclopedia of German Resistance to the Nazi Movement*, New York 1997, pp. 151–155.

[15]Joseph Walk (ed.), *Das Sonderrecht für die Juden im NS-Staat. Eine Sammlung der gesetzlichen Maßnahmen und Richtlinien – Inhalt und Bedeutung*, Heidelberg 1996, vol. 4, p. 257.

[16]Marie-Luise Kreuter, 'Rettung von Juden im nationalsozialistischen Deutschland 1933–1945. Ein Dokumentationsprojekt mit Datenbank am Zentrum für Antisemitismusforschung der Technischen Universität Berlin', in *Zeitschrift für Geschichtswissenschaft*, vol. 46 (1998), pp. 445–451.

Germany could vary from a warning or fine[17] to a term in a concentration camp –
the latter sometimes leading to the death of the person concerned. "Jews' helpers"
(*Judenhelfer*) and "Jews' friends" (*Judenfreunde*) could be indicted on different counts
such as violating the *Heimtückegesetz* (the "law against malicious gossip"), financial corruption, or even tuning in to foreign radio programmes.[18]

   The German rescuers' scope for action was severely hampered by the omnipresent
phenomenon of denunciation. Indeed, informing on one's neighbours and colleagues, not necessarily out of antisemitic motives, became a hallmark of German
society under Hitler. The Gestapo's well-earned reputation as a pervasive instrument
of terror did not depend so much on its own efficiency as on the willing collaboration of masses of ordinary Germans. In this sense it is justified to talk about a process
of 'self-policing' and 'self-surveillance' by the German population.[19] The non-political, everyday context of rescue made the rescuers particularly vulnerable. Because
help offered to Jews took place in the private, non-public sphere of home and work,
the only way the authorities could get wind of it was through denunciation.

THE MOTIVATION OF THE RESCUERS

This brings us to the problem at the heart of our discussion: what motivated the rescuers? What made them behave so wholly differently from the vast majority of their
German compatriots? If we reject, as intuitively untenable, the idea of some unique
personality structure they shared, rooted in anomalous upbringing, social background, or political and religious views, what led to their willingness to risk life and
limb on behalf of Jewish victims of Nazi persecution? I would argue that the search
for a single, overarching explanation is in fact misconceived. Rather, we need to try
to understand the rescuers in light of their own historically conditioned societies and
traditions. Despite a complexity of situations and personality-types, it is possible to
suggest a list of – to be sure conceptually differing – categories that acknowledges the
persons involved in their historical individuality: (1) personally-motivated rescuers;
(2) principled rescuers; (3) last-minute rescuers; (4) soldiers and army entrepreneurs
in the occupied countries. These categories are admittedly no more than rough-and-
ready in nature, descriptive rather than analytic. They are not intended to provide a
systematic or exhaustive typology, but only an approximate sense of the range and
singularity of German Holocaust rescuers.

PERSONALLY MOTIVATED RESCUERS

For this sort of rescuer, the dominant impetus for action, or the main predisposing
factor, was some previous personal connection to the rescued person. In more than

---

[17]See *Yad Vashem, YVR*, M-31, file 387 (Theodor Görner).
[18]See *YVR*, M-31, file 970 (Karl and Eva Hermann).
[19]Christl Wickert, 'Popular Attitudes to National Socialist Antisemitism: Denunciations for "Insidious
   Offenses" and "Racial Ignominy"', Bankier (ed.), pp. 282–295.

forty per cent of all cases of rescue that took place inside the German Reich, the rescuers had some pre-war connection to the person they helped – a reflection of the intense interaction of German Jews with their non-Jewish environment. Gerhard Paul has strikingly termed the effect of social closeness as "the central violence-retarding factor, fractures, as it were, in the process of radicalisation".[20] It is as if the unreflective, natural solidarity springing out of close personal contact acted in these cases as a shield, a sort of psychological immunisation, against ideological and emotional Nazi contamination. The personal ties in question could vary widely in quality and intensity and could range from intimate personal friendships and romantic ties, through business partnerships, to passing acquaintance. It is only fair to add, however, that in the great majority of cases "those relationships had not, before the war, reached a level of intensity and commitment in which either party would consider risking their lives for the other as obvious moral obligation".[21]

To an even higher degree than in the other categories, the typical personal rescuers were women. Ursula Büttner's research on so-called mixed couples – as indeed Victor Klemperer's published diary – give us some insight into the human costs involved in keeping faith with a Jewish partner under the conditions imposed by the Nazi regime: the daily humiliations and petty harassment, the social ostracism, the turning away of former friends and acquaintances, the disapproval by your own "Aryan" relatives. Marie Grünberg (born 21 January 1903) lived in such a mixed marriage with the Jewish-born Kurt Grünberg.[22] They owned a small wooden summer house with an adjacent garden in the suburb of Berlin-Blankenburg (Ziegelstraße 30), but were officially registered in another apartment they owned, within the city. After the large Gestapo round-up at the end of February 1943, in the wake of which Berlin was declared *judenfrei*, Marie harboured no less than four "illegals" at her two apartments: her Jewish brother-in-law, Martin Grünberg; his colleague, Ostazcewer; a female relative of the latter, Mrs. Dobriner; and her "Aryan" fiancé, Klinzahn, a military deserter who had escaped from an assignment to the 999 "punishment battalion", which was notorious for recruiting German convicts and concentration camp prisoners and sending them on suicide missions to the eastern front. Marie Grünberg also took it upon herself occasionally to assist and shelter the sixteen-year-old Zwi Abrahamsohn, her husband's nephew.

Starting with the intensified air bombardment of Berlin in the latter phase of the war, it was no longer safe to live in the city apartment, all six individuals thus being forced to move into the little house in Berlin-Blankenburg. The four "illegals" were practically incarcerated there. In addition to the dangers always involved in hiding Jews, Marie had to cope with the daily burden of feeding six adults with two ration cards – one of which was marked with a "J" – and to regulate her purchases so that no one would notice that additional people were living at the house.

In Marie Grünberg's case, the primary bond with a spouse was widened to include his relatives and friends. In contrast, the solidarity shown the Jewish man they were

---

[20]Paul, "'Nein, den kenn ich, der ist Italiener!'", p. 587.
[21]Gushee, p. 385.
[22]*YVR*, M-31, file 2824 (Marie Grünberg).

protecting by the elderly farming couple Heinrich and Maria List (born on 15 February 1882 and 25 February 1881 respectively) should be seen against the background of pre-Nazi economic and social German-Jewish relations in the Odenwald, southern Hesse; this case reveals a complex picture of personal commitment to a Jewish acquaintance, on the one hand, integration into the Nazi mood of the time, on the other hand.[23] The couple's story unfolded in the tiny village of Ernsbach, not far from the ancient market town of Michelstadt, and ended tragically, the sixty-year-old farmer being denounced to the authorities and dying in a concentration camp. Through luck, nearly the entire, extensive police documentation bearing on the case was preserved in the Darmstadt State archives, to be discovered there in the early 1990s by two Michelstadt high school teachers, Hans Winter and Werner König. The documentation allows a reconstruction of the case in some detail.

The Odenwald is a hilly wooded area of southern Germany bordered by the Rhine, Main, and Neckar rivers. While there was no Jewish community in Ernsbach, Michelstadt (4,071 inhabitants in 1933) had a vibrant one with roots reaching back to the seventeenth century. The town's Jews (198 in 1871) were well-integrated, proud of both their Germanness and the legacy of their renowned rabbi, Seckel Loeb Wormser (1768–1847), the *"Ba'al Shem* of Michelstadt". Most of the Jewish breadwinners were either shopkeepers or merchants, with a few cattle dealers.

Despite isolated anti-Jewish incidents in the early nineteenth century, there is no record of any notable social animosity after emancipation. Otto Böckel's antisemitic German Social Reform Party (founded 1887), which enjoyed huge popularity in Upper Hesse, had very few adherents in the Odenwald. The good relations persisted well into the twentieth century, Jews and Germans maintaining close business contacts, their children attending the same schools, and befriending each other in sports and dance clubs "without any racial problems" (*ohne Rassenprobleme*).[24] The tolerant public atmosphere was preserved for the better part of the troubled Weimar period, not least thanks to the enlightened policies of the Social Democratic town mayor, Heinrich Ritzel, who held office from 1919 to 1930. Nevertheless, the economic crisis and soaring unemployment of the late 1920s was reflected in the Nazi Party's rising popularity. In the Reichstag elections of 14 September 1930, the party Nazis polled 31.3% of the votes in Michelstadt (the result for Germany as a whole: 18.3%); in the following elections of 31 July 1932 it gained 45.6% (Germany as a whole: 33.1%).

After the Nazi accession to power, an accelerated Jewish emigration set in. On *"Kristallnacht"*, Jewish shops and houses were vandalised and looted in Michelstadt as elsewhere. The interior of the old synagogue (founded in 1791) was destroyed, but – again as elsewhere – the building was not set ablaze for fear that the nearby barns would catch fire. Arrested by SA thugs, Jewish men were marched through the streets, twenty being sent to Buchenwald, from which they returned in January 1939. By 1942 only fourteen Jews remained in Michelstadt; ten were deported on 18 March 1942, three on 24 September 1942, and the last remaining Jewish person, a woman, in April 1943.[25]

---

[23]*YVR*, M-31, file 5525 (Heinrich and Maria List).
[24]Martin Schmall, *Die Juden in Michelstadt, 1650–1943*, 4th edn., Michelstadt 1988, p. 63.
[25]*ibid.*, p. 87.

Working in the fields – Heinrich List and his wife. Mr. Hans H. Winter of Bad König, Germany, who kindly provided the photograph, adds the following description: "This picture shows the farmer and his wife with his simple tools scratching a living from the poor soil where hardly anything grows. He is nearly sixty years old – this is what they looked like when they were hiding Ferdinand Strauß."

By courtesy of Yad Vashem

The List family, *c.* 1935. The author wishes to thank Mr. Hans H. Winter for his great help in obtaining the List family photographs.

By courtesy of Yad Vashem

The Jewish man protected by the Lists was Ferdinand Strauß (born 1 July 1902); he was probably among those arrested and molested by the SA on the night of the Pogrom (9–10 November 1938). He was the only member of his family remaining in Michelstadt, his father having died in the early thirties and his American-born mother having returned to the States. Sometime in 1939, Strauß left Michelstadt to join his uncle in Frankfurt am Main. In November 1941, however, he showed up without prior warning at the Lists' home in Ernsbach – he had decided to return to the Odenwald after his uncle had died and his aunt had committed suicide by poisoning. The Lists sheltered him from mid-November 1941 to 16 March 1942, concealing his presence from other village residents. Strauß, who participated fully in the daily routine of the List family, sharing their meals and listening with them to the radio, would disappear into his room or hide in the wardrobe whenever the door opened.

The Lists were betrayed by their Polish farmhand, who, because of a petty quarrel with Heinrich List, reported the stranger's presence to a neighbouring farmer. After verifying the story, the farmer notified both village mayor Jakob Bär and the regional gendarmerie in Erbach, which launched an investigation on 23 March, 1942 – that is, exactly a week after Strauß had finally left Ernsbach. List denied the charges at first, but was forced to confess after his wife broke down when confronted with the Polish foreign worker. He was detained by the police and sent to the Dachau concentration camp; his wife was left alone. In October 1942, she received an official letter from the Dachau commandant stating that her husband had died on 5 October in the camp hospital, following an infection in his lower leg. The urn with the remains arrived a few days later. To compound the Lists' tragedy, their only son Jakob was reported missing in action on the Russian front in August 1944. Ferdinand Strauß, had better luck, managing to cross the Swiss border and ending up in Jamaica, where he died in 1983.

Why should a simple German farmer have agreed to shelter a Jewish runaway, putting himself and his family at great risk? This is the same question that perplexed List's police interrogators, Schmidt and Wagner. List was not cast in the mould of a typical anti-Nazi resister. To be sure, he had business connections with the Strauß family before the Nazi takeover and had even bought a few pieces of linen and furniture from Strauß's widowed mother before her emigration to the States. This, however, was hardly exceptional and did not by itself make the farmer a "Jews' friend". In fact, Jakob Bär, obviously at pains to clear himself of any taint of complicity, testified to the police that List had always put himself forward as a "good National-Socialist" and had been one of the first in Ernsbach to vote for the Nazis. This is why, he explained, he had not been at all suspicious at first and had reacted with disbelief to the report that List was hiding a Jew on his farm. He leaned towards holding List's Catholic sister-in-law responsible: Frau Weyrauch had served with the Strauß family for many years as a maid and had remained on friendly terms with them even after the Nazi takeover. Wary of compromising himself, Bär would refuse to pass on a plea for mercy written by List's son-in-law in Würzberg, tearing the letter into pieces. For his part, Schmidt, the *Meister der Gendarmerie*, had little patience with List's reputation as a convinced National-Socialist and "big antisemite" (*großer Judengegner*). Anyone taking it upon himself to hide a Jew in a village of 298 inhabitants, he reasoned in his report to the Gestapo in Darmstadt, "must be regarded without any doubt as a

Jews' friend". But List himself should have the last word. Questioned about his motives for hiding Strauß, he answered simply: "Because I have known him since childhood ... I was seized with pity *(das Mitleid hat mich gepackt)*."[26]

PRINCIPLED RESCUERS (I): RELIGIOUSLY MOTIVATED RESISTERS

With principled German rescuers, the first impetus for action was not a personal relationship to the persecuted individual but rather a well-articulated ideological stand against Nazism. This stand could be rooted either in religious faith or in a secular political *Weltanschauung*. The principled rescuers did not wait for somebody to turn to them for help; they were driven by a sort of inner compulsion to act in face of the barbarism around them.

Among these persons, the religiously motivated could hardly draw inspiration or solace from a resolute moral stand of the organised church, whether Protestant or Catholic. In fact, as has now been amply demonstrated, the silence of the German churches – even, despite post-war German mythologising, the Professing Church *(Bekennende Kirche)* – regarding the ongoing persecution of the Jews, and even their active and passive collaboration with this persecution, was in itself one of the most telling signs of German society's moral bankruptcy under Hitler.[27] Against this backdrop, the sustained resistance that Pastor Hermann Maas offered the regime appears all the more remarkable.[28] Born on 5 August 1877 in Gegenbach/Schwarzwald, Maas was from a family of Protestant pastors in Baden. Having studied theology at the universities of Halle, Strasbourg, and Heidelberg, he became a curate in the autumn of 1900 – the beginning of a life-long career in the Protestant church.

Since the Sixth Zionist Congress in 1903, which Maas had visited out of curiosity while visiting Basel, he had felt friendship with the Jewish people and ardent sympathy with the Zionist movement. At the congress, he witnessed the debate between the proponents of the "Uganda plan" and those faithful to "Zion" and had the opportunity to meet prominent Jewish political leaders such as Herzl and Weizmann, as well as Martin Buber with whom he maintained a life-long connection. As an adherent of the Christian ecumenical movement, he subsequently became an advocate of the cause of understanding among the monotheistic religions and, in particular, of Christian-Jewish reconciliation.

Maas's ecumenical outlook and liberal politics – he was an admirer of Friedrich Naumann and Max Weber and served twice as city councillor representing the German Democratic Party – seems to have rendered him immune to Nazi ideology in all its forms and disguises. In this he differed from other clerical opponents of the

---

[26]*YVR*, M-31, file 5525 (Heinrich and Maria List).

[27]Shelley Baranowski, 'The Confessing Church and Antisemitism: Protestant Identity, German Nationhood, and the Exclusion of Jews', in Robert P. Ericksen and Susannah Heschel (eds), *Betrayal: German Churches and the Holocaust*, Minneapolis 1999, pp. 90–109. For the role of the German churches under Hitler see, among other studies, John S. Conway, *The Nazi Persecution of the Churches, 1933–45*, New York 1968; Ernst C. Helmreich, *The German Churches under Hitler. Background, Struggle, and Epilogue*, Detroit 1979; Volker Fabricius and Georg Denzler, *Christen und Nationalsozialisten*, Frankfurt am Main 1993; Doris L. Bergen, *Twisted Cross: The German Christian Movement in the Third Reich*, Chapel Hill–London 1996.

[28]*YVR*, M-31, file 74 (Dr. Hermann Maas).

regime like Martin Niemöller and Heinrich Grüber, who were at first infatuated with Hitler and his promise of national revival.[29] On 1 April 1933, the same day the Nazis launched their general economic boycott against the Jews of Germany, Maas set sail for Palestine on a three-month tour financed by a grant from the "German Palestine Committee". The sight of the new Jewish settlements, meetings with freshly arrived German-Jewish emigrants, and contacts with Hebrew scholars left an indelible impression on the Protestant theologian, who himself was a fluent Hebrew speaker.

On his return to Heidelberg at the beginning of July, Maas was exposed to a concerted campaign of threats and vilification by local Nazi leaders and the SA, accompanied by demands that the "pastor of the Jews" be dismissed from his duties. However, Maas was a highly respected figure in the Christian world ecumenical movement, and the authorities were reluctant to risk an international scandal. In response to intercession by the Lutheran *Landesbischof* on 14 July 1933, they thus ruled that Maas should be allowed to remain in office. But with demands for his removal gathering momentum the *Stabsleiter* of the Baden *Gau* took up the matter on 2 August. The *Landesbischof* now sent Maas a stern warning, asking him to desist from "comments and actions that might give rise to the impression that you intend to continue with your earlier political and cultural endeavours".[30]

This first serious conflict with the new rulers of Germany seemed only to intensify Maas's defiance and his sense of identification with the Jewish people. He contributed articles to the *Jüdische Rundschau*, translated poems by the Hebrew poet Chaim Nachman Bialik, and even sent his eldest daughter to Palestine to teach young Jewish women the art of hand-weaving. Furthermore, he made a custom of inviting Jewish religious leaders in Heidelberg to join him on Christmas Eve and of participating in the Passover celebration. The expressions of solidarity were so strong and direct that Heidelberg Rabbi Dr. Fritz Pinkuss was forced to ask him not to attend public Jewish prayer services so as not to put himself at risk.

Maas was a member of the *Pfarrernotbund*, the emergency association of dissident Protestant pastors set up by Martin Niemöller in September 1933, and had joined the Professing Church. However, while members of the latter – including Maas's close colleague Heinrich Grüber – were mainly concerned with the plight of the so-called non-Aryan Christians, largely ignoring, at first, the fate of the Jews,[31] Maas was equally committed to both groups. In October 1940, while the Jews of Baden, the Palatinate, and several places in Baden and Württemberg, were being deported

---

[29]Niemöller's early espousal of Hitler and the Nazi movement – which he was to regret deeply later jn life – is well-known and was never denied by him. See James Bentley, *Martin Niemöller, 1892–1984*, New York 1984, p. 41. Grüber briefly joined the Nazi party in early 1933. See Dieter Winkler, *Heinrich Grüber. Protestierender Christ. Berlin-Kaulsdorf, 1933–1945*, Berlin 1993, p. 24.

[30]Cited in Albert Lohrbächer and Claudia Pepperl, 'Der "stadtbekannte Judenfreund"', in Werner Keller, Albrecht Lohrbächer, Eckhart Marggraf, Claudia Pepperl, Jörg Thierfelder, and Karsten Weber (eds.), revised by Matthias Riemenschneider, *Leben für Versöhnung. Hermann Maas. Wegbereiter des christlich-jüdischen Dialoges*, 2nd edn., Karlsruhe 1997, pp. 76–103, here p. 80.

[31]See Hartmut Ludwig, 'Als Zivilcourage selten war. Die evangelische Hilfsstelle "Büro Grüber", ihre Mitarbeiter und Helfer im Rheinland 1938 bis 1940', in Ginzel, pp. 29–54, here pp. 31–32. As late as November 1938, Grübers's 'clientele' consisted almost exclusively of so-called Protestant 'non-Aryans'. See Winkler, p. 111.

to the Gurs concentration camp in southern France, Maas managed to protect some old and frail persons from being included in the deportation. He also kept in contact with the deportees, using his connections to help them obtain exit visas abroad.[32]

In March 1942, the Reich Ministry of Religious Affairs started a campaign against Maas that ended in his forced retirement in mid-1943. One of the most incriminating pieces of evidence against him was a bundle of letters, discovered by the Gestapo, that Maas had written in the 1930s to a Christian woman of Jewish descent in Karlsruhe; in this he expressed abhorrence for the Nazi regime and its racist persecution of the Jews. Confronted with the evidence, the clergyman for once lost heart. The official, duly signed record of his statement on 6 April 1943 to the *Oberkirchenrat* of Karlsruhe makes sad reading, attesting as it does to the ability of violent regimes to intimidate their opponents.[33] In his statement, Maas tried to repudiate the charge of "friendliness to Jews" (*Judenfreundlichkeit*) by claiming a purely spiritual concern for the "Jewish Christians" (the official category of *Judenchristen*). He had, he asserted, never meant to challenge the state's racial principles and political measures. Furthermore, he had always regarded "unconverted Judaism" as a "curse in many respects". Maas also claimed that he had ceased looking after the interests of the "Jewish Christians" after the arrest of Heinrich Grüber in early 1941.[34] These vehement denials – which amounted to a repudiation of all that Maas had believed in – failed to convince the Gestapo, and he was forced to retire. In 1944, the sixty-seven-year-old was sent to a forced-labour camp in France, where he remained until liberation by the Americans.[35]

PRINCIPLED RESCUERS (II): POLITICAL RESISTERS

For the politically motivated German rescuer, offering help to persecuted Jews was just one expression of an overall opposition to Nazism. Nearly all the rescuers in this category were adherents of political parties on the left. With the possible exception of Hans Walz, the general manager of the Robert Bosch corporation in Stuttgart,[36] there are no representatives of the Conservative-Liberal opposition to Hitler on the honour roll-call of Holocaust rescuers. For all the persons involved, the road taken from a general anti-Nazi stance to risking one's life on behalf of Jews was far from simple. It was not made any easier by the fact that by 1939 the regime had long succeeded in breaking the back of every non-Nazi political organisation, incarcerating former political activists in concentration camps or forcing them into exile.

---

[32]See Lohrbächer and Pepperl, pp. 86–97.

[33]The signed *Protokoll* is reprinted in facsimile in Keller, *Hermann Maas*, pp. 102–103.

[34]Grüber was arrested by the Gestapo on 19 December 1940, as he was preparing for a trip to the Gurs camp to investigate the situation of the Jewish deportees from Baden and the Palatinate. See *YVR*, M-31, file 75 (Heinrich Grüber).

[35]After the war, Hermann Maas became the first German officially invited to visit the State of Israel (in 1950). He wrote several books about Israel and the reconciliation between Judaism and Christianity.

[36]Hans Walz (YVR, M-31, file 497) is treated extensively in Joachim Scholtysek, *Robert Bosch und der liberale Widerstand gegen Hitler; 1933–1945*, Munich 1999.

The career of the Communist activist Wilhelm Hammann is a case in point.[37] The eldest of nine siblings, he was born on 25 February 1897 in Biebesheim am Rhein, and grew up in a working-class milieu in the Groß-Gerau district, northwest of Darmstadt. His father was a railway-worker and his mother a midwife. Between 1907 and 1913, he attended secondary school at Gernsheim, where he displayed academic excellence. After graduating, he studied at a teacher-training college in Alzey, being drafted into military service after his final examinations in 1916. He served with the cavalry in Belgium and in Russia and finished the war as a flying cadet in Halle. There he came into contact with German revolutionaries and became fired with enthusiasm for the Russian Revolution – as soon as the war ended, he joined the German Communist Party. After qualifying as a teacher in 1920, he taught in the Darmstadt district between 1922 and 1931. He was greatly beloved by his students, in part for refraining from punishment by flogging, which was still customary at the time. In 1927, Hammann was elected representative of the Hessian *Landtag* and became the Communist Party spokesman; in the 1930–1932 period, he was sentenced to two prison terms for alleged involvement in a political conspiracy and consequently removed from his teaching position.

There is nothing to suggest that Hammann gave much attention to the "Jewish Question" in Germany prior to 1933 or that he did not toe the official Communist line in this respect. His warning in a speech in the Hessian *Landtag* on 7 July 1931 that "The aim of the finance oligarchy is [to bring about] undisguised dictatorship, the handing over of power to the Nazis" does not indicate any special political perspicacity; it was well in tune with the stereotyped Communist interpretation of Nazism as a mere tool of big-money interests. In fact, the German Communist Party's early stand on Nazi antisemitism is – to agree with David Bankier – a glaring example of an ideologically distorted interpretation of reality. Until very late, the party persisted in viewing Nazi persecution of the Jews as merely a diversionary tactic – a way of deflecting attention from the regime's real aims.[38] Such intellectual distortion notwithstanding, Hammann's communist ideology appears to have preserved the potential for resistance within him, preventing him from turning into one of countless Nazi fellow-travellers after 1933.

In the first years after Hitler's ascent to power, Hammann served several prison terms for "preparation of high treason". Finally, on August 27, 1938, he was remanded without trial to Buchenwald, where he remained until the end of the war. He was the 1,224th *Schutzhäftling* (prisoner under preventive detention) to enter the infamous camp. Opened in July 1937 and located on Mount Ettersberg near Weimar, it was one of the first concentration camps set up in Germany primarily for political prisoners, and it maintained this function throughout the war years. Jews only began to arrive there in great numbers in the winter of 1944–45, as the camps in the East were being evacuated in the face of steady progress by the Soviet army. It was the good fortune of these newly-arrived prisoners to find a strongly-organised, Communist-inspired resistance network in the camp.

---

[37]*YVR*, M-31, file 2725 (Wilhelm Hammann).
[38]David Bankier, 'The German Communist Party and Nazi Antisemitism, 1933–1938', in *LBI Year Book*, vol. 32 (1987), pp. 325–339.

From the start, Hammann had been part of the underground resistance that gradually took control of the camp's internal administration. In the summer of 1943, the leaders of the prisoners' organisation[39] succeeded in persuading the camp commandant to set up a special barracks for children and teenagers. One purpose of this Block 8, as it was called, was to accommodate mainly Ukrainian and Russian fourteen and fifteen year olds who had been sent to Germany for forced labour. Through subterfuge and manipulation, it was possible to obtain special concessions for these inmates such as lighter work-loads and exemption from the daily roll calls on the camp parade-ground. Children under fourteen living in Block 8 did not have to go to work at all. In the summer of 1944, the resistance organisation succeeded in secretly moving into the barracks some seventy Jewish children who had arrived with transports of Jews from Hungary; other Jewish children arrived in the first weeks of 1945.

Hammann was appointed *Blockältester* at the end of 1944, after the SS had arrested his Austrian predecessor, Franz Leitner,[40] on suspicion that he had participated in a secret memorial service for the murdered Socialist leader Ernst Thälmann. He treated both Jewish and non-Jewish children with invariable kindness, doing his utmost to protect them from the brutality of the SS guards. During the last days of Buchenwald, when a massive liquidation of Jews was being carried out, the entire children's barrack was ordered to line up outside for a roll call. As reported by a witness, Hammann expressed a preference for death over being implicated in the murder of Jewish children. As the report has it, when the Jewish children were called on to step forward, no one did, one of the SS guards then asking Hammann whether any Jews were present. His response, we read, was that to his knowledge there were children of all nationalities – Czechs, Poles, Ukrainians – but no Jews. The previous night, Hammann had personally distributed national identification patches to the Jewish children in his block and instructed them to remove their stars of David. The gamble succeeded, the SS declining to investigate the matter further. Some ten days later, on 11 April 1945, the Americans liberated Buchenwald.

Hammann's fate after 1945 was a reflection of the ambiguities of the post-war era and the climate of suspicion generated by the Cold War. Following his liberation, he resumed his political activity in Groß-Gerau and was elected *Landrat*. But as a committed Communist, he soon incurred the wrath of black-market racketeers who denounced him to the American military authorities. At the beginning of 1946, he was deposed from his post and incarcerated in Dachau, falsely accused of having been a Nazi sympathiser. He was released fourteen months later, in May 1947, without any trial and without any formal charges having been brought against him. He died in 1955 in Groß-Gerau as the result of a road accident.

The post-war controversy over Wilhelm Hammann and his activities need not concern us here. It was part of German society's troubled process of coming to terms with its recent past. However, the irony of the German Communist Party turn-

[39]Extraordinary as it may seem, the everyday running of Buchenwald was largely in the hands of the (non-Jewish) political prisoners. This provided the underground cells with an opportunity to 'plant' their own members in key posts in the internal administration. See Yehushua R. Büchler, 'Buchenwald', in Israel Gutman (ed.), *Encyclopedia of the Holocaust*, New York–London 1990, vol. 1, pp. 254–256.

[40]Yad Vashem decided to recognize Franz Leitner as one of the Righteous Among the Nations on 29 October 1998.

ing to Yad Vashem, the official Holocaust remembrance authority of the State of Israel, for the sake of honouring their late comrade, should not be missed.[41]

LAST-MINUTE RESCUERS

A third category of rescue acts performed by Germans on German soil involved help to escaped concentration camp inmates or death march survivors in the war's last stages. The category is distinctive on several counts: the Jewish survivors – coming for the most part from Poland and other East European countries – were total strangers to the rescuers; the help extended was of short duration, in no case lasting more than a few weeks; and the German rescuer was confronted with a situation for which he or she was totally unprepared. The gaps in documentation make the historical assessment of these cases especially difficult. Frequently, the Jewish survivors, whose testimony is crucial for reconstructing the story, had only the most fleeting acquaintance with their various German benefactors and knew next to nothing about their circumstances. At times, they could not even recall the names of the rescuers.

The following account illustrates some of the problems involved in reconstructing the events at play in such last-minute rescues. The Gerbrandt family owned a large farm in Steegen, a village, not far from Danzig.[42] The village had itself become part of the concentration-camp complex of Stutthof, now notorious for death marches in the course of which thousands of evacuated prisoners were murdered in the war's last phase. In the winter of 1945, the family offered shelter to three Jewish women – Polish born Chaya Feigin, her mother, and an unnamed third girl – who had managed to slip out of the camp on 27 January 1945, just as it was being evacuated in a final death march. Under the cover of dark the women had managed to wade through snow for two kilometers before Feigin's sick mother collapsed.

At this point Christl Gerbrandt found them and brought them to her parents' farm, where they were given shelter, along with warm clothes and food. Klara Gerbrandt turned away SS men who came searching for Jews. The three women remained on the farm from January until May 1945, and the Gerbrandts' son, himself a member of the Waffen-SS, did not betray them.

This rather dramatic story was recorded by Chaya Feigin for an Israel Radio programme in June 1989. Chaya could not even recall the name of the German family, whose identity only came to light when the daughter of one of the farm's previous employees responded to an appeal published in the German papers. However, it turned out that Chaya's perception of events had been too simple. In 1991 an autobiographical book came out in Germany depicting the *via dolorosa* of Gerda Gottschalk, a native of Leipzig, from her home town to the Riga ghetto and back to Germany via Stutthof.[43] During her incarceration at Stutthof in late 1944, Gottschalk was inducted for work at the Gerbrandts' farm in Steegen. Her story

[41] *Gerechter unter den Völkern: Wilhelm Hammann. Landrat, Lehrer, Kommunist, Widerstandskämpfer. Eine Dokumentation,* edited by the German Communist Party (DKP), Groß-Gerau *c.* 1985.

[42] *YVR,* M-31, file 4507 (Gustav and Klara Gerbrandt; daughter Christl).

[43] Gerda Gottschalk, *Der letzte Weg,* Constance 1991.

(written immediately after liberation) leaves little doubt that the Steegen farm was part of the concentration camp's system of exploitation, taking advantage of cheap slave labour. The owner of the farm, Gustav Gerbrandt, though not his wife or daughter, had in reality been a ruthless slave-driver.

Another such last-minute rescue narrative, taking place at Sorgenau on the Baltic coast, seems free of the ambiguity of the Gerbrandt story. In the last months of the war, the German housewife Erna Härtel (born 2 June 1904) operated a busy road-side inn in Sorgenau.[44] In East Prussia the Germans were retreating before the rap-idly advancing Soviet army and Härtel was busy with a stream of refugees and passers-by spending the night at the inn. Her husband was serving as a soldier on the western front and her only help was a young Polish housemaid. One morning, we are informed in the files, the maid brought a Jewish girl from Lodz to the inn – Frieda, a concentration camp inmate who had managed to escape from a death march. She was dressed in rags, had a closely shaven head, and was bleeding from two freshly inflicted gun wounds. Härtel, it appears, unhesitatingly took it upon her-self to shelter the girl until the war was over. To fend off the two SS-men who came to search the house two days after Frieda's arrival, she explained that the girl was a "foreign worker" sent her from Poland who had lost all her possessions, including papers, during an aerial bombardment, her hair being shaven because of a typhoid infection. Confirmed by a sympathetic elderly *Wehrmacht* man, the story was accept-ed, Frieda allowed to stay at the Härtel inn, where she remained from 31 January 1945 until the Russian arrival at Sorgenau on 14 April.

The common denominator of these last-minute rescue cases is the German res-cuer's need to take a spontaneous decision – to postpone thoughts regarding possi-ble consequences. The sparse documentation does not allow us to connect the deci-sion to a rescuer's personality, previous events in his or her life, or particular religious or political views.

RESCUERS OUTSIDE GERMANY (I): SOLDIERS

Some two thirds of all those classified as "German Righteous" by Yad Vashem were living inside the German Reich, more than sixty-five per cent of these persons being women. This is to be expected, considering that most men of military age were away from home. By contrast most German rescuers outside Germany were men, espe-cially men in uniform – a fact with significant implications. Whereas the typical German rescuer inside the Reich was a private person acting outside the Nazi sys-tem's framework, German Holocaust rescuers in the occupied countries – whether uniformed soldiers or army entrepreneurs – were more often than not implicated in the Nazi extermination machinery, thus treading treacherous moral ground. At the same time, their very complicity in and proximity to that system created possibilities for rescue not open to those on the outside.

The confrontation between the SS and two *Wehrmacht* officers, Lieutenant Albert Battel and Major Max Liedtke, over the deportation of the Jews of Przemyśl is a

---

[44]YVR, M-31, file 243 (Erna Haertel).

unique recorded exception to German army collaboration with the unfolding Holocaust.[45] The moving spirit behind the episode was probably Battel, a reserve officer and lawyer from Breslau, aged fifty-one. With the SS preparing to launch its first large-scale "resettlement" action against the Jews of Przemyśl in southern Poland, Battel, together with his superior Liedtke, ordered the bridge over the River San, the only access to the Jewish ghetto, to be blocked. On 26 July 1942, as an SS squad tried to cross to the other side, the sergeant-major in charge of the bridge threatened to open fire unless they withdrew. All this happened in broad daylight, to the amazement of the local inhabitants. Later that afternoon, an army detachment under Battel's command broke into the ghetto and used army trucks to remove up to a hundred Jewish men and their families to the barracks of the local military command. These Jews were placed under the protection of the *Wehrmacht*, thus being temporarily protected from deportation. In the following days, the remaining ghetto inmates, including the head of the *Judenrat*, Dr. Ignatz Duldig, were taken away for extermination.

In the wake of this embarrassing incident, the SS authorities launched a secret investigation. It turned out that Battel, though himself a member of the Nazi party since May 1933, had already attracted attention through friendly behaviour towards Jews. Before the war he had been indicted by a party tribunal for extending a loan to a Jewish colleague. Later, in the course of his service in Przemyśl, he was officially reprimanded for shaking the hand of Dr. Duldig (whom Battel had recognised as a former university friend from Vienna), the affair reaching the attention of the highest levels of the Nazi hierarchy. In fact, no less a figure than Heinrich Himmler, *Reichsführer* of the SS, took a lively interest in the investigation's results, forwarding a copy of the incriminating documentation to Martin Bormann, chief of the party chancellery and Hitler's right-hand man. In the accompanying letter, Himmler vowed to have the lawyer arrested immediately after the war.

Crucially, however, one must avoid any idealisation of the two *Wehrmacht* officers. In actuality, their confrontation with the SS was set within the context of a conflict of jurisdictions between the SS and the *Wehrmacht* and of the *Wehrmacht*'s desire to keep for itself skilled Jewish workers it deemed vital for the German war effort. Under the distorted normative code of the time, resistance to the SS's treatment of Jews could never be couched in humanitarian terms, but had to be premised on arguments of military expediency: the *Wehrmacht* officers' action was well within the bounds of this utilitarian rationality.[46] The blockade of the bridge over the San was only undertaken after the SS withdrew the special passes of the "*Wehrmacht* Jews" in Przemyśl, in violation of a previous agreement, the standoff being terminated as soon as the hundred or so Jewish workers were secured. In addition, in defying the SS Liedtke and Battel probably reckoned on the support of the military high command in Poland. This turned out to be a miscalculation: on the same day Liedtke was forced to lift his siege, and on the following day the security police were able to

---

[45] *YVR*, M-31, file 1979 (Dr. Albert Battel); file 1979a (Max Liedtke). This entire episode and its ramifications have now been thoroughly analysed by Norbert Haase. See *idem*, 'Oberleutnant Dr. Albert Battel und Major Max Liedtke. Konfrontation mit der SS im Polnischen Przemyśl im Juli 1942', in Wette (ed.), pp. 181–208.
[46] Cf. *ibid.*, p. 201.

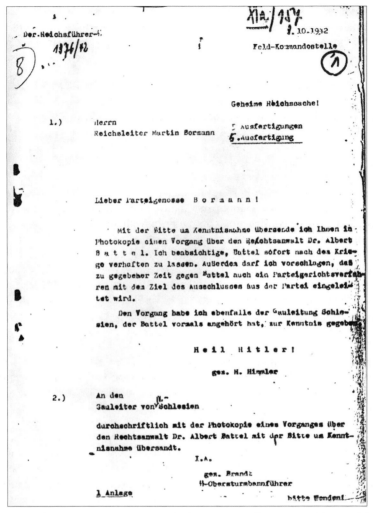

Heinrich Himmler's letter to Martin Bormann, 1 October 1942, apprising
him of his intention to have Dr. Albert Battel arrested "immediately after
the end of the war".

carry out their planned deportation of some 8,000 Jews to the Belzec extermination
camp. In the following months both Battel and Liedtke were moved to other posts.
Battel was discharged from the *Wehrmacht* in 1944 because of poor health, settling
after the war in West Germany. A denazification court disqualified him from practising as a lawyer, and he died destitute in 1952. Liedtke's subsequent war career
casts a grave shadow on his designation as a "righteous gentile". Having served as
the military commander of the town of Kislovodsk in the Stavropol region in southern Russia from November 1942 to January 1943, he was captured by the Soviets

who sentenced him to twenty-five years imprisonment for alleged war crimes. According to the verdict, he personally ordered the execution of more than a thousand "Soviet citizens".[47] Liedtke died in 1955 in a Soviet prison camp in the Urals.

RESCUERS OUTSIDE GERMANY (II): ENTREPRENEURS

In the case of German entrepreneurs working in the occupied countries in the rear of the *Wehrmacht*, the justification for keeping their Jewish workers alive was that they were serving "war-essential" industries. The most celebrated such entrepreneur is Oskar Schindler, the wartime owner of an enamel and ammunitions production plant near Cracow employing some 800 men and women.[48] Others who are well-known are Berthold Beitz, business-manager of the Beskidian Oil Company in Boryslaw, Eastern Galicia, employing many hundreds of Jews; and Hermann Graebe, a large-scale construction contractor in Volhynia, Ukraine.[49]

Let us consider the less well-known case of Alfred Rossner, the "trustee" for Będzin.[50] Although the original German documentation bearing on the case has until now not been located, the pertinent file in Yad Vashem contains a wealth of historical evidence and oral testimonies – some collected immediately after the war – shedding light on the historical context of the rescue case.

Będzin was a middle-sized town in Upper Silesia where a Jewish community had existed since at least the end of the sixteenth century. In 1931 the 21,625 Jewish inhabitants made up forty five per cent of the town's total population. The Germans occupied Będzin on 4 September 1939 and "integrated" it into the German Reich as "Bendsburg". After an initial period of terror in the first days of occupation, during which the Great Synagogue was set on fire and dozens of Jews were burnt alive, conditions became for a time more tolerable. But in 1939 and 1941 thousands of Jews arrived in Będzin from Central Poland and mass deportations started in May and June 1942 with the "resettlement" of 2,400 "non-productive" Jews in Auschwitz. Another 5,000 Jews were deported in August 1942. In January 1943 a ghetto was established in the suburb of Kamionka; its liquidation began in August 1943, lasting two weeks. After that the only Jews in Będzin were employees in the German-supervised workshops producing goods for the army, the final liquidation of these "shops" taking place between 5 and 13 January 1944. The remaining Jews were now sent to Auschwitz. The Będzin *Judenrat*, forming a branch within the umbrella organisation of

---

[47]See Haase, in Wette (ed.), pp. 197–198. Ought we to dismiss this as another instance of "Soviet justice"? As Haase rightly points out, the irregularities of Soviet military justice can hardly justify a wholesale exculpation of an accountable *Wehrmacht* officer. See also the incriminating references to Liedtke in the Nuremberg series, USSR 01, *Prosecution Documents, Trials of War Criminals Before the Nuremberg Military Tribunal*. ('Ueber die Greueltaten der deutsch-faschistischen Okkupanten im Stavropol-Gebiet', Yad Vashem microfilms, reel JM 2154).

[48]*YVR*, M-31, file 20 (Oskar and Emilie Schindler).

[49]*YVR*, M-31, file 299 (Berthold Beitz); *YVR*, M-31, file 116 (Hermann Graebe).

[50]*YVR*, M-31, file 6239, (Alfred Rossner).

Alfred Rossner. Photograph taken in Będzin.

Judenräte in the industrial region of Zagłębie Dąbrowskie, was noted for particular subservience.[51]

The reasons for Rossner's first arrival in Będzin in 1940 had nothing to do with altruism: like Oskar Schindler, he was simply out to make quick and easy money. The German authorities were appointing German *Treuhänder*, "trustees", to take over the management of confiscated Jewish businesses. These "trustees" continued to employ Jewish workers and relied on the expert advice of former Jewish owners. The 34 year old Rossner (born 1906) had been exempted from military service on medical grounds – he was a haemophiliac with a pronounced limp and barely any teeth. His choice of Będzin as the place to do business may have been influenced by his previous acquaintance with Arje Ferleiger, a Polish-born Jew who before the war had owned a textile plant in Berlin, where Rossner worked, and had settled in Będzin after his expulsion from Germany in 1938. Before long, Rossner, who had excellent connections with both the German authorities and local Jewish experts – among them his former Jewish boss, Ferleiger – had become the largest employer in Będzin, responsible for thousands of Jewish workers.

In contrast to the other German "trustees", who were acting as private entrepreneurs, Rossner worked directly under the SS. His chief workshop, the so-called

[51]For a different assessment of the role played by the Będzin *Judenrat* see Avihu Ronen, 'Institutionen, Politik und Identität der Jüdischen Selbstverwaltung im Getto von Zaglembie', in Doron Kiesel, Cilly Kugelmann, Hanno Loewy und Dietrich Neuhaus (eds.), *"Wer zum Leben, wer zum Tod ..."*. *Strategien jüdischen Überlebens im Ghetto*, Frankfurt am Main–New York 1992, pp. 97–114.

Rossner's workshop. Group portrait.

By courtesy of Yad Vashem

Schneidersammelwerkstatt producing uniforms for the *Wehrmacht*, belonged to the Schmelt Organisation, which controlled the forced labour camps in Upper Silesia. The organisation was headed by the SS-*Oberführer* Albrecht Schmelt, Himmler's special representative in Upper Silesia. The tenor of Rossner's relationship to the SS comes out clearly in a letter that he sent to the Berlin headquarters (he reportedly first read it to Kaminski, one of his most trusted Jewish confidantes). According to the testimony of Henrietta (Kicia) Altman, one of the Będzin Jews saved by Rossner, he explained in his letter that "he wanted to serve the Third Reich in the field of War Economy, as his physical disability prevented him from taking up arms in defence of the fatherland. He also said ... that the only justification for continued Jewish existence in Eastern Upper Silesia was the Jews' usefulness for the war economy, and that he intended to exploit them fully for that purpose."[52] With production in the "shops" being considered "war essential", the Jews who worked there were entitled to the protection of a special pass, the Rossner pass – blue in colour – becoming a much-coveted possession: it provided a measure of protection against deportation for the bearer and his family. With the onset of the deportations people were willing to pay large sums of money for these passes, and their provision became a lucrative business. A number of Jewish survivors testified after the war that Rossner profited in this fashion.

At the same time, Rossner stood out from other German "trustees" through the kindness and humane treatment he exhibited toward the Jews under his command. He defended them and their families against the SS by giving them prior warnings of impending "actions" and, dramatically, by sending his German staff to free them at the last moment from the deportation train. According to one testimony, during the first large deportation from Będzin, in May 1942, Rossner drove in his one-horse buggy into the town's poorest quarters shouting to the inhabitants in Yiddish not to be fooled by the summons of the *Judenrat* into reporting for extermination.

Following the final liquidation of the ghetto, in August 1943 the position of Rossner and his depleted Jewish work force became increasingly precarious. In December 1943 he was arrested by the Gestapo, and one month later he was exe-

---

[52]*YVR*, M-31, file 6239, (Alfred Rossner).

Auschwitz deportees arrive in Będzin, April 1941. Photograph by Alfred Rossner,
taken in front of his factory.

By courtesy of Mira Binford

cuted by hanging. The exact nature of the charges brought against him is not known,
but there is little doubt that financial corruption figured prominently.

The overall assessment of Rossner's story must remain ambivalent. Like
Schindler, his life and career before the events in question had revealed few obviously altruistic gestures. The retired Israeli police inspector Michael Gilead, who has
examined the case in some depth, divides Rossner's activity as "trustee" into three
stages: the arrival in Będzin and organisation of the "shops" (1940–1941); with the
onset of deportations to Auschwitz, the emergence of the special Rossner-pass as a
life-saving possession (mid 1942–mid 1943); the decline of the "shops" and their final
liquidation (mid 1943–mid 1944).[53] His conclusion is that Rossner, despite much
sympathy with the persecuted Jews, was mainly driven by greed during the first two
stages. His solidarity with the Jews was only transformed into a positive readiness to
put his life on the line during the last months of his life and activity in Będzin. One
may reflect that a corrupt, underhand dealer could only become one of the "righteous among the nations" in a world where murder had become a new norm.[54]

---

[53]*ibid.*
[54]Cf. Omer Bartov's characterisation of Oskar Schindler in *idem, Murder in Our Midst: The Holocaust,
Industrial Killing, and Representation*, New York–Oxford 1996, pp. 166–171.

CONCLUSION

There were not only "many paths to righteousness" for the German rescuers, but the path itself was strewn with many obstacles and moral ambiguities. There is no need anachronistically to idealise or sanctify these individuals. Rather, they should be judged in the light of their own historically limited horizon: as I have suggested, they were "ordinary Germans" who at a certain point acted counter to the norms of a state organised around mass murder. The examples I have chosen stand for many others: Heinrich List, the Hessian farmer who paid with his life for harbouring an "illegal" Jew, was a self-declared Nazi and Jew-hater. Alfred Rossner, to whom many survivors of the Będzin ghetto owe their lives, was a war-profiteer. The Gerbrandt family's farm at Stutthof, providing a hiding place for death-march escapees, was a functional part of the concentration camp system. The resistance of *Wehrmacht* officers Battel and Liedtke to the policies of the SS was circumscribed by strictly utilitarian concerns. The idea of being able to construct something like a theory of the "rescuer personality", say as a pedagogic blueprint for helping such personalities emerge in the future, seems illusory. We can perhaps educate individuals to become more useful members of a better society; but we can hardly train them to become rescuers in a moral catastrophe. Though some of the most notable such persons did indeed reveal unique and distinctive personalities, many others would have been indistinguishable from their normal countrymen in normal times.

While their actions call into question the notion of "eliminationist antisemitism"[55] as a feature permanently and invariably embedded in the German psyche before 1945, the German rescuers were, self-evidently, too isolated and far too few in number to redeem German society in the face of its perversion of norms and values during the Nazi period. It is instead best to regard them as something like a natural control group against which to test the "normal" stance of the German populace at large. From this perspective, the main meaning of the rescuers' actions involved giving the lie – in the face of all moral ambiguities – to claims of impotence in the face of a totalitarian and terrorist regime – a claim so often reiterated after the war. Demonstrating an enduring capacity for empathy in a context of virtually unprecedented human wickedness, the rescuers' actions underscore how much ordinary people could have, and indeed should have, accomplished to stem the tide.

---

[55]Daniel J. Goldhagen, *Hitler's Willing Executioners: Ordinary Germans and the Holocaust*, New York 1996.

Publications on German-speaking Jewry

A Selected and Annotated Bibliography of Books and Articles 2002

Compiled by

BARBARA SUCHY and ANNETTE PRINGLE

The Bibliography is supported by grants from:

Friends of Bat Hanadiv Foundation

Sheldon and Suzanne Nash Fund

The Rayne Trust

Robert Bosch Stiftung

The Ruben and Elisabeth Rausing Trust

Leo Baeck Institute
4 Devonshire Street
London W1W 5LB

INTRODUCTION

The Bibliography of the Leo Baeck Institute Year Book annually provides an almost complete overview on recent publications about the history of German-speaking Jewry and antisemitism in German-speaking countries. It is not only our pronounced objective to give the reader "fast" and comprehensive bibliographic information about relevant publications of the respective preceding year but also to make the consulting and reading of the bibliography easy and interesting. Without the generous financial help of our supporters this would be impossible.

Over the years the structure and "make-up" of the bibliography has undergone only minor changes. Sometimes compromises have to be made as far as the exceeding of the bibliography's limits is concerned. This is true especially for the Sections III (The Nazi Period), IV. B. (Post-1945/Memorials and Remembrance). We are also well aware that including some titles in Section VII (Participation in Cultural and Public Life) may occasionally cause some surprise or even doubt.

Much effort is taken to trace relevant "hidden" literature. Therefore, we would like to thank those authors who inform us directly about their publications, and we encourage others to do so too (info@leobaeck.co.uk).

The Bibliography 2002 lists books and articles published in 2002 as well as supplementary books and articles published in 2001 and 2000; in a few cases also those published earlier are included. Preference has been giving to entering as many publications as possible. Again, however, some sections had to be curtailed, and review essays have been cut to some extent.

All titles are fully indexed: names, places, periodicals, titles (in some cases), subjects.

Communal and regional histories are listed either in Section I B (Communal and Regional History), or in Section III (The Nazi Period), depending on their main focus. Autobiographies and memoirs are listed either in Section III (The Nazi Period), or in Section VIII (Autobiographies, Memoirs, Letters), again depending on their main focus. Antisemitism including post-1945 antisemitism is listed in Section IX. D (Antisemitism). Section IV. A. (Post-1945. General) includes only titles pertaining to Jewish life in Germany and Austria after the Second World War. The Subsection Prosecution of Nazi Crimes/Restitution has been re-inserted this year.

The consistently high number of publications is striking, considering that 2002 has not been a year of important anniversaries. All together about 1370 titles have been included into the Bibliography 2002, among them some indeed with new themes, perspectives, methods and approaches. Leafing through the pages the reader will, we hope, discover some surprisingly interesting publications. For the first time also selected electronic media have been included. Besides the ongoing productivity of "established" and internationally recognised scholars we find an increasing number of representatives of the younger generation well-versed in the field of German-Jewish historiography, mainly from Germany and other continental European countries, but also some from the United States, Israel and Great Britain, contributing to the history of German-speaking Jewry. The Pre-Enlightenment Period (Middle Ages/Early Modern Period) is represented by a number of excellent publications. Also notable is the increasing attraction which questions of "Jewish identity" seem to exercise, especially German Literature studies. In the field of Communal and Regional History one finds side by side with studies by mostly young academics, the works of lay historians and groups of school students – often remarkably good.

A bibliography of this scope is dependent on the services of numerous institutes and libraries and the help provided by their friendly and cooperative staff for which we would like to express our gratitude: Leo Baeck Institute, New York, The Wiener Library, London, Widener Library at Harvard, Universitäts- und Landesbibliothek/ Heinrich-Heine-Universität, Düsseldorf, Bibliothek Germania Judaica, Cologne, Die Deutsche Bibliothek, Frankfurt am Main.

B.S.

CONTENTS

Bibliography

I. HISTORY

A. General

—— ALTHAUS, HANS PETER: *Mauscheln. Ein Wort als Waffe.* [See No. 42062.]

40834. AWERBUCH, MARIANNE: *Vor der Aufklärung: Die 'Denkwürdigkeiten der Glückel von Hameln' – Ein jüdisches Frauenleben am Ende des 17. und zu Beginn des 18. Jahrhunderts.* [In]: Preußens Himmel breitet seine Sterne ... [see No. 41991]. Bd. 1. Pp. 163–181, notes.

40835. BAADER, MARIA BENJAMIN: *Vom Rabbinischen Judentum zur bürgerlichen Verantwortung: Geschlechterorganisation und "Menschenliebe" im jüdischen Vereinswesen in Deutschland zwischen 1750 und 1870.* [In]: Comparativ, Jg. 2001, H. 5/6, Leipzig, 2002. Pp. 14–29, footnotes.

40836. BARKAI, AVRAHAM: *"Wehr dich!" Der Centralverein deutscher Staatsbürger jüdischen Glaubens (C.V.) 1893–1938.* München: Beck, 2002. 496 pp., notes (379–475), illus., bibl. (478–488), indexes. (Eine Veröffentlichung des Leo Baeck Instituts Jerusalem.) [Cf.: Unbeirrbar patriotisch. Zwischen Antisemitismus und Zionismus: Avraham Barkais beeindruckende Geschichte des Centralvereins deutscher Staatsbürger jüdischen Glaubens (Michael Wildt) [in]: Zeitliteratur [Beilage von] Die Zeit, Nr. 47, Hamburg, Nov. 2002, p. 38.]

40837. BECHTEL, DELPHINE: *La Renaissance culturelle juive en Europe centrale et orientale 1897–1930: langue, littérature et construction nationale.* Paris: Éditions Belin, 2002. 319 pp., index, bibl., gloss., notes. [On the Haskalah, encounter with Eastern Jewry; also on Western Yiddish.]

40838. BEHM, BRITTA L.: *Moses Mendelssohn und die Transformation der jüdischen Erziehung in Berlin.* Eine bildungsgeschichtliche Analyse zur jüdischen Aufklärung im 18. Jahrhundert. Münster; New York: Waxmann, 2002. 309 pp., footnotes, bibl. (275–296), gloss., index. (Jüdische Bildungsgeschichte, Bd. 4.) Zugl.: Hamburg, Univ., Diss., 2001.

40839. BEHM, BRITTA L./LOHMANN, UTA/LOHMANN, INGRID, eds.: *Jüdische Erziehung und aufklärerische Schulreform.* Analysen zum späten 18. und frühen 19. Jahrhundert. München; New York: Waxmann, 2002. 398 pp., footnotes, gloss. (Jüdische Bildungsgeschichte, Bd. 5.) [Incl. (some titles abbr.): Vorwort (eds., 7–12). Der pädagogische Philanthropismus und die jüdische Erziehung (Ernst A. Simon, 13–65; orig. publ. in Hebrew 1953, transl. by Uta Lohmann). I. Moderne jüdische Schulen im Spätaufklärung; cont.: Erziehungsprogramme und gesellschaftliche Ideale im Wandel: Die Freischule in Berlin, 1778–1825 (Shmuel Feiner, 69–106; first publ. in Hebrew 1995, transl. by Miriam A. Goldmann). Moses Mendelssohns Beziehungen zur Berliner jüdischen Freischule zwischen 1778 und 1786. Eine exemplarische Analyse zu Mendelssohns Stellung in der Haskala (Britta L. Behm, 107–136). Religionsunterricht und staatliche Klassifizierung der Berliner Freischule (Uta Lohmann, 137–166). Handlungsstrategien der preußischen Verwaltung gegenüber der jüdischen Freischule in Berlin (1778–1825) und der Königlichen Wilhelmsschule zu Breslau (1791–1848) (Peter Dietrich, 167–212). Die Prager deutsch-jüdische Schulanstalt 1782–1848 (Louise Hecht, 213–252). Jüdische Reformschule im Herzogtum Braunschweig – Die Jacobson-Schule in Seesen von der Spätaufklärung bis zur Reichsgründung (Meike Berg, 253–266). II. Reformansätze und Erziehungsprogramme jüdischer Aufklärer; cont.: Moses Mendelssohn und die Frage der "bürgerlichen Verbesserung" der Juden (Britta L. Behm, 269–290). 'Interkulturalität' in der Bildungskonzeption David Friedländers (Uta Lohmann, 291–306). Aaron Halle-Wolfson the pedadogue (Jutta Strauss, 307–334). Religion, Geschichte, Politik und Pädagogik in Herz Hombergs Lehrbüchern (Rainer Wenzel, 335–358). Lazarus Bendavids Bildungsweg und seine Tätigkeit als Direktor der jüdischen Freischule in Berlin (Dominique Bourel, 359–368). Zur Ambivalenz in den Mädchenbildungskonzepten der Zeitschrift 'Sulamith' (1806–1848) (Michaela Will, 369–387).]

40840. BORCHARDT, KARL: *Das Dekret zur Ausweisung der Juden auf Rhodos 1503.* [In]: Auxilia Historica. Festschrift für Peter Acht zum 90. Geburtstag. Im Auftrag der Kommission für bayerische Landesgeschichte hrsg. von Walter Koch, Alois Schmid und Wilhelm Volkert. Red.: Ludwig

Holzfurtner. München: Beck, 2001. Pp. 21–40, footnotes. [Refers also to expulsions in German-speaking lands.]

40841. BRENNER, MICHAEL, ed.: *Jüdische Sprachen in deutscher Umwelt. Hebräisch und Jiddisch von der Aufklärung bis ins 20. Jahrhundert.* Göttingen: Vandenhoeck & Ruprecht, 2002. 134 pp., notes (109–128), index. (Eine Veröffentlichung der Wissenschaftlichen Arbeitsgemeinschaft des Leo Baeck Instituts in der Bundesrepublik Deutschland.) [Cont.: Jüdische Sprachen und die neuere deutsch-jüdische Geschichte (ed., 7–10). Sprachverhältnisse und Identität der Juden im 18. Jahrhundert (Nils Roemer, 11–18). Vorgeschrieben und umgeschrieben: die "neue heilige Sprache" der jüdischen Aufklärer (Andrea Schatz, 19–27). Vatersprache und Mutterland: Sprache als nationaler Einheitsdiskurs im 19. Jahrhundert (Andreas Gotzmann, 28–42). Hebräische Zeitschriften in Deutschland (1750–1856) (Thomas Kollatz, 43–48). Hebräische Begriffe in der Umgangssprache der südwestdeutschen und elsässischen Juden im 19. und 20. Jahrhundert (Uri R. Kaufmann, 49–67). Wissenschaft des Judentums, in welcher Sprache? (Henry Soussan, 56–67). Hebräisch im zionistischen Berlin (Barbara Schäfer, 68–75). Die Vermittlung der hebräischen Sprache in Deutschland vor 1933 (Rachel Perets, 76–84). Jiddische Literatur und Sprache in Berlin im Kaiserreich und in der Weimarer Republik (Delphine Bechtel, 85–95). Von Kafka bis Celan: Deutsch-jüdische Schriftsteller und ihr Verhältnis zum Hebräischen und Jiddischen (Amir Eshel, 96–108).]

———— BRINKMANN, TOBIAS: *Separierung versus Integration: Ein Vergleich der Funktion jüdischer Wohltätigkeit in Deutschland und in den USA im 19. Jahrhundert.* [See No. 41111.]

40842. CORDES, ODA: *Prozeßrecht im Dienste eines Vorurteils: Der Judeneid.* [In]: Jahrbuch für Antisemitismusforschung 2002, Frankfurt am Main; New York, 2002. Pp. 13–30, footnotes.

40843. DAVIS, JOSEPH: *The reception of the 'Shulhan Arukh' and the formation of Ashkenazic Jewish identity.* [In]: AJS Review, Vol. 26, No. 2, Waltham, MA, 2002. Pp. 251–276, footnotes. [Incl. Askenazic Jewry in the Middle Ages, the 16th and 17th centuries.]

40844. *"… der den Erniedrigten aufrichtet aus dem Staube und aus dem Elend erhöht den Armen". Unvollendetes Leben zwischen Tragik und Erfüllung.* Die Fünfte Joseph Carlebach-Konferenz. Hrsg. von Miriam Gillis-Carlebach und Wolfgang Grünberg. Hamburg: Dölling und Galitz, 2002. 237 pp., notes. (Publications of the Joseph Carlebach Institute.) [Title, table of contents and introd. also in Hebrew at back of book.] Incl. the sections: I. Erinnern und Gedenken (16–73; incl. Julius Carlebach (Mordechai Breuer, 16–18). II. Autobiographische Zeugnisse (74–127). III. Im Schatten des Holocaust (128–177). IV. Das Leiden und die Philosophie (178–216). Selected articles are listed according to subject.]

40845. *Deutsch-jüdischer Parnaß. Rekonstruktion einer Debatte.* [Issue title of] Menora, Bd. 13 [see No. 41150]. Berlin, 2002. [Incl.: Einleitung/Einführung (Red., 9–18). I. Dokumentation (21–199; cont. reprint of articles from 'Ost und West', 'Kunstwart', 'Jüdische Rundschau', 'Allgemeine Zeitung des Judentums', 'Janus' by Moritz Goldstein, Ernst Lissauer, Ferdinand Avenarius, Ludwig Geiger, Cheskel Zwi Klötzel and others, publ. between 1906 and 1913; also an article by Moritz Goldstein written in 1958). II. Kommentare, Essays und Briefe (203–336, notes; cont.: Moritz Goldstein. Ein biographischer Abriß (Elisabeth Albanis, 203–238). Von 1912 bis 1938: Moritz Goldsteins Wandlung und Beharrung (Joachim Schlör, 239–270). Der 'hypereuropäische' Zionist. Moritz Goldstein, die 'Kunstwart'-Debatte und Europa (Manfred Voigt, 271–288). Interpretationen eines kulturellen Zwischenraums. Die Debatte um die deutsch-jüdische Literatur 1900 bis 1933 (Andreas Kilcher, 289–312). Ein jüdisch-christliches Streitgespräch am Vorabend der Katastrophe. Ungedrucktes aus dem 1932 geführten Briefwechsel zwischen Hans Blüher und Hans-Joachim Schoeps (Julius H. Schoeps, 313–336).]

40846. DINER, DAN: *Geschichte der Juden – Paradigma einer europäischen Historie.* [In]: Annäherungen an eine europäische Geschichtsschreibung. Hrsg. von Gerald Stourzh [et al.]. Wien: Verlag der österreichischen Akademie der Wissenschaften, 2002. Pp. 85–103, footnotes.

40847. DUBIN, LOIS C.: *Between toleration and "equalities" – Jewish status and community in pre-revolutionary Europe.* [In]: Jahrbuch des Simon-Dubnow-Instituts, Stuttgart, 2002. Pp. 219–234, footnotes.

40848. ELON, AMOS: *The pity of it all: a history of the Jews in Germany, 1743–1933.* New York: Metropolitan Books/Holt; Engl. edn.: *The pity of it all: a portrait of German Jews, 1743–1933.* London: Allen Lane, 2002. 446 pp., illus., ports., maps, notes, bibl. (405–429), index. [Deals with different intellectual and religious movements from radical assimilation to Zionism. Incl. Ludwig Börne, Heinrich Heine, Moses Mendelssohn.] [Cf.: Review article (Frederic Krome) [in]: Library Journal, Vol. 127, No. 16, New York, Oct. 1, 2002, p. 113. A cold eye on Zion (Jonathan Steele) [in]: The Guardian Review, London, Feb. 1, 2003 (a profile of the author, b. 1926 in Vienna).]

——— FERGUSON, NIALL: *Die Geschichte der Rothschilds.* Propheten des Geldes. [See No. 41980.]

40849. *Geschichte als Falle. Deutschland und die jüdische Welt.* Für die Forschungsstelle deutsch-jüdische Zeitgeschichte [Munich] hrsg. von Michael Wolffsohn und Thomas Brechenmacher. Neuried: ars una, 2001. 322 pp., notes, index. [Incl.: Einleitung. Deutsch-jüdische Zeitgeschichte als Fallenprävention (eds., 7–12; deals with the burden of history and its effects on historiography and German-Jewish relations). Geschichte als Falle. Deutschland und die jüdische Welt (Michael Wolffsohn, 35–44). Further essays are listed according to subject.]

40850. GOTZMANN, ANDREAS: *Gemeinde als Gemeinschaft. Politische Konzepte der deutschen Juden im Absolutismus.* [In]: Jahrbuch des Simon-Dubnow-Instituts, Jg. 1, Stuttgart, 2002. Pp. 375–430, footnotes.

40851. GRAB, WALTER (S.A.): *Ursachen des Scheiterns der Judenemanzipation in Deutschland.* [In]: Preußens Himmel breitet seine Sterne [see No. 41991], Bd. 1. Pp. 429–447.

40852. GRAETZ, MICHAEL: *Jüdische Mentalität zwischen Tradition und Moderne: Der autobiographische Text.* [In]: Judentum zwischen Tradition und Moderne [see No. 41727]. Pp. 117–134.

40853. GRAUS, FRANTISEK: *Ausgewählte Aufsätze (1959–1989).* Hrsg. von Hans-Jörg Gilomen [et al.]. Stuttgart: Thorbecke, 2002. X, 436 pp., port., footnotes. (Vorträge und Forschungen, Bd. LV.) [Incl.: Historische Traditionen über Juden im Spätmittelalter (Mitteleuropa) (261–288). Judenpogrome im 14. Jahrhundert: Der Schwarze Tod (289–302). Randgruppen der städtischen Gesellschaft im Spätmittelalter (303–350; incl. Jews).]

40854. GUESNET, FRANÇOIS: *Strukturwandel im Gebrauch der Öffentlichkeit: Zu einem Aspekt jüdischer politischer Praxis zwischen 1744 und 1881.* [In]: Jörg Requate/Martin Schulze Wessel, eds.: Europäische Öffentlichkeit. Transnationale Kommunikation seit dem 18. Jahrhundert. Frankfurt am Main; New York: Campus, 2002. Pp. 43–62, footnotes.

40855. HAHN, BARBARA: *Die Jüdin Pallas Athene.* Auch eine Theorie der Moderne. Berlin: Berlin Verlag, 2002. 367 pp., notes (311–353), bibl. [Cont. essays on the phenomenon of the German Jewess, incl. Rahel Varnhagen, salonières in early and late 19th-cent. Berlin, Selma Stern, Margarete Susman, Rosa Luxemburg, Hannah Arendt, Elisabeth Blochmann.] [Cf.: Exempel ja, Exemplum nein. Barbara Hahn riskiert eine Kulturgeschichte der deutschen Jüdin (Jakob Hessing) [in]: 'FAZ', Nr. 36, Frankfurt am Main, 12. Feb. 2003, p. 34.]

40856. HAVERKAMP, ALFRED: *Gemeinden, Gemeinschaften und Kommunikationsformen im hohen und späten Mittelalter.* Festgabe zur Vollendung des 65. Lebensjahres. Hrsg. von Friedhelm Burgard, Lukas Clemens und Michael Matheus. Trier: Kliomedia, 2002. XX, 526 pp., frontis., footnotes, bibl. A.H., index (places; persons, 511–526). [Incl.: Tabula Gratulatoria (IX-XIV). Vorwort der Hrsg. (XV-XVI). Zum Geleit (Israel J. Yuval, XVII-XX; deals also with the Arye-Maimon-Institut für Geschichte der Juden in Trier, founded by A. Haverkamp in 1997 at the Univ. of Trier, and its accomplishments in the field of medieval Jewish history). Selected articles pertaining to German-Jewish history: Erzbischof Balduin und die Juden (39–88). Die Juden im Erzstift Trier während des Mittelalters (183–207). Die Judenviertel in deutschen Städten während des späten Mittelalters (237–254). Zur Siedlungs- und Migrationsgeschichte der Juden in den deutschen Altsiedellanden während des Mittelalters (255–276). "Concivilitas" von Christen und Juden in Aschkenas im Mittelalter (315–344). Judenvertreibungen in Mittelalter und Frühneuzeit – Erscheinungsformen und Zusammenhänge, Betrachtungsweisen und Erkenntnischancen. Zur Orientierung (375–396). Getaufte Juden im 'regnum Teutonicum' während des 12. Jahrhunderts (447–490).]

40857. HAVERKAMP, ALFRED, ed.: *Geschichte der Juden im Mittelalter von der Nordsee bis zu den Südalpen.* Kommentiertes Kartenwerk. Bearb. von Thomas Bardelle [et al.]. Red.: Jörg R. Müller. Hannover: Verlag Hahnsche Buchhandlung, 2002. 3 vols. (Forschungen zur Geschichte der Juden, A 14.) [*Teil 1: Kommentarband* (428 pp., footnotes, index). Cont.: Vorwort (ed., 7–8). Essays are arranged under the sections: Einleitung: Von der Nordsee bis zu den Südalpen; cont.: Einleitende Bemerkungen zur kartographischen Darstellung mittelalterlicher Geschichte der Juden in einem europäischen Kernraum (Jörg R. Müller, 9–30). Kommentare zur Siedlungsgeschichte der Juden und zur kultisch-kulturellen Ausstattung jüdischer Gemeinden in verschiedenen Regionen des Untersuchungsraums (Kartensequenzen A und B); cont.: Zur Siedlungsgeschichte der Juden im Nordwesten des Reichs während des Mittelalters (Christoph Cluse/Rosemarie Kosche/Matthias Schmandt, 33–54). Zur Siedlungsgeschichte der Juden im mittleren Rheingebiet bis zum Beginn des 16. Jahrhunderts (Rainer Barzen, 55–74). Jüdische Siedlungsgeschichte der Maas-Mosel-Lande mit Ausblick in die östliche Champagne (Friedhelm Burgard/Alexander Reverchon, 75–98). Zur mittelalterlichen Siedlungsgeschichte der Juden im schwäbischen Raum (Jörg R. Müller, 99–128). Die Entwicklung der jüdischen Niederlassungen im Herzogtum und Grafschaft Burgund während des Mittelalters (Annegret Holtmann, 129–142). Die Siedlung der Juden in der Dauphiné während des Mittelalters (Frédéric Chartrain, 143–168). Die Siedlungsgeschichte der Juden in der Grafschaft bzw. im Herzogtum Savoyen-Piemont während des Mittelalters (Thomas Bardelle, 169–186). Kommentare zu Verfolgungen und Vertreibungen (Kartensequenzen C, D und E); cont.: Judenverfolgungen und -vertreibungen zwischen Nordsee und Südalpen im hohen und späten Mittelalter (Jörg R. Müller, 189–222). Zur Chronologie der Verfolgungen zur Zeit des "Schwarzen Todes" (Jörg R. Müller, 223–242). Erste Siedlungsbelege nach 1350 – Siedlungsnetz und "jüdische" Raumperzeption (Rosemarie Kosche, 243–248). Kommentare zu den thematischen Spezialkarten (Kartensequenz F); cont.: Juden und Herrschaft im Mittelalter am Vorabend der Pestpogrome (Bernhard Kreutz, 251–266). Jüdische Geld- und Pfandleihe im Norden der Grafschaft Burgund um die Mitte des 14. Jahrhunderts (Annegret Holtmann, 167–274). Juden und Lombarden im Maas-Rheingebiet während der ersten Hälfte des 14. Jahrhunderts: Siedlungsgefüge und Raumerfassung im Vergleich (Winfried Reichert, 275–292). Regionalorganisationen jüdischer Gemeinden im Reich in der ersten Hälfte des 14. Jahrhunderts (Rainer Barzen, 293–366). Migrationswege von Angehörigen der jüdischen Familie "von Vesoul" in der zweiten Hälfte des 14. Jahrhunderts (Annegret Holtmann, 367–378). Ämter und Judensiedlungen in Kurtrier unter Erzbischof Balduin von Luxemburg (1307–54) (Friedhelm Burgard (379–390). *Teil 2: Ortskatalog* (468 pp., bibl. (407–468); incl. almost 2000 alphabetically listed places (with annotations). *Teil 3: Karten* (104 maps, DIN A 3); cont.: Übersichtskarte. Sequenz A: Siedlingskarten (43 maps). Sequenz B: Kultausstattung (10 maps). Sequenz C: Verfolgungen und Vertreibungen (38 maps). Sequenz D: Zur Chronologie der Verfolgungen zur Zeit des "Schwarzen Todes" (5 maps). Sequenz E: Erste Siedlungsbelege nach 1350 – Siedlungsnetz und "jüdische" Raumperzeption (2 maps). Sequenz F: Thematische Spezialkarten zu weiteren ausgewählten Aspekten (6 maps).]

40858. *L'héroisme au féminin* [issue title of] Les cahiers du judaisme, No. 12, Paris, 2002. [Incl.: Rahel Varnhagen, l'"amie la plus proche" d'Hannah Arendt (Pierre Birnbaum, 4–18, notes). Glückel d'Hameln. Quelques pistes pour une figure d'héroïne juive (Ariel Sion, 20–24, notes). D'Anna O. à Bertha Pappenheim (Daniel Boyarin, 63–73, notes). Friedel Dicker-Brandeis et les enfants de Teresin (Annette Wieviorka, 132–137).]

40859. HESS, JONATHAN M.: *Germans, Jews and the claims of modernity.* New Haven; London: Yale Univ. Press, 2002. XI, 258 pp., frontis., illus., notes (211–240), index. [A collection of essays with the following titles: Introduction: Modernity and the legacy of enlightenment. 1. Rome, Jerusalem and the triumph of Modernity. Christian Wilhelm Dohm and the regeneration of the Jews. 2. Orientalism and the colonial imaginary. Johann David Michaelis and the specter of racial antisemitism. 3. Mendelssohn's Jesus. The frustrations of Jewish resistance. 4. Philosophy, antisemitism and the politics of religious reform. Saul Ascher's challenge to Kant and Fichte. Jewish baptism and the quest for world rule. Perceptions of Jewish power around 1800. Concluding remarks.]

40860. HEYNICK, FRANK: *Jews and medicine: an epic saga.* Hoboken, NJ: Ktav, 2002. VIII, 602 pp., notes, bibl.(559–573), indexes. [Refers also to German-Jewish physicians.] [Cf.: Jewish healers through the centuries (Steven G. Friedman) [in]: Midstream, Vol. 48, No. 7, New York, Nov./Dec. 2002, pp. 41–42.]

40861. HOLMES, VIRGINIA IRIS: *Integrating diversity, reconciling contradiction: the 'Jüdischer Friedensbund' in late Weimar Germany.* [In]: Leo Baeck Institute Year Book 2002, Vol. XLVII, Oxford, 2002. Pp. 175–194, footnotes.

40862. HYMAN, PAULA E.: *Two models of modernization: Jewish women in the German and the Russian Empires.* [In]: Studies in Contemporary Jewry [with the issue title] *Jews and gender. The challenge to hierarchy*, Vol. XVI, Oxford, 2000. Pp. 39–53.

40863. *Jewish studies at the Central European University, II, 1999–2001.* Ed. by Andras Kovács and Eszter Andor. Budapest: Central European Univ., Jewish Studies Project, 2002. [Incl.: Jewish culture in contemporary America and Weimar Germany: parallels and differences (Michael Brenner, 15–29). A virtual Jewish world (Ruth Ellen Gruber, 65–73; deals with Jews in post-1945 Europe, incl. Germany). The 'People of the Book' and denominational inequalities of access to primary school libraries in early twentieth-century Hungary (Victor Karády, 93–101). Business success and tax debts: Jewish women in late medieval Austrian towns (Martha Keil, 103–23). Samson Raphael Hirsch and the Revolution of 1848 (Michael I. Miller, 223–238). Between emancipation and antisemitism: the Jewish presence in parliamentary politics in Hungary 1867–1884 (Árpád Welker, 239–279). Jewish politics in Central Europe: the case of the Jewish party in interwar Czechoslovakia (Marie Crhova, 271–301). Other contribs. also on Israeli policies of immigration; Hungarian Zionists.]

40864. *Judentum und Aufklärung. Jüdisches Selbstverständnis in der bürgerlichen Öffentlichkeit.* Hrsg. von Arno Herzig, Hans Otto Horch, Robert Jütte. Göttingen: Vandenhoeck & Ruprecht, 2002. 244 pp. [Incl. (some titles abbr.): Einleitung (eds., 7–29). Hofjuden als Vorreiter? Bedingungen und Kommunikationen, Gewinn und Verlust auf dem Weg in die Moderne (Rotraud Ries, 30.65). Die jüdische Freischule in Berlin im Spiegel ihrer Programmschriften (1803–1826) (Ingrid Lohmann/Uta Lohmann, 66–90). Die jüdische Gemeinde Altona zwischen Tradition und Moderne. Aufklärung und der Umgang mit dem Tod (Gabriele Zürn, 91–118). Jüdische Ärzte und Rabbiner als ungleiche Partner in der Debatte um die Beschneidungsreform zwischen 1830 und 1850 (Eberhard Wolff, 119–149). Diskurse über den Wandel auf dem Lande anlässlich der israelitischen Kreisversammlungen im Königreich Bayern (Eva Groiss-Lau, 150–177). Zur Huldigungs-Rede von Rabbiner Israel Deutsch anlässlich der Inthronisation des Geburtstages [sic] des Preußenkönigs Friedrich Wilhelm IV (Hans-Michael Haußig, 178–193). Synagogendiskussion. Architekten und die Modernisierung des Judentums (Saskia Rohde, 194–215). Der Lehrer als Autor und Akteur in der deutschsprachigen Ghettoliteratur (Gabriele von Glasenapp, 216–240).]

40865. *Judentum: Wege zur geistigen Befreiung.* Materialien der Dessauer Herbstseminare 2000 und 2001 zur Geschichte der Juden in Deutschland. Im Auftrag der Moses-Mendelssohn-Gesellschaft Dessau e.V. herausgegeben von Eva J. Engel und Bernd Gerhard Ulbrich. Dessau: Moses-Mendelssohn-Gesellschaft Dessau e.V., 2002. 248 pp., illus., notes. [Incl. (some titles abbr.): Vorwort (Eva J. Engel, 3). Judith: eine biblische Heldin als Identifikationsfigur (Marion Kobelt-Groch, 5–17). Jüdische Frauen an der Schwelle zur Moderne am Beispiel der Glückel Hameln (Maike Strobel, 18–29). Quellen und Zeugnisse zum aschkenasischen Synagogenbau im Mittelalter (Simon Paulus, 30–43). Architektur und Ritus der Synagoge (Katrin Keßler, 44–58). Preußisches zur Judengesetzgebung (Hermann Klenner, 102–138). Further contribs. are listed according to subject.]

40866. *Jüdische Geschichtsschreibung heute.* Themen, Positionen, Kontroversen. Ein Schloss Elmau-Symposion. Hrsg. von Michael Brenner und David N. Myers. München: Beck, 2002. 308 pp., notes (265–300), index. (Zugl.: Eine Veröffentlichung der Abt. für Jüdische Geschichte und Kultur an der Ludwig-Maximilians-Universität München.) [Papers presented at an international conference in July 2000. Incl.: Einleitung (Daniel N. Myers (7–16). Essays are arranged under the sections: 1. Ideologie und Objektivität; cont.: Von einer jüdischen Geschichte zu vielen jüdischen Geschichten (Michael Brenner, 17–35). Streitfragen in der zeitgenössischen jüdischen Historiographie (Michael A. Meyer, 36–43). Ohne jüdische Identität keine jüdische Geschichte (Georg G. Iggers, 44–54). 2. Geschichte und Gedächtnis; cont.: Selbstreflexion im modernen

Erinnerungsdiskurs (David N. Myers, 55–74). Jüdische Historiographie und Postmodernismus: Eine abweichende Meinung (Yosef Hayim Yerushalmi, 75–94). Geschichte und Gedächtnis: Moderne Theorien und alte Ursprünge (Jan Assmann, 95–104). 3. Religion und Modernisierung; cont.: Eine traumatische Begegnung: Das jüdische Volk in der europäischen Moderne (Shmuel Feiner, 105–122). Jüdische Religion zwischen Tradition und Transformation (Steven M. Lowenstein, 123–129). Was heißt: "Religion modernisieren"? (Friedrich Wilhelm Graf, 130–138). 4. Jüdische Geschichte und Frauengeschichte; cont.: Nicht nur Opfer und Heldinnen (Susannah Heschel, 139–162). Die Theorie und ihre Grenzen (Paula Hyman, 163–171). Geschlechtergeschichte: Rück- und Ausblicke (Ute Frevert, 172–180). 5. Zionismus und Nationalismus; cont.: Geschichte, Nationalismus, Eingedenken (Amnon Raz-Krakotzkin, 181–206). Historische Anthropologie nationaler Geschichtsschreibung (Dan Diner, 207–216). Nationalistische Mythen und eine post-nationalistische Perspektive (Rogers Brubaker, 217–228). 6. Der Holocaust und historisches Denken; cont.: Kann es zu viel Geschichte geben? Zur Diskussion über den Stellenwert des Holocaust in der Neueren Geschichte (Yfaat Weiss, 229–246). Deutsche und jüdische Geschichtsschreibung über den Holocaust (Ulrich Herbert, 247–258). Von der Mikro- zur Makroebene: Chancen und Risiken der Holocaustforschung (Saul Friedländer, 259–264).] [Cf.: Meisternarrativ gesucht: Zum Stand jüdischer Geschichtsschreibung (Jakob Hessing) [in]: 'FAZ', Nr. 236, Frankfurt am Main, 11. Okt. 2002, p. 40.]

40867. KATZ, JACOB: *Tradition und Krise. Der Weg der jüdischen Gesellschaft in die Moderne.* Aus dem Engl. von Christian Wiese. Mit einem Vorwort von Michael Brenner. München: Beck, 2002. 382 pp., notes, bibl., index. [Orig. publ. in Hebrew 1958; this first German edn. is based on the Engl. edn. of 1993, see No. 31402/YB XL.] [Cf.: Jacob Katz und sein Meisterwerk zur jüdischen Gesellschaft in der Zweiten Moderne (Friedrich Niewöhner) [in]: 'FAZ', Nr. 233, Frankfurt am Main, 8. Okt. 2002, p. L 31.]

40868. KIESEL, HELMUTH: *Woraus resultiert die außerordentliche kulturelle Leistung des Judentums zu Beginn der Moderne?* [In]: Das Judentum im Spiegel seiner kulturellen Umwelten. Symposium zu Ehren von Saul Friedländer [see No. 41864.] Pp. 71–110, bibl, notes.

40869. KOSCHE, ROSEMARIE: *Studien zur Geschichte der Juden zwischen Rhein und Weser im Mittelalter.* Hannover: Hahnsche Buchhandlung, 2002. VII, 423 pp., footnotes, bibl. (361–395), index (places, persons; 396–423), 9 maps. (Forschungen zur Geschichte der Juden, Abt. A: Abhandlungen, Bd. 15.) [Incl. chaps.: II. Siedlungsgeschichte. III. Die Gemeinde Dortmund im zentralörtlichen Gefüge des jüdischen Siedlungsnetzes: Dortmund als Unterzentrums Kölns. IV. Verfolgungen und Vertreibungen. VI. Die Rechtsgrundlagen der jüdischen Ansiedlungen. VII. Wirtschaftliche Tätigkeitsfelder. VIII. Feme. Anhang: 1. Schutzbriefe bis 1519. 2. Textanhang: Juden und Femegerichtsbarkeit, nach gedruckten Quellen.]

40870. KROCHMALNIK, DANIEL: *Die aschkenasische Spiritualität.* [In]: Hoch- und Spätmittelalter. Hrsg. und verfaßt von Peter Dinzelbacher. Mit einem Beitrag von Daniel Krochmalnik, Paderborn: Schöningh, 2000. (Handbuch der Religionsgeschichte im deutschsprachigen Raum, Bd. 2.) Pp. 376–396, illus., gloss., notes (481–488). [Incl. the sections: Der Holocaust des 1. Kreuzzuges. Die Spiritualität Israels. Die Frommen von Deutschland.]

40871. *L'Europe et les juifs.* Ed. by Esther Benbassa and Pierre Gisel, in collaboration with Lucie Kaennel. Geneva: Labor et Fides, 2002. 215 pp. (Religion en perspective, 11.) [Incl. Germany. Selected essays: L'Europe et les juifs. Introduction (Pierre Gisel, 7–24). Kabbale et christianisme du Moyen Age à l'aube de la modernité (Karen de Léon-Jones, 61–78). La Réforme et les juifs (Lucie Kaennel, 79–94; incl. Luther, Calvin). La formation des identités juives modernes en Europe (Esther Benbassa, 129–140). Rejet identitaire et quête de "spiritualité": Raissa Maritain, Edith Stein, Simone Weil (Silvie Courtine-Denamy, 141–166).] L'Allemagne nazie et les juifs (Philippe Burrin, 167–174).]

40872. *Die Landjudenschaften in Deutschland als Organe jüdischer Selbstverwaltung von der frühen Neuzeit bis ins neunzehnte Jahrhundert.* Eine Quellensammlung. Hrsg. von Daniel J. Cohen. Band 3. Jerusalem: Israel. Akad. der Wissenschaften, 2001. VIII, pp. 1377–2033. [Last vol. of the edn., for previous vols. see Nos. 34680/YB XLIII and 38420/YB XLVI.]

40873. MATTI, SIEGFRIED: *Walled cities und die Konstruktion von Communities. Das europäische Ghetto als urbaner Raum.* [In]: Wiener Jahrbuch für Geschichte, Kultur & Museumswesen, Bd. 5, Wien, 2000/2001, Wien, 2001. Pp. 9–12. [The title of this essay is also the issue title. Further contribs. are listed according to subject.]

40874. MAZÓN, PATRICIA: *Die Auswahl der "besseren Elemente". Ausländische und jüdische Studentinnen und die Zulassung von Frauen an deutschen Universitäten 1890–1909.* [In]: Jahrbuch für Universitätsgeschichte, Bd. 5, [with the title] Universität und Kunst], Stuttgart, 2002. Pp. 185–198, footnotes.

———— MENTGEN, GERD: *Alltagsgeschichte und Geschichte der Juden. Die Juden und das Glücksspiel im Mittelalter.* [See No. 41718.]

40875. NAGEL, MICHAEL (ed.): *Zwischen Selbstbehauptung und Verfolgung. Deutsch-jüdische Zeitungen und Zeitschriften von der Aufklärung bis zum Nationalsozialismus.* Hildesheim: Olms, 2002. 275 pp., illus., tabs. (Haskala, Bd. 25.) [Cont. (some titles abbr.): Einleitung (ed., 1–4); Erziehung zu Toleranz und Menschenliebe in Volksaufklärung und Publizistik (Holger Böning, 5–24). Zum Bild der Juden in deutschen Zeitschriften zwischen 1750–1806 (Eva Kirn-Frank, 25–66). A. Bernstein, die "Reform-Zeitung" und die Beschlüsse der Rabbinerkonferenzen in Braunschweig, Frankfurt a.M. und Breslau (Julius H. Schoeps, 83–100). Zur Konzessionierung und Zensur deutsch-jüdischer Periodika in den Königreichen Preußen und Sachsen bis 1850 (Johannes Valentin Schwarz, 101–138). Das Ghetto der "ewigen Stadt" im Urteil deutschsprachiger Publizisten (1846–1870) (Aram Mattioli, 159–186). Die jüdische musikalische Fachpresse im 19. Jahrhundert (Esther Schmidt, 187–216). Die Begriffe der jüdischen und der deutschen Kultur und ihre Differenzierung in der frühen deutsch-zionistischen Presse (Mark Gelber, 217–232). Julius Moser, der "Generalanzeiger für die gesamten Interessen des Judentums" (1902–1910) und der "Schlemiel" (1903–1906) (Kurt Nemitz, 233–252). Die "Wiener Morgenzeitung" und Robert Stricker. Jüdischnational-zionistischer Journalismus in Wien (Dieter Josef Mühl (253–268). Deutsch-jüdische Publizistik (Nicolaus Heutger, 269–280). Der jüdische Kinderkalender 1928–1936. Ein Beitrag zur Geschichte der deutsch-jüdischen Kinderliteratur (Dieter Richter, 281–294). Zwischen Selbstbehauptung und Diskriminierung. Deutsch-jüdische Turn- und Sportzeitungen (Moshe Zimmermann, 295–314). "Kinder-Rundschau", Beilage der "Jüdischen Rundschau" zwischen 1933 und 1938 (Michael Nagel, 315–350). Compact memory. Ein DFG-Projekt zur retrospektiven Digitalisierung jüdischer Periodika im deutschsprachigen Raum (Hans-Otto Horch/Kay Heiligenhaus/Till Schicketanz, 351–360); Register der deutsch-jüdischen Zeitungen, Zeitschriften, Kalender und Almanache (361–364).]

40876. NOWAK, KURT: *Kirchliche Zeitgeschichte interdisziplinär. Beiträge 1984–2001.* Hrsg. von Jochen-Christoph Kaiser. Stuttgart: Kohlhammer, 2002. XIV, 504 pp., frontis. (Konfession und Gesellschaft, Bd. 25.) [Incl.: Judenpolitik in Preußen. Eine Verfügung Friedrich Wilhelms III. aus dem Jahr 1821 (143–163). Protestantismus und Judentum im Deutschen Kaiserreich (1870/71–1918). Beobachtungen zum Stand der Forschung (164–185). Das Stigma der Rasse. Nationalsozialistische Judenpolitik und die 'christlichen Nichtarier' (186–202). Deutsch-christliche Kirchenpolitik im Dritten Reich im Zeichen des Antisemitismus (203 ff).]

40877. OLTMER, JOCHEN: *Flucht, Vertreibung und Asyl im 19. und 20. Jahrhundert.* [In]: Migration in der europäischen Geschichte seit dem späten Mittelalter. Vorträge auf dem Deutschen Historikertag in Halle a.d. Saale, 11. September 2002. Hrsg. von Klaus J. Bade, Osnabrück, 2002. Pp. 107–134, footnotes. [Deals briefly with the immigration of Jews seeking asylum in Germany after World War I.]

40878. RAUSCHENBERGER, KATHARINA: *Jüdische Tradition im Kaiserreich und in der Weimarer Republik. Zur Geschichte des jüdischen Museumswesens in Deutschland.* Hannover: Hahn, 2002. 332 pp., footnotes, index, bibl. (Forschungen zur Geschichte der Juden, Abt. A, Abhandlungen, Bd. 16.) Zugl.: Berlin, Techn. Univ., Diss., 2000.

40879. REINKE, ANDREAS: *Ethnic solidarity and national allegiance – B'nai B'rith in Germany.* [In]: Jahrbuch des Simon-Dubnow-Instituts, Jg. 1, Stuttgart, 2002. Pp. 321–342, footnotes. [Also in this vol.: Community in modernity – Jewish solidarity and the order B'nai B'rith (Cornelia Wilhelm, 297–320). From inclusion to exclusion – B'nai B'rith in Chicago, 1857–1881 (Tobias Brinkmann, 343–374).]

40880. RIES, ROTRAUD/BATTENBERG, FRIEDRICH, eds.: *Hofjuden – Ökonomie und Interkulturalität. Die jüdische Wirtschaftselite im 18. Jahrhundert*. Hamburg: Christians, 2002. 395 pp., illus., notes, index. (Hamburger Beiträge zur Gechichte der deutschen Juden, Bd. XXV.) [Cont. contribs. delivered at a conference at the Moses-Mendelssohn-Akademie in Halberstadt, Sept. 1999. Cont.: Vorwort (eds., 9–10). The sections: I. Grundlagen; incl: Hofjuden – Funktionsträger des absolutistischen Territorialstaates und Teil der jüdischen Gesellschaft. Eine einführende Positionsbestimmung (Rotraud Ries, 11–39). Interkulturalität, Akkulturation oder Protoemanzipation? Hofjuden und höfischer Habitus (Michael Schmidt, 40–58). Hofjuden und Wirtschaft im Merkantilismus (Rainer Gömmel, 59–65). II. Funktion und Wandel der jüdischen Wirtschaftselite in zentraleuropäischen Metropolen; incl.: Einführung (Wilhelm Kreutz, 67–70). Wiener Hofbankiers und ökonomische Modernisierung (Natalie Burkhardt, 71–86). Kontinuität und Wandel im ökonomischen Verhalten preußischer Hofjuden – Die Familie Itzig in Berlin (Thekla Keuck, 87–101). Jüdische Wechselmakler am Börsenplatz Frankfurt am Main und die Wirtschaftspolitik des reichsstädtischen Rates (Gabriela Schlick, 102–114). Sefardische Residentenfamilien in Amsterdam (Hiltrud Wallenborn, 115–133). III. Jüdische Wirtschaftselite – jüdische Gemeinde – jüdische Kultur; incl.: Einführung (Birgit Klein, 135–142). Creating an elite norm of behavior – court Jews as patrons and collectors of art (Richard I. Cohen, 143–153). "Es residiren in Hamburg Minister fremder Mächte" – Sefardische Residenten in Hamburg (Michael Studemund-Halévy, 154–176). Spuren der Realität in der Erinnerung? Zu Grabsteininschriften und Memorbucheinträgen für Hofjuden (Martina Strehlen, 177–190). Individueller Ruhm und kollektiver Nutzen – Berend Lehmann als Mäzen (Lucia Raspe, 191–208; on the Saxonian court Jew in Halberstadt). Hofjuden auf dem Lande und das Projekt der Moderne (209–229). IV. Väter und Söhne, Aufsteiger und Nachfolger: Wandel in der Generationenfolge; incl.: Einführung (J. Friedrich Battenberg, 231–239). Ein Hofjude im Schatten seines Vaters – Wolf Wertheimer zwischen Wittelsbach und Habsburg (J. Friedrich Battenberg, 240–255). Die Familien May und Mayer in Mannheim (Britta Waßmuth, 256–273). Die Rothschild-Brüder und die Bewahrung des Judentums (Fritz Backhaus, 274–280). V. Zwischen Stadt und Land, zwischen Hof und Gemeinde: Hofjuden in deutschen Kleinterritorien; incl.: Einführung (Jörg Deventer, 281–288). "Hier ist ein kleiner Ort und eine kleine Gegend" – Hofjuden in Lippe (Dina von Faassen, 289–306). "Man will ja nichts als Ihnen dienen, und das bisgen Ehre" – Die Hofjuden Herz und Saul Wahl im Fürstentum Pfalz-Zweibrücken (Dieter Blinn, 307–331). Madame Kaulla und ihr Clan – Das Kleinterritorium als individuelle Nische und ökonomisches Sprungbrett (Kerstin Hebell, 332–348). VI. Der reiche und verlustreiche Weg in die Moderne: Kommentare, Exempel und Perspektiven; incl.: The messages from the roosters (Deborah Hertz, 349–353). Hofjuden und Identitätswandel – ein Konstrukt? Die Deszendenz der Familie Wertheimer (Felicitas Heimann-Jelinek, 354–368). Court Jews, tradition and modernity (Steven Lowenstein, 369–381).]

——— RÜRUP, REINHARD: *Jüdische Geschichte in Europa zwischen Aufbruch und Katastrophe*. [See in No. 41357.]

40881. SABEAN, DAVID WARREN: *Kinship and prohibited marriages in Baroque Germany: Divergent strategies among Jewish and Christian populations*. [In]: Leo Baeck Institute Year Book 2002, Vol. XLVII, Oxford, 2002. Pp. 91–103, footnotes.

40882. SACHAR, HOWARD M.: *Dreamland: Europeans and Jews in the aftermath of the Great War*. New York: Knopf (distrib. by Random House), 2002. XII, 385 pp., maps, notes, bibl.(345–367), index. [Incl.: Chap. VI: The professor and the prophet: Imperial Prague and Jewish memory (132–160; incl. Kafka's Jewish circle). Chap. VII: Notes from a shattered dream: the case of Anna O. (161–204; incl. Austrian-Jewish culture, Freud's circle and writers such as Arthur Schnitzler, Jakob Wassermann, Stefan Zweig). Chap. VIII: The age of assassins (205–254; incl. the 1919 Revolution, assassination of Walther Rathenau, also Jewish women, Rosa Luxemburg, Bertha Pappenheim). Chap. IX: Minerva's owl at Weimar's twilight: Weimar in cultural memory (255–282; on the declining political situation, the work of the 'Centralverein' and other defense organisations. Also on Martin Buber, Hermann Cohen, Ismar Elbogen, Franz Rosenzweig, Karl Kraus, Franz Werfel, Albert Einstein, Fritz Haber.]

40883. SCHOEPS, JULIUS H.: *Die mißglückte Emanzipation. Wege und Irrwege deutsch-jüdischer Geschichte*. Berlin: Philo, 2002. 418 pp., footnotes, bibl., index. [Orig. publ. 1996 with the title Deutsch-jüdische Symbiose oder Die mißglückte Emanzipation. Essays are arranged under the sections:

Aufklärung, Judentum und bürgerliche Gleichstellung (15–148). Antisemitismus, Abwehrkampf und Identitätskrise (149–272). Nationaljudentum, Autoemanzipation und Selbsthilfe (273–382). Anhang: Autobiographische Anmerkungen und Notizen (383–399).]

40884. SCHULTE, CHRISTOPH: *"Diese unglückliche Nation" – Jüdische Reaktionen auf Dohms 'Über die bürgerliche Verbesserung der Juden'.* [In]: Zeitschrift für Religions- und Geistesgeschichte, Jg. 54, H. 4, Leiden, 2002. Pp. 352–365, footnotes. [See also No. 42067.]

40885. SCHULTE, CHRISTOPH: *Kindheit statt Vorsehung. Vom Verschwinden Gottes in der Biographik der Haskala: Jacob Emden, Isaak Euchel, Sabbatia Wolff.* [In]: Preußens Himmel breitet seine Sterne .... [see No. 42991], Bd. 1. Pp. 259–272, notes.

40886. SCHULTE, CHRISTOPH: *Die jüdische Aufklärung. Philosophie, Religion, Geschichte.* München: Beck, 2002. 279 pp., illus., notes (223–246), bibl. (247–266), chronol., gloss., index. [Cont. the sections: I. Europäische Aufklärung und Haskala. II. Moses und die Tora. III. Das Verhältnis der Maskilim zum Talmud: Historisierung statt Haß. IV. Haskala und Kabbala. V. Die Entdeckung des Chassidismus. VI. Kant und die jüdische Aufklärung. VII. Die politische Philosophie der Haskala. VIII. Die Erfindung der Orthodoxie. IX. Jüdischer Sokrates und jüdischer Diogenes.]

40887. SCHULTE, CHRISTOPH: *Zur Debatte um die Anfänge der jüdischen Aufklärung.* [In]: Zeitschrift für Religions- und Geistesgeschichte, Jg. 54, H. 2, Leiden, 2002. Pp. 122–137, footnotes.

40888. SIEG, ULRICH: *Kriegserfahrungen jüdischer Intellektueller im Ersten Weltkrieg.* [In]: Wissenschaften und Wissenschaftspolitik. Bestandsaufnahmen zu Formationen, Brüchen und Kontinuitäten im Deutschland des 20. Jahrhunderts. Hrsg. von Rüdiger vom Bruch und Brigitte Kaderas. Steiner: Stuttgart, 2002. Pp. 142–161, footnotes.

40889. SIEG, ULRICH: *Jüdische Intellektuelle im Ersten Weltkrieg. Kriegserfahrungen, weltanschauliche Debatten und kulturelle Neuentwürfe.* Berlin: Akademie, 2001. 400 pp., footnotes, bibl. (333–380), indexes (persons, places/subjects, 381–400). Zugl.: Marburg, Habil.-Schr., 1999. [Cf.: Wessen Moderne? Ulrich Sieg über jüdische Debatten zur Zeit des Ersten Weltkriegs (Thomas Meier) [in]: Süddeutsche Zeitung, Nr. 30, München, 5. Feb. 2002, p. 16.

40890. SORKIN, DAVID: *Port Jews and the three regions of emancipation.* [In]: Jewish Culture and History, Vol. 4, No. 2 [with the issue title] Port Jews: Jewish communities in cosmopolitan maritime trading centres, 1550–1950, London, Winter 2001. Pp. 31–46, notes. [Incl. emancipation in Germany; also deals with the Jews in Hamburg.]

40891. STEMBERGER, GÜNTER: *Jüdische Apokalyptik in Spätantike und Mittelalter.* [In]: Jahrbuch der Oswald von Wolkenstein Gesellschaft, Bd. 13, 2001/2002, Frankfurt am Main, 2002. Pp. 21–28, bibl.

40892. STERN, FRANK: *Dann bin ich um den Schlaf gebracht.* Ein Jahrtausend jüdisch-deutsche Kulturgeschichte. Berlin: Aufbau, 2002. 239 pp., illus., notes (219–228), index.

40893. *Studien zum jüdischen Mittelalter* [issue title of] Trumah, Bd. 12, Heidelberg: Winter, 2002. VIII, 231 pp., frontis., footnotes. [This vol. is dedicated to the memory of Prof. Julius Carlebach (1922–2001), the former Rector of the Hochschule für Jüdische Studien, Heidelberg; for data J.C. see No. 40841/YB XLVII. Selected essays: Tzidduq ha-Din und Kaddisch. Beobachtungen zur Entwicklung der jüdischen Begräbnisliturgie im Mittelalter (Andreas Lehnardt, 1–34). Die Fortschreibung der Aggada. Zur Verwendung rabbinischer Literatur im Piyyut-Kommentar (Elisabeth Hollender, 35–54). Frauen, Bildung und Spiritualität: Aspekte jüdischer Binnenakkulturation im christlichen Mittelalter (Gerold Necker, 55–64). Dream narratives in Sefer Hasidim (Book of the Pietists) (Tamar Alexander, 65–78). "Like the turtledove at the thought of His homeland": Exile as a universal paradigm in medieval thought (Yossef Schwartz, 79–96). Other essays are listed according to subject.]

40894. TOCH, MICHAEL: *Kultur des Mittelalters, jüdische Kulturen des Mittelalters.* Das Problem aus der Sicht der Wirtschaftsgeschichte. [In]: Historische Zeitschrift, Beiheft 32 [with the title] Unaufhebbare Pluralität der Kulturen? Zur Dekonstruktion und Konstruktion des mittelalterlichen Europa], München, 2001. Pp. 7–17, footnotes.

40895. TOCH, MICHAEL: *Mehr Licht: Eine Entgegnung zu Friedrich Lotter.* [In]: Aschkenas, Jg. 11/2001, H. 2, Wien, 2002. Pp. 465–487, footnotes. [Continuation of a debate about European Jewry in the early middle age with F.L.; for previous essays by M.T. and F.L. see No. 39625/YB XLVII.]

40896. TREUE, WOLFGANG: *'Verehrt und angespien': Zur Geschichte jüdischer Ärzte in Aschkenas von den Anfängen bis zur Akademisierung.* [In]: Würzburger medizinhistorische Mitteilungen. Bd. 21, Würzburg, 2001. Pp. 139–203, footnotes, bibl. [Incl. Engl. summary.]

40897. VÖLPEL, ANNEGRET/SHAVIT, ZOHAR, eds.: *Deutsch-jüdische Kinder- und Jugendliteratur. Ein literaturgeschichtlicher Grundriß.* In Zusammenarbeit mit Ran HaCohen. Stuttgart: J.B. Metzler, 2002. XII, 465 pp., illus., footnotes, bibl. (415–434), indexes. (Kompendien zur jüdischen Kinderkultur.) [Cont.: Einleitung (eds., 1–5). Juden und die Welt der Bücher in den Jahren 1100–1700: "Schriften für Kinder" und "Kinderbücher" bei den Juden in Deutschland (Simcha Goldin, 6–23). Kinder- und Jugendliteratur der Haskala und der jüdischen Reformpädagogik seit den 1770er Jahren (Zohar Shavit/Ran HaCohen, 24–270). Jüdische Kinder- und Jugendliteratur der Weimarer Republik (Annegret Völpel, 271–340). Jüdische Kinder- und Jugendliteratur unter nationalsozialistischer Herrschaft (Annegret Völpel, 341–414).]

40898. VOLKOV, SHULAMIT: *Talking of Jews, thinking of Germans – The ethnic discourse in 19th century Germany.* [In]: Tel Aviver Jahrbuch für deutsche Geschichte XXX, (2002), Göttingen, 2002. Pp. 37–49, footnotes.

———— WAGNER-KERN, MICHAEL: *Staat und Namensänderung. Die öffentlich-rechtliche Namensänderung in Deutschland im 19. und 20. Jahrhundert.* [See No. 42085.]

40899. WALLENBORN, HILTRUD: *Die Ansiedlung von Juden in Brandenburg-Preußen (1671) im Kontext europäischer Tolerierungsdebatten des 17. Jahrhunderts.* [In]: Preußens Himmel breitet seine Sterne [see No. 41991]. Bd. 1. Pp. 183–202, notes.

40900. WITTE, BERND: *Kulturelles Gedächtnis und Geschichtsschreibung im Judentum.* [In]: Jahrbuch der Heinrich-Heine-Universität Düsseldorf 2001, Düsseldorf, 2001. Pp. 266–278, footnotes, bibl.

40901. *The work of memory: new directions in the study of German society and culture.* Ed. by Alon Confino and Peter Fritzsche. Urbana: Univ. of Illinois Press, 2002. 265 pp., notes, bibl., index. [Incl.: Memory, history, and the Jewish question: universal citizenship and colonization of Jewish memory (Jonathan Hess; 39–61, deals with early German literature on Jewish emancipation, Jewish historiography a.o.). Public relations as a site of memory: the case of West German industry and National Socialism (S. Jonathan Wiesen, 196–212; deals with the industry's attempts at defending or whitewashing their Nazi past).]

40902. *Zeitenwenden. Herrschaft, Selbstbehauptung und Integration zwischen Reformation und Liberalismus.* Festgabe für Arno Herzig zum 65. Geburtstag. Hrsg. von Jörg Deventer [et al.] Münster: Lit Verlag, 2002. 570 pp. (Geschichte, Bd. 39.) [Incl. the sections entitled Grundfiguren neuzeitlichen Geschichtsdenkens; cont.: "Zeitwende" – eine Grundfigur neuzeitlichen Geschichtsdenkens: Richard Koebner im Vergleich mit Francis Fukuyama und Eric Hobsbawm (Dieter Langewiesche, 9–26). Also a contrib. on Norbert Elias (Claudia Opitz, 27–52). Marginalisierung und Akkulturation: Zugänge zur deutsch-jüdischen Geschichte (53–204); incl.: Jüdische Geschichtsschreibung zwischen Mythos und Moderne – eine Verortung der Differenz (Karl E. Grözinger, 53–70). Further selected contribs. are listed according to subject.]

Linguistics/Western Yiddish

40903. ALLERHAND, JACOB: *Jiddisch. Ein Lehr- und Lesebuch.* Wien: Mandelbaum, 2001. 129 & 58 pp. [Hebrew page nos.], illus., notes, gloss., bibl. [Hebrew title on the back cover. First part of book deals with the origins and development of Western Yiddish, the second with Yiddish in the Slavic countries, the third part is a text book.]

———— ALTHAUS, HANS PETER: *Mauscheln. Ein Wort als Waffe.* [See No. 42062.]

40904. ALTHAUS, HANS PETER: *Zocker, Zoff & Zores.* Jiddische Wörter im Deutschen. München: Beck, 2002. 159 pp., illus., notes, bibl., indexes. (Beck'sche Reihe.) Orig.-Ausg.

40905. APTROOT, MARION/NATH, HOLGER: *Einführung in die jiddische Sprache und Kultur.* Hamburg: Buske, 2002. XLII, 465 pp., illus., bibl. [+ 1 CD-ROM.] [Cont. a German introduction and a Yiddish part with 18 lessons (incl. grammar and texts from different periods.]

40906. GOLD, DAVID L.: *The Jewish given name and family name file. The etymology of the Yiddish name of Emperor Francis-Joseph of Austria-Hungary ('fayvl-yosl'), the possible etiology of a Yiddish nickname of his ('papirene hoyzn'), and the etymology of the Yiddish name, in literature, of Queen Victoria of Great Britain ('di mume vite').* [In]: Beiträge zur Namenforschung, Neue Folge, Bd. 37, H. 4, Heidelberg: 2002. Pp. 409–415, footnotes. [Analyses a Yiddish nickname of Austrian Emperor Franz Joseph, trying to determine its etiology; also on his Yiddish given name and the affectionate Yiddish name of Queen Victoria.]

———— *Jüdische Sprachen in deutscher Umwelt.* Hebräisch und Jiddisch von der Aufklärung bis ins 20. Jahrhundert. Hrsg. von Michael Brenner. [see No. 40841.]

40907. NEWMAN, ZELDA KAHAN: *The melody lingers: the Yiddish speech of Ashkenazi Jews.* [In]: Midstream, Vol. 48, No. 5, New York, July/Aug. 2002, pp. 18–21.

———— *The Oldyiddish (jüdisch–deutsche) literature.* [See No. 41151.]

40908. ROSTEN, LEO: *Jiddisch. Eine kleine Enzyklopädie.* München: Deutscher Taschenbuch Verlag, 2002. 638 pp. [Incl.: Woher dieses Buch kommt (Lutz-W. Wolff, 7–10).]

40909. SCHUMACHER, JUTTA: *Aschkenasisch-Romanisch im 18. Jahrhundert.* [In]: Jiddistik-Mitteilungen, Nr. 28, Trier, Nov. 2002. Pp. 1–11, footnotes.

40910. *Storm in the community. Yiddish polemical pamphlets of Amsterdam Jewry 1797–1798.* Selected, translated, and introduced by Jozeph Michman and Marion Aptroot. Cincinnati: Hebrew Union College, 2002. VII, 527 pp., frontis., footnotes, chronol., gloss., bibl. (517–525), index. [Incl. a bilingual edn. of texts (English transl. with annotations) selected from Yiddish pamphlets publ. by a group of enlightened members of the "new" Ashkenazik community and the responses publ. by representatives of the "old" established community.]

———— VOLOJ, JULIAN: *Do mit hat das buch ein end/Das uns got moschiach send. Zur jüdischdeutschen Sprache und Literatur im Mittelalter.* [See in No. 42131.]

40911. WEINSTEIN, MIRIAM: *Yiddish: a nation of words.* South Royalton, VT: Steerforth Press, 2001. XIII, 303 pp., illus., map, notes, bibl. (280–289), index. [Cf.: An informative history (Jack Fischel) [in]: Midstream, Vol. 48, No. 7, New York, Nov./Dec. 2002, pp. 39–40.]

———— WIESEMANN, FALK: *"Kommt heraus und schaut" – Jüdische und christliche Illustrationen zur Bibel in alter Zeit.* [See No. 41733.]

B. Communal and Regional History

1. Germany

40912. ALSBACH. HEINEMANN, HARTMUT: *"Wohltätigkeit rettet vor dem Tod". Die Beerdigungsbruderschaften des Friedhofs in Alsbach an der Bergstraße und ihre Pokale.* [In]: Aschkenas, Jg. 12, H. 1/2, Wien, 2002. Pp. 115–125, illus., footnotes.

40913. ALTONA. ZÜRN, GABRIELE: *Die Altonaer "Findelkindaffäre" 1774 – Rechtskonkurrenz und soziale Praxis im Beerdigungswesen in einer frühneuzeitlichen jüdischen Gemeinde.* [In]: Zeitenwenden [see No. 40902]. Pp. 115–128.

—— ALTONA. Zürn, Gabriele: *Die Jüdische Gemeinde Altona zwischen Tradition und Moderne. Aufklärung und der Umgang mit dem Tod 1772–1875.* [See in No. 40864.]

40914. BADEN. Nolte, Achim: *Jüdische Gemeinden in Baden und Basel. Eine rechtsvergleichende Studie über ihr Recht und ihre rechtliche Stellung.* Berlin: Duncker & Humblot, 2002. 418 pp., footnotes. (Staatskirchenrechtliche Abhandlungen; Bd. 38.) [Deals also with the Nazi period.]

40915. BADEN-WÜRTTEMBERG. *Nebeneinander – miteinander – gegeneinander.* Zur Koexistenz von Juden und Katholiken in Süddeutschland im 19. und 20. Jahrhundert. [Hrsg: Haus der Geschichte Baden-Württemberg]. Gerlingen: Bleicher, 2002. 332 pp., notes (261–287), bibl. (288–320), index. (Laupheimer Gespräche, 2000.) [Incl.: Emanzipation und jüdisches Selbstverständnis im 19. Jahrhundert (Uri Kaufmann, 21–34). Das Judenbild in der katholischen Volksbildung des 19. Jahrhunderts (Michael Langer, 35–62). "Schaddaj" – Hüter der Türen Israels. Jüdische Frömmigkeit in Alltag und Schabbat im 19. Jahrhundert (Karl Erich Grözinger, 63–80). Theologisches und Volkstümliches aus dem synagogalen und kirchlichen Festkreis. Gemeinsamkeiten im jüdischen und christlichen Kalender (Joel Berger, 81–88). "Ich weiß, was sich gehört". Das Zusammenleben von Juden, Katholiken und Protestanten im ländlichen Baden, 1862–1933 (Ulrich Baumann, 89–112). Juden und Katholiken in einer oberschwäbischen Landgemeinde – Beispiel Laupheim (Anna-Ruth Löwenbrück, 113–136). Heimatgeschichte als Harmonielehre? Warum ausgerechnet stets in "unserem" Ort Toleranz herrschte und niemals Judenhass. Erklärungen eines Widerspruchs (Olaf Blaschke, 137–162). Juden im gesellschaftlichen Leben Süd- und westdeutscher Dörfer und Kleinstädte zur Zeit der Weimarer Republik (Jacob Borut, 163–182). Hitlers Wähler in Süddeutschland (Oded Heilbronner, 183–198). Die "Reichspogromnacht" und die Haltung von katholischer Bevölkerung und Kirche. Mentalitätsgeschichte als Schlüssel zu einem neuen Verständnis? (Olaf Blaschke, 199–230). Katholische Kirche, Katholiken und die Juden in der Zeit der nationalsozialistischen Herrschaft (Joachim Köhler, 231–260).]

—— BAVARIA. Groiss-Lau, Eva: *Diskurse über den Wandel auf dem Lande anlässlich der israelitischen Kreisversammlungen im Königreich Bayern (1836).* [See in No. 40864.]

40916. BAVARIA. Mehler, Richard: *Grundzüge der demographischen Entwicklung der bayerischen Juden in der Kaiserzeit 1871–1914.* [In]: Zeitschrift für bayerische Landesgeschichte, Bd. 65, H. 2, München, 2002. Pp. 501–533, footnotes, tabs.

40917. BAVARIA. Müller, Hans-Jürgen/Rudnick, Ursula, eds.: *Christen und Juden – Juden und Christen.* Katalog zur Wanderausstellung in Bayern. Eine Ausstellung von Begegnung Christen und Juden (BCJ). Verein zur Förderung des christl.-jüd. Gesprächs in der Evang.-Luth. Kirche in Bayern. Bonn: VG Bild-Kunst, 2002. 212 pp., illus. [Incl. contribs. on the Jews in Bavaria from the beginnings to the present (Peter Fassl, Monika Berthild-Hilpert (12–31); the Protestant church in Bavaria during the Nazi period (Axel Töllner, 32–47); also on Christian-Jewish relations, Luther, antisemitism.]

40918. BERGHEIM. Friedt, Heinz Gerd: *Justizrat Bernhard Falk. Bergheim – Köln – Brüssel 1867–1944.* [In]: Geschichte in Bergheim. Jahrbuch des Bergheimer Geschichtsvereins, Bd. 11, Bergheim, 2002. Pp. 252–260, port., bibl. [Incl. excerpts from his memoirs.] [B.F., 1867 Bergheim – 1944 Brussels, lawyer, Liberal politician, emigr. from Cologne to Belgium in 1938.]

40919. BERLIN. Battenberg, J. Friedrich: *Tolerierte Juden in Berlin. Zur Ansiedlung von Wiener Juden in der Mark Brandenburg unter dem Großen Kurfürsten.* [In]: Zeitenwenden [see No. 40902]. Pp. 53–70.

—— BERLIN. Behm, Britta L./Lohmann, Uta/Lohmann, Ingrid, eds.: *Jüdische Erziehung und aufklärerische Schulreform.* Analysen zum späten 18. und frühen 19. Jahrhundert. [See No. 40839.]

—— BERLIN. Behm, Britta L.: *Moses Mendelssohn und die Transformation der jüdischen Erziehung in Berlin.* Eine bildungsgeschichtliche Analyse zur jüdischen Aufklärung im 18. Jahrhundert. [See No. 40839.]

40920. BERLIN. Grötzinger, Edith: *Und wieder blüht ein Mandelbaum. Die Geschichte einer Liebe in Berlin 1939–1945.* Berlin: Metropol, 2002. 197 pp., port. (Bibliothek der Erinnerung, Bd. 9.) [Incl.:

Vorwort des Herausgebers (Wolfgang Benz, 7–13). Memoirs; author, b. 1910, daughter of a Jewish mother, married to Jakob G. posthumously after 1945, tells about her illegal life with him, imprisonment, forced labour and futile efforts to save his life. Jakob G. was eventually deported to Auschwitz in 1943.]

40921. BERLIN. HAMMER, KLAUS: *Friedhofsführer Berlin*. Historische Friedhöfe und Grabmale in Kirchenräumen. Mit Fotografien von Jürgen Nagel. Berlin: Jaron, 2001. 280 pp., illus., gloss., index. [Incl. five Jewish cemeteries.]

40922. BERLIN. HELAS, HORST: *Juden in Berlin-Mitte*. Biografien – Orte Begegnungen. Hrsg. vom Verein zur Vorbereitung einer Stiftung Scheunenviertel Berlin e.V. 2., erg. und durchges. Aufl. Berlin: Trafo-Verlag, 2001. 309 pp., illus., bibl. [For orig. edn. see No. 38476/YB XLIV.]

40923. BERLIN. HERTZ, DEBORAH: *Jüdische Mäzene und Persönlichkeiten des öffentlichen Lebens im Berlin des Biedermeier*. [In]: Wiener Jahrbuch für jüdische Geschichte, Kultur & Museumswesen, Bd. 5, 2000/2001, Wien, 2001. Pp. 53–68, notes.

———— BERLIN. HERTZ, DEBORAH: *Theilhaber's "racial suicide" of Scholem's "flight of the avant-garde"? Interpreting conversion rates in 19th Century Berlin*. [See No. 42071.]

40924. BERLIN. KAHMANN, HENNING: *Die Bankiers von Jacquier & Securius 1933–1945. Eine rechtshistorische Fallstudie zur "Arisierung" eines Berliner Bankhauses*. Mit einem Geleitwort von John Kornblum. Frankfurt am Main: Peter Lang, 2002. 243 pp., illus., footnotes, tabs., bibl., index of names. [Partly deals with Jewish merchant bankers in general and Erich and Hermann Frenkel, Eugen and Alfred Panofsky and Max Landesmann in particular.]

———— BERLIN. KEUCK, THEKLA: *Kontinuiät und Wandel im ökonomischen Verhalten preußischer Hofjuden – Die Familie Itzig in Berlin*. [See in No. 40880.]

40925. BERLIN. KURTZE, RALF: *Das jiddische Theater in Berlin um die Jahrhundertwende*. Köln: Teiresias-Verlag, 2001. 174 pp., illus., facsims., footnotes, bibl. (Theaterwissenschaft, 8.)

———— BERLIN. LOHMANN, INGRID/LOHMANN, UTA: *Die jüdische Freischule in Berlin im Spiegel ihrer Programmschriften (1803–1826)*. [See in No. 40864.]

40926. BERLIN. LUSTIGER, ARNO: *Jüdische Kultur im Berlin der 1920er Jahre*. [In]: "Wir werden nicht untergehen". Zur jüdischen Geschichte [see No. 41930]. Pp. 41–55.

40927. BERLIN. NEISS, MARION: *Jiddische Presse im Berlin der Weimarer Republik*. [In]: Judenfeindschaft als Paradigma. Studien zur Vorurteilsforschung [see No. 42134]. Pp. 174–179, footnotes.

40928. BERLIN. NEISS, MARION: *Presse im Transit. Jiddische Zeitungen und Zeitschriften in Berlin von 1919 bis 1925*. Berlin: Metropol, 2002. 240 pp., facsims., footnotes, bibl., index. (Dokumente – Texte – Materialien, Bd. 44.)

40929. BERLIN. WEISSBERG, LILIANE: *Wie schnell kann man verhaftet werden? Benjamin Veitel Ephraim, Preußens erster jüdischer Geheimrat, reflektiert über das Berufsrisiko um 1800*. [In]: Preußens Himmel breitet seine Sterne [see No. 41991], Bd. 1. Pp. 85–105, notes.

40930. BERLIN, JEWISH MUSEUM. STRAUSS, JUTTA: *Das Jüdische Museum Berlin: "Leben nicht Tod"*. [In]: Der Wormsgau, Bd. 21, Worms, 2002. Pp. 165–175, illus., footnotes.

40931. BERLIN-STAHNSDORF. EINHOLZ, SIBYLLE: *Fern vom guten Ort – Spurensicherung auf dem Stahnsdorfer Südwestkirchhof. Eine Projektbeschreibung*. [In]: Der Bär von Berlin, Bd. 2002, Berlin, 2002. Pp. 85–114, notes, illus. [Deals with the numerous graves of Jews of Charlottenburg and Schöneberg.]

40932. BERNBURG. FABER, ROLF: *Salomon Herxheimer 1801–1884. Ein Rabbiner zwischen Tradition und Emanzipation*. Leben und Wirken eines fast vergessenen Dotzheimers. Wiesbaden: Heimat- und

Verschönerungsverein Dotzheim e.V., 2001. 94 pp., frontis., illus., facsims., notes (69–80), bibl. S.H. (81–94). (Schriften des Heimat- und Verschönerungsvereins Dotzheim e.V., Nr. 21.) [Cf.: Bespr. (Christopher R. Friedrichs) [in]: Nassauische Annalen, Bd. 113, Wiesbaden, 2002, pp. 639–640).] [S.H., 1801 Dotzheim – Bernburg, scholar, teacher and Rabbi in Herborn, Wiesbaden and Eschwege, from 1831 "Landesrabbiner" in Anhalt-Bernburg.]

40933. BIEBRICH. FABER, ROLF: *Seligmann Baer 1825–1897. Neue Erkenntnisse zu Leben und Werk des jüdischen Gelehrten aus Wiesbaden-Biebrich.* Biebrich: Verschönerungs- und Verkehrsverein Biebrich am Rhein e.V., 2002. 56 pp., illus., facsims.

40934. BIESENTHAL. KOHNKE, META: *Geschichte der jüdischen Gemeinde in Biesenthal von ihrer Gründung bis zur Auflösung im Jahre 1758.* [In]: Jahrbuch für Brandenburgische Landesgeschichte, Bd. 53, Berlin, 2002. Pp. 90–121, footnotes. [Biesenthal: north-east of Berlin.]

40935. BIRKENFELD. HOEBBEL, KATHARINA: *Die Geschichte und Dokumentation des jüdischen Friedhofs in Birkenfeld.* [In]: Mitteilungen des Vereins f. Heimatkunde im Landkreis Birkenfeld, Jg. 76, Birkenfeld, 2002. Pp. 85–111, illus., footnotes.

40936. BOCHOLT. SUNDERMANN, WERNER: *Drei jüdische Friedhöfe in Bocholt.* [Bocholt: Stadt Bocholt, 2002]. 182 pp., illus., plans. (Bocholter Quellen und Beiträge, Bd. 10.) [Incl.: Dokumentation des Jüdischen Friedhofes an der Vardingholter Straße erstellt von einer Arbeitsgruppe (55–181).]

40937. BONN. RAUHUT-BRUNGS, LEAH/WASSER, GABRIELE/HODDE, PETER [et al.]: *Stadtrundgang durch Bonns jüdische Geschichte.* "Aleff-puff, Beis-puff. Hört er noch nich uff?" Egling an der Paar: Verlag Roman Kovar, 2001. 140 pp., illus., facsims., plan. [Based on the search for traces of two teachers and 14 pupils of the Katholische Hauptschule St. Hedwig, Bonn-Auerberg.]

40938. BRANDENBURG. DIEKMANN, IRENE: *Zur Geschichte der Juden in Brandenburg/Havel im 19. Jahrhundert unter besonderer Berücksichtigung der Familien Frank und Joel.* [In]: Preußens Himmel breitet seine Sterne [see No. 41991], Bd. 1. Pp. 289–306, illus., facsims., geneal. tabs., notes.

40939. BRAUNFELS. FITZLER, ARNO W.: *Juden zu Braunfels. Die Schule, das Bethaus oder die Synagoge.* [In]: Heimatjahrbuch für das Land an der Dill im Lahn-Dill-Kreis, Bd. 45, 2002. Pp. 264–269, notes, illus.

40940. BRAUNSCHWEIG. SCHMID, JOACHIM: *Landrabbinat und Landesrabbiner im Herzogtum Braunschweig.* [In]: Braunschweigisches Jahrbuch für Landesgeschichte, Bd. 81, Braunschweig, 2000. Pp. 102–116, ports., footnotes.

40941. BREMEN. DÜNZELMANN, ANNE E.: *Vom Gaste, den Joden und den Fremden.* Zur Ethnographie von Immigration. Rezeption und Exludierung Fremder am Beispiel der Stadt Bremen vom Mittelalter bis 1948. Hamburg: Lit, 2001. 419 pp., facsims., gloss., notes (344–378), bibl. (Geschichte, 37.) [Incl. Jews settling in Bremen.]

40942. BREMEN. JAKUBOWSKI, JEANETTE: *Geschichte des jüdischen Friedhofs in Bremen.* Bremen: Donat, 2002. 176 pp. (& 40 pp. of photographs), plan, notes (148–157), bibl. (166–176).

40943. BREMKE. MÜLLER, TONIA SOPHIE: *Die jüdische Familie Meyerstein in Bremke und Göttingen.* Eine Dokumentation. Unter Mitarbeit von Eike Dietert. [In]: Göttinger Jahrbuch, Bd. 50, Göttingen, 2002. Pp. 41–73, illus., ports., tabs., facsim., footnotes.

40944. BÜHL. *Jüdisches Leben. Auf den Spuren der israelitischen Gemeinde zu Bühl.* [Red.: Bettina Peter]. Bühl: Stadtgeschichtliches Institut, 2001. 267 pp., illus., facsims., notes. (Bühler Heimatgeschichte, Nr. 15/2001.) [Incl. numerous contribs. by Markus Leukam, Andrea Rumpf, Michael Rumpf, Bettina Peter, Marco Müller and others.]

———— CASTROP. SCHOLZ, DIETMAR: *"Durch die Geburt eines kräftigen Antisemiten wurden hocherfreut…" Zum Antisemitismus in Castrop und Umgebung im ausgehenden 19. Jahrhundert.* [See No. 42151.]

40945. CASTROP. SCHOLZ, DIETMAR: *Der jüdische Friedhof in Castrop (1743–1943/2000).* [In]: Der Märker, Jg. 49, H. 4, Lüdenscheid, 2000. Pp. 165–172, illus., footnotes.

40946. CASTROP-RAUXEL. SCHOLZ, DIETMAR: *Zum Leben und Schicksal der Juden in Castrop/Castrop-Rauxel 1825–1942.* [In]: Vestische Zeitschrift, Bd. 99, Recklinghausen, 2002. Pp. 171–190, footnotes.

40947. CHEMNITZ. DIAMANT, ADOLF: *Ostjuden in Chemnitz 1811 bis 1945. Eine Dokumentation anläßlich der Einweihung des neuen Jüdischen Gemeindezentrums und der Synagoge in Chemnitz.* Chemnitz: [Chemnitzer Geschichtsverein], 2002. XII, 64 pp., illus, graphs.

40948. CHEMNITZ. *Juden in Chemnitz. Die Geschichte der Gemeinde und ihrer Mitglieder. Mit einer Dokumentation des Jüdischen Friedhofs.* Hrsg. von Jürgen Nitsche und Ruth Röcher im Auftrag der Jüdischen Gemeinde Chemnitz. Entstanden in Zusammenarbeit mit dem Salomon Ludwig-Steinheim-Institut für deutsch-jüdische Geschichte Duisburg und dem Stadtarchiv Chemnitz. Dresden: Sandstein, 2002. 497 pp., illus., facsims., notes, bibl., indexes. [Title page and table of contents also in Hebrew. Cont.: Prefaces (Paul Spiegel, Peter Seifert, Ruth Röcher, Michael Brocke, 7–11). Die Gemeinde (13–170; contribs. by Stephan Pfalzer, Michael Schäbitz, Ruth Röcher, Solvejg Höppner, Cornelia Wustmann, Andreas Neubert, Eberhard Hübsch, Jürgen Nitsche, Tilo Richter, Steffen Held, Peter Ambros, Reinhard Kühn, Gabriele Juppe, Jens Kassner, Franziska Specht, Undine Völschow, Siegmund Rotstein). Der Friedhof (171–439; cont. contribs. by Jürgen Nitsche, Isabel Haupt, Dan Bondy, Michael Brocke, Christiane E. Müller). Dokumentation (Jürgen Nitsche/Dan Bondy, 210–439; incl. biographies of 115 families and individual persons). Register (Jürgen Nitsche/Kathrin Grunert, 442–489; cont. eight lists of names, incl. list of Nazi victims.]

40949. COLOGNE. SCHMANDT, MATTHIAS: *'Judei, cives et incole': Studien zur jüdischen Geschichte Kölns im Mittelalter.* Hannover: Hahn, 2002. IX, 319 pp., footnotes, tabs., index, bibl., maps. (Forschungen zur Geschichte der Juden, Abt. A., Abhandlungen, Bd. 11.) Zugl.: Trier, Univ., Diss., 2000. [First part of book covers the period from the beginnings of the medieval community in the 11th cent. to the pogrom of 1349; the second part deals with the resettlement period up to the expulsion (1372–1424).]

40950. CREGLINGEN. HEUWINKEL, CLAUDIA: *Jüdisches Creglingen: ein Gang durch die Stadt.* [Hrsg.: Stadt Creglingen.] Haigerloch: Medien und Dialog, Schubert, 2001. 42 pp., illus. (Orte jüdischer Kultur.)

40951. DESSAU. GROSSERT, WERNER: *David Fränckel (um 1707–1762). Rabbiner, Wissenschaftler und Lehrer Moses Mendelssohns.* [In]: Dessauer Kalender 2003, Jg. 47, Dessau, 2002. Pp. 18–23, facsims, notes. [D.F., Dessau rabbi from 1737 to 1743, not to be confused with his great-nephew David Fränkel (1799–1865).]

——— DOTZHEIM. FABER, ROLF: *Salomon Herxheimer 1801–1884. Ein Rabbiner zwischen Tradition und Emanzipation.* Leben und Wirken eines fast vergessenen Dotzheimers. [See No. 40934.]

40952. DRESDEN. *Der Alte Jüdische Friedhof in Dresden. … daß wir uns unterwinden, um eine Grabes-Stätte fußfälligst anzuflehen…* Hrsg.: HATIKVA – Bildungs- und Begegnungsstätte für Jüdische Geschichte und Kultur Sachsen e.V. Projektgruppe Alter Jüdischer Friedhof [Projektleitung: Heike Liebsch, Erfassung und Übersetzung: Gil Frowald Hüttenmeister.] Teetz: Hentrich & Hentrich, 2002. 299 pp., illus., notes, indexes. [Incl. also contribs. by various other authors on the history of the Dresden Jews.]

40953. DRESDEN. HAGEMEYER, KERSTIN: *Jüdisches Leben in Dresden.* Ausstellung anlässlich der Weihe der neuen Synagoge Dresden am 9. November 2001. Mit einer Dokumentation der Ausstellung Blick/Fragmente: Bilder jüdischen Lebens aus Beständen der Deutschen Fotothek. Dresden: Sächsische Landesbibliothek – Staat- und Universitätsbibliothek Dresden, 2002. 278 pp., illus., facsims., chronol., index, bibl. [On the history of the Dresden community; also on music in the synagogue; artists.]

40954. EAST FRIESLAND. *Quellen zur Geschichte und Kultur des Judentums im westlichen Niedersachsen vom 16. Jahrhundert bis 1945.* Ein sachthematisches Inventar. Teil 1: Ostfriesland. Unter Leitung von

Albrecht Eckhardt, Jan Lokers und Matthias Nistal. Bearb. von Heike Düselder und Hans-Peter Klausch. Göttingen: Vandenhoeck & Ruprecht, 2002. XXX, 520 pp. (Veröffentlichungen der Niedersächsischen Archivverwaltung, Bd. 55.). [See also Nos. 41002, 41020, 41021.]

40955. EMMENDINGEN. GRASSE, CAROLA [et al.]: *Jüdisches Leben in Emmendingen: Orte, Schauplätze, Spuren.* [Hrsg.: Verein für Jüdische Geschichte und Kultur Emmendingen e.V.]. Haigerloch: Medien und Dialog, Schubert, 2001. 34 pp., illus. (Orte jüdischer Kultur.)

40956. ERFURT. ZUCHT, OLAF: *Die Geschichte der Juden in Erfurt von der Wiedereinbürgerung 1810 bis zum Ende des Kaiserreiches. Ein Beitrag zur deutsch-jüdischen Geschichte Thüringens.* Erfurt: [Privately printed], 2001. 341 pp., tabs., graphs., footnotes.

——— FELLHEIM. LÖFFELMEIER, ANTON: *Die Wurzeln der Rosenthals: Fellheim in Bayerisch Schwaben.* [See in No. 41975.]

40957. FLÖRSHEIM/MAIN. SCHIELE, WERNER: *Jüdische Eheverträge und Sponsalienklagen.* [In]: Zwischen Main und Taunus. Jahrbuch des Main-Taunus-Kreises, Jg. 10, 2002. Hofheim/Ts., 2001. Pp. 51–56, facsims, notes. [Deals with Flörsheim marriage contracts dating from 1770–1817.]

40958. FRANKFURT am Main. BONAVITA, PETRA, ed.: *Assimilation, Verfolgung, Exil am Beispiel der jüdischen Schüler des Kaiser-Friedrich-Gymnasiums (heute: Heinrich-von-Gagern-Gymnasium) in Frankfurt am Main.* [Cover title: Assimilation, Verfolgung, Exil am Beispiel der jüdischen Schüler eines Frankfurter Gymnasiums]. Stuttgart: Schmetterling Verlag, 2002. 210 pp., illus., facsims., bibl. [Incl.: Biographien der jüdischen Schüler des Kaiser-Friedrichs-Gymnasium (123–205).]

40959. FRANKFURT am Main. *The Jewish Museum Frankfurt am Main.* Frankfurt am Main: Jewish Museum Frankfurt am Main; Munich; New York: Prestel, 2002. 112 pp., illus, index. [Museum guide book (texts by Georg Heuberger, Annette Weber, Michael Lenarz, Johannes Wachten, Helga Krohn, Cilly Kugelmann, Fritz Backhaus).]

——— FRANKFURT am Main. SCHLICK, GABRIELA: *Jüdische Wechselmakler am Börsenplatz Frankfurt am Main und die Wirtschaftspolitik des reichsstädtischen Rates.* [See in No. 40880.]

40960. FRIEDBERG. HOOS, HANS-HELMUT: *"Kehillah Kedoscha – Spurensuche"* Zur Geschichte der jüdischen Gemeinde in Friedberg und der Friedberger Juden von den Anfängen bis 1942. [Weilburg-Waldhausen]: Hans Helmut Hoos, [2002?]. 384 pp., illus., facsims., notes (345–378)., bibl.

40961. FRITZLAR. LOHMANN, PAULGERHARD: *Hier waren wir zu Hause. Die Geschichte der Juden von Fritzlar 1096–2000 vor dem Hintergrund der allgemeinen Geschichte der deutschen Juden.* [Also on book title: Den ehemaligen Fritzlarer Juden, ihren Kindern und Enkeln gewidmet.] Norderstedt: Books on Demand [2002]. 532 pp., illus., facsims., footnotes, tabs., bibl. [Obtainable at Touristinformation Zwischen den Krämen 5, D-34560 Fritzlar. Incl. numerous lists of names; the synagogue, the cemetery, the inscriptions on the gravestones, Nazi victims.] [Cf.: Bespr. (Uta Löwenstein) [in]: Zeitschrift des Vereins für hessische Geschichte und Landeskunde, Bd. 107, Kassel, 2002, pp. 403–404.]

40962. FULDA. SOMMERLECHNER, ANDREA: *Das Judenmassaker von Fulda 1235 in der Geschichtsschreibung um Kaiser Friedrich II.* [In]: Römische Historische Mitteilungen, Bd. 44, Wien, 2002. Pp. 121–150, footnotes.

40963. GELDERN. *Juden in der Geschichte des Gelderlandes.* Hrsg. von Bernhard Keuck und Gerd Halmanns im Auftrag des Arbeitskreises Jüdisches Bethaus Issum und des Historischen Vereins für Geldern und Umgegend. Geldern: Verl. des Histor. Vereins für Geldern u. Umgegend, 2002. 411 pp., illus., facsims., map, notes. (Veröffentlichungen des Historischen Vereins für Geldern und Umgegend. Bd. 101.) [Incl. contribs. by Bernhard Keuck, Gerd Halmanns, Thekla Keuck, Christoph Nonn, Albert Spitzner-Jahn, Theo Mäschig, Henk Raijer, Johanna Klümpen-Hegmans, Bernd Ingenpass on Geldern, Issum, Hoerstgen, Kamp-Lintfort, Rheurdt, Sevelen, Kerken, Straelen, Kevelaer, Kapellen, Weeze, Arcen (Netherl.).]

40964. GELLIEHAUSEN. DIETERT, EIKE: *"... der Messias werde von hier aus kommen"*. *Die Auseinandersetzungen um den Bau der Synagoge in Gelliehausen in den Jahren 1777 bis 1785*. [In]: Göttinger Jahrbuch, Bd. 50, Göttingen, 2002. Pp. 33–39, footnotes. [Gelliehausen = nr. Hanover.]

40965. GLADBECK. SAMEN, MANFRED: *Ein jüdisches Schicksal*. [In]: Vestischer Kalender 2000, Jg. 71, Recklinghausen, 2001 Pp. 49–52, illus. [On the Daniel family.]

40966. GÖPPINGEN. RUEß, KARL-HEINZ: *Rabbiner Dr. Aron Tänzer*. Stationen seines Lebens. [Göppingen: Jüdisches Museum Göppingen], 2002. 28 pp., illus., facsims., bibl. [A.T., Jan. 30, 1871 Preßburg/Hungary, 1896 – 1907 rabbi in Hohenems and Meran, from 1907 until his death in 1937 in Göppingen.]

40967. GRÖTZINGEN. METZGER, SIGMUND: *Festschrift zum hundertjährigen Jubiläum der Erbauung der Synagoge in Grötzingen*. [Nachdr. der Ausg. Grötzingen: S. Metzger, 1899 [wiederveröffentl. von der Evang. Kirchengemende Karlsruhe-Grötzingen durch Pfarrer Ulrich Schadt mit einem Anh.] Karlsruhe-Grötzingen: Evang. Kirchengemeinde, 2002. 50 pp., illus.

40968. GROSS-KARBEN. WITTENBERGER, G.: *Stammbaum der jüdischen Familie Kirschner aus Groß-Karben*. [In]: Hessische Familienkunde, Jg. 25, H. 5–8, Neustadt/Aisch, 2001. Pp. 281–285.

40969. GROSSKROTZENBURG. *Ihre Seele sei eingebunden in das Bündel des Lebens. Die jüdische Gemeinde und der jüdische Friedhof zu Großkrotzenburg*. Hrsg.: Arbeitskreis "Ehemalige Synagoge Großkrotzenburg. Hanau: CoCon-Verlag, 2002. 182 pp., illus., facsims., notes, bibl., plan. [Großkrotzenburg: Hesse, nr. Hanau; incl. contribs. by Abraham Frank, Heinz Klab, Monika Ilona Pfeifer. Documents the cemetery with Hebrew and German inscriptions (57–176).]

40970. HACHENBURG/WESTERWALD. GÜTH, WERNER A./KEMPF, JOHANNES/FRANK, ABRAHAM: *Zachor. Ein Buch des Gedenkens*. Zur Erinnerung an die jüdische Gemeinde Hachenburg. Hrsg. im Auftrag der Stadt Hachenburg. Hachenburg: Selbstverlag, 2002. 400 pp., illus., facsims., footnotes, docs., gloss., bibl. [Covers the period from the 17th cent. until the present. Documents more than 20 families and their fate during the Nazi period; also the cemetery incl. the inscriptions on 95 gravestones.]

40971. HAINSFARTH. IMMENKÖTTER, HERBERT: *Die israelitische Kultusgemeinde in Hainsfarth (Landkreis Donau-Ries) im 19. und 20. Jahrhundert*. Mit Beiträgen von Rolf Hofmann und Gernot Römer. Augsburg: Wißner-Verlag, 2002. XI, 300 pp., illus., facsims., footnotes, docs., bibl., index. (Veröff. der Schwäbischen Forschungsgemeinschaft Augsburg: Reihe 1, Studien zur Gesch. des bayerischen Schwaben, Bd. 30.) [Hainsfarth = nr. Nördlingen.]

40972. HAMBURG. BRADEN, JUTTA: *"Zur Rechtschaffenheit ermahnt"*. Taufwillige Jüdinnen und Konvertitinnen aus dem Judentum in Hamburg in der zweiten Hälfte des 18. Jahrhunderts. [In]: Zeitenwenden [see No.40902]. Pp. 93–114.

40973. HAMBURG. GUDERIAN, DIETER: *Die Hamburger Familie Isaac. Lebensgeschichte der Volkssänger Gebrüder Wolf*. [28832 Achim, Schwedenschanze 9a]: D. Guderian, 2001. 124 pp., illus., facsims., music. (Familienkundliche Schriften, T. 1.) Hergestellt on demand. [On Ludwig and Leopold Isaac and other members of the family; author is the grandson of Helene, one of the sisters of Ludwig and Leopold.]

40974. HAMBURG. HUCKERIEDE, JENS/MÜLLER, ANGELA: *An de Eck steiht'n Jung mit'n Tüdelband*. Gebrüder Wolf. Hamburger Gesangshumoristen von 1895 bis 1953. Hamburg: Kunstwerk e.V., 2002. 150 pp., illus., facsims., 1 CD. [Book has parallel German and English texts. Tells the story of Ludwig, James and Leopold Isaac (since 1924 family name: Wolf), popular vocal humorists in Hamburg from the 1890s till 1934; also on their fate during the Nazi period, their emigr. to Shanghai and later life in the US; incl. also 20 of their most successful songs and sketches written in the local dialect. Attached to book is a CD with eight songs, five of them orig. productions, one recorded at a performance in Hamburg in 2002.]

40975. HAMBURG. KAUNZNER, FRIEDERIKE: *In der Geschichtsfalle, ohne es zu merken. Vornamengebung und jüdische Identität zwischen Kaiserreich und Nationalsozialismus. Das Beispiel Hamburg.* [In]: Geschichte als Falle. Deutschland und die jüdische Welt [see No. 40849]. Pp. 83–120, notes, tabs.

40976. HAMBURG. LIEDTKE, RAINER: *Germany's door to the world: a haven for the Jews?: Hamburg 1590–1593.* [In]: Jewish Culture and History, Vol. 4, No. 2 [with the issue title] *Port Jews: Jewish communities in cosmopolitan maritime trading centres, 1550–1950,* London, Winter 2001. Pp. 75–86, notes.

40977. HAMBURG. SARRAGA, MARIAN & RAMON F.: *Sephardic epitaphs in Hamburg's oldest cemetery: poetry, riddles, and eccentric texts.* [In]: AJS Review, Vol. 26, No. 1, Waltham, MA, 2002. Pp. 53–92, footnotes.

———— HAMBURG. STUDEMUND-HALÉVY, MICHAEL: *"Es residiren in Hamburg Minister fremder Mächte" – Sefardische Residenten in Hamburg.* [See in No. 40880.]

40978. HAMBURG. STUDEMUND-HALÉVY, MICHAEL/ZÜRN, GABY: *Zerstört die Erinnerung nicht. Der jüdische Friedhof Königstraße in Hamburg.* Hamburg; München: Dölling und Galitz, 2002. 184 pp., frontis., illus., bibl., index.

———— HECHINGEN. HEBELL, KERSTIN: *Madame Kaulla und ihr Clan – Das Kleinterritorium als individuelle Nische und ökonomisches Sprungbrett.* [See in No. 40880.]

40979. HEIDELBERG. LEHMANN, HERMANN W.: *Die sogenannte Judenschule.* Sozialgeschichte eines Hauses. Heidelberg: Kurpfälzischer Verlag, 2001. 251 pp., illus., facsims., footnotes, docs., gloss., bibl., index. (Die Häuser der Judengasse in Heidelberg, H. 2.) [On the house Dreikönigstraße 10/Bussemergasse 1a.]

40980. HEPPENHEIM. JOST, HARALD E.: *Die jüdische Gemeinde Heppenheim und ihr prominentestes Mitglied Martin Buber.* [In]: Aschkenas, Jg. 12, H. 1/2, Wien, 2002. Pp. 141–153, footnotes.

40981. HERNE & WANNE-EICKEL. PIORR, RALF, ed.: *"Nahtstellen, fühlbar, hier…". Zur Geschichte der Juden in Herne und Wanne-Eickel.* Im Auftrag der Stadt Herne. Essen: Klartext, 2002. 264 pp., illus., facsims., lists, tabs., map, bibl., gloss., notes. [Incl. the sections: Zur Geschichte der Juden in Herne und Wanne-Eickel (10–110; contribs. by Kurt Tohermes and Ralf Piorr). Gedenken: Die Opfer der Shoah aus Herne und Wanne-Eickel (113–146). Portaits und Biographisches (148–259; contribs. by Max Fritzler, Ralf Piorr, Leo Schnur, Norbert Ripp, Liesel Spencer, Andreas Eiynck, Jenny Dresen, Hubert Schneider, Channa Birnfeld, Kate Katzki, Jens Hoffmann).]

40982. HERRLINGEN. KRUS, HEINZ, ed.: *"… aber ein Leben lang unvergessen …". Die Landschulheime Herrlingen.* Erinnerungen und Dokumente. Mit Beiträgen von Marga Bell [et al.]. Ulm: Klemm und Oelschläger, 2001. 100 pp. [Incl. the sections: 1. Landschulheim Herrlingen unter Leitung von Anna Essinger (1926–1933) (11–66). Landschulheim Herrlingen unter Leitung von Hugo Rosenthal (1933–1939) (67–89).]

40983. HESSE. *Das achte Licht. Beiträge zur Kultur- und Sozialgeschichte der Juden in Nordhessen. Hrsg. von Helmut Burmeister und Michael Dorhs.* Hofgeismar: Verein für hessische Geschichte und Landeskunde e.V. Kassel 1834 – Zweigverein Hofgeismar, 2002. 320 pp., illus., notes. [A collection of 35 contribs. spanning more than three centuries, some of them not publ. before, others revised.]

40984. HESSE. CASPARY, EUGEN: *Die junge Witwe 'Lea' – ihr zweiter Ehemann 'Abraham Raphael' und ihr Landesherr, der Fürst von Nassau-Weilburg. Über Judenschutz, Judenordnung sowie über die soziale und rechtliche Stellung der Juden im Fürstentum Nassau am Ende des 18. Jahrhunderts.* [In]: Blätter um die Freudenberger Begegnung, Bd. 6 [with the title] Fundstücke … Kristalle …, Offenbach am Main, 2001. Pp. 123–133, facsims., footnotes.

40985. HESSE. SCHWARZ, ANKE: *Jüdische Gemeinden zwischen bürgerlicher Emanzipation und Obrigkeitsstaat.* Studien über Anspruch und Wirklichkeit jüdischen Lebens in kurhessischen Kleinstädten im 19. Jahrhundert. Wiesbaden: Komm. für die Geschichte der Juden in Hessen, 2002. 349 pp., footnotes, bibl. (Schriften der Kommission für die Geschichte der Juden in Hessen, Bd. 19.) Zugl.: Kassel, Univ., Diss., 1999/2000. [Incl. Fritzlar, Grebenstein, Witzenhausen, Wolfhagen.]

40986. HESSE. VOGT, MONIKA: *"Die Zeit ist der Strom, in dem ich fische."* *Begegnungesn mit dem jüdischen Leben in Hessen.* Frankfurt am Main: Sparkassen-Kulturstiftung Hessen-Thüringen, Landesamt für Denkmalpflege Hessen, 2002. 108 pp., illus.

40986a. HOHENLOHE (KREIS). BAMBERGER, NAFTALI BAR GIORA: *Memor-Buch. Die jüdischen Friedhöfe im Hohenlohekreis.* Hrsg. vom Landratsamt Hohenlohekreis. Künzelsau: Swiridoff Verlag, 2002. 2 vols., 1104 pp., illus., plans, indexes. [Vol. 1 incl.: Juden im Hohenlohekreis (Rainer Gross, 11–24). Der jüdische Friedhof Berlichingen (Rainer Gross, 41–42). Die Grabsteine Nr. 1–1013 (43–564). Vol. 2 incl.: Die Grabsteine Nr. 1014–1251 (of the Berlichingen cemetery, 565–697). Indexes (717–774). Incl. also a documentation of the cemeteries Hohebach (775–956), Krautheim (957–1024), Laibach (1025–1038), Öhringen (1039–1076). Opfer der nationalsozialistischen Judenverfolgung (Rainer Gross, 1077–1080).]

40987. HOLZMINDEN. KIECKBUSCH, KLAUS: *Aus dem Besitz des Holzmindeners Stadtmuseums: Judaica.* Mit 4 Abbildungen. [In]: Jahrbuch für den Landkreis Holzminden, Bd. 19, 2001 [2000]. Pp. 137–144.

40988. JENA. HORN, GISELA, ed.: *Die Töchter der Alma mater Jenensis. 90 Jahre Frauenstudium an der Universität von Jena.* Band 2 der Reihe: Quellen und Beiträge der Universität Jena. Rudolstadt: Hain Wissenschafts-Verlag, 1999. 360 pp., illus. [Incl.: Zwischen Schulhof und Parnaß – Künstlerinnen in Jena (Lisa Kerstin Kunert, 115–164; incl. Helene Czapski-Holzman). Anna Auerbach – eine Frau an der Schwelle zur Moderne (Barbara Happe, 199–218; on A.A., née Silbergleit, 1861 Breslau – 1933 Jena (suicide, together with her husband), wife of Felix Auerbach, Prof. of Physics at Jena Univ., around 1900 friend of Elisabeth Förster-Nietzsche.] [Cf.: Bespr. (Dagmar Klein) [in]: Mitteilungen des Oberhessischen Geschichtsvereins Gießen, N.F. Bd. 85, Gießen, 2000, pp. 273–274.]

40989. JÜLICH. DOVERN, WILLI: *Die Juden in Koslar bei Jülich.* [In]: Neue Beiträge zur Jülicher Geschichte, Bd. XIII, Jülich, 2002. Pp. 147–154, illus., footnotes. [In the same vol. by the same author: Bemerkungen zur Namensliste auf dem Denkmal zur Erinnerung an die Jülicher Juden (159–168); incl. list of names.]

40990. KIPPENHEIM. : *Gedächtnis aus Stein. Die Synagoge in Kippenheim 1852–2002.* Hrsg. im Auftrag des Fördervereins Ehemalige Synagoge Kippenheim e.V. von Uwe Schellinger. Heidelberg: Verlag Regionalkultur, 2002. 320 pp., illus., facsims., notes. [Incl. (some titles abbr.): Die Baugeschichte der Kippenheimer Synagoge (Jürgen Stude, 17–60). Die jüdische Gemeinde Kippenheim und ihre Synagoge 1852 bis 1940 (Ulrich Baumann/Uwe Schellinger, 61–110). Das religiöse Leben in der Kippenheimer Synagoge und seine Gestalter (Ruben Frankenstein, 111–142). Die Bedeutung der Zeitzeugen – Erinnerungen an die Synagoge (eingel. und komm. von Uwe Schellinger, 143–164). Further contribs. on the synagogue between 1938 and 2002 by Uwe Schellinger, Monika Müller, Thorsten Mietzner, Renate Kreplin; also one contrib. on former synagogues as memorial places (Konrad Pflug). Incl. list of Nazi victims.]

40991. KLEVE. KRAUS, KERSTIN: *Fundamente der Klever Synagoge neu aufgedeckt.* Eine Grabung des Rheinischen Amtes für Bodendenkmalpflege. [In]: Kalender für das Klever Land auf das Jahr 2003, Kleve, 2002. Pp. 28–31, illus.

40992. KLEVE. KREBS, WOLFGANG: *Das jüdische Lehrhaus von Kleve.* [In]: Kalender für das Klever Land auf das Jahr 2003, Kleve, 2002. Pp. 32–36, illus.

——— KLEVE. KREBS, WOLFGANG: *Tomor – eine koschere Margarine.* [See No. 41714.]

40993. KLEVE. MANDELBAUM, CHANOCH: *"Mögen ihre Seelen eingebunden sein im Bundes des Lebens".* Der jüdische Friedhof in Kleve. Jerusalem: Old City Press, 2002. 255; 33 pp. [in Hebrew], frontis. [Documents the gravestones, incl. the Hebrew inscriptions.] [Ch.M., b. in Kleve in 1923, fled 1938 to the Netherlands, 1942–1945 imprisoned in Westerbork, Bergen-Belsen, from there sent on a "death march" to Theresienstadt, liberated by the Red Army in Tröbitz, in 1946 emigr. illegally via France to Palestine; lives in Jerusalem.]

40994. KÖNIGSBACH. MEHNE, JOACHIM: *Jüdisches Königsbach: Einladung zu einem Rundgang.* [Hrsg.: Gemeinde Königsbach-Stein]. Haigerloch: Medien und Dialog, Schubert, 2001. 34 pp., illus. (Orte jüdischer Kultur.)

——— KONITZ. NONN, CHRISTOPH: *Eine Stadt sucht einen Mörder. Gerücht, Gewalt und Antisemitismus im Kaiserreich.* [See No. 42141.] [See also Nos. 42121, 42124, 42155.]

40995. KREUZNACH. SENNER, MARTIN: *Kleine Geschichte Zelemochums.* Bad Kreuznach: Schloßparkmuseum Bad Kreuznach, 2002. 270 pp., illus., notes, bibl. (230–253), index. (Aus Museen und Archiv, Nr. 3.) [On the Jews of Kreuznach before the Nazi era.]

40996. KRUMBACH-HÜRBEN. SCHÖNHAGEN, BENIGNA/AUER, HERBERT: *Jüdisches Krumbach-Hürben: Einladung zu einem Rundgang.* Haigerloch: Medien und Dialog, Schubert, 2002. 30 pp., illus. (Orte jüdischer Kultur.)

40997. LEIPZIG. GAUDER, DIETMAR: *In der Geschichtsfalle, ohne es zu merken. Vornamengebung und jüdische Identität zwischen Kaiserreich und Nationalsozialismus. Das Beispiel Leipzig.* [In]: Geschichte als Falle. Deutschland und die jüdische Welt [see No. 40849]. Pp. 45–82, notes, tabs. [Based on the evaluation of the May 1939 census.]

40998. LEIPZIG. KOWALZIK, BARBARA: *Das jüdische Schulwerk in Leipzig 1912–1933.* Köln: Böhlau, 2002. VII, 374 pp., frontis., illus., docs., facsims., footnotes, tabs., chronol., bibl. (339–350), indexes. (Geschichte und Politik in Sachsen, Bd. 18.) [On the orthodox schools founded by rabbi Ephraim Carlebach, their director from 1912 until 1936.]

40999. LEIPZIG. LORZ, ANDREA: *Schulhaus H. Nordheimer. Lebensbilder jüdischer Unternehmer in Leipzig.* Hrsg. vom Stadtgeschichtlichen Museum Leipzig und Andrea Lorz. Leipzig: Passagen-Verl., 2002. 86 pp., illus., tabs., facsims., notes.

41000. LICHTENAU. UIBEL, LUDWIG: *Die israelitische Gemeinde in Lichtenau im 19. Jahrhundert.* [In]: Die Ortenau, Bd. 82, Offenburg, 2002. Pp. 487–504, illus., notes.

41001. LINNICH. FRIEDT, GERD: *Das Beschneidungsbuch des Salomon Franck aus Linnich.* Jülich: Verlag Willi Dovern, 2002. 70, XII pp., illus., facsims., bibl., indexes. (Jülicher Genealogische Blätter, H. 17.) [All texts also in English.] [S.F., 1800 Heerenberg/Bergh (Netherlands) – 1864 Arnheim.]

——— LIPPE. FAASSEN, DINA VAN: *"Hier ist ein kleiner Ort und eine kleine Gegend" – Hofjuden in Lippe.* [See in No. 40880.]

41002. LOWER SAXONY. *Quellen zur Geschichte und Kultur des Judentums im westlichen Niedersachsen vom 16. Jahrhundert bis 1945. Ein sachthematisches Inventar.* Teil 4: Indizes. Unter Leitung von Albrecht Eckhardt, Jan Lokers und Matthias Nistal. Bearb. von Heike Düselder und Hans-Peter Klausch. Göttingen: Vandenhoeck & Ruprecht, 2002. 237 pp. [1p.: Errata & Korrigenda]. (Veröffentlichungen der Niedersächsischen Archivverwaltung, Bd. 55.) [See also No. 41021. Cf.: Bespr. (Gerd Steinwascher) [in]: Das Historisch-Politische Buch, Jg. 50, H. 6, Göttingen, 2002, pp. 657–658.]

41003. LUDWIGSBURG. STING, ALBERT: *Ein Rundgang durch Ludwigsburg: Spuren jüdischen Lebens.* [Hrsg.: Stadt Ludwigsburg, Stadtarchiv]. Haigerloch: Medien und Dialog, 2001. 34 pp., illus., facsims., map. (Orte jüdischer Kultur).

41004. LÜBBECKE & HALLE. BECKMANN, VOLKER: *Die jüdische Bevölkerung der Landkreise Lübbecke und Halle i.W. vom Vormärz bis zur Befreiung vom Faschismus (1815–1945).* Lage: Verlag Hans Jacobs, 2001. 594 pp., footnotes, tabs., bibl. (570–594). Zugl.: Bielefeld, Univ. Bielefeld, Dissertation 2001.

——— MANNHEIM. WAßMUTH, BRITTA: *Die Familien May und Mayer in Mannheim.* [See in No. 40880.]

41005. MECKLENBURG. FRANCKE, NORBERT/KRIEGER, BÄRBEL: *Die Familiennamen der Juden in Mecklenburg.* Mehr als 2000 jüdische Familien aus 53 Orten der Herzogtümer Mecklenburg-

Schwerin und Mecklenburg-Strelitz im 18. und 19. Jahrhundert. Schwerin: Verein für jüd. Gesch. und Kultur in Mecklenburg und Vorpommern e.V., 2001. 74 pp., gloss., bibl., index.

41006. MECKLENBURG. FRANCKE, NORBERT/KRIEGER, BÄRBEL: *Schutzjuden in Mecklenburg. Ihre rechtliche Stellung, ihr Gewerbe, wer sie waren und wo sie lebten.* Schwerin: MVJG, 2002. 131 pp., facsims., docs., lists, footnotes, bibl., index. (Schriften des Vereins für Jüdische Geschichte und Kultur in Mecklenburg und Vorpommern e.V.).

41007. MERGENTHEIM. FECHENBACH, HERMANN: *Die letzten Mergentheimer Juden und die Geschichte der Familien Fechenbach.* Mit Holzschnittillustrationen von Hermann Fechenbach. Bad Mergentheim: [Privately printed, 1997]. 216 pp., illus. [Reprint (orig. edn. not previously listed in the bibl.), publ. on the occasion of the author's 100th birthday; based on the author's personal reminiscences; incl. list of Nazi victims.] [H.F., Jan. 11, 1897 in Bad Mergentheim, later has been living in the UK.]

41008. MINDEN. LINNEMEIER, BERND-WILHELM: *Jüdisches Leben im Alten Reich. Stadt und Fürstentum Minden in der Frühen Neuzeit.* Bielefeld: Verlag für Regionalgeschichte, 2002. 831 pp., footnotes, bibl. (769–786), indexes (persons; places, 787–831). Studien zur Regionalgeschichte, Bd. 15.) [From the late 16th to the beginning of the 19th cent.]

—— MÖNCHENGLADBACH. BENARI, ASHER: *Erinnerungen eines Pioniers aus Deutschland.* [See No. 41737.]

41009. MOSELLE. BAUER, UWE F.W./BÜHLER, MARIANNE: *Steine über dem Fluss. Jüdische Friedhöfe an der Mosel.* Trier: Paulinus, 2002. 96 pp., illus., index. [Incl. 24 cemeteries.]

41010. MÜHLHEIM am MAIN. NEUMEISTER-JUNG, JÖRG: *Der jüdische Friedhof in Mühlheim am Main. Die Schicksale der Mühlheimer Juden.* [Hrsg. vom Geschichtsverein Mühlheim am Main e.V.]. Mühheim am Main: Geschichtsverein, 2002. 88 pp., illus. (Zur Geschichte der Stadt Mühlheim; Kleine Reihe, Nr. 6.)

41011. MÜNSTER. FREUND, SUSANNE: *Alexander Haindorf. Grenzgänge zwischen jüdischer und christlicher Kultur.* [In]: Grenzgänge. Festschrift für Diethard Aschoff [see No. 41473]. Pp. 174–194, footnotes.

—— MUNICH. LANDAU, PETER/NIEHLSEN, HERMANN, eds.: *Große jüdische Gelehrte an der Münchener Juiristischen Fakultät.* [See No. 41784.]

41012. NASSAU/LAHN. BECKER-HAMMERSTEIN, WALTRAUD/BECKER, WERNER: *Julius Israel Nassau. Juden in einer ländlichen Kleinstadt im 19. und 20. Jahrhundert.* Bad Honnef: Verlag K.H. Bock, 2002. 304 pp., illus., facsims., bibl. (293–300). [Traces the life of several families, among them many involved in cattle trade; also on their specific dialect with numerous elements of Judaeo-German/Western Yiddish; incl. chaps. on antisemitism and the Nazi period.]

41013. NIDDA. STINGL, WOLFGANG GILBERT: *Jüdisches Leben in Nidda im 19. und 20. Jahrhundert. Untersuchung zur Lokalgeschichte des oberhessischen Landjudentums.* Obertshausen: Context-Verl., 2001. 384 pp., illus., facsims., tabs, notes, bibl., index.

41014. NORDRACH/BADEN. SCHELLINGER, UWE: *Adelheid de Rothschild (1853–1935) und die Gründung der 'M.A. von Rothschild'schen Lungenheilanstalt' in Nordrach.* [In]: Die Ortenau, Jg. 82, Offenburg/Baden, 2002. Pp. 519–528, notes, ports.

41015. NUREMBERG. HAEUSLER, JOCHEN: *Der Hopfenhändler Berthold Bing – ein Förderer Rudolf Diesels.* [In]: Mitteilungen des Vereins für Geschichte der Stadt Nürnberg, Bd. 88, Nürnberg, 2001. Pp. 219–232, illus., footnotes.

41016. NUREMBERG. RUSAM, HERMANN: *Die Geschichte der jüdischen Gemeinde Nürnbergs ab 1850.* Hersbruck: Pfeiffer, 1998. 64 pp., illus. (Schriftenreihe der Altnürnberger Landschaft, Bd. 45.)

41017. OBERWESEL. WOLF, DANIELA: *Ritualmordaffäre und Kultgenese. Der "Gute Werner von Oberwesel".* Bacharach: Bauverein Wernerkapelle Bacharach e.V., [2002?]. 32 pp., illus., footnotes.

41018. OFFENBURG. SCHELLINGER, UWE: *Faszinosum, Filou und Forschungsobjekt: Das erstaunliche Leben des Hellsehers Ludwig Kahn (1873 – ca. 1966).* [In]: Die Ortenau, Jg. 82, Offenburg/Baden, 2002. Pp. 429–468, notes, facsims., ports.

41019. OFFENBURG. STEIN, PETER: *Ein Schiddusch – Eine jüdische Ehevermittlung in Offenburg 1878.* [In]: Die Ortenau, Bd. 82, Offenburg, 2002. Pp. 469–486, facims., illus. [On the Stein family from Diersburg and Reichenberger family from Ichenhausen.]

41020. OLDENBURG. *Quellen zur Geschichte und Kultur des Judentums im westlichen Niedersachsen vom 16. Jahrhundert bis 1945: ein sachthematisches Inventar.* Teil 2: Oldenburg. Unter Leitung von Albrecht Eckhardt [et al.]. Bearb. von Heike Düselder und Hans-Peter Klausch. Göttingen: Vandenhoeck und Ruprecht, 2002. XXX, 471 pp. (Veröffentlichungen der Niedersächsischen Archivverwaltung, Bd. 55.) [See also Nos. 40954, 41002, 41021.]

41021. OSNABRÜCK. *Quellen zur Geschichte und Kultur des Judentums im westlichen Niedersachsen vom 16. Jahrhundert bis 1945.* Ein sachthematisches Inventar. Teil 3: Osnabrück. Unter Leitung von Albrecht Eckhardt, Jan Lokers und Matthias Nistal. Bearb. von Heike Düselder und Hans-Peter Klausch. Göttingen: Vandenhoeck & Ruprecht, 2001. XXXII, 497 pp. (Veröffentlichungen der Niedersächsischen Archivverwaltung, Bd. 55.) [See also Nos. 40954, 41002, 41020.]

41022. PADERBORN. PESCH, ALEXANDRA: *Die Ausgrabung auf dem Gelände der ehemaligen Synagoge an der warmen Pader und die eisenzeitlichen Siedlungsspuren des Stadtgebietes von Paderborn.* [In]: Westfalen, Hefte für Geschichte, Bd. 78, Münster, 2000 [publ. 2002]. Pp. 46–61, footnotes, illus.

41023. PALATINATE. KUKATZKI, BERNHARD/JACOBY, MARIO: *Die jüdischen Friedhöfe in Heuchelheim bei Frankenthal.* Begräbnisstätte für Beindersheim, Dirmstein, Frankenthal, Gerolsheim, Großkarlbach, Heßheim, Heuchelheim, Laumersheim, Obersülzen und Weisenheim am Sand. Schifferstadt: [Privately printed], 2002. 50 pp., illus, footnotes, facsims., index.

41024. PETERSHAGEN/WESTPHALIA. LINNEMEIER, BERND-WILHELM: *Die jüdische Gemeinde Petershagen und ihre Synagogen – Historischer Überblick auf der Grundlage archivalischer Quellen.* [In]: Westfalen, Hefte für Geschichte, Bd. 78, Münster, 2000 [publ. 2002]. Pp. 286–292, footnotes.

41025. PETERSHAGEN/WESTPHALIA. MÜNZ, BIRGIT: *Die Synagoge in Petershagen. Die archäologische Untersuchung der ehemaligen Synagoge einer jüdischen Landgemeinde.* [In]: Westfalen, Hefte für Geschichte, Bd. 78, Münster, 2000 [publ. 2002]. Pp. 293–312, footnotes, illus. [On the remains of a half-timbered synagogue built ca. 1800, in 1845/1846 replaced by a brick one on the same site, at present being transformed into a documentation centre of local and regional Jewish history.]

41026. POSEN. ÖSTREICH, CORNELIA: *Berlin und Hamburg: Mobilitätsalternativen für Posener Juden um die Mitte des 19. Jahrhunderts?* [In]: Zeitenwenden [see No. 40902]. Pp. 181–204.

——— PRUSSIA. WALLENBORN, HILTRUD: *Die Ansiedlung von Juden im Brandenburg-Preußen (1671) im Kontext europäischer Tolerierungsdebatten des 17. Jahrhunderts.* [See No. 40899.]

41027. RATHENOW. KOHNKE, META: *Geschichte der jüdischen Gemeinde in Rathenow bis zum Erlaß des Emanzipationsedikts von 1812.* [In]: Jahrbuch für Brandenburgische Landesgeschichte, Bd. 52, Berlin, 2001. Pp. 81–110, footnotes.

——— RECKLINGHAUSEN. BURNETT, STEPHEN G.: *Christian Gerson of Recklinghausen and Johannes Buxtorf of Kamen: two Christian interpreters of Judaism in the Reformation Era.* [See No. 42110.]

41028. REGENSBURG. CREASMAN, ALLYSON F.: *The Virgin Mary against the Jews: Anti-Jewish polemic in the pilgrimage to the Schöne Maria of Regensburg, 1519–25.* [In]: The Sixteenth Century Journal, Vol. XXXII, No. 4, winter 2002, Kirksville, MS, 2002. Pp. 963–980, footnotes.

41029. REGENSBURG. *Das mittelalterliche Judenviertel.* Eine multimediale Präsentation von europäischem Rang. Ein Projekt der Stadt Regensburg. Projektplanung und -konzeption: Silvia Codreanu-Windauer [et al.]. Regensburg: Stadt Regensburg, 2002 [?]. 1 CD-ROM + booklet.

41030. REMSCHEID. FLEERMANN, BASTIAN: *Von Remscheid nach Kapstadt. Ernst Adolf Landsberg (1903–1976) und sein Weg in die Emigration.* [In]: Ratinger Forum. Beiträge zur Stadt- und Regionalgeschichte, H. 7, Ratingen, 2001. Pp. 283–325, illus., footnotes. [Article is introd. by: Der Nachlaß Landsberg im Stadtarchiv Ratingen (Erika Münster-Schröer, 277–281). Deals with the partly Jewish Landsberg family in general and the life of E.A.L., in particular. E.A.L., 1903 Remscheid-Lennep – 1976 Cape Town, journalist, emigr. 1933 with his Jewish wife to South Africa.]

41031. RHINELAND. ROOS, LENA: *The stranger who lives next door: Jewish-Christian relations in Germany during the High Middle Ages.* Uppsala: Distrib. by Swedish Science Press, 2001. 51 pp., bibl. (47–51). (Studies on inter-religious relations, No.3.) [Deals with the Rhine valley region.]

41032. RHINELAND. ZIWES, FRANZ-JOSEF: *Jüdische Niederlassungen im Mittelalter.* Köln: Rheinland-Verlag, 2002. 37 pp., footnotes, bibl., maps. (Publikationen der Gesellschaft für Rheinische Geschichtskunde, XII. Abteilung 1b Neue Folge, 8. Lieferung: Geschichtlicher Atlas der Rheinlande, Beiheft VIII, 7.) [Incl. a historical essay; alphabetical list of Jewish medieval settlements; six maps.]

41033. ROTH. *Landsynagoge Roth.* [Weimar-Roth: Arbeitskreis Landsynagoge Roth e.V., 2002]. 9 pp. [unpag.], illus. [Roth: a village nr. Marburg/Lahn. Incl. texts on the history of the Jews in Roth, the synagogue and its reconstruction from 1993 – 1998 by Annegret Wenz-Haubfleisch.]

41034. SACHSEN-ANHALT. KNUFINKE, ULRICH: *Jüdische Friedhofsbauten in Sachsen-Anhalt – ein Überblick.* [In]: Judentum: Wege zur geistigen Befreiung [see No. 40865]. Pp. 79–101, illus., notes.

41035. SALZUFLEN. EICHMANN, HERBERT: *Aus dem Leben einer jüdischen Familie im Wilhelminischen Deutschland.* Erzählt von einem Nachfahren. [In]: Bad Salzuflen 2001, Jahrbuch für Geschichte und Zeitgeschehen, Bielefeld, 2001. Pp. 65–72, illus., notes. [Author tells about his father Willy Eichmann and other Jewish family members orig. from Schötmar.]

41036. SALZUFLEN. POHLMANN, KLAUS: *Synagoge und jüdische Gemeinde in Salzuflen zu Anfang des 17. Jahrhunderts.* [In]: Bad Salzuflen 2001, Jahrbuch für Geschichte und Zeitgeschehen, Bielefeld, 2001. Pp. 11–31, illus., notes.

41037. SAXONY. HÖPPNER, SOLVEJG: *Jewish immigration to Saxony, 1834–1933.* An overview. [In]: Jahrbuch des Simon-Dubnow-Instituts, Jg. 1, Stuttgart, 2002. Pp. 135–152, footnotes.

41038. SCHLESWIG-HOLSTEIN. PAUL, GERHARD/GOLDBERG, BETTINA: *Matrosenanzug – Davidstern. Bilder jüdischen Lebens aus der Provinz.* Neumünster: Wachholtz, 2002. 373 pp., illus., facsims., bibl., index. (Quellen und Studien zur Geschichte der jüdischen Bevölkerung Schleswig-Holsteins.) [Incl. numerous documents and photographs selected from family collections, arranged in eight chaps. ranging from 1871 until the present, introd. with historical essays. Residences incl. Flensburg, Friedrichstadt, Lübeck, Rendsburg, Itzehoe, Kiel.]

41039. SCHWÄBISCH HALL. *Spurensuche. Jüdische Geschichte und Nationalsozialismus im Kreis Schwäbisch Hall.* [Hrsg.: Arbeitsgemeinschaft der Gedenkstätten et al.; Texte: Folker Förtsch et. al.] [Schwäbisch Hall: Kreisarchiv, 2001], 39 pp., illus. [A guide to archives, museums, memorial places.]

———— SEESEN. BERG, MEIKE: *Jüdische Reformschule im Herzogtum Braunschweig – Die Jacobson-Schule in Seesen von der Spätaufklärung bis zur Reichsgründung.* [See in No. 40839.]

41040. SILESIA. HERZIG, ARNO: *Konfession und Heilsgewissheit. Schlesien und die Grafschaft Glatz in der Frühen Neuzeit.* Bielefeld: Verlag für Regionalgeschichte, 2002. 192 pp., illus., footnotes, bibl., index. (Religion in der Geschichte, Bd. 9.) [Chap. 6 is entitled: Außerhalb der Konfessionen: Die Juden (137–162; on Glatz and Breslau).]

41041. SIMMERN/HUNSRÜCK. WESNER, DORIS: *Die Jüdische Gemeinde in Simmern/Hunsrück.* Familiengeschichte(n) und Schicksale aus den vergangenen drei Jahrhunderten. 55469 Simmern: D. Wesner, Riesweilerhohl 1 [privately printed], 2001. 335 pp., illus., facsims., footnotes, chronol., gloss., indexes (309–325; places, countries; names), bibl. (326–329). (Schriftenreihe des

Hunsrücker Geschichtsvereins e.V., Nr. 36.) [Incl. alphabetically arranged biographies (37–260); sections on the synagogue, school, cemetery.]

41042. SODEN (BAD). KRAUSKOPF, GUNTHER: *Giacomo Meyerbeer 1843 in Soden.* [In]: Zwischen Main und Taunus. Jahrbuch des Main-Taunus-Kreises, Jg. 10. 2002, Hofheim/Ts., 2001. Pp. 35–40, ports., notes.

41043. SOEST. *Jüdische Nachbarn in Soest bis 1942.* Ein Stadtrundgang. Zusammengestellt im Auftrag des Vereins für Geschichte und Heimatpflege Soest von Ulrike Sasse-Voswinckel und Gerhard Köhn. Soest: Stadtarchiv, 2001. 64 pp., illus., plan.

41044. SOMBORN/HESSE. SCHILLING, RUDOLF: *Die jüdische Gemeinde Somborn im Freigericht.* [Hrsg.: Gemeinde Freigericht und Heimat- und Geschichtsverein Freigericht]. Freigericht: Verl. Frohberg, 2002. 72 pp., illus., facsims. [Somborn: nr. Hanau/Hesse.]

41045. SONSBECK. PETERS, DIETER: *Der jüdische Friedhof in Sonsbeck.* Aachen: Selbstverlag Dieter Peters, 2002. 31 pp., illus., notes. (Jüdische Friedhöfe am Niederrhein, Bd. 4.)

41046. STUTTGART. RALLE, PETRA: *Konsequenz Abriss. Der (un)vermeidbare Ende des Kaufhauses Schocken von Erich Mendelsohn in Stuttgart.* Stuttgart: Archiv der Stadt Stuttgart, 2002. 194 pp., illus., facsims., notes, bibl. (Veröff. des Archivs der Stadt Stuttgart, Bd. 90.) [On the Schocken department store constructed in 1927/1928.]

41047. STUTTGART. SAUER, PAUL/HOSSEINZADEH, SONJA: *Jüdisches Leben im Wandel der Zeit. 170 Jahre Israelitische Religionsgemeinschaft – 50 Jahre neue Synagoge in Stuttgart.* Hrsg. von der Israelitischen Religionsgemeinschaft Württembergs, Körperschaft des öffentlichen Rechts. Gerlingen: Bleicher, 2002. 326 pp., illus., notes (297–320), bibl. (321–323). [Cont.: Grußworte (Erwin Teufel, Wolfgang Schuster, 9–12). Vorwort (Barbara Traub, 13–19). Die Jüdische Gemeinde Stuttgart von ihrer Gründung im Jahr 1832 bis zu ihrer Vernichtung durch das NS-Regime (Paul Sauer, 23–152). "Wir, ein lebendiger Zweig am grünenden Baum unseres Volkes …" (Alfred Marx, 1949): Die jüdische Gemeinde in Württemberg seit 1945. Trotz allem geblieben: Lebensaufgabe, Herausforderung und Perspektiven (Sonja Hosseinzadeh, 155–280). Meine Jahre in Stuttgart. Einsichten – Aussichten (Joel Berger, 281–294).]

41048. THURINGIA. LITT, STEFAN: *Conversions to Christianity and Jewish family life in Thuringia: Case Studies in the sixteenth and seventeenth centuries.* [In]: Leo Baeck Institute Year Book 2002, Vol. XLVII, Oxford, 2002. Pp. 83–90, footnotes.

41049. THURINGIA. LÖWENBRÜCK, ANNA-RUTH: *Die Emanzipation der Juden in Thüringen im 19. Jahrhundert.* [In]: Judentum: Wege zur geistigen Befreiung [see No. 40865]. Pp. 139–157, notes.

——— TRIER. [See in Nos. 40856, 40857.]

——— TRIER. GUMPRICH, BERTHA: *Vollständiges Praktisches Kochbuch für die jüdische Küche.* [See No. 41713.]

41050. TRIER. KANN, HANS-JOACHIM: *Neue Überlegungen zur Trierer Menorah-Öllampe.* [In]: Landeskundliche Vierteljahrsblätter, Jg. 48, H. 4, Trier, 2002. Pp. 177–181, illus., notes.

41051. TRIER. MONZ, HEINZ: *Bertha Gumprich, die Trierer jüdische Köchin, vor 170 Jahren geboren.* Zur Vorstellung eines Trierer jüdischen Kochbuchs. [In]: Neues Trierisches Jahrbuch, Trier, 2002. pp. 133–136. [See also No. 41713.]

41052. ÜBERLINGEN. BURGER, OSWALD/STRAUB, HANSJÖRG: *Die Levingers. Eine Familie in Überlingen.* Eggingen: Edition Isele, 2002. 197 pp., illus., facsims., bibl.

41053. ÜBERLINGEN. NEBE, G. WILHELM: *Die Überlinger jüdischen Grabinschriften.* Ad Monumenta Judaica Medinat Bodase. Heidelberg: Winter, 2002. 84 pp., illus., bibl. (Schriften der Hochschule für Jüdische Studien Heidelberg, Bd. 3.) [Documents 15 fragments of gravestones dating back to 1275–1332 and 1349, which have survived as building material.]

41054. VIERSEN/RHINELAND. NUSSBAUM, ISRAEL: *"Gut Schabbes!". Jüdisches Leben auf dem Lande.* Aufzeichnungen eines Lehrers (1869–1942). Mit einem Geleitwort von Gerry Nussbaum. Hrsg. und mit einem Nachwort versehen von Michael Philipp. Berlin: Jüdische Verlagsanstalt, 2002. 294 pp., illus. [Memoirs, written between 1932 and 1937, by I.N., teacher and "Hilfsvorbeter" in Jewish schools in Padberg and Oelde, and, from 1897 until his retirement in 1932, in Viersen, from where he was deported to Theresienstadt in 1942.]

41055. WARENDORF. ESTER, MATTHIAS M.: *Von der "deutsch-jüdischen Verständigung" zur "christlich-jüdischen Aussöhnung" in Warendorf. Die Verleihung des Bundesverdienstkreuzes an Hugo Spiegel (1970) und des Ehrenbürgerrechts an Paul Spiegel (2001).* [In]: Hans-Joachim Behr/Johann Zilien, eds.: Geschichte in Westfalen – Bewahren, Erforschen, Vermitteln. Festschrift für Paul Leidinger zum 70. Geburtstag. Warendorf: Kreisgeschichtsverein Beckum-Warendorf, e.V., 2002. (Quellen und Forschungen zur Geschichte des Kreises Warendorf, Bd. 40.) Pp. 281–320, illus., facsims., footnotes.

41056. WENDELSHEIM. HOLZER, MILENA: *Zur Geschichte der Juden in Wendelsheim.* [In]: Alzeyer Geschichtsblätter, H. 33, Alzey, 2002. Pp. 93–118, illus., plans, geneal., footnotes. [Slightly abridged version of the author's history essay written as "Facharbeit" at the Gymnasium am Römerkastell, Alzey 1998. Incl. the cemetery, Nazi period.]

41057. WESTPHALIA. BECKMANN, VOLKER: *Die jüdische Bevölkerung der Landkreise Lübbecke und Halle i.W. Vom Vormärz bis zur Befreiung vom Faschismus (1815–1945).* Lage: Verlag Hans Jacobs, 2001. 495 pp., footnotes, tabs., maps, bibl. (570–495). Zugl.: Bielefeld, Univ., Diss., 2001.

41058. WESTPHALIA. LINNEMEIER, BERND-WILHELM: *Innerjüdische Alltagskonflikte der Frühen Neuzeit im Spiegel der obrigkeitlichen Überlieferung Ostwestfalens.* [In]: Grenzgänge. Festschrift für Diethard Aschoff [see No. 41473]. Pp. 143–160, footnotes.

41059. WESTPHALIA. PRACHT-JÖRNS, ELFI: *Jüdisches Kulturerbe in Nordrhein-Westfalen.* Teil IV: *Regierungsbezirk Münster.* Köln: Bachem, 2002. 582; 6 pp., illus., facsims., footnotes, bibl., gloss., maps, index. (Beiträge zu den Bau- und Kunstdenkmälern von Westfalen, Bd. 1.2.)

41060. WOLFENBÜTTEL. DERDA, HANS-JÜRGEN: *Zwischen Aufklärung und Anpassung: Die Samsonschule in Wolfenbüttel.* [In]: Judentum zwischen Tradition und Moderne, [see No. 41727]. Pp. 187–196.

41061. WORMS. BÖNNEN, GEROLD: *Der Durchzug französischer Kreuzfahrer durch Worms im Sommer 1147.* [In]: Der Wormsgau, Bd. 21, Worms, 2002. Pp. 177–184, footnotes. [Refers also to rioting against the Jews.]

41062. WORMS. HOPPE, JENS: *Das Jüdische Museum in Worms.* Seine Geschichte bis 1938 und die anschließenden Bemühungen um die Wiedererrichtung der Wormser Synagoge. [In]: Der Wormsgau, Bd. 21, Worms, 2002. Pp. 81–101, illus., footnotes.

41063. WORMS. *Medinat Worms.* Themenheft. [Issue title of] Aschkenas, Jg. 12, H. 1/2. Hrsg. von Annette Weber. Wien, 2002. 164 + 96 [illus., unpag.] pp., footnotes. [Incl.: Vorwort. Jüdische Geschichte und Kultur in der Medinat Worms (Annette Weber, 9–12). Vom Erwachen des historischen Interesses am jüdischen Worms bis zum Museum des Isidor Kiefer (Fritz Reuter, 13–44). "Hier atmet noch die gute alte Zeit". Das Heimatmuseum der israelitischen Gemeinde Worms (katharine Rauschenberger, 45–51). Der Hort der Mythe – das Museum der israelitischen Gemeinde in der Alten Synagoge zu Worms 1924–1938 (Annette Weber, 53–66). Katalog der Kultgegenstände aus dem Museum der israelitischen Gemeinde Worms anhand der Angaben und Fotos von Isidor Kiefer (Annette Weber, 67–89). "Es ist mein Lebenszweck". Isidor Kiefer und sein Anteil am Wiederaufbau der Wormser Synagoge 1957–1961 (Gerold Bönnen, 91–113). Further essay are listed according to subject/places.]

41064. WÜRTTEMBERG. *Jüdische Gotteshäuser und Friedhöfe in Württemberg.* Stuttgart 1932. Hrsg. vom Oberrat der Israelitischen Religionsgemeinschaft Württembergs. Frankfurt am Main: J. Kauffmann, 1932. 143 pp., illus., map, index. [Reprint edn. publ. 2002 by Verlag Medien und Dialog, Haigerloch. Texts by "Stadtrabbiner Dr. Rieger".]

41065. WÜRZBURG. DETTELBACHER, WERNER: *Dr. Klara Oppenheimer – die erste niedergelassene Kinderärztin Würzburgs.* [In]: Würzburger medizinhistorische Mitteilungen, Bd. 21, Würzburg, 2001. Pp. 43–48, footnotes, bibl. [Incl. Engl. summary.] [K.O., 1869 Paris – 1943 Theresienstadt, lived from 1875 in Würzburg, in 1918 opened a pediatric practice which she was forced to close in 1934.]

41066. WÜRZBURG. GRÜN, KARL: *Die Judensteine aus der Würzburger Pleich.* [In]: Freiburger Rundbrief, N.F., Jg. 9, H. 4, Freiburg, 2002. Pp. 312–314, footnotes. [On the remains of a medieval cemetery from the 13th and 14th cent., consisting of 1504 gravestones and fragments, found in the rubble in 1987 after the pulling-down of an old house in Würzburg-Pleich.]

41067. WÜRZBURG. LEIMKUGEL, FRANK: *Die Würzburger Apotheker-Dynastie Landauer/Friede.* Zum 150. Geburtstag von Robert Landauer, Gründer der Kneipp-Werke. [In]: Geschichte der Pharmazie, Jg. 51, Stuttgart, 1999.Pp. 51–52, illus. [Also, by the same author, on the Landauer family: Die Würzburger Apotheker-Dynastie Landauer/Friede. Zum 100. Geburtstag von Dr. Heinrich und Margarete Friede [in]: Geschichte der Pharmazie, Jg. 54, Stuttgart, 2002. Pp. 26–27.]

——— ZWEIBRÜCKEN. BLINN, DIETER: *"Man will ja nichts als Ihnen zu dienen, und das bisgen Ehre – Die Hofjuden Herz und Saul Wahl im Fürstentum Pfalz-Zweibrücken.* [See in No. 40880.]

1a. Alsace

——— FAUSTINI, PASCAL: *Un procès opposant deux familles juives de 1563 à 1581, ou comment les Grotwohl s'installèrent à Metz en 1567.* [See No. 41706.]

——— KAUFMANN, URI R.: *Hebräische Begriffe in der Umgangssprache der südwestdeutschen und elsässischen Juden im 19. und 20. Jahrhundert.* [See in No. 40841.]

41068. MISKIMIN, PATRICIA BEHRE: *One king, one law, three faiths: religion and the rise of absolutism in seventeenth-century Metz.* Westport, CT: Greenwood Press, 2001. XXIV, 153 pp., map, footnotes, bibl. (139–148), index. [Incl. the Jewish community in Metz and its relationship with both Christian churches. Also chap.: Ritual murder as solace: the case of Raphael Levy.]

41069. SCHMANDT, MATTHIAS: *Straßburg und Köln. Jüdische Beziehungen im Mittelalter.* [In]: Geschichte in Köln. Zeitschrift für Stadt- und Regionalgeschichte, Jg. 49, Köln, 2002. Pp. 27–45, footnotes.

2. Austria

41071. FRIESEL, EVYATAR: *The 'Oesterreichisches Central-Organ', Vienna 1848: A radical Jewish periodical.* [Incl.: In the name of the persecuted Jews in Bohemia, to their persecuted brethren in Hungary (Simon Hock, 146–169; translation of an article publ. in 1948).] [In]: Leo Baeck Institute Year Book 2002, Vol. XLVII, Oxford, 2002. Pp. 117–169, footnotes.

41072. INNSBRUCK. SCHREIBER, HORST, ed.: *Jüdische Geschäfte in Innsbruck.* Eine Spurensuche. Ein Projekt des Abendgymnasiums Innsbruck. Innsbruck: Studienverlag, 2001. 116 pp., illus. (Tiroler Studien zur Geschichte und Politik, Bd. 1.)

41073. *Jüdische Identitäten in Mitteleuropa. Literarische Modelle der Identitätskonstruktion.* Hrsg. von Armin A. Wallas unter Mitwirkung von Primus-Heinz Kucher, Edgar Sallager u. Johann Strutz. Tübingen: Niemeyer, 2002. VI, 325 pp. [Selected essays: Jüdische Identität(en) in Mitteleuropa – Literarische Modelle der Identitätskonstruktion (Armin A. Wallas, 1–16). Tradition, Emanzipation und Erinnerung. Reflexionsebenen von "Ghettogeschichten" in der österreichischen Literatur (Primus-Heinz Kucher, 17–34). "Galizianer" in Wien. Zur Darstellung "östlicher Juden" im jiddischen Theater und Film (Brigitte Dalinger, 35–46). Ludwig Strauß und Ernst Sommer als Vertreter der Jüdischen Renaissance. Ein Beitrag zur Buber-Rezeption (Andreas Herzog, 47–60). Kulturzionismus,

Expressionismus und jüdische Identität. Die Zeitschrift 'Jerubbaal' (1918/19) und 'Esra' (1919/20) als Sprachrohr und Diskussionsforum der zionistischen Jugendbewegung in Österreich (Armin A. Wallas, 61–100). Jüdische Autobiographien und ihre Subtexte. Am Beispiel von Stefan Zweig und Albert Ehrenstein (Hanni Mittelmann, 101–110). Mähren – ein Sonderweg der deutschgeschriebenen jüdischen Literatur? (Ingeborg Fiala-Fürst, 119–126). Jüdische Identität bei Karl Emil Franzos. Glossen zu einem Manuskript aus dem Jahre 1868 (Andrei Corbea-Hoisie, 159–170). Jüdische Identitätssuche im Werk von Alfred Gong (Peter Rychlo, 171–186). "Messianische Zuversicht". Aspekte jüdischen Geschichtsdenkens im Werk von Manès Sperber (Hans Otto Horch, 187–214). Implizites Judentum und Psychoanalyse bei Italo Svevo (Edgar Sallager, 283–300). Other essays are related to Czech, Hungarian, Croatian, Serbian and Italian authors.]

41074. LAPPIN, ELEONORE, ed.: *Jüdische Gemeinden. Kontinuitäten und Brüche.* Berlin: Philo, 2002. 367 pp., notes. [Papers presented at the 11th Int. Sommerakademie St. Pölten organised by the Inst. für Geschichte der Juden in Österreich, July 2001. Incl.: 150 Jahre Wiener Kultusgemeinde (Ariel Muzikant, 11–14). Vorwort (ed., 15–21). I. Das Erbe der Habsburger Monarchie (23–104; with essays on Trieste, Czernowitz, Pressburg/Bratislava, Hungary by Lois C. Dubin, Mykola Kuschnir, Juraij Sedivy, Géza Komoróczy). II. Israelitische Kultusgemeinden in Österreich; cont.: From Habsburg Jews to Austrian Jews: The Jews of Vienna, 1918–1938 (Marsha L. Rozenblit, 105–130). Die Wiener jüdische Gemeinde (Evelyn Adunka, 131–138). Gebrochene Kontinuität – Die Kultusgemeinde Linz nach 1945 (Michael John, 139–178). Die jüdische Gemeinde in Salzburg seit 1867 – Ein Neubeginn nach 369 Jahren Verbannung (Helga Embacher/Albert Lichtblau, 179–198). Eine kleine Gemeinde zwischen Erinnerung und jüdischem Alltag: Die Israelitische Kultusgemeinde für Tirol und Vorarlberg in Innsbruck nach 1945 (Niko Hofinger, 199–210). Jüdische Steiermark – Steirisches Judentum (Dieter A. Binder, 211–244). III. Juden auf Wanderschaft (245–364); essays pertaining to German-speaking Jews are listed according to places.]

41075. RECHTER, DAVID: *Ethnicity and the politics of welfare. The case of Habsburg Austrian Jewry.* [In]: Jahrbuch des Simon-Dubnow-Instituts, Jg. 1, Stuttgart, 2002. Pp. 257–276, footnotes.

41076. SALZBURG. *Juden in Salzburg.* History – cultures [sic] – fates. Hrsg. von Helga Embacher. Mit beiträgen von Heinz Dopsch, Daniela Ellmauer, Helga Embacher, Felicitas Heimann-Jelinek, Albert Lichtblau, Vladimir Vertlib. Salzburg: Pustet, 2002. 124 pp., illus., facsims. [Catalogue for exhibition under the same title at the Museum Carolino Augusteum, July 2002 – Jan. 2003; covers the period from the middle ages to the present, incl. chaps. dealing with "aryanisation", Salzburg Jews in exile. All contribs. also in English.]

41077. SALZBURG. KRIECHBAUMER, ROBERT, ed.: *Der Geschmack der Vergänglichkeit. Jüdische Sommerfrische in Salzburg.* Wien: Böhlau, 2002. 364 pp., illus., footnotes, index. [Cont. (some titles abbr.): "Der Geschmack der Vergänglichkeit" (ed., 7–40). Der Traum vom Dazugehören – Juden auf Sommerfrische (Hanns Haas, 41–58). Judenfreundlichkeit, Judenfeindlichkeit. Spielarten in einem Fremdenverkehrsland (Günter Fellner, 59–126). Antisemitismus am Wallersee (Christian Strasser, 127–152). Arnold Schönberg ist in Mattsee unerwünscht (Harald Waitzbauer, 153–174). Bad Gastein: Die Rolle des Antisemitismus in einer Fremdenverkehrsgemeinde während der Zwischenkriegszeit (Laurenz Krisch, 175–226). Jüdische "Gäste" im Gasteinertal nach 1945 (Helga Embacher, 227–148). Salzburg, die Festspiele und das jüdische Publikum (Harald Waitzbauer, 249–258). Schloss Fuschl. Beutegut des NS-Aussenministers (Jutta Hangler, 259–280). Jüdische Sommerfrischler in St. Gilgen (Albert Lichtblau, 281–316). Dirndl, Lederhose und Sommerfrischenidylle (Ulrike Kammerhofer-Aggermann, 317–334). Jüdische Künstler bei den Salzburger Festspielen (Regina Thumser, 335–356).]

41078. STOURZH, GERALD: *Recognizing Yiddish – Max Diamant and the struggle for Jewish rights in Imperial Austria.* [In]: Jahrbuch des Simon-Dubnow-Instituts, Jg. 1, Stuttgart, 2002. Pp. 153–168, footnotes.

41079. TYROL. POLLACK, MARTIN: *Anklage Vatermord.* Der Fall Philipp Halsmann. Wien: Zsolnay, 2002. 324 pp., illus., bibl. [Documents a famous criminal case in the late 1920s in which Philipp Halsmann, a Jewish student from Riga was charged and finally sent to prison for the alleged murder of his father on a hike in the Tyrol Alps. After his reprieve in 1930 H. went to France, in 1940 fled to the US, where he was able to continue his career as a photographer.]

41080. VIENNA. ARNBOM, MARIE-THERES: *Friedmann, Gutmann, Lieben, Mandl und Strakosch. Fünf Familienporträts aus Wien vor 1938.* Wien: Böhlau. 2002. 248 pp., illus., bibl., geneal., index, notes. [On five families, originating from Jewish communities in Bohemia, Moravia and Hungary, some of whom were baptised.]

41081. VIENNA. BELLER, STEVEN, ed.: *Rethinking Vienna 1900.* Oxford, New York: Berghahn Books, 2001. XI, 292 pp., illus., notes, bibl. (271– 284), index. (Austrian History, Culture and Society, Vol. 3.) [Cont. ten essays, some of them dealing with the participation of Jews in the shaping of modern Viennese society around 1900.]

——— VIENNA. BURKHARDT, NATALIE: *Wiener Hofbankiers und ökonomische Modernisierung.* [See in No. 40880]

41082. VIENNA. HACKEN, RICHARD: *The Jewish community library in Vienna: From dispersion and destruction to partial restoration.* [In]: Leo Baeck Institute Year Book 2002, Vol. XLVII, Oxford, 2002. Pp. 151–172, footnotes, illus.

——— VIENNA. HERRBERG, HEIKE/WAGNER, HEIDI: *Wiener Melange. Frauen zwischen Salon und Kaffeehaus.* [See No. 41780.]

41083. VIENNA. *Sei stark und mutig! Jüdische Jugendbewegungen. Jüdisches Museum Wien.* [Begleitband zur Ausstellung]. Hrsg. im Auftrag des Jüdischen Museums Wien von Naomi Lassar. Wien: Jüdisches Museum, 2001. 176 pp., illus., facsims., gloss. [Incl.: Kampf der Jugend oder Kampf um die Jugend? Zur Geschichte der Jugendbewegung (Peter Melichar, 16–61). Die Ideologen der Jugendbewegungen. Siegfried Bernfeld, Zeev Jabotinsky und Ber Borochow (Johnny Bunz, 62–81). Die zionistische Jugendbewegung als Familienersatz? (Eleonore Lappin, 82–115). Jüdische Jugendbewegungen in der Zwischenkriegszeit und während des Zweiten Weltkriegs (Gabriele Anderl, 116–151). Erinnerungen an den Haschomer Hazair: jüdisch jugendbewegt in Wien (Michael Toch, 152–176).]

41084. VIENNA. STAUDACHER, ANNA L.: *Jüdische Konvertiten in Wien 1782–1868.* Teil 1 & Teil 2. Frankfurt am Main; New York: Lang, 2002. 2 vols., 460; 732 pp., footnotes, bibl., name index (447–460). [Part 1 cont. a socio-historical evaluation of all Viennese baptismal registers; incl. the sections: I. Einleitung, Quellen- & Methodenbeschreibung (13–56). II. Die Konversion (57–156). III. Die neue Identität (157–190). IV. Sozialstruktur (191–250). V. Taufpaten (251–282). Epilog: Die Rückkehr zum Judentum (283–290). Exkurs: Namensveränderungen (291–332). Also indexes (place of birth; profession). Part 2 cont. 'Selektive Edition' (15–559; selected edn. of the baptismal registers). Also chaps. on name changes, baptised Jewish foundlings and their mothers, indexes (profession; place of birth).]

41085. VIENNA. VERAN, TRAUDE: *Das steinerne Archiv. Der alte Judenfriedhof in der Rossau.* Wien: Mandelbaum, 2002. 221 pp., illus., bibl., gloss., index. [On the oldest Jewish cemetery of the Viennese Jews; incl. annotated list of gravestones.]

41086. WOLFSBERG. LAURITSCH, ANDREA: *Die Juden in Wolfsberg. Nationalsozialistische Judenverfolgung am Beispiel Wolfsbergs.* [Hrsg.: Stadtgemeinde Wolfsberg]. Wolfsberg: Kulturamt der Stadtgemeinde, 2002. 52 pp., illus., bibl. [Wolfsberg: in Carinthia.]

3. **Central Europe**

41087. BOHEMIA. KESTENBERG-GLADSTEIN, RUTH: *Heraus aus der "Gasse". Neuere Geschichte der Juden in den Böhmischen Ländern.* Zweiter Teil: 1830–1890. Hrsg. von Dorothea Kuhrau-Neumärker. Münster: Lit, 2002. IV, 162 pp., frontis., footnotes. (Geschichte, Bd. 31.) [Cont.: Vorwort der Herausgeberin: In memoriam Ruth Gladstein (1–5). Six essays, on Wolf Pascheles, Ludwig August Frankl, Selig Korn, Moritz Hartmann, Leopold Kompert, Siegfried Kapper, Leopold Weisel.] [R.K.-G., Oct. 25 1910 Berlin – Feb. 28, 2002 Haifa, daughter of Leo Kestenberg, Historian, emigr. to Prague in 1933, to Palestine in 1939.]

41088. BOHEMIA. KRESTAN, JIRÍ/BLODIGOVÁ, ALEXANDRA/BUBENÍK, JAROSLAV: *Židovské spolky v ceskych zemích v letech 1918–1948.* [In Czech, transl. of title: Jewish organisations in the Bohemian lands 1918–1948.] Praha: Sefer, 2001. 191 pp. (Kniznice Institutu Terezínské Inicativy, Bd. 2.) [Cf.: Bespr. (Helena Srubar) [in]: Bohemia, Bd. 43, H. 1, München, 2002, pp. 252–253.]

41089. BOHEMIA. MATUSIKOVÁ, LENKA: *Die Juden im ersten böhmischen Kataster 1653–1655.* [In]: Judaica Bohemiae, XXXVII, 2001, Praha, 2002. Pp. 5–91, footnotes.

41090. BOHEMIA. NEKULA, MAREK: *Die Juden in den böhmischen Ländern im 19. und 20. Jahrhundert und die Familie Kafka.* [In]: Brücken, Germanistisches Jahrbuch Tschechien-Slowakei 2000, Neue Folge 8, Lidové noviny: Nakladatelství, 2002. Pp. 89–128. [Also in this vol. contribs. on Franz Kafka (Marek Nekula, 129–142); Karl Kraus (Sigurd Paul Scheichl, 223–232.]

41091. BOHEMIA. OTTE, ANTON/KRÍZEK, PETR (HRSG.): *Židé v Sudetech – Juden im Sudetenland.* Prag; München: Ackermann-Gemeinde; Ceská krestanská akademie, 2001. 351 pp. [All contribs. in Czech and in German. Incl.: Tausend Jahre jüdische Geschichte in Böhmen und Mähren (Ferdinand Seibt). Von der antisemitischen Alldeutschen Bewegung Georg Ritter von Schönerers bis zum Genozid (Alena Mísková). Antisemitismus im katholischen Milieu des Sudetenlandes (1918–1938) (Alena Mísková). Die nationale Strömung in der deutschen Gesellschaft und ihre Beziehung zu den Juden (Stanislav Biman). Die deutschen Juden und ihre Wahl politischer Parteien (Fred Hahn). Sudetenjuden oder Juden im Sudetenland (Dieter Schallner). Die jüdischen Gemeinden im Sudetenland und ihre Schicksale nach dem Münchener Abkommen (Helena Krejcová). Einige Anmerkungen zur Position der Juden im Gau Sudetenland 1938–1945 (Ludomír Kocourek; on families from Bilin and Teplitz-Schönau). Die jüdische Gemeinde in Aussig/'Ustí nad Labem im 19. und 20. Jahrhundert (Vladimír Kaiser). Die Juden in Südböhmen in den Jahren 1918–1945 (Jirí Dvorák). Die Juden in Nordostböhmen – Aufstieg und Untergang (Rudolf M. Wlaschek). Die Jüdische Gemeinde im Teplitzer Raum in den Jahren 1850–1938 (Kvetoslava Kocourková). Schulalltag mit jüdischen Lehrern und Mitschülern (Johanna von Herzogenberg). Juden in der Tschechoslowakei (Peter Brod). [Cf.: Bespr.: (Jörg Osterloh) [in]: Bohemia, Bd. 43, H. 1, München, 2002, pp. 240–243.]

41092. BOHEMIA. WOODLE, ALEXANDER: *A journey of discovery.* [In]: Avotaynu, Vol. 18, No. 4, Bergenfield, NJ, 2002. Pp. 8–10, illus. [Author traces his roots back to his great-grandparents in 19th-century Bohemia to a village near Prague; travels there to make a film.]

41093. BOHEMIA & MORAVIA. PEKNY, TOMÁS: *Historie Žideu v Cechách a na Morave.* [In Czech; transl. of title: History of the Jews in Bohemia and Moravia]. 2nd edn. Praha: Sefer, 2001. 702 pp. [Cf.: Bespr. (Jirí Kosta) [in]: Bohemia, Bd. 43, H. 1, München, 2002, pp. 240–243. Also on Bohemian Jewish history and not listed previously: Jitka Chmeliková: The fate of the Jews of Eger. The Jews of Eger from the second half of the 19th century until the present. Cheb: Chebské muzeum, 2000. 148 pp., illus., footnotes, bibl. (in Czech, title transl.)]

41094. BOHEMIA & MORAVIA. SEIBT, FERDINAND: *Deutsche, Tschechen, Sudetendeutsche.* Analysen und Stellungnahmen zu Geschichte und Gegenwart aus fünf Jahrzehnten. Festschrift zu seinem 75. Geburtstag. Hrsg. von Robert Luft [et al.] München: Oldenbourg, 2002. 614 pp., frontis., footnotes. [Incl.: Tausend Jahre jüdische Geschichte in Böhmen und Mähren (49–62). Einige Gedanken über die Juden in Böhmen (63–72).]

41095. BUKOWINA. *An der Zeiten Ränder: Czernowitz und die Bukowina.* Geschichte, Literatur, Verfolgung, Exil. Hrsg. von Cecile Cordon und Helmut Kusdat. Wien: Theodor Kramer Gesellschaft, 2002. 396 pp., illus., ports., facsims., maps. [Collection of texts by various authors, some previously publ. 2000 in 'Zwischenwelt'.]

41096. HUNGARY. HOCHSTRASSER, GERHARDT: *Das Gebetbuch des Ungarischen israelitischen Landeslehrer-Vereins.* [In]: Donauschwäbische Forschungs- und Lehrerblätter, Jg. 47, H. 2, Folge 184, München, 2001. Pp. 25–28, facsims.

41097. HUNGARY. *Juden in Ungarn. Kultur – Geschichte – Gegenwart.* Ausstellung des Ungarischen Jüdischen Museums 23. September bis 31. Oktober 1999. [Red.: Eszter Götz [et al.]. Budapest: Ung. Jüd.

Museum Budapest [1999]. 157 pp., illus. [Incl. the sections: Kunst; Architektur; Photo; Film; Geschichte.]

—— *Jüdische Identitäten in Mitteleuropa. Literarische Modelle der Identitätskonstruktion.* [See No. 41073.]

41098. PRAGUE. GIMPL, GEORG: *Weil der Boden selbst hier brennt. Aus dem Prager Salon der Berta Fanta (1865–1918).* Furth im Wald; Prag: Vitalis, 2001, 432 pp., appendix. [Cf.: Bespr. (Ferdinand Seibt) [in]: Bohemia, Bd. 43, H. 1, 2002, pp. 277–278.]

41099. PRAGUE. GLETTLER, MONIKA/MISKOVÁ, ALENA: *Prager Professoren 1938 – 1948.* Zwischen Wissenschaft und Politik. Essen: Klartext, 2001. 682 pp., footnotes, indexes. (Veröffentlichungen zur Kultur und Geschichte im östlichen Europa, Bd. 17.) [Incl.: Tschechische, jüdische und deutsche Professoren in Prag. Möglichkeiten und Grenzen biographischer Zugänge (Monika Glettler, 13–26). Deutsche Professoren aus den böhmischen Ländern. "Flüchtlinge" in der Zeit vor und nach den Münchner Verhandlungen (Alena Misková, 27–44). Die Professoren der Masaryk-Universität Brünn 1938–1948 (Jiří Pulec/Jirina Kalendovská, 45–70). 30 contribs. on individual Professors, among them some German-speaking Jews.] [Cf.: Beispielhaftes deutsch-tschechisches Projekt: Professoren in Prag (Richard Szklorz) [in]: Das Parlament, Jg. 52, Nr. 33–34, Berlin, 19./26. Aug. 2002, p. 13.]

41100. PRAGUE. GREENBLATT, RACHEL L.: *The shapes of memory: Evidence in stone from the Old Jewish Cemetery in Prague.* [In]: Leo Baeck Institute Year Book 2002, Vol. XLVII, Oxford 2002. Pp. 43–67, footnotes, illus.

—— PRAGUE. HECHT, LOUISE: *Die Prager deutsch-jüdische Schulanstalt 1782–1848.* [See in No. 40839.]

41101. PRAGUE. SHERWIN, BYRON L.: *The legacy of Rabbi Judah Loew of Prague.* [In]: European Judaism, Vol. 34, No. 1, London, Spring 2001. Pp. 124–130.

4. **Switzerland**

—— BASLE. NOLTE, ACHIM: Jüdische Gemeinden in Baden und Basel. Eine rechtsvergleichende Studie über ihr Recht und ihre rechtliche Stellung. [See No. 40914.]

41104. BASLE. SIBOLD, NOEMI: *"… mit den Emigranten auf Gedeih und Verderb verbunden": die Flüchtlingshilfe der Israelitischen Gemeinde Basel in der Zeit des Nationalsozialismus.* München: Pendo, 2002. 161 pp., illus. [unpag.], facsims., notes (126–155), bibl. Zugl.: Basel, Univ., Lizentiatsarbeit, 1999. [Deals also with the Swiss refugee policy, the wave of Jewish refugees from the summer of 1938, the closing of the border in 1942, the subsequent internment of refugees and its effects on the Jewish refugees' aid of the Basle Jewish Community.] [Cf.: Eine Gemeinde und die Flüchtlinge (Esther Müller) [in]: tachles, Jg. 2, Zürich, 30. Aug. 2002, pp. 54–56, illus.]

41105. BLOCH, ROLF: *Die jüdische Gemeinschaft in der Schweiz und ihr Umfeld im Wandel der letzten Jahrzehnte.* [In]: Lesarten des jüdisch-christlichen Dialogs [see No. 42076]. Pp. 33–40, footnotes. [Also in this vol.: Die Hochhuth-Debatte in der katholischen Schweiz 1963 (Urs Altermatt, 19–32).]

—— *Deutschsprachige Schriftsteller im Schweizer Exil 1933–1950.* Eine Ausstellung des Deutschen Exilarchivs 1933–1945 der Deutschen Bibliothek. [See No. 41771.]

41106. FISCHLI, ISABELLA MARIA: *"Dreifuss ist unser Name". Eine Politikerin, eine Familie, ein Land.* Zürich: Pendo, 2002. 409 pp., illus., docs., bibl., index. [Incl.: Nachwort. Bilder einer Bundesrätin. Zur öffentlichen Wahrnehmung von Ruth Dreifuss. Ein Essay (Oswald Sigg, 371–386).] [R. Antoinette D., b. in St. Gallen Jan. 9, 1940, Swiss politician, trade union activist, Social Democrat, 1993 elected into the Federal Government, Federal President 1999 – Dec. 2002.]

—— *Gedächtnis, Geld und Gesetz. Vom Umgang mit der Vergangenheit des Zweiten Weltkrieges.* [See No. 41605.]

C. **German-Speaking Jews in Various Countries**

41107. AVNI, HAIM: *"Insular Jewish communal life": Russian Jews in Argentina and German Jews in Bolivia.* [In]: Eleonore Lappin, ed.: Jüdische Gemeinden – Kontinuitäten und Brüche [see No. 41074]. Pp. 245–266, notes.

41108. BERMAN, JUDITH E.: *Holocaust museums in Australia: the impact of Holocaust denial and the role of the survivors.* [In]: The Journal of Holocaust Education, Vol. 10, No. 1, London, Summer 2001. Pp. 67–88, notes. [On the establishment of Holocaust memorials and museums, mainly promoted by survivors with little help from the local Jewish communities. Also deals with the Holocaust museums in Melbourne, Perth and Sydney.]

41109. BLUM, HEIKO R.: *Meine zweite Heimat Hollywood.* Deutschsprachige Filmkünstler in den USA. Unter Mitarbeit von Sigrid Schmitt und Katharina Blum. Berlin: Henschel, 2001. 288 pp., illus., bibl., index. [Incl.: Pioniere, Emigranten und moderne Goldsucher (11–54). Lexikon der deutschsprachigen Filmkünstler (183–278).]

41110. BRINKMANN, TOBIAS: *Von der Gemeinde zur 'Community'. Jüdische Einwanderer in Chicago 1840–1900.* Osnabrück: Universitätsverlag Rasch, 2002. 488 pp., illus., footnotes, tabs., graphs, maps, bibl. (457–487). (Studien zur Historischen Migrationsforschung (SHM), Bd. 10.) [Also deals with immigrants from Germany; incl. chap.: Die 'German-Jewish community' (1880–1923) (383–454).]

41111. BRINKMANN, TOBIAS: *Separierung versus Integration: Ein Vergleich der Funktion jüdischer Wohltätigkeit in Deutschland und den USA im 19. Jahrhundert.* [In]: Comparativ, Jg. 2001, H. 5/6, Leipzig, 2002. Pp. 81–105, footnotes. [Deals mainly with the Chicago Jewish Community, composed of immigrants from Germany and Bohemia.]

41112. EXILE. BANKIER, DAVID: *Responses of exiled German Socialists in the USA and the UK to the Holocaust.* [In]: The Journal of Holocaust Education, Vol. 10, No. 1, London, Summer 2001. Pp. 1–20, notes. [Deals with the fact that German Social Democrats in exile were reluctant to face the issue of the Holocaust for fear of distracting public opinion from the Nazi persecution of the political opposition.]

41113. EXILE. *Changing countries: the experience and achievement of German-speaking exiles from Hitler in Britain, from 1933 to today.* Ed. by Marian Malet and Anthony Grenville. London: Libris, 2002. XX, 259 pp., gloss., notes, index. [Study, undertaken by the Oral History Project at the Research Centre for German and Austrian Exile Studies; based on 34 interviews with refugees from a wide range of backgrounds. Cont.: Brief biographies of the interviewees (XIII–XX). Introducing the refugees: family backgrounds before emigration (Anthony Grenville, 1–17). Culture, education, politics and the impact of historical developments before emigration (Anthony Grenville and Irene Wells, 18–44). Departure and arrival (Marian Malet, 45–89). Everyday life in prewar and wartime Britain (Stefan Howald, 90–126). Religion (Anthony Grenville, 161–183). Facing the facts: relations with the 'Heimat' (Charmian Brinson, 184–216). Postwar: the challenges of settling down (Marietta Bearman and Erna Woodgate, 217–246).]

41114. EXILE. *German-speaking exiles in Great Britian.* [Issue title of] The Yearbook of the Research Centre for German and Austrian Exile Studies. Vol. 3. Ed. by J.M. Ritchie. Amsterdam; New York: Rodopi, 2001. 196 pp., illus., notes, index. [Cont.: Preface (ed.). Autobiography in exile: the reflections of women refugees from Nazism in British exile, 1933–1945 (Charmian Brinson, 1– 22). 'Hetz- und Greuelpropaganda': Die Überwachung der Deutschen Exilschriftsteller in Großbritannien durch das Auswärtige Amt (Alexander Stephan, 23–40). Die Isle of Man-Lagerzeitungen 'The Camp' und 'The Onchan Pioneer': Kultur im Ausnahmezustand (Jörg Thunecke, 41–58). The Fight for Freedom Publishing Company: a case study of conflicting ideas in wartime (Isabelle Tombs (59–72). Pioniere mit Langzeitwirkung: Der Einfluß der fotografischen Emigration der NS-Zeit auf die englische Fotolandschaft und Bildpresse am Beispiel von Kurt Hutton, Felix H. Man, Wolf Suschitzky und weiteren Fotoschaffenden (Irme Schaber, 73–86). 'Psyche among friends': Michael Hamburger's BBC radio broadcasts (Axel Goodbody, 87– 104). 'Die Pein der Wissenden, aber zum Stummsein Verurteilten – im fremden Land': social and cultural integration of exiles in London: the case of Alfred Kerr (Deborah Vietor-Engländer, 105–120). Esther Simpson und die Aktivitäten der SPSL (Society for the Protection of Science and Learning) im Zusammenhang mit der Emigration deutschsprachiger Wissenschaftler zwischen 1933–1945 (Katharina Scherke, 121–130). Die Karrierechancen von österreichischen Sozial-, Politik- und Rechtswissenschaftlern in der englischen Emigration (Johannes Feichtinger, 131–148). Rückkehr in britischer Uniform respektive: Der Exilweg des Wiener Rechtsanwalts Friedrich Schnek (Elisabeth Lebensaft and Christoph Mentschl, 140–162). Zwischen zwei Kulturen: Ein Portrait der Grenzgängerin Magda Kelber (Beate Bussiek, 163–176). "Still on edge?" Marginality and centrality in exile autobiography: Silvia Rodger's 'Red Saint, Pink Daughter' (Andrea Hammel, 177–188).]

41115. EXILE. HARTMANN, REGINA: *Max Tau im norwegischen und schwedischen Exil*. [In]: Exil, Jg. 21, Nr. 2, 2001, Frankfurt am Main, 2002. Pp. 39–51.

——— EXILE. LANG, MARKUS: *Juristen unerwünscht? Karl Loewenstein und die (nicht-)Aufnahme deutscher Juristen in der amerikanischen Rechtswissenschaft nach 1933*. [See No. 41925.]

41116. FREIL, JOSEPH: *Holocaust testimonies: European survivors and American liberators in New Jersey*. Foreword by Elie Wiesel. New Brunswick, NJ: Rutgers Univ. Press, 2001. XVI, 339 pp., illus., ports., fac-sims., maps, appendixes, notes, index. [Incl. 16 survivors from Germany and Austria who live in New Jersey.]

41117. HEIM, SUSANNE: *Emigration and Jewish identity: 'an enormous heartbreak'*. [In]: The Journal of Holocaust Education, Vol. 10, No. 1, London, Summer 2001. Pp. 21–33, notes. [Article is based on memoirs and interviews with Jewish emigrants who left Germany after 1933; discusses the influence emigration had on their identity.]

41118. HEINEN, UTE: *Gertrude Langer – Kunsthistorikerin und Emigrantin in Australien*. [In]: Exil, Jg. 21, Nr. 2, 2001, Frankfurt am Main, 2002. Pp. 5–19. [G.L., 1908 Vienna – 1984 Binna Burra nr. Brisbane/Australia.]

——— HIRSCH, HELMUT: *Freund von Heine, Marx/Engels und Lincoln. Eine Karl Ludwig Bernays-Biographie*. [See No. 41822.]

41119. *In the land of the gauchos: the history of the Jewish German immigration*. Organized by Gladis Wiener Blumenthal. Transl. by Hedy Lorraine Hofmann. Porto Alegre: SIBRA, 2001. 261 pp., illus., fac-sims., geneal. tabs., gloss., appendixes, bibl., index, index of immigrants. [Incl. immigration in the 19th century, the 1930s, and post-1945.]

41120. KREUTER, MARIA-LUISE: *Exil in Ecuador*. [In]: Judenfeindschaft als Paradigma. Studien zur Vorurteilsforschung [see No. 42134]. Pp. 216–221, footnotes.

41121. KWIET, KONRAD: *The second time around: re-acculturation of German-Jewish refugees in Australia*. The Journal of Holocaust Education, Vol. 10, No. 1, London, Summer 2001. Pp. 34–49, notes. [Discusses the long and eventually successful process of integration of about 10,000 German-speaking refugees into Australian society which, however, brought in its wake the dissolution of a small German-Jewish exile community.]

41122. LEISEROWITZ, RUTH: *Die Illusion der transmigratorischen Existenz. Juden in Memel des 20. Jahrhundert*. [In]: Nordost Archiv. Zeitschrift für Regionalgeschichte [with the issue title]: Im Wandel der Zeiten: Die Stadt Memel im 20. Jahrhundert, Neue Folge Bd. X/2001, Lüneburg, 2002. Pp. 307–335, footnotes.

41123. *Pevsner on art and architecture: the radio talks*. Ed. and introd. by Stephen Games. London: Methuen, 2002. 400 pp., chronol., appendix, bibl. of radio talks, index. [Nikolaus P., 1902 Leipzig – 1983 London. For more data see No. 18956/YB XXVIII.] [Cf.: Pevsner a Nazi? Don't be so ridiculous (Tim Adams) [in]: The Observer, London, Dec. 8, 2002, p. 17; refers to the assertion made by Stephen Games that Pevsner was an admirer of Hitler.]

41124. PLESKOFF, ISABELLE: *Martin et Karl Flinker. De Vienne à Paris*. Paris: Musée d'Art et d'Histoire du Judaisme; Institut Mémoires de l'Édition Contemporaine (IMEC), 2001. 95 pp., illus. [Catalogue publ. for the exhibition with the same title at the Musée d'Art et d'Histoire du Judaisme, Paris, Jan. – May 2002.] [M.F., July 18, 1895 Czernowitz – June 21, 1986 Paris, jurist, book dealer, publisher, lived in Vienna, emigr. via Switzerland to Paris, in 1940 fled via Spain to Tangiers, returned to Paris in 1945, opened his legendary "Librairie Flinker" two years later; Karl F., son of K.F. (died 1991), from 1958 onwards owner of the "Galerie Flinker".] [Cf.: Gottsucher hinter dem Ladentisch. Mitten in der Literatur: Eine Pariser Ausstellung würdigt den Buchhändler Martin Flinker (Joseph Hanimann) [in]: 'FAZ', Nr. 23, Frankfurt am Main, 28. Jan. 2002, p. 48, illus.]

41125. PUCKHABER, ANNETTE: *Ein Privileg für wenige. Die deutschsprachige Migration nach Kanada im Schatten des Nationalsozialismus.* Münster: Lit, 2002. 277 pp., illus. (Studien zu Geschichte, Politik und Gesellschaft Nordamerikas, Bd. 20.) Zugl.: Trier, Univ., Diss., 2000. [For previously listed CD-ROM version and details see No. 40102/XB XLVII.]

41126. RUBINSTEIN, HILARY L.: *Jewish refugees in Britain and in New York.* [In]: The Jewish Journal of Sociology, Vol. 64, Nos. 1–2, London, 2002. Pp. 72–77. [Review article on several books on Jewish refugees, incl. internment in Britain.]

41127. RUTLAND, SUZANNE D.: *Edge of the diaspora: two centuries of Jewish settlement in Australia.* 2nd rev. edn. New York: Holmes and Meier, 2001. XVIII, 485 pp., illus., ports., facsims., notes, bibl. (457–471) [Incl. chaps. on refugees from Germany, internment, Australia's response to the Holocaust. For earlier edn. in 1988 see No. 25218/YB XXXIV.]

41128. RUTLAND, SUZANNE D.: *Subtle exclusions: Postwar Jewish emigration to Australia and the impact of the IRO scheme.* [In]: The Journal of Holocaust Education, Vol. 10, No. 1, London, Summer 2001. Pp. 50–66, illus., appendix, notes. [On the 200,000 DPs admitted into Australia 1947–1950 under the auspices of the International Refugee Organisation; discusses how Jews were initally excluded and had to face discrimination when eventually about 500 were admitted; deals also with the reaction of the Australian-Jewish leadership.]

41129. SCHIRP, KERSTIN EMMA: *Jude, Gringo, Deutscher. Das abenteuerliche Leben des Werner Max Finkelstein.* Berlin: Kerstin Emma Schirp; Books on Demand, 2002. 252 pp. [W.M.F., b. 1925 in Gumbinnen/East Prussia, journalist, went to Sweden in 1938 with a Kindertransport, from there to Bolivia, 1948 to Argentina, 1999 to Berlin.]

41130. SCHMIDT, MONIKA S.: *First language attrition, use and maintenance: the case of German Jews in anglophone countries.* Amsterdam, Philadelphia, PA: John Benjamins Publ. Co., 2002. XIV, 258 pp., tabs., charts, appendixes, notes, bibl. (197–212), index + 1 CD-ROM in pocket. (Studies in bilingualism, No. 24.) [Based on interviews and a questionaire survey of 54 emigrants from Düsseldorf, collected by the Düsseldorf Memorial Center 1995–1997.]

41131. SCHOEPS, WOLFGANG: *Deutsch-jüdische Emigration: Ihre Einflüsse auf die wirtschaftliche und kulturelle Entwicklung in Brasilien.* [In]: Preußens Himmel breitet seine Sterne .... [see No. 41991], Bd. 1. Pp. 393–401, notes.

41132. SNOWMAN, DANIEL: *The Hitler emigrés: the cultural impact on Britain of refugees from Nazism.* London: Chatto & Windus, 2002. XXIII, 466 pp., illus., ports., notes, bibl. (420–439), index. [Deals with the substantial contribution made to many disciplines such as music, art history, psychology, sociology, criminology, nuclear physics, biochemistry, publishing, architecture, film, photography, broadcasting and literature; incl. Ernst Gombrich, Nikolaus Pevsner, Karl Popper, Claus Moser, Max Perutz, Max Born, Hermann Bondi, Arthur Koestler, Elias Canetti, Emeric Pressburger, John Heartfield, Rudolf Bing, Kurt Hahn, George Steiner, George Solti, Gerard Hoffnung, the cartoonist Vicky (Victor Weisz) and the Amadeus String Quartet; also the publishers George Weidenfeld, André Deutsch, Paul Hamlyn, Tom Rosenthal, Robert Maxwell.] [Cf.: What did Hitler ever do for us? (Piers Brendon) [in]: The Daily Telegraph, London, April 28, 2002. Emigré variations (Ian Thomson) [in]: The Guardian, London, May 11, 2002. Some refugees are more invisible than others (David Herman) [in]: The Independent, London, Aug. 1, 2002.]

41133. WALTON-JORDAN, ULRIKE: *Safeguards against tyranny: The impact of German émigré lawyers on British legal policy towards Germany, 1942–1946.* [In]: The Yearbook of the Research Centre for German and Austrian Exile Studies, Vol. 2 [with the issue title] *German-Speaking Exiles in Great-Britain.* Amsterdam; Atlanta, GA, 2000. Pp. 1–23, notes.

II. RESEARCH AND BIBLIOGRAPHY

A. Libraries and Institutes

―――― ARYE-MAIMON-INSTITUT FÜR GESCHICHTE DER JUDEN, TRIER. HAVERKAMP, ALFRED, ed.: *Geschichte der Juden im Mittelalter von der Nordsee bis zu den Südalpen.* Kommentiertes Kartenwerk. [See No. 40857.]

41134. CENTRAL ARCHIVES FOR THE HISTORY OF THE JEWISH PEOPLE. REIN, DENISE: *Die Bestände der ehemaligen jüdischen Gemeinden Deutschlands in den "Central Archives for the History of the Jewish People" in Jerusalem.* Ein Überblick über das Schicksal der verschiedenen Gemeindearchive. [In]: Der Archivar, Jg. 55, H. 4, Düsseldorf, Nov. 2002. Pp. 318–327, footnotes.

41135. CENTRAL ARCHIVES FOR THE HISTORY OF THE JEWISH PEOPLE, JERUSALEM. LITT, STEFAN: *Die Central Archives for the History of the Jewish People in Jerusalem/Israel – Bewahrung und Pflege jüdischen Archivgutes der Diaspora.* [In]: Der Archivar, Jg. 55, H. 1, Düsseldorf, 2002. Pp. 65–67, footnotes.

41136. CENTRE FOR GERMAN-JEWISH STUDIES, SUSSEX. MAUS, NICOLE: *"Die deutsch-jüdische Vergangenheit beginnt nicht mit der Shoa".* Ein Besuch beim Centre for German-Jewish Studies im englischen Sussex. [In]: Aufbau, Vol. 68, No. 5, New York, March 7, 2002. P. 21.

41137. FRIESEL, EVYATAR: *Richtungen jüdischer Studien an deutschen Universitäten.* [In]: Zwischen Wissenschaft und Politik. Studien zur deutschen Universitätsgeschichte [see No. 41796]. Pp. 231–237, footnotes.

41138. HOCHSCHULE FÜR JÜDISCHE STUDIEN, HEIDELBERG: *Beiträge zur jüdischen Philosophie.* Festgabe zum 80. Geburtstag von Ze'ev Levy [issue title of]: Trumah, Bd. 11, Heidelberg: Winter, 2001. VI, 177 pp., footnotes. [Incl.: Ze'ev Levy. Lebenslauf (1–2). Ze'ev Levy. Wissenschaftliches Werk (109–118). Jüdisches Recht – Methode und Ziel seiner Forschung. Festvortrag anlässlich der Einweihung des Ignatz-Bubis-Lehrstuhls für Religion, Geschichte und Kultur des europäischen Judentums (Izhak England, 119–146). Further contribs. are listed according to subject.] [Z.L., b. Jan. 1921 in Dresden, prof. emer. of philosphy at the Univ. of Haifa, emigr. 1934 to Palestine, 1964–1973 studied philosphy, during the 1980s and 1990s Visiting Professor at the Hochschule für Jüdische Studien in Heidelberg, lives in the Kibbuz Hama'apil.]

41139. HONIGMANN, PETER: *Geschichte des jüdischen Archivwesens in Deutschland.* [In]: Der Archivar, Jg. 55, H. 3, Düsseldorf, Juli 2002. Pp. 223–230, footnotes.

41140. HOUGHTON LIBRARY, HARVARD UNIVERSITY, CAMBRIDGE, MA. LIEBERSOHN, HARRY/SCHNEIDER, DOROTHEE: *My life in Germany before and after Jan. 30, 1933: a guide to a manuscript collection at Houghton Library, Harvard Univ.* Philadelphia, PA: American Philosophical Society, 2001. 130 pp., footnotes, bibl., index. (Transactions of the American Philosophical Society, Vol. 91, part 3.) [Description of a collection of about 230 memoirs of refugees from Nazi Germany, mainly written in response to a 1939 competition organised by three Harvard professors.]

41141. INSTITUT FÜR ZEITGESCHICHTE, MÜNCHEN. EICHMÜLLER, ANDREAS: *Die Verfolgung von NS-Verbrechen durch westdeutsche Justizbehörden seit 1945.* Inventarisierung und Teilverfilmung der Verfahrensakten. Ein neues Projekt des Instituts für Zeitgeschichte. [In]: Vierteljahrshefte für Zeitgeschichte, Jg. 50, H. 3, München, 2002. Pp. 507–516, footnotes.

41142. KIRCHHOFF, MARKUS: *Häuser des Buches. Bilder jüdischer Bibliotheken.* Hrsg. vom Simon-Dubnow-Institut für jüdische Geschichte und Kultur an der Universität Leipzig. Leipzig: Reclam, 2002. 191 pp., illus., notes (156–178), bibl. (179–189). [Incl. also South-German genisot, the involvement of German Jews with the Jewish National and University Library in Jerusalem (Heinrich Loewe et al.), libraries in Berlin, the "Kulturwissenschaftliche Bibliothek Warburg", Soncino-Gesellschaft, bookburning and confiscation in the Nazi period; also antisemitic institutions such as the Frankfurt Institut zur Erforschung der Judenfrage.]

41143.   LEO BAECK INSTITUTE, LONDON: *Leo Baeck Institute Year Book 2002.* Vol. XLVII. J.A.S. Grenville, ed., Raphael Gross, assoc. ed., Joel Golb, Gabriele Rahaman, manuscript eds. Oxford: Berghahn Books, 2002. X, 446 pp., frontis., facsims., illus., footnotes, bibl. (269–433), general index (437–446).] [Cont.: Preface (eds., IX-X). Essays are arranged under the sections: I. Jewish intellectual responses to tradition and modernity. II. The Jewish 'Alltag' in the early modern period. Incl.: Introduction (Robert Liberles, 41–42). One essay in this section, 'Neofiti' and their families: or, perhaps, the good of the state (Kenneth Stowe, 105–113) is related to converts in 16th-cent. Italy. III. Jewish life in Austria. IV. Jewish organisations between advocacy and accommodation. V. Memoirs. Individual contribs. are listed according to subject.]

41144.   LEO BAECK INSTITUTE LONDON: *Annual report of activities 2002.* Introd. by Raphael Gross. London: Leo Baeck Institute. 2002. 52 pp., ports.

41145.   LEO BAECK INSTITUTE: *Jüdischer Almanach [2002] des Leo Baeck Instituts* [with the issue title] *Vom Essen.* Hrsg. von Gisela Dachs. Frankfurt am Main: Jüdischer Verlag, 2002. 155 pp., illus. [Articles pertaining to German-speaking Jewry are listed according to subject.]

41146.   LEO BAECK INSTITUTE NEW YORK/BERLIN: *2002 Overview.* New York: Leo Baeck Institute, 2002. 58 pp. [Report on the archive, the library, publications, lectures, events and other activities. Incl.: Overview 2002 (CKS = Carol Kahn Strauss, Executive Director, 2–3.).]

41147.   LEO BAECK INSTITUTE NEW YORK/BERLIN. EBBINGHAUS, FRANK: *Berlin leuchtete. Das Leo Baeck Institut eröffnete eine Dependance in der Hauptstadt.* [In]: Süddeutsche Zeitung, Nr. 85, München, 12. April 2002. P. 15. [On the opening of the LBI branch in the Jewish Museum.]

41148.   LEO BAECK INSTITUTE, NEW YORK.: *Speech of thanks by Federal President Johannes Rau on the occasion of the award of the Leo Baeck Medal, New York, Nov. 13, 2001.* New York: Leo Baeck Institute, 2001. 6 pp. [Transl. of advance text of President Rau's address.]

41149.   MOSES MENDELSSOHN AKADEMIE HALBERSTADT. DICK, JUTTA: *Die Moses Mendelssohn Akademie Halberstadt und das Berend Lehmann Museum in Halberstadt.* [In]: Preußens Himmel breitet seine Sterne .... [see No. 41991], Bd. 1. Pp. 307–318, illus. [Moses Mendelssohn Akademie: founded in 1995; Berend Lehmann Museum: founded in 2001 as part of the MMA.]

41150.   MOSES MENDELSSOHN ZENTRUM FÜR EUROPÄISCH-JÜDISCHE STUDIEN, POTSDAM: *Menora.* Jahrbuch für deutsch-jüdische Geschichte 2002, Bd. 13 [with the issue title] *Deutsch-jüdischer Parnaß. Rekonstruktion einer Debatte.* Im Auftrag des Moses Mendelssohn Zentrums für europäisch-jüdische Studien hrsg. von Julius H. Schoeps, Karl E. Grözinger, Willi Jasper und Gert Mattenklott. Berlin: Philo, 2002. 348 pp., index. [Incl.: Einleitung/Einführung (eds., 9–18). I. Dokumentation (21–199). Kommentare, Essays, Briefe (203–336). Articles are listed according to subject.]

41151.   ROSTOCK UNIVERSITY LIBRARY: *The Hebraica and Judaica of the Tychsen Collection and the Rostock University Library.* [Part 1]: *The Oldyiddish (jüdisch-deutsche) literature.* Prepared by Hermann Süß and Heike Tröger. Erlangen: Harald Fischer, 2001. 846 microfiches in two boxes. [Incl. nearly 400 titles from mid-15th cent. up to the 19th cent.]

41152.   SIMON-DUBNOW-INSTITUT, LEIPZIG.: *Jahrbuch des Simon-Dubnow-Instituts.* Jg. I, 2002. [Red.: Christoph Böwing]. Stuttgart: Deutsche Verlags-Anstalt, 2002. 1 vol., 534 pp., footnotes. [Incl.: Leipzig und Jerusalem (Dan Diner, 9–16). Essays (some English, some German) are arranged under the sections: Schwerpunkt I: Polnische Judenheit der Zwischenkriegszeit (17–134). Allgemeiner Teil (135–218). Schwerpunkt II: Formen jüdischer Selbstorganisation (219–374). Aus der Forschung (375–430). Diskussion (431–456). Dubnowiana (457–474). Literaturbericht (475–532). Selected contribs. pertaining to German-speaking Jewry are listed according to subject.]

41153. STAATSBIBLIOTHEK ZU BERLIN – PREUSSISCHER KULTURBESITZ: *Kitwe Jad/Jüdische Hand-schriften. Restaurieren – Bewahren – Präsentieren.* [Ausstellung der Staatsbibliothek zu Berlin – Preußischer Kulturbesitz, 4. Juli 2002 – 17. Aug. 2002, Ausstellung und Katalog: Petra Werner, Red.: Ursula Hartwieg]. Teil I: *Jüdische Kultur im Spiegel der Berliner Sammlung.* Katalog: Julia Bispinck. Berlin: Staatsbibl. zu Berlin – Preuß. Kulturbesitz, 2002. 200 pp., facsims., gloss., bibl., index. (Ausstellungskataloge N.F., 47a.) [The sections: 'Jüdische Medizin im Mittelalter', 'Der jüdische Jahresablauf in der christlichen Umwelt' and 'Die Haskala: Mithilfe des Verstandes aufklären' incl. Hebrew and Western-Yiddish manuscripts from German-speaking lands.]

41154. STAATSBIBLIOTHEK ZU BERLIN – PREUSSISCHER KULTURBESITZ: *Kitwe Jad/Jüdische Handschriften.* Restaurieren – Bewahren – Präsentieren. Teil 2: *Erste Schritte der Restaurierung der Hebräischen Bibel "Erfurt 1".* Berlin: Staatsbibliothek Berlin – Preußischer Kulturbesitz, 2002. 36 pp., illus. (Ausstellungskataloge N.F., 47b.) [Text by Julia Bispinck.]

41155. UNITED STATES HOLOCAUST MEMORIAL MUSEUM, WASHINGTON: *Archival guide to the collections of the United States Holocaust Memorial Museum.* Prepared by Brewster S. Chamberlin and Carl Modig. Washington, DC: United States Holocaust Memorial Museum, Center for Advanced Holocaust Studies, 2002. XIV, 454 pp., index.

41156. WIENER LIBRARY, LONDON. RAHIM, JOANNA: *An archive of villainy.* Photographs by Paul Wetherell. [In]: The Sunday Telegraph Magazine, London, Nov. 3, 2002. Pp. 27–31, illus. [Also on Alfred Wiener's life.] [Cf.: The power and pain of the truth (Daniel Finkelstein) [in]: The Times, London, Jan. 25, 2002, pp. 8–9. (D.F., Alfred Wiener's grandson, discusses both the family and the library).]

41157. ZENTRUM FÜR ANTISEMITISMUSFORSCHUNG, BERLIN: *Jahrbuch für Antisemitismusforschung 11.* Hrsg. von Wolfgang Benz für das Zentrum für Antisemitismusforschung der Technischen Universität Berlin. Red.: Werner Bergmann, Johannes Heil, Mona Körte. Geschäftsführende Red.: Juliane Wetzel. Berlin: Metropol, 2002. 339 pp., footnotes. [Incl.: Vorwort (Wolfgang Benz, 9–12). Essays are arranged under the sections: Antisemitismus (13–75). Nationalsozialismus (76–197). Auseinandersetzung mit der Vergangenheit (198–248). Minoritäten (249–270). Literatur (271–294). Besprechungsessays (295–324). Berichte (325–335). Selected articles pertaining to German-speaking Jews are listed according to subject.]

41158. ZENTRUM FÜR ANTISEMITISMUSFORSCHUNG, BERLIN. STRAUSS, MONICA: *The Center for Research into Anti-Semitism is twenty.* Berlin Institute celebrates its anniversary. [In]: Aufbau, Vol. LXVIII, No. 21, New York, Oct. 17, 2002. P. 6. [Cf.: Herbert A. Strauss – Gründer (Hans-Joachim Neubauer) [in]: 'FAZ', Nr. 248, Frankfurt am Main, 25. Okt. 2002. P. 44.]

41159. ZENTRUM FÜR ANTISEMITISMUSFORSCHUNG, BERLIN.: *Epilog.* [Section title of] *Judenfeindschaft als Paradigma.* Studien zur Vorurteilsforschung [see in No. 42134]. Pp. 327–365, footnotes. [Incl.: Die Bibliothek des Zentrums für Antisemitismusforschung (Antje Gerlach, 329–334). Das Archiv des Zentrums für Antisemitismusforschung (Claudio Curio/Peter Widmann, 335–338). "Vom Vorurteil zum Völkermord". Gastprofessoren am Zentrum für Antisemitismusforschung (Marion Neiss, 339–347). Die Datenbank zur Judenrettung (Dennis Riffel, 348–354).]

B. Bibliographies, Catalogues and Reference Books

41160. *Biographische Enzyklopädie der deutschsprachigen Aufklärung.* Hrsg. von Rudolf Vierhaus und Hans Erich Bödeker. München: Saur, 2002. XIV, 474 pp. [Incl. numerous entries related to German-speaking Jewry, Haskalah, emancipation.]

41161. BRAHAM, RANDOLPH L.: *The Holocaust in Hungary: a selected and annotated bibliography: 1984–2000.* New York: Rosenthal Institute for Holocaust Studies, Graduate Center/City Univ. of New York; Bolder, CO: Social Science Monographs (distrib. by Columbia Univ. Press), 2001. 252 pp., indexes. (East European Monographs, No. 583, Holocaust studies series.)

41162. COHEN, SUSAN SARAH, ed.: *Antisemitism*. An annotated bibliography. Vol. 15 (1999). [Publ. by] The Vidal Sassoon International Center for the Study of Antisemitism/The Hebrew University of Jerusalem. München: Saur, 2002. XXX, 520 pp., indexes. (The Felix Posen Bibliographic Project on Antisemitism.)

41163. *Encyclopedia of Holocaust literature*. Ed. by David Patterson, Alan L. Berger, and Sarita Cargas Westport, CT: Oryx Press, 2002. XVIII, 263 pp., bibl. (231–251), index. (Oryx Holocaust series.)

41164. GILBERT, MARTIN: *The Routledge atlas of the Holocaust*. 3rd. edn. London: Routledge, 2002. 282 pp., illus., ports., maps, bibl., index.

41165. GILBERT, MARTIN: *The Routledge atlas of Jewish history*. 6th edn. London: Routledge, 2002, 176 pp., maps.

41166. *Die "Judenfrage". Schriften zur Begründung des modernen Antisemitismus 1780 bis 1918*. Mikrofiche Edition. Hrsg. von Wolfgang Benz im Auftrag des Zentrum für Antisemitismusforschung. *Begleitheft zu Lieferung 1 & 2*. München: Saur, 2002. 2 vols., 44; 40 pp. [Bibliography, related to the microfiche edn. of c. 600 antisemitic publications, see No. 42133.]

41167. *Jüdisches biographisches Archiv/Jewish biographical archive*. Editor: Hilmar Schmuck. Advising editor.: Pinchas Lapide. München: Saur, 1994–1998. 690 microfiches & supplement: 127 microfiches. [Cont. c. 75.000 international biographical data from the 18th cent. to 1948. Followed by: *Jüdisches biographisches Archiv. Neue Folge/Series II*, Lfg. 1, 2001. 34 microfiches; focuses on the 20th cent.; to be continued.]

41168. *Jüdischer Biographischer Index/Jewish Biographical Index*. Bearb. von/compiled by Hilmar Schmuck. München: Saur, 1998. 4 vols. [Vol. 1: A-Glass, XIII, 365 pp. Vol. 2: Glassberg-Milch, pp. XIII, 369–730. Vol. 3: Milder-Z, XIII, pp. 733–1092. Vol. 4: Register/Index, XIII, pp. 1095–1491. Separate index vols. related to the microfiches of the Jewish Biographical Archive (see No. 41167), but also a biographical dictionary in its own right; CD-ROM edn. of these vols. publ. 2000.]

41169. KEINTZEL, BRIGITTA/KOROTIN, ILSE, eds.: *Wissenschafterinnen* [sic] *in und aus Österreich*. Wien: Böhlau, 2002. 870 pp., ports. [Incl. 342 bio-bibliographical articles, alphabetically arranged; among them numerous articles about Jewish women scientists.]

41170. *Lexikon deutsch-jüdischer Autoren*. Bd. 11: Hein-Hirs. Red. Leitung: Renate Heuer. Unter Mitarbeit von Jürgen Eglinsky [et al.]. München: Saur, 2002. XXV, 397 pp. (Archiv Bibliographia Judaica.)

41171. *Lexikon des Holocaust*. Hrsg. von Wolfgang Benz. München: Beck, 2002. 264 pp. Orig.-Ausg.

41172. *Nazi-Deutsch/Nazi-German: an English lexicon of the language of the Third Reich*. Comp. by Robert Michael and Karin Doerr. Forewords by Paul Rose, Leslie Morris, Wolfgang Mieder. Westport, CT: Greenwood Press, 2002. XX, 480 pp., bibl., (477–480. [Incl.: The tradition of anti-Jewish language (Robert Michael, 1–25, notes).]

——— NIEWERTH, TONI/PEIFFER, LORENZ: *"Jüdischer Sport in Deutschland" – eine kommentierte Bibliografie*. [See in No. 41721.]

41173. PHILLIPS, ZLATA FUSS: *German children's and youth literature in exile 1933–1950. Biographies and bibliographies*. München: Saur, 2001. 318 pp., footnotes, bibl. (289–294), indexes. [Incl.: Bio-bibliographical entries A – Z (19–288).]

41174. *Publications on German-speaking Jewry*. A selected and annotated bibliography of books and articles 2001. Compiled by Barbara Suchy and Annette Pringle. [In]: Leo Baeck Institute Year Book 2002, Vol. XLVII, Oxford, 2002. Pp. 269–433, index (names, places, subjects, periodicals, 397–433).

41175. *Religion in Geschichte und Gegenwart*. Vierte, völlig neubearb. Aufl. hrsg. von Hans Dieter Betz [et al.]. Bd. 4: I – K; Bd. 5: L – M. Tübingen: Mohr Siebeck, 2001–2002. 2 vols., 1923 cols.; 1703 cols.

[Vol. 4 incl. articles entitled: Judenchristen; Judenmission; Judentum; Judentum und Christentum (602–637; authors: Seth Schwartz, Andreas Gotzmann, Berndt Schaller, Michael A. Meyer, Andreas Lindemann, Michael Beintker). Judenverfolgungen (Christhard Hoffmann, 637–643).]

41176. ROSEN, PHILIP/APFELBAUM, NINA: *Bearing witness: a resource guide to literature, poetry, art, music, and videos by Holocaust victims and survivors.* Westport, CT: Greenwood Press, 2002. XVI, 210 pp. [Incl. many German Jews.]

III. THE NAZI PERIOD

A. General

41177. AHLHEIM, KLAUS/HEGER, BARDO: *Die unbequeme Vergangenheit. NS-Vergangenheit, Holocaust und die Schwierigkeiten des Erinnerns.* Schwalbach/Ts.: Wochenschau-Verlag, 2002. 158 pp., footnotes, bibl. (Studien zu Politik und Wissenschaft.) [Based on a survey conducted among students of Essen Univ. in 2000/2001.]

41178. AHRWEILER. JEFFRÉ, IRMGARD: *Spurensuche: Erich Hertz.* Ein Projekt der Geschichts-Arbeitsgemeinschaft am Peter-Joerres-Gymnasium Ahrweiler. [In]: Heimat-Jahrbuch Kreis Ahrweiler 2003, Jg. 60, Mayen, 2002. Pp. 203–205, notes.

41179. ALLEN, MICHAEL THAD: *The business of genocide: the SS, slave labor and the concentration camps.* Chapel Hill, London: The Univ. of North Carolina Press, 2002. XI, 377 pp., illus., facsims., notes, bibl. (347–365) index.

41180. ALY, GÖTZ: *Enteignung. Was geschah mit den Besitztümern der ermordeten Juden Europas? Zur Ökonomie der Nazis.* [In]: Die Zeit, Nr. 47, Hamburg, 14. Nov. 2002. P. 51.

41181. ALZEY. SCHLÖSSER, ANNELORE: *Von Alzey bis New York.* Das bewegte und bewegende Leben der Sybille Schloß. [In]: Alzeyer Geschichtsblätter, H. 33, Alzey, 2002. Pp. 67–92, illus., notes. [Deals with the fate of the Schloss family from Alzey; in particular with the actress Sybille Sch.] [S.Sch., b. 1910 in Munich, lover of Wolfgang Koeppen in Berlin during the 1920s, the heroine in his first novel 'Eine unglückliche Liebe; emigr. 1933 to Zurich, engagements in Erika Mann's political cabaret 'Pfeffermühle', 1936 emigr. via the Netherlands to the US; lives in New York.]

——— AMÉRY, JEAN: *Jenseits von Schuld und Sühne.* Bewältigungsversuch eines Überwältigten. [See in No. 41800.]

41182. ARNDS, PETER: *On the awful German fairy tale: breaking taboos in representations of Nazi euthanasia and the Holocaust in Günter Grass's 'Die Blechtrommel', Edgar Hilsenrath's 'Der Nazi & und der Friseur', and Anselm Kiefer's visual art.* [In]: The German Quarterly, Vol. 75, No. 4, Riverside, CA, Fall 2002. Pp. 422– 439, notes. [Deals with the use of fairy tales in Nazi racist ideology and how this is reflected in the works cited.]

——— *Archival guide to the collections of the United States Holocaust Memorial Museum.* Prepared by Brewster S. Chamberlin and Carl Modig. [See No. 41155.]

41183. AUSCHWITZ. ASCHOFF, DIETHARD: *Münster – Auschwitz, Auschwitz – Gelsenkirchen. Der bisher unbekannte Auschwitzbericht eines Remscheider Soldaten.* [In]: Westfälische Forschungen, Jg. 52, Münster, 2002. Pp. 555–567, footnotes. [On a manuscript kept in the Wiener Library, London.]

41184. AUSCHWITZ. FRIEDLER, ERIC/SIEBERT, BARBARA/KILIAN, ANDREAS: *Zeugen aus der Todeszone: das jüdische Sonderkommando in Auschwitz.* Gerlingen: Bleicher; Lüneburg: zu Klampen, 2002. 416 pp., illus.

41185. AUSCHWITZ. MEIER, CHRISTIAN: *Von Athen bis Auschwitz.* Betrachtungen zur Lage der Geschichte. München: Beck, 2002. 235 pp., notes. (Krupp-Vorlesungen zu Politik und

Geschichte am Kulturwissenschaftlichen Institut im Wissenschaftszentrum Nordrhein-Westfalen.) [Incl.: V. Auschwitz (132–161, notes: 224–230).]

41186. AUSCHWITZ. PIPER, FRANCISZEK: *Auschwitz Prisoner Labor. The organization and exploitation of Auschwitz concentration camp prisoners as laborers.* Translated [from the Polish] by William Brand. Oswiecim: Auschwitz-Birkenau State Museum, 2002. 467 pp., illus., docs., footnotes, tabs., maps, gloss., bibl., index.

41187. AUSCHWITZ. WHITE, JOSEPH ROBERT: *Target Auschwitz: historical and hypothetical German responses to Allied attack.* [In]: Holocaust and Genocide Studies, Vol. 16, No. 1, Oxford, Summer 2002. Pp. 54–76, notes. [Author concludes that even a successful Allied bombing campaign would not have affected the Final Solution.]

41188. AUSCHWITZ-BIRKENAU. ALLEN, MICHAEL THAD: *The devil in the details: the gas chambers of Birkenau, October 1941.* [In]: Holocaust and Genocide Studies, Vol. 16, No. 2, Oxford, Fall 2002. Pp. 189–216. [Author discusses that as early as Oct. 1941 the SS had adapted the installations at the crematoria for mass murder.]

41189. AUSCHWITZ-BIRKENAU. SCHULTE, JAN ERIK: *Vom Arbeits- zum Vernichtungslager. Die Entstehungsgeschichte von Auschwitz-Birkenau 1941/42.* [In]: Vierteljahrshefte für Zeitgeschichte, Jg. 50, H. 1, München, 2002. Pp. 41–69, footnotes. [Engl. abstract on p. 157.]

41190. AUSTRIA. ADUNKA, EVELYN: *Der Raub der Bücher.* Plünderung in der NS-Zeit und Restitution nach 1945. Wien: Czernin, 2002. 310 pp., notes (241–285), gloss., bibl., index. (Bd. IX der Bibliothek des Raubes.) [Cont. the sections: I. Die Bibliothek von Tanzenberg in Kärnten. II. Bücher aus jüdischem Besitz während der NS-Zeit in Wien. III. Jüdische Bücher und Bibliotheken nach 1945 in Wien. IV. Die Rolle des Staates Israel und weitere internationale jüdische Bemühungen. V. Private Archive und Bibliotheken.]

41191. AUSTRIA. FEICHTLBAUER, HUBERT: *The Austrian dilemma: an inquiry into National Socialism and racism in Austria.* Transl. by Andrew Smith and Penny Senften. Vienna: Holzhausen, 2001. VII, 348 pp., notes, bibl. (343–348), index. [Also deals with post-1945 Austria, incl. restitution claims. German edn. by the same publ. in 2000.]

41192. AUSTRIA. REFAIE, ELISABETH EL: *Keeping the truce? Austrian press politics between the July agreement (1936) and the Anschluß (1938).* [In]: German History, Vol. 20, No. 1, London, 2002. Pp. 44–66, footnotes. [Incl. attitude to Jews.]

41193. AUSTRIA. SEEFRIED, ELKE: *Sozialdemokraten und Sozialisten im österreichischen Exil 1933/34.* [In]: Zeitschrift für Geschichtswissenschaft, Jg. 50, H. 7, Berlin, 2002. pp. 581–602, footnotes.

41194. AUSTRIA. SPUHLER, GREGOR [et al.], eds.: *"Arisierungen in Österreich und ihre Bezüge zur Schweiz.* Beitrag zur Forschung. Hrsg. von der Unabhängigen Expertenkommission Schweiz – Zweiter Weltkrieg. Zürich: Chronos, 2002. 209 pp., tabs., bibl., index. (Veröffentlichungen der Unabhängigen Expertenkommission Schweiz – Zweiter Weltkrieg, Bd. 20.) [Incl. summary in German, French, Italian and English.]

41195. *Autobiographische Zeugnisse* [&] *Im Schatten des Holocaust.* [Section titles of] "… der den Erniedrigten aufrichtet aus dem Staube und aus dem Elend erhöht den Armen [see No. 40844]. Pp. 74–177. [*Autobiographische Zeugnisse*; cont.: The final testimony (Walter Zwi Bacharach, 74–79; on letters written before deportation). Leben und Autobiographie. Warum schreiben Menschen über ihr Leben? (Barbara Vogel, 80–94). Der Breslauer Historiker Willy Cohn (1888–1941) (Arno Herzig, 98–107). "Ich will Zeugnis ablegen bis zum letzten" – Die Schriftsteller Victor Klemperer und Jochen Klepper in ihren Tagebüchern aus der Kriegszeit (Wolfgang Grünberg, 108–127). *Im Schatten des Holocaust*; cont.: Selma Meerbaum-Eisinger (1924–1942): Portrait of the poet as a young woman (Edward Timms, 128–145). Jewish mothers of small children during the Holocaust. The changing tasks – the unchanging motherly role (Miriam Gillis-Carlebach, 146–169). Janusz Korszak und Joseph Carlebach – parallel lives (Ruth Goodman, 170–177).]

41196. BAD EMS. *Bad Emser Hefte.* Nr. 204. Bad Ems: Verein für Geschichte/Denkmal- und Landschaftspflege e.V. Berg/Taunus, 2002. 1 issue. [Incl.: Grandmother and grandchildren relate (Edith Dietz née Königsberger; transl. from the German article (orig. publ. in Bad Emser Hefte No. 136/1995) by a group of school children in Bad Ems. Documents of the suffering of two Bad Ems children (Astrid Pöltz; on two Jewish Euthanasia victims and their family).]

41197. BAD EMS. DIETZ, EDITH: *Den Nazis entronnen. Die Flucht eines jüdischen Mädchens in die Schweiz. Autobiographischer Bericht 1933–1942.* Vorwort von Micha Brumlik. Frankfurt am Main: Brandes & Apsel, 2002. 131 pp., facsims., illus. [First publ. 1990 (Frankfurt am Main: dipa); see No. 18350/YB XXXVI.] [E.D., née Königsberger, b. 1921 in Bad Ems; lives in Karlsruhe.]

41198. BADEN. STOLLE, MICHAEL: *Die Geheime Staatspolizei in Baden. Personal, Organisation, Wirkung und Nachwirken einer regionalen Verfolgungsbehörde im Dritten Reich.* Konstanz: UVK.-Verl.-Ges., 2001. 411 pp., footnotes. (Karlsruher Beiträge zur Geschichte des Nationalsozialismus, Bd. 6.). [Incl. persecution of Jews.]

41199. BADEN & SAARPFALZ. TESCHNER, GERHARD J.: *Die Deportation der badischen und saarpfälzischen Juden am 22. Oktober 1940.* Vorgeschichte und Durchführung der Deportation und das weitere Schicksal der Deportierten bis zum Kriegsende im Kontext der deutschen und französischen Judenpolitik. Frankfurt a.M.; New York: Peter Lang, 2002. 364 pp., footnotes, tabs., docs., chronol., bibl. (Europäische Hochschulschriften. Reihe III, Geschichte und ihre Hilfswissenschaften, Bd. 930.) Zugl.: Heidelberg, Univ., Diss., 2001.

———— BARON, FRANK: *The 'myth' and reality of rescue from the Holocaust: The Karski-Koestler and Vrba-Wetzer reports.* [See in No. 41763.]

41200. BAUMGARTEN, ELISHEVA: *As families remember: Holocaust memoirs and their transmission.* [In]: Studies in Contemporary Jewry, Vol. XVI, Oxford, 2000. Pp. 265–288.

41201. BAVARIA. KERSHAW, IAN: *Popular opinion and political dissent in the Third Reich, Bavaria 1933–1945.* New edn. Oxford: Clarendon Press; New York: Oxford Univ. Press, 2002. XXXIV, 433 pp., tabs., map, footnotes, bibl. (398–411), bibl. of works since 1st edn. (413–419). [Incl. chaps.: Reactions to the persecution of the Jews. Popular opinion and the extermination of the Jews. For orig. edn. 1983 see No. 19945/YB XXIX.]

41202. BACKHAUS, FRITZ/LIEPACH, MARTIN: *Leo Baecks Manuskript über die "Rechtsstellung der Juden in Europa".* Neue Funde und ungeklärte Fragen. [In]: Zeitschrift für Geschichtswissenschaft, Jg. 50, H. 1, Berlin, 2002. Pp. 55–71, footnotes.

41203. BECK-KLEIN, GRETE: *Never forget (The story of a very ordinary family).* Transl. by the author. Haifa: [Privately printed], [2002?]. 128 pp., illus., ports., maps, facsims., geneal., tabs., bibl. [Orig. publ. in 1997 with the title: Was sonst vergessen wird: von Wien nach Shanghai, England und Minsk. For details see No. 34974/YBXLIII.]

41204. BENZ, WOLFGANG/DISTEL, BARBARA, eds.: *Herrschaft und Gewalt. Frühe Konzentrationslager 1933–1945.* Red.: Angelika Königseder, Verena Walter. Berlin: Metropol, 2002. 294 pp., footnotes. (Geschichte der Konzentrationslager 1933–1945, Bd. 2.) [Cont. 13 essays.]

41205. BENZ, WOLFGANG: *Schwierige Ankunft. Jüdische Emigration aus Hitler-Deutschland nach Australien.* [In]: Zeitschrift für Geschichtswissenschaft, Jg. 50, H. 4, Berlin, 2002. Pp. 316–321, footnotes.

41206. BENZ, WOLFGANG/DISTEL, BARBARA, eds.: *Terror ohne System, Die ersten Konzentrationslager im Nationalsozialismus 1933–1935.* Red.: Angelika Königseder. Berlin: Metropol, 2001. 310 pp., footnotes. (Geschichte der Konzentrationslager 1933–1945, Bd. 1.) [Incl. 15 essays.]

41207. BERGEN-BELSEN. BASSERMANN, FRIEDRICH J.: *Als Arzt in Bergen-Belsen.* Ein Bericht über Zeiten und Menschen nach 1945. 2. Aufl. Regensburg: Universitätsverlag Regensburg, 2002. 144 pp., bibl. [First edn. publ. 2000 by Mittelbayerischer Verlag, Regensburg.]

41208.	BERGEN-BELSEN. LAVSKY, HAGIT: *New beginnings: Holocaust survivors in Bergen-Belsen and the British Zone in Germany, 1945–1950.* Detroit: Wayne State Univ. Press, 2002. 311 pp., illus., ports., tabs., notes, bibl. (277–293), index. [Discusses the liberation of Bergen-Belsen and the efforts by the British occupation forces and international Jewish organisations to rebuild the lives of those left behind.]

41209.	BERLIN. BEHAR, ISAAK: *Versprich mir, dass Du am Leben bleibst.* Ein jüdisches Schicksal. Berlin: Ullstein, 2002. 223 pp. [Author, b. 1923 in Berlin to a family orig. from Constantinople, tells about his survival in hiding in Berlin with the help of numerous non-Jews.]

41210.	BERLIN. FISCHER, ERICA: *Das kurze Leben der Jüdin Felice Schragenheim.* "Jaguar" Berlin 1922 – Bergen-Belsen 1945. Mit Fotos von Christel Becker-Rau. München: Deutscher Taschenbuch Verlag, 2002. 199 pp., illus., docs. Orig.-Ausg. [On a young Berlin woman, a niece of Lion Feuchtwanger, and her unsuccessful attempt to avoid deportation by going into hiding. For the author's documentary story about F.Sch. and her "aryan" friend with the title *Aimée & Jaguar* see No. 32836/YB XLI.]

41211.	BERLIN. GAILUS, MANFRED: *Overwhelmed by their own fascination with the ideas of 1933: Berlin's Protestant social milieu in the Third Reich.* [In]: German History, Vol. 20, No. 4, London, 2002. Pp. 462–493, footnotes. [Incl. attitudes to Jews.]

41212.	BERLIN. GÖRLICH, FRANK: *Flucht in den Untergrund. Die Rettung einer jüdischen Familie während der NS-Zeit in Berlin.* [In]: Jahrbuch für Antisemitismusforschung 2002, Frankfurt am Main; New York, 2002. Pp. 114–136, footnotes. [On Lieselotte and Eduard Levy.]

41213.	BERLIN. GRUNER, WOLF: *Die Fabrik-Aktion und die Ereignisse in der Berliner Rosenstraße. Fakten und Fiktionen um den 27. Februar 1943.* [In]: Jahrbuch für Antisemitismusforschung 2002, Frankfurt am Main; New York, 2002. Pp. 137–177, footnotes.

41214.	BERLIN. KÖNIGSEDER, ANGELIKA: *Recht und nationalsozialistische Herrschaft. Berliner Anwälte 1933–1945.* Ein Forschungsprojekt des Berliner Anwaltsvereins. Hrsg. vom Berliner Anwaltsverein. Bonn: Deutscher Anwaltsverein, 2001. 391 pp., footnotes, docs., bibl. [Incl. chaps. dealing with Jewish jurists, their exclusion and fate (focusing on Ludwig Bendix); also a section on female solicitors.]

41215.	BERLIN. LOVENHEIM, BARBARA: *Survival in the shadows: seven hidden Jews in Hitler's Berlin.* London: Peter Owen, 2002. 231 pp., illus., ports., facsims., maps, bibl. [Deals with members of the Arndt, Lewinsky and Gumbel families who survived with the help of more than fifty non-Jews, and who subsequently went to the US.]

41216.	BERLIN. MEYER, BEATE: *Die Inhaftierung der "jüdisch Versippten" in der Berliner Rosenstraße im Spiegel staatsanwaltlicher Zeugenvernehmungen in der DDR.* [In]: Jahrbuch für Antisemitismusforschung 2002, Frankfurt am Main; New York, 2002. Pp. 178–197, footnotes.

41217.	BERLIN. *Vorbei = Beyond call: Dokumentation jüdischen Musiklebens in Berlin, 1933: a record of Jewish musical life in Nazi Berlin, 1933–1945.* Comp. by Horst J.P. Bergmeier, Ejal Jakob Eisler, Rainer E. Lotz. Foreword by Henryk M. Broder. Hambergen: Bear Family records, [2001]. 516 pp., illus., ports., facsims., maps, bibl. (499–505) + 11 CD-ROM and 1 DVD disk. [Book has parallel German and English texts. The discs reproduce recordings from many sources, collected and restored after the Nazi period. Incl. classical music, Yiddish comedians, German-Jewish cabaret artists and singers, Zionist songs, and cantorial recordings. The DVD is a reconstruction of the sound film 'Hebräische Melodie', featuring the violinist Andreas Weissgerber.]

41218.	BERLIN. WEISSBERG-BOB, NEA/IRMER, THOMAS: *Heinrich Richard Brinn (1874–1944). Fabrikant – Kunstsammler – Frontkämpfer. Dokumentation einer "Arisierung"* Mit Beiträgen von Michel Friedman, Hermann Simon und Jacov Tsur. Berlin, Lichtig, 2002. 263 pp., illus., bibl., notes.

41219.	BERLIN. WILLEMS, SUSANNE: *Der entsiedelte Jude. Albert Speers Wohnungsmarktpolitik für den Berliner Hauptstadtbau.* Berlin: Hentrich, 2000. 460 pp., illus., facsims., tabs., footnotes, bibl., index. (Publikationen der Gedenk- und Bildungsstätte Haus der Wannsee-Konferenz, Bd. 10.) Zugl.: Bochum, Univ., Diss., 1999 u.d.T.: Stadtmodernisierung, Wohnungsmarkt und Judenverfolgung in Berlin 1938–1943. [On the persecution of the Berlin Jews, "aryanisation", expulsion from their dwellings, forced labour and eventual deportation as a prerequisite for the enormous construction plans of Albert Speer.]

41220. BERLIN-FRIEDRICHSHAIN. GIROD, REGINA/LIDSCHUN, REINER/PFEIFFER, OTTO: *Juden in Friedrichshain*. [Hrsg.: Kulturring Berlin]. Berlin: Mondial Verlag, 2000. 264 pp., illus., facsims., notes.

41221. BERLIN-KREUZBERG. WETZEL, JÜRGEN: *"Zur Statistik". Zwei Berliner Frauenschicksale*. [In]: Der Bär von Berlin, Bd. 51, 2002, Berlin, 2002. Pp. 115–130, notes, illus., facsims. [On Maria Günzburger, nurse and social worker, and Amalie Loewenberg, teacher, during the Nazi period.]

41222. BERLIN-TEMPELHOF. SCHILDE, KURT: *Bürokratie des Todes. Lebensgeschichten jüdischer Opfer des NS-Regimes im Spiegel von Finanzamtsakten* Mit einem Geleitwort von Hans Eichel, Bundesminister der Finanzen. Berlin: Metropol, 2002. 255 pp., illus., facsims., footnotes, bibl. (224–249). (Reihe Dokumente, Texte, Materialien, Bd. 45.) [Focuses on documents related to Horst Fenichel and his family from Berlin-Tempelhof, also on the Herschkowitz family.]

41223. BERNHEIM-FRIEDMANN, RACHEL: *Ohrringe im Keller: Von Transkarpatien durch Auschwitz-Birkenau nach Israel*. Aus dem Hebr. von Rachel Grünberger-Elbaz. Hrsg. von Erhard Roy Wiehn. Konstanz: Hartung-Gorre, 2002. 170 pp., illus., bibl.

41224. BERNKASTEL. SCHAAF, ERWIN: *Judenverfolgung im Spannungsfeld von Legalität und rasseideologischer Legitimation. Konflikte im Raum Bernkastel-Wittlich 1933 bis 1935*. [In]: Jahrbuch für westdeutsche Landesgeschichte, Jg. 27, Koblenz, 2001. Pp. 373–413, footnotes.

41225. BIERSTECKER, HENK/KAAM, BEN VAN: *Kurt Gerstein und der holländische Widerstand*. [In]: Jahrbuch für Westfälische Kirchengeschichte, Bd. 97, Bielefeld, 2002. Pp. 269–277, footnotes. [Incl. introd. by Matthias Rickling.]

41226. BOCHUM & WATTENSCHEID. STADTARCHIV BOCHUM, ed.: *Vom Boykott bis zur Vernichtung. Leben, Verfolgung, Vertreibung und Vernichtung der Juden in Bochum und Wattenscheid 1933–1945*. Ein Quellen- und Arbeitsbuch (nicht nur) für Schulen. Konzeption und Red.: Ingrid Wölk. Mit einem Vorwort von Paul Spiegel. Bearb. von Rainer Adams, Andreas Halwer, Eberhard Heupel und Ingrid Wölk. Essen: Klartext, 2002. 280 pp., illus., facsims., footnotes, bibl. [Incl. list of Nazi victims; also contribs. on the Jews of Bochum and Wattenscheid before 1933; antisemitic education in schools; "aryanisation".]

41227. BODO, BÉLA: *The role of antisemitism in the expulsion of non-Aryan students, 1933–1945*. [In]: Yad Vashem Studies, Vol. 30, Jerusalem, 2002. Pp. 189–227, footnotes. [Author argues that in some cases opposition by students and administrators to expelling "part-Jewish" students enabled a few to continue taking courses for several years.]

41228. BONN. MEYER, OTTO: *Meine Erlebnisse in den Jahren 1933–1945*. [In]: Bonner Geschichtsblätter, Bd. 49/50, Bonn, 1999/2000 [publ. 2001]. Pp. 473–486, footnotes, facsims. [Memoirs, orig. written in 1946, are introduced by Feeke Meents: Unterdrückung und Verfolgung in Bonn – aber es gab auch die anderen. Zu den Aufzeichnungen von Dr.iur. Otto Meyer (471–473).] [O.M., jurist, owner of the "Bonner Fahnenfabrik", survived thanks to his "mixed marriage" and the help of several people in Bonn.]

41229. BONN. SAMUEL, ARTHUR: *Mein Leben in Deutschland vor und nach dem 30. Januar 1933*. [In]: Bonner Geschichtsblätter, Bd. 49/50, Bonn, 1999/2000 [publ. 2001]. Pp. 399–457, footnotes, illus., facsims., index. [A.S., 1885 Bonn – 1974 Seattle, physician, president of the Bonn Jewish community, emigr. 1939 to the US, participated in the Harvard Univ. competition in 1940, for which these memoirs were written. The text is followed by an essay on A.S. and his family: "Wir waren vogelfrei" (Sylke Bartmann/Detlef Garz, 457–470, bibl.).]

41230. BOSMAJIAN, HAMIDA: *Sparing the child: children's literature about Nazism and the Holocaust*. New York; London: Routledge, 2002. XXVI, 274 pp., notes, bibl. (253–263), index. (Children's literature and culture, Vol. 16.)

41231. BREMEN-NEUSTADT. *Jüdisches Leben in der Bremer Neustadt während der NS-Zeit.* Erschienen anläßlich der Ausstellung in der St. Pauli Gemeinde in der Bremer Neustadt vom 05. – 23. November 2001. Hrsg.: Arbeitsgemeinschaft "Stadtteilgeschichte Bremen-Neustadt" [Kontakt: Birte Schleef]. Bremen: Privately printed (Birte Schleef), 2001. 63 pp., illus.

41232. BROWN, DANIEL PATRICK: *The camp women: the female auxiliaries who assisted the SS in running the Nazi concentration camp system.* Atglen, PA: Schiffer Military History, 2002. 285 pp., illus., ports., facsims., maps, notes, bibl. (245–251), index. [Chiefly a register of personal files of the Nazi camp women or SS overseers (25–234).]

41233. BUCHENWALD. *Stimmen aus Buchenwald.* Ein Lesebuch. Hrsg. von Holm Kirsten und Wulf Kirsten im Auftrag der Stiftung Gedenkstätten Buchenwald und Mittelbau-Dora. Göttingen: Wallstein, 2002. 336 pp., illus., gloss., notes. [Cont.: Vorwort (Wulf Kirsten, 5–12). Texts by sixty former inmates, among them many German-speaking Jews; incl. short biographies.]

41234. *Building history. The Shoah in art, memory, and myth.* Ed. by Peter M. Daly [et al.] New York; Bern: Lang, 2002. XVIII, 284 pp., notes. [Cont. preface, introd., addresses (Peter Kleinmann/Alain Goldschläger/Rudolf Klinger/Claire Miller, XIII-XVIII). Esaays are arranged under the sections: History and the Shoah; incl.: Germany, Israel and the Shoah (Avraham Primor, 9–20). Dachau – as a 'historical sign' (Barbara Distel, 21–34); also a contrib. by Jackie Feldman on Israel (35–66). Kristallnacht: Icon of the Shoah?; cont.: 'Kristallnacht' the icon of the Shoah (Naomi Kramer, 67–72). 'Reichskristallnacht' – 'Reichspogromnacht'. Reflections of a term (Ludwig Eiber, 73–86). Some reflections on the implications of the term 'Kristallnacht' (Peter M. Daly, 87–94). Cultural programming and the Shoah (95–140; contribs. by Naomi Kramer, Saul Balagura). Art: The transformation of the Shoah in film (141–166; contribs. by Peter M. Daly, Naomi Kramer, Alain Goldschläger). The limits of representation (167–190; contribs, by Jean-Jacques van Vlasselaer, Tibor Egervari). Questioning myths. The case of the Swiss neutrality and the Swiss banking system (191–206; contribs. by Claude Altermatt, Irving Abella). The duty of memory (207–248; contribs. by Anna Rosmus, Ronald Headland). Education and the Shoah. The Austrian, Canadian, Swiss and German experiences (contribs. by Bruno Winkler on the Jewish Museum of Hohenems, Margaret Wells on gender aspects, Frieda Miller, Miryam Eser Davolio, Hans-Peter Hagedorn on Dachau).]

41235. BURGER, REINER: *Von Goebbels Gnaden. "Jüdisches Nachrichtenblatt" (1938–1943).* Münster: LIT, 2001. 202 pp., facsims., footnotes, bibl., indexes. (Kommunikationsgeschichte, 15.). [Cf.: Bespr. (Kurt Schilde) [in]: Westfälische Forschungen, Bd. 52, Münster, 2002, pp. 739–740.]

41236. CASTROP-RAUXEL. SCHOLZ, DIETMAR: *Zum Schicksal von Ostjuden aus Castrop-Rauxel. Der Funkspruch S.S.D. Nr. 12–II 50–42 vom 27.10.1938.* [In]: Märkisches Jahrbuch für Geschichte, Bd. 101, Dortmund, 2001. Pp. 251–263, footnotes.

41237. CESARANI, DAVID/LEVENE, PAUL E., eds.: *'Bystanders' to the Holocaust: a re-evaluation.* London: Frank Cass, 2002. 286 pp., illus., notes, bibl., index. [Based on an international colloquium held in Uppsala, Sweden, in Sept. 1999. Deals with how much the USA, Britain, Switzerland and Sweden knew about the Holocaust and their reactions to it.]

41238. CHARGUÉRAUD, MARC-ANDRÉ: *Silences meurtriers. Les Alliés, les neutres et l'holocauste, 1940–1945.* Genève: Labor et Fides; Paris: Cerf, 2001, 298 pp. [Cf.: Compte rendu (Bruno Ackermann) [in]: Schweizerische Zeitschrift für Geschichte, Vol. 52, Nr. 4, Basel, 2002, pp. 534–536.]

41239. CHAUMONT, JEAN-MICHEL: *Die Konkurrenz der Opfer.* Genozid, Identität und Anerkennung. Aus dem Französ. und Amerik. von Thomas Laugstien. Lüneburg: zu Klampen, 2001. 359 pp., footnotes, bibl. [Incl. the author's epilogue for the German edn. (319–342). Orig. edn.: *La concurrence des victimes. Génocide, identité, reconnaissance.* Paris: Éd. La Découverte & Syros, 1997.]

41240. CHURCH. BESIER, GERHARD: *Die Kirchen und das Dritte Reich. Spaltungen und Abwehrkämpfe 1934–1937.* Berlin: Propyläen, 2001. 1262 pp., illus., notes (903–1164), bibl. (1171–1240), index (1241–1262). [Incl.: Kapitel 9. Kirche und NS-Rassenpolitik: Nürnberger Gesetze, Ausgrenzung der Juden und Zwangssterilisierung (1935–1937) (807–902).] [Cf.: Gewaltige Forschungsleistung

(Hans Fenske) [in]: Jahrbuch Extremismus & Demokratie, Jg. 14, Baden-Baden, 2002, pp. 293–295. Bespr. (Winfried Becker) [in]: Zeitschrift für bayerische Landesgeschichte, Bd. 65, H. 2, München, 2002, pp. 688–692.]

41241. CHURCH. BRAKELMANN, GÜNTER: *Evangelische Kirche und Judenverfolgung.* Waltrop: Verlag Hartmut Spenner, 2001. 124 pp., notes. (Schriften der Hans Ehrenberg Gesellschaft, Bd. 7.) [Incl. three lectures given 1998/1999: Kirche und staatliche Judenpolitik 1933; Kirche und Judenpogrom 1938; Kirche und die Frage der Mitschuld 1945–1950.]

41242. CHURCH. BRECHENMACHER, THOMAS: *Der Dichter als Fallensteller. Hochhuth's 'Stellvertreter' und die Ohnmacht des Faktischen – Versuch über die Mechanismen einer Geschichtsdebatte.* [In]: Geschichte als Falle. Deutschland und die jüdische Welt [see No. 40849]. Pp. 217–257, notes.

41243. CHURCH. GOLDHAGEN, DANIEL J.: *A moral reckoning: The role of the Catholic Church in the Holocaust and the unfulfilled duty of repair.* New York: Knopf, 2002. 352 pp., illus., tabs., facsims., notes, bibl., index. [German edn.: *Die katholische Kirche und der Holocaust. Eine Untersuchung über Schuld und Sühne.* Aus dem Engl. von Friedrich Griese. Berlin, Siedler, 2002, 473 pp., illus., bibl., index.] [Cf.: Selected reviews: Die katholische Kirche und der Holocaust. Eine Untersuchung über Schuld und Sühne (István Deák) [in]: Europäische Rundschau, Jg. 31, Nr. 1/2003, Wien, 2003, pp. 107–117, notes. Goldhagens Moralpredigt gegen die katholische Kirche aus der Sicht eines anderen Kritikers ihres Antisemitismus (Olaf Blaschke) [in]: Zeitschrift für Geschichtswissenschaft, Jg. 50, H. 12, Berlin, 2002, pp. 1099–1115). Im Furor des Rechthabens (Jan Ross) [in]: Zeitliteratur [Beilage von] Die Zeit, Nr. 41, Hamburg, Okt. 2002, pp. 61–62. Dostojewski nahm es mit Schuld und Sühne genauer. Hätte Daniel Goldhagen nur José Sánchez gelesen, wäre Goldhagen II nicht passiert (Konrad Repgen) [in]: 'FAZ', Nr. 233, Frankfurt am Main, 8. Okt. 2002, p. L 31; refers to: José M. Sánchez: *Pius XII und der Holocaust. Anatomie einer Debatte.* Aus dem Amerik. von Karl Nicolai. Paderborn: Schöningh, 2002. 182 pp. (for American edn. see No. 39930/YB XLVII). Review (Donald Dietrich) [in]: Holocaust and Genocide Studies, Vol. 16, No. 3, Oxford, Winter 2002, pp. 415–426 (also on several other books on the Catholic church, Pius XII and their role during the Nazi period). See also on this topic: *Pope Pius and the Jews.* New York: Catholic League for Religious and Civil Rights, 2002. 10 pp.]

41244. CHURCH. GOLDHAGEN, DANIEL JONAH: *What would Jesus have done?: Pope Pius XII, the Catholic Church, and the Holocaust.* [In]: The New Republic, Jan. 21, New York, 2002. Pp. 21–45, illus., port., bibl. [Cf.: Pius XII and the Jews: a clash between history and theology (Albert H. Friedlander) [in]: European Judaism, Vol. 35, No. 2, London, Autumn 2002, pp. 131–145.]

41245. CHURCH. *The Holocaust, never to be forgotten: reflections on the Holy See's document 'We Remember'.* Commentaries by Avery Dulles, S.J. and rabbi Leon Klenicki with an address by Edward Idris, Cardinal Cassidy. New York: Paulist Press, 2001. 92 pp., notes. (Studies in Judaism and Christianity.) [Address was directed to the American Jewish Committee.]

41246. CHURCH. REPGEN, KONRAD: *Judenpogrom, Rassenideologie und katholische Kirche im Jahr 1938.* [In]: Rainer Bendel, ed.: Die katholische Schuld? Katholizismus im Dritten Reich zwischen Arrangement und Widerstand. Münster: Lit, 2002. Pp. 56–91.

41247. CHURCH. RUESS, KARL-HEINZ/ZECHA, MARCUS, eds.: *Mutige Christen im NS-Staat.* Elisabeth Braun [et al.]. Göppingen: Stadt Göppingen; Jüd. Museum Göppingen, 2002. 47 pp., illus. [Deals with anti-Nazi Christian pastors in Württemberg, some of whom helped Jews or spoke out against their persecution.]

41248. CHURCH. STEHLIN, STEWART A.: *Päpstliche Diplomatie im Zweiten Weltkrieg: Pius XII., Deutschland und die Juden.* Wolnzach: Kastner, 2002. 28 pp., notes. (Eichstätter Universitätsreden, 109.)

41249. COLOGNE. DERES, THOMAS: *Das Bing-Haus. Ein Fallbeispiel von "Arisierung" und "Wiedergutmachung" durch die Stadt Köln.* [In]: Geschichte in Köln. Zeitschrift für Stadt- und Regionalgeschichte, Jg. 49, Köln, 2002. Pp. 193–204, footnotes. [On a department store originally owned by the wholesale textile firm Gebr. Bing. German and Engl. abstracts on p. 327.]

41250. COLOGNE. MATZERATH, HORST: *Der Weg der Kölner Juden in den Holocaust. Versuch einer Rekonstruktion.* [In]: Nationalsozialismus und Regionalgeschichte. Festschrift für Horst Matzerath. Hrsg. von Barbara Becker-Jákli [et al.]. Köln: Emons, 2002. Pp. 224–246, notes. [First publ. 1995.]

41251. COLOGNE. SCHMITZ, MARKUS/HAUNFELDER, BERND: *Humanität und Diplomatie. Die Schweiz in Köln 1940–1949.* Münster: Aschendorff, 2001. 320 pp., bibl., index. [The second part of the book incl. hitherto unpubl. reports of the long-time Swiss Consul General in Cologne, Franz-Rudolf von Weiss, among them reports referring in detail to the deportation of the Jews in 1941.]

41252. COLOGNE. SERUP-BILFELDT, KIRSTEN: *Auf den Spuren eines Kindermordes in Köln.* [In]: Brigitta Huhnke/Björn Krondorfer, eds.: Das Vermächtnis annehmen. Kulturelle und biographische Zugänge zum Holocaust [see No. 41610]. Pp. 237–250. [Deals with tracing the death of a little Jewish boy, Hans Abraham Ochs, who died in Cologne in Sept. 1936 after violent juvenile attacks.]

41253. CZECHOSLOVAKIA. KÁRNY, MIROSLAV: *Die tschechoslowakischen Opfer der deutschen Okkupation.* [In]: Begegnung und Konflikt. Schlaglichter auf das Verhältnis von Tschechen, Slowaken und Deutschen 1815–1989. Beiträge aus den Veröffentlichungen der Deutsch-Tschechischen und Deutsch-Slowakischen Historikerkommission. Hrsg. von Jörg K. Hoensch und Hans Lemberg. Essen: Klartext, 2001. (Veröff. der Deutsch-Tschechischen und der Deutsch-Slowakischen Historikerkommission, Bd. 12.) (Veröff. zur Kultur und Geschichte im östlichen Europa, Bd. 20.) Pp. 137–146, footnotes.

41254. CZERNOWITZ. BARTFELD-FELLER, MARGIT: *Am östlichen Fenster. Gesammelte Geschichten aus Czernowitz und aus der sibirischen Verbannung.* Hrsg. von Erhard Roy Wiehn. Konstanz: Hartung-Gorre, 2002. 286 pp., illus., facsims., frontis., footnotes. [Autobiographical stories.]

41255. *Dachauer Hefte.* Studien und Dokumente zur Geschichte der nationalsozialistischen Konzentrationslager. Im Auftrag des Comité International de Dachau, Brüssel hrsg. von Wolfgang Benz und Barbara Distel. Jg. 18, H. 18 [with the issue title] *Terror und Kunst. Zeugnis, Überlebenshilfe, Rekonstruktion und Denkmal,* Dachau, 2002. 222 pp., footnotes. [Selected articles (titles abbr.): Kunst und Denkmal als Mittel der Erinnerung (Stefanie Endlich, 3–22). Erinnerungsliteratur (Mona Körte, 23–33). Holocaust-Kunst (Jürgen Kaumkötter, 34–41). Zeichnungen aus dem Konzentrationslager Dachau (Michaela Haibl, 42–64). Poesie in Ravensbrück (Anise Postel-Vinay, 65–72). Kunst im Konzentrationslager Auschwitz (Irena Szymanska, 73–96). Zu den Gedichten in "weiter leben" von Ruth Klüger (Katja Schubert, 109–121). Herbert Zipper (1904–1997), Komponist des "Dachau-Liedes" (Albrecht Dümling, 122–134). Meine letzten Tage im KZ Buchenwald (Robert Jehoshua Büchler, 160–177). Felix Nussbaum – Leben und Werk (Inge Jaehner, 178–199). Todesmarsch von Kaufering ins Ungewisse (Zwi Katz, 200–211).]

41256. DAMBITSCH, DAVID: *Im Schatten der Shoah. Gespräche mit Überlebenden und deren Nachkommen.* Mit einem Vorwort von Wolfgang Benz. Berlin: Philo, 2002. 345 pp., footnotes. [Based on radio interviews conducted between 1985 and 2001; cont.: 1. Teil – Vom Pflichtgefühl nach dem Überleben (19 interviews). 2. Teil – Von Generation zu Generation (11 interviews with representatives of the second generation.]

41257. DEAK, ISTVAN: *Essays on Hitler's Europe.* Lincoln: Univ. of Nebraska Press, 2001. XVIII, 222 pp., notes, bibl. (195–205), index. [Collection of previously publ. essays on various topics of National Socialism and the Holocaust, incl. the Nazi past in the two Germanies, Goldhagen debate, Pope Pius XII.]

41258. DEAN, MARTIN C.: *The development and implementation of Nazi denaturalization and confiscation policy up to the eleventh decree to the Reich citizenship law.* [In]: Holocaust and Genocide Studies, Vol. 16, No. 2, Oxford, Fall 2002. Pp. 217–242, notes. [Traces the development of this policy from 1933 to November 1941, discussing that economic rather than political interests dictated the implementation of the eleventh decree whereby Jewish property could be confiscated.]

41259. DEICHMANN, UTE: *Emigration, isolation and the slow start of molecular biology in Germany.* [In]: Studies in History and Philosophy of Biological and Biomedical Sciences, Vol. 33C, No. 3, Amsterdam, Sept. 2002. Pp. 449–471, notes. [Incl. the forced emigration of Jewish molecular biologists after 1933.]

41260. DEICHMANN, UTE: *Flüchten, Mitmachen, Vergessen. Chemiker und Biochemiker in der NS-Zeit.* Weinheim; New York: Wiley-VCH, 2001. XII, 597 pp., illus., footnotes, bibl. [Four of eight chaps. deal with Jewish scientists, their dismissal in 1933 and emigration; the scientific impact they had in the countries of refuge; also with academic antisemitism.]

41261. *Die Deutsche Reichspost 1933–1945. Eine politische Verwaltungsgeschichte.* Ausgewählte Dokumente. Bearb. von Wolfgang Lotz. Koblenz: Bundesarchiv, 2002. LVIII, 719 pp., index. (Materialien aus dem Bundesarchiv, H. 11.) [Incl.: Einleitung (Wolfgang Lutz, 1–12). Sections entitled: Judenpolitik der Deutschen Reichspost (209–265 & 474–527).]

41262. DINER, DAN: *Über Schulddiskurse und andere Narrative. Epistemologisches zum Holocaust.* [In]: Gedächtnis und Geld. Vom Umgang mit der Vergangenheit des Zweiten Weltkrieges [see No. 41605]. Pp. 179–202, notes.

41263. DOERRY, MARTIN: *"Mein verwundetes Herz". Das Leben der Lilli Jahn 1900–1944.* Stuttgart: Deutsche Verlags-Anstalt, 2002. 351 pp., frontis., illus., chronol. [Based on numerous recently found letters the author tells about his grandparents, the non-Jewish physician Ernst Jahn and the Jewish physician L.J. née Schlüchterer, their five children and the fate of L.J. after their divorce in 1942. Incl. the sections: Eine jüdische Familie in Köln. Jahre der Verfolgung in Immenhausen. Die Verbannung nach Kassel. Im Arbeitslager Breitenau. Der Tod in Auschwitz.] [Selected reviews: Lilli Jahn – ihr Leben – unsere Verantwortung (B. Schirmer) [in]: Das achte Licht. Beiträge zur Kultur- und Sozialgeschichte der Juden in Nordhessen [see No. 40983]. Pp. 292–296. Kaum dreißig Kilometer entfernt und doch unerreichbar. Vergleichbar dem Tagebuch der Anne Frank: Die Briefe der Lilli Jahn sind bewegende Dokumente des Wartens und des Hoffens (Eva Menasse) [in]: 'FAZ', Nr. 184, Frankfurt am Main, 10. Aug. 2002, p. 40. Der Enkel, der Chronist (Verena Walter) [in]: Aufbau, Vol. 68, No. 21, New York, Oct. 17, 2002, p. 16. Ein neues, bewegendes Zeugnis über den Holocaust. Die Briefe der Lilli Jahn an ihre Kinder (Volker Ullrich) [in]: Die Zeit, Nr. 33, Hamburg, 8. Aug. 2002, p. 36.]

41264. DRESDEN. *Aktenzeichen "unerwünscht". Dresdner Musikerschicksale und nationalsozialistische Judenverfolgung 1933–1945.* Bearb. von Agata Schindler. Mit einer Einleitung von Sylvia Rogge-Gau. Dresden: Stiftung Sächsische Gedenkstätten zur Erinnerung an die Opfer politischer Gewaltherrschaft, 1999. 156 pp., illus., facsims. (Lebenszeugnisse – Leidenswege, H. 9.) [Documents the fate of eight musicians resp. families of musicians; incl. chap.: Chronik des kulturellen Lebens der Dresdner Israelitischen Religionsgemeinde 1933–1938 (27–56).]

41265. DRESDEN. ULRICH, MICHAEL: *Nach der Synagoge brannte die Stadt.* Dokumente, Berichte, persönliche Zeugnisse. Leipzig: Evang. Verl.-Anstalt, 2002. 176 pp., illus., footnotes, bibl., index. [Also on the post-1945 Jewish community.]

41265a. DÜSSELDORF. *Augenblick.* Berichte, Informationen und Dokumente der Mahn- und Gedenkstätte Düsseldorf, Nr. 20/21 & 22/23, Düsseldorf, 2002. 48; 48 pp., illus., facsims. [Nr. 20/21 [with the issue title] *Deportationen aus dem Rheinland* incl. contribs., interviews, letters and personal memoirs related to the deportation of Jews from Düsseldorf to the ghetto of Riga (Ingrid Schupetta, Angela Genger, Werner Rübsteck, Barbara Materne, Kurt Düwell); to the ghetto of Lodz (Angela Genger, Gary Wolff, Alfred Mayer); to the ghetto of Minsk (Angela Genger, Günter Katzenstein). Also in this issue contribs. related to Essen and Wuppertal, reports on activities and book reviews. Nr. 22/23 [with the issue title] *Lebens-Brüche. Schilderungen aus einer traumatisierenden Zeit* incl.: Lebens-Brüche im Spiegel von Interviews und Selbstzeugnissen (Angela Genger, 1–6). Letters of Georg and Frieda Lindemeyer (7–18; see also No. 41267). Die Düsseldorfer Deportationen nach Theresienstadt 1942–1944 (Angela Genger, 19–20). Letters of Otto and Paula Mayer (introd. by Hildegard Jacobs, 21–32). Vom "eleganten Dandy" zum "politischen Menschen". Der Schauspieler, Regisseur und Intendant Wolfgang Langhoff (Michael Matzigkeit, 33–37). Zur Erinnerung an Wolfgang Langhoff (1901–1966) (Manfred Weber, 37–38). Also reports on exhibitions and other events.]

41266. DÜSSELDORF. BERSCHEL, HOLGER: *Bürokratie und Terror. Das Judenreferat der Gestapo Düsseldorf 1935–1945.* Essen: Klartext, 2001. 478 pp., illus., footnotes, bibl. (444–466), index. (Düsseldorfer Schriften zur Neueren Landesgeschichte und zur Geschichte Nordrhein-Westfalens, Bd. 58.)

[Incl. the sections III. Die jüdische Bevölkerung Düsseldorf. IV. Die Geheime Staatspolizei auf Reichsebene. V. Die Geheime Staatspolizei im Regierungsbezirk Düsseldorf. VI. Die Tätigkeit der Düsseldorfer Gestapo auf dem Gebiet der Judenangelegenheiten.] [Cf.: Bespr. (Michael Zimmermann) [in]: Essener Beiträge. Beiträge zur Geschichte von Stadt und Stift Essen, Bd. 114, Essen, 2002, pp. 259–262.]

41267. DÜSSELDORF. MOSS, CHRISTOPH: "*... Wir leben doch in Gedanken nur mit Euch ...*". Briefe von Georg und Frieda Lindemeyer 1937 bis 1941. Dokumente der Verfolgung von Christen jüdischer Herkunft in Düsseldorf. Düsseldorf: Archiv der Evang. Kirche im Rheinland/Mahn- und Gedenkstätte Düsseldorf, 2002. V, 243 pp., illus., facsims., footnotes, index.

41268. DÜSING, MICHAEL, Hrsg.: *Wir waren zum Tode bestimmt. Lódz – Theresienstadt – Auschwitz – Freiberg – Oederan – Mauthausen. Jüdische Zwangsarbeiterinnen erinnern sich.* Leipzig: Forum Verl., 2002. 188 pp. [Reminiscences, mainly from Polish women; also some German-speaking ones.]

41269. DWORK, DEBORAH/PELT, ROBERT JAN VAN: *Holocaust: a history.* New York: Norton, 2002. XX, 444 pp., illus., ports., facsims., tabs., maps, notes, bibl. (389–428), index. [Incl. persecution of Jews in Germany; also chaps. on refugees in different countries and rescue efforts.]

41270. EDELSTEIN, ELIESER L./MITTERECKER, INGRID UND CHRISTIAN: *Yoram schlägt sich durch. Eine Jugend in der Nazizeit.* Wien: Czernin, 2002. 135 pp., illus. [E.L.E., author, b. 1922 in Vienna, psychiatrist, emigr. to Palestine in 1938, studied after 1945 in Switzerland, lives in Jerusalem and Vienna.]

41271. EICHMANN, ADOLF. WOJAK, IRMTRUD: *Die Rechtfertigungen des Adolf Eichmann.* [In]: Geschichte in Wissenschaft und Unterricht, Jg. 53, H. 12, Stuttgart, 2002. Pp. 725–736.

41272. *Emigration.* [Section title of] *Judenfeindschaft als Paradigma.* Studien zur Vorurteilsforschung [see No. 42134]. Pp. 185–228. [Incl.: Emigration: Möglichkeiten und Grenzen jüdischer Flucht aus Deutschland (Wolfgang Benz, 187–193). Kindertransporte 1938/39 nach Großbritannien (Claudia Curio, 194–201). Further articles of this section are listed according to subject.]

41273. ENGELKING-BONI, BARBARA: *Holocaust and memory: the experience of the Holocaust and its consequences: an investigation based on personal narratives.* Ed. by Gunnar S. Paulsson. Transl. by Emma Harris. London; New York: Leicester Univ. Press in association with the European Jewish Publication Society, 2001. XX, 348 pp., bibl., notes, index.

41274. ESSEN. ROSEMAN, MARK: *In einem unbewachten Augenblick. Eine Frau überlebt im Untergrund.* Aus dem Engl. von Astrid Becker. Berlin: Aufbau, 2002. 583 pp., illus., notes (518–558), bibl. (559–568), index. [Tells the story of Marianne Ellenbogen née Strauss from Essen. For orig. edn. publ. in 2000 with the title *A past in hiding* and details see No. 40125/YB XLVII.]

41275. ESSNER, CORNELIA: *Die "Nürnberger Gesetze" oder die Verwaltung des Rassenwahns 1933–1945.* Paderborn: Schöningh, 2002. 477 pp., footnotes, bibl. (457–473), index. Zugl.: Berlin, Techn. Univ., Habil.-Schr. 2000. [Incl. chaps.: I. "Der Irrgarten der Rassenlogik" (1871–1935). II. Entwürfe eines Rassenrechts vor den "Nürnberger Gesetzen". III. Die Rekonstruktion des Geschehens auf und nach dem "Reichsparteitag der Freiheit" 1935. IV. Ausbau und Funktionsweise des Systems. V. Rassenrecht und Staatsangehörigkeit: Der lange bürokratische Weg in die Deportation. VI. Vorstösse zur Verschärfung des Judenbegriffs im "Altreich" und den "Besetzten Ostgebieten" 1941/1942. Die "Endlösung der Judenfrage" und das ungelöste "Mischlings"-Problems (1942–1943).]

41276. ESKIN, BLAKE: *A life in pieces: the making and unmaking of Binjamin Wilkomirski.* New York: Norton; London: Aurum, 2002. 251 pp., illus., ports., notes.

41277. ETLIN, RICHARD A., ed.: *Art, culture, and media under the Third Reich.* Chicago: Univ. of Chicago Press, 2002. XXII, 348 pp., illus., ports., facsims., notes, index. [Incl. chaps.: The target of racial purity: the "degenerate music": exhibition in Düsseldorf, 1938 (Albrecht Dümling, 43–71). The impact of antisemitic film propaganda on German audiences: 'Jew Süss' and 'The wandering Jew' (1940) (David Culbert, 139–157). The exile artists from Nazi Germany and their art (Keith Holz, 343–367).]

41278. EVANS, RICHARD J.: *Der Geschichtsfälscher: Holocaust und historische Wahrheit im David-Irving-Prozess.* Aus dem Engl. von Udo Remmert. Frankfurt am Main; New York: Campus, 2001. 390 pp., illus., maps, notes (345–385). [For Engl. edn. see No. 40028/YB XLVII.] [Cf.: Bespr. (Georg Kreis) [in]: Schweizerische Zeitschrift für Geschichte, Vol. 52, No. 3, Basel, 2002, pp. 371–374.]

41279. FACKLER, GUIDO: *Lied und Gesang im KZ.* [In]: Lied und populäre Kultur/Song and popular culture. Jahrbuch des Deutschen Volksliedarchivs Freiburg, Jg. 46, Münster, 2001. Pp. 141–198, footnotes.

41280. FELDMAN, GERALD D.: *Allianz and the German insurance business, 1933–1945.* Cambridge; New York: Cambridge Univ. Press, 2001. XXII, 568 pp., illus., ports., facsims., map, notes, bibl. (539–547), index. [For German edn. and details see No. 39966/YB XLVII.]

41281. FILM. CLINEFELTER, JOAN: *A cinematic construction of Nazi anti-semitism: The documentary 'Der ewige Jude'.* [In]: Cultural history through a National Socialist lens. Essays on the cinema of the Third Reich. Ed. by Robert C. Reimer. Rochester, NY: Camden House, 2000. Pp. 133–154, illus., notes.

41282. FILM. FETSCHER, IRING: *Die Fernsehserie 'Holocaust' und das deutsche Publikum.* [In]: Preußens Himmel breitet seine Sterne …[see No. 41991], Bd. 2. Pp. 539–542.

41283. FILM. FRAHM, OLE: *Von Holocaust zu Holokaust. Guido Knopps Aneignung der Vernichtung der europäischen Juden.* [In]: 1999. Zeitschrift für Sozialgeschichte des 20. und 21. Jahrhunderts, Jg. 17, Sept. 2002, H. 2, Köln, Sept. 2002. Pp. 128–138, footnotes. [On the German TV series 'Holokaust' and the book with the same title (publ. 2000). Also in this issue: Bei Vollmond: Holokaust. Genretheoretische Bemerkungen zu einer Dokumentation des ZDF (Hanno Loewy, 114–127).]

41284. FILM. KNAAP, EWOUT VAN DER: *De verbeelding van nacht en nevel. 'Nuit et Brouillard' in Nederland en Duitsland.* Groningen: Historische Uitgeverij, 2001. 279 pp., illus. [On the Holocaust documentary film by Alain Resnais (1955).] [Cf.: Het beeld van de Holocaust (P.A.C. Caljé) [in]: Tijdschrift voor Geschiedenis, jaargang 115, No. 4, Utrecht, 2002, pp. 636–638.]

41285. FINAL SOLUTION. GRANT, R. GORDON: *Genocide: the Final Solution to the Jewish Question.* Victoria, BC: Trafford, 2002. 83 pp., maps, bibl.

41286. FINAL SOLUTION. LONGERICH, PETER: *The unwritten order: Hitler's role in the final solution.* Stroud: Tempus, 2001. 160 pp., map, bibl., index. [For German edn. see No. 39972/YB XLVII.]

41287. FINAL SOLUTION. ROSEMAN, MARK: *The villa, the lake, the meeting: Wannsee and the final solution.* London: Allen Lane/Penguin, 2002. VII, 152 pp., appendix, notes, index. [American edn.: *The Wannsee Conference and the final solution: a reconsideration.* New York: Metropolitan Books, 2002. 211 pp., notes, bibl. (173–201), index. German edn.: *Die Wannsee-Konferenz. Wie die NS-Bürokratie den Holocaust organisierte.* Aus dem Engl. von Klaus Dieter Schmidt. München: Propyläen, 2002. 221 pp., facsims., bibl., index.] [Cf.: Cognac and genocide (Mark Roseman) [in]: The Guardian Saturday Review, London, Jan. 5, 2002, p. 2. True believers (Saul Friedländer) [in]: TLS, London, March 1, 2002, pp. 4–5.]

41288. FINKENSTEIN, KURT: *Briefe aus der Haft 1935–1943.* Hrsg., kommentiert und eingeleitet von Dietfrid Krause-Vilmar. Mitarbeit: Susanne Schneider. Kassel: Verlag Winfried Jenior, 2002. 480 pp., frontis., illus., facsims., footnotes. (Nationalsozialismus in Nordhessen, Bd. 19.) [K.F., March 27, 1893 Strasbourg – Jan. 29, 1944 Auschwitz, son of a Jewish mother, Auguste Funkenstein (sic), father unknown, dentist, Communist, lived from 1919 in Kassel, 1933–1943 imprisoned in various jails and concentration camps, 1943 deported from Breitenau concentration camp to Auschwitz.]

41289. FISCHER, GERHARD/LINDNER, ULRICH: *Stürmer für Hitler. Vom Zusammenspiel zwischen Fußball und Nationalsozialismus.* Mit Beiträgen von Werner Skrentny und Dietrich Schulze-Marmeling. 2. durchges. Aufl. Göttingen: Verl. Die Werkstatt, 2002. 303 pp., illus., bibl., index, footnotes. [Incl. the chap.: Verfolgt und ermordet: Die Juden im Sport (188–212).]

41290. FLOSSENBÜRG. FÜSSL, BERNHARD/SEIFERT, SYLVIA/SIMON-PELANDA, HANS: *Ihrer Stimme Gehör geben. Zwangsarbeit. Überlebendenberichte ehemaliger Häftlinge des KZ Flossenbürg.* Hrsg.:

Arbeitsgemeinschaft ehemaliges KZ Flossenbürg e.V. Bonn: Pahl-Rugenstein, 2002. 112 pp., illus. [Incl. personal reminiscences of German-speaking Jews. Also on Flossenbürg (same editor, same publ.): Hans Simon-Pelanda: Kunst und KZ. Künstler im Konzentrationslager Flossenbürg und in den Außenlagern. Mit einer Abhandlung von Agnes Rosch und unter Mitarbeit von Sylvia Seifert. Bonn, 2001. 63 pp., illus.]

41291. FORCED LABOUR. BLOXHAM, DONALD: *A survey of Jewish slave labour in the Nazi system.* [In]: The Journal of Holocaust Education, Vol. 10, No. 3, London, Winter 2001. Pp. 25–59, notes.

41292. FORCED LABOUR. LIEDKE, KARL: *Destruction through work: Lodz Jews in the Büssing truck factory in Braunschweig, 1944–1945.* [In]: Yad Vashem Studies, Vol. 30, Jerusalem, 2002. Pp. 153–187, map, appendix, footnotes, [Incl. appendix with names of some prisoners.]

41293. FORCED LABOUR. SPOERER, MARK/FLEISCHHACKER, JOCHEN: *Forced laborers in Nazi Germany: categories, numbers, and survivors.* [In]: The Journal of Interdisciplinary History, Vol. XXXI-II, No. 2, Cambridge, MA, Autumn 2002. Pp. 169–204, footnotes.

41294. FORCED LABOUR. ZUMBANSEN, PEER, ed.: *Zwangsarbeit im Dritten Reich: Erinnerung und Verantwortung/NS-Forced Labor: Remembrance and responsibility.* Juristische und zeithistorische Betrachtungen/Legal and historical oberservations. Baden-Baden: Nomos, 428 pp., footnotes. [Incl. the sections: I. Forced labor during WW II (17–156). II. Public international treaties and payments after 1945 (157–200). III. Individual claims before German and American courts (201–246). IV. The long road to compensation: societal memory, responsibility and the Foundation Law (247–392).]

41295. FRANCE. BURGESS, GREG: *France and the German refugee crisis of 1933.* [In]: French History, Vol. 16, No. 2, Oxford, 2002. Pp. 203–229, footnotes. [Deals with the exclusionary policies of France and its insensitivity to the plight of the refugees.]

41296. FRANCE. EGGERS, CHRISTIAN: *Unerwünschte Ausländer. Juden aus Deutschland und Mitteleuropa in französischen Internierungslagern 1940–1942.* Berlin: Metropol, 2002. 566 pp., tabs., maps, graphs, bibl., index. (Reihe Dokumente, Texte, Materialien, Bd. 42.)

—— FRANCE. HOLL, KARL: *Der lange Weg zur französischen Staatsbürgerschaft. Alfred Falk (1896–1951) im Exil in Frankreich.* [See No. 41856.]

41297. FRANCE. JENNINGS, ERIC: *Last exit from Vichy France: The Martinique escape route and the ambiguities of emigration.* [In]: The Journal of Modern History, Vol. 74, Chicago, IL, 2002. Pp. 289–324, footnotes. [On the escape of Jewish refugees, incl. Anna Seghers, on the 'Paul Lemmerle' to Martinique from Marseille in early 1941; also on the role of Varian Fry and the Emergency Rescue Committee.]

41298. FRANCE. POZNANSKI, RENÉE: *Jews in France during World War II.* Transl. from the French by Nathan Bracher. Hanover, NH: Univ. Press of New England [for] Brandeis Univ. Press in association with the United States Holocaust Memorial Museum, 2001. XXV, 601 pp., illus., tabs., notes, bibl. (579–594), index. (The Tauber Institute for the study of European Jewry series.) [Incl. how French Jews dealt with the influx of Jewish refugees from Germany, Austria, Czechoslovakia. Also deals with Jewish refugees in internment camps.]

41299. FRANCE. SAINT SAUVEUR-HENN, ANNE, ed.: *Fluchtziel Paris: die deutschsprachige Emigration 1933–1945.* Berlin: Metropol, 2002. 336 pp., footnotes. (Reihe Dokumente, Texte, Materialien, Bd. 48.) [Cont.: Vorwort (ed., 9–12). Essays, arranged under the sections: I. Historische und juristische Perspektiven; cont.: Paris in den dreißiger Jahren: Mittelpunkt des europäischen Exils? (ed., 14–28). Frankreichs Haltung gegenüber den deutschsprachigen Emigranten zwischen 1933 und 1940 (Gilbert Badia, 29–40). Die Schaffung eines internationalen Flüchtlingsstatus und die Rolle der Pariser Asylrechts- und Flüchtlingskomitees (Barbara Vormeier, 41–50). Das Pariser Völkerbundinstitut für geistige Zusammenarbeit und die aus Deutschland geflüchteten Intellektuellen (Ute Lemke, 51–60). II. Alltagsgeschichte und Topografie; cont.: "Von Haien umgeben". Existenzerhaltung jüdischer Emigranten in Paris (Julia Franke, 62–72).

Emigrationsalltag im 15. Arrondissement. Walter Benjamin, Arthur Koestler, Lisa Fittko (Catherine Stodolsky, 73–80). Das gewöhnlich-gefährliche Leben Anna Seghers' in Paris (Marie-Laure Canteloube, 81–87). Die Bedeutung der Pariser Cafés für die geflohenen deutschsprachigen Literaten (Anne-Marie Corbin, 88–101). Das Pariser Exil in den Zeichnungen Bil Spiras (1935–1939). III. Politische Zusammenarbeit in europäischer Perspektive; cont.: Zweimal Antifaschismus – zweierlei Antifaschismus? Front populaire und deutsche Volksfrontbewegung in Paris (Ursula Langkau-Alex, 114–128). Deutschsprachige und russische Sozialisten im Pariser Exil (Claudie Weill, 129–136). Das Pariser Auslandssekretariat der KPD im August/September 1939. Ein neuralgischer Punkt in der Geschichte des deutschen Kommunismus (Ulrich Pfeil, 137–152). Paris als Mittelpunkt für deutsche Pazifisten im Exil (Karl Holl, 153–164). Pariser Positionen. Der außenpolitische Diskurs des deutschen Exils 1938/1939 (Boris Schilmar, 165–180). Im Visier der Diplomaten. Die Observierung deutscher Exilanten durch die Botschaft des Dritten Reiches in Paris (Alexander Stephan, 181–189). Kontrolle und Überwachung der deutsch-österreichischen Emigration durch die französische Sûreté Nationale (Michaela Enderle-Ristori, 190–204). IV. Intellektuelle und Politik; cont.: Freitag, 9. Juni 1933, 20. Uhr, Mutualité. Abrechnung und Ausgrenzung als Vorstufen der politischen Einheit unter den Intellektuellen (Valérie Robert, 206–214). "In bewusstem Gegensatz zu der kommunistisch-ullsteinschen Bande". Schwarzschilds Bund Freie Presse und Literatur in Paris (Dieter Schiller, 215–229). Hans Sahl im Pariser Exil (Andrea Reiter, 230–242). V. Paris-Bilder in der Literatur; cont.: Magnet Paris. Das Bild der französischen Metropole in zwei Romanen der frühen dreißiger Jahre (Waltraud Strickhausen, 244–260; on Hilde Spiel's unpubl. novel 'Der Sonderzug' and Peter Mendelssohn's 'Paris über mir', publ. 1931). Zum Paris-Mythos im Pariser Tageblatt/Pariser Tageszeitung. Texte von Franz Hessel, Hermann Wendel, Alfred Wolkenstein, Richard Dyck (Lutz Winckler, 261–270). Wege durch Paris, Schauplätze, Stadtdurchquerungen. Die ersten Sequenzen in Klaus Manns 'Der Vulkan' und in Anna Seghers' 'Transit' (Hélène Roussel, 271–287). "Es gibt keinen Kompromiss mit dem Unrecht". Ernst Lothars Exilroman Die Zeugin. Das Pariser Tagebuch einer Wienerin (Jörg Thunecke, 288–297). Vom Ende des Asyllands Frankreich. Schreiben in Krise und Distanz (Silvia Schlenstedt, 198–305). VI. Erfahrungen im Pariser Exil (307–330; incl. personal reminiscences by Julia Trady-Marcus, Hanna Papanek, Lenka Reinerova).]

41300. FRANK, ANNE. HEYL, MATTHIAS: *Anne Frank*. Dargestellt von Matthias Heyl. Reinbek bei Hamburg: Rowohlt Taschenbuch-Verlag, 2002. 151 pp., illus., facsims., bibl. (Rowohlts Monographien, 50524.)

41301. FRANKFURT am MAIN. DOETZER, OLIVER: *"Aus Menschen werden Briefe". Die Korrespondenz einer jüdischen Familie zwischen Verfolgung und Emigration 1933–1947*. Köln: Böhlau, 2002. 277 pp., footnotes, bibl. (247–266). (Selbstzeugnisse der Neuzeit, Bd. 11.) [Deals with the Rosenberg, Eisenstein and Eichenberg families from Frankfurt on Main two members of whom went with a Kindertransport to England; incl. their correspondence, in detail annotated and analysed by the author.]

41302. FRECHEN. HEEG, EGON: *Die Levys oder Die Vernichtung des Altfrechener Judentums*. Band 2 – Gedenkbuch. Frechen: Stadt Frechen, 2002. 128 pp., illus., facs., maps. [Frechen: nr. Cologne.]

41303. FRIEDLÄNDER, SAUL/FREI, NORBERT/RENDTORFF, TRUTZ/WITTMANN, REINHARD, eds.: *Bertelsmann im Dritten Reich*. Unter Mitarbeit von Hans-Eugen Bühler [et al.]. Gütersloh: Bertelsmann, 2002. 794 pp., notes, index, bibl., illus., facsims., bibl. (712–772), indexes. [Incl.: Antisemitismus im Verlagsprogramm. Theologische Reflexionen und belletristische Stereotype (297–334).]

41304. GANZFRIED, DANIEL:… *alias Wilkomirski. Die Holocaust-Travestie. Enthüllung und Dokumentation eines literarischen Skandals*. Hrsg. im Auftrag des Deutschschweizer PEN-Zentrums von Sebastian Hefti. Berlin: Jüdische Verlagsanstalt, 2002. 270 pp. [Cont. the author's documentary story about the Wilkomirski affair (17–154); also contribs. by Sebastian Hefti, Elsbeth Pulver, Lorenz Jäger, Rafael Newman, Claude Lanzmann, Imre Kertész, Hans Saner, Wanda Schmid, Ruth Klüger, Philip Gourevitch.]

41305. GEIGER, FRIEDRICH: *Die "Goebbels-Liste" vom 1. September 1935*. Eine Quelle zur Komponistenverfolgung im NS-Staat. [In]: Archiv für Musikwissenschaft, Jg. 59, H. 2, Wiesbaden, 2002. Pp. 104–112, footnotes. [Incl. the first publ. of a blacklist containing names of 108 contemporary composers.]

41306. GELSENKIRCHEN. NIEWERTH, ANDREA: *Gelsenkirchener Juden im Nationalsozialismus.* Eine kollektivbiographische Analyse über Verfolgung, Emigration und Deportation. Essen: Klartext, 2002. 392 pp., illus., facsims., tabs., graphs, notes (207–308), bibl. (309–344), docs. (349–392). (Schriftenreihe des Instituts für Stadtgeschichte: Beiträge, Bd. 11.)

41307. GELLATELY, ROBERT: *Hingeschaut und weggesehen. Hitler und sein Volk.* Aus dem Amerik. von Holger Fliessbach. Stuttgart: Deutsche Verlags-Anstalt, 2002. 456 pp., illus., tabs., index, notes (367–438). [Orig. edn.: Backing Hitler. Consent and coercion in Nazi Germany. Oxford, Oxford Univ. Press, 2001. Incl. chap.: Das Unrecht an den Juden (173–212).]

41308. GILBERT, MARTIN: *Nie wieder! Die Geschichte des Holocaust.* Aus dem Engl. übers. von Hans-Ulrich Seebohm. Berlin: Propyläen, 2001. 192 pp., illus., maps. [For Engl. edn. see No. 40022/YB XLVII.]

41309. GILBERT, SHIRLI: *Music in the Nazi ghettos and camps (1939–1945).* Oxford: Oxford Univ. Diss., 2002. 385 pp., gloss., appendixes of musical scores and songs, bibl. (364–385). 2 vols. [Unpubl. ms. available in the Wiener Library, London.]

41310. GOLDHAGEN DEBATE. ULLRICH, VOLKER: *Die Goldhagen-Kontroverse – Ein Rückblick und ein Resümee.* [In]: Preußens Himmel breitet seine Sterne .... [see No. 41991], Bd. 2. Pp. 543–557, notes.

41311. GOLDSMITH, MARTIN: *Die unauslöschliche Symphonie. Musik und Liebe im Schatten des Dritten Reiches – eine deutsch-jüdische Geschichte.* Aus dem Amerik. von Dorothea Brinkmann. Freiburg: Herder, 2002. 380 pp., bibl. [For orig. edn. see No. 38813/YB XLVI.]

41312. GONI, UKI: *The real Odessa: how Peron brought the Nazi war criminals to Argentina.* London: Granta, 2002. XVIII, 382 pp., ports., notes, bibl. (366–374), index. [Author shows that Peron's actions were only possible because of a massive cover-up which involved the Vatican, the Red Cross, as well as the diplomatic corps and the police in several countries.]

41313. GOSLAR. MUELLER, ANDREAS: *Jude – ein Unwort? Die lange Geschichte einer kurzen Straße in Goslar.* Goslar: Geschichtsverein Goslar in Zusammenarb. m. d. Goslarschen Zeitung, [2002]. 40 pp., illus, bibl.

41314. GOSEWINKEL, DIETER: *Einbürgern und Ausschließen. Die Nationalisierung der Staatsangehörigkeit vom Deutschen Bund bis zur Bundesrepublik Deutschland.* Göttingen: Vandenhoeck und Ruprecht, 2001. 472 pp., bibl., index, footnotes. (Kritische Studien zur Geschichtswissenschaft, Bd. 150.) (Zugl.: Berlin, Freie Univ., Habil-Schr.) [Refers also to the naturalisation of Jews in Imperial Germany and to anti-Jewish legislation in the Nazi period.]

41315. GREAT BRITAIN. MOHR, PHILIPP CASPAR: *"Kein Recht zur Einmischung"?* Die politische und völkerrechtliche Reaktion Großbritanniens auf Hitlers "Machtergreifung" und die einsetzende Judenverfolgung. Tübingen: Mohr Siebeck, 2002. XVI, 405 pp., footnotes, bibl. (378–396), indexes. (Beiträge zur Rechtsgeschichte des 20. Jahrhunderts, Bd. 31.) [Focuses on the years 1933–1935.]

41316. GREAT BRITAIN. SHATZKES, PAMELA: *Holocaust and rescue: impotent or indifferent?: Anglo-Jewry 1938–1945.* Basingstoke: Palgrave, 2002. 322 pp., illus., ports., notes, bibl. (289– 304), index. [Author describes the efforts of British Jewry to rescue German Jews as compassionate, and carried out with common sense and administrative expertise. Discusses that Jewish organisations at first supported the internment policy, but made welfare provisions for families left behind.]

41317. GROSS, WOLFF: *Im Gepäck der Davidsstern.* Ein Lebensbericht. Gelnhausen: Triga-Verlag, 2002. 157 pp. [Author, b. 1926 in Kolberg/Pomerania, son of a Jewish father, internist, Professor at Würzburg Univ., tells about the fate of his family during the Nazi period.]

41318. GROHS-MARTIN, SILVIA: *Ich sah die Toten groß und klein. Eine Schauspielerin überlebt den Holocaust.* Aus dem amerik. Englisch von Isabell Lorenz. Berlin: Henschel, 2002. 447 pp., illus. [For American edn. see No. 38814/YB XLVI.] [Cf.: Man kann immer etwas tun (Nora Niemann) [in]: Illustrierte Neue Welt, Nr. 6/7, Wien, Juni/Juli 2002, p. 17.] [S.G-M., née Grohs, b. 1918 in

Vienna, actress, deported from Amsterdam to Auschwitz, later to Ravensbrück, after liberation went to the US. Lives in Los Angeles.]

41319. GRUNER, WOLF: *Öffentliche Wohlfahrt und Judenverfolgung*. Wechselwirkungen lokaler und zentraler Politik im NS-Staat (1933–1942). München: Oldenbourg, 2002. 362 pp., footnotes, tabs., bibl. (343–356), indexes. (Studien zur Zeitgeschichte, Bd. 62.)

41320. GÜTERSLOH. GATZEN, HELMUT: *Befehl zum Abtransport*. *Juden und "Mischlinge 1. Grades" 1933–1945 in und um Gütersloh*. Gütersloh: Flöttmann Verlag, 2001. 144 pp., illus., facsims., notes (126–141), index.

41321. HALLE. KAHLBERG, JOSEF H.: *Deutsche Staatsbürger jüdischen Glaubens. Die Geschichte einer Familie, die Glück hatte*. Halle/Saale: Förderverein Haus des Lebens e.V. Halle (Saale). 43 pp., illus., port. (Schriftenreihe des Fördervereins Haus des Lebens e.V. Halle (Saale), H. 1, Mai 2002.) [Author, b. 1917 in Halle, son of Albert Abraham K., rabbi in Halle 1911–1938, emigr. to Italy in 1936, later to Sweden, from there to Palestine in 1948. Lives in Kibbutz Naot Mordechai.]

41322. HAMBURG. BAJOHR, FRANK: *"Aryanisation" in Hamburg: the economic exclusion of Jews and the confiscation of their property in Nazi Germany*. Transl. by George Wilkes. New York: Berghahn Books, 2002. VII, 344 pp., footnotes, tabs., lists, bibl. (323–335), appendix, index. [Incl.: Register of Jewish firms that were 'aryanised' or liquidated in 1938–39 (292–305). For German edn. in 1997 see No. 35075/YB XLIII.]

41323. HAMBURG. *Die Deportation der Hamburger Juden 1941–1945*. Hrsg. von der Forschungsstelle für Zeitgeschichte in Hamburg und dem Institut für die Geschichte der der deutschen Juden. Mit Beiträgen von Frank Bajohr [et al.]. Hamburg: Forschungsstelle für Zeitgeschichte [et al.], 2002. 80 pp. [Incl. (some titles abbr.): Vorwort (Dorothee Stapelfeldt, 7–12). Die Hamburger und die Deportationen (Frank Bajohr, 13–29). Die Arbeit der Jüdischen Gemeinde 1941 bis 1945 (Ina Lorenz, 30–44). Die Deportationen im Spiegel lebensgeschichtlicher Interviews (Angelika Eder, 45–59). Untergetauchte und gerettete Hamburger Juden (Beate Meyer, 60–76).]

41324. HAMBURG-EIMSBÜTTEL. MEYER, BEATE: *"Goldfasane" und "Nazissen". Die NSDAP im ehemals "roten" Stadtteil Hamburg-Eimsbüttel*. [Hrsg.: Galerie Morgenland]. Hamburg: Selbstverlag, 2002. 166 pp., illus., facsims., notes (138–155), bibl. [Incl. antisemitism; persecution of Jews.]

41324a. HANOVER. HERSKOVITS-GUTMANN, RUTH: *Auswanderung vorläufig nicht möglich. Die Geschichte der Familie Herskovits aus Hannover*. Hrsg., übersetzt und kommentiert von Bernhard Strebel. Göttingen: Wallstein, 2002. 288 pp., notes (241–275), bibl.

41325. HEIDELBERG. MORITZ, WERNER: *Die Aberkennung des Doktortitels an der Universität Heidelberg während der NS-Zeit*. [In]: Zwischen Wissenschaft und Politik. Studien zur deutschen Universitätsgeschichte [see No. 41796]. Pp. 540–562, footnotes. [Incl. name list of ca. 125 people, most of them Jews.]

41326. HEIDELBERG. REMY, STEVEN P.: *The Heidelberg myth: the nazification and denazification of a German university*. Cambridge, MA; London: Harvard Univ. Press, 2002. 329 pp., appendixes, notes (255–322), index. [Incl. antisemitism among faculty, dismissal of Jewish professors, teaching of "Aryan" physics, and the post-war culture of whitewashing.]

41327. HEISTER, HANNS-WERNER, eds.: *"Entartete Musik" 1938 – Weimar und die Ambivalenz*. Ein Projekt der Hochschule für Musik Franz Liszt Weimar zum Kulturstadtjahr 1999. Mit Beiträgen von Albrecht Dümling [et al.]. Saarbrücken: Pfau, 2001. 888 pp., illus., facsims., music, notes, bibl., index. [Selected articles (some titles abbr.): Das "Lexikon der Juden in der Musik" (Silke Wenzel, 740–757). Verfolgung und Vernichtung (Hanns-Werner Heister/Silke Wenzel, 758–762). Das "Horstdussel-Lied" von Paul Dessau (Peter Petersen, 769–773). Spottlieder in und außerhalb von Konzentrationslagern & Musik in Konzentrationslagern (Elisabeth Brinkmann, 774–797). Nachdenken über Musik in Konzentrationslagern (Bernd Sponheuer, 798–822). Other contribs. deal also passim with the banning and persecution of Jewish composers and musicians.]

41328. HERFORD. BRADE, LUTZ: *Die Aberkennung der Menschenrechte in Deutschland zwischen 1933–1945 am Beispiel der Juden aus Herford.* Bad Oeynhausen: Heka-Verlag, 2001. 124 pp., facsims. [Incl. alphabetical list of the Jews in Herford with short texts related to their fate.]

———— HERNE & WANNE-EICKEL. PIORR, RALF, ed.: *"Nahtstellen, fühlbar, hier …". Zur Geschichte der Juden in Herne und Wanne-Eickel.* [See No. 40981.]

41329. HERRMANN, HEINZ J.: *Mein Kampf gegen die Endlösung: von Troppau und Proßnitz durch Theresienstadt, Auschwitz-Birkenau und Dachau nach Israel.* Tschechisch-jüdische Schicksale 1921–1948. Vorwort von Peter Erben. Hrsg. von Erhard Roy Wiehn. Konstanz: Hartung-Gorre, 2002. 202 pp., bibl. (122–140). [For first edn. (Vienna 1994) and details see No. 34057/YB XLII.]

41330. HESSE. *Legalisierter Raub. Der Fiskus und die Ausplünderung der Juden in Hessen 1933–1945.* [Hrsg.: Sparkassen-Kulturstiftung Hessen-Thüringen; Red.: Bettina Hindemith, Susanne Meinl, Mitarbeit: Katharine Stengl, Stephan Wirtz]. Frankfurt am Main: Sparkassen-Kulturstiftung Hessen-Thüringen; Fritz Bauer Institut; Hessischer Rundfunk, 2002. 71 pp., illus., facsims. [Exhibition catalogue.]

41331. HESSE, KLAUS: *Verbrechen der Wehrmacht – Dimensionen des Vernichtungskrieges": Anmerkungen zur Neufassung der "Wehrmachtsausstellung".* In]: Geschichte in Wissenschaft und Unterricht, Jg. 53, H. 10, Stuttgart, 2002. 594–611, notes.

41332. HESSE, KLAUS/SPRINGER, PHILIPP: *Vor aller Augen. Fotodokumente des nationalsozialistischen Terrors in der Provinz.* Für die Stiftung Topographie des Terrors, Berlin hrsg. von Reinhard Rürup. Essen: Klartext, 2002. 216 pp., bibl., illus., indexes, notes. [Incl.: Vorwort (Reinhard Rürup, 7–9). Auf Straßen und Plätzen. Zur Fotogeschichte des nationalsozialistischen Deutschland (Philipp Springer, 11–33). Die Bilder lesen – Interpretationen fotografischer Quellen zur Deportation der deutschen Juden (Klaus Hesse, 185–212). Photographs are arranged under the sections: Der frühe Terror. Antijüdische Aktionen und Diskriminierungen. Der Pogrom im November 1938. Öffentliche Demütigungen von "Rasseschändern". Die Deportationen. Epilog: Die Verwertung jüdischen Eigentums.]

41333. HILBERG, RAUL: *Die Quellen des Holocaust. Entschlüsseln und Interpretieren.* Aus dem Amerik. von Udo Rennert. Frankfurt am Main: S. Fischer, 2002. 256 pp., illus., footnotes, index. [For orig. American edn. see No. 40023/YB XLVII.] [Cf.: Spurensuche. Raul Hilberg entschlüsselt und interpretiert die Quellen des Holocaust (Christoph Jahr) [in]: 'NZZ', Nr. 283, Zürich, 5. Dez. 2002, p. 36.]

41334. HILBRENNER, ANKE/BERG, NICOLAS: *Der Tod Simon Dubnows in Riga 1941 – Quellen, Zeugnisse, Erinnerungen.* [In]: Simon-Dubnow-Jahrbuch, Jg. 1, Stuttgart, 2002. Pp. 457–474, footnotes.

41335. HISTORIOGRAPHY. BODENHEIMER, ALFRED: *Rettung durch Erinnerung? Aufgaben, Ansprüche und Möglichkeiten der Geisteswissenschaften im Umgang mit der Shoa.* [In]: "… der den Erniedrigten aufrichtet aus dem Staube und aus dem Elend erhöht den Armen" [see No. 40844]. Pp. 50–63, notes.

41336. HISTORIOGRAPHY. FRIEDLÄNDER, SAUL: *History, memory and the historian: dilemmas and responsibilities.* [In]: Gedächtnis, Geld und Gesetz. Vom Umgang mit der Vergangenheit des Zweiten Weltkrieges [see No. 41605]. Pp. 63–76, notes.

41337. HISTORIOGRAPHY. FRIEDLÄNDER, SAUL: *Im Angesicht der 'Endlösung'. Die Entwicklung des öffentlichen Gedächtnisses und die Verantwortung des Historikers.* [In]: Das Judentum im Spiegel seiner kulturellen Umwelten. Symposium zu Ehren von Saul Friedländer [see No. 41864]. Pp. 207–223. [Lecture given at Heidelberg Univ., Dec. 5, 2000.]

———— HISTORIOGRAPHY. *Der Holocaust und historisches Denken.* [Section title of] *Jüdische Geschichtsschreibung heute* [see No. 40866.]

41338. HISTORIOGRAPHY. MICHMAN, DAN: *Die Historiographie der Shoah aus jüdischer Sicht.* Konzeptualisierungen, Terminologie, Anschauungen, Grundfragen. Hamburg: Dölling und

Galitz, 2002. 355 pp., indexes, notes. [Incl. the sections: Teil I. Die "Shoah". Teil II. Faschismus und Nationalsozialismus. Teil III. Judenrat. Teil IV. Hilfe, Rettung, Vorhersagbarkeit. Teil V. Widerstand. Teil VI. Die jüdische Religion und gläubige Juden. Teil VII. Shoah und Gründung des Staates Israel. Teil VIII. Historiographie der Shoah: Geschichte und Probleme.]

41339. HISTORIOGRAPHY. STONE, DAN: *Recent trends in Holocaust historiography.* [In]: The Journal of Holocaust Education, Vol. 10, No. 3, London, Winter 2001. Pp. 1–24, notes, bibl. (21–24).

41340. HITLER, ADOLF. GIBLIN, JAMES CROSS: *The life and death of Adolf Hitler.* Boston: Houghton, Mifflin/Clarion Books, 2002. 256 pp., illus., maps, notes, bibl., index.

41341. HITLER, ADOLF. MAUTER, WENDELL: *The great war and the shaping of Adolf Hitler.* [In]: European Studies Journal, Vol. 18/19, Cedar Falls, IA, Fall 2001– Spring 2002. Pp. 39–54, notes.

41342. HOLOCAUST. ALY, GÖTZ/HEIM, SUSANNE: *Architects of annihilation: Auschwitz and the logic of destruction.* Transl. by A.G. Blunden. London: Weidenfeld & Nicolson, 2002. 378 pp., notes (296–356), bibl. (357–378). [For orig. German edn. see No. 28326/YB XXXVII.] [Cf.: The forgotten executioners (Peter Preston) [in]: The Observer Review, London, Jan. 12, 2003.]

41343. HOLOCAUST. BERGER, RONALD J.: *Fathoming the Holocaust.* A social problems approach. New York: Aldine de Gruyter, 2002. 237 pp., notes, bibl. (197–221), index. (Social Problems and Social Issues.) [Incl. chaps. on the politics of Holocaust memory in Israel and Germany, the "Americanization" of the Holocaust.]

41344. HOLOCAUST. FERNEKES, WILLIAM R.: *The Oryx Holocaust sourcebook.* Westport, CT: Oryx Press, 2002. XII, 397 pp. (Oryx Holocaust series).

41345. HOLOCAUST. *Flares of memory: stories of childhood during the Holocaust.* Ed. by Anita Brostoff with Sheila Chamovitz. Oxford; New York: Oxford Univ. Press, 2001. XXXIX, 344 pp., illus., ports., maps, chronol., author index, story index. [Incl. several German-Jewish and Austrian-Jewish survivors.]

41346. HOLOCAUST. GIULIANI, MASSIMO: *Theological implications of the Shoah: caesura and continuum as hermeneutic paradigms of a Jewish theodicy.* New York; Bern: Lang, 2002. 322 pp., notes (279–308), bibl., index. (American university studies. Ser. 7: Theology and religion, Vol. 221.)

41347. HOLOCAUST. *The Holocaust: history and memory: essays presented in honor of Israel Gutman.* Jerusalem: Yad Vashem Martyrs' and Heroes' Remembrance Authority; Hebrew Univ., 2001. XVIII, 123 pp; 246 pp., port. [Festschrift for Israel Gutman, b. 1923 Warsaw, 1975–1993 director of Research Center at Yad Vashem, 1993–1996 director of International Institute for Holocaust Research.] [Texts in English (123 pp.) and Hebrew (246 pp.). Editorial board: Shmuel Almog, David Bankier, Daniel Blatman, Dalia Ofer. Incl. prefaces by the eds. and Sergio DellaPergola. Selected English essays: From Barbarossa to Wannsee: The role of Reinhard Heydrich (Eberhard Jäckel, 1–9). Killing time: Jewish perceptions during the Holocaust (Michael R. Marrus, 10–38). Selected Hebrew essays (titles transl.): Children and youth during the Holocaust (Dalia Ofer, 58–92). A new beginning: The emergence of She'erit Hapletah as a national entity 1945–1950 (Hagit Lavsky, 187–206).]

41348. HOLOCAUST. LAWTON, CLIVE A.: *Die Geschichte des Holocaust.* Deutsch von Mirjam Pressler. Hamburg: Oetinger, 2002. 48 pp., illus. [Orig. title: *The story of the Holocaust; a book for children.*]

41349. HOLOCAUST. RHODES, RICHARD: *Masters of death: the SS-Einsatzgruppen and the invention of the Holocaust.* New York: Knopf, 2002. XII, 335 pp., illus., ports., maps, notes, bibl. (305–319), index.

41350. HOLOCAUST. ROGASKY, BARBARA: *Smoke and ashes: the story of the Holocaust.* Rev. and expanded edn. New York: Holiday House, 2002. 256., illus., ports., map., facsims., chronol., bibl. (231–237), index. [For orig. edn. see No. 25338/YB XXXIV.]

41351. HOLOCAUST. SILVERMANN, JERRY: *The undying flame: ballads and songs of the Holocaust.* 110 songs in 16 languages with extensive historical notes, illus., piano arrangements, guitar chords, and singable English transl. Syracuse, NY: Syracuse Univ. Press, 2002. XXIX, 304 pp., illus., ports., facsims., scores, notes, bibl., index of song titles, index of first lines. [Incl. CD with 14 songs.]

41352. HOLOCAUST. SOLKOFF, NORMAN: *Beginnings, mass murder, and aftermath of the Holocaust: where history and psychology intersect.* Foreword by William Sheridan Allen. Lanham, MD: University Press of America, 2001. XIII, 359 pp., appendix, notes, bibl. (319–340), index. [Incl. chaps. on the history of antisemitism; German support for authoritarianism and conformity; rescuers and bystanders; Holocaust survivors in the postwar world; remembering the Holocaust.]

41353. HOLOCAUST. *Understanding genocide: the social psychology of the Holocaust.* Ed. by Leonard S. Newman and Ralph Erber. Introd. by Christopher Browning. Oxford; New York: Oxford Univ. Press, 2002. XI, 360 pp., illus., bibl., notes, index of persons. [Collection of essays dealing with the psychology of bystanders, perpetrators, rescuers. Incl. chap. on Goldhagen's *Hitler's willing executioners.*]

41354. HOLOCAUST DENIAL. ENDER, WOLFRAM: *"Auschwitz-Lüge?" Wie man rechtsextreme Geschichtsfälscher widerlegt.* Erfahrungen mit einem Unterrichtsprojekt mit jungen Erwachsenen. [In]: Geschichte, Politik und ihre Didaktik, Jg. 30, H. 1/2, Paderborn, 2002. Pp. 100–104, bibl.

41355. HOLOCAUST DENIAL. GUTTENPLAN, D.D.: *The Holocaust on trial: history, justice and the David Irving libel case.* London: Granta; New York: Norton, 2002. XIV, 334 pp., illus., map, notes, index.

41356. HOLOCAUST DENIAL. PELT, ROBERT JAN VAN: *The case for Auschwitz: evidence from the Irving trial.* Bloomington: Indiana Univ. Press, 2002. XV, 570 pp., illus., ports., facsims., notes, bibl. (539–551), index.

41357. *Holocaust. Der nationalsozialistische Völkermord und die Motive seiner Erinnerung.* Hrsg. von Burkhard Asmuss im Auftrag des Deutschen Historischen Museum. Berlin: Deutsches Historisches Museum, 2002. 359 pp., illus., facsims. [Incl.: Vorwort (Hans Ottomeyer, 13). Zur Ausstellung (Burkhard Asmuss, 15–16). Tradition und Moderne; cont.: Jüdische Geschichte in Europa zwischen Aufbruch und Katastrophe (Reinhard Rürup, 17–34). 1. Integration und Antisemitismus in Deutschland (1914–1933). 2. Ausgrenzung und Vertreibung der jüdischen Bevölkerung (1933–1939) (Thomas Rink, 35–102). Dimensionen eines Menschheitsverbrechens; cont.: Die Verfolgung und Ermordung der europäischen Juden 1939–1945 (Dieter Pohl, 103–120). 3. Der Weg in den Völkermord. 4. Der nationalsozialistische Völkermord (1941–1945) (Linde Apel, 121–214). Nach dem Verbrechen; cont.: Nationale Erinnerung an Weltkrieg und Judenmord (Peter Reichel, 215–238). 5. Der Umgang mit dem Holocaust in Deutschland nach 1945 (Kay Kufeke, 239–304). 6. Staatliches Museum Auschwitz-Birkenau, Yad Vashem und United States Holocaust Memorial Museum (Maja Peers, 305–320). Museum und Gedenkstätte Auschwitz-Birkenau. Geschichte, Wahrnehmung und Bedeutung (Teresa Swiebocka, 321–332). Yad Vashem. The Holocaust Martyrs' and Heroes' Remembrance Authority (Avner Shalev, 333–344). United States Holocaust Memorial Museum. Dialog mit der Demokratie (Rabbi Irving Greenberg/Ruth B. Mandel/Sara J. Bloomfield, 345–356). PC-Station. Jüdisches Leben in Deutschland zwischen 1914 und 2001 (Gorch Pieken, 357–359).]

41358. HULLEN, ANTOON: *Erinnerungen an Karl Hilferding, Opfer von Nazi-Judenhass.* [In]: Jahrbuch 2002 [des] Dokumentationsarchivs des österreichischen Widerstandes (DÖW), Wien, 2002. Pp. 99–117. [Deals also with other members of K.H.'s family. Article is followed by: Karl Hilferding und Sir Karl R. Popper (Peter Hilferding-Milford, 118).] [K.H., Sept. 12, 1905 Vienna – Dec. 2, 1942 Strelitz (Auschwitz outcamp), son of Rudolf and Margarethe Hilferding née Hönigsberg, Physical Chemist, Philosopher, baptised (Catholic) 1924, 1935–1938 studied philosophy at Löwen Univ. before joining 'Societas Verbi Divini', lived in monasteries in Belgium and Holland, went into hiding 1942, caught by the French at the French-Swiss border, delivered to the Germans, deported to Auschwitz, from there to Strelitz.]

——— HUNGARY. BRAHAM, RANDOLPH L.: *The Holocaust in Hungary: a selected and annotated bibliography: 1984–2000.* [See No. 41161.]

41359. HUNGARY. GANZENMÜLLER, JÖRG: *Die Motivation zur Vernichtung der ungarischen Juden. Zwischen konstruierten Sachzwängen und europäischen Neuordnungsplänen*. [In]: Ungarn-Jahrbuch, Jg. 26, München, 2002. Pp. 117–138.

——— HUNGARY. GEOFFREY, RENÉ: *Ungarn als Zufluchtsort und Wirkungsstätte deutschsprachiger Emigranten (1933–1938/39)*. [See No. 41726.]

41360. HUNGARY. GERLACH, CHRISTIAN/ALY, GÖTZ: *Das letzte Kapitel. Realpolitik, Ideologie und der Mord an den ungarischen Juden 1944/1945*. Stuttgart: Deutsche Verlags-Anstalt, 2002. 481 pp., footnotes, map, bibl. (449–468), indexes. [Cf.: Endlösung auf magyarisch (Ludger Heid) [in]: Jüdische Literatur, Spezial der Jüdischen Allgemeinen, Jg. 57., Nr. 9, Berlin, 25. April 2002, pp. 24–25.]

41361. HUNGARY. MOLNÁR, JUDIT: *The foundation and activities of the Hungarian Jewish Council, March 20 – July 7, 1944*. [In]: Yad Vashem Studies, Vol. 30, Jerusalem, 2002. Pp. 93–123, footnotes. [On the Jewish Council founded by order of the German occupation authorities, and the futile hope that liberation by the Red Army would come before deportation.]

41362. HUNGARY. STARK, TAMAS: *Hungarian Jews during the Holocaust and after the Second World War, 1939–1949: a statistical review*. Transl. by Christina Rozsnyal. Bolder, CO: East European Monographs, (distrib. by Columbia Univ. Press), 2000. VII, 174 pp., illus., bibl. (East European Monographs, No. 551.)

41363. HUNGARY. ZWEIG, RONALD W.: *The gold train: the destruction of the Jews and the Second World War's most terrible robbery*. London: Allen Lane 2002. XXIII, 311 pp., illus., ports., facsims., tabs., maps, gloss., appendixes, notes, bibl., index. [Deals with the story of a train, organised by Hungarian Nazis, which took Jewish assets from Hungary through Austria to Germany; at the end of the war the train was taken over by the Allies who were later accused of plundering by the victims, who had to fight for restitution.]

41364. ILSAR, YEHIEL: *Der Nationalsozialismus als Religion*. Judenmord als "Erlösungsantisemitismus". [In]: Tribüne, Jg. 41, H. 164, Frankfurt am Main, 2002. Pp. 154–168, footnotes.

41365. ITALY. BREITMAN, RICHARD D.: *New sources on the Holocaust in Italy*. [In]: Holocaust and Genocide Studies, Vol. 16, No. 3, Oxford, Winter 2002. Pp. 402–414, notes.

41366. ITALY. VOIGT, KLAUS: *Villa Emma. Jüdische Kinder auf der Flucht 1940–1945*. [Cover title: *Solidarität und Hilfe für Juden während der NS-Zeit*]. Berlin: Metropol, 2002. 384 pp., illus., footnotes, bibl. (353–371), index. (Solidarität und Hilfe. Rettungsversuche für Juden vor der Verfolgung und Vernichtung unter nationalsozialistischer Herrschaft, Bd. 6.) [Deals with a group of children from Germany and Austria (later also from Yugoslavia) who went with the help of Recha Freier via Zagreb and Lesno Brdo to Nonantola nr. Modena, where they went into hiding in autumn 1943 and later escaped to Switzerland.]

41367. KAHN, SELMA: *Der Weg ins Dritte Reich*. Ein autobiographischer Roman. Eingeführt von Andrea Hammel, bearb. von Marie-Elisabeth Rehn, hrsg. von Erhard Roy Wiehn. Konstanz: Hartung-Gorre, 2002. 260 pp., frontis., gloss., bibl. [Novel was written before and shortly after the author emigr. to Palestine (1934–1938).] [S.K., née Gottlieb, 1888 Berlichingen – 1982 Neustadt, writer, lived in Adelsheim from 1920.]

41368. KAPLAN, MARION A.: *The Jewish response to the Third Reich: Gender at the grassroots*. [In]: Studies in Contemporary Jewry [with the issue title] Jews and gender. The challenge to hierarchy, Vol. XVI, Oxford, 2000. Pp. 70–87.

41369. KASSEL. KRAUSE-VILMAR, DIETFRID: *Korrespondenten der Chicago Herald Tribune berichten im Frühjahr 1933 über die Judenverfolgung in Kassel*. [In]: Zeitschrift des Vereins für Hessische Geschichte und Landeskunde, Bd. 106, Kassel, 2001. Pp. 293–298, footnotes.

41370. KASSEL. RICHTER, GUNNAR: *Die Geheime Staatspolizeistelle Kassel 1933–1945.* [In]: Zeitschrift des Vereins für Hessische Geschichte und Landeskunde, Bd. 106, Kassel, 2001. Pp. 229–270, illus., facsims., notes.

41371. KEHREN, RAPHAELA: *Zwei rostbraune Zöpfe.* Eine wahre Geschichte. Mit Fotos. Weinheim: Beltz, 2001. 131 pp., illus., gloss. (Gulliver Taschenbuch.) [On the Hirsch family from Neumarkt (Hungary).]

41372. KENNA, MICHAEL: *Impossible to forget: the Nazi camps fifty years after.* Photographs by Michael Kenna; texts by Pierre Borhan and Clement Cheroux. Tucson, AZ: Nazraeli Press, 2001. 127 pp., chiefly illus., bibl. [Selection from a collection of photos made by Kenna between 1988–2000 and donated to the French government. Publ. in English and French in association with Editions Marval, Paris.]

41373. KETTLER, DAVID, ed.: *Essays from the "No happy end" workshop, Bard College, Feb. 13–15, 2000, in preparation for the conference "Contested legacies: emigration to the United States and United Kingdom, 1933–1945", Bard College, Aug. 13–15, 2002.* Cambridge, MA; Glienicke/Berlin: Galda & Wilch Verlag, 2002. 62 pp., illus., bibl.

41374. KIESER, HANS-LUKAS/SCHALLER, DOMINIK J., eds.: *Der Völkermord an den Armeniern und die Shoah/The Armenian genocide and the Shoah.* Zürich: Chronos, 2002. 656 pp., illus., notes, chronol., index. [Cont. essays (English, German, French) by the editors and Ronald Grigor Suny, Hilmar Kaiser, Erik Jan Zürcher, Raymond H. Kévorkian, Donald Bloxham, Taner Akcam, Aron Rodrigue, Hamit Bozarslan, Christian Gerlach, Marl Levene, Wolfgang Gust, Martin Tamcke, Hans-Walter Schmuhl, Annette Schaefgens, Yair Auron, Michael de St. Cheron, Peter Wien; incl. abstracts.]

41375. KIEFFER, FRITZ: *Judenverfolgung in Deutschland – eine innere Angelegenheit? Internationale Reaktionen auf die Flüchtlingsproblematik 1933–1939.* Stuttgart: Steiner, 2002. 520 pp., footnotes, bibl. (492–518). (Historische Mitteilungen der Ranke-Gesellschaft, Bd. 44.) Zugl. Mainz, Univ., Diss., 2000.

41376. KINDERTRANSPORT. EMANUEL, MURIEL/GISSING, VERA: *Nicholas Winton and the rescued generation: save one life, save the world.* London; Portland, OR: Vallentine Mitchell, 2002. XXII, 193 pp., illus., ports. [The hitherto unknown story of the English stockbroker N.W. who rescued 669 Czech children before the war by raising money and arranging transportation, as well as finding foster parents for them in England. Co-author V.G. was one of those children.]

41377. KINDERTRANSPORT. SAVILLE, ANNETTE: *Only a kindertransportee.* London: New Millenium, 2002. VIII, 325 pp., illus., ports. [Author, b. in Austria in 1923, went to England on a Kindertransport.]

41378. KNOLLER, FREDDIE (WITH JOHN LANDAW): *Desperate journey: Vienna-Paris-Auschwitz.* London: Metro, 2002. 271 pp., illus., ports., fascims., geneal. table, chronol. [Author, b. Vienna 1921, fled Austria in 1938 via Belgium to France; lived in occupied Paris disguised as a non-Jew; later arrested and deported to Auschwitz, liberated in Belsen in 1945.]

41379. KOSCHEL, ANSGAR, ed.: *Katholische Kirche und Judentum im 20. Jahrhundert.* Mit Beiträgen von Herbert Bettelheim, Ernst-Ludwig Ehrlich, Gabriel Padon, Gerhard Riegner, Herbert Smolinsky und Erich Zenger. Münster: Lit, 2002. 162 pp. (Religion – Geschichte – Gesellschaft. Fundamentaltheologische Studien, Bd. 26.) [Deals mainly with the Nazi period.]

41380. KOCH, EGMONT R.: *Wagners Geständnis. Wie sich ein SS-Mann als Jude tarnte.* München: Bertelsmann, 2001. 382 pp. [On Günter Reinemer/Hans Georg Wagner, formerly involved in crimes in Treblinka, confidence trickster, went to Israel in the 1970s.]

41381. KRAEMER, ERIC RUSSERT: *Holocaust evils and divine limitations: a re-examination.* [In]: Journal of Genocide Research, Vol. 4, No. 4, Basingstoke, Dec, 2002. Pp. 569–580, notes.

41382. KRAUSE, PETER: *Der Eichmann-Prozeß in der deutschen Presse.* Frankfurt am Main: Campus, 2002. 327 pp., footnotes, bibl. (Wissenschaftliche Reihe des Fritz Bauer Instituts, Bd. 8.)

41383. *Kulturelle Repräsentationen des Holocaust in Deutschland und den Vereinigten Staaten.* Hrsg. von Klaus L. Berghahn, Jürgen Fohrmann & Helmut J. Schneider. New York: Lang, 2002. VI, 253 pp., footnotes. (German Life and Civilization, Vol. 38.) [Cont. (most titles abbr.): Eine Gegenüberstellung der Filme 'Der ewige Jude' (1940) und 'Hitlerjunge Salomon' (1990) (Kathrin Bower, 1–22). Gedanken über die Repräsentation und Rezeption des Holocaust am Beispiel des 'Tagebuchs der Anne Frank' (Jolanda Vanderwal Taylor, 23–42). Überlegungen zu 'Holocaust' und 'Schindlers Liste' (Jürgen Fohrmann, 43–58). Schindlers Liste: eine Parabel des kollektiven Narzißmus (Ingeborg Harms, 59–68). Zum Problem der ästhetischen Individualisierung in 'Schindlers Liste' und der 'Holocaust'-Serie (Helmut J. Schneider, 69–82). Erzählstrategische Funktionen der Filmmusik in 'Schindlers Liste' (Bettina Schlüter, 83–96). Steven Spielbergs Film 'Schindlers Liste': "Based on the novel by Thomas Keneally" (Eckart Oehlenschläger, 97–110). Lektüreprotokolle zu Art Spiegelmans Comic 'Maus' (Gerhard Richter, 111–146). Über die Möglichkeiten und Grenzen der dokumentarischen Repräsentation des Holocaust (Klaus L. Berghahn, 147–166). Der schwierige Umgang mit dem Holocaust in der DDR (Thomas Jung, 167–192). "German=Nazi". Der Holocaust im amerikanischen Deutschunterricht (Jennifer Redmann, 193–204). Pädagogische Probleme universitärer Holocaust-Lektüre (Rachel Brenner, 205–232). Gedanken über politische Großverbrechen (Jost Hermand, 233–253).]

41384. *The last expression: art and Auschwitz.* Ed. by David Mickenberg, Corinne Granof, and Peter Hayes. Evanston, IL: Northwstern Univ. Press, 2002. 320 pp., illus. [Catalogue of an exhibition held at Northwestern Univ., Sept.-Dec. 2002, at the Davis Museum in Wellesley MA, Jan.-Feb. 2003. Incl. German-Jewish artists from Theresienstadt and other camps.]

41385. LERNER, BERNICE: *Transcending terror: a study of Holocaust survivors' lives.* Diss. for the Univ. of Michigan, Ann Arbor. Ann Arbor: Univ. of Michigan Dissertation Services, 2001. XIV, 484 pp., notes, bibl.

——— *Lexikon des Holocaust.* [See No. 41171.]

41386. LIEB, PETER: *Täter aus Überzeugung? Oberst Carl von Andrian und die Judenmorde der 707. Infanteriedivision 1941/42.* [In]: Vierteljahrshefte für Zeitgeschichte, Jg. 50, H. 4, München, 2002. Pp. 523–557, footnotes. [Engl. abstract on p. 669. Deals with the ambivalence of a senior German officer towards the mass murder of the Jews he and his troops were involved with as seen in the diary of C.v.A.]

41387. LITTNER, JAKOB: *Mein Weg durch die Nacht.* Mit Anmerkungen zu Wolfgang Koeppens Textadaption. Hrsg. von Roland Ulrich und Reinhard Zachau. Berlin: Metropol, 2002. 245 pp., facsims., footnotes, bibl. (Bibliothek der Erinnerung, Bd. 8.) [Incl. L.'s report (first publ. 1948), also articles by the editors and Alfred Estermann.] [Cf.: "Textverschlechtbesserung". Diskussion über die Aufzeichnungen von Jakob Littner (Miryam Gümbel) [in]: Jüdische Allgemeine, Jg. 58, Nr. 6, Berlin, 13. März 2003, p. 17.]

41388. LODZ (LITZMANNSTADT). FEUCHERT, SASCHA: *Feuilletonistisches aus dem Getto.* Auf den Spuren des Prager Journalisten Oskar Singer. [In]: Aufbau, Vol. 68, No. 10, New York, May 16, 2002. P. 19.

41389. LODZ (LITZMANNSTADT). ROSENFELD, OSKAR: *In the beginning was the ghetto.* Notebooks from Lodz. Ed. and with an introduction by Hanno Loewy. Transl. from the German by Brigitte M. Goldstein. Evanston, Il: Northwestern Univ. Press, 2002. 313 pp. [Editor's note (283–313). For German edn. and details see No. 31803/YB XL.]

41390. LODZ (LITZMANNSTADT). SINGER, OSKAR: *"Im Eilschritt durch den Gettotag …".* Reportagen und Essays aus dem Getto Lodz. Hrsg. von Sascha Feuchert, Erwin Leibfried [et al.]. Berlin: Philo, 2002. 277 pp., illus., footnotes. (Schriftenreihe zur Lodzer Getto-Chronik, Bd. 1.) [Cont.: Oskar Singer und seine Texte aus dem Getto. Eine Hinführung (Sascha Feuchert, 7–26). Im Eilschritt durch den Gettotag … Zum Problem Ost und West – Essays. Pro Domo – Albenblätter (Oskar Singer, 27–232). Notizen zur Sprache der Reportagen und Essays (Jörg Riecke, 233–244). Zur Vorgeschichte und Geschichte des Gettos Lodz (Julian Baranowski, 245–266).] [O.S., Feb. 24, 1893 Friedeck (Bohemia) – Aug. 1944 Auschwitz, journalist, lived and worked in Prague, deported Oct. 1941 to Lodz/Litzmannstadt, leader of the "Statistische Abteilung" in the Ghetto of Lodz, main author of the 'Lodzer Getto-Chronik'.]

41391. LÖHNERT, PETER/GILL, MANFRED: *The relationship of I.G. Farben's Agfa 'Filmfabrik' Wolfen to its Jewish scientists and to scientists married to Jews, 1933–1939.* [In]: The German chemical industry in the twentieth century. Ed. by John E. Lesch. Dordrecht; Boston; London: Kluwer Acad. Publ., 2000. Pp. 123–145, footnotes.

41392. LOEWY, HANNO: *A history of ambivalence: post-reunification German identity and the Holocaust.* [In]: Patterns of Prejudice, Vol. 36, No. 2, London, April 2002. Pp. 3–13, footnotes.

41393. LONGERICH, PETER: *Die Verfolgung und Ermordung der europäischen Juden durch das NS-Regime – ein Überblick.* [In]: Der Nationalsozialismus und die deutsche Gesellschaft. Einführung und Überblick. Hrsg. von Bernd Sösemann. Stuttgart: Deutsche Verlags-Anstalt, 2002. Pp. 239–257.

41394. LORENTZ, BERNHARD: *Die Commerzbank und die "Arisierung" im Altreich. Ein Vergleich der Netzwerkstrukturen und Handlungsspielräume von Großbanken in der NS-Zeit.* [In]: Vierteljahrshefte für Zeitgeschichte, Jg. 50, H. 2, München, 2002. Pp. 237–268, footnotes. [Engl. abstract on p. 336.]

41395. LOZOWICK, YAACOV: *Hitler's bureaucrats: the Nazi security police and the banality of evil.* Transl. by Haim Watzman. London; New York: Continuum, 2002. XX, 297 pp., illus., charts., tabs., notes, bibl. (281–291), index. [Incl. Adolf Eichmann; chaps. on the Final Solution. Orig. German edn.: Hitlers Bürokraten. Eichmann, seine willigen Vollstrecker und die Banalität des Bösen. Aus dem Engl. von Christoph Münz. Zürich: Pendo, 2000. 407 pp., notes (350–386), bibl., index.]

41396. LUDEWIG-KEDMI, REVITAL: *Opfer und Täter zugleich?* Moraldilemmata jüdischer Funktionshäftlinge in der Shoah. Gießen: Psychosozial-Verlag, 2001. 368 pp., notes (343–354), bibl. (Reihe Psyche und Gesellschaft.) Zugl.: Berlin, Techn. Univ., Diss. 2000 u.d. Titel: Moraldilemmata jüdischer Funktionshäftlinge.

———— LUSTIGER, ARNO: *"Wir werden nicht untergehen". Zur jüdischen Geschichte.* [See No. 41930.]

41397. LUXEMBOURG. '… et wor alles net esou einfach'. *Questions sur le Luxembourg et la Deuxième Guerre mondiale. Fragen an die Geschichte Luxemburgs im Zweiten Weltkrieg.* Contributions historiques accompagnant l'exposition/Beiträge zur Ausstellung. Luxembourg: Musée d'Histoire de la Ville de Luxembourg, 2002. 375 pp., illus., facsims. (Publications scientifiques du Musée d'Histoire le la Ville de Luxembourg, tome X.) [Incl. the sections: Résistance et collaboration (106–149). Répression et persécution (150–177; incl.: Luxemburger und Juden im Zweiten Weltkrieg. Zwischen Solidarität und Schweigen (Marc Schoentgen, 150–163). Das SS-Sonderlager/KZ Hinzert im Hunsrück (Barbara Weiter-Matysiak, 178–189).]

41398. LUSTIG, JAN: *Ein Rosenkranz von Glücksfällen. Protokoll einer Flucht.* Hrsg. und mit einem Nachwort von Erich A. Frey. Mit einer Filmographie von Stefan Drößler. Bonn: Weidle, 2002. 157 pp., illus., facsims. [Incl.: Nachwort (Erich A. Frey, 127–142).] [J.L., orig. Gottlieb/Hanns/Jean/Bohumil L., 1902 Brünn – 1979 Munich, journalist, screenwriter, emigr. to France in 1933, via Portugal to the US in 1940, remigr. to Germany in 1959.]

41398a. MAIERHOF, GUDRUN: *Selbstbehauptung im Chaos. Frauen in der jüdischen Selbsthilfe 1933–1943.* Frankfurt am Main; New York: Campus, 2002. 390 pp., illus., footnotes, docs., bibl. (362–386).

41399. MANNHEIM. *Die "Gemeinde-Liste Dr. Neter".* Ein Mitgliederverzeichnis der Jüdischen Gemeinde Mannheim aus dem Jahr 1940. [Red. und Text: Bernhard Kukatzki. Hrsg.: Pfälzisch-Rheinische Familienkunde e.V.]. Ludwigshafen am Rhein: Privately printed, 2001. 1 vol. [unpag.] [Recently found list, presumably compiled by the Mannheim pediatrician, Dr. Eugen Isaak Neter (mixed marriage), after 1938 president of the Mannheim Jewish community.]

41400. MANNHEIM. ZAHLTEN, RICHARD: *Meine Schwester starb in Auschwitz.* Gedenkbuch für Dr. Johanna Geissmar und ihre Familie. Lahr: Johannis-Verlag, 2001. 160 pp., frontis., illus. [On the Heidelberg pediatrician J.G., (1877 Mannheim – 1942 Auschwitz); also on Berta Geissmar, secretary of Wilhelm Furtwängler (1892 Mannheim – 1949 London).]

41401. MARBURG an der Lahn. *Die Marburger Medizinische Fakultät im "Dritten Reich".* Hrsg. von Gerhard Aumüller [et al.]. München: Saur, 2001. 736 pp., illus., footnotes, tabs., graphs, bibl. (669–709), indexes. (Academia Marburgensis, Bd. 8.) [Chap. III incl. a section entitled Antisemitismus, Verfolgung und Opposition (Gerhard Aumüller/Kornelia Grundmann, 205–240).]

41402. MARTIUS, GOETZ-ALEXANDER: *1933–1945. Auch das geschah in Deutschland: Martius zum Beispiel.* [In]: Genealogie, Jg. 51, Bd. 26, Neustadt/Aisch, 2002. Pp. 1–22 [H. 1–2]; 98–115 [H. 3–4]; 244–251 [H. 7–8]; 267–278 [H. 9–10], illus., footnotes. [Deals with the descendants of Friedrich Martius and Martha Leonhard and their fate during the Nazi period. Incl. excerpts from the memoirs of M.L., telling about her Jewish family background, her father's conversion and name change (orig. Levisohn) and the ongoing experience of antisemitism during the 1880s and 1890s.]

41403. MATZERATH, HORST: *Bürokratie und Judenverfolgung.* [In]: Nationalsozialismus und Regionalgeschichte. Festschrift für Horst Matzerath. Hrsg. von Barbara Becker-Jákli [et al.]. Köln: Emons, 2002. Pp. 128–147, notes. [First publ. 1992.]

41404. MAYER, MICHAEL: *NSDAP und Antisemitismus: 1919–1933.* München: Volkswirtschaftliche Fakultät der Ludwig-Maximilians-Universität München, 2002. 19 pp. (Münchener wirtschaftswissenschaftliche Beiträge.)

41405. MAYNARD, MICHAEL: *Michael Maynard, Erinnerungen eines jüdischen Jungen an die Jahre 1933–1939: Alsfeld – Frankfurt – Gambach – KZ-Buchenwald.* [In]: Mitteilungen des Oberhessischen Geschichtsvereins Gießen, Neue Folge, Bd. 86. Gießen, 2001. Pp. 69–88, illus. [Memoirs, introd. by Monica Kingreen; author, 1922 b. as Manfred Moses in Alsfeld, fled after the November Pogrom and inprisonment in Buchenwald to England; lives in London.]

41406. MECKEL, CHRISTOPH: *Sieben Blätter für Monsieur Bernstein/Sept dessins pour Monsieur Bernstein.* Traduit de l'allemand par Nicole Bary. München: Christian Pixis Verlag, 2000. 55; VII; 19 pp., illus. [Text also in Hebrew; tells and illustrates the story of an Auschwitz survivor living in France, orig. from the Rhineland.]

41407. *Medicine and medical ethics in Nazi Germany: origins, practices, legacies.* Ed. by Francis R. Nicosia and Jonathan Huener. Oxford; New York: Berghahn Books, 2002. VII, 160 pp., illus., ports., tabs., notes, appendix, bibl. (142–150), index. [Incl. chaps.: Physicians as killers in Nazi Germany: Hadamar, Treblinka and Auschwitz (Henry Friedlander, 59–76). A criminal profession in the Third Reich: toward a group portrait of physicians (Michael H. Kater, 77–91). Pathology of memory: German medical science and the crimes of the Third Reich (William E. Seidelman, 93–111). Further contribs. by G. Allen, R. Proctor, M. Burleigh.]

41408. MEIER, AXEL: *"Ein Nazi fährt nach Palästina." Der Bericht eines SS-Offiziers als Beitrag zur "Lösung der Judenfrage".* [In]: Jahrbuch für Antisemitismusforschung 2002, Frankfurt am Main; New York, 2002. Pp. 76–90, footnotes. [On Leopold v. Mildenstein, who, together with the Zionist Kurt Tuchler, visited Palestine after 1933 and wrote a report on the negotiations between the Zionists and the Nazis; first printed in 'Der Angriff' Sept./Oct. 1934, 1938 as a book.]

41409. MOLLER, SABINE/RÜRUP, MIRIAM/TROUVÉ, CHRISTEL, eds.: *Abgeschlossene Kapitel? Zur Geschichte der Konzentrationslager und der NS-Prozesse.* Tübingen: edition diskord, 2002. 224 pp., footnotes. (Studien zum Nationalsozialismus, Bd. 5.) [Incl. 14 articles.]

41410. MOMMSEN, HANS: *Auschwitz, 17. Juli 1842. Der Weg zur europäischen "Endlösung der Judenfrage".* München: Deutscher Taschenbuch Verlag, 2002. 236 pp., notes (191–218), bibl. (220–232), index. Orig.-Ausg.

————— *Nazi-Deutsch/Nazi-German: an English lexicon of the language of the Third Reich.* Comp. by Robert Michael and Karin Doerr. [See No. 41172.]

41411. *The Nazi Germany sourcebook: an anthology of texts.* Comp. by Roderick Stackelberg and Sally A. Winkle. London; New York: Routledge, 2002. XXXI, 455 pp., illus., maps, chronol., list of docs., bibl., index. [Collection of documents and source material, incl. a section on Holocaust; also a chap. on the "Historians' Debate".]

41412. NIEMANN, INGMAR: *Japan, Deutschland und die Juden Asiens.* [In]: Geschichte als Falle. Deutschland und die jüdische Welt [see No. 40849]. Pp. 121–144, notes. [Deals also with the Nazi period and the Second World War incl. Shanghai.]

41413. NIVEN, WILLIAM JOHN: *Facing the Nazi past: united Germany and the legacy of the Third Reich.* London, New York: Routledge, 2002. XXII, 266 pp., illus., chronol., notes, bibl. (246–256), index. [Incl. memorial sites, Holocaust Memorial in Berlin, crimes of the Wehrmacht, Walser-Bubis debate, Goldhagen debate, Victor Klemperer.]

41414. NIZNANSKY, EDUARD: *Die Aktion Nisko, das Lager Sosnowiec (Oberschlesien) und die Anfänge des Judenlagers in Vyhne (Slowakei).* [In]: Jahrbuch für Antisemitismusforschung 2002, Frankfurt am Main; New York, 2002. Pp. 325–335, footnotes.

——— NOWAK, KURT: *Kirchliche Zeitgeschichte interdisziplinär. Beiträge 1984–2001.* [See No. 40876.]

41415. *NS-Zeit und Holocaust.* [Section title of] *Judenfeindschaft als Paradigma.* Studien zur Vorurteilsforschung [see No. 42134.]. [Cont. (some titles abbr.): Holocaustforschung (Wolfgang Benz, 115–121). Zeugnisliteratur (Monika Körte, 122–129). Die Verfolgung der deutschen Juden im NS-Staat 1933–1945. Wechselwirkungen lokaler und zentraler Politik (Wolf Gruner, 130–136). Geschichte der nationalsozialistischen Konzentrationslager. Gesamtdarstellung der Lagertopographie als Desiderat der Wissenschaft und der politischen Bildung (Wolfgang Benz/Angelika Königseder, 137–140). Solidarität und Hilfe. Interaktionen von Juden und Nichtjuden in Europa 1933–1945 (Juliane Wetzel/Wolfgang Benz, 141–146). Rettung von Juden im nationalsozialistischen Deutschland (Claudia Schoppmann, 147–155). Trauma und Erinnerung (Beate Kosmala, 156–162; on Poland).]

41416. NUREMBERG. *Gedenkbuch für die Nürnberger Opfer der Schoa.* Ergänzungsband. Hrsg. von Michael Diefenbacher und Wiltrud Fischer-Pache. Bearb. von Gerhard Jochem und Ulrike Kettner. Mit einem Beitrag von Kurt Kellermann s.A. Nürnberg: Selbstverlag des Stadtarchivs Nürnberg. XIII, 194 pp. (Quellen und Forschungen zur Geschichte und Kultur der Stadt Nürnberg, Bd. 30.) [Sequel to No. 36394/YB XLIV.]

41417. NUREMBERG. GREGOR, NEIL: *'Vergangenheitspolitik', CSU-style: the memory of forced labour in Nuremberg.* [In]: The Journal of Holocaust Education, Vol. 10, No. 3, London, Winter 2001. Pp. 83–104, notes. [Deals with the scandal surrounding the industrialist Karl Diehl between 1997 and 1999, who was made honorary citizen of the city of Nuremberg before it became known that he had used forced labour in his factories during the Nazi period.]

41418. OBERURSEL. RIEBER, A.: *"Anständig"? Das Novemberpogrom 1938 in Oberursel.* [In]: Mitteilungen des Vereins für Geschichte und Heimatkunde Oberursel (Taunus), Jg. 40, Oberursel, 2000. Pp. 1–12.

41419. OFFENBURG. RUCH, MARTIN: *"Ich bitte noch um ein paar Sterne …". Jüdische Stimmen aus Offenburg.* Band 2. Offenburg: KulturAgentur, 2002. 155 pp., list of names. [Chronicles the fate of 85 Jews from Offenburg; incl. also: Ahasverus. Eine Schau in zehn Bildern (Sylvia Cohn née Oberbrunner, 152–150).]

41420. OLDENBURG. *Ein offenes Geheimnis. 'Arisierung' in Alltag und Wirtschaft in Oldenburg zwischen 1933 und 1945.* Katalog zur Ausstellung. Oldenburg: Werkstattfilm e.V., 2001. 136 pp., illus., facsims., bibl. [Katalogred. und Bearb.: Mathias Krispin, Patricia Mühr, Melanie Pust, Tanja Schäfer.]

41421. OLDENBURG. *Erinnerungsbuch.* Ein Verzeichnis der von der nationalsozialistischen Judenverfolgung betroffenen Einwohner der Stadt Oldenburg 1933–1945. [Wiss. Bearbeitung: Jörg Paulsen, Beratung und Koordination: Ahlrich Meyer, Mitwirkung: Frauke Chava J. Kuchenbuch et al.] Bremen: Ed. Temmen, 2001. 212 pp., illus., indexes (persons; streets; professions; deportations, 163–204), bibl. [Incl. 585 short biographical articles.]

41422. OPFERMANN (GUTHMANN), CHARLOTTE: *The art of darkness.* Houston: Univ. Trace Press, 2002. 158 pp., bibl., index. [Author, b. Wiesbaden 1925, writer, playwright, daughter of a prominent lawyer and leader of the Jewish community, 1943 deported from Frankfurt am Main; recounts her years in Theresienstadt, her return to Germany and subsequent emigration to the US.]

41423. OSTERHOLZ-SCHARMBECK. *Ein Denkmal für Familie Cohen, die in Osterholz-Scharmbeck in Niedersachsen gelebt hat, errichtet im Jahr 2001 von Klaus Beer.* Mit einem Grußwort von Brigitte Eschershausen, Bürgermeisterin der Stadt Osterholz-Scharmbeck und einem Vorwort von Professor Dr. Wolfgang Benz, Leiter des Zentrums für Antisemitismusforschung an der Technischen Universität Berlin. 27711 Osterholz-Scharmbeck: Verlag FH. Saade, 2001. 180 pp., illus., facsims., geneal., bibl. [Author, a jurist, traces his ancestors.]

41424. PALESTINE. BALKE, RALF: *Hakenkreuz im Heiligen Land. Die NSDAP-Landesgruppe Palästina.* Erfurt: Sutton Verlag, 2001. 221 pp., illus., notes (185–206), bibl. (215–221). [Deals also with the anti-Judaism and antisemitism of the German settlers in Palestine.]

41425. PASSAU. ROSMUS, ANNA ELISABETH: *Against the stream: growing up where Hitler used to live.* Transl. by Imogen von Tannenberg. Columbia: Univ. of South Carolina Press, 2002. VIII, 158 pp. [Orig. publ. in German in 1995 with the title "Was ich denke". Author tells how she overcame resistance in her hometown of Passau when she decided to research the fate of the Jews and the Nazi period; chronicles censorship, lawsuits and death threats she had to face. The 1989 film *The Nasty Girl* is based on her story.]

41426. PEISER, HORST: *Letzte Minute – doch erfolgreich. Geschichte eines Emigranten.* Frankfurt am Main: R.G. Fischer, 2002. 152 pp. [Author, b. in Breslau 1930, emigr. 1939 to Bolivia, 1971 to Israel.]

41427. PEGELOW, THOMAS: *"German Jews", "National Jews", "Jewish Volk", or "Racial Jews"? The constitution and contestation of "Jewishness" in newspapers of Nazi Germany, 1933–1938.* [In]: Central European History, Vol. 35, No. 2, Boston; Leiden, 2002. Pp. 195–221, footnotes. [Examines Nazi and Jewish papers.]

41427a. PERRY, GEOFFREY H.: *When life becomes history.* Stanford-in-the-Vale/Oxon.: Guidon Ltd. in assoc. with White Mountain Press, 2002. 135 pp., illus., facsims., docs., index. [Autobiography.] [G.H.P., orig. Horst Pinschewer, b. 1922 in Berlin, press photographer, magazine publisher, emigr. 1936 to the UK, after Word War II as member of the British Task Force radio broadcaster in Hamburg and producer of the first German-language newspapers publ. for the German population in Northern Germany; on May 28, 1945 captured William Joyce ("Lord Haw-Haw") near Flensburg.]

41428. PLIENINGER, KONRAD: *"Ach, es ist alles ohne Ufer ...".* Briefe aus dem Warschauer Ghetto. [Göppingen: Jüdisches Museum Göppingen], 2002. 51 pp., illus., footnotes. [Incl. letters written by Josef Gelbart (b. 1914 in Altona) to his employer Hans Stockmar in Kaltenkirchen, from where he was expelled to Zbaszyn in Oct. 1938.]

————— POTTER, PAMELA M.: *Die 'deutscheste' der Künste. Musikwissenschaft und Gesellschaft von der Weimarer Republik bis zum Ende des Dritten Reichs.* Aus dem Amerikanischen von Wolfram Ette. [See No. 41786.]

41429. PRAGUE. Jewish Museum. POTTHAST, JAN BJÖRN: *Das jüdische Zentralmuseum der SS in Prag. Gegnerforschung und Völkermord im Nationalsozialismus.* Frankfurt am Main; New York: Campus, 2002. 503 pp., notes, bibl. (472–489), index.

41430. PRAGUE. Jewish Museum. RUPNOW, DIRK: *"Ihr müsst sein, auch wenn ihr nicht mehr seid": The Jewish Central Museum in Prague and historical memory in the Third Reich.* [In]: Holocaust and Genocide Studies, Vol. 16, No. 1, Oxford, Summer 2002. Pp. 23–53, notes. [Deals with the history of the establishment of the Jewish Central Museum in Nazi-occupied Prague and the purpose behind this.]

41431. PRAGER, PETER: *From Berlin to England and back: experiences of a Jewish Berliner.* London; Portland, OR: Vallentine Mitchell, 2002. XIV, 186 pp., illus., ports., facsims., chronol. (The library of Holocaust testimonies.) [Author, b. in Berlin 1923, tells his family story growing up in Berlin before and during the Nazi period; went to England on a Kindertransport, later became a teacher and spent a year in Germany as an exchange teacher.]

41432. *Privatbanken in der NS-Zeit. Rundschreiben der Wirtschaftsgruppe Privates Bankgewerbe 1934–1945.* Hrsg. in Verbindung mit der Gesellschaft für Unternehmensgeschichte/Ed. in association with the Gesellschaft für Unternehmensgeschichte. Erschließungsband zur Mikrofiche-Edition mit einem Vorwort von Harold James/Guide to the Microfiche edition with a foreword by Harold James. München: Saur, 2002. XXXIV, 757 pp., footnotes. [Incl.: Die 'Rundschreiben der Wirtschaftsgruppe Privates Bankgewerbe' als Quelle zur Geschichte des nationalsozialistischen Deutschlands (Harold James, XV-XXII; Engl. transl. XXIII-XXX); also deals with the significance of the "circulars" in relation to "aryanisation" and the looting of Jewish property.]

41433. PROSS, HARRY: *"Exil 1933" – Nachwort zu einem Essay von Leopold Schwarzschild.* [In]: Preußens Himmel breitet seine Sterne .... [see No. 41991], Bd. 1. Pp. 375–391, notes. [On L. Sch.'s essay entitled 'Exit 1933'; publ. in his 'Das Neue Tage-Buch' (Paris-Amsterdam) in Dec. 1933.]

41434. RECKLINGHAUSEN. *Pogrom in Recklinghausen.* Recklinghäuser Bürger erinnern an den 9./10. November 1938. Hrsg. von Georg Möllers und Horst D. Mannel aus Anlaß der 40-Jahr-Feier der Gesellschaft für christlich-jüdische Zusammenarbeit. 5., verb. und erg. Aufl. Recklinghausen: Privately printed, 2001. 96 pp., illus., facsims.

41435. REEMTSMA, JAN PHILIPP, ed.: *Dimensionen des Vernichtungskrieges 1941–1944.* Ausstellungskatalog. [Hrsg.: Hamburger Institut für Sozialforschung]. [Konzeption: Jan Philipp Reemtsma et al., Gesamtredaktion: Ulrike Jureit]. Hamburg: Hamburger Edition, 2002. 749 pp., illus. [Catalogue accompanying the revised exhibition under the title Verbrechen der Wehrmacht. Dimensionen des Vernichtungskrieges 1941–1944; documents and also analyses the controversial discussion between 1995 and 1999 which followed the first exhibition before its withdrawal in 1999.]

41436. *Die Reichsfinanzverwaltung im Nationalsozialismus.* Darstellung und Dokumente. Hrsg. von Martin Friedenberger [et al.]. Bremen: Ed. Temmen, 2002. 287 pp., facsims., docs., chronol., notes. [Incl.: Die Rolle der Finanzverwaltung bei der Vertreibung, Verfolgung und Vernichtung der deutschen Juden (Martin Friedenberger, 10–94). Der Reichsfinanzhof und seine Rechtsprechung in steuerlichen Angelegenheiten von Juden (Johann Heinrich Kumpf, 143–185).]

41437. REINFELDER, GEORG: *MS "St. Louis". Die Irrfahrt nach Kuba – Frühjahr 1939. Kapitän Gustav Schröder rettet 906 deutsche Juden vor dem Zugriff der Nazis.* Teetz: Hentrich & Hentrich, 2002. 270 pp., illus., facsims., bibl., index. [Incl.: Tagebuch von Erich Dublon (218–134). Namens-Liste zur Verteilung der "St. Louis"-Passagiere in Antwerpen (235–259).]

41438. *Remembering the Holocaust in Germany. German Strategies and Jewish responses.* Ed. by Dan Michman. New York; Bern: Lang, 2002. 172 pp., notes, index. (Studies in Modern European History, Vol. 48.) [Papers presented at an international conference held at Bar-Ilan University, Ramat-Gan, Dec. 1999. Cont.: Introduction (ed., 1–5). Part I: Fifty years of debating in Germany; cont.: The Holocaust and the competition of memories in Germany, 1945–1999 (Jeffrey Herf, 9–30). Divided memory? Expressions of a united German memory (Gilad Margalit, 31–42). The uncanny clatter: The Holocaust in Germany before its mass commemorations (Y. Michal Bodemann, 43–54). Memory and amnesia: a comment on the lectures by Gilad Margalit and Michal Bodemann (Inge Marszolek, 55–58). Border-crossings: some reflections on the role of German historians in recent public debates on Nazi history (Chris Lorenz, 59–94). The irreconcilability of an event: integrating the Holocaust into the narrative of the century (Dan Diner, 95–107). Part II: Jewish perceptions; cont.: The changing role of the Holocaust in the German-Jewish public voice (Michael Brenner, 111–120). Constantly disturbing the German conscience: the impact of American Jewry (Shlomo Shafir, 121–142). Ambivalent cooperation: The German-Israeli Joint Committee on schoolbooks (Yehuda Ben-Avner, 143–148). The vague echoes of German discourse in Israel (Yfaat Weiss, 149–158).]

41439. RESCUE OF JEWS. HUNEKE, DOUGLAS K.: *In Deutschland unerwünscht. Hermann Gräbe.* Biographie eines Judenretters. Aus dem Amerik. von Adrian Seifert und Robert Lasser. Lüneburg: zu Klampen, 2002. 325 pp., illus., notes. [Incl. epilogues by Horst Sassin and

Wolfgang Heuer. H.G., 1900 Solingen – 1986 San Francisco, engineer, saved the life of hundreds of Jews in the Ukraine during the German occupation, also prosecution witness to Nazi mass murderers for the Nuremberg trials.]

41440. RESCUE OF JEWS. KOSMALA, BEATE/SCHOPPMANN, CLAUDIA, eds.: *Überleben im Untergrund. Hilfe für Juden in Deutschland 1941–1945* [cover title: Solidarität und Hilfe für Juden während der NS-Zeit, Band 5: Überleben im Untergrund. Hilfe für Juden in Deutschland 1941–1945]. Berlin: Metropol, 2002. 408 pp., illus., footnotes, index. (Solidarität und Hilfe. Rettungsversuche für Juden vor der Verfolgung und Vernichtung unter nationalsozialistischer Herrschaft, Bd. 5.) [Cont.: Solidarität mit Juden während der NS-Zeit (Wolfgang Benz, 5–16). Überleben im Untergrund. Zwischenbilanz eines Forschungsprojekts (eds., 17–31). Zwischen Ignoranz, Wissen und Nicht-glauben-Wollen. Gerüchte über den Holocaust und ihre Diffusionsbedingungen in der deutschen Bevölkerung (Karl-Heinz Reuband, 33–62). Was wußten die Deutschen vom Holocaust? (David Bankier, 63–87). Denunziation im Dritten Reich. Kommunikationsformen und Verhaltensweisen (Inge Marzolek, 89–126). Die anderen Christen. Ihr Einsatz für verfolgte Juden und "Nichtarier" im nationalsozialistischen Deutschland (Ursula Büttner, 127–150). Grenzüberschreitende Flucht und Fluchthilfe (1941–1945): Ereignisse, Interessen und Motive (Kurt Schilde, 151–165). Verfolgung und Rettung in Frankfurt am Main und der Rhein-Main-Region (Monica Kingreen, 167–190). "Bruderring" und "Lucknerkreis": Rettung im deutschen Südwesten (Angelika Borgstedt, 191–203). Mißglückte Hilfe und ihre Folgen: Die Ahndung der "Judenbegünstigung" durch NS-Verfolgungsbehörden (Beate Kosmala, 205–221). "Er besaß den Eifer eines wahren Gläubigen." August Sapandowski (1882–1945), ein Retter von Juden in Berlin (Christoph Hamann, 223–240). Zur Problematik des Begriffes "Retter" (Isabel Enzenbach, 241–256). Widerstand von Juden im nationalsozialistischen Deutschland. Rahmenbedingungen und weiterführende Fragen (Johannes Tuchel, 257–272). Das unausweichliche Dilemma: Die Reichsvereinigung der Juden in Deutschland, die Deportationen und die untergetauchten Juden (Beate Meyer, 273–296). Hilfe für Juden und jüdische Selbsthilfe in Warschau (1940–1945) (Gunnar S. Paulsson, 297–308). Wehrmachtangehörige als Retter von Juden (Peter Steinkamp, 309–316). "Unbesungene Helden": Der Umgang mit "Rettung" im Nachkriegsdeutschland (Dennis Riffel, 317–334). Entstehungszusammenhang und Ergebnisse von Manfred Wolfsons Retterstudie (1945–1975) (Emil Walter-Busch, 335–361). Moraldilemmata von Rettern von Juden. Sozialpsychologische Interpretation und pädagogische Umsetzung (Revital Ludewig-Kedmi, 363–379). "Uropa war ein Guter." Retten und Überleben im Nationalsozialismus als Thema des Geschichtsunterrichts (Christoph Hamann, 381–393).]

41441. RESCUE OF JEWS. LÜTGEMEIER-DAVIN, REINHOLD: *"… like a sunshine in the darkness". Karl Laabs (1896–1979), ein Judenretter im polnischen Krenau.* [In]: Zeitschrift des Vereins für Hessische Geschichte und Landeskunde, Bd. 106, Kassel, 2001. Pp. 271–292, footnotes.

41442. RESCUE OF JEWS. RAU, JOHANNES, ed.: *Hilfe für Verfolgte in der NS-Zeit. Jugendliche forschen vor Ort.* Ein Lesebuch. Hamburg: Edition Körber-Stiftung, 2002. 324 pp., illus. [Incl. contribs. from a history competition initiated by the President of the Fed. Rep. of Germany.]

41443. RESCUE OF JEWS. RIFFEL, DENNIS: *Datenbanken in der Geschichtswissenschaft. Das Projekt "Rettung von Juden im nationalsozialistischen Deutschland 1933–1945".* [In]: Zeitschrift für Geschichtswissenschaft, Jg. 50, H. 5, Berlin, 2002. Pp. 436–446.

41444. RESCUE OF JEWS. SCHMALZ-JACOBSEN, CORNELIA: *Zwei Bäume in Jerusalem.* Hamburg: Hoffmann und Campe, 2002. 223 pp., illus. [Author tells the story of her parents, Donata and Eberhard Helmrich, who both – in Berlin and in Drohobycz – helped and often rescued numerous Jews.]

41445. RESCUE OF JEWS. THOMPSON, BRUCE, ed.: *Oskar Schindler.* San Diego, CA: Greenhaven Press, 2002. 258 pp., notes, bibl., index. (People who make history.)

41446. RESCUE OF JEWS. WETTE, WOLFRAM, ed.: *Retter in Uniform.* Handlungsspielräume im Vernichtungskrieg der Wehrmacht. Mit Beiträgen von Norbert Haase [et al.]. Frankfurt am Main: Fischer Taschenbuch Verlag, 2002. 238 pp., ports., notes, indexes. (Die Zeit des Nationalsozialismus.) Orig.-Ausg. [Cont.: Geleitwort (Fritz Stern, 7–8). Helfer und Retter in der Wehrmacht als Problem historischer Forschung (ed., 11–31). Der Judenretter und seine Kameraden. Gemeinschaftsmoral und Gemeinschaftsterror in der Wehrmacht (Thomas Kühne, 32–44). Essays on Anton Schmid (Arno Lustiger, 45–68), Wilm Hosenfeld (Dirk Heinrichs, 69–88), Karl von Bothmer (Manfred Messerschmidt, 89–104), Reinhold Lofy (Hermine Wüllner, 105–113), Erich Heyn (Peter Steinkamp, 114–122), Willi Schulz (Johannes Winter, 123–141), Dr. Fiedler (Florian Rohdenburg, 142–156), Karl Laabs (Reinhold Lütgemeier-Davin, 157–180), Albert Battel & Max Liedtke (Norbert Haase, 181–208), Heinz Drossel (ed., 209–232; deals with Berlin 1945).] [On Willi Schulz see also: Aktenkundige Liebe, die niemand verstehen konnte (Johannes Winter) [in]: 'FAZ', Nr. 10, Frankfurt am Main, 12. Jan. 2002. P. 44.]

41447. RESISTANCE BY NON-JEWS. FRANCK, DIETER: *Youth protest in Nazi Germany.* [In]: Leo Baeck Institute Year Book 2002, Vol. XLVII, Oxford, 2002. Pp. 247–267, illus., facsims. [D.F., b. 1926 in Kaiserlautern (non-Jewish), journalist, television producer, writer, wrote and distributed anti-Nazi handbills in Stuttgart during World War II, 6 of which have been reproduced according to his personal recollections.]

41448. RESISTANCE BY NON-JEWS. STEINBACH, PETER: *"Sie sind wie Chamäleons..." Helmuth James Graf von Moltke in den Wochen vor der "Wannseebesprechung" des 20. Januar 1942.* [In]: Preußens Himmel breitet seine Sterne .... [see No. 41991], Bd. 2. Pp. 787–804, notes.

41449. RHEINLAND-PFALZ. *"Dem Reich verfallen" – "den Berechtigten zurückzuerstatten".* Enteignung und Rückerstattung jüdischen Vermögens im Gebiet des heutigen Rheinland-Pfalz 1938–1953. Bearbeitet von Walter Rummel und Jochen Rath. Koblenz: Verlag der Landesarchivverwaltung Rheinland-Pfalz, 2001. XX, 547 pp., illus., footnotes, docs., bibl. (503–520), index (places, persons, 521–534). (Veröffentlichungen der Landesarchivverwaltung Rheinland-Pfalz, Bd. 96.) [Incl.: Teil A: Enteignung jüdischen Vermögens (Walter Rummel, 1–224). Teil B: Rückerstattung (Jochen Rath, 225–304). Teil C: Dokumente (305–486). Teil D: Beschreibung der Überlieferung (Walter Rummel/Jochen Rath, 487–500).]

41450. RHEINZ, HANNA: *Verdächtige und verdächtigte Biographien. Der Identitäts-Schwindler und seine Leser.* [In]: Kursbuch, H. 148, Berlin, 2002, Pp. 138–148. [On the Wilkomirski affair.]

41450a. RIGA. SCHEFFLER, WOLFGANG: *Das Schicksal der deutschen Juden im Ghetto Riga und Umgebung.* Vortrag für die Tagung der Lettischen Historischen Kommission in Riga am 29. November 2001. [In]: Die Mahnung, Jg. 49, Berlin, 1. Feb. 2002. Pp. 1–3.

41451. RIGG, BRYAN MARK: *Hitler's Jewish soldiers: the untold story of Nazi racial laws and men of Jewish descent in the German military.* Lawrence: Univ. Press of Kansas, 2002. XXI, 433 pp., illus., ports., facsims., tabs., notes, bibl. (383–404), index. [Cf.: Some Nazi soldiers' secret (David Rodman) [in]: Midstream, Vol. 48, No. 7, New York, Nov./Dec. 2002, 37.]

41452. RÖMER, GERNOT, ed./ERLANGER, ARNOLD: *Ein Schwabe überlebt Auschwitz. Arnold Erlanger aus Ichenhausen.* Aus dem Engl. von Thilo Jörgl. Augsburg: Wißner, 2002. 128 pp., illus. (Lebenserinnerungen von Juden aus Schwaben, Bd. 5.) [Author lives in Australia.]

41453. ROGASKY, BARBARA: *Smoke and ashes: the story of the Holocaust.* Rev. and expanded edn. New York: Holiday House, 2002. 256., illus., ports., map, facsims., chronol., bibl. (231–237), index. [For orig. edn. see No. 25338/YB XXXIV.]

41454. ROLEFF, TAMARA L., ed.: *The Holocaust: death camps.* San Diego: Greenhaven Publ., 2002. 224 pp., illus., maps, index. (History Firsthand.) [Incl. accounts by survivors.]

41455. ROMANIA. HAUSLEITNER, MARIANA, eds.: *Rumänien und der Holocaust. Zu den Massenverbrechen in Transnistrien 1941–1944.* Berlin: Metropol, 2001. 180 pp., footnotes. (Nationalsozialistische Besatzungspolitik in Europa 1939–1945, Bd. 10.) [Selected essays pertaining also to the German-speaking Jews of Bukowina: Der "vergessene" Holocaust". Der Sonderfall Rumänien: Okkupation und (Wolfgang Benz, 9–14). Großverbrechen im rumänischen Transnistrien (ed., 15–24). The deportation of the Jews to Transnistria (Radu Ioanid, 69–100). Rumänien, die SS und die Vernichtung der Juden (Andrej Angrick, 113–138).]

——— ROSEN, PHILIP/APFELBAUM, NINA: *Bearing witness: a resource guide to literature, poetry, art, music, and videos by Holocaust victims and survivors.* [See No. 41176.]

41456. ROTH, HARALD, ed.: *Mit falschem Pass und fremden Namen. Junge Menschen im Holocaust.* Mit einem Vorwort von Paul Spiegel. Gerlingen: Bleicher, 2002. 324 pp. [Anthology of texts from previously publ. memoirs, some by German-speaking authors.]

41457. RUSCHENBUSCH, EBERHARD: *Dönitz, die Konzentrationslager und der Mord an den Juden.* [In]: Schiff und Zeit/Panorama maritim, Nr. 52, Hamburg, Herbst 2000. Pp. 20–26, notes.

41458. SACKETT, ROBERT: *Memory by way of Anne Frank: enlightenment and denial among West Germans, circa 1960.* In]: Holocaust and Genocide Studies, Vol. 16, No. 2, Oxford, Fall 2002. Pp. 243–265, notes.

41459. *Salvaged pages: young writers' diaries of the Holocaust.* Collected and ed. by Alexandra Zapruder. New Haven, CT: Yale Univ. Press, 2002. XVIII, 481 pp., appendixes, notes, sources. [Incl. several German-Jewish and some Czech diarists, two incarcerated in Terezin, and some who were refugees in France.]

41460. SALZKOTTEN. WACKER, BERND/WACKER, MARIE-THERES: *Ausgelöscht. Erinnerung an die jüdische Gemeinde Salzkotten.* Salzkotten: Judentum in Salzkotten e.V., 2002. 320 pp., facsims., footnotes. [Salzkotten: between Lippstadt and Paderborn.]

41461. SAXONY. HELD, STEFFEN: *Von der Entrechtung zur Deportation: Die Juden in Sachsen.* [In]: Sachsen in der NS-Zeit. Hrsg. von Clemens Vollnhals. Leipzig: Kiepenheuer, 2002. Pp. 200–223.

41462. SCHARON, SAMI: *Gestritten, gekämpft und gelitten. Von Danzig nach Erez Israel, bei der britischen Armee in Nordafrika, mit der 'Jewish Brigade Group' durch Italien, Deutschland, Holland und Belgien, dann Offizier in der israelischen Armee 1923–1948.* Hrsg. von Erhard Roy Wiehn. Konstanz: Hartung-Gorre, 2002. 320 pp., illus.

——— SCHMIDT, ESTHER: *Nationalism and the creation of Jewish music: the politicization of music and language in the German-Jewish press prior to the Second World War.* [See No. 41731.]

41463. SCHNAUBER, JENS: *Die Arisierung der Scala und Plaza: Varieté und Dresdner Bank in der NS-Zeit.* Berlin: Weidler, 2002. 143 pp., bibl. (Kleine Schriften der Gesellschaft für Unterhaltende Bühnenkunst, Bd. 8.) [Deals with the "aryanisation" and restitution proceedings of the Berlin entertainment company and its theatres Scala-Theater, Scala-Palast and Plaza run by Jules Marx, Karl Wolffsohn, Max Loewenthal and Ben Blumenthal.]

41464. SCHNAUBER, JENS: *Deutsche Unternehmen in der Geschichtsfalle. Rückerstattungsakten als historische Quelle.* [In]: Geschichte als Falle. Deutschland und die jüdische Welt [see No. 40849]. Pp. 197–216, notes. [Deals with the "Varieté" theatres Scala and Plaza in Berlin and the Dresdner Bank.]

41465. SCHULLE, DIANA: *Das Reichssippenamt: eine Institution nationalsozialistischer Rassenpolitik.* Berlin: Logos Verlag, 2001. 416 pp., footnotes, bibl. Zugl.: Greifswald, Univ., Diss., 1999.

41466. SCHWARZ, EGON: *Refuge: chronicle of a flight from Hitler.* Transl. by Philip Böhm [et al.] Riverside, CA: Ariadne Press, 2002. (Studies in Austrian literature, culture, and thought.) [E.Sch., b. in Vienna 1922, Professor of German, escaped via Czechoslovakia, France, Bolivia to the US, taught at Washington Univ.] [For orig. German edn. in 1979, see No.16799/YB XXV.]

41467. SCHREUDER, SASKIA: *Würde im Widerspruch. Jüdische Erzählliteratur im nationalsozialistischen Deutschland 1933–1938.* Tübingen: Max Niemeyer Verl., 2002. VII, 321 pp., footnotes, bibl. (285–314), index. (Conditio Judaica, 39.) Zugl.: Münster, Univ., Diss., 2001. [Examines works by Gerson Stern, Jacob Picard, Rudolf Frank.]

41468. SCHWEITZER, SIMON/CHARON, MILLY: *Simons langer Weg.* Frankfurt am Main: Edition Büchergilde, 2002. 250 pp., frontis., illus., facsims. [Original edn.: Simon's Quest, 1997.] [Author, b. in Upper Silesia, describes his years in various forced labour and concentration camps, and his survival through the help of 'SS-Hauptsturmführer' Willi Michael. Lives in Montreal. See also a CBC documentary entitled "Behind the uniforms" (1994).]

41469. SHANGHAI. *The Jews in China*. Comp. and ed. by Pan Guang. Beijing: China Intercontinental Press, 2002. 194 pp., illus., ports., facsims., maps, notes, bibl. (186–191) [Incl.: Haven for Holocaust victims from Nazi Europe (86–128). Deals with the Shanghai Ghetto.]

41470. SHANGHAI. KAPLAN, VIVIAN JEANETTE: *Ten green bottles: Vienna to Shanghai – journey of fear and hope.* Toronto: Robin Brass Studio, 2002. X, 285 pp., illus., ports. [Author tells the story of her Viennese mother, Nini Karpel, and the family's experiences in Nazi Austria, later in Shanghai where they had sought refuge and where the author was born in 1946. In the late 1940s the family moved to Toronto.] [Cf.: Kristallnacht (Vivian J. Kaplan) [in]: Midstream, Vol. 47, No. 7, New York, Nov./Dec. 2002, pp. 9–12 (excerpt from the book).]

41471. SHANGHAI. RISTAINO, MARCIA R.: *Port of last resort: the diaspora communities of Shanghai.* Stanford, CA: Stanford Univ. Press, 2001. XVIII, 369 pp., illus., maps, notes, bibl. (287–357). [Deals with the Jewish refugees who found a safe haven in Shanghai during World War II.]

41472. SHANGHAI. RUBIN, EVELYN PIKE: *Ghetto Schanghai: von Breslau nach Schanghai und Amerika.* Erinnerungen eines jüdischen Mädchens 1943–1947, 1995 und 1997. Hrsg. von Erhard Roy Wiehn. Konstanz: Hartung-Gorre, 2002. 94 pp., illus. [For a previous American version see No. 31669/YB XL.]

41473. SIEGERT, FOLKER, ed.: *Grenzgänge. Menschen und Schicksale zwischen jüdischer, christlicher und deutscher Identität.* Festschrift für Diethard Aschoff. Münster: Lit, 2002. 455 pp., frontis., footnotes, bibl. D. Asch., index. (Münsteraner Judaistische Schriften, 11.) [Section 2, entitled Deutsch-jüdische Geschichte bis zur Gegenwart, incl. (some titles abbr.): Der Antisemitismus der Hitlerjugendführer und die "Endlösung der Judenfrage in Europa" (Heinz Schreckenberg, 270–306). Ernst Gerson, ein katholischer "Nichtarier" (Margit Naarmann, 307–327). Angehörige "Privilegierter Mischehen" während des 'Dritten Reiches'. Die Beispiele Litten und von Szily aus Münster (Gisela Möllenhoff, 343–366). Die Zwangsausweisung polnischer Juden aus Münster 1938/39 (Rita Schlautmann-Overmeyer, 367–387). Das Projekt "Jüdische Familien in Münster 1918–1945". Rückblick und Bilanz (Franz-Josef Jakobi, 392–401). Eine Rückkehr von Auschwitz. Imo Moszkowicz erinnert sich (Hans W. Gummersbach). Gespräch mit Marga Spiegel (Michael J. Rainer, 415–422). Incl. also a section entitled Antikes Judentum und Neues Testament (12–129). Further articles pertaining to German-speaking Jewry are listed according to subject.]

41474. SLOVAKIA. BÜCHLER, YEHOSHUA: *"Certificates" for Auschwitz.* [In]: Yad Vashem Studies, Vol. 30, Jerusalem, 2002. Pp. 125–152, facsims., footnotes. [Deals with how members of the Slovakian-Jewish resistance managed to reach Palestine and were able to persuade the Jewish Agency to issue visas for Slovakian Jews in various camps, incl. Auschwitz, in some cases with success.]

41475. SLOVAKIA. MEIRI-MINERBI, HAYA: *Juden in Kesmark und Umgebung zur Zeit der Schoáh. Jüdisches Leben und Leiden in der Slowakei.* Aus dem Hebr. von Magali Zibaso. Hrsg. von Erhard Roy Wiehn. Konstanz: Hartung-Gorre, 2002. 60 pp., illus., footnotes.

41476. SLOVAKIA. *The tragedy of the Jews of Slovakia.* 1938–1945: Slovakia and the "Final Solution of the Jewish Question". Oswiecim; Banská Bystrica: Auschwitz-Birkenau State Museum; Museum of the Slovak National Uprising, 2002. 320 pp., notes, illus., gloss., bibl., index. [Cont.: Introduction (Dezider Toth, 7–10). 16 contribs.]

41477. SPAIN. ROTHER, BERND: *Spanien und der Holocaust.* Tübingen: Niemeyer, 2001. VI, 359 pp., footnotes, bibl., index. [Incl. the fate of German-Jewish refugees.]

41478. STERN, GUY: *Altruismus im Dienste der Kunst: Die Rettung von Kulturgütern während der Nazizeit.* [In]: Preußens Himmel breitet seine Sterne … [see No. 41991], Bd. 1. Pp. 415–427, notes.

41479. SWEDEN. KIEM, THOMAS: *Das österreichische Exil in Schweden 1938–45.* Innsbruck: Studien-Verlag, 2001. 136 pp., illus., bibl., notes (111–127). [Deals mainly with Jewish emigrants.]

41480. SWITZERLAND. BÉRÈS, LOUIS RENÉ: *An open letter to the people of Switzerland.* [In]: Midstream, Vol. 48, No. 6, New York, Sept./Oct. 2002. Pp. 28–29. [Swiss-Jewish author, son of Austrian-Jewish refugees, discusses the dilemma of Switzerland's maintaining neutrality during the Second World War.]

——— SWITZERLAND. *Deutschsprachige Schriftsteller im Schweizer Exil 1933–1950.* [See No. 41771.]

41481. SWITZERLAND (JEWISH ASSETS). FINKELSTEIN, NORMAN: *Whither the Holocaust industry?* [In]: The Jewish Quarterly, Vol. 49, No. 1, London, Spring 2002. Pp. 60–61. [Deals with restitution claims against Switzerland.]

41482. *Die Täter der Shoah. Fanatische Nationalsozialisten oder ganz normale Deutsche?* Hrsg. von Gerhard Paul. Göttingen: Wallstein, 2002. 276 notes, bibl. (Dachauer Symposien zur Zeitgeschichte, Bd. 2.) [Cont.: Introd. and an essay on the historiography of Nazi perpetrators (ed., 7–92). Six contribs. on individual perpetrators by Karin Orth, Klaus-Michael Mallmann, Jürgen Matthäus, Walter Manoschek, Bogdan Musial, Dieter Pohl (93–236). Comments by Harald Welzer and Hanno Loewy (237–264).]

41483. *Theatre and war, 1933–1945: performance in extremis.* Ed. by Michael Balfour. Oxford; New York: Berghahn Books, 2001. IX, 189 pp., notes, bibl., index. [Incl. chaps.: German refugee theatre in British internment (Alan Clarke). Cabaret in concentration camps (Peter Jelavich).]

41484. THERESIENSTADT. FEUSS, AXEL: *Das Theresienstadt-Konvolut.* Altonaer Museum in Hamburg – Norddeutsches Landesmuseum. Hamburg: Dölling und Galitz, 2002. 128 pp., port., side notes, bibl. [Publ. in conjunction with an exhibition with the same title in the "Heine Haus", Hamburg, Feb. – April 2002; incl.: Jüdische Selbstverwaltung Theresienstadt – Prominente (16–78; first complete reproduction of the so-called "Prominenten-Album" (produced in Jan. 1944 and owned by Käthe Stark) with 92 short biographies of "prominent" Theresienstadt inmates). Also water colours and drawings from Theresienstadt.]

——— THERESIENSTADT. KRAUS, OTA B.: *Die bemalte Wand.* Roman. [See No. 42196.]

41485. THERESIENSTADT. KÁRNY, MIROSLAV/MILOZOVÁ, JAROSLAVA/KEMPER, RAIMUND/ WÖGERBAUER, MICHAEL, eds.: *Theresienstädter Studien und Dokumente 2001.* Prag: Institut Theresienstädter Initiative; Academia, 2001. 397 pp., facsims., notes, index. [Inl.: Luftwurzeln. Die Tausendjährige Geschichte der Juden im Böhmen und Mähren in den Namen der Deportierten (Ruth Bondy, 11–48). Die Vorbereitungen zur Konzentrierung der Juden im Protektorat. Die 'Vorgeschichte' des Theresienstädter Ghettos (Anita Franková, 49–74). Die Theresienstädter Außenkommandos (Pavla Zemanová, 75–105). Die Postverbindung zwischen dem Protektorat und dem Ghetto Theresienstadt (Patricia Tosnerová, 106–147). Die Geschichte des Theresienstädter Transports "Be" nach Estland (Lukás Pribyl, 148–229). Die acht Transporte aus dem Reichskommissariat Niederlande nach Theresienstadt (Anna Hájková, 230–251). Das prominente Ehepaar Gutmann und die diplomatischen Bemühungen zu seiner Befreiung (Michael Wögerbauer, 252–268). Möglichkeiten und Grenzen schweizerischer Schutzmachtpolitik im Protektorat Böhmen und Mähren 1939–1945 (Daniel C. Schmid, 287–304).]

41485a. THERESIENSTADT. MILOTOVÁ, JAROSLAVA/RATHGEBER, ULF/KALINOVÁ, GABRIELA, eds.: *Theresienstädter Studien und Dokumente 2002.* Prag: Institut Theresienstädter Initiative; Academia, 2002. 375 pp., notes. [This vol. is dedicated to Miroslav Kárny, the late co-founder of the "Theresienstädter Initiative" and co-editor of the "Theresienstädter Studien und Dokumente" from 1994 until his death, May 9, 2001. Incl. (some titles abbr.): Vorwort (eds., 7–12). Sieben Monate in Kaufering (Miroslav Kárny, 13–24). Miroslav Kárny (obit. and bibl. M.K., 25–44). Überlegungen zur Wahrnehmung und Rezeption des Ghettos Theresienstadt (Wolfgang Benz, 45–56). Die Vergangenheit ist unvergangen. Der Einfluss des Theresienstädter Ghettos auf das Leben seiner ehemaligen Häftlinge (Ruth Bondy, 57–74). Zur Geschichte der Verordnung Konstantin von Neuraths über das jüdische Vermögen (Jaroslava Milotová, 75–115). Zur "Arisierung" der jüdischen Malzfabriken im Protektorat Böhmen und Mähren (Daniel C. Schmid, 116–134; on M. Reiser & Söhne, Prague, Ed. Hamburger & Sohn, Olmütz). Die Juden aus den Niederlanden in Theresienstadt (Anna Hajková, 135–201). Schwarzheide – Aussenlager des KZ-Lagers Sachsenhausen (Jakov Tsur, 202–220). Zur ersten authentischen Nachricht über den Beginn der Vernichtung der europäischen Juden (Livia Rothkirchen, 338–346; followed by the German transl. of "The Nazi Plan. A stony road to extermination" by "a correspondent" = Lewis B. Namier, orig. publ. in 'The Times', Dec. 16, 1939).]

41486. THERESIENSTADT. LANGER, LAWRENCE L.: *The art of atrocity.* [In]: Tikkun, Vol. 17, No. 4, Berkely, CA, July-Aug. 2002. Pp. 67–70, illus. [On the art and culture in Theresienstadt; also deals with the Nazi propaganda film made there.]

41487. THERESIENSTADT. WEISS, OTTO: *Und Gott sah, daß es schlecht war.* Erzählung aus Theresienstadt. Übers. von Jiri Burgerstein, illustriert von Helga Weissová. Mit einem Nachwort von Stefana Sabin. Hrsg. vom Niedersächsischen Verein zur Förderung von Theresienstadt/Terezin. Göttingen: Wallstein, 2002. 62 pp., illus. [A satirical story about life in the ghetto written 1943 by the author in Theresienstadt before being deported to Auschwitz, with illustrations by his then twelve year old daughter.]

41488. TOMASZEWSKI, JERZY: *Auftakt zur Vernichtung. Die Vertreibung polnischer Juden aus Deutschland im Jahre 1938.* Aus dem Polnischen von Victoria Pollmann. Osnabrück: Fibre Verlag, 2002. 331 pp., footnotes, bibl., indexes. (Deutsches Historisches Institut Warschau: Klio in Polen, 9.) [Orig. publ. 1998.]

41489. *Totentanz. Kabarett im KZ.* CD-Edition "Vertriebene deutsch-jüdische Schauspieler". Hrsg. in Zusammenarbeit mit Volker Kühn [et al.] von Wolfgang M. Schwiedrzik. Neckargemünd: Edition Mnemosyne, 2000. 1 CD + 1 DVD. [Booklet (51 pp., illus., facsims.) incl.: Lächeln im Angesicht des Todes (Volker Kühn, 6–40). CD: Die Welt ist eng geworden. Chansons, Conferencen, Texte und Lieder von Künstlern, die in Auschwitz, Dachau, Theresienstadt, Westerbork und anderen Lagern eingesperrt und ermordet wurden. Gesammelt und ausgewählt von Volker Kühn. DVD: Totentanz – Kabarett hinter Stacheldraht. Ein Film von Volker Kühn. Mit deutscher und englischer Tonspur. Eine Fernsehproduktion des Hess. Rundfunks, 1990.]

41490. TRAHAN, ELIZABETH WELT: *Evidence – memory – perspective: the genesis of a Holocaust memoir.* [In]: International Studies in Philosophy, Vol. XXXIV, No. 1, New York, 2002. Pp. 175–184. [Deals with the author's book *Walking with ghosts – a Jewish childhood in wartime Vienna*; see Nos. 33881/YB LII and 36478/YB XLIV.]

41491. UEBACH-PALENBERG. KLOSA, JÜRGEN: *Zur Geschichte der Juden in Übach-Palenberg.* [In]: Heimatkalender des Kreises Heinsberg 2002. Heinsberg, 2002. Pp. 148–154, facsims., illus.

41492. UEBERSCHÄR, GERD R., ed.: *NS-Verbrechen und der militärische Widerstand gegen Hitler.* Darmstadt: Primus, 2000. X, 214 pp., notes, index. (Gleichzeitig: Bd. 18 der Schriftenreihe des Fritz Bauer Instituts.) [Cont.: Vorwort (ed., VII-X). I. Antisemitische Einstellungen im Widerstand gegen Hitler (3–43); cont.: Der Widerstand zwischen unbequemer Erinnerung und nationalem Mythos (Hanno Loewy, 3–13). Der "Aufstand des Gewissens" und die "Judenfrage" . Ein Rückblick (Christof Dipper, 14–18). Reichswehr, Wehrmacht, Antisemitismus und militärischer Widerstand (1933–1939) (Wolfram Wette, 19–30). Der militärische Widerstand, die antijüdischen Maßnahmen, "Polenmorde" und NS-Kriegsverbrechen in den ersten Kriegsjahren (1939–1941) (Gerd R. Ueberschär, 31–43). II. Die Konfrontation militärischer Verschwörer mit den NS-Verbrechen im Vernichtungskrieg an der Ostfront (47–103); cont. contribs. by Peter Steinkamp, Christian Gerlach, Winfried Heinemann, Christian Streit. III. Antisemitismus und NS-Verbrechen als Motive für den Umsturz gegen Hitler am 20. Juli 1944 (107–134); cont.: Motive der militärischen Verschwörer gegen Hitler (Manfred Messerschmidt, 107–118). Die Stellung der Militäropposition im Rahmen der deutschen Widerstandsbewegung gegen Hitler (Hans Mommsen, 119–103). IV. Ausgewählte Dokumente (137–206); cont.: Die Haltung militärischer Verschwörer zum Antisemitismus und zu den NS-Verbrechen im Spiegel von Dokumenten (Peter Steinkamp/Gerd R. Ueberschär).]

———— "*Uns hat keiner gefragt*". *Positionen der dritten Generation zur Bedeutung des Holocaust.* [See No. 42084.]

41493. VALENT, PAUL: *Child survivors of the Holocaust.* New York; London: Brunner-Routledge, 2002. XIII, 288 pp., ports. [Based on interviews with ten survivors, all living in Australia; incl. some from Germany, Austria, Czechoslovakia.]

41494. VARGA, ERVIN: *Requiem für Sternträger. Die Lebenserinnerungen eines ungarischen Juden bis zu seiner Befreiung 1945.* Mit einem Geleitwort von Bert Wallace. Hrsg. vom Bund gegen Anpassung. [Aus dem Amerik. übers.] Freiburg: Ahriman, 2000. 104 pp., illus., bibl. (Ketzerbriefe 95, Flaschenpost für unangepaßte Gedanken.) [Book deals also with the background of the Richter, Reich and Weisz families.] [E.V., orig. Weisz, b. 1935 in Budapest, physician, raised in a partly German-speaking family, survived several slave labour camps and death marches, lives in New York.]

41495. VECHTA. BEHNE, ULRICH: *Die Viehhändlerfamilien Gerson und das Schicksal der jüdischen Gemeinde zu Vechta.* Diepholz: Schrödersccher Buchverlag, 2001. 204 pp., illus., facsims., notes, bibl. (Veröffentlichungen des Museums im Zeughaus, Stadt Vechta, Bd. 4.)

41496. *Vergessen kann man es nie …: Erinnerungen an Nazi-Deutschland.* Hrsg. von Klaus W. Tofahrn. Frankfurt am Main; New York: Lang, 2002. 150 pp., footnotes. [Incl. personal reminiscences of Sophoni and Susi Herz about the November Pogrom in Bonn and in Dinslaken.]

41497. VIENNA. CLARE, GEORGE: *Last waltz in Vienna.* London: Pan Books, 2002. VIII, 278 pp., illus., bibl. (259–263), index. [Story of the Klaar family right through the "Anschluss". For first Engl. edn. 1981 see No. 18675/YB XXVII and for new German edn. and details see No. 39815/YB XLVII.]

41498. VIENNA. FALK, SUSANNE: *Die "Arisierung" Wiener Zeitungsverlage. Das Verlagshaus Canisiusgasse 8–10.* Mit einem Geleitwort von Prof. Dr. Murray G. Hall. Taunusstein: Driesen, 2002. 215 pp., illus., footnotes, bibl. (Driesen Edition Wissenschaft.) Zugl.: Wien, Univ., Diplomarbeit. [Incl. a chap. on the publisher of various Viennese papers, Maximilian Schreier, 1875 Brünn – 1942 Vienna (suicide – to avoid deportation).]

41499. VIENNA. NEUGEBAUER, WOLFGANG: *Juden als Opfer der NS-Euthanasie in Wien 1940–1945.* [In]: Eberhard Gabriel/Wolfgang Neugebauer, eds.: Von der Zwangssterilisierung zur Ermordung. Zur Geschichte der NS-Euthanasie in Wien. Teil II, Wien: Böhlau, 2002. Pp. 99–112, footnotes.

41500. VILNA. KRUG, HERMAN: *The last days of the Jerusalem of Lithuania: chronicles from the Vilna ghetto and the camps, 1939–1944.* Ed. and introd. by Benjamin Harshav. Transl. by Barbara Harshav. New Haven, CT: Yale Univ. Press; New York: YIVO Institute for Jewish Research, 2002. LII, 732 pp., illus., maps, bibl. (713–714), index. [Earlier edn. was publ. in Yiddish in 1961. Three copies of the orig. ms. were prepared inside the ghetto; almost half of the typecripts were retrieved from the bunker where they had been hidden although the author did not survive.] [Cf.: Death foretold (Abraham Brumberg) [in]: TLS, London, Dec. 27, 2002.]

41501. *Voices and views: a history of the Holocaust.* Ed. and with introds. by Deborah Dwork. New York: Jewish Foundation for the Righteous, 2002. XXVI, 687 pp., illus., facsims., maps, bibl., index. [Essays by various authors giving a historical overview of the Holocaust with special focus on rescuers; incl. also first-person accounts and original speeches.]

41502. WAGNER, PATRICK: *Hitlers Kriminalisten.* Die deutsche Kriminalpolizei und der Nationalsozialismus zwischen 1920 und 1960. München: C.H.Beck, 2002. 218 pp., notes, bibl., index. [Deals also with activities related to the Jews.]

41503. WALSER-BUBIS-DEBATE. FUCHS, ANNE: *Towards an ethics of remembering: the Walser-Bubis debate and the other of discourse.* [In]: The German Quarterly, Vol. 75, No. 3, Riverside, CA, Summer 2002. Pp. 235– 246, notes.

41504. WARMBOLD, NICOLE: *Zur Lagersprache der Häftlinge von Sachsenhausen, Dachau und Buchenwald.* [In]: Judentum: Wege zur geistigen Befreiung [see No. 40865]. Pp. 170–180, notes.

41505. *The war crimes of the Deutsche Bank and the Dresdner Bank: Office of Military Government (U.S.) reports.* Ed. and introd. by Christopher Simpson. New York: Holmes and Meier, 2002. XIV, 417 pp., illus., tabs., charts, notes, bibl., index. [A United States Military Government report, first issued in 1946. Incl. confiscation of Jewish property, slave labour.] [Cf.: Wer spinnt? (Gerald D. Feldman) [in]: German Politics and Society, Vol. 20, No. 3, New York, Fall 2002, pp. 40–55, notes.]

41506. WACHS, PHILIPP-CHRISTIAN: *Der Fall Theodor Oberländer (1905–1998). Ein Lehrstück deutscher Geschichte.* Frankfurt am Main; New York: Campus, 2000. 533 pp., bibl. Zugl.: München, Univ. der Bundeswehr, Diss., 1999. [See also the author's essay entitled Ein deutscher Fall: Konrad Adenauer und Theodor Oberländer [In]: Geschichte als Falle. Deutschland und die jüdische Welt [see No. 40849]. Pp. 173–196, notes.]

41507. WEGNER, ARMIN T.: *Brief an Hitler.* Geleitwort von Wolfgang Thierse. Wuppertal: Peter Hammer Verl., 56 pp. [Open letter (1933) protesting against the persecution of the Jews; incl. Engl. and French transl.]

41508. WEISS, YFAAT: *The racialization of the Jews – historical anthropology of the Nuremberg Laws.* [In]: Jahrbuch des Simon-Dubnow-Instituts, Jg. 1, Stuttgart, 2002. Pp. 201–218, footnotes.

41509. WEISZ FAMILY. WEISZ, PAUL B. ed.: *Family in war: a personal chronicle.* Lanham, MD: Univ. Press of America, 2001. 108 pp. [Mainly family letters from different countries with editorial comments, transl. by Paul Weisz. The chronicle starts in 1938 when the family leaves Vienna and is separated. Author went via England to Canada where he was interned. Later he was sponsored by a Canadian family to study and became professor in Montreal. Now lives in the US.]

41510. WELZER, HARALD/MOLLER, SABINE/TSCHUGGNALL, KAROLINE: *"Opa war kein Nazi". Nationalsozialismus und Holocaust im Familiengedächtnis.* Unter Mitarbeit von Olaf Jensen und Torsten Koch. Frankfurt am Main: Fischer Tadchenbuch Verlag, 2002. 247 pp., notes, tabs. Orig.-Ausg. [Documents the results of a research project based on interviews with three generations.]

41511. WESTPHALIA. MECKING, SABINE: *Verfolgung und Verwaltung. Die wirtschaftliche Ausplünderung der Juden und die westfälischen Finanzbehörden.* Hrsg.: Geschichtsort Villa ten Hompel in Kooperation mit der Oberfinanzdirektion Münster. Münster: Selbstverlag, 2001. 100 pp., facsims., docs., footnotes, chronol., bibl. (Villa ten Hompel – Didaktische Bausteine, 1.) [Incl. problems related to restitution.] [Cf.: Bespr. (Ansgar Weißer) [in]: Westfälische Forschungen, Bd. 52, Münster, 2002, pp. 739–740.]

41512. WETTE, WOLFRAM: *Die Wehrmacht. Feindbilder, Vernichtungskrieg, Legenden.* Frankfurt am Main: S. Fischer, 2002. 376 pp., bibl., indexes, notes. [Incl. the sections: Teil II. Antisemitismus im deutschen Militär (36–94; from the 1890s to 1939). Teil III. Wehrmacht und Judenmorde (95–196).]

41513. WIESEN, JONATHAN: *Morality and memory: reflections on business ethics and National Socialism.* [In]: The Journal of Holocaust Education, Vol. 10, No. 3, London, Winter 2001. Pp. 60–82. [Deals with the attitudes of West Germany's business leaders towards World War II and the Holocaust in the context of their own collaboration with the Nazis. Author argues that post-war business leaders believe that their behaviour was both pragmatic and ethical.] [Cf.: Holocaust assets and German business history: beginning or end (Gerald D. Feldman) [in]: German Studies Review, Vol. 25, No. 1, Northfield, MN, Feb. 2002, pp. 23–34, notes.]

41514. *Das Wilkomirski-Syndrom. Eingebildete Erinnerungen oder: Von der Sehnsucht, Opfer zu sein.* Hrsg. von Irene Diekmann und Julius H. Schoeps. Zürich: Pendo, 2002. 367 pp., notes. [Papers given at a conference, Potsdam, May 2001 at the Moses Mendelssohn-Zentrum. Cont.: Vorwort (eds., 7–12). Das Phänomen der eingebildeten Erinnerung. Zum Fall Wilkomirski (Sander L. Gilman, 13–27). Essays are arranged under the sections: Der Fall Wilkomirski – das Buch "mit dem Gewicht dieses Jahrhunderts" (NZZ vom 14.11.1995); cont. (titles abbr.): Das Opfer Wilkomirski [&] Aufregung um Wilkomirski (Stefan Mächler, 28–131). Wilkomirski, ein Lehrstück aus dem Holocaust-Zirkus (Daniel Ganzfried, 132–156). Das Trauma als Faszinosum (Hans Stoffels, 157–179). Wilkomirski und die Schweiz (Eva Lezzi, 180–215). Andere Verwandlungsfälle; cont.: Zum Phänomen "falscher" Identitäten (Gabriele Rosenthal, 216–236). Jakob Littners Erinnerungen und Wolfgang Koeppens "Roman" (Barbara Breysach, 236–261). Eine Christin als "Rabbinerin": Karin Mylius (Lothar Mertens, 262–272). Norman G. Finkelstein, die Nachgeborenen und die paranoiden Züge unserer Gedenkkultur (Julius H. Schoeps, 273–287). Von Lea, von Jakob, von Edith und einer Lebenslüge (Klaus Harpprecht, 288–292). Über die unglaubliche Geschichte der Misha Defonseca (Henryk M. Broder, 293–300). Mundus vult decipi (Elke Liebs, 301–334). Diskussion mit Julius H. Schoeps, Daniel Ganzfried, Stefan Mächler, Henryk M. Broder, Gabriele Rosenthal (335–361).]

41515. WILDT, MICHAEL: *Geld und Weltanschauung. Über unterschiedliche Rationalitäten bei der Verfolgung und Ermordung der europäischen Juden.* [In]: Gedächtnis, Geld und Gesetz. Vom Umgang mit der Vergangenheit des Zweiten Weltkrieges [see No. 41605]. Pp. 251–268, notes.

41516. WILDT, MICHAEL: *Generation des Unbedingten.* Das Führungskorps des Reichssicherheitshauptamtes. Hamburg: Hamburger Edition, 2002. 964 pp., ports., footnotes, bibl. (878–930), index.

41517. WIRSCHING, ANDREAS: *Jüdische Friedhöfe in Deutschland 1933–1957.* [In]: Vierteljahrshefte für Zeitgeschichte, Jg. 50, H. 1, München, 2002. Pp. 1–40, footnotes. [Engl. abstract on p. 157.]

41518. WORMS. SCHLÖSSER, KARL: *Die Wormser Juden 1933–1945.* Dokumentation. Worms: Stadtarchiv Worms, 2002. 1 CD-ROM. [Documents the fate of hundreds of families; incl. anti-semitism, photographs of Jewish Worms.]

41519. WORPSWEDE. MEINERS-DETROY, CHRISTA: *Kindheitserinnerungen.* Gegen das Vergessen – eine persönliche Geschichte. [In]: Tribüne, Jg. 41, H. 164, Frankfurt am Main, 2002. Pp. 178–186. [Deals with the author's attempts to trace details about a former neighbour, Julie Abraham, and her family in Worpswede.]

41520. YAHIL, LENI: *A selection of articles on the fate of European Jewry during the Holocaust.* Presented to Prof. Leni Yahil on the occasion of her 90th birthday. Jerusalem: Yad Vashem; The International Institute for Holocaust Research, 2002. 237, 182 pp., facsims., footnotes, appendixes. [Book has a section in Hebrew (237 pp.), and a section in English and German (182 pp.), cont. previously publ. articles by L.Y.] [L.Y., née Westphal, b. 1912 in Düsseldorf, author, Prof. of History, joined the "Werkleute", went to Palestine in 1934, has been Professor of Jewish history at several Israeli and American universities.]

41521. ZUCKMAYER, CARL: *Geheimreport.* Hrsg. von Gunther Nickel und Johanna Schrön. Göttingen: Wallstein, 2002. 527 pp., frontis., illus., notes (189–406), bibl., index. (Zuckmayer-Schriften.) [Incl.: Carl Zuckmayers 'Geheimreport' für das 'Office of Strategic Services' (eds., 407–477; deals with the historical context). First complete publ. of ca. 150 portrayals of prominent Germans inside Nazi Germany, written in 1943/1944 for the Field Unit of Biographical Records of the OSS in New York.]

41522. ZWICKAU. *Zum Schicksal der Zwickauer Juden.* Die Zerstörung des Weimarer Rechtsstaates durch die Nationalsozialisten. Zwickau: Gerhart-Hauptmann-Gymnasium – Projektgruppe Geschichte [Ltg.: D. Seichter], 2001. 53 pp., illus., facsims. [Incl. personal memoirs by Jews from Zwickau.]

41523. ZYNDUL, JOLANTA: *Ausgesetzte Bürger – Polen und polnischstämmige Juden in Deutschland 1933–1939.* [In]: Jahrbuch des Simon-Dubnow-Instituts, Jg. 1, Stuttgart, 2002. Pp. 93–106, footnotes.

B. Jewish Resistance

41524. PALTER, ROBERT M.: *Jewish resistance during the Holocaust.* [In]: Jewish Spectator, Vol. 66, No. 2, Calabasas, CA, Fall 2001. Pp. 17–25.

——— TUCHEL, JOHANNES: *Widerstand von Juden im nationalsozialistischen Deutschland.* Rahmenbedingungen und weiterführende Fragen. [In]: Beate Kosmala/Claudia Schoppmann, eds.: Überleben im Untergrund [see No. 41440.]

IV. POST-1945

A. General

41525. ARMBORST, KERSTIN: *Ablösung von der Sowjetunion. Die Emigrationsbewegung der Juden und Deutschen vor 1987.* Münster: Lit, 2001. XIII, 452 pp., footnotes, bibl. (425–452). (Arbeiten zur Geschichte Osteuropas, 10.) Zugl.: Münster, Univ., Diss., 1999.

41526. *Aufbau.* The Transatlantic Jewish Paper. Vol. 68, No. 22, New York; Berlin, Oct. 31, 2002. [Incl. a focus section entitled *To be a Jew in today's Germany/Gepackte Koffer ?* Pp. 8–11; cont. a general report (Robert B. Goldmann) and several personal essays.]

41527. AUSTRIA. *Escape through Austria: Jewish refugees and the Austrian route to Palestine.* Ed. by Thomas Albrich and Ronald W. Zweig. London; Portland OR: Frank Cass, 2002. VIII. 136 pp., footnotes, index. [Deals with Jewish DPs in Austria who tried to get to Palestine by various routes and means. Incl. contribs. by Christine Oertel, Michael John, Susanne Rolinek, Norbert Ramp, Eva Pfanzelter, Thomas Albrich.]

41528. AUSTRIA. NAQVI, FATIMA: *Dialectic at a standstill: the discourse of victimhood in Thomas Bernhard's 'Heldenplatz'.* [In]: The German Quarterly, Vol. 75, No. 4, Riverside, CA, Fall 2002. Pp. 408–421, notes.

41529. BEHRENS, KATJA, ed.: *Ich bin geblieben – warum? Juden in Deutschland – heute.* Gerlingen: Bleicher, 2002. 198 pp. [Cont.: Zwischen Antisemitismus und Philosemitismus. Juden in Deutschland nach 1945 (Wolfgang Benz, 7–34). Contribs. by Jurek Becker, Johannes Mario Simmel, Katja Behrens, Peter Finkelgruen, Ralph Giordano, Esther Dischereit, Benjamin Korn, Salomon Korn, Ulrike Maria Hund.] [Cf.: Doch die Antwort bleiben sie uns schuldig (Robert Schopflocher) [in]: Aufbau, Vol. 68, No. 25, New York, Dec. 12, 2002, p. 16.]

41530. BERLIN. GLÖCKNER, OLAF/VOGT, BERNHARD: *"Die Menschen brauchen Zeit". Chancen und Probleme russisch-jüdischer Zuwanderer in der neuen Hauptstadt Berlin.* [In]: Preußens Himmel breitet seine Sterne …. [see No. 41991], Bd. 2. Pp. 641–652, notes.

——— BRANDT, HENRY G.: *Freude an der Tora – Freude am Dialog.* [See No. 41627.]

41531. BROCKE, EDNA: *Jüdisches Leben in der Bundesrepublik Deutschland.* [In]: Eleonore Lappin, ed.: Jüdische Gemeinden – Kontinuitäten und Brüche [see No. 41074]. Pp. 267–282, notes.

41532. CHURCH. OSTMEYER, IRENA: *Zwischen Schuld und Sühne. Evangelische Kirche und Juden in SBZ und DDR 1945–1990.* Mit einem Geleitwort von Julius H. Schoeps. Berlin: Inst. Kirche und Judentum, 2002. 400 pp., footnotes, chronol., docs., bibl., index. (Studien zu Kirche und Israel, Bd. 21) Zugl.: Potsdam, Univ., veränd. Diss., 1998.

——— DÜSSELDORF. SCHMALHAUSEN, BERND: *Josef Neuberger (1902–1977). Ein Leben für eine menschliche Justiz.* [See No. 41945.]

41533. DÜSSELDORF. TYE, LARRY: *Home lands: portraits of the new Jewish diaspora.* New York: Holt, 2001. 336 pp., illus., ports., bibl., index. [Incl. chap.: Düsseldorf: in the land of the murderers (13–58; deals with the present-day Jewish community and specifically with Paul Spiegel, chairman of the Düsseldorf community from 1984 until 2000, since then president of the "Zentralrat der Juden in Deutschland").]

41534. FRANCONIA. TOBIAS, JIM G.: *Vorübergehende Heimat im Land der Täter. Jüdische DP-Camps in Franken 1945–1949.* Mit einem Vorwort von Arno Lustiger und einem Beitrag von Dr. Albrecht Bald. Nürnberg: Antogo, 2002. 287 pp., illus., bibl., gloss., notes.

41535. GAY, RUTH: *Safe among the Germans: liberated Jews after World War II.* New Haven, CT: Yale Univ. Press, 2002. XIV, 347 pp., illus., ports., facsims., bibl., index. [Deals with DPs, incl. German Jews who remained in Germany after the war; also covers Jews in the former GDR as well as the present-day Jewish community in Berlin.]

41536. GELLER, JAY HOWARD: *Representing Jewry in East Germany, 1945–1953: Between advocacy and accommodation.* [In]: Leo Baeck Institute Year Book 2002, Vol. XLVII, Oxford, 2002. Pp. 195–214, footnotes.

41537. GOLDBERG, J.R.: *A brief memoir of a house, Germany, and prejudice by Jews.* [In]: Midstream, Vol. 48, No. 7, New York, Nov./Dec. 2002. Pp. 12–15. [American-Jewish author describes his four years in Germany with the US Army in the 1970s, as he confronts the Holocaust and his own anti-German prejudices.]

—— GOLDFEIN, ALAN: Jews and Germans – Germans and Jews. A novella and short stories. [See No. 42193.]

41538. GRUBER, SABINE/RÜSSLER, HARALD: *Hochqualifiziert und arbeitslos.* Jüdische Kontingentflüchtlinge in Nordrhein-Westfalen. Problemaspekte ihrer beruflichen Integration. Eine empirische Studie. Opladen: Leske + Budrich, 2002. 242 pp., notes, tabs.

41539. GRUBER, RUTH ELLEN: *Virtually Jewish: reinventing Jewish culture in Europe.* Berkeley: Univ. of California Press, 2002. XIII, 304 pp., illus., discography, notes, bibl. (275–286), index. (The S. Mark Taper foundation imprint in Jewish studies.) [Discusses how aspects of Jewish culture (i.e. Kletzmer music) are flourishing in Europe (incl. Germany) amongst non-Jews, often in the absence of a large Jewish community. Deals also with Jewish communities; "Vergangenheitsbewältigung".]

—— HAMBURG. BAHNSEN, UWE: *Die Weichmanns in Hamburg. Ein Glücksfall für Deutschland.* [See No. 42017.]

41540. HAMBURG. LOHALM, UWE, ed.: *"Schließlich ist es meine Heimat …"* Harry Goldstein und die Jüdische Gemeinde Hamburg in persönlichen Dokumenten und Fotos. Hamburg: Ergebnisse-Verlag, 2002. 148 pp., frontis., illus., facsims., bibl., index. [Incl.: Vorwort (Arno Herzig, 7–10). Harry Goldsteins Bericht über den Wiederbeginn jüdischen Lebens in Hamburg 1945–1948 aufgezeichnet von seinem Sohn Heinz Goldstein (14–45). Berichte zur Lage der Juden und der Jüdischen Gemeinde in Hamburg während der nationalsozialistischen Verfolgung und in der Nachkriegszeit (46–69). Also short biographies of Harry and Heinz Goldstein; docs. and photographs.] [Harry G. orig. Heimann G., July 20, 1880 Waldenburg/Silesia – June 10, 1977 Hamburg, settled in Hamburg in 1907.]

41541. HAMBURG. LORENZ, INA S.: *Gehen oder Bleiben. Neuanfang der Jüdischen Gemeinde in Hamburg nach 1945.* Hamburg: Landeszentrale für politische Bildung, 2002. 70 pp., illus., facsims., tabs., notes, bibl.

41542. JAHN, JÜRGEN: *Erinnerung an Bernhard Steinberger. (Geb. 17.09.1917 in München, gest. 16.12.1990 in Berlin).* [In]: Jahrbuch für Historische Kommunismusforschung 2002, Berlin, 2002. Pp. 358–369, footnotes.] [B.St., technician, economist, member of the KPD, emigr. 1936 to Italy, later to Switzerland, returned to Munich in 1945, 1947 to Leipzig, 1949 imprisoned, and later sentenced to 15 years forced labour in the Soviet Union, released in 1955, one year later again imprisoned for four years, charged with being allegedly involved in espionage, in 1990 finally succeeded in quashing the 1957 judgement.]

41543. KATLEWSKI, HEINZ-PETER: *Judentum im Aufbruch.* Von der neuen Vielfalt jüdischen Lebens in Deutschland, Österreich und der Schweiz. Berlin: Jüd. Verlagsanstalt Berlin, 2002. 199 pp., illus., bibl. [Incl. list of addresses (185–199).]

41544. KÖNIGSEDER, ANGELIKA/WETZEL, JULIANE: *Jüdische Displaced Persons im Nachkriegsdeutschland.* [In]: Judenfeindschaft als Paradigma. Studien zur Vorurteilsforschung [see No. 42134]. Pp. 180–184, footnotes.

41545. KORN, SALOMON: *Die fragile Grundlage.* Das Dilemma der jüdischen Kultur in Deutschland. [In]: Tribüne, Jg. 41, H. 161, Frankfurt am Main, 2002. Pp. 152–164, footnotes. [Slightly abbr. reprint of a lecture held at Schloss Elmau, Dec. 13, 2001.]

41546. LEVINSON, NATHAN PETER: *Das Judentum in Deutschland nach 1945 – Zur Psychologie des deutsch-jüdischen Miteinander.* [In]: Preußens Himmel breitet seine Sterne …. [see No. 41991], Bd. 2. Pp. 631–640.

41547. LOCHER, LIESELOTTE: *Jewish and German emigration from the former Soviet Union in the 1990s.* Berlin: dissertation de – Verlag im Internet, 2002. 129 pp., tabs., graphs, footnotes. Zugl.: Bonn, Univ., Diss., 2002.

41548. LUBICH, FREDERICK A.: *Jews in Germany today – contradictions in progress.* [In]: Wendewelten. Paradigmenwechsel in der deutschen Literatur- und Kulturgeschichte nach 1945 [see No. 42002]. Pp. 111–120, footnotes. [First publ. 1997.]

41549. LUSTIGER, ARNO: *Jüdische Widerstandskämpfer und Soldaten. Verleugner des Widerstandes, Jüdischer Selbsthass, Antizionismus.* [Section titles of *"Wir werden nicht untergehen". Zur jüdischen Geschichte"*, see No. 41930]. [Incl.: Jüdischer Widerstand in Europa (162–179). Lassen wir uns nicht wie Schafe zur Schlachtbank führen (180–188). Das Ende einer Stadt – Aufstand im Warschauer Ghetto (189–199). Harold Werner. Ein jüdischer Partisan in Polen (200–209). General Pattons verlorene Schlacht. Captain Baums Abenteuer (210–219). Meine Kontroverse mit Raul Hilberg (220–231). Jüdischer Selbsthass und meine Debatten mit Erich Fried (232–239).]

41550. MEINING, STEFAN: *Kommunistische Judenpolitik.* Die DDR, die Juden und Israel. Mit einem Vorwort von Michael Wolffsohn. Münster: Lit, 2002. 562 pp., notes, bibl. (Diktatur und Widerstand, Bd. 2.) Zugl.: Neubiberg, Univ. der Bundeswehr, Diss., 2000. [Incl. the sections: Der Fall Paul Merker und die Ursprünge des SED-Antifaschismus (1930–1955). Instrumentalisierte Juden: Die deutschjüdische Gemeinschaft im Machtkalkül der SED (1945–1990). Frontstaat gegen Israel: Die DDR im Nahostkonflikt (1950–1989). Im Schatten der NS-Vergangenheit: Ostdeutsch-amerikanisch-jüdische Beziehungen (1970–1989). Letzte Wendemanöver: Die Judenpolitik der Regierung Hans Modrow (1989–1990).]

41551. *Nur wenn ich lache.* Neue jüdische Prosa. Hrsg. von Olga Mannheimer und Ellen Presser. München: deutscher Taschenbuch Verlag, 2002. 377 pp., gloss. Orig.-Ausg. [Cont. texts by 31 authors, some of them from Germany and Austria.]

41552. PINTO, DIANA: *Jüdisches Leben am deutschen "Kreuzweg" zwischen Vergangenheit, Gegenwart und Zukunft.* [In]: Preußens Himmel breitet seine Sterne … [see No. 41991], Bd. 2. Pp. 561–569, notes.

——— POSENER, JULIUS: *In Deutschland 1945 bis 1946.* [See No. 42005.]

——— RIFFEL, DENNIS: *"Unbesungene Helden": Der Umgang mit "Rettung" im Nachkriegsdeutschland.* [In]: Beate Kosmala/Claudia Schoppmann, eds.: Überleben im Untergrund [see No. 41440]

41553. ROGGENKAMP, VIOLA: *Tu mir eine Liebe. Meine Mamme.* Jüdische Frauen und Männer in Deutschland sprechen von ihrer Mutter. Mit einem Essay über nachgeborene Juden in Deutschland und ihr Erbe. Berlin: Verlag Jüd. Presse, 2002. 261 pp. [Based on interviews with 26 persons.]

41554. ROSENFELD, ALVIN H.: *"Feeling alone, again": the growing unease among Germany's Jews.* New York: American Jewish Committee, 2002. II, 27 pp., notes.

41555. ROSS, JAN: *Russen und Reformer.* Eine Reise durch die jüdischen Gemeinden Deutschlands im Schatten des Nahostkonflikts. [In]: Die Zeit, Nr. 21, Hamburg, 16. Mai 2002. P. 11.

41556. *So einfach war das. Jüdische Kindheit und Jugend in Deutschland seit 1945.* Hrsg. von Cilly Kugelmann und Hanno Loewy. Berlin: Dumont; Jüdisches Museum Berlin, 2002. 96 pp., illus. (Zeitzeugnisse aus dem Jüdischen Museum Berlin.) [Cont.: "So einfach war das" (eds., 6–22). 26 autobiogr. essays.]

41557. STERN, SUSAN: *Jews in Germany 2001.* [In]: derekh. judaica urbinatensia, No. 0, Trieste, 2002. Pp. 7–34, notes.

——— STUTTGART. SAUER, PAUL/HOSSEINZADEH, SONJA: *Jüdisches Leben im Wandel der Zeit.* 170 Jahre Israelitische Religionsgemeinschaft – 50 Jahre neue Synagoge in Stuttgart. [See No. 41047.]

41558. TAKEI, AYAKA: *The "Gemeinde Problem": The Jewish restitution successor organization and the postwar Jewish communities in Germany, 1947–1954.* [In]: Holocaust and Genocide Studies, Vol. 16, No. 2, Oxford, Fall 2002. Pp. 266–288, notes.

41559. *Unlikely history: the changing German-Jewish symbiosis, 1945–2000.* Ed. by Leslie Morris and Jack Zipes. New York: Palgrave, 2002. XVI, 335 pp., illus., notes, bibl. (307–325), index. [Cont.: Preface:

German and Jewish obsession (Leslie Morris and Jack Zipes, XI-XVI. 1. Encounters across the void: rethinking approaches to German-Jewish symbiosis (Karen Remmler, 3–29). 2. The rift and not the symbiosis (Katja Behrens, 31–45). 3. The transformation of the German-Jewish community (Michael Brenner, 49–61). 4. Home and displacement in a city of bordercrossers: Jews in Berlin 1945–1948 (Atina Grossman, 63–99). 5. Jewish existence in Germany from the perspective of the non-Jewish majority: daily life between anti-Semitism and philo-Semitism (Wolfgang Benz, 101–117). 6. Austrian exceptionalism: Haider, the European Union, the Austrian past and present: an inimical world for the Jews (Andrei S. Markovits, 119–140). 7. Anti-Semitism in East Germany, 1952–1953: denial to the end (Mario Kessler, 141–154). 8. Reading "between the lines": Daniel Libeskind's Berlin Jewish Museum and the shattered symbiosis (Noah Isenberg, 155–179, illus.). 9. The critical embracement of Germany: Hans Mayer and Marcel Reich-Ranicki (Jack Zipes, 183–201). 10. Return to Germany: German-Jewish authors seeking address (Pascale R. Bos, 203–233; incl. Ruth Beckermann, Esther Dischereit, Barbara Honigmann, Ruth Klüger, Grete Weil). 11. The Janus-faced Jew: Nathan and Shylock on the postwar German stage (Anat Feinberg, 233– 250). 12. Fritz Kortner's last illusion (Robert Shandley, 251–261). 13. Comic vision and "negative symbiosis" in Maxim Biller's 'Harlem Holocaust' and Rafael Seligmann's 'Der Musterjude' (Rita Bashaw, 263–276). 14. German and Austrian Jewish women's writing at the millenium (Dagmar Lorenz, 277–290). 15. Postmemory, postmemoir (Leslie Morris, 291–306).]

41560. WEISS, KARIN: *Zwischen Integration und Ausgrenzung: Jüdische Zuwanderer aus der ehemaligen Sowjetunion in Deutschland.* [In]: Jahrbuch für Antisemitismusforschung 2002, Frankfurt am Main; New York, 2002. Pp. 249–270, footnotes.

41561. SCHNEIDER, RICHARD CHAIM: *Wir sind da!" Juden in Deutschland nach 1945.* Mit Orig.-Beiträgen von Ignatz Bubis [et al.], Red.: Marion Glück-Levi. Sprecher: Richard Chaim Schneider und Gert Heidenreich. München: Der Hörverl., 2001. 5 CDs + booklet (7 pp.) (Zur Sache.)

41562. *Zwischen Politik und Kultur – Juden in der DDR.* Hrsg. von Moshe Zuckermann. Göttingen: Wallstein, 2002. 246 pp., footnotes. [Incl. preface and addresses (ed., Dan Laor, Joseph Kostiner, 7–16). Ein ambivalentes Verhältnis – Juden in der DDR und der Staat Israel (Angelika Timm, 17–33). Verdrängung der Geschichte – Antisemitismus in der SED 1952/53 (Mario Kessler, 34–37). Die Loyalitätsfalle – Jüdische Kommunisten in der DDR (Karin Hartewig, 48–62). Der Schauspieler Gerry Wolf – Ein Beispiel kollektiver Erfahrungsgeschichte jüdisch-deutscher Remigranten (Wolfgang Herzberg, 69–81). "Das hat in der DDR keine Rolle gespielt, was man war" – "Ostalgie" und Erinnerungen an Antisemitismus in der DDR, 1949–1960 (Cora Granata, 81–100); Nation und Identität – Erzählungen von Exil und Rückkehr (Barbara Einhorn, 101–119). Ahasver und Bauernstaat – Stefan Heyms Bibel-Lektüren (Stephan Braese, 123–131). "Auf Druckpapier erzeugte Juden" – Antisemitismus und Judentum im Spätwerk Arnold Zweigs (Alfred Bodenheimer, 132–140). Real existierende Juden im DEFA-Film – Im Kino der subversiven Widersprüche (141–156). Die kulturelle Opposition in der DDR – Der Fall Jurek Becker (Sander L. Gilman, 157–183). "Genosse Klemperer" – Kommunismus, Liberalismus und Judesein in der DDR (Steven E. Aschheim, 184–209). Thomas Braschs "Ich-Drama" ohne "Ich" – Jüdische Perspektiven zur Darstellung deutscher Nicht-Identität (Gad Kaynar, 210–226). Musik und Politik – Paul Dessau und Hanns Eisler (Hans-Jürgen Nagel, 227–238). Incl. also documentation of the discussions.]

41563. *Zwischen den Stühlen? Remigranten und Remigration in der deutschen Medienöffentlichkeit der Nachkriegszeit.* Hrsg. von Claus-Dieter Krohn und Axel Schildt. Hamburg: Christians, 2002. 431 pp., illus., footnotes, index. [Selected essays (titles partly abbr.): Remigranten in der Medienpolitik der USA und der US-Zone (Jessica C.E. Gienow-Hecht, 23–49). Remigranten in der Kultur und Medienpolitik der Britischen Zone (Gabriele Clemens, 50–65). Medienpolitik der französischen Besatzungspolitik und die Rolle von Remigranten (Edgar Wolfrum, 66–92). Remigranten in der Medienpolitik der sowjetischen Besatzungsmacht (Jan Foitzik, 93–114). Emigranten in Nachkriegszeitschriften 1945–1949 (Claus-Dieter Krohn, 115–144). Remigranten über den Nürnberger Prozess (Bernd Greiner, 145–160). Remigration und Remigranten im deutschen Film nach 1945 (Helmut G. Asper, 161–179). Remigranten im Umfeld der Zeitschrift 'Der Monat' und des 'Congress for Cultural Freedom (CCF)' (Michael Hochgeschwender, 180–206). Journalisten im südamerikanischen Exil als Korrespondenten deutscher Zeitungen (Patrik von zur Mühlen, 207–215). Die Rolle der Remigranten auf dem Heidelberger Soziologentag 1964 und die Interpretation des Werkes von Max Weber (Uta Gerhardt, 216–244). Hans Habe, Ernst

Friedlaender, Hermann Budzislawski – drei Zonen, drei Städte, drei Schicksale (Marita Krauss, 245–266). Alfred Kantorowicz – Wanderer zwischen Ost und West (Wolfgang Gruner, 267–293).]

B. **Prosecution of Nazi Crimes. Restitution**

—————— ADUNKA, EVELYN: *Der Raub der Bücher.* Plünderung in der NS-Zeit und Restitution nach 1945. [See No. 41190.]

41564. *"Arisierung" und Restitution.* Die Rückerstattung jüdischen Eigentums in Deutschland und Österreich nach 1945 und 1989. Hrsg. von Constantin Goschler und Jürgen Lillteicher. Göttingen: Wallstein, 2002. 268 pp., footnotes, index. [Cont. (some titles abbr.): "Arisierung" und Restitution jüdischen Eigentums in Deutschland und Österreich (eds., 7–28). I. "Arisierung" und Enteignung; cont.: Einleitung (Patrick Wagner, 33–38). "Arisierung" und Rückerstattung. Eine Einschätzung (Frank Bajohr, 39–60). Zur Bedeutung des "Wiener Modells" für die antijüdische Politik des "Dritten Reiches" im Jahr 1938 (Hans Safrian, 61–92). II. Rückerstattung in Westdeutschland und Österreich; cont.: Einleitung (Bernd A. Rusinek, 93–98). Die Politik der Rückerstattung in Westdeutschland (Constantin Goschler, 99–126). Rechtsstaatlichkeit und Verfolgungserfahrung. "Arisierung" und fiskalische Ausplünderung vor Gericht (Jürgen Lillteicher, 127–160). Die Rückstellungsproblematik in Österreich (Brigitte Bailer-Galanda, 161–190). III. Rückerstattung in der DDR und in Ostdeutschland; cont.: Einleitung (Reinhard Rürup, 191–196). Interne Wiedergutmachungsdebatten im Osten Deutschlands – die Geschichte eines Mißerfolges (Ralf Kessler, 197–214). Die DDR und die Wiedergutmachungsforderungen Israels und der Claims Conference (Angelika Timm, 215–240). Der Umgang der DDR mit dem "arisierten" Vermögen der Juden und die Gestaltung der Rückerstattung im wiedervereinigten Deutschland (Jan Philipp Spannuth, 241–264). Die Entwicklung der Rückerstattung in den neuen Bundesländern seit 1989. Eine juristische Perspektive (Christian Meyer-Seitz, 265–280).]

41565. AUTHERS, JOHN/WOLFFE, RICHARD: *The victim's fortune: inside the epic battle over the debts of the Holocaust.* New York: HarperCollins, 2002. XV, 458 pp., notes, bibl. (389–430), index. [Deals with restitution claims, confiscation of Jewish property in Switzerland; also Swiss banking practices and the holding of Jewish assets.]

41566. *Beiträge öffentlicher Einrichtungen der Bundesrepublik Deutschland zum Umgang mit Kulturgütern aus ehemaligem jüdischem Besitz.* Hrsg. von der Koordinierungsstelle für Kulturgutverluste Magdeburg. Bearb. von Ulf Häder. Magdeburg: Koordinierungsstelle für Kulturgutverluste Magdeburg, 2001. 378 pp., bibl., index. (Veröffentlichungen der Koordinierungsstelle für Kulturgutverluste, 1.) [Incl. 23 contribs. and docs.]

41567. BINDENAGEL, J.D.: *Entschädigung und Wiedergutmachung im Zusammenhang mit der deutschen Stiftung 'Erinnerung, Verantwortung, Zukunft'.* [In]: Europäische Rundschau, Jg. 30, Nr. 2/2002. Wien, 2002. Pp. 93–105.

41568. BLOXHAM, DONALD: *Genocide on trial: war crimes and the formation of Holocaust history and memory.* Oxford, New York: Oxford Univ. Press, 2001. XIX, 273 pp., notes, bibl. (233–261), index. [Deals mainly with the Nuremberg Trials.]

41569. COHEN, AKIBA [et al.]: *The Holocaust and the press: Nazi war crimes trials in Germany and Israel.* Co-authors: Tamar Zemach-Marom, Jürgen Wilke, Birgit Schenk. Cresskill, NJ: Hampton Press, 2002. VII, 184 pp., chart, tabs., appendix, bibl. (167–174), author index, subject index. (The Hampton Press communication series.) [Deals with the press coverage of war crimes trials in Germany and Israel. Incl. the Nuremberg, Eichmann, Auschwitz trials; incl. chaps. on 'The Holocaust and Israeli and German societies'.]

41570. *DDR-Justiz und NS-Verbrechen. Sammlung ostdeutscher Strafurteile wegen nationalsozialistischer Tötungsverbrechen.* Verfahrensregister und Dokumentationsband. Bearb. im Seminarium voor Strafrecht en Strafrechtspleging 'Van Hamel' der Universität Amsterdam von C.F. Rüter. Mit einer Darstellung der Ahndung von NS-Verbrechen in Ostdeutschland von Günther Wieland. Amsterdam: Amsterdam Univ. Press; München: Saur, 2002. XIII, 606 pp.

41571. *DDR-Justiz und NS-Verbrechen. Sammlung ostdeutscher Strafurteile wegen nationalsozialistischer Tötungsverbrechen.* Bearb. im Seminarium voor Strafrecht en Strafrechtspleging 'Van Hamel' der Universität Amsterdam von C.F. Rüter unter Mitwirkung von L. Hekelaar Gombert und D.W. De Mildt. Amsterdam: Univ. Press; München: Saur, 2002. 2 vols., XXIV, 758; XXIV, 769 pp.

41572. FERENCZ, BENJAMIN B.: *Less than slaves: Jewish forced labor and the quest for compensation.* Bloomington: Indiana Univ. Press in association with the United States Holocaust Memorial Museum, 2002. XII, 272 pp., map, bibl., index. [Reprint of 1979 edn., see No. 17219/YB XXVI.]

41573. FLEITER, RÜDIGER: *Die Ludwigsburger Zentrale Stelle und ihr politisches und gesellschaftliches Umfeld.* [In]: Geschichte in Wissenschaft und Unterricht, Jg. 53, H. 1, Stuttgart, 2002. Pp. 32–50, notes.

41574. FORSTER, DAVID: *Wiedergutmachung in Österreich und der BRD im Vergleich.* Innsbruck: Studien-Verl., 2001. 284 pp., bibl. (259–281).

41575. FREUDIGER, KERSTIN: *Die juristische Aufarbeitung von NS-Verbrechen.* Tübingen: Mohr Siebeck, 2002. XI, 446 pp. (Beiträge zur Rechtsgeschichte des 20. Jahrhunderts, Bd. 33.)

41576. FREI, NORBERT: *Der Nürnberger Prozess und die Deutschen.* [In]: Gedächtnis, Geld und Gesetz. Vom Umgang mit der Vergangenheit des Zweiten Weltkrieges [see No. 41605]. Pp. 231–250, notes.

41577. HIRSCH, RUDOLF: *Um die Endlösung. Prozeßberichte.* Berlin: Dietz, 2001. 315 pp. [Incl. the Auschwitz, Majdanek and Lischka trials.] [R.H., 1907 Krefeld – 1998 Berlin, writer, court correspondent, for further data see No. 30372/YB XLIV.]

41578. HÖLSCHER, CHRISTOPH: *NS-Verfolgte im "antifaschistischen Staat": Vereinnahmung und Ausgrenzung in der ostdeutschen Wiedergutmachung (1945–1989).* Berlin: Metropol, 2002. 256 pp., footnotes, bibl. (235–252), index.

41579. HORN, SABINE: *"Jetzt aber zu einem Thema, das uns in dieser Woche alle beschäftigt."* Die westdeutsche Fernsehberichterstattung über den Frankfurter Auschwitz-Prozeß (1963–1965) und den Düsseldorfer Majdanek-Prozeß (1975–1981) – ein Vergleich. [In]: 1999. Zeitschrift für Sozialgeschichte des 20. und 21. Jahrhunderts, Jg. 17, Sept. 2002, H. 2, Köln, Sept. 2002. Pp. 13–43, footnotes.

41580. *Jahrbuch 2001 [des] Dokumentationsarchivs des österreichischen Widerstandes.* [Title on back cover: *Schwerpunkt Justiz.*] Wien: Dokumentationsarchiv d. österr. Widerstandes (DÖW), 2001. 224 pp., footnotes, tabs. [Selected essays: Politische NS-Strafjustiz in Österreich und Deutschland – ein Projektbericht (Wolfgang Form, 13–34). Der Dachauer Mauthausenprozess (Florian Freund, 35–66). Organisatoren und Nutznießer des Holocaust, Denunzianten, "Illegale" ... Eine erste Auswertung der bisher verfilmten Akten von Wiener Gerichtsverfahren wegen NS-Verbrechen (Winfried R. Garscha, 91–123).]

41581. KASTNER, KLAUS: *Von den Siegern zur Rechenschaft gezogen. Die Nürnberger Prozesse.* Nürnberg: Hofmann, 2001. 259 pp., illus., facsims., notes.

41582. KRAUSE, PETER: *Der Eichmann-Prozeß in der deutschen Presse.* Frankfurt am Main; New York: Campus, 2002. 327 pp., footnotes.

41583. MEINING, STEFAN: *Mit der Geschichtswaffe in die Geschichtsfalle. Der ostdeutsch-jüdisch-amerikanische Widergutmachungspoker (1970–1976).* [In]: Geschichte als Falle. Deutschland und die jüdische Welt [see No. 40849]. Pp. 259–292, notes.

41584. MELTZER, BERNARD D.: *The Nuremberg Trial: a prosecutor's perspective.* [In]: Journal of Genocide Research, Vol. 4, No. 4, Basingstoke, Dec, 2002. Pp. 561–568, notes.

41585. MEUSCH, MATTHIAS: *Von der Diktatur zur Demokratie. Fritz Bauer und die Aufarbeitung der NS-Verbrechen in Hessen (1956–1968)*. Wiesbaden: Historische Kommission für Nassau, 2001. VIII, 431 pp., port., illus., footnotes, bibl. (386–424), index. (Politische und parlamentarische Geschichte des Landes Hessen, Bd. 26; Veröffentlichungen der Historischen Kommission für Nassau, Bd. 70.) Zugl.: Gießen, Univ., Diss. 1998. [Cf.: Bespr. (Wolfgang Form) [in]: Nassauische Annalen, Bd. 113, Wiesbaden, 2002, pp. 607–609. Bespr. (Uta George) [in]: Zeitschrift des Vereins für hesssische Geschichte und Landeskunde, Bd. 107, Kassel, 2002, pp. 395–396. Bespr. (Wolfgang Form) [in]: Hessisches Jahrbuch für Landesgeschichte, Bd. 52, Marburg, 2002, pp. 343–345.] [F.B., July 16, 1903 Stuttgart – June 30, 1968 Frankfurt am Main, attorney, Social Democrat, emigr. 1936 to Denmark, 1943 fled to Sweden, 1949 returned to Germany, since 1956 Attorney General in Frankfurt am Main.]

———— MEYER, BEATE: *Die Inhaftierung der "jüdisch Versippten" in der Berliner Rosenstraße im Spiegel staatsanwaltlicher Zeugenvernehmungen in der DDR*. [See No. 41216.]

41586. *Museen im Zwielicht*. Ankaufspolitik 1933–1945. Kolloquium vom 11. und 12. Dezember 2001 in Köln./Die eigene Geschichte. Provenienzforschung an deutschen Kunstmuseen im internationalen Vergleich. Tagung vom 20. bis 22. Februar 2002 in Hamburg. Hrsg. von der Koordinierungsstelle für Kulturgutverluste Magdeburg. Bearb. von Ulf Häder [et al.]. Magdeburg: Koordinierungsstelle für Kulturgutverluste, 2002. 503 pp., illus., index. (Veröff. der Koordinierungsstelle für Kulturgutverluste, 2.) [Incl. 26 contribs. dealing with German and Austrian museums, incl. Jüdisches Museum Franken – Fürth & Schnaittach (Bernhard Purin, 403–418).]

41587. RENZ, WERNER: *Der 1. Frankfurter Auschwitz-Prozeß*. Zwei Vorgeschichten. [In]: Zeitschrift für Geschichtswissenschaft, Jg. 50, H. 7, Berlin, 2002. Pp. 622–641, footnotes.

41588. RENZ, WERNER: *Opfer und Täter: Zeugen der Schoah*. Ein Tonbandmitschnitt vom ersten Frankfurter Auschwitz-Prozess als Geschichtsquelle. [In]: Tribüne, Jg. 41, H. 162, Frankfurt am Main. Pp. 126–136, footnotes.

———— RHEINLAND-PFALZ: *"Dem Reich verfallen"* – *"den Berechtigten zurückzuerstatten"*. Enteignung und Rückerstattung jüdischen Vermögens im Gebiet des heutigen Rheinland-Pfalz 1938–1953 bearbeitet von Walter Rummel und Jochen Rath. [See No. 41449.]

41590. SCHEULEN, ANDREAS: *Ausgrenzung der Opfer – Eingrenzung der Täter*. Berlin: Berliner Wissenschafts-Verlag, 2002. 293 pp., footnotes, bibl., index. (Berliner Juristische Universitätsschriften, Grundlagen des Rechts, Bd. 24.) [Incl. chap.: Die gesetzlichen Regelungen zur Entschädigung und Versorgung der Opfer der nationalsozialistischen Gewaltherrschaft.]

41591. WIESEN, S. JONATHAN: *West German industry and the challenge of the Nazi past, 1945–1955*. Chapel Hill; London: Univ. of North Carolina, 2001. XVI: 329 pp., illus., ports., facsism., glossary, notes, bibl. (291–313), index. [Deals with war crimes, slave labour, restitution, "Vergangenheitsbewältigung"; incl. Siemens, Krupp.]

41592. WITTMANN, REBECCA: *The wheels of justice turn slowly: the pretrial investigations of the Frankfurt Auschwitz trial, 1963–65*. [In]: Central European History, Vol. 35, No. 3, Boston; Leiden, 2002. Pp. 345– 378, footnotes.

C. **Education and Teaching. Memorials and Remembrance**

41593. AHLHEIM, KLAUS/HEGER, BARDO: *Die unbequeme Vergangenheit*. NS-Vergangenheit, Holocaust und die Schwierigkeiten des Erinnerns. Schwalbach/Ts.: Wochenschau Verlag, 2002. 158 pp., bibl. (Studien zu Politik und Wissenschaft.) [Book presents the results of a survey conducted in 2000; incl. debate about Martin Walser, remembrance, antisemitism, knowledge about the Holocaust.]

41594. AUSTRIA. HORVÁTH, MARTIN/LEGERER, ANTON/PFEIFER, JUDITH/ROTH, STEPHAN, eds.: *Jenseits des Schlussstrichs*. Gedenkdienst im Diskurs über Österreichs nationalsozialistische Vergangenheit. Wien: Löcker, 2002. 335 pp., notes. [A collection of essays, interviews and memoirs publ. on the occasion of the tenth jubilee of the Austrian association 'Gedenkdienst'. Cont.: Vorwort (eds., 9–13). I. Schlussstrich? Strategien im Umgang mit dem Nationalsozialismus und Holocaust (17–74; essays by Norbert Frei, Margit Reiter, Dan Bar-On, Briguitte Bailer-Galanda, Alexander Joskowicz, interview with Franz Vranitzky). II. Im Dienste des Gedenkens. "Österreicher haben in Auschwitz nichts zu sühnen" (essays by Josef Teichmann, Anton Legerer, Christian Staffa, Judith Pfeifer, Christian Klösch, Irma Wulz, interview with Jan Erik Dubbelman). III. "Wir sind die Letzten, fragt uns aus …". Begegnungen mit vertriebenen ÖsterreicherInnen (essays by Albert Lichtblau, Martin Horváth, Roman Kopetzky, Dorit B. Whiteman, Anton Pelinka). IV. Zwischen Schlussstrich und Hochkonjunktur. Die Zeitgeschichtsforschung mehr als fünfzig Jahre "danach" (essays by Margit Reiter, Heidemarie Uhl, Dieter Josef Mühl, Georg Mayer, Christian Klösch, Oliver Kühschelm, Philipp Mettauer, Regula Nigg). V. "Versucht gute Menschen zu werden …". Nationalsozialismus und Holocaust als pädagogische Herausforderung (essays by Robert Streibel, Bernhard Schneider, Norbert Hinterleitner, Gottfried Prasenc, Dieter Josef Mühl). VI. Anhang (incl.: Beschreibung der Gedenkdienst-Einsatzstellen. Gedenkdienst-Tagungen. Gedenkdienst-Zeitung).]

41595. BERLIN. HECKNER, ELKE: *Berlin remake: building memory and the politics of capital identity.* [In]: The Germanic Review, Vol. 77, No. 4, Washington, Fall 2002. Pp. 304–325, notes. [Incl. the controversy surrounding the construction of the Jewish Museum; also on the revitalisation of the former Jewish quarters.]

41596. BERLIN, DEUTSCHES HISTORISCHES MUSEUM. KIRSCH, JAN-HOLGER: *Angemessen dargestellt? Die Ausstellung "Holocaust" des Deutschen Historischen Museums in Berlin.* [In]: Werkstatt Geschichte, Jg. 11, H. 32, Hamburg, 2002. Pp. 98–102, footnotes.

41597. BERLIN, HOLOCAUST MEMORIAL. *Auf dem Weg zur Realisierung. Das Denkmal für die ermordeten Juden Europas und der Ort der Information. Architektur und historisches Konzept.* Hrsg. von Sibylle Quack. Stuttgart: Deutsche Verlags-Anstalt, 2002. 296 pp., illus. (Schriftenreihe der Stiftung Denkmal für die ermordeten Juden Europas, Bd. 1.) [Incl.: Vorwort (Wolfgang Thierse, 9–12). Einleitung (ed., 13–20). Prolog: Das Denkmal und die Erinnerung nach dem 11. September 2001 (Peter Eisenman, 21–30). Grußwort (Julian Nida-Rümelin, 31–33). Der Ort der Information (Dagmar von Wilcken, 36–41). Book further incl. contribs. by Winfried Nerdinger, Christoph Stölzl, Ulrich Herbert, Eberhard Jäckel, Peter Steinbach, Reinhard Rürup presented at an international symposium held in Berlin, Nov. 2001; documents also statements and comments by Silke Wenk, Tilmann Buddensieg, Friedhelm Boll, Hanno Loewy, Barbara Distel, Werner Durth, Wolfgang Benz, Harald Welzer, David Bankier, Ruth Wodak, Philippe Burrin, Norbert Frei.]

41598. BERLIN, HOLOCAUST MEMORIAL. MEIER, CHRISTIAN: *Das Problem eines Berliner Denkmals.* [In]: Christian Meier: Das Verschwinden der Gegenwart. Über Geschichte und Politik, München; Wien, Hanser, 2001. Pp. 96–122, notes (247). [Also in this vol.: Erinnern – Verdrängen – Vergessen (70–95, notes (247–248); on problems related to "Vergangenheitsbewältigung".]

41600. BERLIN, HOLOCAUST MEMORIAL. STAVGINSKI, HANS-GEORG: *Das Holocaust-Denkmal. Der Streit um das "Denkmal für die ermordeten Juden Europas" in Berlin (1988–1999).* Paderborn: Schöningh, 2002. 357 pp., illus., footnotes. Zugl.: Berlin, Freie Univ., Diss., 2001.

41601. DECKERT, PEACEMAN, HEIKE: *Holocaust als Thema für Grundschulkinder?* Ethnographische Feldforschung zur Holocaust education am Beispiel einer Fallstudie aus dem amerikanischen Grundschulunterricht und ihre Relevanz für die Grundschulpädagogik in Deutschland. Frankfurt am Main; New York: Lang, 2002. 355 pp. (Europäische Hochschulschriften: Reihe 11, Pädagogik, Bd. 862.) Zugl.: Frankfurt am Main, Univ., Diss., 2001.

——— *Education and the Shoah. The Austrian, Canadian, Swiss, and German experiences* [section title of] Building history. The Shoah in art, memory, and myth [see No. 41234.]

41602. EHMANN, ANNEGRET: *Holocaust in Politik und Bildung.* [In]: Grenzenlose Vorurteile. Antisemitismus, Nationalismus und ethnische Konflikte in verschiedenen Kulturen [see No. 42123.] Pp. 41–68, notes.

41603. ENGELHARDT, ISABELLE: *A topography of memory: representation of the Holocaust at memorials/museums at Dachau and Buchenwald in comparison with those at Auschwitz, Yad Vashem and Washington, DC.* Brussels; New York: Lang, 2002. 237 pp., illus., footnotes, bibl. (217– 237).

41604. FÜRTH. BERTHOLD-HILPERT, MONIKA: *Orte der Verfolgung und des Gedenkens in Fürth.* Einladung zu einem Rundgang. Haigerloch: Verlag Medien und Dialog, 2002. 24 pp., illus.

41605. *Gedächtnis, Geld und Gesetz.* Vom Umgang mit der Vergangenheit des Zweiten Weltkrieges. Hrsg. von Jakob Tanner und Sigrid Weigel. Beiträge von Michael Böhler [et al.]. Zürich: vdf, Hochschul-Verlag an der ETH, 2002. 376 pp., illus., notes. (Zürcher Hochschulforum, Bd. 29.) [Incl.: Gedächtnis, Geld und Gesetz in der Politik mit der Vergangenheit des Zweiten Weltkriegs und des Holocaust (eds., 7–18). 13 essays, focusing on "Vergangenheitsbewältigung" in Switzerland, restitution, historiography of the Nazi period and related matters by the Jakob Tanner, Sigrid Weigel, Saul Friedländer, Jacques, Picard, Daniel Thürer, Michael Böhler, Dan Diner, Raphael Gross, Werner Konitzer, Norbert Frei, Michael Wildt, Peter Hug, Birgit R. Erdle, Daniel Wildmann. Selected essays are listed according to subject.]

41606. GRUNENBERG, ANTONIA: *Die Lust an der Schuld.* Von der Macht der Vergangenheit über die Gegenwart. Berlin: Rowohlt, 2001. 223 pp. [On the problems arising from numerous manifestations of "Vergangenheitsbewältigung".]

41607. HASS, MATTHIAS: *Gestaltetes Gedenken. Yad Vashem, das U.S. Holocaust Memorial Museum und die Stiftung Topographie des Terrors.* Frankfurt am Main; New York: Campus, 2002. 405 pp., footnotes, bibl. (384–403).

41608. HISTORIOGRAPHY. LANGENBACHER, ERIC: *Competing interpretations of the past in contemporary Germany.* [In]: German Politics and Society, Vol. 20, No. 1, New York, Spring 2002. Pp. 92–106, notes. [Review essay of recently publ. books dealing with the topics of "Vergangenheitsbewältigung", the Walser-Bubis affair, the debate about the Holocaust memorial, a.o.]

———— *Holocaust. Der nationalsozialistische Völkermord und die Motive seiner Erinnerung.* [See No. 41357.]

41609. HOLTSCHNEIDER, HANNAH K.: *German Protestants remember the Holocaust: theology and the construction of collective memory.* Münster: Lit; New Brunswick, NJ: Transaction Books, 2001. 225 pp., bibl. (200– 225). (Religion, Geschichte, Gesellschaft, Bd. 24.)

41610. HUHNKE, BRIGITTA/KRONDORFER, BJÖRN, eds.: *Das Vermächtnis annehmen.* Kulturelle und biographische Zugänge zum Holocaust. Beiträge aus den USA und Deutschland. Gießen: Psychosozial-Verlag, 2002. 365 pp. (Reihe "Psyche und Gesellschaft".) [Incl.: Einleitung (eds., 9–42). Zum Geleit. Deutsche Existenz nach Auschwitz (Hildegard Hamm-Brücher, 43–52). I. Der nationale Kontext: Erinnerungskultur in den USA (contribs. by James Young, Hilene Flanzbaum, 53–112). II. Der nationale Kontext: Erinnerungskultur in Deutschland (contribs. by Robert Moeller, Brigitta Huhnke, Irmgard Wagner, 113–216). III. Erinnerungen im regionalen Kontext (contribs. by Alan E. Steinweis, Kirsten Serup-Bilfeldt, 217–236). IV. Erinnerungen im (familien-)biographischen Kontext (contribs. by Dori Laub, Katharina von Kellenbach, Marianne Hirsch, Björn Krondorfer, 217–344). Nachwort. Die Gegenwärtigkeit des Holocaust in interkulturellen Begegnungen: Stimmen der dritten Generation (Björn Krondorfer, 345–364).]

41611. KNOCH, HABBO, ed.: *Das Erbe der Provinz. Heimatkultur und Geschichtspolitik nach 1945.* Göttingen: Wallstein, 2001. 303 pp., footnotes. (Veröffentlichungen des Arbeitskreises Geschichte des Landes Niedersachsen (nach 1945), Bd. 18.) [Section entitled 'Die ferne Heimat der Verbrechen' cont.: Das Verschwinden der Lager. Mittelbau-Dora und seine Außenlager im deutsch-deutschen Grenzbereich nach 1945 (Jens-Christian Wagner, 171–190). Vom Stigma zum Standortfaktor. Die Gemeinde Flossenbürg und das Erbe des Konzentrationslagers (Jörg Skriebeleit, 191–217). Seismographen der Vergangenheitsbewältigung. Regionalbewußtsein und Erinnerungsort der NS-Verbrechen am Beispiel des ehemaligen KZ Neuengamme (Detlef Garbe, 218–234).]

41612. LAWTON, CLIVE A.: *Die Geschichte des Holocaust.* Deutsch von Mirjam Pressler. Hamburg: Oetinger, 2002. 48 pp., illus., facsims., chronol., gloss., index. [For children and young people; orig. edn. with the title *The story of the Holocaust* publ. 1999 in the UK.]

41613. MEISSEN. *Gedenkstätten und Gedenkorte für die Opfer des Nationalsozialismus 1933 bis 1945 im Landkreis Meißen.* Eine Übersicht. [Hrsg. vom] Verband der Verfolgten des Naziregimes – Bund der Antifaschisten e.V., Regionalverband Meißen, [Red.: Rudi Müller]. Meißen: VVN, Regionalverband Meißen, 2002. 48 pp., illus.

41614. *Nationalsozialismus im Geschichtsunterricht.* Beobachtungen unterrichtlicher Kommunikation. Bericht zu einer Pilotstudie. Oliver Hollstein [et al.]. Pilotstudie gefördert mit Mitteln des American Jewish Committee. Frankfurt am Main: Univ., Fachbereich Erziehungswiss., 2002. 173 pp. (Frankfurter Beiträge zur Erziehungswissenschaft, Reihe Forschungsberichte, 3.) [Focuses on the Holocaust and related themes.]

——— NIVEN, WILLIAM JOHN: *Facing the Nazi past: united Germany and the legacy of the Third Reich.* [See No. 41413.]

41615. PFUNGSTADT. LEHMANN, F.: *Die Wiederherstellung der ehemaligen Synagoge Pfungstadt, Denkmalpflege zwischen Konservierung und Restaurierung.* [In]: Denkmalpflege & Kulturgeschichte, Wiesbaden, 2001. Pp. 2–6.

41616. *Recasting German identity: culture, politics, and literature in the Berlin Republic.* Ed. by Stuart Taberner and Frank Finlay. Rochester, NY: Camden House, 2002. VI, 276 pp., notes, bibl., index. (Studies in German literature, linguistics, and culture.) [Collection of 15 essays, incl. the Bubis-Walser debate, the controversy surrounding the Jewish Museum and the building of a Holocaust memorial; also on normalising the relationship between Germans and Jews in the 1990s.]

41617. SCHMITZ, HELMUT: *Malen nach Zahlen: Bernhard Schlinks 'Der Vorleser' und die Unfähigkeit zu trauern.* [In]: German Life and Letters, Vol. 55, No. 3, Oxford, July 2002. Pp. 296–311, footnotes. [Deals with Schlink's novel in the wider context of the united Germany coming to terms with its past ("Vergangenheitsbewältigung"), the Walser-Bubis affair, the debate about the Holocaust memorial.]

41618. STEFFEN, FRIEDERIKE: *Theaterstücke zum Thema Holocaust in didaktischer Perspektive.* [In]: Mitteilungen des Deutschen Germanistenverbandes, Jg. 48, H. 3/2001, Bielefeld, 2001. Pp. 420–450, footnotes.

41619. THOMA, CLEMENS: *Nationalsozialismus und Schoa im Geschichts- und Religionsunterricht.* [In]: Freiburger Rundbrief, N.F., Jg. 9, H. 2, Freiburg, 2002. Pp. 276–285.

41620. *Verbrechen erinnern. Die Auseinandersetzung mit Holocaust und Völkermord.* Hrsg. von Volkhard Knigge und Norbert Frei unter Mitarbeit von Anett Schweitzer. München: C.H. Beck, 2002. XII, 450 pp., illus., index, notes. [Incl. the chaps.: II. Nationalsozialismus und Zweiter Weltkrieg. Berichte zur Geschichte der Erinnerung; incl. essays on Germany and Austria by Edgar Wolfrum, Bertrand Perz. III. Nationalsozialismus und Zweiter Weltkrieg. Berichte zur Gegenwart der Erinnerung; incl. essays on Germany and Austria by Franziska Augstein and Karl Stuhlpfarrer. IV. Tendenzen der Gedenkkultur. Sondierungen; cont. essays by Dan Diner, Heinz D. Kittsteiner, Charles S. Maier, Harald Welzer, Rudolf Herz. V. Die Zukunft der Erinnerung. Geschichtswissenschaft, Gedenkstätten, Medien; cont. essays by Norbert Frei, Volkhard Knigge, Detlef Hoffmann, Gertrud Koch. Statt eines Nachworts: Abschied der Erinnerung. Anmerkungen zum notwendigen Wandel der Gedenkkultur in Deutschland (Volkhard Knigge, 423–440).]

41621. VIENNA. KNALLER, SUSANNE: *Das Gedächtnis der Allegorie. Am Beispiel von Rachel Whitereads Holocaust-Mahnmal.* [In]: Arcadia, Zeitschrift für Allgemeine und Vergleichende Literaturwissenschaft, Bd. 37, H. 1, Berlin, 2002. Pp. 113–128, illus., footnotes.

41622. WESTPHALIA. KELLER, MANFRED: *Jüdische Gedenkstätten in Westfalen.* [In]: Hartmut Steinecke/Günter Tiggesbäumker, eds.: Jüdische Literatur in Westfalen. Vergangenheit und Gegenwart [see No. 41791]. Pp. 195–212, illus., footnotes.

41623. WIESBADEN. FRITZSCH, W.: *Das ehemalige jüdische Badhaus "Zum Rebhuhn" in Wiesbaden.* [In]: Denkmalpflege & Kulturgeschichte, Wiesbaden, 2001. Pp. 7–11.

41624. WILLICH. MEISTER, HORST: *Ein Mahnmal für die ermordeten Willicher Juden.* [In]: Heimatbuch des Kreises Viersen 2003, Folge 54, Viersen, 2002. Pp. 303–307, illus.

——— *The work of memory: new directions in the study of German society and culture.* Ed. by Alon Confino and Peter Fritzsche. [See No. 40901.]

V. JUDAISM

A. Jewish Learning and Scholars

41625. BAECK, LEO. FRIEDLANDER, ALBERT H.: *Leo Baeck: the teacher.* [In]: European Judaism, Vol 34, No. 1, London, Spring 2001. Pp. 40–43.

41626. BAECK, LEO: *Nach der Schoa – Warum sind Juden in der Welt?* Schriften aus der Nachkriegszeit. Hrsg. von Albert H. Friedlander und Bertold Klappert. Gütersloh: Gütersloher Verlagshaus, 2002. 558 pp. (Leo Baeck Werke, Bd. 5.) [Cont. the sections: Wiederbegegnung mit Deutschland. Entdeckungen und Epochen der jüdischen Geschichte. Brücken zwischen Judentum, Christentum und Islam. Die Sendung des Judentums in die Welt.] [Cf.: Warum die Schoa für ihn kein Thema war: Leo Baecks Geschichtsdeutung als Kunst des Ausweichens (Friedrich Niewöhner) [in]: 'FAZ', Nr. 104, Frankfurt am Main, 6. Mai 2002, p. 50.]

41627. BRANDT, HENRY G.: *Freude an der Tora – Freude am Dialog.* Hrsg. von Manfred Heller und Andreas Nachama. Bochum: Kamp, 2002. 239 pp., illus. [A collection of texts by and also some on Henry G. Brandt. Incl. addresses by Johannes Rau and Paul Spiegel, preface by the eds. (9–16). Geboren unter weißblauem Himmel. Autobiographische Skizzen (17–29).] [H.G.B., orig. Heinz Georg B., b. in Munich Sept. 25, 1927, economist, rabbi, emigr. via England to Palestine in 1939, rabbi in the UK (Leeds), Switzerland (Geneva), Sweden since 1983, thereafter in Germany (Hanover and Dortmund).]

41628. BREUER, ISAAC. MORGENSTERN, MATTHIAS: *From Frankfurt to Jerusalem. Issac Breuer and the history of the secession dispute in modern Jewish Orthodoxy.* Leiden; Boston: Brill, 2002. XIV, 348 pp., bibl. (340–373). (Studies in European Judaism, Vol. 6.) [For German edn. publ. in 1995 see No. 33144/YB XLI.]

41629. BUBER, MARTIN. BUBER, MARTIN: *Between man and man.* Transl. by Ronald Gregor-Smith. With and introd. by Maurice Friedman. London: Routledge, 2002. XX, 268 pp. (Routledge classics.) [Orig. publ. 1947 by K. Paul, London.]

41630. BUBER, MARTIN. BUBER, MARTIN: *Ten rungs: collected Hasidic sayings.* Transl. by Olga Marx. London: Routledge, 2002. 96 pp.

41631. BUBER, MARTIN. BUBER, MARTIN: *The way of man: according to the teaching of Hasidism.* London: Routledge, 2002. 48 pp.

41632. BUBER, MARTIN. BUBER, MARTIN: *The legend of Baal-Shem.* Transl. by Maurice Friedman. London: Routledge, 2002. 224 pp. [New edn. of the transl., which was first publ. in 1955.]

41633. BUBER, MARTIN. CISSNA, KENNETH N./ANDERSON, ROB: *Moments of meeting: Buber, Rogers and the potential for public dialogue.* Albany, NY: State Univ. of New York Press, 2002. XXV, 323 pp., notes, bibl. (267–307), author index, subject index. [Based on a 1957 meeting between Martin Buber and Carl S. Rogers (1902–1987,) American psychologist and psychotherapist.]

41634. BUBER, MARTIN. KOREN, ISRAEL: *Between Buber's 'Daniel' and his 'I and Thou': a new examination.* [In]: Modern Judaism, Vol. 22, No. 2, Cary, NC, May 2002. Pp. 169–198, notes.

41635. BUBER, MARTIN. MENDES-FLOHR, PAUL, ed.: *Martin Buber, a contemporary perspective : proceedings of an international conference held at the Israel Academy of Sciences and Humanities.* Syracuse, N.Y.: Syracuse Univ. Press; Jerusalem: 2002. X, 191 pp., bibl., index of names; index of works by Buber.(The library of Jewish philosophy.) [Incl. chap. on Buber's friendship with S.J. Agnon.]

41636. CARLEBACH, JOSEPH. GILLIS-CARLEBACH, MIRIAM: *Readiness for death – choice for life: Franz Rosenzweig, Erich Buchholz and Rudolf Bleiweiss as reflected in the eulogies of Joseph Carlebach.* [In]: "… der den Erniedrigten aufrichtet aus dem Staube und aus dem Elend erhöht den Armen" [see No. 40844]. Pp. 19–33, notes. Also in this vol.: Franz Rosenzweig (Nachruf 1927) (Joseph Carlebach, 217–225).]

41637. CARLEBACH, JOSEPH: *Ausgewählte Schriften.* Band III. Hrsg. von Miriam Gillis-Carlebach. Hildesheim; New York: Olms, 2002. 526 pp., frontis., notes (460–474), gloss., index, bibl. (513–526). [Incl.: Einleitung (Alfred Bodenheimer, 14–27). Cont. the setions: Teil I. Standpunkte. Teil II. Predigt und Erbauung. Teil III. Festtage. Teil IV. Zum Gebet. Teil V. Erziehung. Teil VI. Zu Büchern. Teil VII. Würdigungen. For Vol. 1 and 2 (in 1 vol.) publ. 1982 see No. 19134/YB XXVIII.]

41638. COHEN, HERMANN. WIEDEBACH, HARTWIG: *Aesthetics in religion: remarks on Hermann Cohen's theory of Jewish existence.* [In]: The Journal of Jewish Thought and Philosophy, Vol. 11, No.1, Chur, Philadelphia, May 2002. Pp. 63–73, footnotes.

41639. DEUBER-MANKOWSKY, ASTRID: *Walter Benjamin's "Theological-Political Fragment" as a response to Ernst Bloch's "Spirit of Utopia".* [In]: Leo Baeck Institute Year Book 2002, Vol. XLVII, Oxford, 2002. Pp. 3–19, footnotes, illus.

41640. FACKENHEIM, EMIL: *In memory of Leo Baeck, and other Jewish thinkers "in dark times": once more, "after Auschwitz, Jerusalem".* [In]: Judaism, Vol. 51, No. 3, New York, Summer 2002. Pp. 282–292, notes. [Incl. also Martin Buber, Franz Rosenzweig, Leo Strauss.]

41641. GOODMAN-THAU, EVELINE: *Aufstand der Wasser.* Jüdische Hermeneutik zwischen Tradition und Moderne. Berlin: Philo, 2002. 330 pp., footnotes. [A collection of articles by the present rabbi in Vienna, where the author was born; some of them previously publ. between 1994 and 2000.

41642. GOODMAN-THAU, EVELINE: *Fremd in der Welt, zu Hause bei Gott. Bruch und Kontinuität in der jüdischen Tradition.* Münster: Lit, 2002. 66 pp. notes. (Forum Jüdische Kulturphilosophie. Studien zu Religion und Moderne, Bd. 1.) [Incl. Franz Rosenzweig, Martin Buber, Walter Benjamin.]

41643. HASIDISM. MAGID, SHAUL, ed.: *God's voice from the void: old and new studies in Bratslav Hasidism.* Albany: State Univ. of New York Press, 2002. XI, 298 pp., notes, bibl. refs., index. [Cont. transl. of three studies on Rabbi Nahman of Bratslav from German, Hebrew and Yiddish as well as six new studies by scholars in various fields. Contribs.: Shaul Magid; David G. Roskies; Elliot R. Wolfson; Yakov Travis; Nathaniel Deutsch; Martin Kavka; Hillel Zeitlin; Samuel Abba Horodetzsky; Joseph Weiss.]

41644. HASKALA. HECHT, LOUISE: *"How the power of thought can develop within a human mind". Salomon Maimon, Peter Beer, Lazarus Bendavid: Autobiographies of 'maskilim' written in German.* [In]: Leo Baeck Institute Year Book, Vol. XLVII, Oxford, 2002. Pp. 21–38, footnotes.

41645. HASKALAH. FEINER, SHMUEL: *Haskalah and history: the emergence of a modern Jewish historical consciousness.* Transl. by Chaya Naor and Sondra Silverton. Oxford; Portland, OR: Littman Library of Jewish Civilization, 2002. X, 404 pp., footnotes, gloss., bibl. (353–396), index. [Section 1 is entitled: From traditional history to Maskilic history in late eighteenth-century Germany (9–70; refers to Marcus Herz, Salomon Maimon, Moses Mendelssohn, Naphtali Herz Wessely. Also deals with Austria, Galicia.]

41646. HASKALAH. FEINER, SHMUEL: *Seductive science and the emergence of the secular Jewish intellectual.* [In]: Science in Context, Vol. 15, No. 1, Cambridge, 2002. Pp. 121–135, footnotes. [On the attraction the "forbidden" knowledge outside the boundaries of Jewish culture had on the early 'maskilim' and the traumatic conflicts resulting from the crossing of barriers of language and social norms.]

41647. HASKALAH. LEHNARDT, ANDREAS: *Rabbi Nachman Krochmal. Eine Biographie zwischen Tradition und Aufklärung.* [In]: Grenzgänge. Festschrift für Diethard Aschoff [see No.41473]. Pp. 130–142, footnotes.

—— HASKALAH. *Reformansätze und Erziehungsprogramme jüdischer Aufklärer.* [See in No. 40839.]

—— HERXHEIMER, SALOMON. FABER, ROLF: *Salomon Herxheimer 1801–1884. Ein Rabbiner zwischen Tradition und Emanzipation.* Leben und Wirken eines fast vergessenen Dotzheimers. [See No. 40932.]

41648. HESCHEL, ABRAHAM JOSHUA. DRESNER, SAMUEL: *Heschel, Hasidism and Halakha.* New York: Fordham Univ. Press, 2002. XIII, 133 pp., notes, bibl. (125–130), index.

41649. HOFFMANN, JACOB. ZUR, YAAKOV: *Rabbi Dr. Jacob Hoffmann. The man and his era.* Jerusalem: Inst. for Advanced Torah Studies, Bar-Ilan Univ., 2001. 318 pp. [Hebrew part], 141 pp. [English part]. [Cf.: Ein Rabbinerleben. Yaakov Zurs Biographie des Frankfurter Toragelehrten Jacob Hoffmann (Yizhak Ahren) [in]: Jüd. Allgemeine, Jg. 57, Nr. 18, Berlin, 29. Aug. 2002, p. 38.] [J.H., 1881 Papa (Hungary) – 1956 Tel Aviv, 1923–1937 Rabbi in Frankfurt am Main (Börneplatz Synagogue), founder and director of the Rabbiner-Lehranstalt Frankfurt, 1938 emigr. to the US, in 1953 went to Israel.]

41650. JACOB, BENNO. *Die Exegese hat das erste Wort. Beiträge zu Leben und Werk Benno Jacobs.* Hrsg. von Walter Jacob und Almuth Jürgensen. Stuttgart: Calwer, 2002. 200 pp., footnotes. [Incl.: Introduction (eds., 7–10). The life and work of Benno Jacob (Walter Jacob, 11–32). "Nur das Persönliche tut wohl …". Familie Jacob/Loewenthal im Grindelviertel (Christiane Pritzlaff, 32–48). Ein "Schrei ins Leere"? Die Wissenschaft des Judentums und ihre Auseinandersetzung mit protestantischer Theologie und ihren Judentumsbildern als Kontext des Werkes Benno Jacobs (Christian Wiese, 49–69). The fascination of Benno Jacob and his critique of Christian scholarship (Almuth Jürgensen, 70–84). Benno Jacob's concept of a "Wissenschaft des Judentums" (Maren Ruth Niehoff, 85–97). Six further contribs. on B.J. and exegesis by Shimon Gesundheit, Yaakov Elman, Almuth Jürgensen, W. Gunther Plaut, Herbert Marks, Walter Jacob.] [B.J., Sept. 7, 1862 Breslau – Jan. 24, 1945 London, Rabbi, biblical scholar, 1906–1929 Rabbi in Dortmund, also lecturer at the Frankfurt Lehrhaus, settled in Hamburg 1929, emigr. 1938 to the UK.]

41651. KROCHMALNIK, DANIEL: *Modelle jüdischen Philosophierens.* [In]: Trumah, Bd. 11, Heidelberg, 2001. Pp. 89–107, footnotes. [Incl. Abraham Joshua Heschel, Franz Rosenzweig, Hermann Cohen.]

41652. LAZARUS, MORITZ. HEITMANN, MARGRET: *Moritz Lazarus (1824–1903): Erziehung unter dem Primat der "sittlichen Berechtigung Preußens in Deutschland".* [In]: Preußens Himmel breitet seine Sterne …. [see No. 41991.], Bd. 1. Pp. 107–119, notes.

41653. MAIER, JOHANN: *Fremdes und Fremde in der jüdischen Tradition und im Sefär* [sic] *Chasidim.* 4. "Arye-Maimon-Vortrag" an der Universität Trier, 7. Nov. 2001. Trier: Kliomedia, 2002. Pp. 2–59, footnotes, bibl. J.M. (60–64). (Kleine Schriften des Arye-Maimon-Instituts, H. 5.) [Also in this vol.: Verzeichnis der Veröffentlichungen des Arye-Maimon-Instituts für jüdische Geschichte (65–89).]

41654. MAIMON, SALOMON. BARNOUW, DAGMAR: *Origin and transformation: Salomon Maimon and German-Jewish Enlightenment culture.* [In]: Shofar, Vol. 20, No. 4, Lincoln, NE, Summer 2002. Pp. 64–80, footnotes.

41655. MAYBAUM, IGNAZ: *Ignaz Maybaum: a reader.* Ed. by Nicholas de Lange Oxford; New York: Berghahn Books, 2001. XXX, 224 pp., bibl. (216–220), indexes. [Incl. the essays: Samson Raphael Hirsch and Abraham Geiger; Jewish self-hatred (on Sigmund Freud); Freud's Vienna; Leo Baeck in Terezin.]

—— MENDELSSOHN, MOSES. BEHM, BRITTA L.: *Moses Mendelssohn und die Transformation der jüdischen Erziehung in Berlin.* Eine bildungsgeschichtliche Analyse zur jüdischen Aufklärung im 18. Jahrhundert. [See No. 40838.]

41656. MENDELSSOHN, MOSES. BOUREL, DOMINIQUE: *Zur Mendelssohn Legende in Frankreich.* [In]: Preußens Himmel breitet seine Sterne …. [see No. 41991], Bd. 1. Pp. 203–213, notes.

41657. MENDELSSOHN, MOSES. ERLIN, MATT: *Reluctant modernism: Moses Mendelssohn's philosophy of history.* [In]: Journal of the History of Ideas, Vol. 63, No. 1, Baltimore, 2002. Pp. 83–104, footnotes.

41658. MENDELSSOHN, MOSES. *Judentum: Wege zur geistigen Befreiung* [see No. 40865]. [Incl.: Die Bildnisproduktion um den Philosophen Moses Mendelssohn (Gisbert Porstmann, 181–195, illus., notes). Mendelssohn: Förderer der Literaturwissenschaft (Eva J. Engel 196–214, notes). Moses Mendelssohn und das Seidengewerbe (Brigitte Meier, 215–230, notes; focuses on the Berlin manufacturing family Bernhard). Carl Wilhelm Ramler: Sulamith und Eusebia, eine Trauerkantate auf den Tod Moses Mendelssohns (1786) (231–237; reprint).]

41659. MENDELSSOHN, MOSES. *Moses Mendelssohn: the first English biography and translations.* Introd. by James Schmidt. Bristol: Thoemmes, 2002. 3 vols. XXI, 578; VII, 329; IX, 371 pp. [Facsimile reprints.] Vol. 1: *Memoirs of Moses Mendelsohn* [sic], the Jewish philosopher, including the celebrated correspondence on the Christian religion with J.C. Lavater. By M.[oses] Samuels [sic]. 2nd edn. London: Printed for Sainsbury and Co. and sold by Longman and Co. and all booksellers, 1827. Vol. 2 & 3: Moses Mendelssohn: *Jerusalem.* A treatise on ecclesiastical authority and Judaism. Transl. by M.[oses] Samuel. London: Longman, Orme, Brown & Longmans, 1838. 2 vols. in 1.]

41660. MENDELSSOHN, MOSES: *Sefer Netiwot ha-Schalom. Die Tora nach der Übersetzung von Moses Mendelssohn mit den Prophetenlesungen im Anhang.* Hrsg. im Auftrag des Abraham Geiger Kollegs und des Moses Mendelssohn Zentrums Potsdam von Annette Böckler. Berlin: Jüd. Verlagsanstalt, 2001. 528 pp. [Cf.: Ins 21. Jahrhundert katapultiert. Moses Mendelssohn in neuer Gesellschaft. Zu zwei Neuausgaben seiner Toraübersetzung (Christiane E. Müller) [in]: Kalonymos, Jg. 4, H. 4, Duisburg, 2001, pp. 7–11.]

41661. MENDELSSOHN, MOSES: *Die Tora in jüdischer Auslegung.* Hrsg. von Gunther W. Plaut. Mit einer Einleitung von Landesrabbiner Walter Homolka. Autorisierte Übersetzung und Bearbeitung von Annette Böckler. Gütersloh: Chr. Kaiser Gütersloher Verl.-Haus, 2001. (Gesamtwerk.) [For review see No. 41660.]

41662. *Polin. Studies in Polish Jewry.* Vol. 15 [with the title] *Focusing on Jewish religious life, 1500–1900.* Oxford; Portland, OR, 2002. I issue. [Part I, entitled Jewish religious life, 1500–1900, incl. numerous articles on the Frankist Movement and Hasidism; incl.: Rabbi Jonathan Eibeschuetz's attitude towards the Frankists (Sid Z. Leiman, 145–152).]

41663. ROSENZWEIG, FRANZ: *Zur jüdischen Erziehung. Drei Sendschreiben.* Hrsg. und mit einem Nachwort versehen von Daniel Weidner. Berlin: Jüd. Verlagsanstalt Berlin, 2002. 94 pp. (JVB Klassiker, Bd. 4.) [Orig. publ. between 1917 and 1924.]

41664. ROSENZWEIG, FRANZ. DAGAN, HAGGAI: *The motif of blood and procreation in Franz Rosenzweig.* [In]: AJS Review, Vol. 26, No. 2, Waltham, MA, 2002. Pp. 241–249, footnotes.

41665. ROSENZWEIG, FRANZ. RASHKOVER, RANDI: *Rosenzweig's return to biblical theology: an encounter between the 'Star of Redemption' and Jon Levenson's 'Sinai and Zion'.* [In]: The Journal of Jewish Thought and Philosophy, Vol. 11, No.1, Chur, Philadelphia, May 2002. Pp. 75–88, footnotes. [J.D. Levenson: professor of Jewish studies at the Harvard Divinity School.]

41666. SEIDLER, MEIR: *Hebräisches Recht – Wunschtraum oder Realität?* [In]: Aschkenas, Jg, 11/2001, H. 2, Wien, 2002. Pp. 515–529, footnotes.

41667. SOLOVEITCHITZ, HAYM: *Piety, pietism and German pietism: 'Sefer Hasidim' and the influence of Hasidei Ashkenas.* [In]: The Jewish Quartely Review, Vol. 92, Nos. 3–4, Philadelphia, Jan.-April, 2002. Pp. 455–493, notes.

41668. *Spinoza im Deutschland des achzehnten Jahrhunderts.* Zur Erinnerung an Hans-Christian Lucas. Hrsg. von Eva Schürmann, Norbert Waszek und Frank Weinreich. Stuttgart-Bad Cannstadt: Frommann-Holzboog, 2002. 590 pp., footnotes. (Spekulation und Erfahrung, Texte und

Untersuchungen zum Deutschen Idealismus, Abt. II: Untersuchungen, Bd. 44.) [Selected essays: Mendelssohns schwierige Beziehung zu Spinoza (Ursula Goldenbaum, 265–318). Salomon Maimons Einsicht in die Unausführbarkeit seines Versuchs einer Vereinigung von Kantischer Philosophie und Spinozismus (Wolfgang Bonsiepen, 377–406).]

41669. UNGER, ERICH. UNGER, ERICH: *Erich Unger's "The natural order of miracles".* Transl. and introd. by E.J. Ehrman. I. The Pentateuch and the vitalistic myth. II. The world of nature and miracles in the Pentateuch. Transl. and introd. by E.J. Ehrman. [In]: The Journal of Jewish Thought and Philosophy, Vol. 11, No. 2, Chur, Nov. 2002. Pp. 135–152; 153–189. [Essays were written in 1940.] [E.U. 1887 Berlin – 1950 England, philosopher.]

41670. VELTRI, GIUSEPPE: *Jüdische Einstellung zu den Wissenschaften im 16. und 17. Jahrhundert: Das Prinzip der praktisch-empirischen Anwendbarkeit.* [In]: Judentum zwischen Tradition und Moderne [see No. 41727]. Pp. 149–160.

41671. WEIDNER, DANIEL: *Gershom Scholem, die Wissenschaft des Judentums und der 'Ort' des Historikers.* [In]: Aschkenas, Jg. 11/2001, H. 2, Wien, 2002. Pp. 435–464, footnotes.

41672. WIENER, MAX: *Jüdische Religion im Zeitalter der Emanzipation.* Hrsg. und mit einem Nachwort versehen von Daniel Weidner. Berlin: Jüd. Verlagsanstalt, 2002. 296 pp. [First publ. 1933; incl.: Nachwort (283–295).]

——— WISSENSCHAFT DES JUDENTUMS. *Chajim H. Steinthal. Sprachwissenschaftler und Philosoph im 19 Jahrhundert/Linguist and philosopher in the 19th century.* [See No. 42001.]

41673. WISSENSCHAFT DES JUDENTUMS. SEIDEL, ESTHER: *Women pioneers of Jewish learning.* Ruth Liebrecht and her companions at the "Hochschule für die Wissenschaft des Judentums" in Berlin 1930–1934. Berlin: Jüdische Verlagsanstalt, 2002. 175 pp., illus., facsims., notes (137–166), bibl., index. [One part of book focuses on R.L.s biography, the other on the history of the 'Hochschule'.] [R.L., née Capell, 1911 Wiesbaden – 1998 London, music teacher, emigr. to the UK in 1939.]

——— WISSENSCHAFT DES JUDENTUMS. SOUSSAN, HENRY: *Wissenschaft des Judentums, in welcher Sprache?* [See in No. 40841.]

41674. WISSENSCHAFT DES JUDENTUMS. WASSERMANN, HENRY: *The 'Wissenschaft des Judentums' and Protestant theology: a review essay.* [In]: Modern Judaism, Vol. 22, No. 1, Cary, NC, Feb. 2002. Pp. 83–98. [On Christian Wiese's book on the subject; for details see No. 37917/YB XLV.]

B. **Perception and Identity**

41675. ALBANIS, ELISABETH: *German-Jewish cultural identity from 1900 to the aftermath of the First World War.* A comparative study of Moritz Goldstein, Julius Bab and Ernst Lissauer. Tübingen: Niemeyer, 2002. VIII, 310 pp., footnotes, bibl. (279–304), index. (Conditio Judaica, 37.) [Based on the author's PHD diss. at Oxford Univ. Incl. chaps.: II. Moritz Goldstein: An example of the German-Jewish cultural dilemma: a cultural Zionist stance. III. Julius Bab: An example of a "prosymbiotic" stance on German-Jewish culture and identity. IV. Ernst Lissauer: An example of a German nationalist with a Jewish background.]

41676. BAND, ARNOLD: *The Moses complex in modern Jewish literature.* [In]: Judaism, Vol. 51, No. 3, New York, Summer 2002. Pp. 302–314, notes. [Deals with Naftali Herz Wessely, Nahman of Bratzlav, Ahad Ha'Am, Sigmund Freud.]

41677. BÖRNE, LUDWIG. RIPPMANN, INGE: *Emanzipation und Akkulturation. Ein nicht ganz typisches Beispiel: Ludwig Börne.* [In]: Heine-Jahrbuch 2002, Jg. 41, Stuttgart, 2002. Pp. 161–187, notes. [Focuses on questions of Jewish and German identy and self-perception.]

41678. GEBHARDT, MIRIAM: *Zur Psychologie des Vergessens. Antisemitismus in jüdischen Autobiographien vor und nach 1933.* [In]: Clemens Wischermann, ed.: Vom kollektiven Gedächtnis zur Individualisierung der Erinnerung. Stuttgart: Steiner, 2002. (Studien zur Geschichte des Alltags, Bd. 18.) Pp. 53–64, footnotes.

41679. GILMAN, SANDER L.: *Private knowledge and Jewish diseases.* [In]: Preußens Himmel breitet seine Sterne … [see No. 41991], Bd. 2. Pp. 587–597, notes. [On the function of certain diseases as part of a social group's identity, e.g. Tay-Sachs for American Jews of Eastern European origin, or diabetes for Western European Jews in late 19th cent.]

41680. GOODMAN-THAU, EVELINE: *Zwischen Gestern und Morgen – Jude-Sein an der Schwelle zum 21. Jahrhundert.* [In]: Preußens Himmel breitet seine Sterne …. [see No. 41991]. Pp. 653–667, notes. [Extended version of a lecture given in Nov. 1996 in Vienna.]

41681. HEIDRICH, CHRISTIAN: *Die Konvertiten.* Über religiöse und politische Bekehrungen. München: Hanser, 2002. 382 pp., notes (338–377), index. [Cont. nine essays on conversions; incl.: Afred Döblin, Heinrich Heine, Arthur Koestler, Edith Stein.]

41682. HEINE, HEINRICH. FINGERHUT, KARLHEINZ: *"Manchmal nur, in dunklen Zeiten".* Heine, Kafka, Celan. Schreibweisen jüdischer Selbstreflexion. [In]: Heine-Jahrbuch 2002, Jg. 41, Stuttgart, 2002. Pp. 83–129, port., notes.

41683. HEYM, STEFAN. BODENHEIMER, ALFRED: *Gottes Erwählter. Davids Herrschaftslegitimation und Dynastiegründung – eine Reflexion, ausgehend von Stefan Heyms Roman "Der König David Bericht".* [In]: Kirche und Israel, Neukirchener Theologische Zeitschrift, Jg. 17, H. 1, Neukirchen-Vluyn, 2002. Pp. 20–30, notes.

41684. HEYM, STEFAN. GELLERMANN, HERMANN: *Stefan Heym: Judentum und Sozialismus. Zusammenhänge und Probleme in Literatur und Gesellschaft.* Berlin: Wiss. Verl. Berlin, 2002. 172 pp., bibl. (151–161).

41685. HOFFMANN, DANIEL: *"Im neuen Einband Gott gereicht". Liturgische Poesie in der deutsch-jüdischen Literatur des 20. Jahrhunderts.* Berlin: Jüd. Verlagsanstalt Berlin, 2002. 237 pp., footnotes, bibl., index. (Wissenschaftliche Reihe, Bd. 6.) [Focuses on works by Else Lasker-Schüler, Joseph Roth, Franz Werfel, Theodor Lessing, Alfred Döblin, Karl Wolfskehl.]

——— *Jüdische Identitäten in Mitteleuropa.* Literarische Modelle der Identitätskonstruktion. [See No. 41073.]

41686. KAFKA, FRANZ. LOEB, SARA: *Franz Kafka: a question of Jewish identity: two perspectives.* Transl. by Sondra Silverston and Chaya Naor. Lanham, MD; Oxford: Univ. Press of America, 2001. XIV, 273 pp., illus., notes, bibl. (239–266), index.

41687. KAFKA, FRANZ. MELLER, MARIUS: *Die Mechanik der Schrift in Franz Kafkas 'Strafkolonie'.* [In]: Das Judentum im Spiegel seiner kulturellen Umwelten. Symposium zu Ehren von Saul Friedländer [see No. 41864]. Pp. 181–204, notes. [Examines the hidden Jewish allusions in the 'Strafkolonie', a story written in 1914.]

41688. LANGGÄSSER, ELISABETH. GELBIN, CATHY S.: *An indelible seal: race, hybridity and identity in Elisabeth Langgässer's writing.* Essen: Verlag Die Blaue Eule, 2001. 168 pp., notes, bibl. (158–168). (Literaturwissenschaft in der Blauen Eule.) [Deals with L.'s relation to Jews and Judaism as reflected in her writings; with her own conflicts of identity as a "Mischling" under the Nazis. Also discusses her relationship with her daughter Cornelia Edvardson, an Auschwitz survivor.]

41689. MAIMON, SALOMON. DAMKEN, MARTIN: *Theoretischer und praktischer Gott.* Versuch einer Annäherung an Salomon Maimons vielfach zerrissene Einstellung zum Judentum. [In]: Antisemitische und antijudaistische Motive bei Denkern der Aufklärung. Susanne Miller zum 85. Geburtstag [see No. 42113]. Pp. 81–88.

41690. MEYER, THOMAS: *Ernst Cassirer und Albert Lewkowitz*. Was heißt und zu welchem Ende studiert man Philosophiegeschichte? [In]: Trumah, Bd. 11, Heidelberg, 2001. Pp. 71–87. footnotes. [On Cassirer's "acculturated" Jewish identity.]

41691. MÜHSAM, ERICH. *Erich Mühsam und das Judentum*. Zwölfte Erich-Mühsam-Tagung in der Gustav-Heinemann-Bildungsstätte in Malente, 25.-27. Mai 2001. [Malente: Erich-Mühsam-Gesellschaft, 2002]. 194 pp., frontis., ports., footnotes. (Schriften der Erich-Mühsam-Gesellschaft, H. 21.) [Incl.: I. Texte von Erich Mühsam (7–29; on Jewish themes). II. Dokumentation der Erich Mühsam-Tagung vom 25.-27. Mai 2001; cont.: Jüdische Neo-Orthodoxie 1870 bis 1919 in Lübeck. Zur religiös-geistigen Situation der Juden während des Rabbinats von Salomon Carlebach (Peter Guttkuhn, 31–37). Siegfried Seligmann Mühsam und seine Erzählungen zum jüdischen Leben um die Mitte des 19. Jahrhunderts. "Die Killeberger" und "Die Neu-Killeberger" (Ingaburgh Klatt, 38–51). Erich Mühsam und das Judentum (Chris Hirte, 52–70). An-archie und (talmudisches) Gesetz. Erich Mühsams Judentum (Thomas Dörr, 71–84). "… der Geist ist die Gemeinschaft, die Idee ist der Bund". Gustav Landauers Judentum (Siegbert Wolf, 85–116). Judentum und Anarchie (Chaim Seeligmann, 117–135). Assimilation und Antisemitismus im Kaiserreich (Erika Hirsch, 136–148). Elf Jahre Arbeit im Jüdischen Museum Rendsburg und Dr. Bamberger-Haus. Ein Erfahrungsbericht (Frauke Dettmer, 149–155). III. Anhang: Zwei ältere Beiträge; cont.: Erich Mühsams jüdische Identität (Lawrence Baron, 157–170). Zur jüdischen Tradition im romantisch-anarchistischen Denken Erich Mühsams und Gustav Landauers (Rolf Kauffeldt, 171–192).]

41692. NOOR, ASHRAF/WOHLMUTH, JOSEF, eds.: *'Jüdische' und 'christliche' Sprachfigurationen im 20. Jahrhundert*. Paderborn: Schöningh, 2002. 305 pp., bibl., index. [Selected sections/contribs.: Weichenstellung; cont: Juden und Christen am Ende des 20. Jahrhunderts (R.J. Zwi Werblowsky, 33–40). Franz Rosenzweig und das hebräische Seinsverständnis (incl. contrib. by Bernhard Casper, 111–124). Walter Benjamin – noch einmal gelesen; incl. contribs. by Francesca Albertini (125–140); Irving Wohlfahrth (141–214); Werner Hamacher (215–244).]

41693. ROTH, JOSEPH & ZWEIG, ARNOLD. RAFFEL, EVA: *Vertraute Fremde: das östliche Judentum im Werk von Joseph Roth und Arnold Zweig*. Tübingen: Narr, 2002. 330 pp., bibl., footnotes. (Mannheimer Beiträge zur Sprach- und Literaturwissenschaft, Bd. 54.)

41694. SCHENKE, MANFRED FRANK: *… und nächstes Jahr in Jerusalem?* Darstellung von Juden und Judentum in den Texten von Peter Edel, Stephan Hermlin und Jurek Becker. Frankfurt am Main; New York: Lang, 2002. 501 pp., footnotes, bibl. (Studien zur Reiseliteratur- und Imagologieforschung, B.) Zugl.: Chemnitz, Techn. Univ., Diss., 2001. [Examines some texts of the three authors dealing with the Holocaust against the background of their writing in the former Soviet Zone/German Democratic Republic between 1947 and 1986.]

41695. SCHNITZLER, ARTHUR. RIEDMANN, BETTINA: *"Ich bin Jude, Österreicher, Deutscher": Judentum in Arthur Schnitzlers Tagebüchern und Briefen*. Tübingen: Niemeyer, 2002. VI, 475 pp., footnotes, bibl. (435–460), index. (Conditio Judaica, 36.)

41696. SCHÖNBERG, ARNOLD. BRILL, ANDREA: *Geschichtsprozesse als Identitätsstifter? Holocaust und jüdische Identität bei Arnold Schönberg und Alexandre Tansman*. [In]: Geschichte als Falle. Deutschland und die jüdische Welt [see No. 40849]. Pp. 145–173, notes.

41697. SCHURZMÜLLER, JEANETTE: *Von den Männern und dem Mammon, von der Macht und dem Malheur. Lebensentwürfe und jüdische Identität bei Lisette Molinari und anderen jüdischen Schauspielerinnen in der Weimarer Republik*. [In]: Rollenspiele. Studien über Frau und Bühne im 20. Jahrhundert. Hrsg. von Margaretha Thünen. Oldenburg: Edition Farfadette, 2001. Pp. 27–41, notes.

41698. SONINO, CLAUDIA: *Exil, Diaspora, Gelobtes Land? Deutsche Juden blicken nach Osten*. Aus dem Italienischen von Ute Lipka. Berlin: Jüdische Verlagsanstalt Berlin, 2002. 156 pp., footnotes, bibl., index. (Wissenschaftliche Reihe, Bd. 7.) [Deals with Heinrich Heine, Theodor Lessing, Martin Buber, Arnold Zweig, Alfred Döblin, Joseph Roth; incl. also chaps. on German Jews and Eastern Jewry, antisemitism, "Nitzscheanism".]

41699. SUSMAN, MARGARETE. PÖDER, ELFRIEDE: *Lebendige Dialektik: Sprache und [jüdische] Identität bei Margarete Susman*. Zur Charakteristik ihrer Essays der Weimarer Republik. [In]: Literatur der Weimarer Republik. Kontinuität und Brüche. Hrsg. von Michael Klein [et al.]. Innsbruck: Inst. für deutsche Sprache, Literatur und Literaturkritik, 2002. (Innsbrucker Beiträge zur Kulturwissenschaft: Germanistische Reihe, Bd. 64.) Pp. 145–172, notes.

41700. TUCHOLSKY, KURT. HUTH, MARIO: *Kurt Tucholsky und das Judentum*. Versuch einer Deutung. Potsdam: Linden-Verlag, 2002. 29 pp., illus. (Die besondere Reihe, 5.)

41701. WEILL, KURT. KUHNT, CHRISTIAN: *Kurt Weill und das Judentum*. Saarbrücken: Pfau, 2002. 184 pp., footnotes, musical score, bibl. Zugl.: Hamburg, Univ., Diss., 2000.

41702. WOLFF, THEODOR. GOLDBACH, CHRISTEL: *Distanzierte Beobachtung: Theodor Wolff und das Judentum*. "… es sind zwar nicht meine Kerzen, aber ihr Licht ist warm". Oldenburg: Bis, Bibliotheks- und Informationssystem der Univ. Oldenburg, 2002. 269 pp., footnotes. (Oldenburgische Beiträge zu jüdischen Studien, Bd. 11.) Zugl.: Oldenburg, Univ., Magisterarbeit, 2000. [Incl.: Nochmals zur Frage jüdisch-deutscher Identität (Werner Boldt, 13–18).]

41703. ZWEIG, STEFAN. FRAIMAN, SARAH: *Das tragende Symbol: Ambivalenz jüdischer Identität in Stefan Zweigs Werk*. [In]: German Life and Letters, Vol. 55, No. 3, Oxford, July 2002. Pp. 248–265, footnotes.

41704. ZWEIG, STEFAN & WERFEL, FRANZ. LANGENHORST, GEORG: *Jeremia als literarische Identifikationsfigur*. Jüdische Selbst- und Zeitdeutung bei Stefan Zweig und Franz Werfel. [In]: Kirche und Israel, Neukirchener Theologische Zeitschrift, Jg. 17, H. 1, Neukirchen-Vluyn, 2002. Pp. 45–61, notes.

C. Jewish Life and Organisations. Genealogy

41705. ADLER, BENJAMIN BENNO: *Esra. Die Geschichte eines orthodox-jüdischen Jugendbundes zur Zeit der Weimarer Republik*. Wiesbaden: Harrassowitz, 2001. 487 pp., notes (425–470), bibl., index (Jüdische Kultur. Studien zur Geistesgeschichte, Religion und Literatur, Bd. 8.) [Incl. prefaces by Manfred Voigts and Lea Dasberg.] [Author, b. in Beuthen, rabbi, emigr. 1938 to Palestine.]

41706. *Archiv für Familiengeschichtsforschung*. H. 4, Sonderheft jüdische Genealogie. Limburg: C.A.Starke, 2001. 315 pp., footnotes. [Incl.: Vom Solidarverband ins jüdische Großbürgertum: Zur Geschichte der Familie Mosse im Kaiserreich (Elisabeth Kraus, 242–263). Zur Genealogie von Jacques Offenbach (Josef Heinzelmann, 264–275). Un procès opposant deux familles juives de 1563 à 1581, ou comment les Grotwohl s'installèrent à Metz en 1567 (Pascal Faustini, 276–294).]

41707. BAADER, MARIA B.: *Die Entstehung jüdischer Frauenvereine in Deutschland*. [In]: Organisiert und engagiert. Vereinskultur bürgerlicher Frauen im 19. Jahrhundert. Hrsg. von Rita Huber-Sperl unter Mitarbeit von Kerstin Wolff. Königstein/Ts.: U. Helmer Verlag, 2002. (Aktuelle Frauenforschung.) Pp. 99–116, notes.

———— BAADER, MARIA BENJAMIN: *Vom Rabbinischen Judentum zur bürgerlichen Verantwortung: Geschlechterorganisation und "Menschenliebe" im jüdischen Vereinswesen in Deutschland zwischen 1750 und 1870.* [See No. 40835.]

———— BARKAI, AVRAHAM: *"Wehr dich!" Der Centralverein deutscher Staatsbürger jüdischen Glaubens (C.V.) 1893–1938.* [See No. 40836.]

41708. BAR-LEVAV, AVRIEL: *Ritualisation of Jewish life and death in the early modern period*. [In]: Leo Baeck Institute Year Book 2002, Vol. XLVII, Oxford, 2002. Pp. 69–82, footnotes.

41709. BERGBAUER, KNUT/SCHÜLER-SPRINGORUM, STEFANIE: *"Wir sind jung, die Welt ist offen"*. Eine jüdische Jugendgruppe im 20. Jahrhundert. Berlin: Haus der Wannsee-Konferenz, 2002. 131 pp., biographies, illus., bibl., list of archives. (Begleitbuch zur Ausstellung in der Gedenk- und Bildungsstätte

Haus der Wannsee-Konferenz ab 8. September 2002.) [Publ. on the occasion of an exhibition held under the same title in Sept. 2002; deals with "Der Schwarze Haufen – Bund Jüdischer Jugend".]

41710. BERGER, RUTH: *Tanzt der Teufel mit? Vergnügungen und Zerstreuung in der jüdischen Gesellschaft des späten Mittelalters und der frühen Neuzeit.* [In]: Kalonymos, Jg. 5, H. 1, Duisburg, 2002. Pp. 2–7, notes.

41711. FRAENKEL, LOUIS & HENRY: *Genealogical fragments of the history of the Fraenkel family.* 2nd revised and enlarged edn. Ed. by Georg Simon on behalf of The Memorial Foundation of Eva and Henry Fraenkel. München: Saur, 1999. 2 vols. Vol. 1: Text and indexes. 189 pp., ports., illus., facsims., gloss. Vol. 2: Genealogical tables. 198 pp. + suppl. [Incl. the Fränkel, Behrens, Hameln, Gumperz families.]

41712. GROSSERT, WERNER: *Sulamith (1806–1848), die erste jüdische Zeitschrift in deutscher Sprache und deutscher Schrift.* [In]: Judentum: Wege zur geistigen Befreiung [see No. 40865]. Pp. 158–169, illus., notes. [Also in this issue: Sulamith – Inhaltsliste des 1. Jahrgangs (1806/07) (238). (Joseph) Wolf: Erklärung der Titelvignette (aus Sulamith, 1. Jahrgang) (239–241, notes).]

41713. GUMPRICH, BERTHA: *Vollständiges Praktisches Kochbuch für die jüdische Küche.* Selbstgeprüfte und bewährte Rezepte zur Bereitung aller Speisen, Getränke, Backwerke und alles Eingemachten für die gewöhnliche und feinere Küche. [Hrsg. von Annette Haller und Heinz Monz]. Trier: WVT Wissenschaftlicher Verlag Trier, 2002. 289 pp., gloss. [First publ. in 1888, further edns. were publ. in 1896 and 1900; incl.: Bertha Gumprich – Biographische Notizen (Heinz Monz, 7–12). Erläuterungen zu den jüdischen Speisegesetzen (Annette Haller, 13–20).] [B.G. née Mayer, 1832 Nickenich – 1901 Trier, cook.]

——— HOLMES, VIRGINIA IRIS: *Integrating diversity, reconciling contradiction: The 'Jüdischer Friedensbund' in late Weimar Germany.* [See No. 40861.]

41714. KREBS, WOLFGANG: *Tomor – eine koschere Margarine.* [In]: Jüdischer Almanach [2002] des Leo Baeck Instituts, Frankfurt am Main, 2002. Pp. 116–124.

41715. *Le Juif errant. Un temoin du temps.* Paris: Biro, 2001. 238 pp., illus. [Catalogue book publ. on the occasion of the exhibition under the same title in the Musée d'Art et d'Histoire du Judaisme, Oct. 2001 – Feb. 2002. Text: Pierre Birnbaum (et al.).] [Cf.: "Der Ewige Jude – Zeuge der Zeit": Das Pariser Museum für Jüdische Kunst und Geschichte zeigt die Bilder einer folgenreichen Legende (Jürgen Müller) [in]: 'FAZ', Nr. 7, Frankfurt am Main, 9. Jan. 2002, p. 7.]

41716. LOWENSTEIN, STEVEN M.: *Jüdisches Leben – jüdischer Brauch.* Internationale jüdische Volkstraditionen. Aus dem Amerik. von Alice Jakubeit. Düsseldorf: Patmos, 2002. 269 pp., illus., maps, notes, bibl. [Orig. publ. 2000 under the title *The Jewish Cultural Tapestry. Jewish folk traditions.* Refers passim to traditions, language, names, music, cookery (with recipes), antisemitism in Aschkenaz resp. German-speaking countries.]

41717. *Marcus Beer Friedenthal und Raphael Gabriel Prausnitzer. Familienbande seit 1760.* Zusammengestellt von Michael Müller-Stüler. Meerbusch: Michael Müller-Stüler; Books on Demand, 2002. 201 pp., illus., footnotes. [Incl. the genealogy of two families orig. from Glogau and Liegnitz (Silesia) compiled by a descendant.]

41718. MENTGEN, GERD: *Alltagsgeschichte und Geschichte der Juden. Die Juden und das Glücksspiel im Mittelalter.* [In]: Historische Zeitschrift, Bd. 274, München, 2002. Pp. 25–60, footnotes.

41719. PELLI, MOSHE: *The genre of the fable in Haskalah literature in Germany.* [In]: Preußens Himmel breitet seine Sterne ... [see No. 41991], Bd. 1. Pp. 229–257, notes. [Discusses mainly 'Hame'asef', the first Hebrew journal in Germany (late 18th cent.).]

41720. *Source-documentation Jewish families of Northern Germany: index of documented families and locations/Quellendokumentation jüdischer Familien in Norddeutschland: Index der dokumentierten Familien.* Compiled by Egmar Ruppert. Hildesheim: Gesine Hasselhoff, Edition Materialien zur Sozialgeschichte, 9. Jg., 2002. 84 pp., tabs., indexes. [Incl. the genealogy of the Northern

German-Jewish families Dux, Meyerhof, Rothgiesser and Wolfers. Material covers about 1,000 towns in Hesse, Lower Saxony and North Rhine-Westphalia.]

41721. *SportZeit. Sport in Geschichte, Kultur und Gesellschaft.* Jg. 1, H. 2, Göttingen, 2001. 120 pp., illus., facsims., footnotes. [Incl.: Ausgegrenzt – ausgebootet – zur Flucht getrieben. Die Lebensgeschichte der jüdischen Hochspringerin Gretel Bergmann (Claudia Diederix, 5–30). Zwischen alljüdischem Olympia und nationaljüdischem Sportfest. Zur Entstehungsgeschichte der Makkabiaden (Toni Niewerth, 53–30). "Jüdischer Sport in Deutschland" – eine kommentierte Bibliografie (Toni Niewerth/Lorenz Peiffer, 81–108).]

41722. *Stammbaum.* The Journal of German-Jewish Genealogical Research. Issue 20 + 21. New York: Leo Baeck Institute, Winter/Summer 2002. 51; 41 pp., illus., facsims., maps, tabs. [Incl. contribs. on genealogical matters, also book reviews, reports on projects, and other material related to German-speaking Jewry. Issue 20 focuses on refugees in Shanghai (contribs. by Ralph B. Hirsch, Horst Eisfelder, Claus W. Hirsch, 1–14). 19th century Hamburg Jewish residence registration (Peter W. Landé, 28–29). Where to find clues as to how early your ancestors were in Berlin (Edward David Luft, 17–19). Selected essays of Issue 21: German Jewish genealogical research. New sources and old questions (Karen Franklin/Peter Landé/Jürgen Sielemann, 1–4). The persistence of Schneidemühl (Peter Simonstein Cullman, 6–10). Shanghai HIAS lists (Peter Nash, 11–15).]

41723. STEIN, PETER: *Jüdische Genealogie.* [In]: Schweizerische Gesellschaft für Genealogie, Jahrbuch 2001, Zürich, 2001. Pp. 125–147, illus., facsims. [Deals mainly with Switzerland.]

41724. WEISS, NELLY: *The origin of Jewish family names.* Morphology and History. Bern; New York: Lang, 2002. 216 pp. [Mostly about names from Germany and Austria.]

41725. WIESEMANN, FALK: *Hygiene des jüdischen Körpers. Der Pavillon "Hygiene der Juden" auf der Düsseldorfer Gesolei-Ausstellung 1926.* [In]: 1926 – 2002/ GE SO LEI. Kunst, Sport und Körper. Hrsg. von Hans Körner und Angela Stercken. Ostfildern-Ruit: Hatje Cantz Verlag, 2002. Pp. 200–208, illus., notes.

D. Jewish Art and Music

41726. GOLDMAN-IDA, BATSHEVA: *'Chanukka-Eisen' und der Aufbruch zur Urbanisation – Das Landjudentum im Zeitalter der Industrialisierung.* [In]: Aschkenas, Jg. 12, H. 1/2, Wien, 2002. pp. 127–139, illus., footnotes. [On Hanukah chandeliers.]

41727. *Judentum zwischen Tradition und Moderne.* Hrsg.: Gerd Biegel, Michael Graetz. Heidelberg: C. Winter, 2002. VIII, 197 pp. (Schriften der Hochschule für Jüdische Studien Heidelberg, Bd. 2.) [Selected essays: Das architektonische Konzept der neuzeitlich-modernen Synagoge (Harmen H. Thies, 31–48). Bauwerke jüdischer Friedhöfe in Deutschland – eine Skizze (Ulrich Knufinke, 31–48). Architektur zwischen Repression und Emanzipation – Zur Dokumentation und Erforschung jüdischer Ritualbauten in Mitteleuropa (Katrin Kessler/Simon Paulus, 49–66). Wandel und Kontinuität jüdischer Grabkunst am Beispiel von Prag und Ouderkerk (Manja Altenburg, 85–94).]

41728. MELL, JULIE: *Die befestigte Stadt in der deutsch-jüdischen Kunst in der Zeit vor der Entstehung des Ghettos.* [In]: Wiener Jahrbuch für jüdische Geschichte, Kultur & Museumswesen, Bd. 5, 2000/2001, Wien, 2001. Pp. 25–42, illus., notes.

41729. OTT, NORBERT: *Die Mär vom Bilderverbot.* Zur Illustration hebräischer und jiddischer Handschriften im europäischen Mittelalter. [In]: Süddeutsche Zeitung, Nr. 85, München, 12. April 2002. P. 17, illus.

41730. SCHALIT, HEINRICH. KAHN, ELIOTT: *Heinrich Schalit and Weimar Jewish music.* [In]: Musica Judaica: Journal of the American Society for Jewish Music, Vol. 15, New York, 2000–2001. Pp. 32–67, port., footnotes, bibl. (63–67). [H.Sch., 1886 Vienna – 1976 Evergreen, CO, composer of Jewish music, studied in Vienna, then lived in Munich where he was organist and music director of the Hauptsynagoge from 1927–1933. Emigr. via Rome and London to the US in 1940.

Worked as organist and composer of liturgial music in Providence, RI, Hollywood, CA; finally settled in Evergreen, CO. Essay also deals with other Jewish composers.]

41731. SCHMIDT, ESTHER: *Nationalism and the creation of Jewish music: the politization of music and language in the German-Jewish press prior to the Second World War.* [In]: Musica Judaica: Journal of the American Society for Jewish Music, Vol. 15, New York, 2000–2001. Pp. 1–31, bibl. (28–31).

41732. URY, LESSER. *Lesser Ury. Bilder der Bibel – Der Malerradierer.* Begleitbuch zu den Ausstellungen im Käthe-Kollwitz-Museum Berlin und in der Stiftung "Neue Synagoge Berlin – Centrum Judaicum". Hrsg. im Auftrag der Stiftung "Neue Synagoge Berlin – Centrum Judaicum" von Chana C. Schütz. [Gesamtredaktion: Bernd Rottenburg, Chana C. Schütz, Hermann Simon.] Berlin: Jüd. Verlagsanstalt Berlin, 2002. 125 pp., illus. [Selected essays: Lesser Ury – Bilder der Bibel (Chana C. Schütz, 12–24). Jüdische Identität und Großstadt. Symbolismus im Werk von Lesser Ury (Emily D. Bilski, 25–41). Lesser Ury – ein Berliner Jude (Hermann Simon, 69–73).]

41733. WIESEMANN, FALK: *"Kommt heraus und schaut" – Jüdische und christliche Illustrationen zur Bibel in alter Zeit.* [Katalog zur Ausstellung: "Kommt heraus und schaut" – Jüdische und christliche Illustrationen zur Bibel aus alter Zeit]. Mit Beiträgen von Marion Aptroot und William L. Gross. Essen: Klartext, 2002. 148 pp., illus. [Incl.: Das "Volk des Buches" und die Bilder zur Bibel vom 16. bis zum 19. Jahrhundert (Falk Wiesemann, 9–34). Die Holzschnitte der Tsene-rene-Ausgaben Sulzbach 1796 mit den jiddischen und den ins Deutsche übersetzten Überschriften (Marion Aptroot, 35–46). Biblical illustrations on Judaica objects: The Gross Family Collection (William L. Gross, 143–147).]

41734. STUDEMUND-HALÉVY, MICHAEL: *Sefardische Grabkunst.* [In]: Michael Studemund-Halévy/Gaby Zürn: Zerstört die Erinnerung nicht. Der Jüdische Friedhof Königstrasse in Hamburg [see No. 40978]. Pp. 104–128, illus.

VI. ZIONISM AND ISRAEL

41735. ADUNKA, EVELYN: *Exil in der Heimat. Über Österreicher in Israel.* Innsbruck: Studien-Verl., 2002. 272 pp., illus., gloss., notes (221–245), bibl., index. (Österreich-Israel-Studien, Bd. 2.) [Cont. chaps.: I. Die Situation der deutschsprachigen Juden in Palästina/Israel. II. Lebensgeschichten (41 biogr. portraits).]

41736. BAUMANN, ODETTE: *70 Jahre MB – eine positive Bilanz.* [In]: 'MB', Jg. 70, Nr. 170, Tel Aviv, Feb. 2002. pp. 1–2, facsim. [On the Mitteilungsblatt des Irgun Olei Merkas Europa ("MB"), the first issue of which was publ. with the name Mitteilungsblatt der Hitachduth Olei Germania in Sept. 1932, at times a weekly, at present a monthly paper incl. also Hebrew contribs.]

41737. BENARI, ASHER: *Erinnerungen eines Pioniers aus Deutschland.* Privately printed by the Benari family [2002]. V, 152 pp. [Available at the Bibliothek Germania Judaica, Cologne.] [Author, orig. Arnold Löwisohn, b. Dec. 11 1911 in München-Gladbach, member of the "Werkleute", emigr. 1934 to Palestine, co-founder of Kibbuz Hasorea; covers childhood and youth in M.-Gladbach and the history of Hasorea up to the present.]

41738. BERKOWITZ, MICHAEL: *Die Schaffung einer jüdischen Öffentlichkeit: Theodor Herzl und der Baseler Kongress von 1897.* [In]: Jörg Requate/Martin Schulze Wessel, eds.: Europäische Öffentlichkeit. Transnationale Kommunikation seit dem 18. Jahrhundert. Frankfurt am Main; New York, 2002. Pp. 79–91, footnotes.

41739. BRENNER, MICHAEL: *Geschichte des Zionismus.* München: Beck, 2002. 128 pp., illus., bibl., chronol., index. (C.H. Beck Wissen in der Beck'schen Reihe, 2184.) Orig.-Ausg.

—— GERSON, MANFRED MOSCHE: *Ein Leben im 20. Jahrhundert.* Von Westpreußen über Berlin und Hannover durch Amerika, NS-Deutschland und Lettland nach Israel 1906–1982. [See No. 42039.]

41740. HALBRONN, JACQUES: *Prophetica Judaica Beith: Le Sionisme et ses avatars au tournant du XXe siècle*. Suivi d'un dossier de documents sionistes et pseudo sionistes comportant notamment 'L'Etat Juif' de Théodore Herzl (Paris 1896) & divers textes relatifs aux 'Protocoles des Sages de Sion'. Préface de Hervé Gabrion. Feyzin: Editions Ramkat, 2002. 440 pp., illus., facsims., chronol., footnotes, appendixes, bibl. (431–437).

41741. KAGAN, GENNADI E.: *Der Ruf aus Wien*. Die zionistische Bewegung Theodor Herzls unter dem Zarenadler. Wien: Böhlau, 2002. 412 pp., facsims., bibl., index. [Incl. 40 docs. (transl. from the Russian), among them letters addressed to Th.H., also other texts by Th.H.]

41742. KREPPEL, KLAUS: *Israels fleißige Jeckes. Zwölf Unternehmerportraits deutschsprachiger Juden aus Nahariya*. Mit einem Vorwort von Paul Spiegel. Bielefeld: Westfalen Verl., 2002. 192 pp., illus., gloss., bibl., index. [Incl. chap.: Die "Fünfte Aliyah" 1933–1939 (12–34).]

41743. KRUPP, MICHAEL: *Die Geschichte des Zionismus*. Ein Nes Ammim Buch. Gütersloh: Gütersloher Verlagshaus, 2001. 128 pp.

——— MEIER, AXEL: *"Ein Nazi fährt nach Palästina." Der Bericht eines SS-Offiziers als Beitrag zur "Lösung der Judenfrage"*. [See No. 41408.]

41744. RUBINSTEIN, W.D.: *Zionism and the Jewish people, 1918–1960: from minority to hegemony*. [In]: The Jewish Journal of Sociology, Vol. 63, Nos. 1–2, London, 2001. Pp. 5–36, tabs., notes. [Incl. German Zionism.]

41745. SEELIGMANN, CHAIM: *Es war nicht nur ein Traum*. Autobiographische und kibbuzgeschichtliche Skizzen. Bad Tölz: Verlag Urfeld, 2002. 167 pp., frontis., illus., gloss. [Incl. Vorwort (Traudl Wallbrecher/Rudolf Pesch, 8–11). Author, orig. Heinz S., b. in 1902 in Karlsruhe, lives in Givat Brenner/Israel.]

41746. SEGENREICH, BEN: *Herzl und das Schnitzel – zwei verflochtene Erfolgsgeschichten*. [In]: Jüdischer Almanach [2002] des Leo Baeck Instituts, Frankfurt am Main, 2002. Pp. 98–114.

41747. VOIGTS, MANFRED: *Aktivistischer oder zionistischer Geist? Eine Debatte zwischen Kurt Hiller und Siegmund Kaznelson aus den Jahren 1916/17*. [In]: Aschkenas, Jg. 11/2001, H. 2, Wien, 2002. Pp. 351–434, footnotes. [Reprint of 9 letters and articles orig. publ. in 'Die Selbstwehr. Unabhängige jüdische Wochenschrift', Prague, 'Jerubbaal, Eine Zeitschrift der jüdischen Jugend, Berlin/Vienna. Incl. an introd. by M.V. (351–367).]

41748. ZABEL, HERMANN: *In der Erinnerung liegt das Geheimnis der Erlösung*. Gespräche mit Israelis deutscher Muttersprache. Essen: Klartext, 2002. 606 pp., ports., facsims., bibl. (Beiträge zur Förderung des christlich-jüdischen Dialogs, Bd. 19.) [Incl. a preface by Johannes Rau; an introductory chap. and 30 interviews.]

——— ZERTAL, IDITH: *Judaism and Zionism – Between the pariah and the parvenu*. [See No. 41811.]

41749. *Der Zionist Georg Goldstein fotografiert Palästina/Israel (1936–1953)*. Begleitbuch zur Ausstellung des S.L. Steinheim-Instituts für deutsch-jüdische Geschichte in der Volkshochschule der Stadt Duisburg vom 13. Mai – 14. Juni 2002. Duisburg: S.L. Steinheim-Inst.; Volkshochschule d. Stadt Duisburg, 2002. 74 pp., illus. [Based on the Goldstein collection, S.L. Steinheim Inst. Incl.: Vorwort (Michael Brocke, 4–5). Texts by Margret Heitmann, Hiltrud Metzmacher, Suzanne Zittartz.] [G.G., Aug. 10, 1898 Proskurow/Ukraine – 1980 Düsseldorf, Physician, Photographer, lived from 1907 in Germany, from 1930 in Düsseldorf, emigr. 1936 to Palestine, remigr. 1953 to Düsseldorf.]

VII. PARTICIPATION IN CULTURAL AND PUBLIC LIFE

A. General

41750. ALBANIS, ELISABETH: *German-Jewish cultural identity from 1900 to the aftermath of the First World War: a comparative study of Moritz Goldstein, Julius Bab and Ernst Lissauer.* [See No. 41675.]

41751. *Apokalypse und Erinnerung in der deutsch-jüdischen Kultur des frühen 20. Jahrhunderts.* Hrsg. von Jürgen Brokoff und Joachim Jacob. Göttingen: Vandenhoeck & Ruprecht, 2002. 223 pp., footnotes. (Formen der Erinnerung, Bd. 13.) [Incl. essays on Hermann Cohen (Astrid Deuber-Mankowsky, 9–18). Walter Benjamin (Jürgen Brokoff, 39–58), Gershom Scholem (Elisabeth Hamacher, 59–74), Georg Simmel (Joachim Jacob, 75–98), Ernst Bloch (Christian Senkel, 99–130). Elias Bickermann (Christoph Schmidt, 147–170), Jacob Taubes (Jens Mattern, 171–186), Elias Canetti (Bernhard Greiner, 187–200), Hannah Arendt (Claudia Althaus, 201–220); also one entitled "Braune Apokalypse" (Gerhard Kurz, 131–146).]

41752. BODENHEIMER, ALFRED: *Wandernde Schatten. Ahasver, Moses und die Authentizität der jüdischen Moderne.* Göttingen: Wallstein-Verl., 2002. 282 pp., illus., notes (219–264), bibl. (265–282). [Incl. Heinrich Heine, Theodor Herzl, Fritz Mauthner, Ernst Toller, Jakob Wassermann, Karl Wolfskehl, Else Lasker-Schüler, Hedwig Caspari, Rudolf Kayser, Arnold Schönberg, Sigmund Freud, Gertrud Kolmar, Stefan Heym.]

41753. BRAUN, CHRISTINA VON: *Ist die Sexualwissenschaft eine "jüdische Wissenschaft"? – Säkularisierung und die Entstehung der Sexualwissenschaft.* [In]: Preußens Himmel breitet seine Sterne ... [see No. 41991], Bd. 2. Pp. 697–714, notes. [Examines Jewish and Christian concepts of sexuality, the development of the sexology of Freud, Hirschfeld and others and its antisemitic defamation as a "Jewish science".]

41754. *Contemporary Jewish writing in Germany.* An anthology. Ed. by Leslie Morris & Karen Remmler. Lincoln, Ill; London: Univ. of Nebraska Press, 2002. VIII, 248 pp., facsims., notes, gloss. (Jewish Writing in the Contemporary World.) [Incl.: Introduction (eds., 1–31). Texts by Katja Behrens, Barbara Honigmann, Esther Dischereit, Maxim Biller.]

41755. DALBY, HANNAH-VILLETTE: *German-Jewish historiography in the work of Hannah Arendt, Eva G. Reichmann and Selma Stern from Weimar Germany to the post-war period.* Southhampton: Univ. of Southhampton, MA dissertation, 2001. 96 pp., bibl. [Available at the Wiener Library, London.]

41756. SCHOLZ, ALBRECHT/HEIDEL, CARIS-PETRA, eds.: *Das Bild des jüdischen Arztes in der Literatur.* Frankfurt am Main: Mabuse-Verl., 2002. 176 pp., illus., notes. (Schriftenreihe Medizin und Judentum, Bd. 6.) [With Engl. summaries. Selected essays.: Das Bild des jüdischen Arztes in der Literatur (Klaus Stiebert, 12–21). Der Juden-Arzt in der Contra-Judaeos Literatur (17.-18. Jahrhundert) (Samuel S. Kottek, 22–31). "Sänger Israels". Isachar Falkensohn Behrs literarische Akkulturation (Andreas Wittbrodt, 32–43). Von Dr. Sammet (Thomas Mann) bis Dr. Semig (Uwe Johnson). Das Scheitern der deutsch-jüdischen Assimilation im Spiegel literarischer Arztfiguren (Peter Voswinckel, 44–63). Ernst Weiß "Mensch gegen Mensch" und Stefan Zweigs "Clarissa": Parallelen und Tangenten im Lebensweg der Schriftsteller und medizinrelevante Reflexionen in diesen Werken zum Ersten Weltkrieg (Susanne Hann, 80–91). Der Regimentsarzt Dr. Demant in Joseph Roths "Radetzkymarsch" (Ingrid Kästner, 92–101). Frieda Fromm-Reichmann (1889–1957). Jüdische Ärztin, ehemalige Dresdnerin, emigrierende Psychoanalytikerin, verfilmte Romanfigur (Thomas Müller, 102–119). Ärzte, Heiler und Patienten im Werk des Arztes und Dichters Friedrich Wolf (Albrecht Scholz/Werner Kohlert, 120–129). Mamlok und Mamlock 1937: Eine Literaturgestalt wurde lebendig. – Der Berliner Zahnarzt Hans-Jacques Mamlok und Friedrich Wolfs Drama "Professor Mamlock" (Peter Schneck, 130–139). Würdevoll bleiben – der Widerstand des Kardiologen Kirschbaum im Roman "Jakob der Lügner" von Jurek Becker (Joanna Obrusnik, 140–149). Three further contribs. on Polish-Jewish authors.]

———— *Deutsch-jüdischer Parnaß. Rekonstruktion einer Debatte.* [See No. 40845.]

41757. *Engagierte Literatur zwischen den Weltkriegen*. Hrsg. von Stefan Neuhaus [et al.] Würzburg: Königshausen & Neumann, 2002. 410 pp., footnotes. (Schriften der Ernst-Toller-Gesellschaft, Bd. 2.) [Cont. 27 papers given at an international symposium in Neuburg/Austria, Nov. 29. – Dec. 2, 2001. Contribs. incl. nine essays dealing with Ernst Toller; others also on Alfred Döblin, Kurt Tucholsky, Erwin Piscator, Josef Breitenbach by Volker Ladenthin, Anke Detken Rolf Selbmann, Stefan Neuhaus, Gordana-Dana Grozdanic, Erika Jäger, Cecil Davies, Andreas Meier, Wolfgang Schopf.]

41758. ERLER, HANS/EHRLICH, ERNST LUDWIG, eds.: *Judentum verstehen*. Die Aktualität jüdischen Denkens von Maimonides bis Hannah Arendt. Frankfurt am Main; New York: Campus, 2002. 363 pp., notes, bibl. [A collection of 20 essays arranged under the sections: Vorwort: Judentum für Nichtjuden – Die Aktualität des jüdischen Gedankens (Hans Erler, 7–16). Teil 1: Der Weg der Aufklärung, 17–108; incl. Moses Mendelssohn (Martina Thom, 86–108). Teil 2: Emanzipation und Selbstvergewisserung, 109–230; cont.: Samson Raphael Hirsch (Yizhak Ahren), Heinrich Graetz (Michael Graetz), Hermann Cohen (Hartwig Wiedebach), Leo Baeck (Ernst Ludwig Ehrlich), Martin Buber (Kalman Yaron), Franz Rosenzweig (Heinz-Jürgen Görtz), Walter Benjamin (Astrid Deuber-Mankowsky). Teil 3: Der jüdische Gedanke, 231–322; incl.: Günther Anders (Gabriele Althaus), Theodor W. Adorno (Heinz Adam), two essays on Hannah Arendt (Claudia Schulze, Ingeborg Nordmann), Abraham J. Heschel (Ernst Ludwig Ehrlich). Statt eines Nachworts: Das politische Universum des Judentums: Leo Baeck, Martin Buber, Theodor W. Adorno, Hannah Arendt (Hans Erler, 323–360).]

———— EXILE. DEICHMANN, UTE: *Flüchten, Mitmachen, Vergessen. Chemiker und Biochemiker in der NS-Zeit*. [See No. 41260.]

41759. EXILE. EAKIN-THIMME, GABRIELA ANN: *Die emigrierten Historiker als Vermittler sozialgeschichtlicher Ansätze?* [In]: Comparativ, Jg. 12, H. 1, Leipzig, 2002. pp. 63–85, footnotes.

41760. EXILE. *Emigration*. [Section title of] *Judenfeindschaft als Paradigma*. Studien zur Vorurteilsforschung [see No. 42134]. Pp. 185–228, footnotes. [Incl.: Über die Emigration hinaus. Perspektivische Überlegungen anhand der Gruppe der Politikwissenschaftler (Alfons Söllner, 202–207). Quantitative Emigrationsforschung am Beispiel der Physik (Klaus Fischer, 208–215). Drei Jahre im Gelobten Land. Wolfgang Steinitz' Exil in der Sowjetunion (Annette Leo, 222–228).]

41761. EXILE. *Exil. Forschung, Erkenntnisse, Ergebnisse*. Hrsg. von Edita Koch und Frithjof Trapp. Jg. 21 & 22, Frankfurt am Main, 2001/2002. 4 issues, illus., notes, index. [Jg. 21, Nr. 1 incl.: Spielerlaubnis mit Sondergenehmigung im "Dritten Reich" – jüdische Schauspieler in der Nazizeit (Bärbel Schrader, 5–13). Nr. 2 (publ. 2002): Selected contribs. are listed according to subject. Jg. 22, Nr. 1 incl.: München und der Geist der Erzählung (Marcel Reich-Ranicki, 5–10). "… die von uns geforderte Bewährungsprobe nicht bestanden …" – Die Situation emigrierter Schriftsteller in der Schweiz der Jahre 1933 bis 1950 (Charles Linsmayer, 11–22). Alfred Döblin, Hans Siemsen und der Bund Neues Deutschland 1938/1939 (Dieter Schiller, 44–61). Vom alten Österreich nach Kalifornien – Der Schriftsteller und Herausgeber Paul Elbogen (Günter Rinke, 62–71). "Seine Zeit wird noch kommen" … – Hans Sahl: ein Porträt in Zitaten (Momme Brodersen, 77–86). Nr. 2 (publ. 2003) incl.: "Where do we go from here?". Die Geschwister Eleonora und Francesco von Mendelssohn (Thomas Blubacher, 21–40). Die Schweiz, Singapur, Australien – Exilstationen des Künstlerehepaares Slawa und Karl Duldig (Ute Heinen, 41–57; on two sculptors and art teachers from Vienna, b. 1902 in Galicia). One further essay is listed according to subject.]

41762. EXILE. GEOFFREY, RENÉ: *Ungarn als Zufluchtsort und Wirkungsstätte deutschsprachiger Emigranten (1933–1938/39)*. Frankfurt am Main; New York: Europ. Verlag der Wissenschaften, 2001. 486 pp., footnotes, docs., bibl., appendix. (Studien zur deutschen und europäischen Literatur des 19. und 20. Jahrhunderts, Bd. 45.) [Appendix incl. list of names of refugees (314–356), contribs. to Hungarian periodicals, German books publ. in Hungary 1933–1944 and other documents.]

41763. EXILE. *German-speaking exiles in Great Britain*. [Issue title of] The Yearbook of the Research Centre for German and Austrian Exile Studies, Vol. 2, ed. by Anthony Grenville. Amsterdam; Atlanta, GA., 2000. 276 pp., notes, index. [Cont. (some titles abbr.): Preface (Anthony Grenville). The impact of German emigré lawyers on British legal policy towards Germany, 1942–1946

(Ulrike Walton-Jordan, 1–24). Frederick Lindemanns Rolle bei der Emigration der aus Deutschland vertriebenen Physiker (Stefan Wolff, 25–58). The refugee historian Hans Baron and the Society for the Protection of Science and Learning (Kay Schiller, 59–76). The education of the Cologne Jawne Gymnasium children and the Berlin ORT school boys in Germany and England (Monica Lowenberg, 77–98). From 'Emil' to 'Alice': the hiatus in the childhood reading of exiles from Germany and Austria, 1933–45 (Gillian Lathey, 99–122). Hans Vogel, the flight of the exiled German Social Democrats from France, 1940–41, and the British Labour Party (Jennifer Taylor, 123–142). Eva Kolmer and the Austrian emigration in Britain, 1938–1946 (Charmian Brinson, 143–170). The 'myth' and reality of rescue from the Holocaust: The Karski-Koestler and Vrba-Wetzler reports (Frank Baron, 171–208). The Austrian exile theatre Laterndl (Richard Dove, 209–230). Deutsch-jüdische Emigranten, nach England geflohen, in Australien interniert (231–258). Peter de Mendelssohns und Hilde Spiels Kulturaufbau im Dienst des britischen Re-Educationsprogramms (Esther Schneider Handschin, 259–276).]

41764. EXILE. *German literature, Jewish critics.* The Brandeis Symposium. Ed. by Stephen D. Dowden and Meike G. Werner. Rochester, NY: Camden House, XXIV, 321 pp., illus., ports., notes, bibl., index. [Papers presented at Brandeis Univ. in 1997. Incl.: (some titles abbr.): Introduction: Positions to defend (eds., XV–XXIV). On the role of Jewish critics in exile (Hinrich C. Seeba, 1–24). Reminiscences of a UFO (Egon Schwarz, 25–33; see also No. 41466). Margarete Susman, Bertha Badt-Strauss und Hannah Arendt in der Emigration (Barbara Hahn, 99–120). Eine Klassikerin der Literaturtheorie: Käte Hamburger (Gesa Dane, 121–130). A Jewish critic from Germany: Hermann Levin Goldschmidt (Willi Goetschel, 149–166; followed by a response by Thomas Sparr, 167–170). Part of an intellectual autobiography (Walter H. Sokel, 189–206; followed by a response by Marc A. Weiner, 207–212). An appreciation of the work of J.P. Stern, Siegbert Prawer, and George Steiner (Ritchie Robertson, 237–262; followed by a response by David Suchoff, 263–270). Incl. also the panelists' comments and discussions. Further contribs. are listed according to subject.]

41765. EXILE. HAARMANN, HERMANN: *Wie deutsche Schriftsteller und Publizisten aus dem Exil gegen Hitler kämpften.* [In]: Der Nationalsozialismus und die deutsche Gesellschaft. Einführung und Überblick. Hrsg. von Bernd Sösemann. Stuttgart: Deutsche Verlags-Anstalt, 2002. Pp. 298–311.

41766. EXILE. *Metropolen des Exils.* [Issue title of] Exilforschung. Ein Internationales Jahrbuch, Bd. 20. Hrsg. im Auftrag der Gesellschaft für Exilforschung von Claus-Dieter Krohn [et al.]. München: edition text + kritik, 2002. 309 pp., notes. (Exilforschung, Bd. 20.) [Incl. (some titles abbr.): Migrationen und Metropolenkultur in Berlin vor 1933 (Claus-Dieter Krohn, 14–35). Die literarische Moderne im Exil. Kontinuitäten und Brüche der Stadtwahrnehmung (Sabina Becker, 36–52). Die Großstadtfotografie der fotografischen Emigration im NS-Zeit in Paris, London und New York (Irme Schaber, 53–73). Exil des Intellektuellen und Großstadt /Zu Walter Benjamin (Chryssoula Kambas, 74–96). Siebzehn Tage in Israel: Paul Celan "auf Lichtsuche" (Lydia Koelle, 97–130). Zur Topographie des literarischen und publizistischen Exils in Paris (Hélène Roussel/Lutz Winckler, 131–158; incl. name lists of authors and journalists). Metropole des Exils Prag 1933–1939 (Peter Becher, 159–177). Metropole New York (Michael Winkler, 178–198). Los Angeles als Zentrum der Exilkultur und die Krise des Modernismus (Ehrhard Bahr, 199–212). Struktur und Leistung deutschsprachiger Exilanten in México Ciudad (Markus G. Patka, 213–241). Buenos Aires, eine unbekannte und vielseitige Exilmetropole (1933–1945) (Anne Saint Sauveur-Henn, 242–268). Shanghai. Rettung am "schlechtest möglichen Ort" der Welt? (Astrid Freyeisen, 269–293).]

41767. EXILE. MEYER, MICHAEL A.: *Refugees from Hitler's Germany. The creative elite and its middle class audience in Los Angeles in the 1930's and 1940's – Film Noir and orders of "sunny-side up".* [In]: Preußens Himmel breitet seinen Sterne ... [see No. 41991], Bd. 1. Pp. 357–374, notes.

41768. EXILE. SOKOLOFF, LEON: *Refugees from Nazism and the biomedical publishing industry.* [In]: Studies in History and Philosophy of Biological and Biomedical Sciences, Vo. 33, Amsterdam, 2002. Pp. 315–324, notes.

41769. EXILE. STERN, FRANK: *Von Berlin nach Hollywood und zurück. Bilder des deutsch-jüdischen Films.* [In]: Preußens Himmel breitet seine Sterne ... [see No. 41991], Bd. 1. Pp. 403–414, notes. [On the contribs. of Ernst Lubitsch, Fritz Lang, Fritz Kortner, Billy Wilder.]

41770. EXILE. STOFFREGEN, MATTHIAS: *Kämpfen für ein demokratisches Deutschland. Emigranten zwischen Politik und Politikwissenschaft.* Opladen: Leske + Budrich, 2002. 320 pp., footnotes, bibl. (297–320). [Incl. Ernst Fraenkel, A.R.L. Gurland, John H. Herz, Henry Holborn, Henry Kellermann, Hans Kelsen, Robert W. Kempner, Otto Kirchheimer, Karl Loewenstein, Franz L. Neumann, Sigmund Neumann, Hans Simons, Hans Speier et al.]

——— EXILE. *Zwischen den Stühlen? Remigranten und Remigration in der deutschen Medienöffentlichkeit der Nachkriegszeit.* [See No. 41563.]

41771. EXILE LITERATURE. *Deutschsprachige Schriftsteller im Schweizer Exil 1933–1950.* Eine Ausstellung des Deutschen Exilarchivs 1933–1945 Der Deutschen Bibliothek. [Begleitbuch: Frank Wende, Mitarbeit: Gesa M. Valk, Brita Eckert, Marlis Staehli.] Wiesbaden: Harrassowitz, 2002. 344 pp., illus., facsims., notes. (Gesellschaft für das Buch, Bd. 8.) [Documents 21 writers, among them numerous Jews.]

41772. EXILE LITERATURE. THUNECKE, JÖRG: *Von Soma Morgensterns 'Flucht in Frankreich' zu Fred Wanders 'Hotel Baalbek'.* [In]: Exil, Jg. 21, Nr. 2, 2001, Frankfurt am Main, 2002. Pp. 82–87.

41773. FRANKFURT SCHOOL. *Rethinking the Frankfurt School: alternative legacies of cultural critique.* Ed. by Jeffrey T. Nealon and Caren Irr. Albany, NY: State Univ. of New York Press, 2002. VII, 227 pp., notes, bibl., index. [A re-examination of the key Frankfurt School thinkers, such as Walter Benjamin, Max Horkheimer, Ludwig Marcuse.]

41774. FREIDENREICH, HARRIET PASS: *Female, Jewish and educated: the lives of Central European university women.* Bloomington: Indiana Univ. Press, 2002. 296 pp., illus., ports., maps, tabs., glossary, notes, bibl. (263–280), index. [Deals mainly with German- and Austrian-Jewish women from different periods. Incl. chaps.: Emancipation through higher education. University years – Jewish women and German academia. Interrupted lives – persecution and emigration.]

41775. *Gestalten um Alfred Adler.* Pioniere der Individualpsychologie. Alexandra Adler – Rudolf Allers – Rudolf Dreikurs – Viktor Frankl – Carl Furtmüller – Otto Glöckel – Henry Jacoby – Fritz Künkel – Sofie Lazarsfeld – Friedrich Liebling – Isa Löwy – Alice Rühle-Gerstel – Oswald Schwarz – Manès Sperber – Oskar Spiel – Wilhelm Stekel – Erwin Wexberg. Hrsg. von Alfred Lévy und Gerald Mackenthun. Würzburg: Königshausen & Neumann, 2002. 332 pp., notes. [Cont. contribs. by Katharina Kaminski, Alfred Lévy, Hartmut & Sabine Siebenhüner, Gisela Deising, Gerhard Danzer, Irmgard Fuchs, Gerald Mackenthun, Dorothee Friebus, Josef Rattner, Margarete Eisner, Ullrich Kümmel.]

41776. GREINER, BERNHARD/SCHMIDT, CHRISTOPH, eds.: *Arche Noah. Die Idee der 'Kultur' im deutsch-jüdischen Diskurs.* Freiburg: Rombach, 2002. 413 pp., frontis., footnotes. (Rombach Wissenschaften, Reihe Cultura, Bd. 26.) [Incl. English and German papers presented at a conference held under the title 'Noah's Ark: Jewish-German concepts of culture' at the Hebrew Univ. Jerusalem, Nov. 14–16, 2000; cont. (only selected essays fully listed): Vorwort (eds., 9–24). "Cultur ist ein Fremdling in der Sprache". Zu Moses Mendelssohns Kulturbegriff (Carola Hilfrich, 25–48). Salomon Maimon. Christianity, Judaism and Geometry (Meir Benaglo, 49–58). Kultur als Weltanschauung. Der Kulturbegriff der Begründer der „Wissenschaft des Judentums" (Rachel Livneh-Freudenthal, 59–84). Der Raum der Nation im jüdischen Kulturdenken zwischen Idealismus und Zionismus (Philipp Theisohn, 95–124). Also essays on Karl Marx (Moshe Zuckermann), Edmund Husserl and Hermann Cohen (Ashraf Noor), Ernst Cassirer (Gideon Freudenthal), Franz Kafka (Bernhard Greiner), Arnold Zweig (Hanswalther Staeubli), Gershom Scholem (Moshe Idel), Walter Benjamin (Liliane Weissberg), Theodor Lessing (Yotam Hotam), German-Jewish identity and the 'Schocken Bücherei' (Antony Skinner), Anton Kuh/Karl Kraus (Lothar Müller), Kairos and culture. Some remarks on the formation of the cultural sciences in Germany and the emergence of a Jewish political thought (Christoph Schmidt), Ernst Bloch (Michael Eckert), Elias Canetti (David Roberts), Susan Taubes (Sigrid Weigel). Nachwort: Text und Arche. Die Arche Noah zwischen Mythologie und Theologie (Christoph Schmidt).]

41777. *Grenzgänge. Menschen und Schicksale zwischen jüdischer, christlicher und deutscher Identität.* Festschrift für Diethard Aschoff [see No. 41473]. [Incl.: Der Vater, der Sohn und das Heilige Russland.

Biographische Notizen zu Leonid und Boris Pasternak (Julian Voloj (212–232). Josef
Rabinowitschs messianisches Judentum (Arnulf H. Baumann, 195–211). "Ich habe das
Empfinden und das Bewußtsein, ein posenscher Jude zu sein, nicht verloren". Der Historiker
Täubler und sein Verhältnis zum Ostjudentum (Heike Scharbaum, 233–244). Else Lasker-
Schülers jüdischer Jesus (Rainer Kamplimg, 245–254).]

41778. GÜRTLER, CHRISTA/SCHMID-BORTENSCHLAGER, SIGRID: *Erfolg und Verfolgung. Österreichische
Schriftstellerinnen 1918–1934. Fünfzehn Porträts und Texte.* Salzburg: Residenz, 2002. 319 pp., ports,
bibl. [Incl.: Else Feldmann, Alma Johanna Koenig, Vicki Baum, Maria Leitner, Paula Grogger,
Mela Hartwig, Gina Kaus, Veza Canetti, Lili Körber, Adrienne Thomas (Hertha A. Strauch,
married Lasser), Paula Ludwig.]

41779. GUSY, CHRISTOPH, ed.: *Demokratisches Denken in der Weimarer Republik.* Baden-Baden: Nomos,
2000, 681 pp., footnotes. (Interdisziplinäre Studien zu Recht und Staat, Bd. 16.) [Incl.:
Demokratisches Denken in der Weimarer Verfassungsdiskussion – Hugo Preuß und die
Nationalversammlung (Jörg-Detlef Kühne, 115–134). Der Beitrag von Hans Kelsen und Hugo
Preuß zum modernen Demokratieverständnis (Detlef Lehnert, 221–255). Von Max Adler zu
Ernst Fraenkel. Demokratie und pluralistische Gesellschaft in der sozialistischen
Demokratietheorie der Weimarer Republik (Hubertus Buchstein, 534–606).]

41780. HERRBERG, HEIKE/WAGNER, HEIDI: *Wiener Melange. Frauen zwischen Salon und Kaffeehaus.* Berlin:
Ed. Ebersbach, 2002. 239 pp., illus., notes, index. [Deals with 20 women; incl. Veza Canetti,
Trude Fleischmann, Anna Freud, Dora Kallmus alias Madame d'Ora, Gina Kaus, Gertrud
Kraus, Eugenie Schwarzwald, Hilde Spiel, Grete Wiesenthal, Berta Zuckerkandl.]

41781. HOFFMANN, DANIEL, ed.: *Handbuch der deutsch-jüdischen Literatur des 20. Jahrhunderts.* Paderborn:
Schöningh, 2002. 488 pp., footnotes, index. [Cont. 16 essays by different authors (with annota-
tions and bibl. references) arranged under the sections: I. Die jüdische Renaissance im 20.
Jahrhundert (13–78). II. Jüdische Schriftsteller und die deutsche Literatur. Erste Hälfte des 20.
Jahrhunderts (79–398). III. Deutsch-jüdische Literatur nach dem Zweiten Weltkrieg (399–440).]

——— HORN, GISELA, ed.: *Die Töchter der Alma mater jenensis. 90 Jahre Frauenstudium an der Universität von
Jena.* [See No. 40988.]

41782. KEßLER, MARIO: *Exil und Nach-Exil. Vertriebene Intellektuelle im 20. Jahrhundert.* Hamburg: VSA-
Verl., 2002. 206 pp., footnotes. [Cont. 12 essays previously publ. between 1991 and 2001; incl.
Albert Einstein, Ernst Bloch, Hans Mayer, Leo Kofler, Alfred Kantorowicz, Arthur Rosenberg,
Walter Grab, Ossip K. Flechtheim, Richard Löwenthal, Leo Löwenthal, Stefan Heym.]

41783. KROBB, FLORIAN: *Kollektivautobiographien – Wunschautobiographien. Marranenschicksal im deutsch-jüdischen Roman.* Würzburg: Königshausen & Neumann, 2002. 174 pp., footnotes, bibl., index. [Deals
with novels by Phöbus Philippson, Markus Lehmann, Hermann Sinsheimer, Lion Feuchtwanger,
Robert Menasse.]

41784. LANDAU, PETER/NEHLSEN, HERMANN, eds.: *Große jüdische Gelehrte an der Münchener Juristischen
Fakultät.* Ebelsbach: Aktiv Druch & Verlag, 2001. VIII, 111 pp., footnotes. [Incl. essays on Hans
Nawiasky (Hans F. Zacher, 1–19), Erich Kaufmann (Peter Lerche, 20–31), Karl Loewenstein (Peter
Badura, 32–44), Theodor Loewenfeld (Peter Landau, 45–62), Leo Rosenberg (Bruno
Rimmelspacher, 63–76), Ernst Rabel (Dagmar Coester-Waltjen, 77–96), Karl Neumeyer (Klaus
Vogel, 97–111).]

41785. MEISSNER, KURT: *Der große Beitrag zur deutschen Kultur. Jüdisches Denken in Deutschland zwischen
Aufklärung und Holocaust.* Münster: Hansen & Hansen, 2002. 200 pp., bibl. (Sylter Beiträge,
Schriftenreihe der Volkshochschule Klappholttal auf Sylt, 11.) [Incl. seven essays on German-
Jewish history, Zionism, antisemitism.]

41786. POTTER, PAMELA M.: *Die 'deutscheste' der Künste.* Musikwissenschaft und Gesellschaft von der
Weimarer Republik bis zum Ende des Dritten Reiches. Aus dem Amerik. von Wolfram Ette.
Stuttgart: Klett-Cotta, 2000. 416 pp. [Orig. publ. with the title 'Most German of the arts.

Musicology and society from the Weimar Republic to the end of Hitler's Reich', New Haven; London: Yale Univ. Press, 1998. Deals also with Jewish Musicologist and antisemitism.]

41787. REICH-RANICKI, MARCEL: *Die verkehrte Krone oder Juden in der deutschen Literatur*. [In]: Preußens Himmel breitet seine Sterne … [see No. 41991], Bd. 2. Pp. 571–586. [Lecture held in Jan. 1995 in Heidelberg.]

41788. REICH-RANICKI, MARCEL: *Sieben Wegbereiter*. Schriftsteller des zwanzigsten Jahrhunderts. Arthur Schnitzler, Thomas Mann, Alfred Döblin, Robert Musil, Franz Kafka, Kurt Tucholsky, Bertolt Brecht. Stuttgart: Deutsche Verlags-Anstalt, 2002. 300 pp., notes.

41789. SCHUBERT, KATJA: *Notwendige Umwege: Gedächtnis und Zeugenschaft in Texten jüdischer Autorinnen in Deutschland und Frankreich nach Auschwitz = Voies de traverse obligées*. Hildesheim; New York: Olms, 2001. 438 pp., footnotes, bibl. (423–438). (Haskala, Bd. 23.) Zugl.: Berlin, Humboldt-Univ. und Paris, Univ. de Paris 7 Denis Diderot, Diss., 2000. [Analyses 'Weiter leben. Eine Jugend' (Ruth Klüger), and 'Rue Ordener Rue Labat' (Sarah Kofman), 'Eine Liebe aus nichts' (Barbara Honigmann), 'Joemis Tisch. Eine jüdische Geschichte' (Esther Dischereit, 'La trahison' (Cécile Wajsbrot).]

41790. SCHWANITZ, WOLFGANG G.: *Gold, Bankiers und Diplomaten. Zur Geschichte der Deutschen Orientbank 1906–1946*. Berlin: Trafo-Verlag, 2002. XIX, 426 pp., illus., facsims., notes (333–374), index. (Amerika – Nahost – Europa, Regionalhistorische Komparatistik: Politik, Wirtschaft, Militär und Kultur, Bd. 1.) [Deals also with the founder of the Orientbank, Eugen Gutmann (also founder of the Dresdner Bank), his son Herbert M. Gutmann and other Jewish bankers; "aryanisation"; Jewish assets.]

41791. STEINECKE, HARTMUT/TIGGESBÄUMKER, GÜNTER, eds.: *Jüdische Literatur in Westfalen. Vergangenheit und Gegenwart*. Symposion im Museum Bökerhof 27. bis 29. Oktober 2000. Bielefeld: Aisthesis, 2002. 231 pp., footnotes. (Veröffentlichungen der Literaturkommission für Westfalen, Bd. 4.) [Deals with the research project 'Jüdische Schriftstellerinnen und Schriftsteller in Westfalen'; with contribs. by Hartmut Steinecke, Iris Nölle-Hornkamp, Michael Voigt, Thomas Dörr, Arie Goral-Sternheim, Petra Rennecke, Jenny Alon, Walter Gödden, Jochen Grywatsch, Heinrich Stiewe, Manfred Keller. Incl. list of Jewish writers in Westphalia. One further contrib. is listed according to subject.]

————— *Unlikely history: the changing German-Jewish symbiosis, 1945–2000*. Ed. by Leslie Morris and Jack Zipes. [See No. 41559.]

41793. *Vom Salon zur Barrikade. Frauen in der Heinezeit*. Hrsg. von Irina Hundt. Mit einem Geleitwort von Joseph A. Kruse. Stuttgart: Metzler, 2002. 460 pp., illus., notes, index. (Heine Studien.) [Incl.: Rahel Varnhagen von Ense (1771–1833). Eine "Sévigné prussienne"? Französische Echos auf Rahel Varnhagens Briefwerke (Volker Schindler, 17–46). Lea Mendelssohn Bartholdy (1777–1842). "In voller geistiger Lebendigkeit" (Cornelia Bartsch, 61–74). Jeanette Strauß-Wohl (1783–1861). "Die bekannte Freyheitsgöttinn". Versuch eines Porträts der Freundin Ludwig Börnes (Inge Rippmann, 75–90). Fanny Hensel (1805–1847). Heine-Lieder (Cornelia Bartsch, 241–254).]

41794. *(Les) voyages de l'intelligence*. Passages des idées et des hommes, Europe, Palestine, Israel. [Issue title of] CRFJ Mélanges, Vol. 4, Paris, 2002. 333 pp., footnotes. [Cont.: Introd. (Gabriel Motzkin/Dominique Bourel, 9–12). Selected papers: Le passage en France des Juifs de Bohème au milieu du XIXe siècle (Michel Espagne, 13–28). Brody, Leipzig, Lyon: les relations commerciales européennes et leurs acteurs (Katharina Middell, 29–58). Eduard Gans: Berlin – Paris – Berlin (Norbert Waszek, 59–80). De Breslau à Francfort: l'itinéraire de l'historien Isidor Kracauer (Olivier Agard, 81–104). La Bucovine de Rose Ausländer entre Vaterland et Muttersprache (Florence Heymann, 105–124). De Vienne à Bruxelles, de Hanovre à New York: Jean Améry, Hannah Arendt et la langue allemande (Marc Crépon, 143–160). Livres, exil et retour (Anthony David Skinner, 161–174). Leo Strauss: du sionisme judéo-allemand à la vie en diaspora (Marc de Launay, 175–190). Les usages juifs de l'historicisme allemand. Naissance et professionnelisation d'une discipline judéo-allemande, 1871–1914 (Jacques Ehrenfreund, 203–228). Les racines allemandes de l'Université hébraique (Dominique Trimbur, 247–268). A propos des influences allemandes sur le droit israélien (Claude Klein, 269–280). Les médecins de formation allemande et leur influsence sur le développement de la profession et de son enseigne-ment en Palestine-Israel (Samuel S. Kottek/Gerhard Baader, 281–294). Demeures freudiennes en Palestine-Eretz-Israel (Guido Liebermann, 295–313). La résistance aux transferts: le rejet des auteurs "diasporiques" dans la culture israélienne (Stéphane Mosès, 314–324).]

41795. WOLIN, RICHARD: *Heidegger's children: Hannah Arendt, Karl Löwith, Hans Jonas, and Herbert Marcuse.* Princeton, NJ: Princeton Univ. Press, 2001. XVI. 276 pp., notes, bibl., index.

41796. *Zwischen Wissenschaft und Politik. Studien zur deutschen Universitätsgeschichte.* Festschrift für Eike Wolgast zum 65. Geburtstag. Hrsg. von Armin Kohl und Frank Engehausen. Steiner: Stuttgart, 2001. VIII, 605 pp., footnotes. [Section 4, entitled Biographisches, incl.: Adolf Fischhof – ein jüdischer Akademiker an der Spitze der Revolution von 1848 (Michael Graetz, 296–308; deals with the involvement of A.F., a medical student, in the Revolution in Vienna in 1848). Alfred Hessel (1877–1939), Mediävist und Bibliothekar in Göttingen (Wolfgang Petke, 387–414; A.H., brother of Franz Hessel, dismissed from Göttingen Univ. in 1935). Mayer versus Meyer. Gustav Mayers gescheiterte Habilitation in Berlin 1917/18 (Gottfried Niedhart, 329–344). "Das Verhältnis von Forschung und Lehre kehrt sich um". Eugen Rosenstock als erster Leiter der Frankfurter Akademie der Arbeit 1921/22 (Hermann Jakobs, 345–386). Further essays are listed according to subject.]

41797. *Zwischen Adaption und Exil. Jüdische Autoren und Themen in den romanischen Ländern.* Hrsg. von Brigitte Sändig. Wiesbaden: Harrassowitz, 2001. 175 pp., footnotes, index. (Jüdische Kultur. Studien zur Geistesgeschichte, Religion und Literatur, Bd. 7.) [Incl.: In zwei Sprachen schreiben und in zwei Kulturen leben? Georges-Arthur Goldschmidt zwischen Frankreich und Deutschland (Wolfgang Asholt, 45–60). Jüdische Gelehrte in der Wissenschaftsgeschichte der deutschsprachigen Romanistik (Gerda Haßler, 153–171; deals with Else Richter, Leo Spitzer, Victor Klemperer et al.).]

B. **Individual**

41798. ADORNO, THEODOR W. *In practice: Adorno, critical theory and cultural studies.* Ed. by Holger Briel and Andreas Kramer. Oxford; New York: Lang, 2001. 205 pp., bibl. (German linguistic and cultural studies, Vol. 9.) [Papers presented at an international conference held at the Univ. of Surrey in Jan. 1999. Incl.: Adorno, Auschwitz, and the contradictions of representation (Josh Cohen).]

41799. ADORNO, THEODOR W. & HORKHEIMER, MAX. STEIN, EVA: *Subjektive Vernunft und Antisemitismus bei Horkheimer und Adorno.* Oldenburg: Bis, 2002. 177 pp., footnotes, bibl. [M.A. Thesis; analyses section entitled 'Elemente des Antisemitismus' in 'Dialektik der Aufklärung'. Incl.: Die Subversion der Negation (Martin Deppner, 11–16). Appendix cont.: Erinnerungen an Theodor W. Adorno (Leo Löwenthal, 153–166). Über den Begriff der Geschichte (Walter Benjamin, 167–177).]

41800. AMÉRY, JEAN: *Werke.* Hrsg. von Irene Heidelberger-Leonard. Bd. 2: *Jenseits von Schuld und Sühne. Unmeisterliche Wanderjahre. Örtlichkeiten.* Hrsg. von Gerhard Scheit. Stuttgart: Klett-Cotta, 2002. 856 pp., appendices (492–853; a collections of essays, many of them autobiographical; incl. additional texts by J.A., epilogues by Gerhard Scheit and annotations related to the works, first publ. 1966, 1971, 1980). [J.A. (orig. Hans Mayer), 31. Oct. 1912 Vienna – Oct. 17, 1978 Salzburg (suicide), author, essayist, emigr. 1938 to Belgium, active in the Belgian resistance movement, 1943–1945 in Auschwitz, Buchenwald and Bergen-Belsen, after liberation returned to Brussels.]

41801. AMÉRY, JEAN. RISARI, GUIA: *Jean Améry. Il risentimento come morale.* Milano: Franco Angeli, 2002. 158 pp., bibl. [Incl. preface by Davide Bigalli; postscript by Armando Gnisci.]

41802. AMÉRY, JEAN. SIGUAN, MARISA: *Über Sprache und ihre Grenzen: einige Beispiele zur Bewältigung von Sprachlosigkeit in der Literatur (Jean Améry, Primo Levi, Jorge Semprún).* [In]: Ulrike Haß-Zumkehr [et al.], eds.: Ansichten der deutschen Sprache. Festschrift für Gerhard Stickel zum 65. Geburtstag. Tübingen: Gunter Narr Verlag, 2002. (Studien zur Deutschen Sprache, Bd. 25 – 2002.) Pp. 605–622, footnotes.

41803. ANDERS, GÜNTHER. GREFFRATH, MATHIAS: *Lob der Sturheit.* Eine Erinnerung an Günther Anders – den Philosophen und Pamphletisten, den Analytiker und Kämpfer, der am 12. Juli 100 Jahre geworden wäre. [In]: Die Zeit, Nr. 28, Hamburg, 4. Juli 2002. P. 80.

41804. ANDERS, GÜNTHER. HOLBEIN, ULRICH: *Noch bevor der Morgen graut.* Der Weltnachtwächter, der aller Zeit voraus war: Zum hundertsten Geburtstag von Günther Anders. [In]: 'FAZ', Nr. 160, Frankfurt am Main, 13. Juli 2002. P. 40.

41805. ANDERS, GÜNTHER. LIESSMANN, KONRAD PAUL: *Günther Anders. Philosophieren im Zeitalter der technologischen Revolutionen.* München: Beck, 2002. 208 pp., notes, chronol., bibl. [Deals with A.'s life and work.]

41806. ANDERS, GÜNTHER. SCHUBERT, ELKE: *Zur Aktualität des Philosophen Günther Anders.* [In]: Die Neue Gesellschaft/Frankfurter Hefte, Nr. 7/8, Frankfurt am Main, Juli/Aug. 2002. Pp. 473–475.

41807. ARENDT, HANNAH. CHRISTOPHERSEN, CLAUDIA: *"… es ist mit dem Leben etwas gemeint". Hannah Arendt über Rahel Varnhagen.* Königstein/Ts.: Ulrike Helmer Verlag, 2002. 328 pp., footnotes, bibl. (287–318), index. [On *Rahel Varnhagen*, first publ. 1958; deals also with how the book came to be written, its publishing history and reception; A.'s Jewish identity.]

41808. ARENDT, HANNAH. KLOTZ, ANDREAS TASSILO: *Juden und Judentum bei Hannah Arendt unter besonderer Berücksichtigung des Briefwechsels mit Karl Jaspers.* Frankfurt am Main: Haag und Herchen, 2001. 166 pp., footnotes. Zugl.: Frankfurt am Main, Univ., Diss., 2001.

41809. ARENDT, HANNAH. NEWMAN, JEFFREY: *Hannah Arendt – thinking in circles.* [In]: European Judaism, Vol 34, No. 1, London, Spring 2001. Pp. 44–56.

41810. ARENDT, HANNAH. *The philosophy of Hannah Arendt.* [Issue title of] International Journal of Philosophical Studies, Vol. 10, No. 2, London, 2002. 1 issue. [Special issue editor: Amy Allen. Cont.: Introduction (Amy Allen, 119–207). Six essays by Amy Allen, Elizbeth Kamarck, Dianna Taylor, Johanna Meehan, Bat-Ami Bar On; incl.: Martin Heidegger, Hannah Arendt and the politics of remembrance (Jeffrey Andrew Barash, 171–182).]

41811. ARENDT, HANNAH. ZERTAL, IDITH: *Judaism and Zionism – Between the pariah and the parvenu.* [In]: Tel Aviver Jahrbuch für deutsche Geschichte XXX (2002). Ethnizität, Moderne und Enttraditionalisierung. Gerlingen, 2002. Pp. 341–357, footnotes. [Analyses A.'s concept of the Jewish people and Zionism.]

41812. ANHEIM, RUDOLF: *Rundfunk als Hörkunst und weitere Aufsätze zum Hörfunk.* Mit einem Nachwort von Helmut H. Diederichs. Frankfurt am Main: Suhrkamp, 2001. 236 pp. [Incl.: Radio als Kunst. Rudolf Arnheims rundfunktheoretische Schriften im biographischen Zusammenhang (Helmut H. Diederichs, 217–237, footnotes).] [R.A., b. 1904 in Berlin, journalist, broadcaster, emigr. to Italy in 1933, to UK in 1938, to the US in 1940, since 1974 has been living in Ann Arbor, MI.]

41813. ARONSFELD, CAESAR CASPAR. *Caesar Aronsfeld: Fugitive from Hitler whose documentation of Nazi atrocities proved invaluable to historians.* [In]: The Times, London, Sept. 25, 2002. [Obituary.] [C.C.A. July 15, 1910 Exin – Aug. 28, 2002 London, author, editor, former director of the Wiener Library.]

41814. AUSLÄNDER, ROSE. *"Immer zurück zum Pruth".* Dokumentation des Czernowitzer Symposiums 2001 "100 Jahre Rose Ausländer". Hrsg. von Michael Gans und Harald Vogel. Baltmannsweiler: Schneider-Verlag Hohengehren, 2002. 220 pp., illus., footnotes. [Incl. 10 contribs. in German, also with Russian transl.]

41815. AUSLÄNDER, ROSE. *"Wörter stellen mir nach, ich stelle sie vor".* Dokumentation des Ludwigsburger Symposiums 2001 "100 Jahre Rose Ausländer". Hrsg. von Michael Gans. Baltmannsweiler: Schneider-Verlag, 2002. 221 pp., illus., facsims., footnotes. (Ludwigsburger Hochschulschriften, 23.) [A collection of 17 contribs. dealing with various aspects of A.'s life and work; also some on Czernowitz, Paul Celan.]

41816. BAB, JULIUS: *Leben und Tod des deutschen Judentums.* Essays, Briefe und 'vita emigrationis'. Hrsg. von Klaus Siebenhaar. Berlin: Bostelmann & Siebenhaar, 2002. 174 pp., illus., footnotes. (akte exil, Bd. 6.) [Incl.: Vorbemerkung (Hermann Haarmann, 7–8). "weil ich eben ein 'Deutscher' bin" – Julius Bab und die deutsche Kultur (ed., 9–18). 'Leben und Tod des deutschen Judentums' (19–148; written in Paris in 1939. Also letters and the autobiographical fragment 'vita emigrationis' (159–166).]

41817. BARBAKOFF, TATJANA. *Tatjana Barbakoff. Tänzerin und Muse.* Hrsg. vom Verein August Macke Haus e.V. Mit Beiträgen von Klara Drenker-Nagels [et al.]. Katalog und Ausstellung Hildegard Reinhardt unter Mitarbeit von Günter Goebbels. Bonn: August Macke Haus, 2002. 206., frontis., notes. (Schriftenreihe Verein August Macke Haus Bonn, Nr. 43.) [Incl.: Vorwort (Klara Drenker-Nagels, 5–8). Tatjana Barbakoff – Tänzerin zwischen den Welten (Günter Goebbels, 9–88). "Aus dem Osten wird Rausch und Schönheit zu uns kommen" – Tatjana Barbakoff als Modell bildender Künstler (Hildegard Reinhardt, 89–139). Offenbarung des Rätsels Asien – Tatjana Barbakoff im Spiegel der zeitgenössischen Fotografie (Anja Hellhammer, 140–159). Also personal reminiscences.] [T.B., orig. Cilly Edelberg, 1899 Libau, Latvia – 1944 Auschwitz, at times well-known dancer of the German "Ausdruckstanz" in the 1920s and 1930s, model and muse of a number of European painters, sculpturers, graphic artists and photographers, lived in Germany, performed in different European countries, since 1926 close friend of the painter Gert Wollheim, emigr. with him to France in 1933, interned in 1940, deported to Auschwitz in 1944.]

41818. BECKER, JUREK. *"Wenn ich auf mein bisheriges Leben zurückblicke, dann muß ich leider sagen." Jurek Becker 1937–1997.* Dokumente zu Leben und Werk aus dem Jurek-Becker-Archiv. Zusammengestellt und hrsg. von Karin Kiwus. Berlin: Akademie der Künste, 2002. 238 pp., illus., facsims. [Cf.: Der heitere Grübler. Der Schriftsteller Jurek Becker würde diesen Monat 65 (Janko Tietz) [in]: Aufbau, Vol. 68, No. 19, New York, Sept. 19, 2002, p. 16, port.]

41819. BENJAMIN, WALTER. *Walter Benjamin* [Issue title of] New German Critique, No. 83, New York, Spring-Summer 2001. 191 pp., footnotes. [Cont.: Walter Benjamin or: the commodity as phantasmagoria (Gyorgy Markus, 3– 42). The true politician (Uwe Steiner, 43–88). Art's fateful hour: Benjamin, Heidegger, art and politics (Christopher P. Long, 89–118). The work of Walter Benjamin in the age of information (Noah Isenberg, 119–150). Beyond use, within reason: Adorno, Benjamin and the question of theology (David Kaufmann, 151–176). Messianism in the early work of Gershom Scholem (Michael Löwy, 177–190).]

41820. BENJAMIN, WALTER. VALERO, VICENTE: *"Experiencia y pobreza". Walter Benjamin en Ibiza. 1932–1933.* Barcelona: Península, 2001. 215 pp. [Cf.: Hitlerjugend auf Ibiza. Zwischeneinkehr: Vicente Valero folgt Walter Benjamin ins Exil (Klaus Englert) [in]: 'FAZ', Nr. 152, Frankfurt am Main, 4. Juli 2002, p. 38.]

41821. BERMANN, RICHARD A. OPITZ, ALFRED: *"Zuviel Heine gelesen …". Der "Bimini"-Roman von Richard A. Bermann.* [In]: Literarische Fundstücke [see No. 41884]. Pp. 214–223, footnotes.

41822. BERNAYS, KARL LUDWIG. HIRSCH, HELMUT: *Freund von Heine, Marx/Engels und Lincoln. Eine Karl Ludwig Bernays-Biographie.* Mit einer Genealogie der Familie Bernays von Marianne Hirsch und René Löb sowie einem Nachwort von Lars Lambrecht. Frankfurt am Main; New York: Lang, 2002. 184 pp., illus., footnotes, bibl., index. (Forschungen zum Junghegelianismus, Bd. 6.) [Biography, interwoven with numerous insertions related to the author's own life and the bookwriting process; incl.: Nachwort. H.H. – Ein wirklicher 'homme de lettres' (Lars Lambrecht, 149–154; for data H.H. see No. 32338/YB XL. Book incl. also K.L.B.' essay entitled 'Mein Judentum'.] [K.L.B., orig. Lazarus B., Nov. 16, 1815 Mainz – June 22, 1879 St. Louis, MS, jurist, political journalist, US diplomat, with his sibling became baptised (Protestant) before leaving school, lived in the mid-1840s in Paris, contrib. to the 'Deutsch-Französische Jahrbücher' and the 'Vorwärts', started his diplomatic career in Vienna 1848 before emigr. 1849 to the US.]

41823. BLOCH, EDUARD. BLOCH, EDUARD: *The autobiography of 'Obermedizinalrat' Eduard Bloch.* [In]: Leo Baeck Institute Year Book 2002, Vol. XLVII, Oxford, 2002. Pp. 217–245, footnotes, illus. [Memoirs, transl. from the German by H.J. Schmeller; orig. written and partly publ. in 1941.] [E.B., 1872 Frauenberg/Bohemia – 1945 New York, physician (of Hitler and his mother in Linz before World War I), emigr. 1941 to the US.]

41824. BLOCH, ERNEST. KUSHNER, DAVID Z.: *The Ernest Bloch companion.* Westport, CT: Greenwood Press, 2002. XIV, 198 pp., illus., bibl. (179–189), index. [E.B., 1880 Geneva – 1959 Agate Beach, OR, composer, studied in Brussels and Frankfurt, emigr. to the US in the 1920s and became director of the Cleveland Institute of Music and later the San Francisco Conservatory of Music. Also taught at the Univ. of California, Berkeley.]

41825. BLOCH, ERNST. DIECKMANN, FRIEDRICH: *Ernst Bloch in Leipzig.* [In]: ndl, neue deutsche literatur, Jg. 50, H. 546, Berlin, Nov./Dez. 2002. Pp. 8–27.

41826. BLOCH, ERNST. DURST, DAVID: *Ernst Bloch's theory of nonsimultaneity.* [In]: The Germanic Review, Vol. 77, No. 3, Washington, Summer 2002. Pp. 171–194, notes.

41827. BLOCH, ERNST. *Stefan Moses fotografiert Ernst Bloch.* Hrsg. von Klaus Kufeld. Ludwigshafen: Ernst-Bloch-Zentrum der Stadt Ludwigshafen; Ostfildern: Quantum Books, 2001. 71 pp., illus. [Also incl. texts by and on E.B. See also No. 41944.]

41828. BLUM, KLARA. YANG, ZHIDONG, ed.: *Klara Blum.* Kommentierte Auswahledition. Wien: Böhlau, 2001. 652 pp., illus., facsims., bibl. K.B. (636–642), indexes. [Incl.: Einleitung (13–26; biographical essay). Der Hirte und die Weberin (31–224; autobiographical novel). Lebenszeugnisse, Briefe (507–560); also essays, stories and poetry written during her years in Vienna and Moscow, some dealing with Jewish themes.] [For data on K.B. see No. 34425/XLII.]

41829. BLUMENTHAL, MICHAEL W. ROMBERG, OTTO R.: *Ich wollte den Holocaust verstehen.* Tribüne-Gespräch mit Michael W. Blumenthal, Direktor Jüdisches Museum Berlin. [In]: Tribüne, Jg. 41, H. 161, Frankfurt am Main, 2002. Pp. 85–94.

41831. BORCHARDT, RUDOLF. *Stefan George: Werk und Wirkung seit dem "Siebenten Ring".* Für die Stefan-George-Gesellschaft hrsg. von Wolfgang Braungart [et al.]. Tübingen: Niemeyer, 2001. XI, 456 pp., footnotes. [Incl. two essays on Rudolf Borchardt: Kopf statt Ohr. Rudolf Borchardt als Kritiker Stefan Georges (Dieter Burdorf, 353–377). "Restauration deutscher Kulturtotalität aus ihren gesamten geschichtlichen Beständen". Rudolf Borchardt Anthologien (Gerhard R. Kaiser, 378–395).]

41832. BORCHARDT, RUDOLF: *Prosa I.* Textkritisch revidierte, chronologisch geordnete und erweiterte Neuedition der Ausgabe von 1957. Hrsg. von Gerhard Schuster. Stuttgart: Klett-Cotta, 2002. 610 pp., notes (525–592), index (593–610). (Gesammelte Werke in Einzelbänden.)

41833. BROCH, HERMANN. STEINECKE, HARTMUT: *Von Lenau bis Broch.* Studien zur österreichischen Literatur – von außen betrachtet. Tübingen: Francke, 2002. 215 pp., footnotes. (Edition Patmos, Bd. 7.) [Incl.: Hermann Broch: Erkenntnis und Menschlichkeit. Ein Portrait (141–158). Broch und Goethe. oder: Goethe im österreichischen Exil (159–170). "Unpersönlich bin ich ein Opfer". Jüdische Spuren im Spätwerk Hermann Brochs (171–184). Incl. also one contrib. on Karl Emil Franzos: Karl Emil Franzos. Plädoyer für einen "mittleren" galizischen Erzähler (107–116).]

41834. BUBER, MARTIN: *Meetings: autobiographical fragments.* Ed. and introd. by Maurice Friedman. 3rd edn. London: Routledge, 2002. 113 pp., bibl. (75–113).

41835. BUBER, MARTIN: *Frühe kulturkritische und philosophische Schriften 1891–1924.* Bearb., eingel. und kommentiert von Martin Treml. Gütersloh: Gütersloher Verlagshaus, 2001. 396 pp. (Martin Buber Werkausgabe, Bd. 1.)

41836. CANETTI, VEZA. *Veza Canetti.* [Issue title of] Text + Kritik, H. 156, München: Richard-Boorberg-Verl., 2002. 111 pp., bibl. [Guest ed.: Helmut Göbel.] [A collection of articles on V.C.]

41837. CELAN, PAUL. BUCK, THEO: *Celan und Frankreich.* Darstellung mit Interpretationen. Celan-Studien V. Aachen: Rimbaud, 2002. 107 pp., illus., notes, index. Orig.-Ausg.

41838. CELAN, PAUL. FELSTINER, JOHN: *Translating Paul Celan.* [In]: Midstream, Vol. 48, No. 3, New York, April 2002. Pp. 30–33. [Also deals with Celan's life.]

41839. CELAN, PAUL. GLENN, JERRY: *Paul Celan 2000.* [In]: Shofar, Vol. 20, No. 2, West Lafayette, IN, Winter 2002. Pp. 122–128. [Review essay of books and articles publ. in 2000 on the occasion of Celan's 80th anniversary.]

41840. CELAN, PAUL. HAWKINS, BETH: *Paul Celan and the language of sanctification.* [In]: Shofar, Vol. 20, No. 4, Lincoln, NE, Summer 2002. Pp. 36–63, footnotes.

41841. CELAN, PAUL. PIERCY, MARGE: *Celan, the poet of painful 'Yahrzeit'.* [In]: Midstream, Vol. 48, Nr.7,. New York, Nov./Dec. 2002. Pp. 25–27.

41842. CELAN, PAUL: *"Du mußt versuchen, auch den Schweigenden zu hören".* Briefe an Diet Kloos-Barendregt. Handschrift – Edition – Kommentar. Hrsg. von Paul Sars unter Mitwirkung von Laurent Sprooten. Frankfurt am Main: Suhrkamp, 2002. 142 pp., frontis., illus., facsims.

41843. COHN, OSKAR. HEID, LUDGER: *Oskar Cohn. Ein Sozialist und Zionist im Kaiserreich und in der Weimarer Republik.* Frankfurt am Main; New York: Campus, 2002. 450 pp., footnotes, gloss., bibl. (419–450). (Campus Judaica, Bd. 19.) [O.C., Oct. 15, 1869 Guttentag/Upper Silesia – Oct. 31, 1934 Geneva, Politician, lived in Berlin from the 1890s in Berlin, emigr. via Palestine, France to Switzerland in 1933.]

41844. COHN, VALLY. HEITMANN, MARGRET/KAUFHOLD, BARBARA: *"… mein höchster Stolz ist, dass meine Kunst weiblich sei".* Vally Cohn und ihre geretteten Briefe. [In]: Kalonymos, Jg. 5, H. 4, Duisburg, 2002. Pp. 5–9, illus., notes. [V.C., married Wygodzinski, 1873 Görlitz – 1905 Bonn, author, painter, sister of the philosopher Jonas Cohn.]

41845. COHEN, HERMANN: *Werke.* Im Auftrag des Hermann-Cohen-Archivs am Philosophischen Seminar der Universität Zürich und des Moses-Mendelssohn-Zentrums für Europäisch-Jüdische Studien, Universität Potsdam hrsg. von Helmut Holhey [et al.]. Bd. 17: *Kleinere Schriften.* Bearb. und eingel. von Hartwig Wiedebach. Hildesheim; New York: Olms, 2002. XLI, 766 pp.

41846. DÖBLIN, ALFRED. SANDER, GABRIELE: *Alfred Döblin.* Stuttgart: Reclam, 2001. 397 pp., footnotes. (Universal-Bibliothek, Bd. 17632.) [Incl. the sections: I. Leben; II. Das dichterische Werk; Das theoretische und essayistische Werk.]

41847. DÖBLIN, ALFRED. TSCHÖRTNER, H.D.: *Döblin versus Hauptmann.* [In]: ndl, neue deutsche literatur, Jg. 50, H. 542, Berlin, März/Apr. 2002. Pp. 147–152. [On Döblin's vitriolic criticism of Gerhart Hauptmann.]

41848. DRACH, ALBERT. SCHOBEL, EVA: *Albert Drach. Ein wütender Weiser.* Salzburg: Residenz, 2002. 555 pp., illus., notes (499–526), bibl., index. [Biography.] [A.D., Dec. 17, 1907 Vienna – March 11, 1995 Vienna, Lawyer, writer, further data see No. 33333/YB XLI.]

41849. DRACH, ALBERT: *Untersuchung an Mädeln. Kriminalprotokoll.* Werke in zehn Bänden, Bd. 1. Hrsg. von Ingrid Cella. Wien: Zsolnay, 2002. 446 pp. [Cf.: Regennaß und ohne Geld. Eine Biographie und eine Werkausgabe erinnern an Albert Drach (Thomas Rietzschel) [in]: 'FAZ', Nr. 293, Frankfurt am Main, 17. Dez. 2002, p. 36. Amtliches aus dem vorletzten Abgrund. Aus Anlass des 100. Geburtstags von Albert Drach beginnt der Zsolnay-Verlag mit einer Werkausgabe (Burkhard Müller) [in]: Süddeutsche Zeitung, Nr. 291, München, 17. Dez. 2002, p. 16.]

41850. EINSTEIN, ALBERT. FISCHER, KLAUS: *Einstein.* Freiburg: Herder, 1999. 206 pp., bibl., index (Spektrum: Meisterdenker.)

41851. EISENMAYER, ERNST. *"About the dignity of man": Ernst Eisenmayer, Leben und Werk.* Hrsg. von Gabriele Kohlbauer-Fritz im Auftrag des Jüdischen Museums Wien. Vienna: Jüdisches Museum Wien, 2002. 107 pp., illus., ports., bibl. [Parallel German and English texts. Catalogue of an exhibition held at the Jüd. Mus. March 12–June 16, 2002.] [E.E. b. 1920 Vienna, painter, sculptor, deported to Dachau in 1938, escaped to England in 1939. Incl. "About the dignity of man": der Maler und Bildhauer Ernst Eisenmayer (Gabriele Kohlbauer-Fritz, 11–27). Contrasts and contradictions: Gedanken zum Werk Ernst Eisenmayers (Gretchen Sylvia Simms, 29–57).]

41852. EISLER, HANNS. AMZOLL, STEFAN: *"Mein armes Deutschland"*. Hanns Eisler und der 13. August 1961. [In]: Dreigroschenheft, H. 1, Augsburg, 2002. Pp. 24–28.

41853. ELIAS, NORBERT. KRIEKEN, ROBERT VAN: *Norbert Elias*. London; New York, Routledge, 1998. VIII, 212 pp., notes, bibl., index. [Deals also with N.E.'s life.]

41854. ELIAS, NORBERT: *Frühschriften*. [Bearb. von Reinhard Blomert]. Frankfurt am Main: Suhrkamp, 2002. 191 pp., index. (Norbert Elias Gesammelte Schriften, Bd. 1.) [Incl.: articles orig. publ. in 'Blau-Weiss-Blätter'; a "Singspiel", performed in 1930 by Nina Rubinstein, Boris Goldenberg, Richard Löwenthal under the author's direction in Heidelberg on the occasion of a farewell ceremony for Karl Mannheim; Zur Soziologie des deutschen Antisemitismus.]

41855. ELIAS, NORBERT: *Gesammelte Schriften*. Hrsg. im Auftrag der Norbert Elias Stichting Amsterdam von Reinhard Blomert [et al.]. Bd. 2: *Die höfische Gesellschaft. Untersuchungen zur Soziologie des Königtums und der höfischen Aristokratie*. Mit einer Einleitung: Soziologie und Geschichtswissenschaft. Bearb. von Claudia Opitz. Frankfurt am Main: Suhrkamp, 2002. 549 pp. Bd. 13: *Symboltheorie*. Aus dem Englischen von Rainer Ansen. Bearb. von Helmut Kuzmics. Frankfurt am Main: Suhrkamp, 2001. 236 pp.

41856. FALK, ALFRED. HOLL, KARL: *Der lange Weg zur französischen Staatsbürgerschaft. Alfred Falk (1896–1951) im Exil in Frankreich*. [In]: Krieg, Frieden und Demokratie. Festschrift für Martin Vogt zum 65. Geburtstag. Hrsg. von Christof Dipper [et al.]. Frankfurt am Main, 2002. Pp. 153–168, footnotes. [A.F., orig. Cohn, 1896 – 1951 Nizza, journalist, pacifist, leading member of the Deutsche Friedensgesellschaft and the Deutsche Liga für Menschenrechte, 1933 fled via Czechoslovakia, Switzerland to France.]

41857. FRAENKEL, ERNST. SÖLLNER, ALFONS: *Ernst Fraenkel und die Verwestlichung der politischen Kultur in der Bundesrepublik Deutschland*. [In]: Leviathan, Jg. 30, H. 1, Wiesbaden, März 2002. Pp. 132–154, footnotes. [Engl. abstract: p. 156.]

41858. FRANK, OTTO. LEE, CAROL ANN: *The hidden life of Otto Frank*. New York; London: Viking, 2002. XIII, 364 pp., illus., ports., facsims., glossary, appendixes, refs., bibl. (336–343), index. Deals with the father of Anne Frank (1889–1980), his personal life and family background, his years in Amsterdam, and his time in Westerbork and Auschwitz. Incl. his life-long involvement in the various publications of Anne's diaries.]

41859. FREUD, MARTHA. BEHLING, KATJA: *Martha Freud. Die Frau des Genies*. Mit einem Vorwort von Anton W. Freud. Berlin: Aufbau-Taschenbuch-Verlag, 2002. 266 pp., illus., bibl. [M.F., née Bernays, 1861 Hamburg – 1951 London, wife of Sigmund F.]

41860. FREUD, SIGMUND. DANLER, HUBERT: *Sigmund Freud in seiner Epoche (1856–1939)*. Achenkirch 551: H. Danler; [Norderstedt]: Books on Demand, 2001. 275 pp., footnotes, bibl. (270–275).

41861. FREUD, SIGMUND & HERZL, THEODOR. LIPPMAN, ROBERT L.: *Sigmund Freud avoids his double, Theodor Herzl*. [In]: Midstream, Vol. 48, No. 7, New York, Nov./Dec. 2002. Pp. 22–24, notes.] [Deals with the impact of Herzl's work on Freud, specifically interpreting Freud's and Herzl's different approaches to the "Jewish Question" and antisemitism.]

41862. FRIEDENTHAL, RICHARD. WAGENER, HANS: *Richard Friedenthal. Biographie eines großen Biographen*. Gerlingen: Bleicher, 2002. 316 pp., illus., notes, bibl., index. [Incl. bibl. R.F.] [R.F., June 9, 1896 Munich – Oct. 19, 1979 (on trip), author, 1938 emigr. to the UK.]

41863. FRIEDJUNG, HEINRICH. FELLNER, FRITZ: *Biographische Skizzen. Heinrich Friedjung – ein österreichischer Ahnherr der "Oral History"*. [In]: Fritz Fellner: Geschichtsschreibung und nationale Identität. Probleme und Leistungen der österreichischen Geschichtswissenschaft. Wien: Böhlau,

2002. Pp. 293–322, footnotes. [Orig. publ. 1988.] [H.F., Jan. 18, 1851 Rostschin/Moravia – July 13, 1920 Vienna, teacher, Journalist, historian.]

41864. FRIEDLÄNDER, SAUL. *Das Judentum im Spiegel seiner kulturellen Umwelten.* Symposium zu Ehren von Saul Friedländer. Mit Beiträgen von Jan Assmann [et al.]. Hrsg. von Dieter Borchmeyer und Helmuth Kiesel. Neckargemünd: Edition Mnemosyne, 2002. 227 pp., notes. (Reihe 'GegenSatz', Bd. 5.) [Based on papers presented at a symposium in Dec. 2000, initiated by the Germanistisches Seminar at Heidelberg Univ. in honour of S.F. Incl.: Vorwort (eds., 5–9; on S.F.). Saul Friedländer und die Zukunft der Erinnerung (Hans Rudolf Vaget, 11–32). Two essays: on anti-judaism in Hellenistic literature (Jan Assmann, 33–54) and in the New Testament (Klaus Berger, 55–70). Further essays are listed according to subject.]

41865. FRIEDLANDER, ELIZABETH. PAUCKER, PAULINE: *Elizabeth Friedlander: The art of understatement.* [In]: Imprimatur. Ein Jahrbuch für Bücherfreunde, Neue Folge XVII – 2002, München, 2002. Pp. 196–218, illus., notes. [On E.F.'s life and work.] [E.F., graphic designer, data see No. 36827/YB XLIV.]

41866. FROMM, ERICH. LÉVY, ALFRED: *Erich Fromm. Humanist zwischen Tradition und Utopie.* Würzburg: Königshausen & Neumann, 2002. 265 pp., footnotes. [Cont. the sections: I. Von der Psychoanalyse zur analytischen Sozialpsychologie. II. Vom Judentum und Christentum zur Religion ohne Gott. Mythen und Träume; incl. also a biographical chap.] [E.F., March 23, 1900 Frankfurt am Main – March 18, 1980 Muralto/Switzerland, Psychoanalyst, in 1934 emigr. to the US, in 1949 to Mexico City, since 1974 in Switzerland.]

——— FROMM-REICHMANN, FRIEDA. MÜLLER, THOMAS: *Frieda Fromm-Reichmann (1889–1957)* Jüdische Ärztin, ehemalige Dresdnerin, emigrierende Psychoanalytikerin, verfilmte Romanfigur. [See in No. 41756.]

——— GANS, EDUARD. WASZEK, NORBERT: *Eduard Gans: Berlin – Paris – Berlin.* [See in No. 41794.]

41867. GANS, EDUARD. : *Eduard Gans (1797–1839). Politischer Professor zwischen Restauration und Vormärz.* Hrsg. von Reinhard Blänkner, Gerhard Göhler und Norbert Waszek. Leipzig: Leipziger Univ.-Verl., 2002. 410 pp., illus. (Deutsch-französische Kulturbibliothek, Bd. 15.) [Cont. 15 papers presented at a symposium of the Werner Reimers Stiftung, Bad Homburg, in June 1995; selected essays (some titles abbr.): Einleitung: Eduard Gans (eds., 9–20). Börne, Heine, Gans: Drei deutsch-jüdische Intellektuelle zwischen Deutschland und Frankreich im Spannungsfeld von Akkulturation, Politik und Kulturtransfer (Michael Werner, 41–56). Hegel und die jüdische Intelligenz (Willi Jasper, 57–70), Eduard Gans und die hegelianischen Ursprünge der 'Wissenschaft des Judentums' (Norbert Waszek, 71–104).]

41868. GEIGER, LUDWIG. KÖNIG, CHRISTOPH: *Aufklärungsgeschichte: Bemerkungen zu Judentum, Philologie und Goethe bei Ludwig Geiger.* [In]: German literature, Jewish critics [see No. 41764]. Pp. 59–78, notes. [Article is followed by: Vom wahren Weg: Eine Respondenz (Amir Eshel, 79–86); also by the panelists' commentary and discussion (87–99).]

41869. GEIST, EDWIN. KAISER, REINHARD: *Man soll Träumende nicht wecken.* Auf der Suche nach Edwin Geist: Ein bislang vergessener deutscher Komponist, den die Nazis um Leben, Familie und Werke brachten, findet seinen Weg zurück in die Opernhäuser. [In]: 'FAZ', Nr. 46, Frankfurt am Main, 23. Feb. 2002. P. 49, port. [Edwin Ernst Moritz G., July 31, 1902 Berlin – Dec. 1942 Ghetto of Kaunas/Lithuania, composer.]

——— GOLDSTEIN, MORITZ. *Deutsch-jüdischer Parnaß. Rekonstruktion einer Debatte.* [See No. 40845.]

41870. GOLDSTÜCKER, EDUARD: *Die russische Revolution. Hoffnung und Enttäuschung.* Eduard Goldstücker zum Gedenken. Hrsg. von Erhard Roy Wiehn. Konstanz: Hartung-Gorre, 2001. 52 pp., frontis. [Cont.: Nüchterne Hoffnung (ed., 7–12). Die russische Revolution (personal reminiscences of the years 1935–1968 (lecture given at Konstanz Univ. in 1984). Über "Metamorphosen der Demokratie" (Maria Schorpp, 28–30). Zum Verlust eines Freundes (Karoline von Graevenitz, 31–33). Eduard Goldstücker: Vita und Schriften (34–35).] [E.G., May 30, 1913 Podbiel

(Slovakia) – Oct. 24, 2000 (?) Prague, Diplomat, Prof. of German literature, emigr. 1939 via Poland to the UK, 1945 returned to Prague, 1953–1955 imprisoned, 1968 emigr. via Vienna to the UK, 1969–1978 Prof. at Sussex Univ., 1991 returned to Prague.]

41871. GOMBRICH, ERNST. DOD, BERNARD [et al.]: *In memoriam: Sir Ernst Gombrich.* [In]: Tate: the art magazine, Vol. 28, London, Spring 2002.

41872. GOMBRICH, ERNST. WIEGAND, WILFRIED: *Der Lessing der Kunst. Zum Tod von Ernst Gombrich.* [In]: Deutsche Akademie für Sprache und Dichtung, Jahrbuch 2001, Göttingen, 2001. Pp. 201–204. [E.G., art historian, for data see No. 40519/YB No. XLVII.]

41873. GRAB, WALTER. DINER, DAN: *Weder Heimat noch Exil – Walter Grab zum Gedenken.* [In]: Tel Aviver Jahrbuch für deutsche Geschichte XXX, (2002) Göttingen, 2002. Pp. 361–368.

41874. GRADENWITZ, PETER. RIETHMÜLLER, ALBRECHT: *Zum Gedenken an Peter Gradenwitz (1910–2001).* [In]: Die Musikforschung, Jg. 55, H. 3, Kassel, 2002. P. 237. [P.G., Jan. 24, 1910 Berlin – July 27, 2001, Tel Aviv, musicologist, composer, emigr. to the UK in 1934, to Palestine in 1936, 1980–2000 Hon. Prof. at Freiburg Univ.]

41875. GRAETZ, PAUL. *Heimweh nach Berlin. Paul Graetz (1890–1937).* CD-Edition "Vertriebene Deutsch-jüdische Schauspieler. Neckargemünd: Edition Mnemosyne, 2002. 2 CDs. [Booklet (51 pp., illus., facsims.) incl. texts by Paul Graetz, Walter Mehring; Paule Graetz – ein Stück Berlin (Volker Kühn, 8–32). CD 1: Heimweh nach Berlin (texts by Paul Graetz, Friedrich Hollaender, Walter Mehring, Karl Schnog, Kurt Tucholsky et al., and chansons from orig. recordings of the 1920s and early 1930s). CD 2: Und wo hab ick Murmeln jespielt? Feature über Paul Graetz von Volker Kühn. Eine Produktion des DeutschlandRadio/DLF Köln 2002.] [P.G., 1890 Berlin – Feb. 1937 Hollywood, actor, cabaret singer, member of Max Reinhardt's cabaret "Schall und Rauch", emigr. in 1933 to the UK, in 1935 to the US, attempting unsuccessfully a new film career in Hollywood.]

41876. GUMBEL, EMIL JULIUS. BRENNER, ARTHUR DAVID: *Emil J. Gumbel: Weimar German pacifist and professor.* Boston: Brill, 2001. XVIII, 227 pp., appendixes, footnotes, bibl. (199– 220), index. (Studies in Central European histories.) [E.J.G., 1891 Munich – 1966 New York, mathematician, pacifist, socialist, studied in Munich and Heidelberg where he was suspended because of his political activities, worked in France during the 1930s, emigr. to New York in 1940 where Einstein interceded on his behalf and secured him a position as professor of statistics at the New School for Social Research.]

41877. HABERER, OSCAR. RUCH, MARTIN: *Der Offenburger Künstler Oscar Haberer (1867–1932): "Prototyp des Besten, das in der jüdischen Seele lebt …"* [In]: Die Ortenau, Bd. 82, Offenburg, 2002. Pp. 505–518, illus., port., notes. [O.H., 1867 Offenburg – 1932 Berlin, painter, designer, illustrator, lived in Berlin from 1914.]

41878. HARTWIG, MELA. FRAISL, BETTINA: *Mela Hartwig.* Wien: Passagen, 2002. 366 pp., bibl. (347–366). (Studien zur Moderne, 17.) [See also the first publ. of M.H.'s first novel (written in 1930/1931) dealing with a female office worker: Bin ich ein überflüssiger Mensch? Roman. Mit einem Nachwort von Bettina Fraisl. Graz: Droschl, 2001. 171 pp. (Nachwort (157–171, notes) deals with M.H.'s life.).] [M.H., Oct. 10, 1893 Vienna – April 24, 1967 London, orig. Melanie Herzl, daughter of the the author Theodor Herzl, who in 1895 converted to Catholicism with her family, actress, writer, emigr. with her husband Robert Spira 1938 to London.]

41879. HASE, ANNEMARIE. *Annemarie Hase (1900–1971).* CD-Edition "Vertriebene deutsch-jüdische Schauspieler". Hrsg. im Zusammenarbeit mit Volker Kuhn [et al.] von Wolfgang M. Schwiedrzik. Neckargemünd: Edition Mnemosyne, 1999. 2 CDs. [Booklet (51 pp., illus., facsims.) incl. a biographical essay (Wolfgang M. Schwiedrzik, 11–50). CD 1: Das Zersägen einer lebenden Dame. Chansons von Friedrich Hollaender, Klabund, Marcellus Schiller, Kurt Tucholsky et al. (incl. two chansons recorded in 1931, others were recorded 1959/1960 in the GDR). Frau Wernecke. Sendungen der BBC – Aus dem Londoner Exil. Texte von Bruno Adler und Egon Larsen. Wo kommen die Löcher im Käse her? Texte von Kurt Tucholsky und Joachim Ringelnatz. CD 2: Das

Zersägen einer lebenden Dame. Die Kabarettistin Annemarie Hase. Feature von Wolfgang M. Schwiedrzik. Eine Produktion des DeutschlandRadio/DLF Köln (broadcasted March 19, 1999).] [A.H., orig. Hirsch, 1900 Berlin – Feb. 22, 1971 Berlin (West), actress, cabaret singer, member of Max Reinhardt's "Wilde Bühne", after 1933 performed in the Jüdischer Kulturbund, emigr. in 1936 to the UK, active member of "Freier Deutscher Kulturbund" in London, 1940–1944 speaker ("Frau Wernecke") in the German BBC radio programme, returned to Berlin in 1947.]

41880. HEINE, HEINRICH. *A companion to the works of Heinrich Heine.* Ed. by Roger Cook. Rochester, NY: Camden House, 2002. XII, 373 pp., notes, bibl., index. (Studies in German literature, linguistics, and culture.) [Incl. chaps.: Troubled apostate: Heine's conversion and its consequences (Robert C. Holub). Heine and Jewish culture: the poetics of appropriation (Jeffrey A. Grossman).]

41881. HEINE, HEINRICH. *Heinrich Heines Werk im Urteil seiner Zeitgenossen. Bd. 7: Rezensionen und Notizen zu Heines Werken aus den Jahren November 1841 bis Dezember 1843. Bd. 8: Rezensionen und Notizen zu Heines Werken aus den Jahren 1844 bis 1845.* Hrsg. und eingel. von Sikander Singh. Stuttgart: Metzler, 2002. 2 vols., XXII, 423 pp.; XXV, 524 pp. (Heine Studien.)

41882. HEINE, HEINRICH. *Heinrich Heine auf Helgoland.* Briefe, Berichte und Bilder aus den ersten Jahren des Seebads Helgoland. Gesammelt und hrsg. von Pastor Eckhard Wallmann, Helgoland. Helgoland: Verlag der ev. Kirchengemeinde, 2002. 48 pp., illus., footnotes.

41883. HEINE, HEINRICH. HOFMANN, MICHAEL: *Götter im Exil im Vor- und Nachmärz. Bruch oder Kontinuität? Zur Entwicklung eines Motivs bei Heinrich Heine.* [In]: Vormärz – Nachmärz. Bruch oder Kontinuität? Vorträge des Symposions des Forum Vormärz Forschung e.V. vom 19. bis 21. November 1998 an der Universität Paderborn. Hrsg. von Nobert Otto Eke [et al.]. Bielefeld: Aisthesis Verl., 2000. (Vormärz-Studien V.) Pp. 169–184. [Also in this book: Heine's geschichtsphilosophisches Denken im Kontext von Vor- und Nachmärz (Jürgen Ferner, 185–212).]

41884. HEINE, HEINRICH. *Literarische Fundstücke. Wiederentdeckungen und Neuentdeckungen.* Festschrift für Manfred Windfuhr. Hrsg. von Ariane Neuhaus-Koch, Gertrude Cepl-Kaufmann. Heidelberg: Universitätsverlag C. Winter, 2002. 527 pp., footnotes. [Incl.: "auf Requisizion unserer Regierung konfiszirt". Heine und der Zensurfall Hoffmann (Hartmut Steinecke, 88–106). Ein Lichtstrahl aus dem Dunkeln. Zur Judenkritik in Heines "Lutezia" (Hiroshi Kiba, 107–142. See also No. 41940.]

41885. HEINE, HEINRICH. PETERS, GEORGE F.: *The highways and byways of Heine research today.* Review essay. [In]: German Studies Review, Vol. 25, No. 3, Northfield, MN, Oct. 2002. Pp. 569–576.

41886. HEINE, HEINRICH. SINGH, SIKANDER: *Die zeitgenössische Rezeption der Werke Heinrich Heines (1821–1856).* Düsseldorf: Privately printed, 2002. XXII, 349 pp., footnotes, bibl. (333–347). Düss., Univ., Diss., 2002. [Available at Düsseldorf Univ. Library.]

41887. HEINE, HEINRICH & MARX, KARL. TAUBER, ZVI: *Remarks on the relationship between Heine and Marx in 1844.* [In]: Tel Aviver Jahrbuch für deutsche Geschichte XXX (2002), Göttingen, 2002. Pp. 402–413. [Lecture, delivered in honour and memory of Walter Grab.]

41888. HENSEL, FANNY. BORCHARD, BEATRIX/SCHWARZ-DANUBER, MONIKA: *Fanny Hensel geb. Mendelssohn Bartholdy. Komponieren zwischen Gesellschaftsideal und romantischer Musikästhetik.* Stuttgart: Metzler, 1999. XXV, 341 pp., illus., music. [Cont. 23 essays, some dealing with the Jewish background of Fanny and Felix and its sociological impact (Julius H. Schoeps, Eva Maria Thimme).] [Cf.: Bespr. (Thomas Schmidt-Beste) [in]: Die Musikforschung, Jg. 54, Kassel. 2001, pp. 85–87.]

41889. HEYM, STEFAN. BELTZ, WALTER: *Träumen von Himmel und Erde.* Theologische Fragen an das Werk von Stefan Heym. [In]: Freiburger Rundbrief, N.F., Jg. 9, H. 4, Freiburg, 2002. Pp. 269.

41890. HIRSCH, KARL JAKOB. *Karl Jakob Hirsch. Expressionistische Grafik.* Stationen im Leben eines deutsch-jüdischen Künstlers. [Hrsg.: Altonaer Museum in Hamburg – Norddeutsches Landesmuseum. Ausstellung und Katalog: Anne Mahn]. Hamburg: Altonaer Museum in Hamburg – Norddeutsches Landesmuseum, 2002. 67 pp., illus., notes, bibl. [Incl. biography K.J.H. (11–59); see also No. 42194.]

41891. HOFMANNSTHAL, HUGO VON. *A companion to the works of Hugo von Hofmannsthal.* Ed. by Thomas A. Kovach. Rochester, NY: Camden House, 2002. XVII, 265 pp., illus., notes, bibl., index. (Studies in German literature, linguistics, and culture.) [Incl. 12 essays on different aspects of H.'s work.]

41892. HOHENEMSER, KURT. RAMMER, GERHARD: *Der Aerodynamiker Kurt Hohenemser.* Befragt von Gerhard Rammer. [In]: 'N.T.M.', Internationale Zeitschrift für Geschiche und Ethik der Naturwissenschaften, Technik und Medizin, Vol. 10, Nr. 2, Boston, 2002. Pp. 78–101, footnotes. port. [K.H., Jan. 3, 1906 Berlin – April 7, 2001, St. Louis, MO, son of a Jewish father, Prof. of Aerodynamics, expelled from Göttingen Univ. in Oct. 1933, emigr. 1947 to the US.]

41893. JACOBS, DORE. ROSEMAN, MARK: *Ein Mensch in Bewegung: Dore Jacobs (1894–1978).* [In]: Essener Beiträge, Bd. 114, Essen, 2002. Pp. 73–108, footnotes, illus. [D.J., née Marcus, 1894 Essen – 1979 Essen, teacher of rhythmics, together with her husband Arthur founder and leader of the Socialist community 'Bund. Gemeinschaft für sozialistisches Leben'.]

41894. KAFKA, FRANZ. ADLER, JEREMY: *Franz Kafka.* Woodstock, NY: Overlook Press, 2002. IX, 164 pp., illus., ports., facsims., chronol., bibl. (153–158). (Overlook illustrated lives.)

41895. KAFKA, FRANZ. *A companion to the works of Franz Kafka.* Ed. by James Rolleston. Rochester, NY: Camden House, 2002. XVI, 372 pp., notes, bibl., index. (Studies in German literature, linguistics, and culture.) [A collection of articles by 15 authors; incl.: A dream of Jewishness denied: Kafka's tumor and 'Ein Landarzt' (Sander L. Gilman).]

41896. KAFKA, FRANZ. *The Cambridge companion to Kafka.* Ed. by Julian Preece. Cambridge; New York: Cambridge Univ. Press, 2002. XIX, 254 pp., chronol., bibl., index. (Cambridge companions to literature.)

41897. KAFKA, FRANZ. PREECE, JULIAN: *Practising 'binding girls with writing': Kafka's failed correspondence with Hedwig Weiler.* [In]: Journal of European Studies, Vol. 32, Nos. 125–126, Chalfont St. Giles, June/Sept. 2002. Pp. 209–221, notes.

41898. KAFKA, FRANZ. SOKEL, WALTER H.: *The myth of power and the self: essays on Franz Kafka.* Detroit, MI: Wayne State Univ. Press, 2002. 334 pp., notes, bibl., index. [Incl. biographical essays.]

41899. KAFKA, FRANZ. STACH, REINER: *Kafka. Die Jahre der Entscheidungen.* Frankfurt am Main: S. Fischer, 2002. XXVII, 671 pp., illus., bibl. (646–658). [Biography, covers the years 1910–1915.]

41900. KAFKA, HANS: *Hollywood calling. Die Aufbau-Kolumne zum Film-Exil.* Ausgewählt und eingeführt von Roland Jaeger. Hamburg: ConferencePoint Verlag; Norderstedt: Books on Demand, 2002. 129 pp., illus., facsims., index. [Incl.: Hans (John) Kafka und seine Hollywood-Kolumne im 'Aufbau' (Ronald Jaeger, 7–42). Auszüge aus der 'Aufbau'-Kolumne 'Hollywood calling – Hans Kafka speaking' (43–122; texts written between 1941 and 1947).] [H.K., Dec. 26, 1902 Vienna – Feb. 5, 1974 Munich (suicide), author, film critic, screenwright, lived in the 1920s in Berlin, emigr. 1936 to the UK, 1937 to France, 1940 to the US, returned 1958 to Munich on assignment of 'Variety'.]

41901. KAHN, LUDWIG. SCHELLINGER, UWE: *Faszinosum, Filou und Forschungsobjekt: Das erstaunliche Leben des Hellsehers Ludwig Kahn (1873 – ca. 1966).* [In]: Die Ortenau, Bd. 82, Offenburg/Baden, 2002.Pp. 429–468, illus., facsims., notes. [1873 Offenburg – 1966 New York, clairvoyant, at times rather dubious representative of Parapsychology and swindler, lived in numerous European countries and in the US.]

41902. KAHN, OTTO. COLLINS, THERESA M.: *Otto Kahn: art, money, and modern time.* Chapel Hill; London: Univ. of North Carolina Press, 2002. XII, 383 pp., illus., ports., notes, bibl. (343–366), index. [Based on author's Ph.D. thesis, New York Univ., 1998.] [O.K., 1867 Mannheim – 1934 New York, banker, philanthropist, legendary patron of the arts, trained in London, went to the US in 1893, joined Kuhn, Loeb & Co in New York, helped reorganise the US railway system; also a major financial contributor to the Metropolitan Opera and to many artists as well as Hollywood films.]

41903. KALISCHER, CLEMENS. *Clemens Kalischer.* Ed. by/Hrsg. von Denis Brudna & Norbert Bunge. Ostfildern-Ruit: Hatje Cantz, 2002. 176 pp. [Incl. mostly photographs; introd. essay by Miles Unger, interview with the artist in 1999 conducted by Norbert Bunge. All texts in German and English.] [C.K., b. 1921 in Lindau/Lake Constance, photographer, emigr. 1933 from Berlin via Switzerland to Paris, 1939–1942 imprisoned in several French internment camps, 1942 escaped to the US through the help of Varian Fry; is living in Stockbridge, MA.]

41904. KALLMANN, FRANZ JOSEF. MILDENBERGER, FLORIAN: *Auf der Spur des "scientific pursuit".* *Franz Josef Kallmann (1897–1965) und die rassehygienische Forschung.* [In]: Medizinhistorisches Journal, Jg. 37, Jena, 2002. Pp. 183–200, footnotes. [Article examines K.'s involvement with Eugenics and his close co-operation with the Reach Foundation for Psychiatry in Munich and its head Ernst Rüdin.] [F.J.K., 1897 Neumarkt/Silesia – 1965 New York, psychiatrist, emigr. 1936 to the US.]

41905. KANTOROWICZ, ERNST H.. SERRIER, THOMAS: *D'ou sortira Kantorowicz? Historiens juifs à Posen avant 1914: figures et milieu.* [In]: Les cahiers du judaisme, No. 11, Paris, 2002. Pp. 83–96, notes. [On. E.K., Jacob Caro, Adolf Warschauer, Arthur Kronthal.]

——— KESTENBERG-GLADSTEIN, RUTH. KUHRAU-NEUMÄRKER, DOROTHEA: *In memoriam Ruth Gladstein.* [See in No. 41087.]

41906. KLEMPERER, VICTOR. CHAMBERLIN, BREWSTER: *The American reception of the Klemperer diaries.* [In]: WerkstattGeschichte, Jg. 9, H. 26, Hamburg, 2000. Pp. 80–86, footnotes.

41907. KLEMPERER, VICTOR. REUTER, BERNARD: *"Der leidet wie ein ganz deutscher Deutscher": Interview mit Dr. Hadwig Klemperer, Dresden, über Victor Klemperer und die DDR.* [In]: The German Quarterly, Vol. 75, No. 4, Riverside, CA, Fall 2002. Pp. 361– 378, port., notes. [Interview given by K.'s second wife on July 23, 2001.]

41908. KLÜGER, RUTH. BRAUN, MICHAEL: *"Für ein Kind war das anders".* Kindheit in der Holocaust-Literatur: Louis Begleys 'Lügen in den Zeiten des Krieges' (1991/94) und Ruth Klügers 'weiter leben. Eine Jugend' (1992). [In]: Internationales Archiv für Sozialgeschichte der deutschen Literatur, Bd. 27, H. 1, Tübingen, 2002. Pp. 96–115, footnotes.

41909. KOFLER, LEO. JÜNKE, CHRISTOPH, ed.: *Am Beispiel Leo Koflers. Marxismus im 20. Jahrhundert.* Münster: Westfälisches Dampfboot, 2001. 329 pp., notes. [Cont. essays on K.'s life and work by Wolfgang Fritz Haug, Ulrich Brieler, Michael R. Krätke, Jakob Moneta, Günter Brakelmann, Hartmut Krauss, Rüdiger Dannemann, Sebastian herkommer, Werner Seppmann, Hans Heinz Holz, Wilfried Korngiebel, Horst Müller, Christoph Jünke, Reinhart Kößler, Roger Behrens.] [L.K., April 26, 1907 Chocimierz (Galicia) – July 29, 1995 Cologne, sociologist, philosopher, lived since 1915 in Vienna, 1938 fled to Switzerland, 1947 remigr. to Germany (East), professor at Halle University, 1950 dismissed, fled to West Germany, settled in Cologne, lecturer at the Kunstakademie, Cologne, and the Ruhr-Universität Bochum.]

41910. KOLMAR, GERTRUD. GOLDSMITH-REBER, TRUDIS: *"Vom einsamen Gebet in den Nächten des Herbstes 1940." Gertrud Kolmar (1894–1943) und Chaim Nachman Bialik (1873–193).* [In]: Preußens Himmel breitet seine Sterne ... [see No. 41991], Bd. 1. Pp. 319–337, notes.

41911. KOMPERT, LEOPOLD. VIVANCO, PABLO: *Leopold Kompert – Ein "jüdischer Volksschriftsteller"?* [In]: Trumah, Bd. 11, Heidelberg, 2001. Pp. 147–166, footnotes.

41912. KORTNER, FRITZ. *König Lear – Fritz Kortner.* CD-Edition "Vertriebene deutsch-jüdische Schauspieler". Produktion: Wolfgang M. Schwiedrzik. Neckargemünd: Edition Mnemosyne, 1999. 1 CD. [Booklet (51 pp., illus., facsims.) incl. one text by F.K., numerous texts on F.K. by Peter Stein, Klaus Völker, Alfred Braun. CD: König Lear (transl. by Wolf Graf Baudissin, directed by Wilhelm Semmelroth, with F.K. as King Lear); a radio production of the WDR Köln, 1958.]

41913. KRONSTEIN, ILI. *Die Welt der Ili Kronstein – the world of Ili Kronstein: Werke 1938–1943.* Hrsg. von Werner Hanak im Auftrag des Jüdischen Museums Wien. Vienna: Jüdisches Museums Wien,

2000. 112 pp., illus., port. [Catalogue of an exhibition held at the Jüdisches Museum Wien, Dec. 13 – March 25, 2001.] [I.K. 1897 Vienna – 1948 Switzerland, painter, fled to Liechtenstein in 1938, then Nice, 1940 detained in Gurs internment camp, managed to return to Liechtenstein, died from multiple sclerosis in 1948.]

41914. KUH, EPHRAIM MOSES. HORCH, HANS-OTTO: *Unvollendete 'Hedschra'. Zu Leben und Werk des Breslauer Lyrikers Ephraim Moses Kuh (1731–1790)*. [In]: Zeitenwenden [see No. 40902]. Pp. 143–162.

41915. LANDAUER, GUSTAV. KAUFFELDT, ROLF: *"Rückkehr in die Großstadt". Bemerkungen zu einem früh-expressionistischem Text Gustav Landauers*. [In]: Literarische Fundstücke [see No. 41881]. Pp. 224–235, footnotes.

41916. LANDAUER, GUSTAV. WILLEMS, JOACHIM: *Der "Passionsweg, den du Untergang nennst …" – Fragmentisierung und Vollendung in Gustav Landauers Biographie und Philosophie*. [In]: "… der den Erniedrigten aufrichtet aus dem Staube und aus dem Elend erhöht den Armen" [see No. 40844]. Pp. 194–216, notes.

41917. LANG, FRITZ. *Fritz Lang. Leben und Werk*. Bilder und Dokumente. Hrsg. von Rolf Aurich, Wolfgang Jacobsen, Cornelius Schnauber. Berlin: Filmmuseum Berlin – Deutsche Kinemathek; jovis Verlag, 2001. 512 pp., illus., facsims. [All texts in German, English and French.] [F.L., Dec. 5 1890 Vienna – Aug. 2, 1976 Los Angeles, son of a Jewish mother, scriptwriter, film director, producer, emigr. to France in 1933, to the US in 1934, returned to Germany for a few years during the 1950s.]

41918. LANIA, LEO: *Gewehre auf Reisen*. München: Andreas Krings/R & A, 2002. 125 pp., illus. [First publ. in the early 1920s; incl. a review of Kurt Tucholsky (1923).] [L.L., orig. Lazar Herman, 1896 Charkow – 1961 Munich, investigative journalist, since 1904 in Vienna, since 1921 in Berlin, emigr. 1933 to France, 1940 to the US, remigr. in the 1950s to Germany.]

41919. LASKER-SCHÜLER, ELSE: *Prosa. Das Hebräerland*. Bearb. von Karl Jürgen Skrodzki und Itta Shedletzky. Frankfurt am Main: Jüdischer Verlag, 2002. 580 pp., frontis., notes (471–580). (Else Lasker-Schüler Werke und Briefe, Kritische Ausgabe Bd. 5.)

41920. LEVETT, OSWALD . WINTHROP-YOUNG, GEOFFREY: *Am Rand der Uchronie: Oswald Levetts Verirrt in den Zeiten und die Frühphase der alternate history*. [In]: Modern Austrian Literature, Vol. 34, No. 3–4, Bowling Green OH, 2001. Pp. 21–43, notes, bibl. [On a novel orig. publ. 1933, new edns. 1984, 1996.] [O.L., orig. Oswald Franz Löwith, June 15, 1884, Baden nr. Vienna – 1942 Minsk (?), lawyer, writer, some-time collaborator of Leo Perutz, converted to Catholicism in 1933, publ. his science fiction novel 'Verirrt in den Zeiten', escaped to Belgium, 1942 deported to Minsk.]

41921. LEWALD, FANNY. VAN ORNAM, VANESSA: *Fanny Lewald and nineteenth-century construction of femininity*. New York; Frankfurt am Main: Lang, 2002. X, 192 pp., bibl. (North American studies in nineteenth-century German literature, Vol. 29.)

41922. LEWY, FRITZ: *Fritz Lewy – ein Leben für die Form*. Hrsg. von Michael Matzigkeit und Birgit Bernard. Düsseldorf: Theatermuseum, Dumont-Lindemann-Archiv, 2002. 358 pp., frontis., illus., bibl., chronol., facsims., footnotes. (Dokumente zur Theatergeschichte, Bd. 12.) [Cont.: Vorwort (Dietrich Schwarzkopf, 7). Fritz Lewy – ein Werk von Bedeutung (Michael Matzigkeit/Birgit Bernard, 8–10). Zwischen Bühne, Kunst und Business 1911–1926 (Michael Matzigkeit, 12–60). Fritz Lewy – Gebrauchsgraphik und Avantgarde (Ute Brüning, 181–205). Beim Westdeutschen Rundfunk 1927–1933 (207–271; contribs. by Birgit Bernard, Renate Schumacher, Ute Brüning, Anne Gantefürher-Trier). Exil 1933–1950 (273–335; contribs by Patrik von zur Mühlen, Ingrid L. Severin, Noel Martin). Werkverzeichnis (337–344).] [F.L., May 22, 1893 Essen – June 12, 1950 Cincinnati, graphic artist, set designer, emigr. 1933 to Spain, fled 1938 via France and Belgium to the US, settled in Cincinnati.]

41923. LIEBERMANN, MAX. GRONAU, DIETRICH: *Max Liebermann*. Eine Biographie. Frankfurt am Main: Fischer Taschenbuch Verlag, 2001. 414 pp., illus., notes (379–388), bibl., chronol. index. Orig.-Ausg.

41924. LIND, JAKOV. *Writing after Hitler: the work of Jakov Lind*. Ed. by Andrea Hammel, Silke Hassler and Edward Timms. Cardiff: Univ. of Wales Press, 2001. XII, 222., illus., ports., facsims., notes, bibl. (199–213). [Collection of essays by various authors, some dealing with L.'s literary career, his refugee years in the Netherlands, Zionism; the representation of the Holocaust in his fictional writings; his reception in Austria and Germany.] [J.L., b. 1927 in Vienna, writer, artist, went to England in 1954 after having spent some of the war years in the Netherlands and some post-war years in Palestine and Austria; now lives in London.]

41925. LÖWENSTEIN, KARL. LANG, MARKUS: *Juristen unerwünscht? Karl Loewenstein und die (nicht-)Aufnahme deutscher Juristen in der amerikanischen Rechtswissenschaft nach 1933*. [In]: Politisches Denken. Jahrbuch 2003. Hrsg. von Karl Graf Ballestrem [et al.], Stuttgart, 2002. Pp. 55–84, footnotes, bibl. [K.L., Nov. 9, 1891 Munich – July 10, 1973 Heidelberg, prof. of law and political science, lawyer, emigr. to the US in 1933, from the 1950ies prof. at various universitites in Germany, Japan, Mexico.]

41926. LÖWENTHAL, LEO. JANSEN, PETER-ERWIN: *Leo Löwenthal – ein optimistischer Pessimist*. [In]: Zeitschrift für kritische Theorie, Jg. 8, H. 15, Lüneburg, 2002. Pp. 7–40, illus., footnotes. [L.L., 1900–1993, for data see No. 31087/YB XXXIX.]

41927. LOEWY, HANNO: *Taxi nach Auschwitz*. Feuilletons. Berlin: Philo, 2002. 191 pp., illus. (Philo Litera.) [H.L., April 24, Krefeld – Sept. 17, 2002 Frankfurt am Main, librarian, archivist, publicist, initiator and author of exile studies, emigr. 1936 to Palestine, remigr. to Germany 1956, 1995–2000 founding director of the Fritz Bauer Institute, Frankfurt am Main, Dr.hc. Univ. of Osnabrück 1989.]

41928. LOWENFELD, HENRY. MÜLLER, THOMAS: *Von Charlottenburg zum Central Park West. Henry Lowenfeld und die Psychoanalyse in Berlin, Prag und New York*. Frankfurt am Main: Edition Déjà-vu, 2000. 344 pp., footnotes, facsims., ports., bibl., index. (Edition Déjà-vu Reihe Übertragung, Bd. 1.)

41929. LUKÁCS, GEORG. KÓKAI, KÁROLY: *Im Nebel. Der junge Georg Lukács und Wien*. Wien: Böhlau, 2002. 272 pp., footnotes, bibl. [Deals with the years 1909–1918; incl. an essay entitled 'Die Frage nach dem Judentum' (169–179).]

41930. LUSTIGER, ARNO: *"Wir werden nicht untergehen". Zur jüdischen Geschichte*. München: Ullstein, 2002. 272 pp. [A collection of essays arranged under the sections: Biographisches (cont.: Lebenslauf (7–8). Die KZ, die Todesmärsche und meine Befreiung (9–40). Jüdische Arbeiterbewegung und Kultur (41–55). Spanischer Bürgerkrieg (56–82). Juden in Polen (83–91). Juden in der Sowjetunion (92–114). Schoa und Judenretter (115–161). Jüdische Widerstandskämpfer und Soldaten (162–219). Verleugner des Widerstandes, jüdischer Selbsthass, Antizionisten (220–253). Jüdische Widerstands- und Arbeiterlieder (254–270).] [A.L., b. May 7, 1924 in Bedzin/Poland, during World War II member of the Polish Underground Movement, survived various forced labour camps, after liberation lived in a DP-camp in Frankfurt-Zeilsheim, founding member of the post-1945 Frankfurt Jewish community, for many years Chairman of the 'Freunde und Förderer des Leo Baeck Instituts in Deutschland'. Selected essays are listed according to subject.]

41931. LUXEMBURG, ROSA. ITO, NARIHIKO [et al.], eds.: *Rosa Luxemburg im internationalen Diskurs*. Internationale Rosa-Luxemburg-Gesellschaft in Chicago, Tampere, Berlin und Zürich (1998–2000). Berlin: Dietz, 2002. 303 pp., notes. [Incl. 38 contribs.]

41932. LUXEMBURG, ROSA. SCHARRER, MANFRED: *Rosa Luxemburg – "Die Revolution ist großartig, alles andere ist Quark"*. [In]: Jahrbuch für Historische Kommunismusforschung 2000/2001, Berlin, 2001. pp. 391–408. [In the same issue: Rosa Luxemburg – demokratische Sozialistin oder Bolschewistin? (Ottokar Luban, 409–420).]

41933. LUXEMBURG, ROSA. SCHARRER, MANFRED: *"Freiheit ist immer …". Die Legende von Rosa & Karl*. Berlin: Transit, 2002. 190 pp., illus., footnotes.

41934. MAHLER, GUSTAV. MITCHELL, DONALD: *Gustav Mahler: songs and symphonies of life and death*. Rochester, NY: Univ. of Rochester Press; Woodbridge, Suffolk (UK): Boydell and Brewer, 2002. 664 pp., illus., ports., facsims., scores, bibl. (639–643), indexes. [For orig. 1985 edn. which appeared as vol. 3 of a Mahler series see No. 22649/YB XXXI.]

41935. MARCUSE, HERBERT: *Nachgelassene Schriften*. Band 3: *Philosophie und Psychoanalyse*. Hrsg. und mit einem Vorwort von Peter-Erwin Jansen. Mit einer einleitenden Studie von Alfred Schmidt. Aus dem Amerik. von Cornelia Lösch. Lüneburg: zu Klampen, 2002. 233 pp., illus. [Incl.: Einleitende Studie (Alfred Schmidt, 15–94).]

41936. MARX, KARL. MEHRING, FRANZ: *Karl Marx*. Geschichte seines Lebens. Essen: Arbeiterpresse-Verl., 2001. 523 pp., notes (503–511), chronol., index. [First publ. 1918. Incl.: Vorwort des Herausgebers (Wolfgang Zimmermann, 9–13).]

41937. MEIDNER, LUDWIG & ELSE. *Ludwig und Else Meidner*. [Hrsg.: Georg Heuberger, Bearb.: Erik Riedel]. Frankfurt am Main: Jüd. Museum der Stadt Frankfurt am Main, 2002. 111 pp., ports., illus., bibl. [Catalogue for exhibition held in Jüdisches Museum, Frankfurt am Main and in The Ben Uri Gallery, London; incl. contribs. on life and work of the two artists and on their biographies (in German and English).]

41938. MEITNER, LISE. SEXL, LORE/HARDY, ANNE: *Lise Meitner*. Dargestellt von Lore Sexl und Anne Hardy. Reinbek bei Hamburg: Rowohlt Taschenbuch Verlag, 2002. 155 pp., illus., notes, bibl. (rowohlts monographien.) Orig.-Ausg.

41939. MENDELSSOHN, FELIX. STINSON, RUSSELL: *Mendelssohns große Reise. Ein Beitrag zur Rezeption von Bachs Orgelwerken.* [In]: Bach-Jahrbuch, Jg. 88, Leipzig, 2002. Pp. 119–137, footnotes, music.

41940. MERZ, KONRAD. BIERWIRTH, SABINE: *Der fast vergessene Schriftsteller Konrad Merz und sein Lieblingsdichter Heinrich Heine – zwei Deutsche, zwei jüdische Emigranten.* [In]: Literarische Fundstücke [see No. 41884]. Pp. 333–358, footnotes. [K.M., orig. Kurt Lehmann, April 2, 1908 Berlin – Nov. 30, 1999 Pumerend, Netherlands, writer, emigr. to the Netherlands in 1934, survived in hiding in Ilpendam.]

41941. MEYER, KLAUS. WOOD, ANTONY: *Klaus Meyer*. A gifted printmaker, he found new ways of showing how a work of art takes shape. Obituary. [In]: The Guardian, London, June 24, 2002. P. 20, illus. [K.M., Sept. 16, 1918 Berlin – June 7, 2002 London, graphic artist, painter, printmaker, emigr. to the UK in 1938.]

41942. MILLER, SUSANNE. LEMKE-MÜLLER, SABINE: *Susanne Miller – ein Porträt.* [In]: Antisemitische und antijudaistische Motive bei Denkern der Aufklärung. Susanne Miller zum 85. Geburtstag [see No. 42113.]. Pp. 13–20. [S.M., b. 1915 in Sofia, Socialist, historian, follower of the philosopher Leonard Nelson, grew up in Vienna, emigr. in the 1930s to London, 1946 returned with Willi Eichler, the Leader of the Internationaler Sozialistischer Kampfbund (ISK), to Cologne, since then leading member of the SPD.]

41943. MORGENSTERN, SOMA. NACHBAUR, PETRA: *Soma Morgenstern und Max Riccabona: ein Briefwechsel.* [In]: Exil, Jg. 21, Nr. 2, 2001, Frankfurt am Main, 2002. Pp. 74–81.

41944. MOSES, STEFAN. *Stefan Moses*. Die Monographie. Hrsg. von Ulrich Pohlmann und Matthias Harder. Mit Texten von Marion Ackermann [et al.]. München: Schirmer/Mosel, 2002. 334 pp. [See also No. 41827.] [St.M., b. 1928 in Liegnitz, son of a Jewish father, portrait and theatre photographer, has lived in Munich since 1950.]

41945. NEUBERGER, JOSEF. SCHMALHAUSEN, BERND: *Josef Neuberger (1902–1977)*. Ein Leben für die menschliche Justiz. Baden-Baden: Nomos, 2002. IX, 141 pp., illus., footnotes, bibl. (Juristische Zeitgeschichte, Abt. 4: Leben und Werk – Biographien und Werkanalysen, Bd. 6.) [J.N., Oct. 11, 1902 Antwerp – Jan. 12, 1977 Düsseldorf, jurist, Social Democrat, Zionist, lived since 1914 in Düsseldorf, emigr. Nov. 1938 via Netherlands to Palestine, remigr. 1952 to Düsseldorf, Minister of Justice of North-Rhine-Westphalia 1966–1972.]

41946. NEUMANN, FRANZ. KELLY, DUNCAN: *Rethinking Franz Neumann's Route to 'Behemoth'.* [In]: History of Political Thought, Vol. XXIII, No. 3, London, 2002. Pp. 458–496, footnotes. [Incl. summary.]

41947. NOETHER, EMMY. HARGITTAI, ISTVÁN/HARGITTAI, MAGDOLNA: *Homage to Emmy Noether.* [In]: The Mathematical Intelligencer, Vol. 24, No. 1, New York, 2002. Pp. 48–49, illus.

41948. NOETHER, EMMY. KOREUBER, MECHTHILD/TOBIES, RENATE: *Emmy Noether. Begründerin einer mathematischen Schule.* [In]: Mitteilungen der Deutschen Mathematiker-Vereinigung, H. 3, Berlin, 2000. Pp. 8–21, illus., facsims., footnotes, bibl.

41949. NORDAU, MAX. UJVÁRI, HEDVIG: *Die exemplarische Schulkarriere eines 'deutschen' Juden im Pest des 19. Jahrhunderts: Max Nordau.* [In]: Zeitschrift für Religions- und Geistesgeschichte, Jg. 54, H. 2, Leiden, 2002. Pp. 138–153, footnotes.

41950. NORDEN, ALBERT. PODEWIN, NORBERT: *Der Rabbinersohn im SED-Politbüro. Albert Norden – Stationen eines ungewöhnlichen Lebens.* Berlin: Edition Ost, 2001. 437 pp., illus., notes, index. [A.N., Dec. 4, 1904 Myslowitz/Oppeln – May 30. 1982 Wandlitz, Communist, son of the Elberfeld Rabbi Joseph N., journalist, politician, in 1933 emigr. to Paris, after internment in 1940 failed to emigr. to Mexico, from 1941–1946 lived in the US, in 1946 returned to Berlin/East.]

41951. NOUSSIMBAUM, LEO. SAID, KURBAN: *Das Mädchen vom Goldenen Horn.* Roman. Mit einer biographischen Notiz des Autors und einem Nachwort von Radhia Shukrullah. München: Matthes & Seitz, 2001. 255 pp., frontis. [Incl.: Über den Autor: Kurban Said alias Leo Noussimbaum alias Muhammed Essad Bey (247–255). See also: Essad Bey: Mohammed. Biographie. Mit einem Vorwort von Barbara Frischmuth. Berlin: Aufbau Taschenbuch Verlag, 2002. IX, 435 pp. [Leo Noussimbaum/Lev Abramovic Nussenbaoum, pseudonym: Essad Bey, 1905 Baku/Aserbaidjan – 1942 Positano/Italy, writer, in his youth converted to Islam, fled via Istanbul, Rome and Paris to Berlin in the early 1920s, went to Austria in 1933, fled to Italy in 1938, author of 16 books in German, since 1935 with the pseudonym of Kurban Said.]

41952. NUSSBAUM, JAKOB. MÜLLER, CLAUDIA C.: *Jakob Nussbaum (1873–1936). Ein Frankfurter Maler im Spannungsfeld der Stilrichtungen.* Frankfurt am Main: Kramer, 2002. 412 pp., illus. (Studien zur Frankfurter Geschichte, Bd. 47.) Zugl.: Frankfurt am Main, Univ., Diss., 1999. [Part 2 = 1 CD-ROM, Catalogue Raisonnée.] [J.N., 1873 Rhina (Hesse) – 1936 Moshava Kinneret, painter, lived and worked from 1904 in Frankfurt am Main, 1933 emigr. to Palestine.]

41953. PAPPENHEIM, BERTHA: *Literarische und politische Texte.* Hrsg. von Lena Kugler und Albrecht Koschorke. Wien: Turia und Kant, 2002. 327 pp., notes, bibl., bibl. B.P. (Texte von Bertha Pappenheim.)

41954. PAPPENHEIM, BERTHA. BRENTZEL, MARIANNE: *Anno O. – Bertha Pappenheim.* Biographie. Göttingen: Wallstein, 2002. 319 pp., illus., notes, bibl., bibl. B.P., chronol., index. [B.P., Feb. 27, 1859 Vienna – May 28, 1936 Neu-Isenburg, writer, feminist, lifelong campaigner against the White Slave Trade, founder of the Jüdischer Frauenbund and the Mädchenheim des Jüdischen Frauenbundes, Neu-Isenburg.]

41955. PAULI, WOLFGANG. ENZ, CHARLES P.: *No time to be brief.* A scientific biography of Wolfgang Pauli. Oxford: Oxford Univ. Press, 2002. 581 pp. [W.P., 1900 Vienna – 1958 Zurich, nuclear physicist, Nobel Prize winner in Physics (1945).]

41956. PERUTZ, MAX FERDINAND. CRICK, FRANCIS: *Max Ferdinand Perutz.* [In]: Physics today, Vol. 55, No. 8, College Park, MD, Aug. 2002. Pp. 62–63, port. [Obituary.] [M.F.P., May 9, 1914 Vienna – Feb. 6, 2002 Cambridge, UK, Nobel Prize winner in chemistry (1962).]

41957. POPPER, KARL. MORGENSTERN, MARTIN/ZIMMER, ROBERT: *Karl Popper.* München: Dt. Taschenbuch-Verl., 2002, 191 pp., frontis., illus., facsims., bibl. [Biography.]

41958. POPPER, KARL. MORSCHER, EDGAR, ed.: *Was wir Karl R. Popper und seiner Philosophie verdanken.* Zu seinem 100. Geburtstag. Sankt Augustin: Academia Verlag, 2002. 501 pp., frontis., notes, index. (ProPhil, Projekte zur Philosophie, Bd. 4.) [Incl. 15 contribs.; also chap.: V. Persönliche Erinnerungen und Briefe (Paul Weingartner, 467–478; letters (479–494).]

41959. POPPER, KARL. OESER, ERHARD: *Sir Karl Popper 1902 – 1994.* [In]: Illustrierte Neue Welt, Nr. 6/7, Wien, Juni/Juli 2002. P. 12. [Biographical essay.]

41960. PRESSBURGER, EMERIC (EMMERICH). HERMAN, DAVID: *Three kinds of silence: the career of Emeric Pressburger.* [In]: The Jewish Quarterly, Vol. 49, No. 3, London, Autumn 2002. Pp. 39–45, illus. [E.P., 1902–1988, Hungarian-Jewish film director who worked in Germany with Billy Wilder and Max Ophüls, later made his name in England with films such as "The Red Shoes", "The Tales of Hoffmann".]

41961. PREUSS, HUGO. STIRK, PETER: *Hugo Preuss, German politicical thought and the Weimar Constitution.* [In]: History of Political Thought, Vol. XXIII, No. 3, London, 2002. Pp. 497–516, footnotes.

41962. RABINOVICI, DORON: *Credo und Credit.* Einmischungen. Frankfurt am Main: Suhrkamp, 2001. 157 pp., frontis., footnotes. (edition suhrkamp.) [A collection of essays, some previously publ.; most of them dealing with Jewish themes; incl. first publ. of following essays (some titles abbr.): 'Credo und Kredit. Oder Einige Überlegungen zum Antisemitismus (67–80). Ein Nocturno für Leo Perutz (22–47). Gedanken zur Leugnung der Vergangenheit (122–129; on Holocaust denial); also essays on Elias Canetti.]

41963. RATHENAU, FRITZ. RINK, THOMAS: *Fritz Rathenau als deutscher Beamter und Jude.* Hildesheim; New York: Olms, 2002. 307 pp., index, bibl. (279–301), index. (Haskala, Bd. 24.) Zugl.: Potsdam, Univ., Diss., 2001. [F.R., July 9, 1874 Berlin – Dec. 15, 1949 Bilthoven/Netherlands, cousin of Walther Rathenau, Prussian senior civil servant, member of the DVP, emigr. to the Netherlands in 1939, deported to Theresienstadt in 1943, after liberation returned to the Netherlands.]

41964. RATHENAU, WALTHER: *Die schönste Stadt der Welt.* Mit einem Nachwort von Rolf Sachsse. Berlin: Philo, 2002. 91 pp., illus., chronol. [On Berlin around 1900, first publ. 1902 in a collection of essays entitled 'Impressionen'.]

41965. RATHENAU, WALTHER. MICHALKA, WOLFGANG: *"Wir müssen unsere Wiedergeburt in uns selbst finden." Rathenau über Krieg und Katastrophe, Einkehr und Wiedergeburt.* [In]: Krieg, Frieden und Demokratie. Festschrift für Martin Vogt zum 65. Geburtstag. Hrsg. v. Christof Dipper [et al.]. Frankfurt am Main, 2001. Pp. 119–136, footnotes.

41966. RATHENAU, WALTHER. PAPPAS, CHARALAMBOS ALEXANDROS: *Den Krieg lenken: Walther Rathenau zwischen Wirtschaft und Krieg.* [In]: Helmut Konrad, ed.: Krieg, Medizin und Politik. Der Erste Weltkrieg und die österreichische Moderne. Wien: Passagen Verlag, 2000. Pp. 255–278, notes.

41967. RATHENAU, WALTHER. REICHEL, PETER: *Der Tod als Anti-Republikaner – Totenfeiern als Demonstration für die Republik: Friedrich Ebert, Walther Rathenau, Gustav Stresemann.* [In]: … der den Erniedrigten aufrichtet aus dem Staube und aus dem Elend erhöht den Armen" [see No. 40844]. Pp. 34–49, notes.

41968. REICH, WILHELM. *Der "Fall" Wilhelm Reich.* Beiträge zum Verhältnis von Psychoanalyse und Politik. Hrsg. von Karl Fallend und Bernd Nitschke. Überarb. und mit einem aktuellen Vorwort vers. Neuaufl. Gießen: Psychosozial-Verlag, 2002. 385 pp., notes, chronol., bibl., index. (Bibliothek der Psychoanalyse.) [First publ. 1997; incl. (some titles abbr.): Vorwort zur Neuausgabe (13–28, bibl.) I. Verfolgung, Vertreibung, Verleugnung. Historische Anmerkungen zum Schicksal eines 'Linksfreudianers'; cont.: Otto Fenichel und Wilhelm Reich. Wege einer politischen und wissenschaftlichen Freundschaft zweier 'Linksfreudianer' (Karl Fallend, 31–82). "Ich muß mich dagegen wehren, still kaltgestellt zu werden". Voraussetzungen, Begleitumstände und Folgen des Ausschlusses Wilhelm Reichs aus der DPG/IPV in den Jahren 1933/34 (Bernd Nitzschke, 83–140). Der "Fall" Reich als Exempel für Freuds Umgang mit abweichenden Schülertypus (Johannes Cremerius, 141–172). Psychoanalytiker in Deutschland 1933–1951. Ein unglückseliger Verein und eine Geschichte, die sich nicht selber schreibt (Helmut Dahmer, 173–193). II. Hommage und Kritik. Wilhelm Reichs körpertherapeutisches und (sexual-)politisches Erbe (197–345; cont. six contribs.). Bibliographie der Schriften Wilhelm Reichs (347–360).]

41969. REICH-RANICKI, MARCEL. DEMETZ, PETER: *On Marcel Reich-Ranicki*. [In]: German literature, Jewish critics [see No. 41764]. Pp. 289–302, notes.

41970. REICH-RANICKI, MARCEL. FRANZEN, GÜNTER: *Über Marcel Reich-Ranicki*. [In]: Die Neue Gesellschaft/Frankfurter Hefte, H. 10, Frankfurt am Main, 2002. Pp. 618–621, ports. [Cf.: Was ich empfinde. Über eine neue deutsche Mordphantasie, München und den Geist der Erzählung. Dankesrede zur Verleihung der Ehrendoktorwürde (Marcel Reich-Ranicki) [in]: 'FAZ', Nr. 159, Frankfurt am Main, 12. Juli 2002. P. 41.]

41971. REICH-RANICKI, MARCEL. MATT, PETER VON: *Der Kampf für die Literatur ist auch ein Kampf für die Freiheit*. [In]: 'FAZ', Nr. 208, Frankfurt am Main, 7. Sept. 2002. P. [Laudatio held on the bestowment of the Goethe Prize of the city of Frankfurt am Main to M. R.-R.]

41972. REICH-RANICKI, MARCEL. *Reich-Ranicki: seine Sprüche, seine Verrisse, seine Weisheiten: "der Reißwolf der Literatur"*. Ausgew. von Matthias Ohnsmann. Illus. von Beck. Hamburg: Europa-Verl., 2002. 77 pp.

41973. REICHE, FRITZ. WEHEFRITZ, VALENTIN: *Verwehte Spuren. Prof. Dr. phil. Fritz Reiche (1883–1969)*. Ein deutsches Gelehrtenschicksal im 20. Jahrhundert. Dortmund: Univ. Dortmund, 2002. 55 pp., frontis., facsims., footnotes, bibl. F.R. (Universität im Exil. Biografisches Archiv verfolgter Universitätsprofessoren 1933–1945 an der Universitätsbibliothek Dortmund, Nr. 5.) [F.R., July 4, 1883 Berlin – Jan. 1, 1969 New York, Prof. of Theoretical Physics, 1921–1933 Prof. at Breslau univ., 1934–1935 visiting Prof. at the German Univ., Prague, 1941 emigr. to the US.]

41974. ROBERT, LUDWIG. WEISSBERG, LILIANE: *Das Drama eines preußischen Patrioten: Ludwig Roberts 'Jephthas Tochter'*. [In]: Judentum zwischen Tradition und Moderne [see No. 41727]. Pp. 95–116. [L.R., 1778–1832, brother of Rahel Varnhagen.]

41975. ROSENTHAL FAMILY. *Die Rosenthals. Der Aufstieg einer jüdischen Antiquarsfamilie zu Weltruhm*. Mit Beiträgen von Elisabeth Angermair, Jens Koch, Anton Löffelmeier, Eva Ohlen und Ingo Schwab. Wien: Böhlau, 2002. 262 pp., illus., facsims., notes, bibl., indexes. [Cont.: Grußwort (Bernard Rosenthal, 9). Vorwort (Tichard Bauer, 11–12). Der Münchner Antiquariatsbuchhandel in der ersten Hälfte des 19. Jahrhunderts (Ingo Schwab, 13–46). Die Wurzeln der Rosenthals: Fellheim in Bayerisch-Schwaben (Anton Löffelmeier, 47–164). Generationenwechsel in den Antiquariatshäusern Rosenthal (Elisabeth Angermair, 165–202; deals also with the fate of the Rosenthal family and their firms during the Nazi period). Gabriella Rosenthal, Enkelin von Jacques Rosenthal und Ehefrau von Schalom Ben-Chorin (Eva Ohlen, 203–207). Hans Koch und die Firma Rosenthal (Jens Koch, 208–213). Die Antiquariatshäuser Rosenthal nach 1945 – ein Ausblick (Elisabeth Angermair, 215–230; on the firms in the Netherlands, in Munich, Switzerland, the US and Oxford). Katalogverzeichnisse der Antiquariatshäuser Ludwig und Jacques Rosenthal (231–244).]

41976. ROSENZWEIG, FRANZ. BLAHA, JOSEF: *Der Begriff der Erlösung bei Franz Rosenzweig*. [In]: Freiburger Rundbrief, N.F., Jg. 9, H. 4, Freiburg, 2002. Pp. 260–263, footnotes.

41977. ROSENZWEIG, FRANZ. CESARE, DONATELLA DI: *Die Grammatik der Zukunft. Ich, Du, Wir in Rosenzweigs Sprachdenken*. [In]: Trumah, Bd. 11, Heidelberg, 2001. Pp. 51–69, footnotes.

41978. ROSENZWEIG, FRANZ. MEIR, EPHRAIM: *The unpublished correspondence between Franz Rosenzweig and Gritli Rosenstock-Huessy on the 'Star of Redemption'*. [In]: Jewish Studies Quarterly, Vol. 9, No. 1, Tübingen, 2002. Pp. 21–70, footnotes. [See also No. 42053.]

41979. ROTH, JOSEPH. FRONK, ELEONORE/ANDREAS, WERNER: *"Besoffen, aber gescheit". Joseph Roths Alkokolismus in Leben und Werk*. Oberhausen: Athena, 2002. 197 pp., bibl. (Übergänge – Grenzfälle, Österreichische Literatur in Kontexten, B. 5.)

41980. ROTHSCHILD FAMILY. FERGUSON, NIALL: *Die Geschichte der Rothschilds*. Propheten des Geldes. Aus dem Englischen von Irmela Arnsperger und Boike Rehbein. Stuttgart: Deutsche Verlags-

Anstalt, 2002. 2 vols., 709 pp., illus., family trees, tabs., graphs., notes (581–709); 830 pp., illus., family trees, tabs., notes (607–720), bibl. (721–751), indexes (persons; subjects, places, 753–830). [For English orig. edn. see No. 36762/YB XLIV.] [Cf.: Magie verträgt kein Tageslicht. Niall Ferguson entwirrt die Bank- und Familiengeschichte (Jürgen Jeske) [in]: 'FAZ', Nr. 233, Frankfurt am Main, 8. Okt. 2002, p. L 44. Ein Meisterwerk der Wirtschaftsgeschichte: Niall Ferguson erzählt vom Aufstieg des Hauses Rothschild zur führenden europäischen Finanzdynastie (Julius H. Schoeps) [in]: Zeitliteratur [Beilage von] Die Zeit, Nr. 41, Hamburg, Okt. 2002, S. 68.]

41981. RUBEN, PAUL. BIESTER, BJÖRN: *Der innere Beruf zur Wissenschaft: Paul Ruben (1866–1943).* Studien zur deutsch-jüdischen Wissenschaftsgeschichte. Berlin: Reimer, 2001. 315 pp., illus. [P.R., 1866 Hamburg – 1943 Hamburg, philologist, scholar on his own account, friend of Aby M. Warburg, participated in establishing the 'Warburg Library'.] [Cf.: Bespr. (Frank Leimkugel) [in]: Berichte zur Wissenschaftsgeschichte, Bd. 25, H. 4, Weinheim, Dez. 2002, p. 282.]

41982. SAHL, HANS. REITER, ANDREA: *Repräsentant eines Jahrhunderts. Hans Sahl wäre am 20. Mai 100 Jahre alt geworden.* [In]: Aufbau, Vol. 68, No. 10, New York, May 16, 2002. P. 21

41983. SAMUEL, HERBERT. PERRY, WARREN: *A biography of Professor Richard Herbert Samuel 1900–1983.* Melbourne: Univ. of Melbourne, 1997. XII, 352 pp. [H.S., March 23, 1900 Elberfeld – Oct. 28, 1983 Melbourne, Prof. of German, teacher at a Grammar School in Berlin, assistant at Berlin univ. until 1933, 1934 emigr. to Cambridge, UK, in 1947 went to Australia to be head of the German Dept., Univ. Melbourne.] [Cf.: Eine Biographie: Richard Herbert Samuel (Horst Häker) [in]: Beiträge zur Kleist-Forschung, Frankfurt (Oder), 2002. Pp. 339–347.]

41984. SCHLEGEL, DOROTHEA. BECKER-CANTARINO, BARBARA: *Dorothea Veit-Schlegel als Schriftstellerin und die Berliner Romantik.* [In]: Arnim und die Berliner Romantik: Kunst, Literatur und Politik [see No. 42163]. Pp. 123–134, footnotes.

41985. SCHNITZLER, ARTHUR. *Arthur Schnitzler: Zeitgenossenschaften/Contemporaneities.* Hrsg. von/Ed. by Ian Foster, Florian Krobb. Bern; New York: Lang, 2002. 410 pp. (Wechselwirkungen, Bd. 4.) [Incl. 26 contribs., some in German, some in English, on different aspects of Schnitzler's life and work.]

41986. SCHNITZLER, ARTHUR. GAY, PETER: *Schnitzler's century. The making of middle-class culture 1815–1914.* New York: Norton, 2002. XXIX, 334 pp., illus., bibl., index. [German edn.: *Das Zeitalter des Doktor Arthur Schnitzler. Innenansichten des 19. Jahrhunderts.* Aus dem Amerik. von Ulrich Enderwitz, Monika Noll und Rolf Schubert. Frankfurt am Main: S. Fischer, 2002. 381 pp., illus., notes, index. Cont. essays on the "biography of the bourgoisie", throughout interwoven with quotations from the works, correspondence, diaries and autobiography of Arthur Schnitzler.] [Cf.: Eine Liebeserklärung. Peter Gay rettet das Viktorianische Zeitalter (Ludger Lütkehaus) [In]: Zeitliteratur [Beilage von] Die Zeit, Nr. 41, Hamburg, Okt. 2002, pp. 96–97.]

41987. SCHNITZLER, ARTHUR. NUY, SANDRA: *Arthur Schnitzler ferngesehen.* Ein Beitrag zur Geschichte des Theaters im Fernsehen der Bundesrepublik Deutschland (1953–1989). Münster; New York: Waxmann, 2002. 360 pp., footnotes (Internationale Hochschulschriften, Bd. 338.) (Zugl.: Siegen, Univ., Diss., 1999.)

41988. SCHÖNBERG, ARNOLD. *Arnold Schönberg 1874–1951 zum fünfzigsten Todestag.* Ein Komponist im Abseits. Zusammengestellt von Bettina v. Seyfried. Begleitheft zur Ausstellung des Deutschen Musikarchivs Berlin vom 13. Sept. 2001 bis 13. Dez. 2001. Leipzig: Die Deutsche Bibliothek, 2001. 73 pp., illus., facsims. [Incl. selected discography (48–73).]

41989. SCHÖNBERG, ARNOLD. RINGER, ALEXANDER L.: *Arnold Schönberg: das Leben im Werk.* Mit einem Nachwort von Thomas Emmerig. Stuttgart: Metzler; Kassel: Bärenreiter, 2002. IX, 342 pp., footnotes, music, chronol. of works, bibl., index. [Cf.: Zum Gedenken an Alexander L. Ringer (1921–2002) (Albrecht Riethmüller) [in]: Die Musikforschung, Jg. 55, H. 4, Kassel, 2002. Pp. 361–362.] [A.L.R., Feb. 3, 1921 Berlin – May 3, 2002 Urbana, Ill, Prof. of musicology, emigr. to the Netherlands in 1938, 1943–1945 in various concentration camps, emigr. to the US in 1947, since 1958 faculty member at the Univ. of Illinois School of Music.]

41990. SCHÖNBERG, ARNOLD. SHAWN, ALLEN: *Arnold Schoenberg's journey.* New York: Farrar, Straus & Giroux, 2002. XX, 340 pp., illus., notes, bibl., index. [Discusses Sch.'s music in the context of his life and times.]

――――― SCHOEPS, HANS-JOACHIM. SCHOEPS, JULIUS H.: *Ein jüdisch-christliches Streitgespräch am Vorabend der Katastrophe.* Ungedrucktes aus dem 1932 geführten Briefwechsel zwischen Hans Blüher und Hans-Joachim Schoeps. [See in No. 40845.]

41991. SCHOEPS, JULIUS H.. JASPER, WILLI/KNOLL, JOACHIM H., eds.: *Preußens Himmel breitet seine Sterne ... Beiträge zur Kultur-, Politik- und Geistesgeschichte der Neuzeit.* Festschrift zum 60. Geburtstag von Julius H. Schoeps. Hildesheim; New York: Olms, 2002. 2 vols., 915 pp., illus., notes, bibl., index. (Haskala. Wissenschaftliche Abhandlungen, Bd. 26.) [Incl. Vorwort (eds., 11–12). Vol. 1 cont. the sections: I. Zur Lage der Zeit; incl. essays by Michael Salewski, Arnulf Baring, Hilmar Hoffmann. II. Zur Geschichte Preußens. III Zum Verhältnis von Aufklärung und Judentum. IV. Zur Geschichte des deutschen Judentums im 19. und 20. Jahrhundert. Vol. 2 cont. the sections: V. Zu Antisemitismus, jüdischem Abwehrkampf und deutscher Befindlichkeit. VI. Zum jüdischen Selbstverständnis im europäischen Zusammenhang. VII. Zur Geistes- und Zeitgeschichte im 19. und 20. Jahrhundert. VIII. Zur Biographie von Julius H. Schoeps; cont.: Ein Leben in der doppelten Identität: Julius H. Schoeps zum 60. Geburtstag (Joachim H. Knoll, 839–845). Schriftenverzeichnis von Julius H. Schoeps, 1965–2001, zus.-gest. von Karin Bürger und Ursula Wallmeier (847–854). Selected contribs. are listed according to subject.] [Cf.: Julius H. Schoeps wird 60 (Joachim Knoll et al.) [In]: Zeitschrift für Religions- und Geistesgeschichte, Jg. 54, H. 2, Leiden, 2002. pp. 1–2.] [J.H.Sch., b. June 1, 1942 in Djursholm/Sweden, Prof. of Political Science and History, Director of the Moses Mendelssohn Zentrum, Potsdam, founding Director of the Jewish Museum in Vienna (1993–1997), editor of Zeitschrift für Religions- und Geistesgeschichte.]

――――― SCHOLEM, GERSHOM. LÖWY, MICHAEL: *Messianism in the early work of Gershom Scholem.* [See in No. 41819.]

41992. SEGHERS, ANNA. *Anna Seghers im Rückblick auf das 20. Jahrhundert.* Studien und Diskussionsbeiträge. Leipzig: Rosa-Luxemburg-Stiftung Sachsen, 2001. 181 pp., footnotes. (Texte zur Literatur, H. 9.) [Incl.: Prämissen einer Leipziger Anna-Seghers-Ehrung (Klaus Pezold, 5–10). 13 contribs. on A.S.'s work; also texts by A.S.]

41993. SEGHERS, ANNA. FEHERVARY, HELEN: *Anna Seghers: the mythic dimension.* Ann Arbor: Michigan Univ. Press, 2001. XI, 275 pp., illus., notes, bibl. (219– 267), index. (Social history, popular culture, and politics in Germany.)

41994. SINGER, PAUL. REUTER, URSULA: *Nicht fragen, wer ist der Mann, sondern: Wie ist der Mann.* Paul Singer (1844–1911): Bürger, Kaufmann, Sozialdemokrat. [In]: Kalonymos, Jg. 5, H. 1, Duisburg, 2002. Pp. 1–3, illus., notes.

41995. SONNENSCHEIN, HUGO. WILDE, DIETER: *Der Aspekt des Politischen in der frühen Lyrik Hugo Sonnenscheins.* Frankfurt am Main; New York: Lang, 2002. 322 pp., frontis., footnotes, bibl. (291–314), gloss., indexes. (Literarhistorische Untersuchung, Bd. 34.) Zugl.: Wien, Univ., Diss., 2001. [H.S. (pseud.: Sonka), May 25, 1885 Gaya (Kyjov) – July 20, 1953 Mirov (prison), Moravian poet, wrote and publ. in German, lived from 1908 until his expulsion in 1934 in Vienna, later deported to Auschwitz. After his liberation returned to Czechoslovakia where he was sentenced to 20 years imprisonment because of alleged cooperation with the Gestapo.]

41996. STEIN, EDITH. *Edith Stein Jahrbuch.* Jahreszeitschrift für Philosophie, Theologie, Pädagogik, andere Wissenschaften, Literatur und Kunst. Hrsg. im Auftrag des Teresianischen Karmel. Würzburg: Echter. Bd. 8, Würzburg: Echter, 2002. 400 pp., footnotes. [Section V, entitled Edith-Stein-Forum (317–394) cont. eight contribs. on E. St.]

41997. STEIN, EDITH. OBEN, FREDA MARY: *The life and thought of St. Edith Stein.* New York: Alba House, 2001. 164 pp., illus., bibl. (159–164).

41998. STEINHARDT, JACOB. *Jakob Steinhardt: Zeichnungen/Drawings.* Schenkung/Donation Josefa Bar-On Steinhardt. [Ausstellung 24. Juni 2000 – 3. Sept. 2000, Stiftung Stadtmuseum Berlin et al.] Berlin: Stiftung Stadtmuseum Berlin, 2000. 131 pp., illus. [Katalog: Dominik Bartmann]. [Incl. biography (Kathrin Conrad, 9–26).] [J.St., May 24, 1887 Zerkow/Posen – Feb. 11, 1968 Nahariya, Artist, Student of Lovis Corinth, emigr. 1934 to Palestine, Teacher at the Jerusalem New Bezalel School.]

41999. STEINHARDT, JACOB. *Jakob Steinhardt (1887–1968), Druckgraphik.* Bestandskatalog Stiftung Wilhelm-Lehmbruck-Museum – Zentrum Internationale Skulptur, Duisburg, Salomon-Ludwig-Steinheim-Institut für Deutsch-Jüdische Geschichte, Duisburg. [Ausstellungen in der großen Kundenhalle der Stadtsparkasse Duisburg an der Königsstraße (22. April-6. Mai 2002) und in der Stiftung Wilhelm-Lehmbruck-Museum – Zentrum Internationale Skulptur (14. Mai-28. Juli 2002]. Duisburg: Stiftung Wilhelm-Lehmbruck-Museum, 2002. 54 pp., illus. [Incl. contribs. by Christoph Brockhaus, Michael Brocke and Katharina Lepper.]

42000. STEINHARDT, JACOB. KAUFMANN, DOROTHEE: *Einflüsse auf das Frühwerk Jakob Steinhardts. Zur geistesgeschichtlichen Verortung eines jüdischen Expressionisten mit einem Ausblick auf sein Gesamtwerk.* Egelsbach; New York: Hänsel-Hohenhausen, 2000. 5 microfiches. (Deutsche Hochschulschriften, 2719.) Zugl.: Heidelberg, Univ., Diss., 2000.

42001. STEINTHAL, CHAJIM H.. *Chajim H. Steinthal. Sprachwissenschaftler und Philosoph im 19. Jahrhundert/Linguist and philosopher in the 19th century.* Ed. by Hartwig Wiedebach & Annette Winkelmann. Leiden; Boston: Brill, 2002. XXII, 283 pp., footnotes. (Studies in European Judaism, Vol. 4.) [Papers presented at an Internat. Conference held on the occasion of the hundredth anniversary of St.'s death at the Centre of Education of the Konrad Adenauer Foundation at Wendgräben Castle/Anhalt-Zerbst, Dec. 1999, organised jointly by the Museum Synagoge Gröbzig and the Leopold-Zunz-Zentrum zur Erforschung des europäischen Judentums, Wittenberg. Cont.: Einleitung & Introduction (eds., IX-XVIII). Three essays in English, ten in German, arranged in four sections: Sprachwissenschaft und Sprachphilosophie/Linguistics and philosophy of language (3–112; with contribs. by Craig Christy, Bogdan Bovtyk, Joan Leopold, Hans-Ulrich Lessing, Manfred Ringmacher, Hartwig Wiedebach). Jüdische Fragestellungen/Jewish questions (cont.: H. Steinthal und der Begriff der "Wissenschaft des Judentums" (Dieter Adelmann, 113–134). Steinthal, the Jewish orientalist (Ivan Kalmar, 135–152). H. Steinthals 'Über Juden und Judentum' im Kontext des aufkommenden Antisemitismus (Cornelie Kunze, 153–170). Ethischer Monotheismus und Prophetie: Zu Steinthals dynamischer Deutung der Schöpfung (Guiseppe Veltri, 171–185). Ethik/Ethics; cont.: Steinthals 'Allgemeine Ethik' (Ingrid Belke, 189–236). Materialien/Documentation (cont.: Ein Brief Steinthals aus der alten Heimat, mit einer biographischen Vorbemerkung (Marion Méndez, 239–246). Der Nachlaß von H. Steinthal in der Jüdischen National- und Universitätsbibliothek in Jerusalem (Silke Schaeper, 247–280).] [Chajim H. Steinthal, May 16, 1823 Gröbzig/Anhalt-Dessau – March 14, 1899 Berlin, Linguist Scholar, Philosopher, Orientalist, Proponent of Wissenschaft des Judentum.]

42002. STERN, GUY. LUBICH, FREDERICK A.: *"You can('t) go home again" – tragisch-triumphale Stationen einer deutsch-jüdischen Lebensgeschichte.* Interview mit Prof. Guy Stern (New York: 1996; update: 2000). [In]: Frederick A. Lubich: Wendewelten. Paradigmenwechsel in der deutschen Literatur- und Kulturgeschichte nach 1945. Würzburg: Königshausen & Neumann, 2002. Pp. 165–206. [One further article from this vol. is listed according to subject.] [G.St., orig. Günter, b. in Hildesheim Jan. 14, 1922, Prof. emer. of German Languages and Literature (Wayne State Univ., Detroit), Visiting Prof. at various German universities, emigr. in 1937 to the US.]

42003. STERN, GUY. LUBICH, FREDERICK A.: *'You can ('t) go home again' – Tragisch-triumphale Stationen einer deutsch-jüdischen Lebensgeschichte: Interview with Guy Stern.* [In]: Monatshefte, Vol. 93, No. 1, Madison, WI, 2001. Pp. 1–19.

42004. STERN, LEO.: *Leo Stern (1901–1982). Antifaschist, Historiker, Hochschullehrer und Wissenschaftspolitiker.* Hrsg. von Helmut Meier. Berlin: Trafo-Verl. Weist, 2002. 189 pp., illus., bibl. (Gesellschaft – Geschichte – Gegenwart, Bd. 30.) [L.St., orig. Jonas Leib, March 27, 1901 Woloka/Galicia – 1982 Halle, Communist, historian, lived in Vienna 1921–1936, fought in the Spanish Civil War, moved to the Soviet Union in 1939, returned to Vienna in 1945 as an officer of the Red Army, in 1950 accepted a chair as Prof. of History at Halle Univ., GDR.]

42005. STERN, SELMA. HOFFMANN, CHRISTHARD: *Zerstörte Geschichte. Zum Werk der jüdischen Historikerin Selma Stern.* [In]: Judenfeindschaft als Paradigma: Studien zur Vorurteilsforschung [see No. 42134]. Pp. 165–173, footnotes.

42006. STRAUSS, LEO: *The early writings (1921–1932).* Transl. and ed. by Michael Zank. Albany: State Univ. of New York Press, 2002. XIX, 238 pp., bibl., indexes. (SUNY series in the Jewish writings of Leo Strauss.)

42007. TABORI, GEORGE. FRIEDBERG, LILIAN: *Mule minus forty million acres: topographies of geographic disorientation and redface minstrels in George Tabori's "Weismann und Rotgesicht".* [In]: New German Critique, No. 84, Ithaca, NY, Fall 2001. Pp. 55–86, footnotes. [Deals with Tabori's Jewish Western play (1990) as an example of how Jews often identify with the plight of the American Indians. Discusses also other examples found in works of Else Lasker-Schüler and Rafael Seligmann.]

42008. TABORI, GEORGE. PASCAL, JULIA: *Scenes from the cemetery: the life and dramas of George Tabori.* [In]: The Jewish Quarterly, Vol. 48, No. 3, London, Autumn 2001. Pp. 57–60, illus.

42009. TERGIT, GABRIELE: *Frauen und andere Ereignisse.* Publizistik und Erzählungen von 1915 bis 1970. Hrsg. und mit einem Nachwort von Jens Brüning. Berlin: Das Neue Berlin, 2002. 224 pp., notes. [Nachwort (213–217; deals with T.'s biography.]

42010. TUCHOLSKY, KURT. *Kurt Tucholsky. Das literarische und publizistische Werk.* Hrsg. von Sabina Becker und Ute Maack. Darmstadt: Wiss. Buchgesellschaft, 2002. 317 pp., notes, bibl. [Cont.: Kurt Tucholsky. Das literarische und publizistische Werk (eds., 7–16). Nine essays by the eds., Sascha Kiefer, Günter Häntzschel, Dieter Mayer, Walter Delabar, Hermann Korte, Renke Siems, Gerhard Kraiker.]

42011. ULLMANN, VIKTOR. NAEGELE, VERENA: *Viktor Ullmann. Komponieren in verlorener Zeit.* Köln: Dittrich, 2002. 496 pp., illus., notes (441–463), bibl. (464–474), bibl. V.U. (475–485), index. [Biography.] [V.U., Jan. 1, 1898 Teschen/Moravia – Oct. 18, 1944 Auschwitz, composer, baptised (Catholic), grew up in Vienna, in 1919 moved to Prague, in 1942 deported to Theresienstadt, in Oct. 1944 to Auschwitz.]

42012. ULLSTEIN FAMILY. *125 Jahre Ullstein. Presse- und Verlagsgeschichte im Zeichen der Eule.* Hrsg. vom Axel Springer Verlag. Berlin: Springer, 2002. 180 pp., illus., facsims., chronol., bibl., index. [Esays are arranged under the sections.: Einführung (6–13; contribs. by Mathias Döpfner and Christoph Stölzl). Familie Ullstein (14–33; contribs. by Marion von Rautenstrauch, Bartholomew Ullstein, Klaus Saalfeld, Sir Paul Lever, Sten Nadolny on Karl, Rudolf, Elisabeth Ullstein). Verlagsepoche bis 1945 (34–99; contribs. on various Ullstein papers; also: Georg Bernhard zwischen Weimarer Republik und Exil (Johannes Mikuteit, 70–73). "Arisierung", Gleichschaltung, Zwangsarbeit. Ullstein 1934–1945 (Erik Lindner, 74–81). Solidarität und Hilfe für verfolgte Kollegen in der NS-Zeit (Beate Kosmala, 82–87). Ullstein in Wien (Isabella Matauschek, 88–91). Amerikanische Lizenzpolitik und die Berliner Presse (Peter de Mendelssohn, 92–99). Verlagsepoche bis 2002 (100–137; some contribs. deal also with Axel Springer's relation to members of the Ullstein family). Anhang (140–180; incl.: Stammbaum der Familie Ullstein (140–141).]

42013. URY, LESSER. ROSENBACH, DETLEV: *Lesser Ury. Das druckgraphische Werk.* Berlin: Ed. Rosenbach Hannover im Gebr. Mann Verlag Berlin, 2002. 152 pp., illus., notes. [Incl.: Der Künstler als Mensch, 7–18). Vita (148–149).] [L.U., Nov. 7, 1861 Birnbaum/Posen – Oct. 18, 1931 Berlin, artist.] [See also No. 41732.]

42014. VARNHAGEN, RAHEL. HAHN, BARBARA: *"Eine Impertinenz": Rahel Levin liest Achim von Arnim.* [In]: Arnim und die Berliner Romantik: Kunst, Literatur und Politik [see No. 42163]. Pp. 223–232, footnotes.

42015. WARBURG, ABY M.. DIDI-HUBERMANN, GEORGES: *L'image survivante. Histoire de l'art et temps des fantômes selon Aby Warburg.* Paris: Les Éditions de Minuit, 2002. 592 pp., illus. [Cf.: Pathosformeln eines Erlösungssuchers. Der große Wurf: Georges Didi-Hubermanns kongeniale Biographie des einverleibenden Aby Warburg (Werner Hofmann) [in]: 'FAZ', Nr. 209, Frankfurt am Main, 9. Sept. 2002, p. 37.]

42016. WARBURG, ABY M.: *Tagebuch der Kulturwissenschaftlichen Bibliothek.* Mit Einträgen von Gertrud Bing und Fritz Saxl. Hrsg. von Karen Michels und Charlotte Schoell-Glass. Berlin: Akademie, 2001. XXXIX, ports., 681 pp., footnotes, (Aby Warburg Gesammelte Schriften, Studienausgabe, Siebte Abt., Bd. VII.) [Diary covers the years 1926–1929. Incl.: Zur Einführung (IX-XXXVII). Bio-bibliographischer Anhang (557–648).] [Cf.: Der Cäsarenwahn steckt im Detail: Das jetzt erstmals edierte Tagebuch Aby Warburgs protestiert gegen die Verharmlosung unserer Bildkultur (Henning Ritter) [in]: 'FAZ', Nr. 125, Frankfurt am Main, 31. Mai 2001, p. 62. Das Tagebuch des Warburg-Instituts erzählt mit Esprit, wie Kunstwissenschaft neu entsteht (Wolfgang Kemp) [in]: Die Zeit, Nr. 27, Hamburg, 28. Juni 2001, pp. 37–38. "Fräulein Bing! please: Sing!" Das Logbuch der Kulturwissenschaftlichen Bibliothek Warburg (Barbara von Reibnitz) [in]: 'NZZ', Nr. 54, Zürich, 6. März 2002, p. 34.]

42017. WEICHMANN, HERBERT. BAHNSEN, UWE: *Die Weichmanns in Hamburg. Ein Glücksfall für Deutschland.* [Hrsg. von der Herbert und Elsbeth Weichmann Stiftung]. Hamburg: Christians, 2001. 517 pp., illus., notes (494–510), index. [For first vol. of biography covering the years 1896–1948 by Anneliese Ego and data H.W. see No. 38236/YB XLV.]

42018. WEILL, ALBERT. SCHELLINGER, UWE: *Kantor Albert Weill und sein Lebensweg von Südbaden nach Israel 1867–1950.* Teil II. [In]: Dessauer Kalender 2003, Jg. 47, Dessau, 2002. Pp. 38–51, illus., notes. [For part I see No. 40669/YB XLVII.]

42019. WEISS, LEOPOLD/ASAD, MUHAMMAD. WINDHAGER, GÜNTHER: *Leopold Weiss alias Muhammad Asad.* Von Galizien nach Arabien 1900–1927. Böhlau: Wien, 2002. 230 pp., illus., footnotes [Incl.: Ein Löwe im Gegenlicht. Vorwort (Andre Gingrich (11–19).] [L.W., July 2, 1900 Lemberg – 1992 Andalusia/Spain, journalist, author, orientalist, Muslim Philosopher, Pakistani diplomat, lived from 1914 in Vienna, from 1920 in Berlin, 1923–1927 Middle East correspondent of 'Frankfurter Zeitung', 1926 converted to Islam in Berlin, 1932–1952 lived in British India/Pakistan, 1952–1987 in USA, Germany, Syria, Pakistan, Switzerland, Marocco, Portugal, from 1987 in Spain.]

42020. WEISS, PETER. BEISE, ARNDT: *Peter Weiss.* Stuttgart: Reclam, 2002. 296 pp., illus., bibl. (263–284), indexes. (Universal-Bibliothek, Nr. 17633.) [Incl.: Heimatloses Leben (ed., 10–21; biographical essay).] [P.W., Nov. 8, 1916 Nowawes – May 10, 1982 Stockholm, graphic artist, author, playwright, baptised 1921, lived since 1921 in Berlin, emigr. in the late 1930s with his family to Sweden, remigr. to Germany.]

42021. WEISSKOPF, VICTOR. TELEGDI, VALENTIN: *Nachruf auf Victor Weisskopf.* [In]: Physik Journal, Jg. 1, Nr. 7/8, Weinheim, Juli/Aug. 2002. P. 118. [V.W., Sept. 19, 1908 Vienna – April 21, 2002, theoretical physicist, for further data see No. 28839/YB XXXVII.]

42022. WILDER, BILLY. NICODEMUS, KATJA: *Das kleine Menschsein.* Mit dem Tod von Billy Wilder verschwindet die Kunst der subversiven Pointe. [In]: Die Zeit, Nr. 15, Hamburg, 4. April 2002. P. 36, port.

42023. WOLPE, STEFAN. SCHAD, MARGIT: *Konzert für stehende Musik.* Zum hundertsten Geburtstag von Stefan Wolpe (1902–1972). [In]: Kalonymos, Jg. 5, H. 4, Duisburg, 2002. Pp. 1–4. [St.W., Aug. 25, 1902 Berlin – April 4, 1972 New York, composer, emigr. to Palestine in 1934, to the US in 1939.]

42024. ZOHN, HARRY. *Obituaries:* In memoriam (Pam Saur) [in]: Modern Austrian Literature, Vol. 34, No. 1–2, Bowling Green, OH, 2001. Pp. 125–128. Professor Zohn dies at Boston at age 77 [in]: Aufbau, New York, June 21, 2001.] [H.Z., Nov. 21, 1923 Vienna – June 3, 2001 Boston, Germanist and translator, emigr. to England in 1938, to the US in 1940, 1951 – 1996 Professor for modern German literature at Brandeis Univ.; editor and transl. of Karl Kraus, Stefan Zweig, Kurt Tucholsky, Sigmund Freud, Gershom Scholem, Walter Benjamin and many others.]

42025. ZWEIG, ARNOLD. KAMNITZER, HEINZ: *Ein Mann sucht seinen Weg. Über Arnold Zweig.* Schkeuditz: GNN Verlag, 2001. 146 pp.

42026. ZWEIG, STEFAN. KLAGHOFER, WOLFGANG: *Zwischen Gottestraum und Untergang. Zum 120. Geburtstag von Stefan Zweig.* [In]: Freiburger Rundbrief, N.F., Jg. 9, H. 1, Freiburg, 2002. Pp. 41–49, port., footnotes.

VIII. AUTOBIOGRAPHIES, MEMOIRS, LETTERS

42027. ABELES, PETER WITH TOM HICKS: *Otto, the boy at the window.* Berkeley, CA: Creative Arts Books, 2001. 161 pp., illus. [Memoirs; on life in Austria under the Nazis, escape to the US, Army service. Author became a business man in Chicago; is now living in Maryland.]

42028. ADORNO, THEODOR W.: *Theodor W. Adorno / Thomas Mann: Briefwechsel 1943–1955.* Hrsg. von Christoph Gödde und Thomas Sprecher. Frankfurt am Main: Suhrkamp, 2002. 179 pp., notes, index. (Theodor W. Adorno, Briefe und Briefwechsel, Bd. 3.). [Incl. Anhang: Adornos Aufzeichnungen zum "Doktor Faustus" (155–162). Nachbemerkung (eds., 163–170).] [Cf.: Der Teufel als Förderer. Zum Briefwechsel von Thomas Mann und Theodor W. Adorno (Lorenz Jäger) [in] 'FAZ', Nr. 92, Frankfurt am Main, 20. Apr. 2002, p. 54.]

——— AMÉRY, JEAN: *Werke.* Bd. 2: Jenseits von Schuld und Sühne. Unmeisterliche Wanderjahre. Örtlichkeiten. [See No. 41800.]

42029. ARENDT, HANNAH: *Denktagebuch. 1950 bis 1973.* Hrsg. von Ursula Ludz und Ingeborg Nordmann in Zusammenarbeit mit dem Hannah-Arendt-Institut, Dresden. München: Piper, 2002. 2 vols.: Bd. 1: VIII, 613 pp., illus. Bd. 2: Pp. 617–1230, illus., notes (907–1167), indexes, bibl. [Cf.: Im Raum der Einsamkeit. Das "Denktagebuch" der großen Philosophin Hannah Arendt erscheint in einer hervorragenden Edition (Barbara Hahn) [in]: Zeitliteratur [Beilage von] Die Zeit, Nr. 47, Hamburg, Nov. 2002, pp. 33–34.]

42030. *Aus Widersprüchen zusammengesetzt.* Das Tagebuch der Gertrud Bleichröder aus dem Jahr 1888. Hrsg. von Karin H. Grimme mit einem Vorwort von Monika Richarz und einer Erzählung von Lena Kugler. Köln: Dumont, 2002. 191 pp., illus., facsims., bibl., annot. index (names, places, 158–180). (Zeitzeugnisse aus dem Jüdischen Museum Berlin.) [Cont.: Vorwort (Monika Richarz, 7–17). Das Tagebuch der Gertrud Bleichröder aus dem Jahr 1888 (18–82). Editorische Notiz (83). "Ein kurzes Tagebuch zu führen": Die Aufzeichnungen aus dem Jahr 1888 (Karin H. Grimme, 84–155). Liebe Cleo (Lena Kugler, 181–189).] [Gertrud Arons, née Bleichröder, 1865 Berlin – 1917 Berlin, niece of Gerson von Bleichröder.]

42031. BEER-HOFMANN, RICHARD: *Der Briefwechsel mit Paula 1896–1937.* Unter Mitwirkung von Peter Michael Braunwarth hrsg., kommentiert und mit einem Nachwort versehen von Richard M. Sheirich. Übers. des Nachworts von Maria E. Clay-Jorda. Oldenburg: Igel Verlag Literatur, 2002. 511 pp., frontis., illus., notes (388–450), bibl., tabs., index. (Richard Beer Hofmann, Werke, Bd. 8.) [Paula: R.B.-H.s wife; b. 1879, became converted to Judaism and married R.B.-H. in 1898, died Oct. 30, 1938 in Zurich on the couple's way to the US, three days before R.B.-H. was expelled from Switzerland.]

——— BENARI, ASHER: *Erinnerungen eines Pioniers aus Deutschland.* [See No. 41737.]

42032. BORCHARDT, RUDOLF: *Rudolf Borchardts Leben von ihm selbst erzählt.* Nachwort Gustav Seibt. Frankfurt am Main: Suhrkamp, 2002. 168 pp. [Cf.: Als Häuptling der Goten in Lucca. Eine Reise zu den italienischen Villen, in denen der Dichter Rudolf Borchardt die Nazis überlebte – Exil als historische Selbsterfahrung (Martin Mosebach) [in]: Die Zeit, Nr. 28, Hamburg, 4. Juli 2002. P. 36.]

42033. BORCHARDT, RUDOLF: *Briefe 1936–1945.* Bearb. von Gerhard Schuster in Verbindung mit Christoph Ziermann. München: Edition Tenschert bei Hanser, 2002. 723 pp., indexes. (Gesammelte Briefe / Rudolf Borchardt, Bd. 7.)

42034. BUBER, MARTIN. KROME, FREDERIC: *Correspondence between Martin Buber, Hans Kohn, Abraham J. Heschel and Adolph Oko, 1939–1944.* [In]: Jewish Culture and History, Vol. 5, No. 1, London,

Summer 2002. Pp. 121 ff. [Letters are part of the A. Oko collection at the American Jewish Archives where Oko was librarian; they deal with Buber's wish to publish some of his works in English, and with Kohn and Heschel trying to help and intercede on his behalf.]

42035. EINHORN, ERICH & CELAN, PAUL. *Einhorn: du weißt um die Sterne.* Briefwechsel. Hrsg. und kommentiert von Marina Dmitrieva-Einhorn. Berlin: Friedenauer Presse, 2002. 31 pp. [Incl.: Nachwort (ed., 25–31, footnotes; on the life of E.E. and his fate. Cont. 16 letters written between 1944 and 1967.] [E.E., 1920 Czernowitz – 1974 Moscow, translator, lecturer, friend of Paul Celan, 1941 deported by the Soviets from Czernowitz to the Soviet Union.]

42036. *Feldpostbriefe jüdischer Soldaten 1914–1918.* Gemeinsam hrsg. von der Stiftung "Neue Synagoge Berlin" – Centrum Judaicum" und dem Militärgeschichtlichen Forschungsamt, Potsdam. Bearbeitet, kommentiert und eingeleitet von Sabine Hank und Hermann Simon, Centrum Judaicum. Teetz: Hentrich & Hentrich, 2002. 2 vols., 735 pp., frontis., illus., facsims., footnotes, index. (Jüdische Memoiren, Sonderausgabe.) [Cont. 754 letters/cards written by 81 soldiers, most of them former boarders or educators of the Berlin Jewish orphanage; incl. also annotations on their families and their later life after World War I. Vol.I incl.: Geleitwort (Hermann Simon/Jörg Duppler, 7). Einleitung (eds., 8–25). Das Reichenheimsche Waisenhaus (Karl-Heinz Noack, 26–31). Direktor Dr. Sigmund Feist und seine Familie (Karl Kilian, 32–36). Bemerkungen zur Edition (eds., 37–38).]

42037. FISCHL, MOSCHE ROBERT: *Wiener – Jude – Israeli. Jüdische Familiengeschichte in Österreich und Israel 1928–1964.* Hrsg. von Erhard Roy Wiehn. Konstanz: Hartung-Gorre, 2002. 116 pp., illus.

42038. FREUD, ANNA. *"… als käm ich heim zu Vater und Schwester". Lou Andreas-Salomé – Anna Freud. Briefwechsel 1919–1937.* Hrsg. von Daria A. Rothe und Inge Weber. Transkription: Dorothee Pfeiffer. 2 vols. Göttingen: Wallstein, 2001/2002. 442 pp.; pp. 443–907, notes (677–837), bibl. (838–852), chronol., index.

42039. GERSON, MANFRED MOSCHE: *Ein Leben im 20. Jahrhundert.* Von Westpreußen über Berlin und Hannover durch Amerika, NS-Deutschland und Lettland nach Israel 1906–1982. Hrsg. von Erhard Roy Wiehn. Konstanz: Hartung-Gorre, 2002. 332 pp., frontis., illus., footnotes, bibl. [M.M.G., 1906 Czarnikau, Posen – 1982 Moshav Habonim, Israel, agriculturist, emigr. to Palestine in 1935.]

42040. GOLDZIHER, IGNAZ. *"Machen Sie doch unseren Islam nicht gar zu schlecht." Der Briefwechsel der Islamwissenschaftler Ignaz Goldziher und Martin Hartmann 1894–1914.* Hrsg. und kommentiert von L. Hanisch. Wiesbaden: Harrassowitz, 2000, XXVII, 465 pp., illus. (Akademie der Wissenschaften und der Literatur Mainz. Veröffentl. d. Orientalischen Kommission, Bd. 45.). [I.G., 1850–1921, Orientalist, for data see No. 40518/YB No. XLVII.] [Cf.: Bespr. (Friedrich Niewöhner) [in]: Zeitschrift für Religions- und Geistesgeschichte, Jg. 54, H. 1, Leiden, 2002. Pp. 89–90.]

42041. GRONEMANN, SAMMY: *Erinnerungen.* Aus dem Nachlaß herausgegeben von Joachim Schlör. Berlin: Philo, 2002. 350 pp., port., gloss. (Philo Litera.) [Incl.: Vorwort (ed., 7–9); also contribs. by students of Potsdam Univ., tracing the different places of G.'s life. Memoirs cover the author's life until he settled in Berlin in 1906.] [S.G., March 21, 1875 Strasburg/West Prussia – March 6, 1952 Tel Aviv, Jurist, Zionist activist, humorist, playwright, son of the Hanover Rabbi Selig G., attended the rabbinical seminaries in Frankfurt am Main, Halberstadt and Berlin before becoming a lawyer, emigr. 1933 to France, 1936 to Palestine.]

42042. HOBSBAWM, ERIC: *Interesting times: a twentieth-century life.* London, New York: Allen Lane, 2002. XV, 447 pp., illus., ports., bibl., index. [E.H., b. 1917 in Alexandria of Austrian-Jewish descent, Marxist historian, lived in Vienna, Berlin, went to the UK in the early 1930s, prof. at the Univ. of London, Birbeck College until retirement.] [Cf.: No regrets (Matthew Price) [in]: Boston Sunday Globe, Boston, March 2, 2003, pp. E 1, E 5.]

42043. HOLENDER, IOAN: *Von Temesvar nach Wien. Der Lebensweg des Wiener Staatsoperndirektors.* Bearb. von Marie-Theres Arnbom. Böhlau: Wien, 2002. 231 pp., illus. [I.H., b. July 18, 1935 Temesvar (Romania) into a German-speaking Sephardic family orig. from Constantinople, opera singer, opera director, dismissed from Romanian universities for political reasons in 1956, in 1959 emigr. to Austria, since 1991 Director of the Wiener Staatsoper & Volksoper (jointly with Eberhard Waechter).]

42044. HUDSON-WIEDENMANN, URSULA: *Pauline statt Rahel? Von der Wiederentdeckung einer Schriftstellerin zur Entdeckung einer Liebenden.* [In]: Internationales Jahrbuch der Bettina-von-Arnim-Gesellschaft, Bd. 13/14, 2001/2002, Berlin, 2002. Pp. 205–214, footnotes. [Deals with various recent editions of the correspondence of Rahel Varnhagen and Pauline Wiesel.]

42045. IGGERS, WILMA/IGGERS, GEORG: *Zwei Seiten einer Geschichte.* Lebensbericht aus unruhigen Zeiten. Göttingen: Vandenhoeck & Ruprecht, 2002. 320 pp., illus. [W.I., née Abeles, b. in Mirschikau/Bohemia (Czechoslovakia) March 23, 1921, historian, grew up in Bischofteinitz, emigr. with her family to Canada in 1938; G.I., orig. Igersheimer, b. in Hamburg Dec. 7, 1916, emigr. with his family to the US in 1938, Prof. emer. of History, State Univ. of New York, Buffalo, both associated with Göttingen Univ. and the Göttingen Max-Planck-Inst. for History through numerous research visits since the early 1960s.]

42046. KLIBANSKY, RAYMOND: *Erinnerungen an ein Jahrhundert.* Gespräche mit Georges Leroux. Aus dem Französ. von Petra Willim. Frankfurt am Main: Insel, 2001. 287 pp., notes (259–274), gloss., bibl. R.K., index. [Orig. publ. 1998 under the title 'Le philosophe et la mémoire du siècle.'] [Cf.: Die Macht des Wissens, das Wissen der Macht. Der Philosoph Raymond Klibansky erzählt aus einem Leben (Martin Meyer) [in]: 'NZZ', Nr. 149, Zürich, 30. Juni 2001, pp. 49–50.] [R.K., b. Oct. 15, 1905 Paris to German-Jewish parents, Prof. of philosophy, lived until 1933 in Frankfurt am Main, Heidelberg and Hamburg, helped in transferring the "Warburg Library" to London, emigr. 1933 to Oxford, 1946 went to Montréal, professor at McGill University.]

42047. KOSTA, JIŘÍ: *Nie aufgeben. Ein Leben zwischen Bangen und Hoffen.* Berlin: Philo, 2001. 184 pp., illus. [J.K., orig. Heinrich Georg Kosta (Kohn), b. Oct. 2, 1921 in Prague, Auschwitz survivor, economist, emigr. from Prague to the FRG after 1968, lives in Frankfurt am Main.] [Cf.: Bespr. (Ferdinand Seibt) [in]: Bohemia, Bd. 43, H. 1, München, 2002, pp. 245–247.]

42048. KRAUS, KARL: *"Verehrte Fürstin".* Karl Kraus und Mechtilde Lichnowsky. Briefe und Dokumente 1916–1958. Hrsg. von Friedrich Pfäfflin und Eva Dambacher in Zusammenarbeit mit Volker Kahmen. Göttingen: Wallstein, 2001. 256 pp., illus., notes, index.

42049. KREISLER, GEORG: *Lola und das Blaue vom Himmel.* Eine Erinnerung. Hrsg. von Thomas B. Schumann. Hürth bei Köln: Ed. Memoria, 2002. 136 pp., frontis. [Incl. personal reminiscences and the play 'Lola Blau'.] [Cf.: Liedervergiften in Wien. Pessimistischer Optimist: Dem singenden Kritiker Georg Kreisler zum achtzigsten Geburtstag (Dietmar Polaczek) [in]: 'FAZ', Nr. 164, Frankfurt am Main, 18. Juli 2002. P. 39.]

42050. LASSALLE, FERDINAND. HEXELSCHNEIDER, ERHARD/SCHWENDLER, GERHILD, eds.: *"Auf ehrliche und anständige Gegnerschaft…" Ferdinand Lassalle und der F.A. Brockhaus-Verlag in Briefen und Kommentaren.* Wiesbaden: Harrassowitz, 2000. 195 pp. (Veröffentlichungen des Leipziger Arbeitskreises zur Geschichte des Buchwesens. Schriften und Zeugnisse zur Buchgeschichte, Bd. 13.) [Incl. the correspondence and articles, one on Lassalle's political development (Wolfgang Schröder).]

42051. MEYERBEER, GIACOMO. *The diaries of Giacomo Meyerbeer.* Transl., ed., and annot. by Robert Ignatius Letellier. Madison, NJ: Fairleigh Dickinson University Press, 1999–2002. 3 vols., 578; 446; 481 pp. illus., bibls., indexes. [Transl. of the untitled and unpubl. German diaries. Cont.: Vol. 1: 1791–1839. Vol. 2: The Prussian years and le prophete, 1840–1849. Vol. 3: The years of celebrity, 1850–1856.] [For earlier German edns. of correspondence and diaries covering different years see No. 9127/YB XVI and No.13308/YB XXI.]

42052. NEWTON, HELMUT: *Helmut Newton.* Autobiographie. Aus dem Englischen übertragen von Rudolf Hermstein. München: Bertelsmann, 2002. 335 pp., illus. [H.N., orig. H. Neustädter, b. 1920 in Berlin, photographer, emigr. to Singapore in 1938, 1940–1942 interned in Australia, later in the Australian Army, 1961–1981 worked for 'Vogue' in Paris, is living in Monte Carlo.]

42053. ROSENZWEIG, FRANZ: *Die "Gritli"-Briefe. Briefe an Margrit Rosenstock-Huessy.* Hrsg.: Inken Rühle, Reinhold Mayer. Tübingen: Bilam-Verlag, 2002. VI, 860 pp., footnotes, indexes (841–860). [Incl.: Vorwort (Rafael Rosenzweig, III-VI). More than 1.000 love letters written by F.R. between

1917 and 1929 to the wife of his best friend, Eugen Rosenstock (1–825).] [Cf.: Bespr. (Ernst Ludwig Ehrlich) [in]: Freiburger Rundbrief, N.F., H. 4, Jg. 9, Freiburg, 2002, pp. 286–287.]

42054. PINTZKA, WOLFGANG: *Von Sibirien in die Synagoge.* Erinnerungen aus zwei Welten. Berlin: Hentrich & Hentrich, 2002. 340 pp., frontis., illus. (Jüdische Memoiren, Bd. 8.) [Author, b. 1928, tells about five years imprisonment in Bautzen and forced labour in Soviet coal mines, his career as assistant at the Berliner Ensemble, friendship with Helene Weigel and eventual conversion to Judaism. Lives in Oslo.]

42055. POSENER, JULIUS: *In Deutschland 1945–1946.* Kommentierte Ausgabe mit einem Nachwort von Alan Posener. Berlin: Siedler, 2002. 207 pp. [First publ. with a pseudonym in Jerusalem 1947. Deals with his experiences as Garrison Engineer and later, as Political Intelligence Officer, travelling through the British Occupied Zone. Incl.: Nachwort (Alan Posener, 193–207; also on the two brothers of J.P. and their fate: Karl and Ludwig.] [J.P., Nov. 4, 1904 Berlin – Jan. 29, 1996 Berlin, architect, architecture historian, emigr. to Palestine in 1935, to the UK in 1941, returned to Germany in 1961, accepting a professorship at the Hochschule für Künste, Berlin.]

42056. RIES, HENRY: *Ich war ein Berliner. Erinnerungen eines New Yorker Fotojournalisten.* Berlin: Parthas, 2001. 220 pp., illus. [Memoirs, illustrated mainly with the author's photographs.] [H.R., data see No. 38196/YB XLV.]

42057. SELIGMANN, CAESAR: *Erinnerungen eines Grossvaters (A grandfather remembers).* [In]: European Judaism, Vol. 35, No. 2, London, Autumn 2002. Pp. 73–89, notes. [Incl. introduction (Albert Friedlander). Transl. (by Francis Clark-Lowes) of one chapter of Rabbi Seligmann's memoirs written in 1941.] [C.S., 1860 Landau – 1950 London, rabbi in Hamburg and Frankfurt (1902–1939), editor of 'Liberales Judentum', emigr to the UK in 1939.]

42058. SONNENFELD, SONJA: *Es begann in Berlin. Ein Leben für Gerechtigkeit und Freiheit.* Bremen: Donat, 2002. 142 pp., illus. [Memoirs.] [S.S. née Krenzisky, b. in Sweden 1912, grew up in Berlin, returned to Sweden in 1938.]

42059. STEIN, EDITH: *Aus dem Leben einer jüdischen Familie und weitere autobiographische Beiträge.* Neu bearb. und eingel. von Maria Amata Neyer OCD. Fußnoten und Stammbaum unter Mitarbeit von Hanna-Barbara Gerl-Falkovitz. Freiburg: Herder, 2002. XIX, 393 pp., footnotes. (Edith Stein Gesamtausgabe, 1.) [Incl.: Geleitwort (Klaus Mass, V-VIII). Einführung (Maria Amata Neyer, IX-XVII). Memoirs, ending 1916, written between 1933 and 1939 in Breslau, Cologne and Echt/Netherlands.]

42060. SÜSSHEIM, KARL: *The diary of Karl Süssheim (1878–1947). Orientalist between Munich and Istanbul.* Ed. by Barbara Flemming & Jan Schmidt. Stuttgart: Steiner, 2002. 334 pp., illus., chronol., bibl., index, footnotes. (Verzeichnis der orientalischen Handschriften in Deutschland, Suppl., Bd. 32.) [Diary covers the years 1908–1924, 1936–1940.] [K.S., Jan. 21, 1878 Nuremberg – Jan. 13, 1947 Istanbul, orientalist, historian, 1919–1933 prof. at Univ. of Munich, 1937 prof. at Istanbul Univ.]

42061. TABORI, GEORGE: *Autodafé.* Erinnerungen. Aus dem Amerikanischen von Ursula Grützmacher-Tabori. Berlin: Wagenbach, 2002. 96 pp. [G.T., b. 1914 in Budapest, writer, theater and film director, in the 1930s emigr. to the UK and USA, has frequently lived and worked in Germany since 1969.]

IX. GERMAN-JEWISH RELATIONS

A. **General**

42062. ALTHAUS, HANS PETER: *Mauscheln. Ein Wort als Waffe.* Berlin; New York: de Gruyter, 2002. 501 pp., facsims., notes (425–456), bibl. (457–485), index. [Covers 400 years of German-Jewish relations as reflected in the history of the word family 'Mauscheln', incl. its meaning in inner-Jewish assimilation debates and as an antisemitic battle word.]

42063. ANDERSON, MARK M.: *German intellectuals, Jewish victims: a politically correct solidarity.* [In]: The Chronicle of Higher Education, Vol. 48, No. 8, Washington, DC, Oct. 19, 2001, B7–B10. [Deals with present-day attitudes in Germany towards Jews and the Nazi past.]

42064. BROCKMANN, STEPHEN: *Martin Walser and the presence of the German past.* [In]: The German Quarterly, Vol. 75, No. 2 Riverside, CA, Spring 2002. Pp. 127– 43, notes.

—— BURDEKIN, HANNAH: *The ambivalent author. Five German writers and their Jewish characters, 1848–1914.* [See No. 42165.]

42065. CARDELLE DE HARTMANN, CARMEN: *Drei Schriften mit dem Titel `Pharetra fidei'.* [In]: Aschkenas, Jg. 11, 2001, H. 2, Wien, 2002. Pp. 327–349, footnotes. [On anti-Jewish texts distributed widely among the 'clerus minor' in German-speaking lands between the mid-13th to the 15th cent.]

42066. DETERING, HEINRICH: *"der Wahrheit, wie er sie erkennt, getreu" Aufgeklärte Toleranz und religiöse Differenz bei Christian Wilhelm Dohm.* [In]: Zeitschrift für Religions- und Geistesgeschichte, Jg. 54, H. 4, Leiden, 2002. Pp. 326–351, footnotes. [See also No. 40884.]

—— *Deutsch-jüdischer Parnaß. Rekonstruktion einer Debatte.* [See No. 40845.]

42067. FERTIG, MICHAEL/SCHMIDT, CHRISTOPH M.: *The perception of foreigners and Jews in Germany.* A structural analysis of a large opinion survey. Heidelberg: Heidelberg Univ., 2002. 31 pp. (Discussion paper series, Department of Economics, Universität Heidelberg, 368.)

42068. *Freiburger Rundbrief.* Zeitschrift für christlich-jüdische Begegnung. Neue Folge. Hrsg.: Freiburger Rundbrief e.V. Jg. 9. Hauptschriftleiter: Clemens Thoma. Geschäftsführende Schriftleiterin: Elisabeth Weidinger. Freiburg, 2002. 4 issues. [Incl. essays and book reviews pertaining to theological and historical aspects of Christian-Jewish relations. Selected articles and reviews are listed according to subject.]

42069. FRIEDLANDER, ALBERT H.: *Der Dialog in den Religionen: Begegnungen im 21. Jahrhundert.* [In]: Preußens Himmel breitet seine Sterne … [see No. 41991.], Bd. 1. Pp. 65–75, notes.

42070. HERTZ, DEBORAH: *Theilhaber's "racial suicide" of Scholem's "flight of the avant-garde"? Interpreting conversion rates in 19th Century Berlin.* [In]: Preußens Himmel breitet seine Sterne … [see No. 41991], Bd. 1. Pp. 339–355, notes.

42071. HOPPE, JENS: *Jüdische Geschichte und Kultur in Museen. Zur nichtjüdischen Museologie des Jüdischen in Deutschland.* Münster: Waxmann, 2002. 395 pp., footnotes, gloss., bibl., index. Zugl.: Münster/Westf., Univ., Diss., 2001.

42072. *Juden in der deutschen Literatur des Mittelalters: religiöse Konzepte – Feindbilder – Rechtfertigungen.* Hrsg. von Ursula Schulze. Tübingen: Niemeyer, 2002. 19, 290 pp., illus.

42073. *Le juif errant: un témoin du temps.* Paris: Biro, 2001. 238 pp., illus. [Texts by Pierre Birnbaum (et al.), coord. ed.: Juliette Braillon-Philippe. Catalogue publ. on the occasion of the exhibition with the same title at the Musée d'Art et d'Histoire du Judaisme in Paris, Oct. 2001 – Feb. 2002.]

42074. *Juden in der deutschen Literatur des Mittelalters.* Religiöse Konzepte – Feindbilder – Rechtfertigungen. Hrsg. von Ursula Schulze. Tübingen: Niemeyer, 2002. VI, 290 pp., illus., footnotes, indexes. [Cont. (some titles abbr.): Einleitung (ed., 1–10). I. Religionsgespräche; cont.: Christlich-jüdischer Disput in der Silvesterlegende der 'Kaiserchronik' (Vera Milde, 13–34). Ecclesia und Synagoge in fortwährendem Streit (Monika Wolf, 35–58). II. Anschein kultureller Integration der Juden; cont.: Süßkind von Trimberg – ein jüdischer Autor in der Manessischen Handschrift (Ricarda Bauschke, 61–86). Die Judeneide (Annette Schmidt, 87–106). III. Judenbilder in verschiedenen literarischen Gattungen; cont.: Predigten zur Judenfrage vom 12. bis 16. Jahrhundert (Ursula Schulze, 109–134). 'Das Jüdel' – Judenfiguren in christlichen Legenden (Cordula Hennig von Lange, 135–162). Antijüdische Motive in Schwänken und Fastnachtsspielen von Hans Folz (Matthias Schönleber, 163–182). Judenfeindliche Vorstellungen im Passionsspiel des Mittelalters

(Florian Rommel, 183–208). IV. Rechtfertigung von Pogromen; cont.: Legendenbildung um Simon von Trient – ein Ritualmordkonstrukt (Nicole Spengler, 211–232). Das Lied von Deggendorf – Fiktion eines Hostienfrevels (Björn Berghausen, 233–254). V. Der Ewige Jude; cont.: Das Volksbuch von Ahasver (Stefan Nied, 257–278).]

42075. KÄPPELI, SILVIA: *Lesarten des jüdisch-christlichen Dialogs.* Festschrift zum 70. Geburtstag von Clemens Thoma. Bern; New York: Lang, 2002. 369 pp., frontis., footnotes. (Judaica et Christiana, Bd. 20.) [Incl. 26 contribs. dealing mainly with Christian-Jewish relations and theological themes; selected articles are listed according to subject.]

42076. KLESSMANN, CHRISTOPH, ed.: *The divided past: re-writing post-war German history.* Oxford; New York: Berg, 2001. VII, 200 pp., tabs., notes. (German Historical Perspectices, 15.) [Incl.: Antisemitism and philosemitism in the divided Germany (Wolfgang Benz, 149–169). Orig. edn.: Deutsche Vergangenheiten: eine gemeinsame Herausforderung. Der schwierige Umgang mit der doppelten Nachkriegsgeschichte. Berlin: Links, 1999. 338 pp.]

42077. KORN, SALOMON: *Erbschaft der Nachgeborenen.* [In]: Preußens Himmel breitet seine Sterne … [see No. 41991], Bd. 2. Pp. 599–609, notes. [Lecture given in May 2000 in Frankfurt am Main; deals with German-Jewish relations, antisemitism, "Vergangenheitsbewältigung".]

42078. LEVENSON, ALAN: *Missionary Protestants as defenders and detractors of Judaism: Franz Delitzsch and Hermann Strack.* [In]: The Jewish Quarterly Review, Vol. 92, Nos. 3–4, Philadelphia, Jan.-April 2002. Pp. 383–420, footnotes. [Deals with Delitzsch and Strack as leaders in the fight against antisemitism.]

42079. LEVENSON, ALAN: *The problematics of philosemitic fiction.* [In]: The German Quarterly, Vol. 75, No. 4, Riverside, CA, Fall 2002. Pp. 379–393, notes. [Examines literature from Imperial and Weimar Germany with "philosemitic" contents, such as novels by Hans Siemer and Emil Felden, revealing subtle problems in the Jewish-Christian relationship.]

42080. PFANNER, HELMUT F.: *Jewish outsiders in two dramas by Felix Mitterer.* [In]: Modern Austrian Literature, Vol. 34, No. 1–2, Bowling Green OH, 2001. Pp. 89–101, notes. [Examines 'Kein schöner Land' (1989) and 'In der Löwengrube' (1998).]

——— *Recasting German identity: culture, politics, and literature in the Berlin Republic.* Ed. by Stuart Taberner and Frank Finlay. [See No. 41616.]

42081. SCHÖNER, PETRA: *Judenbilder im deutschen Einblattdruck der Renaissance. Ein Beitrag zur Imagologie.* Baden-Baden: Koerner, 2002. 328 pp., illus., footnotes, bibl. (Saecvla spiritalia; Bd. 42.) Zugl.: Univ. Bamberg, Diss., 1999. [Among the objects depicted are biblical themes, "Ecclesia & Synagoga", "ritual murder", desecration of hostages, magic, the Jew's sow, usury.]

42082. SCHMITT, HANNO: *Philanthropismus und Toleranz gegenüber Juden in der Spätaufklärung.* [In]: Preußens Himmel breitet seine Sterne … [see No. 41991], Bd. 1. Pp. 273–285, notes. [Incl. a text by Christian Gotthilf Salzmann.]

——— *Unlikely history: the changing German-Jewish symbiosis, 1945–2000.* Ed. by Leslie Morris and Jack Zipes. [See No. 41559.]

42083. SEEMANN, BIRGIT/WOLF, SIEGBERT: *"Eine hingestreckte Hand …".* Jüdische Autorinnen und Autoren der Tribüne – eine Erinnerung. [In]: Tribüne, Jg. 41, H. 161. [Incl. Robert Neumann, Hilde Rubinstein, Hans Lamm, Eleonore Sterling, Schalom Ben-Chorin.]

42084. *"Uns hat keiner gefragt". Positionen der dritten Generation zur Bedeutung des Holocaust.:* Hrsg. von Jens Fabian Pyper. Berlin: Philo, 2002. 281 pp., notes. [A collection of essays resulting from a tutorial of students (average year of birth 1972) at the Berlin Humboldt Univ. 2000/2001. Incl.: Vorwort (Meike Herrmann, 7–11). Selected essays (some titles abbr.): Die Bedeutung des Holocaust für unsere Generation (ed., 7–12). "Ich bin nicht religiös. Ich bin Kommunist". Ein gemeinsamer Nenner zwischen Juden und Nichtjuden in der DDR. Erfahrungen dreier Generationen im Umgang mit der Vergangenheit (Charlotte Misselwitz, 41–66). Holocaust-

Erinnerung in der jüdischen Tradition (Meike Herrmann, 119–150). Die Schoah als "staatsbürgerliche Religion"? Sakralisierung des öffentlichen Gedenkens in Israel und Deutschland (Johannes Valentin Schwarz, 151–186). Psychologisch inspirierte Anmerkungen zur Bedeutung des Holocaust in der dritten Generation (Gesine Grossmann, 245–272). Also contribs. by Nina Leonhard, Fabian Rüger, Fabian Goppelsröder, Peter Rigney, Gesine Grossmann, Caterina Klusemann on Holocaust memorials, commemoration and related matters.]

42085. WAGNER-KERN, MICHAEL: *Staat und Namensänderung. Die öffentlich-rechtliche Namensänderung in Deutschland im 19. und 20. Jahrhundert.* Tübingen: Mohr Siebeck, 2002. XIII, 459 pp., footnotes, bibl. (419–454), indexes. (Beiträge zur Rechtsgeschichte des 20. Jahrhunderts, Bd. 35.) [Discusses in detail the legislation of giving of names for Jews from the emancipation period to the Nazi era and the influence of antisemitism on it during these periods.]

42086. WEIGEL, SIGRID: *"Generation" as a symbolic form: on the genealogical discourse of memory since 1945.* [In]: The Germanic Review, Vol. 77, No. 4, Washington, Fall 2002. Pp. 264–277, notes. [On the younger generation's preoccupation with Judaism, also on "Vergangenheitsbewältigung".]

B. German-Israeli Relations

42087. AUSTRIA. REITER, MARGIT: *Unter Antisemitismusverdacht. Die österreichische Linke und Israel nach der Shoah.* Innsbruck: Studien-Verlag, 2001. 515 pp., notes (404–484), bibl. (488–515). [Incl. chaps. entitled: VI. Exkurs: Zionismus und Antizionismus Wandel der Begriffe vor und nach Auschwitz. VII. Bruno Kreisky und Israel – ein schwieriges Verhältnis. IX. Exkurs: Antisemitismus der Linken? Traditionen – Kontinuitäten – Ambivalenzen (deals also with philosemitism).] [Cf.: An der schönen blauen Donau? Die österreichische Linke stand in den ersten Jahren nach 1945 zu Recht unter Antisemitismus-Verdacht (Rolf Steininger) [in]: 'FAZ', Nr. 2, Frankfurt am Main, 3. Jan. 2002, p. 11.]

———— BEN-AVNER, YEHUDA: *Ambivalent cooperation: The German-Israeli Joint Committee on schoolbooks.* [See in No. 41438.]

42088. *Challenging ethnic citizenship: German and Israeli perspectives on immigration.* Ed. by Daniel Levy and Yfaat Weiss. New York; Oxford: Berghahn Books, 2002. IV, 282 pp., tabs., charts, notes, chap. bibls., index. [Deals with the concept of dual citizenship. Some parts are contribs. to an international conference "Citizenship and Identity: German and Israeli perspectives" held at Haifa Univ. in March 2000.]

42089. *Deutsch-israelische Begegnungen.* [Issue title of] Psychosozial, Jg. 24, Nr. 83, H. 1, Gießen, 2001. Hrsg. von Roland Kaufhold und Till Lieberz-Groß. 143 pp., illus., notes. [Incl. 16 contribs.]

42090. HANSEN, NIELS: *Aus dem Schatten der Katastrophe. Die deutsch-israelischen Beziehungen in der Ära Konrad Adenauer und David Ben Gurion.* Ein dokumentierter Bericht. Mit einem Geleitwort von Shimon Peres. Düsseldorf: Droste, 2002. 891 pp., footnotes, chronol., gloss., bibl., indexes. (Forschungen und Quellen zur Zeitgeschichte, Bd. 38.)

42091. *Israel und Deutschland. Voraussetzungen und Anfänge einer komplizierten Partnerschaft.* Im Auftr. der Forschungsstelle für Zeitgeschichte in Hamburg und der Katholischen Akademie hrsg. von Angelika Eder und Günter Gorschenek. Hamburg: Kath. Akad., 2002. 198 pp., footnotes. (Publikationen der Katholischen Akademie Hamburg, Bd. 17.) [Incl.: Vorworte (eds. and Arnold Sywottek, 3–8). Das politisch-religiöse Syndrom in den Beziehungen zwischen Deutschen und Israelis (Martin Stöhr, 9–35). Der Jischuw und der Holocaust (Yfaat Weiss, 36–47). She'erit Hapletah – Die Vorbereitung der jüdischen Displaced Persons in Westdeutschland auf das "gelobte Land" (Angelika Eder, 48–62). Die Gründung des Staates Israel und das Aufkommen von Reparationsforderungen in Eretz Israel (Yeshayahu A. Jelinek, 63–72). Vor 50 Jahren: Die Gründung der Gesellschaften für Christlich-Jüdische Zusammenarbeit (Josef Foschepoth, 101–115). Die Vorgeschichte der "Friedensbitte an Israel". Zur Erinnerung an Erich Lüth (Arnold Sywottek, 116–127). Die DDR und Israel – Zur Geschichte eines belasteten Verhältnisses (Angelika Timm, 128–151). Israel und die Jüdischen Gemeinden in der DDR

(Lothar Mertens, 152–168). Der Holocaust in der ost- und westdeutschen Geschichtsschreibung (Joachim Käppner, 169–186). Historiker und Zeitgenossen: eine komplizierte Partnerschaft. Schlusswort (Siegfried von Kortzfleisch, 187–191).]

42092. KANIUK, YORAM: *Der letzte Berliner.* Aus dem Hebr. von Felix Roth. München: List, 2002. 269 pp. [Based on the author's visits to Germany, stories deal with German-Israeli/German-Jewish relations.] [Cf.: Bespr. (Daniel Jütte) [in]: 'MB', Jg. 70, Nr. 178, Tel Aviv, Dez. 2002, p. 12. Yoram Kaniuk rechnet mit den deutschen Intellektuellen ab (Ralf Balke) [in]: Jüdische Literatur, Spezial der Jüdischen Allgemeinen, Jg. 57, Nr. 9, Berlin, 25. April 2002, p. 28.]

42093. MARGALIT, GILAD: *Israel through the eyes of West German Press 1947–1967.* [In]: Jahrbuch für Antisemitismusforschung 2002, Frankfurt am Main; New York, 2002. Pp. 235–248, footnotes.

42094. SHEFFI, NA'AMA: *Der Ring der Mythen. Die Wagner-Kontroverse in Israel.* Aus dem Englischen übersetzt von Liliane Granierer. Göttingen: Wallstein, 2002. 192 pp., footnotes, bibl., index. (Schriftenreihe des Instituts für deutsche Geschichte der Universität Tel Aviv, Bd. 22.) [For Engl. edn. and further details see No. 40741/YB XLVII.]

42095. WEINGARDT, MARKUS A.: *Deutsche Israel- und Nahost-Politik.* Die Geschichte einer Gratwanderung seit 1945. Frankfurt am Main; New York: Campus, 2002. 504 pp., footnotes, chronol., index (persons; subjects), bibl. (485–504).

42096. WOLFFSOHN, MICHAEL: *Geschichte als Falle. Deutschland und die jüdische Welt.* [In]: Preußens Himmel breitet seine Sterne … [see No. 41991], Bd. 2. Pp. 669–677, notes. [Deals mainly with German-Israeli relations.]

42097. WOLFFSOHN, MICHAEL: *Endlos nach der "Endlösung". Deutsche Juden.* [In]: Aus Politik und Zeitgeschichte [Beilage zu] Das Parlament, Jg. 52, Berlin, 2. Sept. 2002. Pp. 3–8. [Deals mainly with the relations between Germans and Israelis.]

C. **Church and Synagogue**

42098. BELL, DEAN PHILLIP: *Sacred communities: Jewish and Christian identities in fifteenth-century Germany.* Boston; Leiden: Brill, 2001. XI, 301 pp., map, notes, bibl. (261–283), index. (Studies in Central European histories.) [Compares developments in the Christian communities with that of the emerging Jewish communities and discusses interactions between them.]

42099. BURNETT, STEPHEN G.: *Christian Gerson of Recklinghausen and Johannes Buxtorf of Kamen: two Christian interpreters of Judaism in the Reformation Era.* [In]: Vestische Zeitschrift, Bd. 99, Recklinghausen, 2002. Pp. 35–59, footnotes. [Article is introduced by: Christianus Gerson aus Recklinghausen und Johannes Buxtorf aus Kamen. Zwei Beispiele humanistischer Gelehrsamkeit im Reformationszeitalter (Peter Borggraefe, 31–34)] [Chr. Gerson, data see No. XLVI/YB 38580.]

——— CHURCH. KOSCHEL, ANSGAR, ed.: *Katholische Kirche und Judentum im 20. Jahrhundert.* [See No. 41379.]

42100. DETMERS, ACHIM: *Reformation und Judentum.* Israel-Lehren und Einstellungen zum Judentum von Luther bis zum frühen Calvin. Stuttgart: Kohlhammer, 2001. VII, 392 pp., illus. (Judentum und Christentum, Bd. 7.) [Cf.: Bespr. (M. Tilly) [in]: Blätter für Pfälzische Kirchengeschichte und religiöse Volkskunde, Jg. 69, Großbundenbach, 2002, pp. 450 (86)-452 (88).]

42101. ELUKIN, JONATHAN: *Judaism: From heresy to pharisee in Early Medieval Christian literature.* [In]: Traditio, Studies in Ancient and Medieval History, Vol. 57, New York, 2002. Pp. 49–66, footnotes.

42102. FREY, WINFRIED: *Das Motiv der Zerstörung Jerusalems als Exempel in deutschen Texten des 16. Jahrhunderts.* Ein Versuch. [In]: derekh. judaica urbinatensia, Vol. 0, Trieste, 2002. Pp. 35–57, notes.

42103. HEIL, JOHANNES: *Deep enmity" and/or "close ties"?: Jews and Christians before 1096: sources, hermeneutics, and writing history in 1996.* Jewish Studies Quarterly, Vol. 9, No. 3, Tübingen, 2002. Pp. 259–306, footnotes. [Incl. Rhineland, Alsace.]

42104. HENRIX, HANS HERMANN/KRAUS, WOLFGANG, eds.: *Die Kirchen und das Judentum.* Bd. II. Dokumente von 1986 bis 2000. Paderborn: Bonifatius, 2001. XXX, 1036 & CD-ROM. [Cf.: Bespr. (Clemens Thoma) [in]: Freiburger Rundbrief, N.F., Jg. 9, H. 1, Freiburg, 2002, pp. 50–54. First vol. publ. 1988.]

42105. LEMKE, HELLA: *Judenchristentum. Zwischen Ausgrenzung und Integration.* Zur Geschichte eines exegetischen Begriffs. Münster: Lit, 2001. X, 329 pp., footnotes, bibl. (Hamburger Theologische Schriften, Bd. 25.) [Incl. chaps.: V. Die Einführung unseres Begriffs in die deutsche Theologie durch Theologen des 18. und frühen 19. Jahrhunderts. VI. Der Begriff des "Judenchristentum" bei Ferdinand Christian Baur.]

42106. LOTTER, FRIEDRICH: *Die Abwendung von der augustinischen Lehre jüdischer Zeugenschaft in der mittelalterlichen Theologie bis zum 13. Jahrhundert: Jeremy Cohen: "Lebende Buchstaben des Gesetzes. Vorstellungen von den Juden in der mittelalterlichen Christenheit".* [In]: Aschkenas, Jg. 11/2001, H. 2, Wien, 2002. Pp. 531–538, footnotes. [Review of Jeremy Cohen: Living letters of the law. Ideas of the Jew in medieval Christianity. Berkeley: Univ. of California Press, 1999. X, 451 pp.]

42107. PANGRITZ, ANDREAS: *"Auf einem Schul-Weg".* Zu Friedrich-Wilhelm Marquardts Arbeit an der Erneuerung des christlich-jüdischen Verhältnisses. [In]: Kirche und Israel, Neukirchener Theologische Zeitschrift, Jg. 17, H. 2, Neukirchen-Vluyn, 2002. Pp. 175–181. [F.-W. Marquardt, 1928–2002, Protestant theologian, publ. of 'Auf einem Schul-Weg. Kleinere christlich-jüdische Lerneinheiten, Berlin, Orient & Okzident Verl., 1999. 308 pp.]

42108. PINNOCK, SARAH K.: *Beyond theodicy: Jewish and Christian continental thinkers respond to the Holocaust.* Albany: State Univ. of New York Press, 2002. XII, 195 pp., notes, bibl. (175–188), index. (SUNY series in theology and continental thought.) [Author focuses on Martin Buber, Ernst Bloch, Gabriel Marcel, Johann Baptist Metz.]

42109. RISSE, SIEGFRIED: *Die Juden in deutschsprachigen katholischen Psalmenerklärungen des 16. Jahrhunderts.* [In]: Freiburger Rundbrief, N.F., Jg. 9, H. 2, Freiburg, 2002. Pp. 105–113, footnotes.

42110. SCHNITZLER, NORBERT: *Der Vorwurf des "Judaisierens" in den Bilderkontroversen des späten Mittelalters und der frühen Neuzeit.* [In]: Macht und Ohnmacht der Bilder. Reformatorischer Bildersturm im Kontext der europäischen Geschichte. Hrsg. von Peter Blickle [et al.]. München, Oldenbourg, 2002. Pp. 333–358, footnotes, illus. [Also in this book: Das biblische Kultbildverbot und seine Auslegung im rabbinisch-orthodoxen Judentum und im Christentum (Othmar Keel, 65–96).]

42111. VASEL, STEPHAN: *Philosophisch verantwortete Christologie und christlich-jüdischer Dialog.* Schritte zu einer doppelt apologetischen Christologie in Auseinandersetzung mit den Entwürfen von H.-J. Kraus, F.-W. Marquardt, P.M. van Buren, P. Tillich, W. Pannenberg und W. Härle. Gütersloh: Chr. Kaiser, Gütersloher Verl.-Haus, 2001. Zugl.: Suegen, Univ., Diss., 2000. 768 pp., footnotes, bibl. (743–768).

42112. *Wie Juden und Christen einander sehen.* Ein Seminar an der Universität Augsburg. Hrsg. von Herbert Immenkötter. Mit Beiträgen von Edna Brocke [et al.]. Augsburg: Wißner-Verlag, 2001. 72 pp. [Incl.: Juden und Judentum in Kollegstufe und Grundstudium. Fragen an ein deutschsprachiges Unterrichtswerk (Herbert Immenkötter, 37–42).]

D. **Antisemitism**

——— ALTHAUS, HANS PETER: *Mauscheln. Ein Wort als Waffe.* [See No. 42062.]

42113. *Antisemitische und antijudaistische Motive bei Denkern der Aufklärung.* Susanne Miller zum 85. Geburtstag. Hrsg. im Auftrag der Philosophisch-Politischen Akademie von Horst Gronke, Thomas Meyer,

Barbara Neißer. Münster: Lit, 2001. 89 pp., footnotes. (PPA-Schriften, Bd. 1.) [Incl.: Laudatio zur Preisschrift von Frau Dr. Bettina Stangneth 'Antisemitische und antijudaistische Motive bei Immanuel Kant' (Micha Brumlik, 33–46; for B.St.'s "Preisschrift" see No. 40793/YB XlVII). Dankesrede der Ersten Preisträgerin (Bettina Stangneth, 47–58). Kontexte antijüdischen Denkens bei Jakob Friedrich Fries und anderen Denkern des deutschen Idealismus (Gerald Hubmann, 59–70). Adolf Freiherr von Knigge und die Juden (Almut Rüllmann, 71–80). Further contribs. are listed according to subject.]

42114. BENZ, WOLFGANG: *Antisemitismus ohne Antisemiten?* Anmerkungen zur Möllemann-Affäre 2002. [In]: Tribüne, Jg. 41, H. 163, Frankfurt am Main, 2002. Pp. 84–92.

42115. BERGSDORF, HARALD: *Von Antisemiten und ihrer Sprache.* Deutsche "Republikaner" (REP) und die französische "Front National" (FN). [In]: Tribüne, Jg. 41, H. 162, Frankfurt am Main, 2002. Pp. 180–185.

42116. BERGMANN, WERNER: *Geschichte des Antisemitismus.* München: Beck, 2002. 143 pp., bibl., index. (Beck Wissen.) Orig.-Ausg. [Focuses on 19th and 20th cent.] [Cf.: Bespr. (Christoph Nonn) [in]: neue politische literatur, Jg. 47, H. 2, Frankfurt am Main, 2002, pp. 323–324.

42117. BRANTZ, DOROTHEE: *Stunning bodies: animal slaughter, Judaism, and the meaning of humanity in Imperial Germany.* [In]: Central European History, Vol. 35, No. 2, Boston: Leiden, 2002. Pp. 167–194, footnotes. [Deals also with antisemitism in the animal protection societies and their fight against Shehitah.]

42118. COHN-SHERBOK, DAN: *Anti-Semitism: a history.* Stroud: Sutton, 2002. X, 357., illus., facsims., bibl. (343–346), index. [Incl. German antisemitism in different periods; deals also with Nazi anti-semitism, the Holocaust, post-1945 antisemitism, antisemitism and Zionism.]

42119. COLIN-BURNS, CHRISTINE A.: *Richard Wagner, Adolf Hitler and the rise of the new Germanic religion.* [In]: European Studies Journal, Vol. 18/19, Cedar Falls, IA, Fall 2001– Spring 2002. Pp. 110–136, notes.

42120. DEFENCE. MEHNERT, GOTTFRIED: *Der Verein zur Abwehr des Antisemitismus.* Seine Anfänge in Marburg 1891/1892. [In]: Freiburger Rundbrief, N.F., Jg. 9, H. 4, Freiburg, 2002. Pp. 270–275, footnotes.

42121. *Exclusionary violence: antisemitic riots in modern German history.* Ed. by Christhard Hoffmann, Werner Bergmann, and Helmut Walser Smith. Ann Arbor: University of Michigan Press, 2002. VII, 210 pp., illus., facsims., map, footnotes, index. (Social history, popular culture, and politics in Germany.) [Revised papers, orig. presented at the 21st annual conference of the German Studies Association, Washington, DC, Sept. 1997. Cont.: Introd. (eds., 1– 24). The "Hep Hep" riots of 1819: anti-Jewish ideology, agitation, and violence (Stefan Rohrbacher, 23–42). Anti-Jewish emotion and violence in the 1848 crisis of German society (Manfred Gailus, 43–65). Political culture and violence against minorities: the antisemitic riots in Pomerania and West Prussia (Christhard Hoffmann, 67–92). Konitz, 1900: ritual murder and antisemitic violence (Helmut Walser Smith, 93–122). "Out with the Ostjuden": the Scheunenviertel riots in Berlin, Nov. 1923 (David Clay Large, 123–140). The November pogrom of 1938: Participation, applause, disapproval (Wolfgang Benz, 141–159). Exclusionary riots: some theoretical considerations (Werner Bergmann, 161–184). Continuities and discontinuities of anti-Jewish violence in modern Germany, 1819–1938 (Richard S. Levy, 185– 202).]

42122. FRIEDRICH, NORBERT: *Die Christlich-soziale Bewegung und Wilhelm II.* [In]: Wilhelm II. und die Religion. Facetten einer Persönlichkeit und ihres Umfelds. Hrsg. von Stefan Samerski. Berlin: Duncker & Humblot, 2002. (Forschungen zur Brandenburgischen und Preussischen Geschichte, N.F., Beiheft 5.) Pp. 105–131, footnotes. [Deals also mit Adolf Stoecker's antisemitism.]

42123. *Grenzenlose Vorurteile. Antisemitismus, Nationalismus und ethnische Konflikte in verschiedenen Kulturen.* Hrsg. im Auftrag des Fritz Bauer Instituts von Irmtraud Wojak und Susanne Meinl. Frankfurt am Main; New York: Campus, 2002. 304 pp., notes. (Fritz Bauer Institut, Jahrbuch 2002 zur Geschichte und Wirkung des Holocaust.) [Incl.: Der transatlantische Sklavenhandel, das Entstehen des modernen

Rassismus und der Antisemitismus. Plädoyer für eine auch pädagogisch folgenreiche Synthese (Micha Brumlik, 69–86, notes). One further essay is listed according to subject.]

42124. GROSS, JOHANNES T.: *Ritualmordbeschuldigungen gegen Juden im Deutschen Kaiserreich (1871–1914).* Berlin: Metropol, 2002. 240 pp., footnotes, bibl. (Dokumente – Texte – Materialien, Bd. 47.) [Deals with the Skurz, the Xanten, and the Konitz blood libel affairs. See also Nos. 42141, 42155.]

42125. HAASE, RICARDA: *"Judenreine" Berge.* Antisemitismus in den Alpenvereinen. [In]: Tribüne, Jg. 41, H. 164, Frankfurt am Main, 2002. Pp. 170–177.

—— HALBRONN, JAQUES: *Prophetica Judaica Beith. Le Sionisme et ses avatars au tournant du XXe siècle.* [See No. 41740.]

42126. HAMANN, BRIGITTE: *Winifred Wagner oder Hitlers Bayreuth.* München; Zürich: Piper, 2002. 687 pp., illus. [Incl. numerous references to the antisemitism of W.W. and her entourage.]

—— HARTWICH, WOLF-DANIEL: *Jüdische Gespenster: E.T.A. Hoffmann und der romantische Antisemitismus.* [See No. 42172.]

42127. HAURY, THOMAS: *Antisemitismus von links.* Kommunistische Ideologie, Nationalismus und Antizionismus in der frühen DDR. Hamburg: Hamburger Edition, 2002. 527 pp., footnotes, bibl., index. [Cf.: Das "Gift des Kosmopolitismus". Thomas Haury über Antisemitismus von links (Christoph Jahr) [in]: 'NZZ', Nr. 99, Zürich, 30. April 2003, p. 36.]

—— HESS, JONATHAN M.: *Germans, Jews and the claims of modernity.* [See No. 40859.]

42128. HILLERBRAND, HANS J.: *"Deutsche" und "Juden": Betrachtungen zum Thema christlicher Antisemitismus von Luther bis Stoecker.* [In]: Preußens Himmel breitet seine Sterne … [see No. 41991], Bd. 2. Pp. 455–472, notes.

42129. JENSEN, UFFA: *"Die Juden sind unser Unglück!"* Das verkündete 1879 der liberale Berliner Geschichtsprofessor Heinrich von Treitschke – und löste damit den ersten Antisemitismusstreit der deutschen Geschichte aus. [In]: Die Zeit, Nr. 25, Hamburg, 13. Juni 2002, P. 82.

42130. JÖCHLER, CHRISTINE: *Lo scandalo dell'ebraicità nella prospettiva antisemita.* [In]: Derekh, Judaica Urbinatensia, Vol. 0, Trieste, 2002. Pp. 76–88.

42131. *Judentum und Antijudaismus in der deutschen Literatur im Mittelalter und an der Wende zur Neuzeit.* Ein Studienbuch. Hrsg. von Arne Domrös, Thomas Bartoldus und Julian Voloj. Berlin: Jüdische Verlagsanstalt Berlin, 2002. 282 pp., illus., facsims., plans., notes, index. [Incl.: Geleitwort (Paul Spiegel, 7–8). Einführung (eds., 9–14). Do mit hat das buch ein end/Das uns got moschiach send. Zur jüdischdeutschen Sprache und Literatur im Mittelalter (Julian Voloj, 15–30). All other chaps. cont. annotated sources related to anti-judaism in plays, blood libel, desecration of the hostages, Martin Luther.]

42133. *Die "Judenfrage". Schriften zur Begründung des modernen Antisemitismus 1780 bis 1918.* Mikrofiche-Edition. Lieferung 1 & 2. Hrsg. von Wolfgang Benz im Auftrag des Zentrums für Antisemitismusforschung. München: Saur, 2002. 369 microfiches. [Cont. ca. 600 antisemitic publications; for "Begleitheft" (bibliography) see No. 41166.]

42134. *Judenfeindschaft als Paradigma. Studien zur Vorurteilsforschung.* Hrsg. von Wolfgang Benz und Angelika Königseder. Berlin: Metropol, 2002. 365 pp., footnotes. [Publ. on the occasion of the 20th anniversary of the Zentrum für Antisemitismusforschung Berlin. Incl.: Antisemitismusforschung als Vorurteilsforschung (Wolfgang Benz, 15–21). Antisemitismusforschung als Wissenschaft. Aus der Antrittsvorlesung 1982 (Herbert A. Strauss, 22–28). Section entitled 'Antisemitismus' cont. (some titles abbr.): Zur Einschätzung des Antisemitismus in der Bundesrepublik Deutschland (Werner Bergmann, 31–39). Kontinuität und Wandel im Konstrukt der jüdischen Weltverschwörung (Johannes Heil, 40–48). Antijüdische Gewalt im frühen 19. Jahrhundert (Stefan Rohrbacher, 49–57). Ritualmordbeschuldigung (Rainer Erb, 58–64). Visueller Antisemitismus in populären Medien (Julia

Schäfer, 65–69). Was das Theater erfindet und was es vermeidet (Hans-Joachim Neubauer, 70–78). Juden und "unehrliche Leute" im Werk Wilhelm Raabes (Michael Schmidt, 79–88). Der Berliner Antisemitismusstreit 1879–1881 (Karsten Krieger, 89–85). Zur Sozialgeschichte jüdischer Studenten im Deutschen Kaiserreich (Norbert Kampe, 96–101). Antisemitismus im Vergleich: Italien und Deutschland 1870–1914 (Ulrich Wyrwa, 102–105). Der Jude als Bolschewist (Daniel Gerson, 106–112). Sections entitled 'NS-Zeit und Holocaust' (113–162), 'Jüdische Geschichte' (165–184), Emigration (185–228), 'Epilog' (327–354) are listed according to subject. Rechtsextremismus (289–326; incl.: Holocaustleugnung im Rechtsextremismus (Wolfgang Benz, 312–317). Schändungen jüdischer Friedhöfe in Deutschland (Marion Neiss, 318–26). Also sections entitled 'Minderheiten' (229–288) and 'Rechtsextremismus' (289–326).]

———— KLESSMANN, CHRISTOPH, ed.: *The divided past: re-writing post-war German history.* [See No. 42077.]

42135. KLEIN, RALPH: *Der Wille zur Reinheit: Antisemitismus und hygienischer Furor.* [In]: Zeitschrift für Geschichtswissenschaft, Jg. 50, H. 7, Berlin, 2002. Pp. 603–621, footnotes.

42136. KOCH, URSULA E.: *Attacken gegen den jüdischen "Geist" und "Witz" in der Hochburg des Liberalismus: Berlin. Ein Mosaikstein zur Rezeptions- und Antisemitismusforschung am Beispiel ausgewählter Satire-Journale des 19. Jahrhunderts.* [In]: Preußens Himmel breitet seine Sterne … [see No. 41991], Bd. 2. Pp. 483–511, illus., notes.

42137. LEY, MICHAEL: *Holokaust als Menschenopfer. Vom Christentum zur politischen Religion des Nationalsozialismus.* Münster: Lit, 2002. 186 pp., footnotes, bibl., index.

42138. MARKOVITS, ANDREI S.: *Terror and clandestine anti-semitism: thoughts on German and American reactions to Sept. 11, 2001.* [In]: Partisan Review, Vol. 69, No. 1, Boston, 2002. Pp. 19–24. [Deals with anti-semitism (and anti-Americanism) expressed in e-mails, internet connections and letters to news-papers after Sept. 11.]

42139. NAUMANN, MICHAEL, ed.: *"Es muß doch in diesem Lande wieder möglich sein …".* Der neue Antisemitismus-Streit. München: Ullstein, 2002. 246 pp. (Orig.-Ausg.) [Cont.: Vorwort (ed., 9–12). 40 newspaper articles documenting the public debate arising from the antisemitic state-ments of the FDP-politician Jürgen Möllemann and the publication of Martin Walsers 'roman à clef' *Tod eines Kritikers.*]

42140. NEAMAN, ELLIOT: *European right-wing populism and anti-Semitism.* [In]: Tikkun, Vol. 17, No. 4, Berkeley, CA, July-Aug. 2002. Pp. 53–55, illus. [Incl. Germany.]

42141. NONN, CHRISTOPH: *Eine Stadt sucht einen Mörder. Gerücht, Gewalt und Antisemitismus im Kaiserreich.* Göttingen: Vandenhoeck & Ruprecht, 2002. 258 pp., notes (206–237). bibl., index. [On the Konitz (West Prussia) "ritual murder" affair following the murder of a young man in 1900.]

42142. PERI, ANAT: *Jörg Haider's antisemitism.* Jerusalem: Vidal Sassoon International Center for the Study of Antisemitism, The Hebrew University of Jerusalem, 2001. 35 pp., bibl. (Analysis of current trends in antisemitism, No. 18.)

42143. PFAHL-TRAUGHBER, ARMIN: *Antisemitismus in der deutschen Geschichte.* [Hrsg.: Landeszentrale für politische Bildungsarbeit Berlin]. Opladen: Leske + Budrich, 2002. 168 pp., bibl. (Beiträge zu Politik und Zeitgeschichte.)

42144. PIPER, ERNST: *Die Ära Bismarck und die Formierung des modernen Antisemitismus.* [In]: Preußens Himmel breitet seine Sterne … [see No. 41991], Bd. 2. Pp. 513–526, notes.

42145. PLANERT, UTE: *Reaktionäre Modernisten? Zum Verhältnis von Antisemitismus und Antifeminismus in der völkischen Bewegung.* [In]: Jahrbuch für Antisemitismusforschung 2002, Frankfurt am Main; New York, 2002. Pp. 31–51, footnotes.

42146. PRIMOR, AVI: *Gibt es eine neue Welle des Antisemitismus in Deutschland?* [In]: Europäische Rundschau, Jg. 30, Nr. 4, 2002, Wien, 2002. Pp. 79–83.

42147. REDNER, HARRY: *Philosophers and anti-Semitism.* [In]: Modern Judaism, Vol. 22, No. 2, Cary, NC, May 2002. Pp. 115–141, notes. [Incl. Martin Heidegger, Georg Lukacs, Ludwig Wittgenstein.]

42148. ROHRMOSER, GÜNTER: *Deutschlands Tragödie. Der geistige Weg in den Nationalsozialismus.* Hrsg. von Michael Grimminger. München: Olzog, 2002. 442 pp. [Incl. a chap. entitled Rassismus, Antisemitismus und die deutsche Angst vor der Moderne (62–76).]

42149. SCHOEPS, JULIUS H.: *Die Angst geht wieder um.* Mit der Gewalt im Nahen Osten nimmt der Antisemitismus in Deutschland zu. [In]: Dialog, H. 17, Potsdam, April 2002. Pp. 1–2.

42150. SCHULZE WESSEL, ALMUT: *Antisemitismus in der Schule im Spiegel der "C.V.-Zeitung".* [In]: Jahrbuch für Antisemitismusforschung 2002, Frankfurt am Main; New York, 2002. Pp. 91–113, footnotes. [Deals with the period before 1933.]

42151. SCHOLZ, DIETMAR: *"Durch die Geburt eines kräftigen Antisemiten wurden hocherfreut…". Zum Antisemitismus in Castrop und Umgebung im ausgehenden 19. Jahrhundert.* [In]: Märkisches Jahrbuch für Geschichte, Bd. 101, Dortmund, 2001. Pp. 219–250, footnotes.

42152. STIBBE, MATTHEW: *Nineteenth century German antisemitic propagandists.* London: Holocaust Educational Trust, 2001. II, 27 pp., illus., facsims., glossary, notes. [Incl. Adolf Stoecker, Ernst Henrici, Theodor Fritsch.]

42153. STÖCKEL, SIGRID, ed.: *Die "rechte Nation" und ihr Verleger. Politik und Popularisierung im J.F. Lehmanns Verlag 1890–1979.* Berlin: Lehmanns Media, 2002. 328 pp., illus., footnotes, indexes. [Cont. 11 essays, some dealing also with antisemitism of the publisher Julius Friedrich Lehmann and several of his nationalistic and racist periodicals and books.]

42154. TRAPP, FRITHJOF: *Traditionen des Antisemitismus in Deutschland – Die Zeitschrift 'Das Zwanzigste Jahrhundert'.* [In]: Exil, Jg. 22, Nr. 2, 2002, Frankfurt am Main, [2003]. Pp. 95–106, notes. [Also deals with Heinrich Mann's involvement with the periodical in 1895/1896.]

——— WAGNER-KERN, MICHAEL: *Staat und Namensänderung. Die öffentlich-rechtliche Namensänderung in Deutschland im 19. und 20. Jahrhundert.* [See No. 42085.]

42155. WALSER SMITH, HELMUT: *Die Geschichte des Schlachters. Mord und Antisemitismus in einer deutschen Kleinstadt.* Aus dem Amerikanischen von Udo Rennert. Göttingen: Wallstein, 2002. 301 pp., notes, illus. [On the Konitz (West Prussia) "ritual murder" affair arising from the murder of a young man in 1900. American edn.: The butcher's tale. Murder and anti-semitism in a German town. New York; London: Norton, 2002. 270 pp., illus., notes, bibl., index.]

42156. WASSERMANN, HEINZ P.: *Naziland Österreich?* Studien zu Antisemitismus, Nation und Nationalsozialismus im öffentlichen Meinungsbild. Innsbruck: Studien-Verl., 2002. 230 pp., tabs., notes (204–230), bibl. (Schriften des Centrums für Jüdische Studien, Bd. 2.) [Based on surveys from the late 1940s to the present.]

42157. *"Was ich den Juden schon immer mal so sagen wollte …".* Beiträge und Gespräche. Mit einem Vorwort von Klaus Schütz. Hrsg. von Nea Weissberg-Bob. Berlin: Lichtig-Verl., 2002. 267 pp. [Deals with various recent manifestations of antisemitism launched by the politician Jürgen Möllemann.]

42158. WEINKE, WILFRIED: *Deutschland, Deutschland … über alles?* Antisemitismus, Rechtsradiaklismus und Rassismus nach 1945. [In]: Tribüne, Jg. 41, H. 161, Frankfurt am Main, 2002. Pp. 130–151, footnotes.

——— WETTE, WOLFRAM: *Die Wehrmacht. Feindbilder, Vernichtungskrieg, Legenden.* [See No. 41512.]

42159. WHITFIELD, STEPHEN J.: *Where they burn books.* [In]: Modern Judaism, Vol. 22, No. 3, Cary, NC, Oct. 2002. Pp. 213–233, notes. [On the burning of Jewish books throughout the ages, incl. Nazi Germany.]

42160. WIESEN, S. JONATHAN: *The Richard Willstätter controversy: The legacy of Anti-Semitism in the West German chemical industry.* [In]: The German Chemical Industry in the Twentieth Century. Ed. by John E. Lesch. Dordrecht; Boston; London, 2000. Pp. 347–266, footnotes. [On a post-1945 discussion about antisemitism amongst chemists before and during the Nazi era launched by the posthumous memoirs of Richard Willstätter.]

42161. WULF, PETER: *Antisemitismus in bürgerlichen und bäuerlichen Parteien und Verbänden in Schleswig-Holstein (1918–1924).* [In]: Jahrbuch für Antismitismusforschung 2002, Frankfurt am Main; New York, 2002. Pp. 52–75, footnotes.

42162. ZIEGE, EVA-MARIA: *Mythische Kohärenz: Diskursanalyse des völkischen Antisemitismus.* Konstanz: UVK-Verl.-Ges., 2002. 301 pp. Zugl.: Potsdam, Univ., Diss., 2001. [Covers the period 1918–1934.]

E. **Noted Germans and Jews**

42163. ARNIM, ACHIM von. PAPE, WALTER, ed.: *Arnim und die Berliner Romantik: Kunst, Literatur und Politik.* Berliner Kolloquium der Internationalen Arnim-Gesellschaft. Tübingen: Niemeyer, 2001. XI, 252 pp., illus., footnotes, bibl. (235–246), index. (Schriften der Internationalen Arnim-Gesellschaft, Bd. 3.). [Incl.: Arnims "Judengeschichte". Eine biographische Rekonstruktion (Hildegard Baumgard, 71–94). Further selected articles are listed according to person.] [Cf.: Bespr. (Marco Puschner) [in]: Aurora, Jahrbuch der Eichendorff-Gesellschaft, Bd. 62, Tübingen, 2002, pp. 215–219.]

42164. ARNIM, ACHIM von. WINTER, HANS-GERD: *Der geldgierige Nathan und der Bekehrer Ahasver. Aspekte der Judenfeindschaft in der deutschen Romantik am Beispiel Achim von Arnims.* [In]: Zeitenwenden [see No. 40902]. Pp. 163–180.

42165. BURDEKIN, HANNAH: *The ambivalent author. Five German writers and their Jewish characters 1848–1914.* Oxford; New York: Lang, 2002. 338 pp., footnotes, bibl., index. [Deals with Gustav Freytag, Wilhelm Raabe, Leopold von Sacher-Masoch, Theodor Fontane, Thomas Mann.]

42166. DROSTE-HÜLSHOFF, ANNETTE. BONHEIM, GÜNTHER: *Von der Würde der Lebenden und der Toten.* Annette von Droste-Hülshoffs 'Die Judenbuch'. [In]: Jahrbuch des Freien Deutschen Hochstifts 2002, Tübingen, 2002. Pp. 212–239, footnotes.

42167. DROSTE-HÜLSHOFF, ANNETTE VON. GOSSMANN, WILHELM: *"Die Judenbuche" – zum dritten Mal neu angeeignet.* [In]: Literarische Fundstücke [see No. 41884]. Pp. 183–198, footnotes.

42168. GEORGE, STEFAN. MATTENKLOTT, GERT/PHILIPP, MICHAEL/SCHOEPS, JULIUS H., eds.: *"verkannte brüder"? Stefan George und das deutsch-jüdische Bürgertum zwischen Jahrhundertwende und Emigration.* Hildesheim; New York: Olms, 2001. 278 pp., illus., notes, index. (Haskala, Bd. 22.) [Cont. (some titles abbr.): Vorwort (eds., 9–12). Judentum, Politik und Gesellschaft. der George-Kreis im 1. Drittel des 20. Jahrhunderts; cont.: Georges Haltung zum Judentum (Jürgen Egyptien, 15–30). Die Thematisierung des "Jüdischen" im George-Kreis vor und nach 1933 (Michael Philipp (31–54). "verkannte brüder", "entjudete Juden". George-Kreis, deutsch-jüdisches Bürgertum und die politische Rechte 1918–1933 (Rainer Kolk, 55–68). Ein Versuch über Männerliebe und Judentum (Marita Keilson-Lauritz, 69–82). Deutsch-jüdische Beziehungen im George-Kreis. Die jüdischen Kreismitglieder; cont.: Der Kammergerichtsrat Dr. Ernst Morwitz (Carola Groppe, 85–100). Friedrich Gundolf und Heinrich Heine (Claudia Sonino, 101–116). Karl Wolfskehl (Richard Faber, 117–134). Karl Wolfskehls Deutung des Exodus in 'Die Stimme spricht' (Daniel Hoffmann, 135–152). Stefan George und die Familie Landmann (Manfred Durzak, 153–162). Zu Erich Kahler und der jüdischen George-Rezeption (Geret Luhr, 163–178). Ernst Kantorowicz und das 'Geheime Deutschland' (Ulrich Raulff, 179–198). Stefan George in der Diskussion und Rezeption. Zwischen Antisemitismus und deutsch-jüdischer Symbiose; cont.: Verkünder eines 'heidnischen' Antisemitismus. Die Kosmiker Ludwig Klages und Alfred Schuler (Elke-Vera Kotowski, 201–218). Stefan George und jüdische Musiker (Wolfgang Osthoff, 219–230). Gershom Scholem über Stefan George. Mit einem Seitenblick auf Werner Kraft (Daniel Weidner, 231–246). Charisma und Vergemeinschaftung im George- und Horkheimer-Kreis (Günter C. Behrmann, 247–264).]

42169. GEORGE, STEFAN. NORTON, ROBERT E.: *Secret Germany: Stefan George and his circle.* Ithaca, NY: Cornell Univ. Press, 2002. XVII, 847 pp., notes, bibl. (815–820), index. [Incl. Jews in Stefan George's circle; his attitude on Jews, antisemitism, Nazism.]

42170. GRILLPARZER, FRANZ. BORCHMEYER, DIETER: *Franz Grillparzers Bild des Judentums in seiner 'Jüdin von Toledo'.* [In]: Das Judentum im Spiegel seiner kulturellen Umwelten. Symposium zu Ehren von Saul Friedländer [see No. 41864]. Pp. 155–179, notes.

42171. GRILLPARZER, FRANZ. HELFER, MARTHA B.: *Framing the Jew: Grillparzer's 'Die Jüdin von Toledo'.* [In]: The German Quarterly, Vol. 75, No. 2 Riverside, CA, Spring 2002. Pp. 160– 180, notes.

42172. HOFFMANN, E.T.A.. HARTWICH, WOLF-DANIEL: *Jüdische Gespenster: E.T.A. Hoffmann und der romantische Antisemitismus.* [In]: Das Judentum im Spiegel seiner kulturellen Umwelten. Symposium zu Ehren von Saul Friedländer [see No. 41864.]. Pp. 111–153, notes.

42173. KOTOWSKI, ELKE-VERA: *"Wahnmoching" und die "Kosmiker". Ein Beispiel für alternative Formen der "Erleuchtung" im Fin de siècle des 19. Jahrhunderts.* [In]: Preußens Himmel breitet seine Sterne ... [see No. 41991], Bd. 2. Pp. 741–756, notes. [Deals with Stefan George, Karl Wolfskehl, Alfred Schuler and Ludwig Klages in Munich-Schwabing in the late 1890s; also with the antisemitism of the latter two.]

42174. LESSING, GOTTHOLD EPHRAIM. JASPER, WILLI: *Lessing und Mendelssohn – ein Briefwechsel der Freundschaft.* [In]: Preußens Himmel breitet seine Sterne ... [see No. 41991], Bd. 1. Pp. 215–227, notes.

42175. LESSING, GOTTHOLD EPHRAIM. LÖTZSCH, FRIEDER: *Ein Jude, das Luthertum und die "Luthertümer" in Lessings 'Nathan'.* [In]: Grenzgänge. Festschrift für Diethard Aschoff [see No. 41473]. Pp. 161–173, footnotes.

42176. LUTHER, MARTIN. SPÄTH, ANDREAS: *Luther und die Juden.* Bonn: Verl. für Kultur und Wissenschaft, 2001. 137 pp., footnotes, bibl. (121–137). (Biblia et symbiotica, Bd. 18.)

42177. NIETZSCHE, FRIEDRICH. KOFMAN, SARAH: *Die Verachtung der Juden. Nietzsche, die Juden und der Antisemitismus.* Aus dem Französ. übersetzt von Bernhard Nessler. Berlin: Diaphanes, 2002. 97 pp., footnotes, bibl. [Orig. title publ. 1994 with the title *Le mépris des Juifs. Nietzsche, les Juifs, l'antisémitisme.*]

42178. NIETZSCHE, FRIEDRICH. MITTMANN, THOMAS: *Friedrich Nietzsche. Judengegner und Antisemitenfeind.* Erfurt: Sutton Verlag, [2002]. 159 pp., frontis., illus., notes (115–143), bibl. (144–159).

42179. NIETZSCHE, FRIEDRICH. WISTRICH, ROBERT S.: *Friedrich Nietzsche: Proto-fascist, anti-Semite or judeophile?* [In]: Preußens Himmel breitet seine Sterne ... [see No. 41991], Bd. 2. Pp. 527–537.

———— RAABE, WILHELM. SCHMIDT, MICHAEL: *Marginalität als Modus der ästhetischen Reflexion. Juden und "unehrliche Leute" im Werk Wilhelm Raabes.* [In]: Judenfeindschaft als Paradigma [see No. 42134.]

42180. SALOMON, ERNST VON. HERMAND, JOST: *Der "Preuße" Ernst von Salomon. Ein antisemitischer Nationalrevolutionär?* [In]: Preußens Himmel breitet seine Sterne ... [see No. 41991]. Pp. 121–132, notes. [E.v.S., involved in the assassination of Walther Rathenau, 1922.]

42181. SAVIGNY, FRIEDRICH CARL VON. HENNE, THOMAS/KRETSCHMANN, CARSTEN: *Der christlich fundierte Antijudaismus Savignys und seine Umsetzung in der Rechtspraxis.* [In]: Zeitschrift der Savigny-Stiftung für Rechtsgeschichte, Germanistische Abteilung, Bd. 119, Wien, 2002. Pp. 250–315, footnotes.

42182. SAVIGNY, FRIEDRICH CARL VON. HENNE, THOMAS/KRETSCHMANN, CARSTEN: *Friedrich Carl von Savignys Antijudaismus und die 'Nebenpolitik' der Berliner Universität gegen das preußische Emanzipationsedikt von 1912. Anmerkungen zu einem berühmten Fall der Universitätsgerichtsbarkeit.* [In]: Jahrbuch für Universitätsgeschichte, Bd. 5, [with the issue title] *Universität und Kunst*, Stuttgart, 2002. Pp. 217–226, footnotes. [Deals with the case of a Jewish medical student, Joseph Brogi.]

42183. SCHLEIERMACHER, FRIEDRICH ERNST DANIEL. *Letters on the occasion of the political theological task and the Sendschreiben (Open letter) of Jewish heads of households.* Transl. and introd. by Gilya G. Schmidt. Lewiston: Edwin Mellen Press, 2001. 90 pp., bibl. (87–90). (Schleiermacher studies and translations, Vol. 21.) [Schleiermacher's open letters orig. publ. by Friedrich Franke, Berlin, 1799, under the title: Briefe bei der Gelegenheit der politisch theologischen Aufgabe und des Sendschreibens jüdischer Hausväter, von einem Prediger, ausserhalb Berlins.]

42184. STIFTER, ADALBERT. METZ, JOSEPH: *The Jew as sign in Stifter's 'Abdias'.* [In]: The Germanic Review, Vol. 77, No. 4, Washington, Fall 2002. Pp. 219–233, notes.

42185. STORM, THEODOR. GOLDAMMER, PETER: *Theodor Storm zwischen Philosemitismus und Antisemitismus.* [In]: Schriften der Theodor-Storm-Gesellschaft, Bd. 51, Heide, 2002. Pp. 101–115, notes.

42186. VIRCHOW, RUDOLF. GOSCHLER, CONSTANTIN: *Rudolf Virchow. Mediziner – Anthropologe – Politiker.* Köln: Böhlau, 2002. 556 pp., illus., notes (400–508), bibl. (509–551). Zugl.: Berlin, Humboldt-Univ., Habil.-Schrift. [Chap. III, 3, entitled Vererbung und Verbesserung, also deals with V.'s attitude to Jews and antisemitism; incl. the debate on his "Schulkinderuntersuchung".]

42187. WAGENSEIL, JOHANN CHRISTOPH. BLASTENBREI, PETER: *Johann Christoph Wagenseil (1633–1705). Barockgelehrter, Philosemit und wissenschaftlicher Entdecker des Jiddischen.* [In]: Jiddistik-Mitteilungen, Nr. 27, Trier, April 2002. Pp. 8–13, footnotes.

42188. WEBER, MAX. OTTO, ECKART: *Max Webers Studien des Antiken Judentums.* Historische Grundlagen einer Theorie der Moderne. Tübingen: Mohr Siebeck, 2002. XII, 371 pp., bibl., index, footnotes.

X. FICTION AND POETRY. HUMOUR

42189. APPELFELD, AHARON: *Alles, was ich liebte.* Roman. Aus dem Hebr. übersetzt von Anne Birkenhauer. Berlin: Alexander Fest, 2002. 287 pp. [Cf.: In der Schule des Todes wird das Leben nicht gelehrt. Der Holocaust-Überlebende Aharon Appelfeld sucht in der Leere seines Gedächtnisses die Heimat, die er nie besaß (Jakob Hessing) [in]: 'FAZ', Nr. 119, Franfurt am Main, 25. Mai 2002, p. 54.]

42190. BECKER, JUREK. *The boxer: a novel.* Transl. from the German by Alessandra Bastagli. New York: Arcade Publ., 2002. 277 pp. [For orig. edn. in 1976 see No. 14537/YB XXIII.]

42191. EDELMAN, GWEN: *Erzähl mir vom Krieg.* Roman. Aus dem Amerik. von Carina von Enzenberg. München: Piper, 2002. 179 pp. [Orig. publ. 2001 with the title *War story*; love story; the protagonist, a Jew from Vienna, playwright and womaniser, tells his life story of childhood, flight to Amsterdam, Palestine, return to Europe to his lover, a young German woman.]

42192. FRISTER, ROMAN: *Impossible love: Ascher Levy's longing for Germany.* Transl. by Alisa Jaffa. London: Weidenfeld and Nicolson, 2002. 359 pp., illus., ports., facsims., geneal. tab. [Fictionalised account about the authentic story of the Levy family from Pomerania going back to 1775. (Ascher Levy, 1815–1897). For German edn. see No. 38384/YB XLV.]

42193. GOLDFEIN, ALAN: *Jews and Germans – Germans and Jews.* A novella and short stories. Heidelberg: American Editions, 2002. 240 pp. [Author, an American Jew, is living in Berlin.]

42194. HIRSCH, KARL JAKOB: *Manhattan-Serenade.* Hrsg. und mit einem Nachwort v. Helmut Pfanner. Bern [et al.]: Lang, 2001. 159 pp. (Exil-Dokumente, Bd. 4.) [Political novel, orig. publ. 1939 in New York in 'Neue Volkszeitung'. See also No. 41890.] [Data K.J.H. see No. 31204/YB XXXIX.]

—— KAHN, SELMA: *Der Weg ins Dritte Reich.* Ein autobiographischer Roman. [See No. 41367.]

42195. KOCH, ERICH: *Earrings*. Baden-Baden 1883. A novel. Niagara Falls, NY: Mosaic Press, 2002. 222 pp. [Historical novel set in late 19th-century Baden-Baden; author, b. 1919 in Frankfurt am Main, integrated authentic elements of his family history.] [Cf.: Surprising encounters in nine-teenth-Century Baden-Baden. Canadian writer Erich Koch uses the figure of his grandfather to create a tale that showcases the intricacies of Baden-Baden society (Monica Strauss) [in]: Aufbau, Vol. 68, New York, May 16, 2002, p. 17.]

42196. KRAUS, OTA B.: *Die bemalte Wand*. Roman. Aus dem Englischen von Jutta R. Witthoefft. Mit einem Nachwort von Pavel Stránsky. Köln: Dittrich Verlag, 2002. 298 pp. [Based on the author's own experience in Theresienstadt.] [O.B.K., 1921 – Prague – 2000 Netanya, Israel, teacher, writer, survived deportation into several concentration camps, emigr. to Israel in 1949.]

42197. KULBACH-FRICKE, KARINA: *Der Kaufmann von Köln*. Historischer Roman. Köln: Emons, 2002. 351 pp. [Novel, based on authentic sources, deals with a Jewish merchant, his four daughters and their descendants between 1096 and 1150.]

42198. ROTH, JOSEPH. ROTH, JOSEPH: *The Radetzky march*. Transl. by Michael Hofman. London: Granta, 2002. XVI, 363 pp.

42199. ROTH, JOSEPH: *The collected stories of Joseph Roth*. Transl. and introd. by Michael Hofman. New York: Norton, 2002. 281 pp., illus. [Cf.: Review article (Stephen H. Garrin), [in]: Jewish Book World, Vol. 20, No. 1, New York, 2002, pp. 28–29; deals with Roth's life.]

42200. ROTH, JOSEPH: *Weights and measures*. Transl. by David Le Vay. London: Peter Owen, 2002. 150 pp., illus.

42201. SCHNITZLER, ARTHUR: *Casanova's journey home and other late stories*. Transl. and with an afterword by Norman M. Watt. Riverside, CA: Ariadne Press, 2002. 270 pp. (Studies in Austrian literature, culture and thought.) [Selection of short stories. 'Casanova's journey home' orig. publ. in 1918.]

42202. WEISS, RUTH: *Meine Schwester Sara*. Augsburg: Maro, 2002. 258 pp. [Novel, dealing with a girl born at the end of World War II in Bergen-Belsen to a Jewish mother from Cologne and later adopted by a Boer family in South Africa.]

42203. WISSE, RUTH R.: *Some serious thoughts about Jewish humour*. New York: Leo Baeck Institute, [2001]. 18 pp., bibl. (Leo Baeck Memorial Lecture, 45.)

42204. WILHELM, ULRIKE MIRJAM: *Die Theaterprinzessin*. Roman. Berlin: Aufbau Taschenbuch Verlag, 2002. 400 pp. Orig.-Ausg. [Deals with the actress Rachel (Elsa) Félix and the author's great-grandmother Elisa Glücklich, both born in Metz.] [Cf.: Sehnsucht nach der eigenen Vergangenheit. Ulrike Mirjam Wilhelm – eine deutsche Schriftstellerin und ihre jüdische Spurensuche (Eva Magin-Pelich) [in]: Aufbau, Vol. 69, No. 8, New York, April 17, 2003, p. 12.]

——— YANG, ZHIDONG, ed.: *Klara Blum*. Kommentierte Auswahledition. [See No. 41828.]

42205. ZIELINSKI, ADAM: *Jan war Jossele (und andere Erzählungen)*. Klagenfurt: Wieser, 2002. 119 pp. [Author, b. 1929 in Drohobycz, has lived in Austria since 1957, 1989 started a new career as an author of Polish and German books.]

Index to Bibliography

List of Contributors

BRÄMER, Andreas, Ph.D., b. 1964 in Lüneburg, Germany. Wissenschaftlicher Mitarbeiter, Institut für die Geschichte der deutschen Juden, Hamburg. Publications include: *Rabbiner und Vorstand. Zur Geschichte der jüdischen Gemeinde in Deutschland und Österreich 1809-1871* (1999); *Rabbiner Zacharias Frankel. Wissenschaft des Judentums und konservative Reform im 19. Jahrhundert* (2000); *Judentum und religiöse Reform. Der Hamburger Tempel 1817-1938* (2000). (Contributor to *LBI Year Book* vols. 42 and 45).

BREUER, Edward, Ph.D., b. 1960 in Montreal, Canada. Associate Professor of Jewish Studies at Loyola University, Chicago. Publications include: *The Limits of Enlightenment* (1996). (Contributor to *LBI Year Book* vol. 44).

FEINBERG, Anat, b. 1951 in Tel Aviv, Israel, Ph.D., Professor for Hebrew and Jewish Literature at the Hochschule für jüdische Studien in Heidelberg. Recent publications include: *Embodied Memory: The Theatre of George Tabori* (1999); German translation: *George Tabori* (2003); 'The Janus-faced Jew: Nathan and Shylock on the Post-War German Stage' in L. Morris and J. Zipes (eds.) *Unlikely History, German-Jewish Symbiosis, 1945-2000* (2002). (Contributor to *LBI Year Book* vol. 29).

FRAENKEL, Daniel, Ph.D., b. 1945 in Haifa, Israel. Editor of the *Yad Vashem Encyclopaedia of the Jewish Communities in Germany*. Publications include: *On the Edge of the Abyss. Zionist Policy and the Plight of the German Jews, 1933-1938* (1994, in Hebrew); 'Jewish Self-Defense under the Constraints of National Socialism. The Final Years of the Centralverein', in David Bankier (ed.), *Probing the Depths of German Antisemitism. German Society and the Persecution of the Jews, 1933-1941* (2000); 'Reichsvertretung der Deutschen Juden' in Walter Laqueur (ed.), *The Holocaust Encyclopedia* (2001).

JAHR, Christoph, Dr. Phil., b. 1963 in Freiburg i. Breisgau, Germany. Wissenschaftlicher Assistent at the Institut für Geschichtswissenschaften, Humboldt-Universität, Berlin. Co-editor of *Feindbilder in der deutschen Geschichte. Studien zur Vorurteilsgeschichte im 19. und 20. Jahrhundert* (1994); author of *Gewöhnliche Soldaten. Desertion und Deserteure im deutschen und britischen Heer 1914-1918* (1998).

KAPLAN, Marion, Ph.D., b. 1946 in New Jersy. Skirball Professor of Modern Jewish History, New York University. Publications include: *The Jewish Feminist Movement in Germany: Th Campaigns of the Jüdischer Frauenbund, 1904-1938* (1979); Translation: *Die Jüdische Frauenbewegung in Deutschland: Organisation und Ziele des Jüdischen Frauenbundes, 1904-1938* (1981). *The Making of the Jewish Middle Class: Women, Family and Identity in Imperial Germany* (1991); Translation: *Jüdisches Bürgertum: Frau, Familie und Identität im Kaiserreich* (1997); *Between Dignity and Despair: Jewish Life in Nazi Germany* (1998); Translation: *Der Mut zum Überleben: Jüdische Frauen und ihre Familien in Nazideutschland* (2001). (Contributor to *LBI Year Book* vols. 27, 28 and 45).

MIRON, Guy, Ph.D., b. 1966 in Jerusalem, Israel. Lecturer at the Schechter Institute of Jewish Studies, Jerusalem and researcher at Yad Vashem International Institute for Holocaust Research. Publications include: 'Autobiography as a Source for Social History–German Jews in Palestine as a Test Case' in *Tel Aviv Jahrbuch für deutsche Geschichte,* 29 (2000), 'Between History and "useful past picture": Representations of the Jewish and the German past in the Jewish Liberal historical discourse in Weimar Germany' in *Zion,* vol. 66 (2001, Hebrew). *From 'There' to 'Here' in First Person: Memory Representations and Past Images in the Autobiographies of German Jews in Israel,* (forthcoming, in Hebrew).

SACKS, Adam J., B.A., b. 1978 in New York, USA. German Academic Exchange Fellow; Journalist; extended work affiliation with the Jewish Museum, Berlin.

SCHÖLZEL, Christian, Ph.D., b. 1964 in Hamburg, Germany. Museum profession-al (Wissenschaftlicher Mitarbeiter) at Haus der Bayerischen Geschichte, Augsburg. Publications include: 'Walther Rathenau. Von der Assimilation zur Depression' in Barbara Danckwortt *et al.* (eds.) *Historische Rassismusforschung* (1995); *Brücken und Brüche. Streifzug durch die deutsch-jugoslawische Beziehungsgeschichte. Schauplatz Berlin* (1999); 'Zeitgenössische Wahrnehmungen von Speziallagern 1945-1950. Das Lager Nr. 2 in Buchenwald' in *Deutschland-Archiv 32* (1999), No. 3; 'Walther Rathenau und die Veränderlichkeit des Menschen. Ansichten zu Bildung und Erziehung', in *Tribüne 42* (2003) [in print].

SCHÜLER-SPRINGORUM, Stefanie, Ph.D., b. 1962 in Hamburg, Germany. Director of the Institut für die Geschichte der deutschen Juden, Hamburg. Publications include: *Die jüdische Minderheit in Königsberg/Pr. 1871-1945* (1996); 'Fear and Misery in the Third Reich: From the Files of the Collective Guardianship Office of the Berlin Jewish Community, in *Yad Vashem Studies* XXVII (1999); co-author: *"Wir sind jung, die Welt ist offen..." Eine Jüdische Jugendgruppe im 20. Jahrhundert* (2002); co-editor: *Home/Front. The Military, War and Gender in Twentieth-Century Germany* (2002).

SORKIN, David, Ph.D., b. 1953 in Chicago, USA. Frances and Laurence Weinstein Professor of Jewish Studies, University of Wisconsin-Madison. Publications include: *The Transformation of German Jewry* (1987); *Moses Mendelssohn and the Religious Enlightenment* (1996); *The Berlin Haskalah and German Religious Thought* (2000). (Contributor to *LBI Year Book* vols. 32, 35, 37, 40).

General Index to Year Book XLVIII
of the Leo Baeck Institute

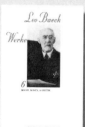

El olivo y la espada

Estudios sobre el antisemitismo en España
(siglos XVI–XX)
Editados por PERE JOAN I TOUS y HEIKE NOTTEBAUM

XXVI, 516 Seiten. 7 Abb. Kart. ca. € 124.– (fPr). ISBN 3-484-57006-7 (Romania Judaica. Band 6)

¿Cuáles han sido los avatares del antisemitismo en España, cuando ésta, a partir del edicto de expulsión (1492), dejó de ser un ámbito de convivencia étnica? Tal fue el tema del coloquio de Constanza (mayo 2000), cuyas actas se reúnen aquí y en el que participaron antropólogos, historiadores y filólogos. Desde este enfoque pluridisciplinar se analizan momentos, espacios, figuras y voces del discurso antijudáico y por ende antisemita, tanto en sus contextos históricos como en su representación literaria, estudiándose ésta con igual atención en su vertiente apologética y en su vertiente crítica.

Zeitgenössische Jüdische Autobiographie

Herausgegeben von CHRISTOPH MIETHING

XII, 200 Seiten. Kart. ca. € 64.–. ISBN 3-484-57007-5 (Romania Judaica. Band 7)

Die Akten des gleichnamigen Kongresses vereinigen Beiträge vor allem zur französisch-jüdischen Autobiographie der letzten Jahrzehnte. Aber auch die einschlägige deutsch- und englischsprachige Literatur wird berücksichtigt. Drei italienische Autoren von Autobiographien kommen ebenfalls zu Wort und nehmen zu ihrem Werk Stellung. Die theoretische Reflexion, die die Analyse einzelner Werke begleitet oder auch selbständig durchgeführt wird, betrifft einerseits das Verhältnis von Autobiographie und ›Autofiktion‹, und andererseits die grundsätzliche Frage, was es heißt, von ›jüdischen Autobiographien‹ zu reden.

Bettina Riedmann
»Ich bin Jude, Österreicher, Deutscher«

Judentum in Arthur Schnitzlers Tagebüchern und Briefen
2002. VI, 477 Seiten. 18 Abb. Kart. € 82.–. ISBN 3-484-65136-9 (Conditio Judaica. Band 36)

Elisabeth Albanis
German-Jewish Cultural Identity from 1900 to the Aftermath of the First World War

A comparative study of Moritz Goldstein, Julius Bab and Ernst Lissauer
2002. VIII, 310 Seiten. Kart. € 60.– (fPr). ISBN 3-484-65137-7 (Conditio Judaica. Band 37)

By illustrating the quintessentially different self-perceptions of three contemporary German writers of Jewish background, this book examines a range of German-Jewish identities in a socio-cultural context in Wilhelmine Germany. Its recognition of the ways in which the individual's cultural identity – Moritz Goldstein's (1880–1977) cultural Zionism, Julius Bab's (1880–1955) synthesis of ›Deutschtum‹ and ›Judentum‹ and Ernst Lissauer's (1882–1937) advocacy of complete assimilation – was constantly refashioned in response to the challenges of increasing anti-Semitism, enables one to reach a fuller understanding of the evolving self-perception of German Jews.

Jüdische Identitäten in Mitteleuropa

Literarische Modelle der Identitätskonstruktion
Herausgegeben von ARMIN A. WALLAS unter Mitwirkung von PRIMUS-HEINZ KUCHER,
EDGAR SALLAGER und JOHANN STRUTZ

2002. VI, 325 Seiten. Kart. € 68.–. ISBN 3-484-65138-5 (Conditio Judaica. Band 38)

Saskia Schreuder
Würde im Widerspruch

Jüdische Erzählliteratur im nationalsozialistischen Deutschland 1933–1938
2002. IX, 321 Seiten. Kart. € 68.–. ISBN 3-484-65139-3 (Conditio Judaica. Band 39)

Jacques Darmaun
Thomas Mann, Deutschland und die Juden

Aus dem Französischen von JACQUES DARMAUN
2003. X, 319 Seiten. Kart. € 72.–. ISBN 3-484-65140-7 (Conditio Judaica. Band 40)

Anatol Schenker
Der Jüdische Verlag 1902–1938

Zwischen Aufbruch, Blüte und Vernichtung
2003. VII, 615 Seiten. 24 Abb. Kart. € 120.–. ISBN 3-484-65141-5 (Conditio Judaica. Band 41)

Brigitte Dalinger
Quellenedition zur Geschichte des jüdischen Theaters in Wien

2003. V, 281 Seiten. Kart. € 64.–. ISBN 3-484-65142-3 (Conditio Judaica. Band 42)

Max Niemeyer Verlag

Max Niemeyer Verlag GmbH · Postfach 2140 · 72011 Tübingen
Tel 07071-989494 · Fax 989450 · E-mail order@niemeyer.de

New Books from Mohr Siebeck

Towards Normality?
Acculturation and Modern
German Jewry
Edited by Rainer Liedtke and
David Rechter

The authors of this volume endeavour to bring a fresh perspective to the study of the diverse efforts of German-speaking Jews to acculturate and »normalise« from the Enlightenment until the Nazi period.

2003. XI, 353 pages (Schriftenreihe wissenschaftlicher Abhandlungen des Leo Baeck Instituts 68). ISBN 3-16-148127-5 cloth € 74.00

Ulrich Wyrwa
Juden in der Toskana und in Preußen im Vergleich
Aufklärung und Emanzipation in Florenz, Livorno, Berlin und Königsberg in Preussen

Woran scheiterte die Emanzipation der Juden in Deutschland? Dieser Frage geht Ulrich Wyrwa nach und untersucht die spezifischen Errungenschaften und der besonderen Behinderungen der Juden im Zeitalter der Emanzipation am Beispiel preußischer und toskanischer Städte.

2003. X, 493 pages (Schriftenreihe wissenschaftlicher Abhandlungen des Leo Baeck Instituts 67). ISBN 3-16-148077-5 cloth € 54.00

Hans Dieter Betz
The »Mithras Liturgy«
Text, Translation, and Commentary

Hans Dieter Betz provides the first complete English commentary on one of the most important texts of the history of religions in late antiquity: the so-called »Mithras Liturgy«, a magic Graeco-Egyptian papyrus from the 4th century AD, written from the inner perspective by an initiated devotee of the god Helios-Mithras-Aion and containing an esoteric ritual instruction for an ascension to and consultation with the god. In addition to an introduction into the history of research since Albrecht Dieterich's famous work »Eine Mithraslithurgie« (1903), the volume contains the Greek text and the English translation, an analysis of the literary composition, and a commentary establishing the text and contextualizing it in relation to Egyptian religion, Mithraism, hermeticism and gnosticism. At the end of the book there is a bibliography and a Greek word-index.

2003. Est. 280 pages (Studien und Texte zu Antike und Christentum). ISBN 3-16-148128-3 cloth est. € 80.00 (August)

Mohr Siebeck
P.O. Box 2040
D-72010 Tübingen

Fax +49 / 7071 / 51104
e-mail: info@mohr.de
www.mohr.de

Up-to-date information via e-mail – to register now, go to www.mohr.de/form/eKurier_e.htm